SECOND EDITION

# STATISTICAL ANALYSIS

## FOR PUBLIC ADMINISTRATION

LAWRENCE L. GIVENTER, PHD
Professor
Department of Politics and Public Administration
California State University–Stanislaus
Turlock, California

JONES AND BARTLETT PUBLISHERS
*Sudbury, Massachusetts*
BOSTON TORONTO LONDON SINGAPORE

*World Headquarters*
Jones and Bartlett Publishers
40 Tall Pine Drive
Sudbury, MA 01776
978-443-5000
info@jbpub.com
www.jbpub.com

Jones and Bartlett Publishers Canada
6339 Ormindale Way
Mississauga, Ontario L5V 1J2
Canada

Jones and Bartlett Publishers International
Barb House, Barb Mews
London W6 7PA
United Kingdom

Jones and Bartlett's books and products are available through most bookstores and online booksellers. To contact Jones and Bartlett Publishers directly, call 800-832-0034, fax 978-443-8000, or visit our website www.jbpub.com.

Substantial discounts on bulk quantities of Jones and Bartlett's publications are available to corporations, professional associations, and other qualified organizations. For details and specific discount information, contact the special sales department at Jones and Bartlett via the above contact information or send an email to specialsales@jbpub.com.

**Library of Congress Cataloging-in-Publication Data**
Giventer, Lawrence L.
    Statistical analysis for public administration / By Lawrence L. Giventer.
        p.   cm.
    Includes bibliographical references and index.
    ISBN 978-0-7637-4076-4 (pbk.)
    1. Public administration—Statistical methods.   2. Statistics.   I. Title.
    JA71.7.G59  2008
        519.5024'351—dc22                                    2007032442
6048

**Production Credits**
Acquisitions Editor: Jeremy Spiegel
Editorial Assistant: Lisa Gordon
Production Director: Amy Rose
Production Editor: Renée Sekerak
Production Assistant: Julia Waugaman
Associate Marketing Manager: Jennifer Bengtson
Manufacturing and Inventory Control Supervisor: Amy Bacus
Cover Design: Kristin E. Ohlin
Interior Design: Publishers' Design and Production Services, Inc.
Composition: ATLIS Graphics
Text Printing and Binding: Malloy Incorporated
Cover Printing: Malloy Incorporated

Printed in the United States of America
11 10 09 08 07   10 9 8 7 6 5 4 3 2 1

*To Mary*

# Contents

# Preface

The *Second Edition* provides a well-designed, updated, and relatively affordable text which addresses an important aspect of public management—the use of statistical methods to help understand and respond to public problems.[1] Its intended audience is the prospective or practicing professional in public sector management, planning, or policy analysis.

Although public administrators are sometimes stereotyped as cynical bureaucrats, most are really idealists. Whether in government or nonprofit organizations, they work to maintain a better state of affairs today than existed yesterday and to strive for a better tomorrow. Pragmatic and rational, they respond to perceived problems by formulating alternatives, making decisions, and implementing programs. Statistical analysis provides a formal, explicit, rational basis for decision making. Before public administrators can formulate, plan, or act, they need to describe what the state of affairs has been, might be now, and is likely to be in the future. They also need to evaluate the differences between what they observe and what they expect. Statistical methods are tools for observing, recording, and drawing lessons from events. With statistical analysis, public administrators do not need perfect information in order to describe and reach judgments about what is happening. They can learn what has happened, what is happening, and what is likely to happen within a known degree of error and a known degree of certainty. Public-sector professionals should learn which statistical techniques to apply to the problems at hand, how the different tools work, and how to interpret and apply the results.

---

[1]The term "statistics" is used very loosely. Depending on the context, "statistics" will refer in a collective sense to the complete set of quantitative methods covered in this text. "Statistics" can also refer to very specific numbers that are calculated to describe and summarize the characteristics of a large number of observations.

## *Pedagogical Features*

This book addresses problem solving. It is oriented toward *applications* of statistical analysis in the public sector, not just statistical computation. The text directly addresses one of the most confusing aspects of statistical analysis for the beginning student—the difficulty of identifying which statistical method to apply to a given problem. Like the tools in a carpenter's box, each statistical technique has a specific application to a particular kind of problem. This text is organized by the type of problems that are encountered. Type of problem is identified first—description, evaluation, or estimation. Then the appropriate statistical techniques are introduced. The text begins with problems that involve only one variable. Later, problems with two variables and then more than two variables are covered. Within each problem area the selection of the appropriate statistical method continues with the identification of the level of measurement for each variable. A series of unique reference tables guide the user to the applicable statistical methods for each type of problem.

The examples and exercises in this book feature actual public sector problem situations and realistic data in such areas as health care, environmental quality, transportation, public finance and budgeting, equal opportunity, unemployment, housing, education, public safety, and aging. Each problem is presented in terms of a policy or program dilemma with a brief explanation about the context of the problem and why the answer is important—what will be "done" with the result/conclusion. This provides the student with the rationale for using quantitative methodology to address policy/management questions as well as some guidance in foreseeing the interpretation/application of results. It is through such examples that students learn to recognize similar problem situations in which quantitative methods may be useful and apply the methods studied in the classroom to the problems they encounter as public service professionals.

The text includes extensive homework exercises for each chapter. Understanding the appropriate use of statistical methods in public administration comes only with practice. Homework exercises are an integral part of the quantitative methods course. The problems in this text have a public sector context and use "real world" data. They are not repetitive, and each contains its own lesson. Answers are included immediately after the problem statement so students can check their work. Both numeric results and appropriate management/policy interpretations and utility are presented. Sometimes students, with the questions at one hand and the answer at the other, will "work backwards" to "discover" the reasoning or computational procedure for solving the problem.

# Acknowledgments

I wish to thank the many students in politics and public administration I have met over the years whose excitement, optimism, perseverance, and commitment to public service inspired, and from time-to-time reinvigorated, the text. My friends and colleagues in the California State University, especially the Department of Politics and Public Administration at CSU, Stanislaus provided invaluable encouragement. My wife Mary, Sarah and Doug, Dominion, Cindy, and Jasmine were constantly supportive. I wish to thank the excellent staff at Jones and Bartlett Publishers. They have worked hard to fulfill my vision of the text while keeping the final cost to students as low as possible.

The result, I think, is a text for undergraduate and graduate students and a useful reference that they will want to keep on hand as a public administration practitioner. You be the judge. I invite your reactions.

*Lawrence L. Giventer*
California State University–Stanislaus

# About the Author

Lawrence L. Giventer is a professor in the Department of Politics and Public Administration at California State University, Stanislaus. He teaches post-baccalaureate level courses in public sector quantitative methods and public policy analysis and undergraduate courses in American government. Professor Giventer is also the author of *Governing California,* 2nd ed. (McGraw-Hill, 2008). Prof. Giventer joined CSU, Stanislaus in 1975 and soon afterward founded the university's nationally accredited Master of Public Administration (MPA) program, which he directed for 20 years. He has served as department chairperson, Speaker of the Faculty, consultant and advisory committee chair for state and local government agencies, book reviewer, and accreditation site-visitor. He has a PhD degree from the University of Pittsburgh in public administration and engineering degrees from the New Jersey Institute of Technology and Massachusetts Institute of Technology. He is often called upon as a political analyst by radio, television, print, and Internet media.

# CHAPTER 1

# Statistical Analysis: Description, Evaluation, and Estimation

The public sector is *Where the action is!* Every issue that excites people's highest hopes and aspirations—or deepest fears and frustrations—is addressed first and foremost in the public sector. Problems in such areas as health care, unemployment, environmental quality, crime and safety, education, transportation, aging, housing, land use, equal opportunity, and emergency preparedness compete for our attention and resources. They demand answers—answers developed by men and women in public administration.

*Public problems* have been defined as ". . . needs, deprivations, or dissatisfactions, self-identified or identified by others, for which relief is sought."[1] In other words, policy makers and public administrators react when they perceive a mismatch between observed social or environmental conditions and their expectation of the way things should be—a difference between what they see and what they want. Addressing a public problem means taking action that will reduce the mismatch and in so doing create a better future state of affairs—one that is perceived as more closely meeting needs, fulfilling aspirations, and being consistent with societal values.

**Observations** of social and environmental conditions—the perceived current state of affairs—are called **data**. Data describe the status quo. Public problems are defined by differences between data and expectations. The analysis of data is critical both to defining and understanding the nature of a public problem and determining how to relieve the public problem.

Statistical analysis helps public administrators address public problems because it provides a set of standardized mathematical procedures to systematically summarize and interpret data. Statistical procedures are like the various tools in a carpenter's workbox. Each tool has a special application to a particular type of problem and kind of data. There are basically three different types of problems: (1) description, (2) evaluation, and (3) estimation. There are also basically three

---

[1]Charles O. Jones. 1970. *Introduction to the Study of Public Policy*, Belmont, CA: Wadsworth Publishing Company, Inc. p. 17.

different kinds of data: (1) nominal, (2) ordinal, and (3) interval observations. To use statistical analysis the public manager needs to select the appropriate statistical tool for the job. Once deciding what tool to use, the analyst needs to learn how to use it.

The use of a computer will be particularly important to this objective. Modern computer technology has made it possible to acquire, store, organize, and utilize more data more rapidly and accurately than ever before. By using computers to alleviate the tedium of extensive calculations, public managers can focus their attention on the most important aspects of problem solving: identification of the appropriate method, and interpretation of results.

## 1.1  Relationship between Statistics and Management—A Conceptual Model

It is important to start with an overview of the role that statistical analysis can play in the process of public management. Consider the conceptual model of the management process in Exhibit 1–1. There are six parts as indicated by the numbers on the diagram.

### 1.1.1  Events

The conceptual model starts with **events**. They are the center of attention. An event is an action—an occurrence—a physical or social change in our society and environment—the product of management action. Societal conditions—the status quo or state of affairs—is the cumulative result of many events.

Despite their characterization as "bureaucrats," public managers try to make this world a better place in which to live—a world characterized by safety, opportunity, reward, security, and all the other elements of a desirable quality of life. Most public sector managers have a vision of a more desirable—a more perfect—tomorrow. They also have the ego, idealism, intelligence, dedication, arrogance, and perseverance to work toward this goal. To this end, managers attempt to formulate policies, acquire and allocate resources, and maneuver power and authority relationships—all in order to control events in such a way that the future, when compared to the present, will be judged as more desirable, more satisfying, more secure—in short, better!

### 1.1.2  Transactions

Decision making in management is a process of reaction. Managers react to perceived societal or organizational conditions. They react to differences between observations and expectations. They react to change (and sometimes to the lack of change). Their reactions are based on what they know or perceive about past

## Exhibit 1–1

**A Conceptual Model of the Management Process**

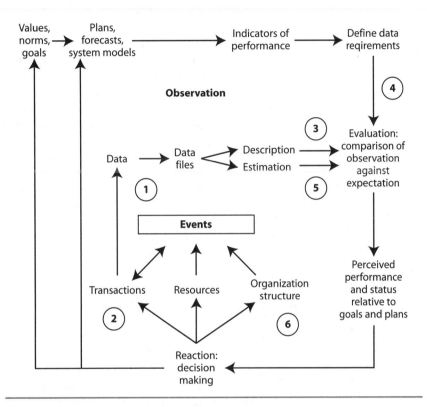

**Expectation**

Values, norms, goals → Plans, forecasts, system models → Indicators of performance → Define data reqirements

**Observation**

Data → Data files → Description / Estimation → Evaluation: comparison of observation against expectation

Events

Transactions    Resources    Organization structure

Perceived performance and status relative to goals and plans

Reaction: decision making

events.[2] They obtain these data by devising, designing, and implementing bureaucratic systems and procedures called **transactions**. Transactions are the means of learning about and remembering events.

*Transactions generate data.* Each transaction contributes to a data record—a set of observations about a single **event**. A "data file," in turn, is a collection of

---

[2]There is always a time delay between an event's occurrence and its perception. Sometimes this delay may be only microseconds. Other times this delay may be a matter of months, years, or even longer. Further, all observations, no matter how thorough, always to some degree contain errors, inaccuracies, and misrepresentations about what "really happened." Thus, public managers and policy makers attempt to control the future—tomorrow—by making decisions in the present—today—based on error-ridden information about yesterday. It is like driving a car while focusing only on the rear-view mirror—reacting only to past events.

data records about many related events. Data are often acquired in a piecemeal and haphazard manner. To be useful, observations must be assembled to form data records, and, in turn, the data records of many similar events must be aggregated and organized to form the all-important files of the bureaucratic state.

The complete set of all related events of interest for which observations could possibly be obtained is called the **population**. A data file that contains observations of fewer events than the number that constitutes the population (that is, a subset of the population) is called a **sample**.

Remember when you registered for this course? Several observations were made about that event. Most likely the registration process involved providing pertinent data such as your name, address, and course identification (and finally, paying good money). That was a transaction. As a result of the transaction, a data record was created in which you are noted as a student in this course. When data about related events are organized, a data file can be created (such as a list of all students who acted in a similar manner by registering for this course).

In addition to generating data, transactions are used by managers to implement policy and regulate events. For example, the operation of motor vehicles is controlled in part by the requirement that each driver obtain a license issued by the state. Through the licensing process, the state can not only obtain information about each driver, but also enforce certain rules about the minimum physical abilities, skill, and knowledge required of each driver.

### 1.1.3  Description

**Description** is one of the three purposes of statistical analysis. If management is a process of reaction, the analyst needs to learn about what is going on—has already occurred—before recommending changes for tomorrow! Even a description of the "present"—the status quo—is actually a summary of the recent past.

Description questions ask for "facts." What is going on? What happened? Who was involved? How often? How much? How many? How fast? What kind? Where? When? The answers are important. The way an analyst describes (or perceives) a problem can influence the public management response to that problem.

Statistics can help describe a public problem by summarizing the characteristics of data about a large number of events. For example, is crime a problem in your community? An analyst might begin by asking questions such as, How many crimes were reported to the police last year? How many arrests were made? How many convictions obtained? What is the ratio of felony to misdemeanor offenses? Or, more subjectively, to what extent do people feel safe walking the streets at night?

### 1.1.4  Evaluation

The central question for the public manager and policy analyst is, "Did it work?" The answer to this question requires a comparison of the *description* of the *observed* state of affairs against the **expectation** of what that state of affairs should have been. Expectations are founded in moral, religious or ethical precepts, in dreams for the future, in political ideologies, or in managerial plans, forecasts, or models. All of these describe what is meant by the good, the more desirable, the better future to which we aspire. They define the ultimate goals and purpose for public administrators and policy analysts. The extent to which there is a match between the expected intention and observed result can be inferred to be the extent to which a program "worked." The process of comparing observation against expectation is called **evaluation**.

The process of evaluation has two parts. The first part is determining the extent of difference between observation and expectation. The second part is *judgment* as to whether the extent of any difference is *unusual*. Is the mismatch between observation and expectation small or large? Can the mismatch be attributed to observational errors or is it systematic? Statistical analysis can be regarded as a means for searching for unusual differences between observation and expectation. The ability to separate the unusual from the happenstance is extremely important to the public manager. It allows the manager to define and monitor *change* in our society. By precisely defining change, a public manager can either work toward maintaining continuity, stability, and order—that is, no change—a constant "steady-state"—or purposely work to bring about change toward a more desirable future state of affairs.

Statistics allows analysts to define what is meant by the concept *unusual*. Any observed difference between observation and expectation could conceivably be due to chance. Sometimes an event outcome is affected by random interference or occurs merely by chance. Other "event outcomes" may be the products of errors in observation and measurement or our own faulty perceptions. We are interested in the likelihood—the "probability"—of the event outcomes that we have observed and described. Suppose that an event could result in one of several possible outcomes. Suppose further that upon observation we see that one event outcome occurs more often than the others. How likely is this? Is this unusual? The answer to these questions depends upon what we expected. Perhaps we expected each outcome to occur about as often as any other outcome (such as rolling a die). On the other hand, we may have expected certain outcomes to occur more often (such as the speed of cars on the street outside). Probability expresses the likelihood of observed event outcomes in relation to expectation. If the probability is small enough we credit the observations not to chance but to some underlying systematic societal, biological, or mechanical process. Using statistics we are able to determine whether a set of event outcomes differs from our expectation by finding the probability of the outcomes occurring by chance.

### 1.1.5  Estimation

The third purpose of statistics is **estimation**. Ideally, decisions should be made on the basis of reacting to estimations rather than reacting to past event outcomes. Managers should not only evaluate where they are today—that is, compare what they perceive against what they expect—but also should judge differences between predicted future states of affairs against desired future expectations. This requires that managers attempt to anticipate the future. What managers need, of course, is a certified, 100 percent accurate, crystal ball that would imbue them with the prescience and clairvoyance to forecast all of the future effects of any decision. Unfortunately there is no such device. But all is not lost! Some statistical techniques (as well as other quantitative methods in the fields of operations research or modeling and simulation methods) encourage managers to use data about past events to glimpse the future.

Estimation methods allow analysts to make inferences about what is or will be happening in our community, our society, our world, or our universe without requiring us to be omniscient. Analysts can closely estimate current conditions—we can learn what is going on in a group or population—without having to be all-seeing and all-knowing about the characteristics and attributes of each and every person, object, and event outcome in that population. Estimations are not perfect. There will be a plus-minus error, which can be determined. And there will be a known degree of certainty that the actual status-quo condition, were we to have perfect knowledge, lies within that error range. Estimations open the door for managers to react to anticipated rather than past event outcomes.

### 1.1.6   Reaction—Decision Making

What can public managers do to change event outcomes? Management is a lot like operating a backhoe. There are only a limited number of levers that can be pushed or pulled—whether singly or in combination—in order to "control" the machine. Similarly, there are only four types of actions a manager can take to influence future events.

(1) A manager can decide to change the *transactions* system. Transactions can be used not only to report event outcomes but to affect (control) behavior. This is accomplished by means of **policies**. Policies are rules for behavior. They are statements of intended action. They prescribe what shall be done under a specified set of circumstances. Policies should not be confused with broad statements of intent, purpose, or goals. Policies are more specific. They look like IF-THEN statements. IF "such-and-such" a condition exists THEN "something-or-other" shall be the response. If you want to receive credit for this class toward a public administration degree, then you must be admitted to the degree program, register for the class, and pass it with a certain minimum grade. Policies prescribe future behavior. Thus policies can be used to control future events. Exhibit 1–2 is an example of a federal policy taxpayers encounter every year.

(2) A manager can decide to reallocate *resources*. Resources include people, money, materials, technology, and time—more food, more police, more money, new equipment, a revised schedule.

(3) A manager can decide to reorganize—to change *organizational structure*—such as creating a new agency with new authorities—changing power

## Exhibit 1–2

**Example of a Policy as an IF-THEN Statement**

IF:

Your marital status at the end of 2006 was "married and living with your spouse," and:

- your filing status is "married filing jointly," and
- at the end of 2006 you and your spouse were under 65, and
- your gross income was at least $16,900,

THEN:

You must file a tax return.

*Source:* Department of the Treasury, Internal Revenue Service, *2006 1040 Instructions,* 2007.

and responsibility relationships. Purposeful public action—changing event outcomes—occurs through concerted action—that is, through the action and behavior of organizations.

(4) Finally, and perhaps most important, managers can decide to change their minds—to change their expectations against which they evaluate the present and the future.

Taken together, events, outcomes, data, expectations, and decisions about organizational power, resources, and policies are the critical elements by which managers affect our lives and work to control the future. Statistical analysis can be a useful, even integral, means of coping and functioning effectively in this world.

# CHAPTER 2

# What's the Problem? Problem Identification, Variables, and Measurement

Using statistical methods to address public problems basically involves the four steps listed in Exhibit 2–1: (1) problem identification, (2) problem setup, (3) computation, and (4) interpretation of results. The first step, problem identification, is often the most difficult. Not all public problems, even those that seemingly have a quantitative focus, are amenable to statistical analysis. And of those that are, there are many types—each requiring a specific statistical technique for analysis. The analyst is a diagnostician. Confronted with a complex set of symptoms, the analyst identifies the type of problem and selects the appropriate "treatment." This is done by following a diagnostic routine that leads to the correct problem identification. The principal diagnostic questions are these:

1. What are the units of analysis? How many units of analysis have been observed? How many cases—data records—are in the sample?
2. What kind of problem do we have: description, evaluation, or estimation?
3. What variables are being measured for each unit of analysis? How many variables are involved in the problem: one, two, or more than two?
4. What is the level of measurement for each variable in the problem: nominal, ordinal, or interval?

The answers to these questions will help identify particular types of problems and appropriate statistical methods.

The second step in the problem-solving process is *setup*. In this step the analyst acquires data, and organizes these data so that the statistical technique can be used. The third step is *computation*. This usually involves calculating the value of a *test statistic* using a mathematical formula. The final step is *interpretation of results*. Here we will refer back to the policy and management context of the problem and use the numeric *statistical* results to draw a conclusion that will influence our decisions.

## Exhibit 2–1

**The Problem-Solving Process**

1. Problem identification
   - What are the units of analysis?
   - What kind of problem is it?
   - How many variables are there?
   - What is the level of measurement for each variable?
2. Problem setup—Acquire data and apply statistical method.
3. Computation—Work out a numeric solution.
4. Interpretation of results—Interpret and apply the results to the problem at hand.

## 2.1 What Are the Units of Analysis? How Many Units of Analysis Have Been Observed?

An event is an opportunity for something to happen. Something occurs, behaves, changes, or is changed. This *something*, the focus of our attention, is called a **unit of analysis** or a **case**. It can be any item that can be separately and uniquely identified. It might be a person (a student, a woman, a tenant, a prison inmate), a place (a city, a street intersection, or a river), an object (a car, or a power plant), an organization (a school, a corporation, or a city administration), an incident (a birth, a traffic accident, or an election), or a time period (a day, a season, or a year). Data originate when we look at a unit of analysis and observe *what happened*.

A statistical **population** is a complete set of related units of analysis. The units of analysis in a statistical population have certain characteristics and attributes in common. Suppose, for example, we are interested in finding out what elected county policymaking officials think is the most pressing problem facing their counties. The relevant statistical population is *every* member of a county board of supervisors (or commissioners) in our state and we might proceed to mail a questionnaire to each one.

For various reasons not every questionnaire will be returned. A data file that contains fewer units of analysis than the number that comprise the statistical population is called a statistical **sample**. A sample is a subset of a population.

## 2.2 What Kind of Problem Is Presented?

There are three kinds of statistical problems: (1) description, (2) evaluation, and (3) estimation. Selection of an appropriate statistical method depends, in part, upon the kind of problem. Description problems *summarize* observations and define the perceived current state of affairs. Evaluation problems *compare observation against expectation*. Estimation problems use observations of past event outcomes to extrapolate or infer the characteristics of a total statistical population.

Suppose that we heard someone complain about the number of people receiving welfare—perhaps advocating a "workfare" program. How many public assistance (welfare) recipients can potentially work? [1] Description problems address inquiries such as "how many," "how much," "how fast," or "how often."

Suppose that an economic development commission is being proposed for your city. Do communities with such organizations do more to promote commercial and industrial development than other communities? This is an evaluation question. It seeks to compare observations against some expected result.

Suppose that a school district's contract with its teachers calls for a maximum of 31 students in a sixth grade classroom. How many classrooms and teachers will be needed for the sixth grade next year? This is an estimation question. The school district records include the enrollment in each grade, kindergarten through sixth, for the past twenty years. In estimation problems the analyst seeks to forecast the future on the basis of past observations.

## 2.3  *What Are the Variables? How Many Variables Are in the Problem?*

The types of characteristics, attributes, and occurrences that we observe—measure—about each unit of analysis are called **variables**. The observed units of analysis will have some common characteristics and attributes in the sense that they are all part of the specified statistical population or sample. Other characteristics and attributes will differ—vary—from one unit of analysis to the next.

For example, suppose that we focus our attention on driver license applications. The units of analysis are the persons who apply for a driver's license. When the license is issued some relevant information—variables—about the applicant will be obtained (name, address, date of birth).

A **value** is the specific observed measurement obtained for a variable. **Data** are recorded values. A **record** preserves the observations about each unit of analysis in the form of a *value* for each variable. The records about a number of related units of analysis comprise a *data file, data set*, or *data base*. All records in a data

---

[1]The Social Security Administration maintains summaries regarding the principal categories of public assistance funded by the federal government: Temporary Assistance to Needy Families (TANF, formerly Aid to Families with Dependent Children, AFDC). The Social Security Administration reported that during 2004 the number of TANF recipients averaged 4,738,000 per month of whom 3,595,000 (about 76 percent) were children. *Annual Statistical Supplement, 2005* (February 2006).

file have the same variables. The values for the respective variables will differ from one unit of analysis—one record—to the next.

Exhibit 2–2 shows a sample driver's license. It is a data record for one unit of analysis—one authorized driver in California—Mr. John J. Smith. What are the variables common to each driver's license and what are the unique values on this particular record?

The name, address, and identification number of every person who has been issued a driver's license in a given county comprise a data file (that is useful, for example, in selecting people for jury service). In fact, we could regard the state department of motor vehicles as an organization whose principal mission is to maintain the massive data file, with millions of records, of all licensed drivers and registered vehicles in the state.[2]

Here are a few other examples of events and data records:

■ Washington, DC operates cameras at more than 40 intersections that photograph the rear, and the license plate, of any cars that run red lights. Tickets carrying a $75 fine are sent to the vehicle's owner. Offenders may view their violation images and pay their fine online.

■ Illinois has a Gender and Racial Balanced Appointments Act. It provides that "All appointments to boards, commissions, committees and councils of the State created by the laws of this State and after the effective date of this Act shall be gender and racially balanced to the extent possible and to the extent that appointees are qualified to serve on those boards, commissions, committees and councils."[3] The planning commission in one city might have three female members, while another city may have none. The variable *number of female members* would have the values 3 and 0, respectively.

■ "Record snowfall buries New York City: 'Dangerous storm' wallops East Coast, snarls travel. . . . Central Park in New York City had recorded nearly 27 inches by about 4:15 p.m. Sunday, breaking a record of 26.4 inches set in December 1947, according to the National Weather Service."[4] The units of analysis are the snowstorms that occur from time to time during the winter. The variable of interest is the depth of snowfall from each storm.

■ The Consumer Confidence Survey, conducted for The Conference Board by the research company TNS, asks an adult in about 5,000 U.S. households every month to express his or her opinion regarding current business and employment

---

[2]Data files can be internally organized in different ways. For example, we might want a list of the names of everyone licensed to drive in a particular city—in alphabetical order—along with their address and identification number. In this example the variable *last name* was used to organize the data file. The cases were assembled in such a way that the values of the variable appear in ascending (alphabetical) order.

[3]5 ILCS 310/2 (2003).

[4]———, "Record snowfall buries New York City," *CNN.com*, February 12, 2006, www.cnn.com/2006/WEATHER/02/12/northeast.snow/

## Exhibit 2–2

**Example of a Record**

Look at your state-issued driver's license or identification card. This is the most common form of official identification in the United States. The REAL ID Act of 2005 effectively establishes the basis for a national identification card by prohibiting federal agencies from accepting a driver's license or state-issued identification that does not meet the requirements of the Act. In March 2007, the Department of Homeland Security proposed a list of variables that must be included on each state-issued driver's license or identity card: (1) Full legal name; (2) Address of principal residence; (3) Date of birth; (4) Gender; (5) Driver's license or identification card number; (6) Issue date; and (7) Expiration date.

**CALIFORNIA**
DRIVER LICENSE

Z1234567
ISSUED: 10-08-06    EXPIRES: 11-09-11
JOHN JAMES SMITH
5555 POBLANO RD
APT E
SAN FRANCISCO    CA    94102-0000
SEX: M    HAIR: BLK    EYES: BRN
HT: 5-09    WT: 175
DOB: 11-09-75
CLASS: C    RSTR: NONE
*John J Smith*

**Required by REAL ID Act of 2005**

| | |
|---|---|
| Full legal name | John James Smith |
| Street address | 5555 Poblano Rd. Apt. E |
| City address | San Francisco |
| State address | California |
| Zip code address | 94102-0000 |
| Date of birth | November 9, 1975 |
| Gender | Male |
| Issue date | October 8, 2006 |
| Expiration date | November 9, 2011 |
| Identification number | Z1234567 |

**Optional**

| | |
|---|---|
| Eye color | Brown |
| Hair color | Black |
| Height | 5 ft 9 inches |
| Weight | 175 pounds |
| Class | C |
| Restrictions | None |

*Source for photo:* © Rui Vale de Sousa/ShutterStock, Inc.

conditions, as well as expectations for business and employment conditions, and family income over the next six months. Respondents answer *positive*, *neutral*, or *negative*.

## 2.4   What Is the Level of Measurement for Each Variable?

Values for the variables of interest are obtained by *measurement* using a transactions process designed by managers. The specific detailed step-by-step procedure by which values are obtained and recorded for each variable is called the **operational definition** of that variable. When we implement the operational definition, we *measure* the variable. Thus, *observation* is *measurement*.

The essence of measurement is classification. There are basically three ways in which the values of a variable can be classified. These **levels of measurement** are called *nominal*, *ordinal*, and *interval*.

A **nominal** level of measurement classifies event outcomes by unique categories. Think of bins, each labeled with a different integer value (a whole number such as 1, 2, 3). The numbers simply identify the discrete categories. The cases are sorted by type when they are placed in one or another category. No case can be placed in more than one bin and there are enough bins to represent all possible categories, so that no case is left unclassified.

For example, the Home Mortgage Disclosure Act requires that financial institutions (lenders) report the racial characteristics and gender of loan applicants. The data are obtained by responses to the following statement on a loan application:

> The following information is requested by the Federal government for certain types of loans related to a dwelling, in order to monitor the lender's compliance with equal credit opportunity, fair housing and home mortgage disclosure laws. You are not required to furnish this information, but are encouraged to do so. The law provides that a lender may neither discriminate on the basis of this information, nor on whether you choose to furnish it. However, if you choose not to furnish it, under federal regulations this lender is required to note race and sex on the basis of visual observation or surname. If you do not wish to furnish the above information, please check the box below.
>
> ☐ I do not wish to furnish this information.
>
> Race or national origin.
> ☐ White
> ☐ Black/African American
> ☐ Asian
> ☐ American Indian/Alaskan Native
> ☐ Native Hawaiian/ Other Pacific islander

☐ American Indian /Alaskan Native and White
☐ Asian and White
☐ Black/African American and White
☐ American Indian/Alaskan Native and Black/African American
☐ Other Multi Racial
☐ Hispanic

Sex

☐ Male
☐ Female

Here are some other variables that have a nominal level of measurement with only a few categories or bins:[5]

Marital status
Region of the country
Race/ethnicity
Religion
Income tax bracket
Occupation
Blood type

Classifying a variable into only two possible categories is called a **dichotomous** nominal level of measurement. The dichotomy describes either opposites (1 = *yes* versus 0 = *no*; 1 = *male* versus 2 = *female*) or the presence versus absence of a certain characteristic or attribute (1 = *65 years of age or older* versus 0 = *not 65 years of age or older*).

An **ordinal** level of measurement classifies event outcomes by ranked categories. Like a nominal level of measurement, the cases can be classified into discrete categories. But there is also an implicit order among the categories. The cases in one category possess more or less of some quality associated with the variable being observed than the cases in another category. Officers in the U.S. Army, for instance, can be classified thus:

1 = General
2 = Colonel
3 = Lieutenant Colonel
4 = Major
5 = Captain
6 = First Lieutenant
7 = Second Lieutenant

---

[5]Some variables, such as social security number or place of birth, can potentially have thousands or millions of bins.

The variable here is military title, but the implicit underlying order of the values is increasing authority and responsibility.[6] The ordinal value is an index to the "relative amount" of the variable being observed. The integer indicates a *more than* or *less than* placement among the observed events. We can say that a particular value is "greater than" or "less than" another value—but we cannot say "how much" the difference is. Some variables that may have an ordinal level of measurement include the following:

A person's health status
Teaching ability
Moody's rating of municipal bonds
Education (highest diploma or degree attained)
Opinion
Skill
Interest in statistics
State of the economy
Degree of fire protection in a community
Effectiveness of library services
Safety of public mass transit
Impact of cattle grazing in a wilderness area
Water quality
Military strength
Extent of discrimination in employment

An **interval** level of measurement classifies a characteristic, attribute, or outcome on a continuous scale. The scale has an arbitrary zero starting reference point. Because of the scale we can determine how much more or less one value is than another. Theoretically a continuous scale has an infinite number of fractional values. There is a fixed difference between each consecutive major measurement unit on the scale. We could use a clock to measure elapsed time in seconds; a thermometer to measure temperature in degrees Fahrenheit; or a ruler to measure distance in inches. The key to an interval level of measurement is the uniform measurement scale. Zero time on a stopwatch does not mean nothing has happened before; 0°F does not mean a complete absence of heat. An interval level of measurement permits us to make relative rather than absolute comparisons between the values of different cases. In other words, we can determine the magnitude of the difference between two values. Imagine two cars speeding down the highway. If we are in one of the cars, we can measure the relative speed of the

---

[6]High ranks are often assigned low numbers; the team that wins the greatest number of games is "number one" and "3" means "finished in third place."

other and say "It's going 5 miles per hour faster." Some variables with an interval level of measurement include:

Dow Jones Average
Consumer price index
Time of day

A fourth level of measurement, called a **ratio** level of measurement, classifies event outcomes on a continuous scale that has a natural zero origin. A zero measurement indicates a complete absence of the characteristic or attribute being measured. For example, the Kelvin scale of temperature uses Celsius degrees as its scale but starts the measurement at "absolute zero" (equivalent to minus 273.15°C), a point at which there is no heat. If we stood at the side of a highway, we could measure the speed of one car as 60 mph and the speed of another as

## *Exhibit 2–3*

**Text Outline by Kind of Problem**

| Description methods | | |
|---|---|---|
| **One-variable problems** | | **Two-variable problems** |
| Chapter 3 | | Chapter 7 |

| Evaluation methods for one-variable problems | | |
|---|---|---|
| Level of measurement | | |
| *Nominal* | *Ordinal* | *Interval* |
| Chapter 4 | Chapter 5 | Chapter 5 |

| Evaluation methods for two-variable problems | | | |
|---|---|---|---|
| **Level of measurement for second variable** | Level of measurement for first variable | | |
| | *Nominal* | *Ordinal* | *Interval* |
| Nominal | Chapter 8 | — | — |
| Ordinal | Chapter 9 | Chapter 10 | Chapter 10 |
| Interval | Chapter 11 | — | Chapter 12 |

| Estimation methods | | |
|---|---|---|
| **One-variable problems** | | **Two-variable problems** |
| Chapter 6 | | Chapter 13 |

65 mph. Further, we can divide the speed of the second car by that of the first, creating a ratio, and say that the speed of the second car is 1.083 that of the first. For the purposes of problem identification and determining appropriate statistical methods, this text terms a variable as "interval" if it has either an interval or ratio level of measurement.

## Summary

Statistical analysis starts with problem identification. We need to identify each problem by *kind* (description, evaluation, or estimation), the *number of variables* (one, two, or more than two), and the level of measurement for each variable (nominal, ordinal, or interval).

In this text the principal organization is by number of variables—starting with description, evaluation, and prediction problems involving only one variable before proceeding to two-variable problems and, finally, problems with more than two variables. Exhibit 2–3 presents an outline of the text by *kind of problem*.

## Homework Exercises

**2-1**    Provide an operational definition (in terms of a specific management transaction) and specify the level of measurement for each of these variables:

| | |
|---|---|
| height | efficiency |
| temperature | inflation |
| race/ethnicity | time of day |
| gender | date |
| income tax bracket | state of the economy |
| age | degree of fire protection in a community |
| marital status | effectiveness of library services |
| region of the country | safety of public mass transit |
| K–12 educational progress | impact of cattle grazing in a wilderness area |
| income | water quality |
| source of income | military strength |
| intelligence | discrimination in employment |
| education | citizenship |
| occupation | a person's health status |
| skill | teaching ability |
| place of birth | rainfall |
| interest in statistics | highway traffic volume |
| a hospital's daily "census" | urban sprawl |

| Variable | Possible operational definition (not necessarily the "best," or most consistent, accurate, or "valid" measure) | Level of measurement |
|---|---|---|
| Height | Distance from the "floor" | Interval |
| Temperature | Thermometer (mercury or digital) | Interval (°F or °C) |
| Race/ethnicity | Skin color; surname | Nominal |
| Gender | First name; length of hair | Nominal |
| Income tax bracket | Entry on 1040 income tax | Ordinal |
| Age | Birth certificate | Ratio |
| Marital status | Ring on finger | Nominal |
| Region of the country | State | Nominal |
| K–12 educational progress | Average test score, such as the National Assessment of Academic Progress | Interval |
| Income[1] | Entry on W-2 form | Interval or ordinal |
| Source of income | Entry on 1040 income tax return | Nominal |
| Intelligence | IQ test | Interval |
| Education | Diploma or degree; years of formal schooling | Ordinal or ratio |
| Occupation | Entry on 1040 income tax return | Nominal |
| Skill | Test | Ordinal or interval |
| Place of birth | Birth certificate | Nominal |
| Interest in statistics | Course enrollment | Ordinal |
| Hospital's daily "census" | Occupied beds | Ratio |
| Efficiency | Output/input | Interval |

*(continued)*

---

[1]Sometimes a variable's level of measurement can be ambiguous. *Income* is a good example. At first it may seem to have a ratio level of measurement. We have probably all had the experience at one time of having no money in our pockets. But a ratio level of measurement means that one additional dollar is of equal value to every person. Some people in our country live from one monthly check to the next. An increase in income of $100 per month may mean the difference between renting an apartment and being homeless. But an increase in monthly income from $4,000 to $4,100 per month does not have the same importance. Perhaps income, then, should be regarded as an ordinal level of measurement. Therefore, to determine a variable's level of measurement we need to examine both the operational definition of the variable and the context of the problem.

| Variable | Possible operational definition (not necessarily the "best," or most consistent, accurate, or "valid" measure) | Level of measurement |
|---|---|---|
| Inflation | Change in consumer-price-index | Interval |
| Time of day | Clock | Interval |
| Date | Calendar | Interval |
| State of the economy | Interest rates; Dow Jones Average; Unemployment rate | Ordinal or interval |
| Fire protection | Insurance Service Organization rating | Ordinal |
| Effectiveness of library services | Volumes in the library | Ordinal |
| Public transit safety | Incidents per 100,000 miles | Ratio |
| Impact of cattle grazing | Comparison: number of seedlings—grazed v. ungrazed areas | Interval or ratio |
| Water quality | Chemical concentrations | Ratio |
| Military strength | Relative size of armed forces; success on the battlefield | Ordinal |
| Discrimination in employment | Proportion of minorities | Interval |
| Citizenship | Birth certificate, passport, or other approved document | Nominal |
| Health status | Physical exam | Ordinal |
| Teaching ability | Student assessment; classroom observation | Ordinal |
| Rainfall | Rain gauge | Interval |
| Highway traffic volume | Metering device on highway | Ratio |
| Urban sprawl | Residential density | Ordinal or interval |

**2-2**  Define the concepts efficient, effective, and economic. How are they different? How would you measure each one?

Efficiency can be defined as a ratio of output results divided by input resources— "bang" for the "buck." The analyst needs to measure both resource commitment and outcomes. Effectiveness can be defined as a goal accomplishment. The analyst needs to identify project milestones and determine whether they have been achieved. Economy can be defined as least cost. The analyst needs to identify project alternatives and their respective costs in order to determine the minimum.

**2-3**  What formal, written policies (rules for behavior) did you comply with today? Look up the specific policy statements in the appropriate book or compendium.

Today, my wife and I went to the symphony. We have a couple of children. One of the rules is that the baby sitter must be over 16 years of age. I adhered to most of the traffic laws while driving to the city—sometimes driving faster than 55 mph. Admission required a ticket (and so forth).

**2-4**  List all the transactions that monitored or influenced your life today. What data were recorded?

For example, I made a cell phone call, parked my car in a parking garage, and ate at a restaurant. In all cases a record was made and I paid for the service.

**2-5**  What is the role of the computer in the management process?

The computer's role is to aggregate data. This may include several intermediate steps in between individual transactions generating data items and eventual comparison of observation against expectation.

**2-6**  Think about a particular organization or job with which you are very familiar. Perhaps it is a police department, a high school, the intensive care ward of a hospital, your local chapter of the American Society for Public Administration, or your church or synagogue. Write down a definition of either (a) productivity or (b) cost-effectiveness for the organization or job you picked. Now develop an operational definition for this same concept. Specify the level of measurement. Provide an example.

In some universities productivity is measured by the number of full-time-equivalent students enrolled or the number of degrees awarded each year. Whether this is a measure of the quality of education is another question. Cost-effectiveness is student/faculty ratio.

**2-7**  Amazon.com provides a comprehensive catalog of books. What are the records? What are the field names? What are the key field names?

The records are the individual books—displayed as unique web pages. The field names are author, title, subject, publisher, ISBN number. . . . Key field names refer to all the ways the web site can be searched to find a particular record. These include author, title, and subject.

**2-8**  Look at your last public utility bill for electricity or natural gas. Specify the level of measurement of the variables "account number," "meter number," "current meter reading," "prior meter reading," "rate schedule," "total amount due." How is the value of the variable "total amount due" obtained?

Account number, nominal; meter number, nominal; current meter reading, interval; prior meter reading, interval; rate schedule, nominal for type of service and ordinal for categorical class of amount of electricity or gas used; total amount due, ratio. Only the difference counts. Given a particular type of service, such as residential, locate the appropriate ordinal group that this difference falls in, multiply the applicable price for that energy use group by the difference in meter readings, add any past due amount and taxes, subtract any credits.

**2-9**  Double-check, explain, and verify every value of every variable on your most recent communications/entertainment bill (telephone, cell phone, cable, satellite dish, or Internet). (Refer to the telephone directory or your provider's web site.)

Some variables include type of service (such as Internet or text messaging), time of day, length of call, and location.

**2-10**  Consider the following management processes.

**a.**  Which of the following management processes are attempting to change the status quo?

**b.**  Which are attempting to maintain the status quo?

**c.**  What is the "status quo" that public administrators are attempting to change or maintain?

**d.**  What would a public administrator want to observe in order to determine whether change either did or did not occur?

| | |
|---|---|
| affirmative action | Head Start |
| price supports for milk products | welfare |
| zoning | urban redevelopment |
| solar energy tax credits | historic preservation |
| mail delivery | |

a. These management processes are attempting to change the status quo: affirmative action, Head Start, urban redevelopment, tax credits, historic preservation (if restoration).

b. These management processes are attempting to maintain the status quo: zoning, mail delivery, price supports, welfare, historic preservation.

c. For example, affirmative action management processes attempt to change the status quo of disparities and imbalances between the gender or ethnic makeup of the employed work force, on the one hand, and the potential qualified applicant pool, on the other.

d. For example, again with respect to affirmative action, a public administrator might observe the gender and ethnic makeup of the applicants and people hired for certain positions, say before and after implementation of new recruitment efforts or revised position requirements.

**2-11** Is a telephone directory a data file? Explain.

Yes. It is a set of related records.

**2-12** List the goals and criteria that might be used to evaluate the following programs— provide an operational definition.

a. Alternative sentencing for misdemeanors (that is, community service or rehabilitation treatment rather than jail).

b. Recycling program in which a truck is used for weekly curbside pickup of newspapers, glass, and metal cans.

a. Rate of re-arrest within the following year or two, for same or similar offenses, for people sentenced to jail v. alternative sentences.

b. Amount of recyclable refuse collected divided by the number of households that could potentially participate.

**2-13** Which of the following statements are "policies"?

a. A police department's motto: "To serve. To protect. To defend."

b. The fine for an overdue DVD is 10 cents per day.

c. Instructions on a fire alarm: "In case of fire. Break glass. Pull lever."

d. The fine for driving through an intersection against a red light is $253.

**e.** Should this product fail to be in good working order, due to a defect in materials or workmanship, during a period of 90 days from the date of purchase, the company will, at its option, repair or replace this product at no additional charge.

**f.** Good faith efforts shall be made to eliminate barriers that obstruct access by people with physical handicaps to public facilities.

**g.** "The average human being has an inherent dislike of work and will avoid it if he can. Because of this human characteristic of dislike of work, most people must be coerced, controlled, directed, threatened with punishment to get them to put forth adequate effort toward the achievement of organizational objectives."

**h.** A minimum grade point average of 3.00 out of possible 4.00 is required for the award of a Masters degree from this program.

**i.** Our goal is to encourage community participation in the planning and decision making process.

---

| | |
|---|---|
| Policies: | b, c, d, e, h |
| Goals or statement of intent: | a, f, g, i |

---

**2-14** What data (variables) do you need in order to test these statements? For each statement, identify each variable, provide an operational definition for each variable, and specify each variable's level of measurement.

**a.** From a public management text: "Personnel time and costs are the major input to departmental budgeting."

**b.** From a grant application by an MPA program: "More than eighty percent of the students who have participated in the Department's internship program have accepted full-time professional positions in the public sector."

**c.** From a newspaper article summarizing the results of a research study: Civil juries in product liability cases granted higher awards in Chicago than in San Francisco.

**d.** From the Federal Aviation Administration: "the airways are unequivocally safe . . . and indeed becoming safer."

---

**a.** Number of employees assigned to a department; time spent by each employee on a project; salary or hourly rate of each employee.

**b.** Participation in internship program; subsequent full-time employment in the public sector.

**c.** Place; amount of jury award; type of case.

**d.** Number of deaths and injuries per 100,000 miles traveled by air carriers.

**2-15** Here is a question taken from a survey asking citizens about municipal services. What are the variables and what are the values?

> The following is a list of problems that could occur in any neighborhood. Please indicate whether each problem listed is a very serious problem, somewhat serious problem, only a small problem, or not a problem at all for your neighborhood.
>
> Noise
> Junked or abandoned cars
> Overgrown vacant lots
> Abandoned houses
> Stray animals
> Rats, mice, or other rodents
> Traffic
> Surface of the streets
> Burglaries
> Vandalism

The variables are the inquiries about the perceived severity of each mentioned problem. There are ten variables: noise, junked or abandoned cars, overgrown vacant lots, etc. Each variable (inquiry) can take on one of four possible values: (1) very serious problem, (2) somewhat serious problem, (3) small problem, or (4) not a problem.

**2-16** A data file in a public health dental clinic includes these variables for each patient: name, street address, city, state, zip code, birth date, home telephone number, type of dental insurance, dates of dental treatments, type of dental treatments, and other medical prescriptions, ailments, and treatments.

   **a.** Suppose an analyst wants to determine how many patients reside out of the county. What variables are needed?

   **b.** Suppose an analyst wants to contact every patient due for a six-month check-up. What variables are needed?

   **c.** In areas where the public water supply is not fluoridated, pediatricians often prescribe fluoride pills to children as a public health measure to improve tooth development and reduce tooth decay. Suppose an analyst wants to determine how many patients under 10 years old have received such treatments. What variables are needed?

   **a.** City or zip code.

   **b.** Name, street address, city, state, zip code, home telephone number, and the last date of dental treatment.

    **c.** Birth date and other medical prescriptions/treatments (although this is an unreliable operational definition because the prescription of fluoride tablets is so common that parents may easily forget to enter it as part of the child's medical history—unusual things are more likely to be remembered than the commonplace).

# CHAPTER 3

# Who, What, When, and How Much? One-Variable Description

| | |
|---|---|
| Kind of problem | *Description* |
| Number of variables | *One* |
| Level of measurement | *Nominal, ordinal, or interval* |

S tatistical problems involve (1) description, (2) evaluation, or (3) estimation. Statistical problems also involve (1) one variable, (2) two variables, or (3) more than two variables. And each of these variables may have either a (1) nominal, (2) ordinal, or (3) interval (or ratio) level of measurement.

Each combination of purpose, number of variables, and level(s) of measurement is a different type of problem and calls for a different analytical method. This chapter starts with the simplest combination—description problems with one variable. The next two chapters deal with one-variable evaluation and one-variable prediction problems.

Although any event has many characteristics and attributes, sometimes an analyst is only interested in a single variable. In effect, each event is seen with blinders on. One and only one characteristic or attribute is measured. Perhaps an analyst is interested in compliance with a local ordinance establishing a 10 p.m. curfew for minors. Although the people on Main Street can be described by such variables as height, weight, sex, home address, occupation, income, or ethnicity, we are only interested in distinguishing one person from another by age—separating minors (say under the age of 18) from adults.

Description is like a snapshot. People and objects are observed at a particular instant in time. Using the photo the objects can be counted and located with respect to one another. This summary of observed events is called a *distribution*. The descriptive picture is incomplete. It does not include every event, person, or incident that comprises the status quo. It does not include every aspect of every event that we are interested in. Nor does it specify how or why the condition occurred or how it might change from one moment to the next. However, with statistical techniques this partial picture is an indicator of the usual or typical state of affairs.

One variable—a particular characteristic or attribute—can classify the observed events into categories or "types." There are three parts to the complete description of this variable. (1) The analyst needs to *summarize* the data so that observations can be discussed without having to list the measured value for each and every case. (2) The analyst wants to know a typical value—an **average**—a point of *central tendency* among the observed values. (3) The analyst wants to know, *How typical is "typical?"*—the extent to which the data are spread out from the point of central tendency—the **dispersion** of the data. Both central tendency and dispersion need to be reported in order to completely describe a variable.

The methods for summarizing data and describing central tendency and dispersion differ by the variable's level of measurement. The outline in Exhibit 3–1 will be a road map for the rest of the chapter. If the variable has a nominal level of measurement, the data will be summarized by a frequency table or bar chart, using a statistic called the mode to describe its central tendency and another statistic, the relative frequency of the mode, to describe its dispersion. A frequency table or bar chart can also be used to summarize the data for a variable having an ordinal level of measurement. The central tendency is indicated by the median and the dispersion by the interquartile range. An intervally measured variable is summarized by a **grouped frequency table**, a **one-way scatterplot**, a **box plot**, or a special kind of bar chart called a **histogram**. The central tendency and dispersion of an interval variable are described by the *mean* and the *standard deviation*.

## Exhibit 3–1

**One-Variable Description**

| | Level of measurement | | |
|---|---|---|---|
| **Description** | *Nominal* | *Ordinal* | *Interval* |
| Summary of observations | Frequency table<br>Bar chart<br>Dot chart<br>Pie chart | Frequency table<br>Bar chart<br>Dot chart | Grouped frequency table<br>Histogram<br>Box plot<br>One-way scatterplot |
| Central tendency | Mode | Median | Mean<br>Median |
| Dispersion | Relative frequency of the mode | Interquartile range | Standard deviation |

## 3.1   One Variable, Nominal Level of Measurement

How prevalent is the mayor-council form of city government? The problem requires the description of one variable—one observable characteristic or attribute. To address this problem, we should begin with the set of diagnostic questions:

*What are the units of analysis?*
*How many units of analysis have been observed?*
*How many cases (data records) are in the sample?*

The individual event that interests the analyst is the adoption of a particular form of government by a city. How often do different outcomes of this event occur? *Cities* are the units of analysis. For this example the related events—defined by size, space, and time—is the set of all cities with more than 5,000 residents in the state of Washington in 2004. These characteristics fix the scope of the inquiry. That is, they define the **statistical population** (cities in Washington)—the statistical **sample** (cities with a population more than 5,000 in 2004)—and the **operational definition** (the legal framework for policymaking). In 2004 there were 106 cities in Washington with a population over 5,000.

*What kind of problem is presented?*

This is a description problem. We want to know *how often* the mayor-council form of government is observed among the cities in Washington and *how prevalent* the mayor-council form is in relationship to the other possible forms of government.

*What are the variables that are being measured for each unit of analysis?*
*How many variables are involved in the problem: one, two, or more than two?*

Each city has a local government. Although the local governments may differ in many ways, we are interested in only characteristic—one variable—the *form of government*.

*What is the level of measurement for each variable in the problem: nominal, ordinal, or interval?*

*Form of government* is a **categorical variable**—meaning that there are only a limited number of possible forms of government that each city could choose. Among cities in Washington the values for the variable *form of government* are *mayor-council, council-manager*, and *commission*. Each of these designations can be represented by a numeric value. The mayor-council form of government category can be called category 1; the council-manager form of government category 2; and the commission form of government category 3. The numbers are only labels—a summary *name* given to each value and its operational definition. The available choices are mutually exclusive—each city has one, and only one, form of government. Thus, this variable has a nominal level of measurement.

A **data file** lists the measured, recorded observations of a set of related events. Exhibit 3–2 presents the data file for the 106 cities in Washington with more than

## *Exhibit 3–2*

**Data File: Form of Government in Cities over 5,000 Population in Washington**

| | | Form of government | |
| | | --- | --- |
| **City/Town** | **Population** | *Category* | *Numeric code* |
| Seattle | 573,000 | mayor-council | 1 |
| Spokane | 198,700 | mayor-council | 1 |
| Tacoma | 198,100 | council-manager | 2 |
| Vancouver | 154,800 | council-manager | 2 |
| Bellevue | 115,500 | council-manager | 2 |
| Everett | 97,500 | mayor-council | 1 |
| Federal Way | 85,800 | council-manager | 2 |
| Spokane Valley | 85,010 | council-manager | 2 |
| Kent | 84,920 | mayor-council | 1 |
| Yakima | 79,480 | council-manager | 2 |
| Bellingham | 72,320 | mayor-council | 1 |
| Kennewick | 60,410 | council-manager | 2 |
| Lakewood | 58,850 | council-manager | 2 |
| Renton | 56,840 | mayor-council | 1 |
| Shoreline | 52,500 | council-manager | 2 |
| Redmond | 47,600 | mayor-council | 1 |
| Auburn | 47,470 | mayor-council | 1 |
| Kirkland | 45,740 | council-manager | 2 |
| Pasco | 44,190 | council-manager | 2 |
| Richland | 43,520 | council-manager | 2 |
| Olympia | 43,330 | council-manager | 2 |
| Edmonds | 39,860 | mayor-council | 1 |
| Sammamish | 38,640 | council-manager | 2 |
| Puyallup | 35,830 | council-manager | 2 |
| Longview | 35,430 | council-manager | 2 |
| Lynnwood | 34,830 | mayor-council | 1 |
| Bremerton | 34,580 | mayor-council | 1 |
| Lacey | 33,180 | council-manager | 2 |
| Burien | 31,040 | council-manager | 2 |
| Bothell | 31,000 | council-manager | 2 |
| University Place | 30,980 | council-manager | 2 |

*(continued)*

## Exhibit 3–2

**Data File: Form of Government in Cities over 5,000 Population in Washington** *(continued)*

| City/Town | Population | Form of government | |
|---|---|---|---|
| | | *Category* | *Numeric code* |
| Walla Walla | 30,630 | council-manager | 2 |
| Marysville | 29,460 | mayor-council | 1 |
| Wenatchee | 29,320 | mayor-council | 1 |
| Des Moines | 28,960 | council-manager | 2 |
| Mount Vernon | 28,210 | mayor-council | 1 |
| Pullman | 26,590 | mayor-council | 1 |
| SeaTac | 25,140 | council-manager | 2 |
| Bainbridge Island | 22,200 | mayor-council | 1 |
| Oak Harbor | 21,720 | mayor-council | 1 |
| Mercer Island | 21,710 | council-manager | 2 |
| Mountlake Terrace | 20,390 | council-manager | 2 |
| Mukilteo | 19,360 | mayor-council | 1 |
| Kenmore | 19,290 | council-manager | 2 |
| Port Angeles | 18,640 | council-manager | 2 |
| Maple Valley | 17,870 | council-manager | 2 |
| Tukwila | 17,110 | mayor-council | 1 |
| Issaquah | 17,060 | mayor-council | 1 |
| Ellensburg | 16,700 | council-manager | 2 |
| Covington | 16,610 | council-manager | 2 |
| Aberdeen | 16,450 | mayor-council | 1 |
| Moses Lake | 16,340 | council-manager | 2 |
| Monroe | 15,920 | mayor-council | 1 |
| Anacortes | 15,700 | mayor-council | 1 |
| Camas | 15,460 | mayor-council | 1 |
| Centralia | 15,340 | council-manager | 2 |
| Arlington | 14,980 | mayor-council | 1 |
| Battle Ground | 14,960 | council-manager | 2 |
| Sunnyside | 14,710 | council-manager | 2 |
| Bonney Lake | 14,370 | mayor-council | 1 |
| Mill Creek | 14,320 | council-manager | 2 |
| Tumwater | 12,950 | mayor-council | 1 |
| Lake Forest Park | 12,730 | mayor-council | 1 |
| Kelso | 11,820 | council-manager | 2 |
| Washougal | 11,350 | mayor-council | 1 |
| Enumclaw | 11,190 | mayor-council | 1 |
| Lynden | 10,480 | mayor-council | 1 |
| West Richland | 10,210 | mayor-council | 1 |
| Woodinville | 10,140 | council-manager | 2 |

*(continued)*

## Exhibit 3–2

**Data File: Form of Government in Cities over 5,000 Population in Washington (continued)**

| City/Town | Population | Form of government | |
|---|---|---|---|
| | | *Category* | *Numeric code* |
| Cheney | 10,070 | mayor-council | 1 |
| Sedro-Woolley | 9,800 | mayor-council | 1 |
| Ferndale | 9,750 | mayor-council | 1 |
| Edgewood | 9,460 | council-manager | 2 |
| Toppenish | 9,000 | council-manager | 2 |
| Sumner | 8,940 | mayor-council | 1 |
| Newcastle | 8,890 | council-manager | 2 |
| Hoquiam | 8,875 | mayor-council | 1 |
| Port Townsend | 8,745 | council-manager | 2 |
| Shelton | 8,735 | commission | 3 |
| Grandview | 8,705 | mayor-council | 1 |
| Snohomish | 8,700 | council-manager | 2 |
| College Place | 8,690 | mayor-council | 1 |
| East Wenatchee | 8,300 | mayor-council | 1 |
| Port Orchard | 8,250 | mayor-council | 1 |
| Burlington | 7,550 | mayor-council | 1 |
| Poulsbo | 7,450 | mayor-council | 1 |
| Clarkston | 7,280 | mayor-council | 1 |
| Lake Stevens | 7,185 | mayor-council | 1 |
| Chehalis | 6,990 | council-manager | 2 |
| Ephrata | 6,930 | mayor-council | 1 |
| Gig Harbor | 6,765 | mayor-council | 1 |
| Selah | 6,740 | mayor-council | 1 |
| Brier | 6,475 | mayor-council | 1 |
| Normandy Park | 6,385 | council-manager | 2 |
| Snoqualmie | 6,345 | mayor-council | 1 |
| Steilacoom | 6,175 | mayor-council | 1 |
| Othello | 6,120 | mayor-council | 1 |
| Milton | 6,100 | mayor-council | 1 |
| Fircrest | 6,080 | council-manager | 2 |
| Pacific | 5,770 | mayor-council | 1 |
| Union Gap | 5,695 | mayor-council | 1 |
| Duvall | 5,595 | mayor-council | 1 |
| DuPont | 5,410 | mayor-council | 1 |
| Quincy | 5,265 | mayor-council | 1 |
| Liberty Lake | 5,255 | mayor-council | 1 |
| Prosser | 5,045 | mayor-council | 1 |

*Source:* Municipal Research and Services Center of Washington, Seattle, Washington
www.mrsc.org/cityprofiles/citylist.aspx

5,000 residents. Note that the data file is structured so that the data are listed sequentially by another variable—*population*. This is a convenient but not essential aspect of the data file. It eases the task of creating the data file and checking the correctness of the observations.

Mayor-council:      An elected council serves as the legislative body with a separately elected head of government.

Council-manager:      The mayor and the council make policy and an appointed manager is responsible for the administration of the city.

Commission:      A board of elected commissioners serves as the legislative body and each commissioner is also responsible for administration of one or more departments.

*How prevalent is the mayor-council form of government?* The 106 observations are summarized by classifying the cities according to *form of government* and counting the number of cities in each category. The result is a **frequency distribution**—a count of the number of times each value of the variable occurs in a data set. The frequency distribution is shown by means of a **frequency table**. Exhibit 3–3 presents a frequency table for these data. The table lists the *number* of Washington cities having each of the three possible values of *form of government*. The number of observations of each value is also called the **absolute frequency**. Sixty cities in Washington have the *mayor-council* form of government.

*Prevalency* requires that the absolute frequency for each value be expressed as a proportion of the total number of observations. This proportion is called the **relative frequency**. The frequency table lists the relative frequency of each value. Each relative frequency is found by dividing the absolute frequency count for the value by the total count of observations in the data file. The relative frequencies can be expressed as percentages by multiplying each proportion by 100%. The

## *Exhibit 3–3*

**Frequency Table: Form of Government, Washington Cities over 5,000 Population**

| Value | Form of government | Absolute frequency (number of observations) | Relative frequency | |
|---|---|---|---|---|
| | | | *Proportion* | *Percentage* |
| 1 | Mayor-Council | 60 | 0.566 | 56.6% |
| 2 | Council-Manager | 45 | 0.425 | 42.5 |
| 3 | Commission | 1 | 0.009 | 0.9 |
| Total | | 106 | 1.000 | 100.0% |

*Source:* Municipal Research and Services Center of Washington, Seattle, Washington
http://www.mrsc.org/cityprofiles/citylist.aspx

prevalence—the relative frequency—of the mayor-council form of government among cities in Washington is 56.6%.

$$\text{Relative frequency of the mayor-council form of government} = \frac{60}{106} = 0.566$$

A **bar chart** is a common graphic technique for depicting the absolute frequency distribution for one variable having a nominal level of measurement. Each category has a separate bar. The length of each bar against a one-dimensional scale indicates absolute frequency (see Exhibit 3–4). The chart may be oriented so that the bars are either horizontal or vertical. A horizontal bar chart provides more space for labeling the nominal values. The same color or fill pattern should be used throughout. (However, if the frequency of one category is of particular interest, it can be highlighted by a contrasting color or pattern.) The frequency scale should begin at 0 and have no breaks. The overall size of the chart and number of values are the principal determinants of the width and spacing of the bars. In general, the spacing between the bars should be about half the width of the bars. The nominal categories can be arranged in the chart so that the bars are arrayed from largest to smallest. This technique helps us perceive small differences in the absolute frequency between several categories.

## *Exhibit 3–4*

**Bar Chart: Form of Government in Cities over 5,000 Population in State of Washington**

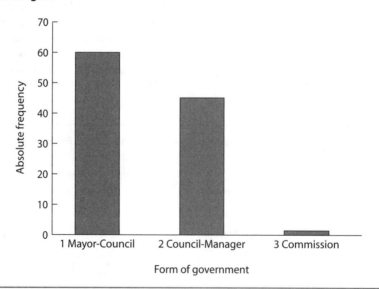

*Source:* Municipal Research and Services Center of Washington, Seattle, Washington
http://www.mrsc.org/cityprofiles/citylist.aspx

## *Exhibit 3–5*

**Dot Chart: Form of Government, Washington Cities over 5,000 Population**

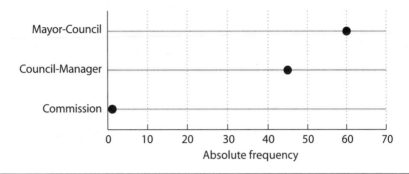

An improved display is the **dot chart**. In this display a bold dot along a faint line indicates the absolute frequency and each data value is given equal visual emphasis (see Exhibit 3–5).

*Mayor-council* is the most frequently occurring value of *form of government* for cities in Washington. This statistic is called the **mode**. But how typical is it? The relative frequency table indicates the dispersion of the distribution. The relative frequency for *mayor-council* of 56.6% indicates that other forms of government are also important (especially *council-manager* with a relative frequency of

## *Exhibit 3–6*

**Pie Chart: Form of Government, Washington Cities over 5,000 Population**

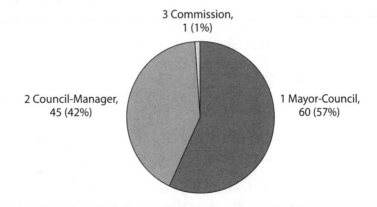

*Source:* Municipal Research and Services Center of Washington, Seattle, Washington
http://www.mrsc.org/cityprofiles/citylist.aspx

42.4%). For a variable with a nominal level of measurement, the **relative frequency of the mode** is the summary indicator of dispersion.

A **pie chart** shows the relative frequency distribution of a variable having several nominal categories. A circle depicts the entire sample. The relative frequency of each nominal category is shown as a slice of this figure, as in Exhibit 3–6. The eye is drawn to the nominal category having the largest relative frequency (the mode). In drawing a pie chart each slice should be labeled with its nominal value and relative frequency (rather than using a legend). The number of units of analysis (sample size) should be indicated in the title so that the reader can reproduce the absolute frequency distribution if needed. The pie chart identifies the modal category and conveys a general sense of the dispersion in the distribution. This, and more, information is shown just as easily, and more accurately, in a frequency table or dot chart.

## 3.2   One Variable—Ordinal Level of Measurement

The tabular and graphic summary of data having an ordinal level of measurement is the same as that for a nominal level of measurement—the frequency table and bar chart.

The Insurance Service Organization (ISO) collects data on the capabilities of more than 44,000 fire-response jurisdictions throughout the United States, ranging from rural fire districts to communities of various population sizes including large cities. ISO assigns a Public Protection Classification (PPC) ranking to each jurisdiction. The PPC classification is on an ordinal scale from 1 to 10. Class 1 represents "exemplary public protection," and Class 10 indicates that the area's fire-suppression program doesn't meet ISO's minimum criteria. The PPC rank affects local fire insurance premiums for businesses and homeowners. Exhibit 3–7 presents the countrywide ISO-PPC frequency distribution and Exhibit 3–8 is a bar chart of this distribution.

The modal ISO category is Class 9 with a relative frequency of 29.04%. However, a better indicator of central tendency for a variable having an ordinal level of measurement is the *median*. The **median** is the value of the case at the "middle-position" of a frequency distribution. One half of the units of analysis will have values that are greater than the median—and the other half will have values less than the median.

To find the median value of a variable, first sort the cases in ascending order so that the values are arranged from lowest to highest. Then find the middle case. The median is the value taken on by that middle case. (With an even number of units of analysis, there are two middle cases. In this situation, the median is the average of the values taken on by these two middle cases.)

The easiest way to find the median value is to construct a **cumulative frequency distribution**. The cumulative frequency for any value is found by adding its relative frequency to the sum of the relative frequencies for all lower values.

## Exhibit 3–7

**Distribution of Insurance Service Organization (ISO) Public Protection Classification (PPC) among U.S. Fire-Response Jurisdictions**

| PPC class | Number of jurisdictions | Relative frequency | Cumulative frequency |
|---|---|---|---|
| 1 | 48 | 0.10% | 0.10% |
| 2 | 453 | 0.97% | 1.07% |
| 3 | 1,691 | 3.62% | 4.69% |
| 4 | 4,154 | 8.90% | 13.59% |
| 5 | 7,460 | 15.98% | 29.57% |
| 6 | 8,702 | 18.64% | 48.20% |
| 7 | 6,258 | 13.40% | 61.60% |
| 8 | 2,601 | 5.57% | 67.17% |
| 8B | 441 | 0.94% | 68.12% |
| 9 | 13,560 | 29.04% | 97.16% |
| 10 | 1,328 | 2.84% | 100.00% |
| Total | 46,696 | | |

## Exhibit 3–8

**Bar Chart: Distribution of Insurance Service Organization (ISO) Public Protection Classification (PPC) among U.S. Fire-Response Jurisdictions**

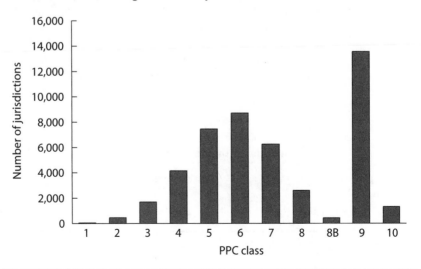

Examine the cumulative frequency distribution and find the category that contains the middle case—that is, the 50% mark of the distribution. The median ISO classification is Class 7.

The indicator of dispersion for a variable having an ordinal level of measurement is the **interquartile range**, $Q_1$ to $Q_3$, where $Q_1$ is the value below which one fourth of the cases fall, with three fourths above, and $Q_3$ is the value below which the values of three fourths of the cases fall, with the remaining 25% of the cases having higher values. ($Q_2$ is the value of the middle case, the median.)

One half, 50%, of the cases will fall between the first and third quartiles. But this does not mean that the range from the median value to $Q_1$ equals the range from the median value to $Q_3$—the median is not necessarily at the midpoint of the interquartile range. The analyst should report the values of both the first and third quartiles. These values make it possible to see whether the clustering of cases above the median is different from that below the median.

The cumulative distribution eases identification of the interquartile range. Look for the value taken on by the cases at the 25th percentile and at the 75th percentile in order to specify the interquartile range. The interquartile range, $Q_1$ to $Q_3$, is Class 5 to Class 9.

## 3.3  One Variable—Interval or Ratio Level of Measurement

The indicator of central tendency for a variable having an interval or ratio level of measurement is the arithmetic **mean**. This is our conventional notion of the average (the mode and median are also averages).

The value of the mean is computed by dividing the sum of the values for all the cases in the data set by the number of cases. The equations in Exhibit 3–9 show this computation. The subscript "$i$" identifies each case. The symbol "$i$" takes on the value 1 for the first case, 2 for the second case, 3 for the third case, and so on up to however many cases there are in the data set—which we will designate by "$N$" if the data set includes the entire population and by "$n$" if the data set is a

## Exhibit 3–9

**Computation of the Arithmetic Mean**

| Data | Observation | Size | Mean |
|---|---|---|---|
| Population | $x_i$ | $N$ | $\mu = \dfrac{\Sigma x_i}{N}$ |
| Sample | $x_i$ | $n$ | $\bar{x} = \dfrac{\Sigma x_i}{n}$ |

sample. The symbol "$x$" stands for the value of the variable and "$\Sigma$" (the upper-case Greek letter *sigma*) indicates the arithmetic operation "find the sum." The resultant value of the mean is represented by "$\mu$" (the lowercase Greek letter *mu*) if we are describing a statistical population and by "$\bar{x}$" (pronounced $x$-bar) when our observations are a statistical sample.

Radon is a colorless, odorless radioactive gas produced by the radioactive decay of uranium and radium in soil and rocks. If inhaled in large quantities, it can cause lung cancer. In houses with little ventilation, the concentration of radon can build up to relatively high levels. The U.S. Environmental Protection Agency estimates that from 5,000 to 20,000 lung cancer deaths per year in the United States are due to radon exposure. In 1989–1990 a team from the California Department of Health Services measured residential radon concentrations in Ventura County and northwestern Los Angeles County by installing radon samplers for one year in participating households. Exhibit 3–10 presents data for eight households in one zip code area—Beverly Hills 90210. (Altogether, 862 households participated—among 49 zip code areas.) A radon concentration exceeding 4 picocuries (pCi) per liter is considered to be "high."

The mean radon concentration is the sum of the individual observations ($\Sigma \, x_i = 14.25$) divided by the number of observations ($n = 8$).

$$\bar{x} = \frac{\Sigma \, x}{n} = \frac{14.25}{8} = 1.78125$$

$$\bar{x} \approx 1.78 \text{ pCi/liter}$$

## *Exhibit 3–10*

**Radon Concentration: Eight Residences in Beverly Hills 90210**

| Household | Radon concentration (picocuries per liter) |
|---|---|
| 1 | 1.50 |
| 2 | 3.50 |
| 3 | 0.50 |
| 4 | 2.00 |
| 5 | 0.50 |
| 6 | 4.60 |
| 7 | 0.75 |
| 8 | 1.00 |

*Source:* Kai-Shen Liu, Yu-Lin Chang, Steven B. Hayward, and Fan-Yen Huang, Survey of Residential Radon Levels in Ventura County and Northwestern Los Angeles County, Indoor Air Quality Program, California Department of Health Services, 2151 Berkeley Way, Berkeley, CA 94704, September 1991.

The indicator of dispersion for a variable having an interval or ratio level of measurement is based upon the deviation, or difference, between each observed value and the central tendency value, the mean—$(x_i - \mu)$. Some units of analysis (not necessarily half) will have observed values greater than the mean—resulting in a positive value for the deviation; and some will be less than the mean—and thus have negative values for the deviation. However, the net deviation—the sum of all deviations about the mean—will always be zero. The positive deviations will be balanced by the negative deviations just like bringing a see-saw or weighing scale into balance with different weights at different distances. Many small deviations in one direction are needed to offset a single large deviation in the other. In order to give greater weight to the larger deviations and avoid the problem of the net deviation being zero, each deviation is squared (multiply each value of deviation by itself). The mean of the squared deviations is found by summing and dividing by the number of cases. This is a measure of dispersion called the **variance**—symbolized by "$\sigma^2$" (the lowercase Greek letter *sigma*, squared) for a statistical population and $s^2$ for a statistical sample.

However, another indicator of dispersion is more useful—the **standard deviation**. The standard deviation is the square root of the variance. Its usefulness can be realized by looking at the "units" of variance and standard deviation. If a variable, say height, were measured in feet, then the variance would be represented in feet squared, suggesting area rather than distance. The standard deviation would have units of feet and is conceptually easier to understand as an indicator of dispersion.

The equations in Exhibit 3–11 define the variance and standard deviation for population and sample data. Defining the sample variance with $n - 1$ as the divisor rather than $n$ is a common convention. The reason is that we will want to use the sample variance as an estimate of the population variance. If $n$ were used in the denominator this estimate would be biased. Imagine an infinitely large population from which we draw all possible samples of size $n$, compute the dispersion of each sample, and then average these values. With $n$ in the denominator the final result

## *Exhibit 3–11*

**Computation of the Variance and Standard Deviation**

| Data | Variance | Standard deviation |
|---|---|---|
| Population | $\sigma^2 = \dfrac{\Sigma (x_i - \mu)^2}{N}$ | $\sigma = \sqrt{\dfrac{\Sigma (x_i - \mu)^2}{N}}$ |
| Sample | $s^2 = \dfrac{\Sigma (x_i - \bar{x})^2}{(n - 1)}$ | $s = \sqrt{\dfrac{\Sigma (x_i - \bar{x})^2}{(n - 1)}}$ |

## Exhibit 3–12

**Computation of the Sample Standard Deviation: Radon Concentration—Eight Residences in Beverly Hills 90210**

| Household | Radon concentration (pCi/liter) | Deviation | Squared deviation |
|-----------|-------------|-----------|-------------------|
| 1 | 1.50 | $(1.50 - 1.78125) = -0.28125$ | 0.079102 |
| 2 | 3.50 | $(3.50 - 1.78125) = 1.71875$ | 2.954102 |
| 3 | 0.50 | $(0.50 - 1.78125) = -1.28125$ | 1.641602 |
| 4 | 2.00 | $(2.00 - 1.78125) = 0.21875$ | 0.047852 |
| 5 | 0.50 | $(0.50 - 1.78125) = -1.28125$ | 1.641602 |
| 6 | 4.60 | $(4.60 - 1.78125) = 2.71875$ | 7.391602 |
| 7 | 0.75 | $(0.75 - 1.78125) = -1.03125$ | 1.063476 |
| 8 | 1.00 | $(1.00 - 1.78125) = -0.78125$ | 0.610352 |
| Mean | 1.78125 | | |
| Total | | | 15.42969 |

*Standard deviation*

$$s = \sqrt{\frac{\Sigma (x_i - \bar{x})^2}{n - 1}}$$

$$s = \sqrt{\frac{15.42969}{8 - 1}}$$

$s \approx 1.48$ pCi/liter

would be less than the population dispersion. However, if $n - 1$ is used as the divisor the result would exactly equal the population dispersion.[1]

Exhibit 3-12 shows the computation of standard deviation for the observed radon concentration in the eight Beverly Hills residences.

The radon example only has eight observations. However, many description problems involve data sets with hundreds or thousands of cases. Consider, for example, how the U.S. Internal Revenue Service might summarize data on the assets of private foundations.

---

[1]CAUTION: Many pocket calculators and computer programs allow us to compute the variance and standard deviation with a simple press of a button or a short command. Be sure to understand exactly what the calculator or computer program does. Is the computational result the population variance or the sample variance? Is the denominator $N$ or $n - 1$?

Private foundations, organized for charitable purposes, are exempt from income taxes. About 6,300 "operating foundations" conduct their own charitable activities, such as museums, while more than 70,000 "nonoperating foundations" provide charitable support indirectly, principally by grants to charitable organizations.

Constructing a frequency table would not help summarize the data because each foundation has its own unique value for the variable *assets*. Each value of *assets* has a frequency count of one. Thus, all of the foundations would be listed, just as they are in the data table—a cumbersome, confusing, and disorganized presentation. The analyst needs some means of describing a large data set short of listing every case.

One way to present a summary description is to change the level of measurement—from ratio to ordinal—by *grouping* the data. Grouping is accomplished by dividing the scale of measurement—in this case, dollars—into ranges called *classes*. The ranges are selected so that there are no gaps between any of the classes and the "width" of each class range (distance along the scale) is constant. The frequency distribution is described by sorting the cases into the selected classes and then counting the frequency with which each class is observed. There should be a sufficient number of classes so that the cases do not all fall into only two or three groups, yet not so many that small absolute frequency counts of only 0, 1, or 2 are commonplace. The dividing point between one class and the next should be unambiguous (for example, 0 up to 10, 10 up to 20, 20 up to 30, . . . or $0 \leq x < 10$, $10 \leq x < 20$, $20 \leq x < 30$, . . . . Not 0 to 10, 10 to 20, 20 to 30, . . . .). The ranges should be chosen so that the class midpoints are easily identified (for example, class midpoint values of 5, 15, 25 are preferable to 2.5, 7.5, 12.5, 17.5, . . .).

Exhibit 3–13 presents the data on nonoperating private foundations grouped into seven ranges of assets ranging from foundations reporting assets less than $100,000 to foundations reporting assets exceeding $100 million. Exhibit 3–14 shows a bar chart of these data. When drawing a bar chart for grouped data, the bars should not be separated—but should be drawn side by side—because the interval or ratio scale for the variable is continuous. This special type of bar chart—for one-variable, grouped data—is called a *histogram*. The range of values for the variable of interest is shown on the horizontal scale. The height of the respective bars indicate the absolute frequency (number of observations) in each group. A histogram shows both the typical and unusual aspects of a frequency distribution. The tallest bar indicates the modal value. The several adjacent tall bars indicate the approximate central tendency of the distribution. The shape of the histogram shows the dispersion of the observations. In Exhibit 3–14 the modal central tendency is the $100,000 to $1 million class and there are comparatively few foundations reporting assets more than $25 million.

A *box-whisker graph* and a *one-way scatterplot* are two other methods to graphically describe intervally measured data. A box-whisker graph uses a one-dimensional continuous scale. Its general structure is shown in Exhibit 3–15. The central tendency is indicated by the median value of the data, marked by a line. The dispersion of the data is indicated by a rectangle outlining the interquartile

## Exhibit 3–13

**Frequency Distribution: Assets of Nonoperating Private Foundations**

| Nonoperating foundations | Number of returns |
|---|---|
| $1 to under $100,000 | 18,900 |
| $100,000 to under $1,000,000 | 26,319 |
| $1,000,000 to under $10,000,000 | 17,869 |
| $10,000,000 to under $25,000,000 | 2,472 |
| $25,000,000 to under $50,000,000 | 1,025 |
| $50,000,000 to under $100,000,000 | 522 |
| $100,000,000 or more | 509 |
| Zero or unreported | 2,387 |
| Total | 70,004 |

*Source:* Internal Revenue Service, Domestic Private Foundations: Number and Selected Financial Data, by Type of Foundation and Size of Fair Market Value of Total Assets, Tax Year 2003 www.irs.gov/taxstats/charitablestats/article/0,,id=96996,00.html

## Exhibit 3–14

**Histogram: Assets of Nonoperating Private Foundations**

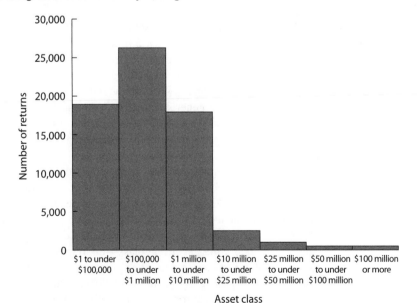

## Exhibit 3–15

**Structure of a Box-Whisker Graph**

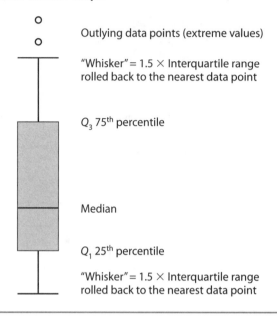

Outlying data points (extreme values)

"Whisker" = 1.5 × Interquartile range
rolled back to the nearest data point

$Q_3$ 75th percentile

Median

$Q_1$ 25th percentile

"Whisker" = 1.5 × Interquartile range
rolled back to the nearest data point

range. The range of values in the data set is indicated by lines extending from the rectangle to data points that are up to 1.5 times the interquartile range above, and below, the median. Any very extreme outlying data points are marked individually. A one-way scatterplot is drawn by creating a one-dimensional continuous scale and marking each observed value in the data set with a hash mark. The resulting picture provides a general indication of both the central tendency and spread of the data. Exhibit 3–16 displays a one-way scatterplot and a box-whisker graph for nonoperating private foundations reporting more than $10 million of assets.

The mean of an intervally measured variable should be computed from absolute, ungrouped data. However, sometimes the only data available have already been grouped. We do not have access to the absolute ungrouped values. In effect, the level of measurement has been changed from interval to ordinal. For grouped data, the analyst will have to approximate the mean. Let "$m_i$" be the midpoint of a class and "$f_i$" be the frequency of that class—the number of cases that have observed values within that class range. The approximate value for the mean can be found by multiplying each midpoint value by the respective class frequency, finding the sum of these products for all classes in the distribution, and dividing this sum by $N$, the number of cases. The symbol "$\approx$" reads "approximately equals."

## *Exhibit 3–16*

**One-Way Scatterplot and Box-Whisker Graph: Assets of the Largest Nonoperating Private Foundations** (specific data points in this example are hypothetical)

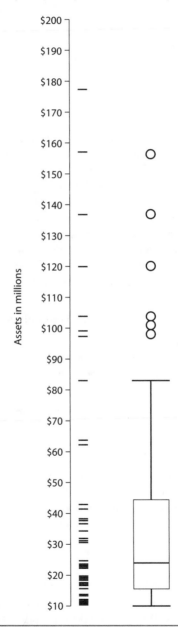

## Exhibit 3–17

**Computation of the Mean and Standard Deviation for Grouped Data**

| Data | Mean | Standard deviation |
|------|------|--------------------|
| Population | $\mu \approx \dfrac{\Sigma f_i \cdot m_i}{N}$ | $\sigma \approx \sqrt{\dfrac{\Sigma f_i \cdot (m_i - \mu)^2}{N}}$ |
| Sample | $\bar{x} \approx \dfrac{\Sigma f_i \cdot m_i}{n}$ | $s \approx \sqrt{\dfrac{\Sigma f_i \cdot (m_i - \bar{x})^2}{n - 1}}$ |

The standard deviation of grouped data also substitutes the product $f_i \cdot m_i$ for $x_i$ in the defining formulas. Equations for calculating the mean and standard deviation of grouped data are in Exhibit 3–17.

Sometimes the dispersion of a frequency distribution is reported as a ratio—dividing dispersion by the mean or the sample size. This helps the analyst assess the relative precision of estimates that may be derived from a sample.

The **standard error of the mean** is the ratio of a sample standard deviation to the square root of the sample size. Standard error will be addressed again in later chapters. For now it is enough to know that reporting standard error and sample size allows the analyst to calculate the standard deviation.

$$\text{Standard error of the mean} = \frac{s}{\sqrt{n}}$$

The *relative standard error* (also called the *coefficient of variation*) is the ratio of the standard deviation to the mean.

$$\text{Relative standard error (RSE) for population data} = \frac{\sigma}{\mu}$$

$$\text{Relative standard error (RSE) for sample data} = \frac{s}{\bar{x}}$$

The relative standard deviation indicates the degree to which the values of the cases in a frequency distribution deviate from the mean—the higher the ratio, the greater the spread of the distribution.

## Homework Exercises

**3-1** Total scores on the Graduate Management Admission Test (GMAT) can range from 200 to 800. Exhibit HW3–1A presents the percentages of candidates who scored below selected total test scores. In other words, the table provides a cumulative distribution of the relative frequencies.

# Exhibit HW3–1A

**Cumulative Distribution of Scores on the Graduate Management Admission Test**

| Total score | Percent below |
|---|---|
| 260 | 2% |
| 280 | 2% |
| 300 | 3% |
| 320 | 4% |
| 340 | 6% |
| 360 | 8% |
| 380 | 11% |
| 400 | 14% |
| 420 | 18% |
| 440 | 22% |
| 460 | 27% |
| 480 | 33% |
| 500 | 39% |
| 520 | 45% |
| 540 | 51% |
| 560 | 58% |
| 580 | 64% |
| 600 | 70% |
| 620 | 76% |
| 640 | 80% |
| 660 | 86% |
| 680 | 89% |
| 700 | 92% |
| 720 | 96% |
| 740 | 98% |
| 760 | 99% |

*Source:* Graduate Management Admission Council, *Sample GMAT® Score Report,* 2006.
www.mba.com/mba/TaketheGMAT/Tools/SampleScoreReport.htm The mean and standard deviation
reported for 622,975 test takers over three years is 526.6 and 117.0, respectively. Calculations in
this example differ due to category grouping and rounding of percentages.

**a.** Draw a cumulative relative frequency histogram.

**b.** Draw a relative frequency histogram.

**c.** What is the mean value?

**d.** What is the median value?

**e.** What is (are) the modal value(s)?

**f.** What is the standard deviation?

**a.** Cumulative relative frequency histogram. See Exhibit HW3–1B.

**b.** Relative frequency histogram. See Exhibit HW3–1C.

**c.** See Exhibit HW3–1D. Mean $\mu \approx 524$.

**d.** Median $\approx 540$.

**e.** Mode $\approx 550$.

**f.** Standard deviation $\approx 114$.

## *Exhibit HW3–1B*

**Cumulative Relative Frequency Histogram**

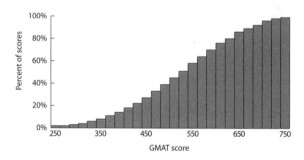

## *Exhibit HW3–1C*

**Relative Frequency Histogram**

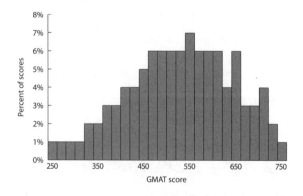

## Exhibit HW3–1D

**Calculations for the Mean and Standard Deviation of the Graduate Management Admission Test Score Distribution**

| Score | Percent below | Class interval | Class midpoint | Relative frequency | $f \cdot m$ | $f \cdot (m - \mu)^2$ |
|---|---|---|---|---|---|---|
| 260 | 2% | < 260 | 250 | 0.01 | 2.5 | 721.9969 |
| 280 | 2% | 260–279 | 270 | 0.01 | 2.7 | 618.5169 |
| 300 | 3% | 280–299 | 290 | 0.01 | 2.9 | 523.0369 |
| 320 | 4% | 300–319 | 310 | 0.01 | 3.1 | 435.5569 |
| 340 | 6% | 320–339 | 330 | 0.02 | 6.6 | 712.1538 |
| 360 | 8% | 340–359 | 350 | 0.02 | 7.0 | 569.1938 |
| 380 | 11% | 360–379 | 370 | 0.03 | 11.1 | 663.3507 |
| 400 | 14% | 380–399 | 390 | 0.03 | 11.7 | 496.9107 |
| 420 | 18% | 400–419 | 410 | 0.04 | 16.4 | 472.6276 |
| 440 | 22% | 420–439 | 430 | 0.04 | 17.2 | 314.7076 |
| 460 | 27% | 440–459 | 450 | 0.05 | 22.5 | 235.9845 |
| 480 | 33% | 460–479 | 470 | 0.06 | 28.2 | 142.3014 |
| 500 | 39% | 480–499 | 490 | 0.06 | 29.4 | 49.4214 |
| 520 | 45% | 500–519 | 510 | 0.06 | 30.6 | 4.5414 |
| 540 | 51% | 520–539 | 530 | 0.06 | 31.8 | 7.6614 |
| 560 | 58% | 540–559 | 550 | 0.07 | 38.5 | 68.5783 |
| 580 | 64% | 560–579 | 570 | 0.06 | 34.2 | 157.9014 |
| 600 | 70% | 580–599 | 590 | 0.06 | 35.4 | 305.0214 |
| 620 | 76% | 600–619 | 610 | 0.06 | 36.6 | 500.1414 |
| 640 | 80% | 620–639 | 630 | 0.04 | 25.2 | 495.5076 |
| 660 | 86% | 640–659 | 650 | 0.06 | 39.0 | 1034.381 |
| 680 | 89% | 660–679 | 670 | 0.03 | 20.1 | 686.7507 |
| 700 | 92% | 680–699 | 690 | 0.03 | 20.7 | 880.3107 |
| 720 | 96% | 700–719 | 710 | 0.04 | 28.4 | 1463.828 |
| 740 | 98% | 720–739 | 730 | 0.02 | 14.6 | 892.9538 |
| 760 | 99% | 740–800 | 750 | 0.01 | 7.5 | 534.9969 |
| Total | | | | 0.99 | 523.9 | 12988.33 |

**3-2** A planner wants to draw a histogram of the age structure of the population in Visalia. Group the values of the variable "age" into ten-year intervals. What level of measurement does the variable "age" have before and after grouping?

---

Let age be symbolized by $x$:

$0 \geq x < 10$   The first group reads "$x$ is greater than or equal to 0 and less than 10."

$0 \geq x < 20$

$0 \geq x < 30$

$0 \geq x < 40$

$0 \geq x < 50$

$0 \geq x < 60$

$0 \geq x < 70$

$x > 70$

Age is a variable with an interval level of measurement. After grouping, the variable has an ordinal level of measurement.

---

**3-3** Suppose that an analyst is interested in how fast vehicles are traveling on Highway 101. The posted speed limit is 55 mph. What is the matter with the following grouping of the variable "speed?"

under 5
5–17
18–20
21–29
31–39
40–45
46–49
50–59
59–65

---

This is a real mess.

■ Groups of unequal size.
■ Discontinuous groups.
■ Some possible values of speed excluded.
■ Overlapping groups.
■ Low range of speeds covered in too much detail while likely range of speeds not covered in enough detail—very high speeds not covered at all.

---

**3-4** A local public radio station is soliciting contributions from its audience during Pledge Week. The announcer states that the average contribution of its members is

$100. Do you think that this average is the mean, median, or mode of the contributions? Why?

The station, since it is seeking contributions, reports the highest average. In this case it would be the mean. The mean would be larger than the median due to the relatively few but substantial contributions made by wealthy donors. The median, a smaller number, would be more representative of what its viewing (and donating) audience contributes—50% of the contributors giving higher and 50% giving lower amounts than the median value reported. The mode is the most frequently occurring contribution amount—for example $35.

**3-5** Exhibit HW3–5A shows expenditures for special education as a percentage of total school operating budget for 327 Massachusetts school districts for one fiscal year.[1]

**a.** What is the average special education expenditure (as a percentage of school operating expenditures)?

**b.** What is the standard deviation?

**c.** Draw a histogram of special education expenditures.

## *Exhibit HW3–5A*

**Special Education Expenditures as a Percentage of Total Operating Budget: Massachusetts School Districts FY2001**

| Special education expenditure percentage | Number of school districts |
|---|---|
| < 5% | 11 |
| 5 to 10% | 22 |
| 10 to 15% | 56 |
| 15 to 20% | 170 |
| 20 to 25% | 60 |
| 25% or more | 8 |
| Total | 327 |

[1]Special Education Expenditures as a Percentage of Total School Budget, Preliminary FY01, Massachusetts Department of Education, finance1.doe.mass.edu/seducation/spedexp01.html

  **a.** Mean ≈ 16.6%.

  **b.** Standard deviation ≈ 5.0%.

  **c.** See Exhibit HW3–5B.

## Exhibit HW3–5B

**Histogram: Special Education Expenditures**

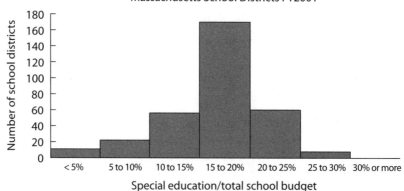

Special Education Expenditures as Percentage of Total Operating Budget: Massachusetts School Districts FY2001

  **3-6** "Congregate housing for the elderly" is defined by the government as age-segregated housing built specifically for the elderly (62 years and over) which provides, at the very least, an on-site meal program. What are the characteristics of congregate facilities beyond provision of a meal program? To answer this question, 27 congregate facilities were asked to list their services (see Exhibit HW3–6A).

  **a.** In what ways is this table different from other frequency tables?

  **b.** How many variables are presented in the table? What are the values of each variable?

  **c.** Can a histogram be drawn?

  **d.** Write a brief statement, based on these data, that summarizes the characteristics of congregate facilities for the elderly.

## Exhibit HW3–6A

**Service Availability on 27 Sample Sites of Congregate Housing for the Elderly**

| Service | Number of sites with service | Percentage of sites with service |
|---|---|---|
| Meal service | 27 | 100% |
| Recreational | 27 | 100 |
| Social | 24 | 89 |
| Educational | 24 | 89 |
| Security | 24 | 89 |
| Transportation | 23 | 85 |
| Commercial | 22 | 81 |
| Medical | 21 | 78 |
| Housekeeping | 18 | 67 |
| Linen | 16 | 59 |
| Protective | 16 | 59 |

**a.** This is a bit tricky. At first glance it appears to be a conventional representation of a frequency distribution for one variable, "service," with 11 values, "meal service, . . . , protective." If each service is examined one at a time, at each of the 27 facilities, and asked the question, "What kind of service is this?", the analyst would indeed get the frequencies shown—27 of the services provide meals, 16 provide linen. Each instance of providing a service would be a separate case ("event" or "unit of analysis"). The variable would have a nominal level of measurement with 11 possible values. But this is not what was done. Instead, each facility was asked, "Which of the following eleven services do you provide?" Each facility is a separate case, and multiple responses are allowed to the inquiry.

**b.** This means that each type of service is a separate variable (there are 11 variables) and the possible values for each variable are "yes" or "no." The relative frequency of the affirmative responses are listed in the table.

**c.** No. The variables have a nominal level of measurement. Strictly speaking, a bar chart, illustrating the frequency distribution, could be drawn for each variable— but it would be redundant (yes and no categories) and not useful in addressing the basic question in the problem—part d. A bar chart could be drawn showing the relative frequency of the 11 different services among the 27 sites.

**d.** "The sample congregate housing sites provide activity and entertainment oriented services more frequently than services to the residents' physical needs."

**3-7** Interview 10 people who are registered to vote. Ask each person about his or her political affiliation. Record the responses as 1. Democratic; 2. Republican; 3. Independent; 4. Other; 5. No Response or Decline to State

   **a.** What is the variable in this problem?

   **b.** What is its level of measurement?

   **c.** How many possible values can the variable take on? What are they?

   **d.** Can a modal value be computed? A median value? A mean value?

   **e.** Set up a table for properly recording these data.

   _____

   **a.** The one variable in this problem is "political affiliation."

   **b.** It is a nominal level of measurement.

   **c.** For each observation the variable can take on any one of five possible values: 1 meaning Democratic; 2 meaning Republican; 3 meaning Independent; 4 meaning Other; 5 meaning Decline to State or No Response.

   **d.** Because the variable has a nominal level of measurement a modal value—the most frequently occurring value—can be found. Median and mean values cannot be found.

   **e.** See Exhibit HW3–7A.

## *Exhibit HW3–7A*

**Hypothetical Data File**

| Observation number | Political affiliation<br>1 = Democratic<br>2 = Republican<br>3 = Independent<br>4 = Other<br>5 = No Response or Decline to State |
|:---:|:---:|
| 1 | 1 |
| 2 | 3 |
| 3 | 2 |
| 4 | 4 |
| 5 | 1 |
| 6 | 2 |
| 7 | 2 |
| 8 | 5 |
| 9 | 1 |
| 10 | 2 |

**3-8** The frequency table shown in Exhibit HW3–8A is part of a study done by an emergency medical services planning agency in order to "delineate the magnitude and character of critical trauma care."

   **a.** What is the population being studied?

   **b.** What variable is being observed?

   **c.** How many observations are there?

   **d.** Draw a histogram of the frequency distribution. (You must exclude cases for which the observation of age is missing.)

   **e.** Another way to display the frequency distribution of a variable inherently having an interval level of measurement is to draw a frequency polygon. The figure is drawn by connecting the points describing the midpoint and frequency of each class with straight lines. Each straight line cuts off a triangular section of one of the histogram bars and seems to add on another triangular area of equal size. Thus the area under the frequency polygon (probability) equals the area of the histogram bars. The tails of the frequency polygon are tied off (brought down to zero) by following the rule of equal areas (a constant interval between midpoint values). Superimpose a frequency polygon on the histogram drawn in part d of this question.

## *Exhibit HW3–8A*

**Number of Trauma Cases by Age in Emergency Services Area 6**

| Age group | Number of cases | EMS-6 population percentages |
|-----------|-----------------|------------------------------|
| Under 1   | 4               | 2.1%                         |
| 1–4       | 11              | 7.8%                         |
| 5–14      | 22              | 16.3%                        |
| 15–24     | 197             | 16.4%                        |
| 25–34     | 150             | 15.9%                        |
| 35–44     | 64              | 10.9%                        |
| 45–54     | 46              | 9.2%                         |
| 55–64     | 40              | 9.5%                         |
| 65–74     | 25              | 7.1%                         |
| 75–84     | 26              | 3.6%                         |
| Over 85   | 4               | 1.0%                         |
| Unknown   | 38              |                              |
| Total     | 627             | 99.8%                        |

    **f.** Find the modal, median, and mean values of the frequency distribution.

    **g.** Find the relative frequency of each group. Compare these to the population relative frequencies shown in the table. Write a brief statement summarizing this comparison. What additional information is needed in order to determine whether this comparison is typical of the rest of the United States or not?

    **h.** Find the standard deviation of the frequency distribution.

    **a.** All trauma cases in emergency services area 6.

    **b.** Age.

    **c.** 627.

**d, e.** See Exhibit HW3–8B.

    **f.** Modal age group: 15 to 24; median age group: 25 to 34; mean age ≈ 34.2.

    **g.** See Exhibit 3–8C. The distribution of trauma victims by age does not match the age distribution of the general population. The incidence of trauma among people less than 15 years old is less than half of its relative frequency in the general population. The incidence of trauma among people from 15 to 35 years old is about double its relative proportion in the general population. Further study would require a similar frequency distribution for trauma cases by age group for the total United States and the age distribution of the U.S. population.

    **h.** Standard deviation ≈ 18.9.

## *Exhibit HW3–8B*

**Frequency Polygon: Trauma Cases by Age**

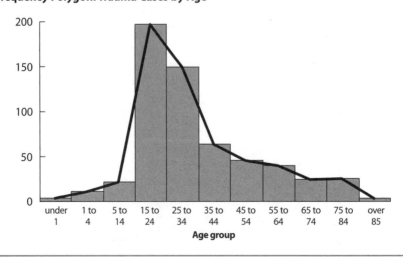

## Exhibit HW3–8C

**Number of Trauma Cases by Age: Emergency Services Area 6**

| Age group | Absolute frequency | Relative frequency |
|---|---|---|
| | | ($n = 589$) |
| Under 1 | 4 | 0.7% |
| 1–4 | 11 | 1.9% |
| 5–14 | 22 | 3.7% |
| 15–24 | 197 | 33.4% |
| 25–34 | 150 | 25.5% |
| 35–44 | 64 | 10.9% |
| 45–54 | 46 | 7.8% |
| 55–64 | 40 | 6.8% |
| 65–74 | 25 | 4.2% |
| 75–84 | 26 | 4.4% |
| over 85 | 4 | 0.7% |
| Unknown | 38 | — |
| Total | 627 | 100.0% |

*Source:* Trauma Study Part I: July 1, 1980–June 30, 1981, Alpine, Mother Lode, San Joaquin Emergency Medical Services Agency, Modesto, California, May 1983.

**3-9** Analysts surveyed cities to obtain information about personnel practices in their police departments. They received responses from 1,250 cities as summarized in Exhibit HW3–9A. What was the average population of cities in the survey?

## Exhibit HW3–9A

**Responses to Survey Regarding Police Personnel**

| Population group | Number of cities reporting |
|---|---|
| Over 1,000,000 | 4 |
| 500,000–1,000,000 | 13 |
| 250,000–499,999 | 27 |
| 100,000–249,999 | 78 |
| 50,000–99,999 | 171 |
| 25,000–49,999 | 310 |
| 10,000–24,999 | 647 |
| Total | 1,250 |

Mean ≈ 59,438 (setting the upper limit of population at 1,500,000).

**3-10** Suppose an analyst is provided the data in Exhibit HW3-10A for a large school district.

**a.** How many teachers does the school district employ?

**b.** How many schools are there in the school district?

**c.** How many variables are presented in the table?

**d.** What are the values of the variables?

**e.** What is the unit of analysis?

**f.** How many observations are in the table?

Using the modal value of the distribution in Exhibit HW3–10A, one colleague guesses that there are about 50 teachers per school. It is anticipated that a salary negotiation settlement will bring a teacher's salary "on the average" up to $50,000 per year. Therefore, your colleague projects that the school district budget for teachers salaries will increase to $100 million.

**g.** Develop another budget estimate using the above data.

**h.** What is the difference between the budget estimates?

## *Exhibit HW3–10A*

**School District Data**

| Number of teachers | Number of schools |
|---|---|
| 0–19 | 3 |
| 20–39 | 12 |
| 40–59 | 20 |
| 60–79 | 5 |

**a.** Do not know from the data given.

**b.** 40 schools.

**c.** One variable—number of teachers.

**d.** Four groups: 0–19, 20–39, 40–59, 60–79.

**e.** Each school is one unit of analysis.

**f.** Forty.

**g.** The first budget estimate was derived by multiplying:

$$(40)(50)(50,000) = \$100 \text{ million}$$

The estimated mean number of teachers per school site is 43.5 (using the formula for estimating the mean of grouped data). Thus a revised budget estimate is

$$(40)(43.5)(50,000) = \$87 \text{ million}$$

**h.** The difference in the budget estimates is $13 million—no small change even for a school district of this size.

---

**3-11** Explain the differences in structure and content between a *data file* and a *frequency table*. Provide an example.

---

A data file lists each observation recorded for a set of related events, case by case. Each line (observation number) represents a separate and unique case (event). The body of the table contains the measured values for each case with respect to the variables of interest. A frequency table lists the possible values that could be measured for a particular variable and the corresponding number of times (number of cases) each value appeared in the data file for that one variable.

---

**3-12** Key words used to describe public policies are important in the development of public opinion and perception. Connecticut officials were interested in developing a baseline of public awareness before launching a new "clean energy" campaign. They were particularly interested in the different connotations of "clean" and "renewable." One group was asked, Have you ever heard of "renewable energy"? Another group was asked, Have you ever heard of "clean energy"? Respondents who replied yes were then asked to explain what the term meant to them or to provide examples. Exhibit HW3–12A provides a few responses to the survey. These data are summarized in Exhibit HW3–12B.

# Exhibit HW3–12A

**Multiple responses to a survey question**

| **Have heard of "renewable energy"** | | **Have heard of "clean energy"** | |
|---|---|---|---|
| *Respondent* | *Response* | *Respondent* | *Response* |
| 1 | 1, 3, 4 | 1 | 2, 4 |
| 2 | 2, 5 | 2 | 2, 5, 7 |
| 3 | 9 | 3 | 1, 6, 9 |
| 4 | 11, 14 | 4 | 2, 14 |
| 5 | 1, 3, 6 | 5 | 13, 16 |
| 6 | 2, 4 | 6 | 17 |
| 7 | 1, 9 | | |
| 8 | 8, 12, 16 | | |

Multiple responses allowed

| | | | |
|---|---|---|---|
| 1 | Reusable/recyclable/won't deplete | 10 | Energy efficiency |
| 2 | Less polluting/cleaner air | 11 | From natural resources |
| 3 | Solar energy/photovoltaics | 12 | Biomass; burning organic matter |
| 4 | Wind power/windmills/wind farms | 13 | Costs more/less |
| 5 | Better for environment | 14 | Hybrid/electric cars |
| 6 | Less fossil fuel/oil | 15 | Hydrogen |
| 7 | Renewable/clean energy | 16 | Other |
| 8 | Water power/hydroelectricity | 17 | Don't know |
| 9 | Recycling | | |

*Source:* http://ctinnovations.com/communities/files/CCEF_survey_report_May_18_2005_Final.pdf
Comparative Assessment of Consumer Awareness for Clean Energy in Connecticut and the United
States, Nexus Market Research, Inc. for the Connecticut Clean Energy Fund.

# Exhibit HW3–12B

**Frequency Distribution: Survey Responses**

| | Definition/Example | Renewable energy | Clean energy |
|---|---|---|---|
| 1 | Reusable/recyclable/won't deplete | 3 | 1 |
| 2 | Less polluting/cleaner air | 2 | 3 |
| 3 | Solar energy/photovoltaics | 2 | 0 |
| 4 | Wind power/windmills/wind farms | 2 | 1 |
| 5 | Better for environment | 1 | 1 |
| 6 | Less fossil fuel/oil | 1 | 1 |
| 7 | Renewable/clean energy | 0 | 1 |
| 8 | Water power/hydroelectricity | 1 | 0 |
| 9 | Recycling | 2 | 1 |
| 10 | Energy efficiency | 0 | 0 |
| 11 | From natural resources | 1 | 0 |
| 12 | Biomass; burning organic matter | 1 | 0 |
| 13 | Costs more/less | 0 | 1 |
| 14 | Hybrid/electric cars | 1 | 1 |
| 15 | Hydrogen | 0 | 0 |
| 16 | Other | 1 | 1 |
| 17 | Don't know | 0 | 1 |

**3-13** Grade point average is one output assessment educational indicator. Some data for students in an MPA program are shown in Exhibit HW3–13A. Compute the appropriate measures of central tendency and dispersion for this frequency distribution.

## Exhibit HW3–13A

**MPA Grade Point Averages**

| Grade point average | Number of students |
|---|---|
| 3.5000–4.0000 | 502 |
| 3.0000–3.4999 | 227 |
| 2.5000–2.9999 | 28 |
| 2.0000–2.4999 | 11 |
| 1.5000–1.9999 | 1 |
| 1.0000–1.4999 | 2 |
| Total | 771 |

Mean ≈ 3.54, standard deviation ≈ 0.34.

**3-14** Consider the following statement from a research report:

> Brush species make up much of the fuel load in forested wildlands. Basic physical and chemical characteristics of these species influence ease of ignition, rate of fire spread, burning time, and fire intensity. Quantitative knowledge in the variations in brush characteristics is essential to progress in fire control and effective use of fire in wildland management.[2]

Five shrub species common to northern California brush fuels were studied. One of the variables measured was ash content. "The amount of ash or minerals in vegetation can affect how well the material burns. . . . Another study showed that the moisture content of living vegetation with high ash content tends to be higher than that with low ash content." The report included the following statement: "Ash content of the woody material [as opposed to plant foliage] was low and did not vary consistently among species or size class of material. Average ash content of the live woody material was 1.6 percent with a coefficient of variation of 25.2 percent. Ash content of the dead material was only slightly lower, averaging 1.4 percent. Variability of the dead fuel ash content was greater, however, with a coefficient of variation of 37.1 percent. The greater variation probably resulted

---

[2]Countryman, Clive M., Physical Characteristics of Some Northern California Brush Fuels, Gen. Tech. Rept. PSW-61, Berkeley, CA: Pacific Southwest Forest and Range Experiment Station, Forest Service, U.S. Department of Agriculture, 1982.

from differences in the amount of weathering among individual samples [cases] rather than from variation among species or size of material." What are the standard deviations of the ash content of the live and dead material that the researcher measured?

The standard deviation for the ash content of the live material is 0.40 percent. The standard deviation for the ash content of the dead material is 0.52 percent.

**3-15** Each civil service employee of the U.S. Government is classified according to grade on a general schedule of employment. The grades indicate increasing levels of expertise, responsibility, or authority—and commensurately higher salaries. A frequency table showing the number of employees by grade in 2004 is shown in Exhibit HW3–15A.

**a.** Summarize these data with a bar chart.

**b.** What is the average GS grade?

## Exhibit HW3–15A

**Full-Time Civilian General Schedule Employment by Grade (2004)**

| GS grade | Number of employees |
|----------|--------------------:|
| 1 | 270 |
| 2 | 955 |
| 3 | 8,445 |
| 4 | 45,327 |
| 5 | 100,984 |
| 6 | 81,255 |
| 7 | 130,828 |
| 8 | 51,413 |
| 9 | 123,437 |
| 10 | 16,975 |
| 11 | 180,333 |
| 12 | 207,566 |
| 13 | 174,575 |
| 14 | 80,205 |
| 15 | 41,845 |
| Total | 1,244,413 |

**c.** To what extent do civil service employees have GS classifications different from the average value?

**a.** See Exhibit HW3–15B Bar Chart: Federal Employment by GS Grade.

**b.** The median GS classification in 2004 was 11 (in 1991 it was 9).

**c.** The interquartile range is 7 to 12.

## Exhibit HW3–15B

**Bar Chart: Federal Employment by GS Grade (2004)**

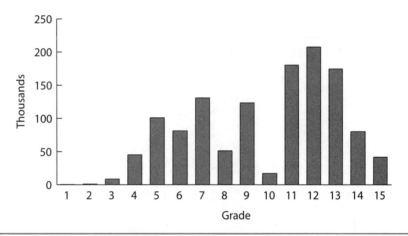

**3-16** How accessible are hospital-provided abortions? To answer this question, activists in one state conducted a survey of every general hospital. Volunteers called each facility. The caller first asked if the hospital had a gynecology department. If it did, the caller asked that the call be transferred to it. The caller stated that she was pregnant and trying to get an abortion, and then asked whether the hospital would perform the procedure. Of the 362 hospitals contacted, 261 (72.1%) replied that they did not provide abortions. Eighteen (5%) did provide abortions. Seventy-two hospitals (19.9%) had restricted abortion policies such as requiring a woman to have a prior relationship with a doctor who will do the procedure and who has surgery rights at the hospital. Eleven hospitals (3%) did not provide clear answers about their abortion accessibility. Present these results in an appropriate table and graph.

## *Exhibit HW3–16A*

**Abortion Accessibility in Hospitals**

| Hospital policy | Number | Relative frequency |
|---|---|---|
| Do not provide abortions | 261 | 72.1% |
| Restricted provision of abortions | 72 | 19.9% |
| Provide abortions | 18 | 5.0% |
| Unknown | 11 | 3.0% |
| Total | 362 | 100.0% |

## *Exhibit HW3–16B*

**Bar Chart: Abortion Accessibility in Hospitals**

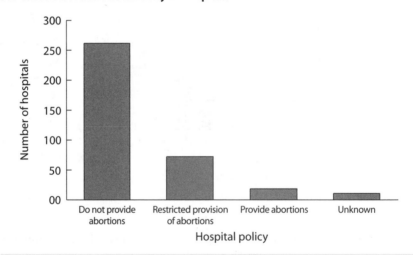

# CHAPTER 4

# What About It? One-Variable Evaluation—Nominal Level of Measurement

| | |
|---:|:---|
| Kind of problem | *Evaluation* |
| Number of variables | *One* |
| Level of measurement | *Nominal* |

The preceding chapter focused on the description of a single variable. The observations were summarized by a frequency distribution and by statistics for the central tendency and dispersion of that distribution. Now the analyst should make some judgments about the observations. Is this what is wanted or not? Is it good or bad—right or wrong—desirable or undesirable? Basically, is the description consistent with *expectation*? This is the essence of evaluation—and evaluation is at the heart of all decision making. Public managers strive to attain goals and objectives, fulfill needs, relieve deprivations, and alleviate dissatisfactions by reacting to perceived differences between observation and expectation.

Traditionally, the topic of evaluation is introduced as hypothesis testing. A **hypothesis** is a proposition that is subjected to analysis in order to test its validity. Consider the rule in American jurisprudence of "Innocent until proven guilty." The initial expectation—hypothesis—is *innocence* (that is, "not guilty"). This hypothesis would be rejected—and the opposite hypothesis—"guilty"—adopted—if the differences between the expectation of innocence and the evidence of guilt were "beyond a reasonable doubt." In evaluation problems the initial hypothesis is that there is *no difference* between observation and expectation. Upon comparison, everything is equal, the same, balanced, fair, and "innocent" (*not guilty*). This is called the **null hypothesis**. If the null hypothesis is rejected, the analyst is compelled to adopt the **alternate hypothesis** that the initial hypothesis is wrong—reality differs from the analyst's initial expectation. But what is the criterion for "beyond a reasonable doubt?" When should the analyst reject the null hypothesis in

**65**

favor of an alternate idea? The answer to this question lies in *probability*. Conventionally, probability is often thought of in such terms as *chance*, *uncertainty*, *doubt*, *likelihood*, or *risk*. Not every difference between observation and expectation should lead to rejecting a null hypothesis. Small differences, attributed to chance or observational error, often occur. Large differences, on the other hand, are uncommon and have a low probability of occurring by chance—they should lead an analyst to doubt that the null hypothesis is an adequate explanation of the status quo.

# *Quick Concepts: Probability*

Doubt, chance, uncertainty, risk, and luck are all expressions of the same concept—**probability**. Probability, represented by a number between 0 and 1, expresses how likely it is that a particular event will occur. It is calculated as the number of times that an event occurred (or might occur) to the number of opportunities there have been (are or will be) for that event to occur. A number close to zero indicates that an event was rarely observed in the past, would be a very unusual occurrence presently, or is unlikely to occur in the future. A number close to 1 indicates that an event has been observed often, is a rather common occurrence, or is likely to happen again. Probability is a very important concept in public administration because our management theories are based on distinguishing unusual events from those that are commonplace happenstance.

$$P = \frac{\text{Number of times one particular event was observed}}{\text{Number of opportunities there were for that event to occur}}$$

$$P = \frac{\text{Number of times one particular event can occur}}{\text{Number of opportunities there are for that event to occur}}$$

$$P = \frac{\text{Number of times one particular event is anticipated}}{\text{Number of opportunities there will be for that event to occur}}$$

Sometimes an analyst is interested in the *net* probability that any one of several possible events will occur. For example, the 2000 census forms listed six racial categories: White; Black; American Indian or Alaskan Native; Asian; Native Hawaiian and other Pacific Islander; and Other.

The ability to choose any combination of two or more races offered each citizen a selection of 63 possible racial classifications. Furthermore, each citizen was asked to designate his or her ethnicity as Hispanic or non-Hispanic. The Hispanic classification included anyone whose familial roots were traceable to a Spanish-speaking nation. Hispanics could belong to any of the 63 possible races, bringing the total number of possible racial-ethnic combinations to

*(continued)*

126. In the 2000 census, about 6.8 million people—2.4% of the total U.S. population—identified themselves as belonging to more than one race.

An individual would be classified as *non-White* if they identify himself/herself as *either* Black *or* American Indian *or* Alaskan Native, *or* Asian, *or* Native Hawaiian, *or* Pacific Islander, *or* Other. Any time an event is described in the form *"either . . . or . . . or,"* think *addition* in order to calculate the *net* probability.

Sometimes an analyst is interested in the *net* probability that a specific series of events will occur. The net probability of a set of successive events is the product of the probabilities of each event. Any time an event is described in the form *". . . and . . . and . . . ,"* think *multiplication* in order to calculate the net probability. This rule works if the events are *independent* or if the probabilities involved are *conditional* probabilities. For example, suppose that an analyst knows that 5% of the cars in a city were red and 8% were blue. The net probability of the first car to turn the corner being red *and* the next car being blue is $p_{red} \times p_{blue} = 0.004$. The two successive events are independent. The color of one car is unrelated to the color of the next, or any other, car.

Now consider a class containing 10 students, categorized as follows: 5 females (2 white graduates, 2 white undergraduates, and 1 nonwhite undergraduate) and 5 males (3 white graduates, 1 nonwhite graduate, and 1 white undergraduate). Thus, $p_{nonwhite} = 0.2$, $p_{female} = 0.5$, and $p_{graduate} = 0.6$. Consider the class to be the population. What is the probability of a student being nonwhite *and* female *and* a graduate student? The events *nonwhite, female*, and *graduate student* are not independent so the analyst cannot simply multiply the proportions of these separate categories to determine the answer.* The analyst should use successive conditional probabilities instead. The proportion of students who are nonwhite is 0.2. Of all the nonwhite students, one half are female. And of all the nonwhite, female students, none is a graduate student. Thus, the nonwhite and female and graduate probability is $0.2 \times 0.5 \times 0.0 = 0$. (If 20% of a student population are nonwhite, 50% of the nonwhite population are female, and 60% of the nonwhite females are graduate students, then the net nonwhite, female, graduate probability would be $0.2 \times 0.5 \times 0.6 = 0.06$.)

There are generally two kinds of evaluation problems that involve a single variable having a nominal level of measurement. First, an analyst could be interested in a single observed value—the recorded observation of the outcome of only one event. The evaluation question is whether this one observation is fairly typical or is the observation out of the ordinary—*unusual*. To answer the question the analyst needs to compare the observed outcome against an expected frequency

*The term "event" includes not only happenings but also *conditions* such as being female or white.

distribution that describes what the analyst thinks about how often possible outcomes of all similar events *should* occur. If the likelihood of the event outcome is high, the analyst judges that it does not differ from the expected outcomes of similar events. Alternatively, if the likelihood is low, the analyst concludes that the event outcome is unusually different. Perhaps the outcome is a rare aberration, but the analyst is justified in inferring that the outcome is all too typical and the initial expectation is wrong.

The second kind of evaluation problem involves a sample—the observed outcomes for a number of related events that are a subset of a statistical population. The evaluation question is whether the observed values for the cases in the sample could reasonably have occurred in light of a known expected frequency distribution. If the likelihood is high, the analyst judges that the expected frequency distribution could indeed describe the target population. If the likelihood is low, then the analyst rejects the expected frequency distribution and concludes that the characteristics of the target population are different from what was initially thought.

Each kind of problem has a statistical method that is most appropriate. This all important recognition is accomplished by answering the following series of questions:

- What are the units of analysis?
- What are the variables that are being observed for each unit of analysis?
- How many variables are in the problem: one, two, or more than two?
- What kind of problem is presented: description, evaluation, or estimation?
- What is the level of measurement of each variable: nominal, ordinal, or interval?

And:

- How many observations are there?
- How many possible values (categories) can the variable take on?

Exhibit 4–1 orients us to the methods for evaluating one nominally measured variable. The binomial test and the normal approximation to the binomial test are

## *Exhibit 4–1*

**One-Variable Evaluation, Nominal Measure**

| Sample size *n* | Two categories | More than two categories |
|---|---|---|
| Small $n \leq 20$ | Binomial test | * |
| Large $n > 20$ | Binomial test Normal approximation to the binomial—*Z* test | Chi-square goodness-of-fit test |

*Either combine categories in order to use the binomial test, or increase the sample size.

used for small and large samples respectively. If the variable can take on values identifying more than two categories, the chi-square (pronounced "ki" square) goodness-of-fit test is used.

## 4.1    *Two Categories*

### 4.1.1    **Binomial Test**

The first problem involves a dichotomous variable—a variable that can take on only two possible values. The values are mutually exclusive. Each event (unit of analysis) is analogous to a flip of a coin—only one of two possible outcomes can occur—the result of each flip is either heads or tails.

To begin, consider an expected frequency distribution. Imagine the hypothetical situation in which every adult in a very large population is registered as either Democrat or Republican and that 40% are registered as Democrat and 60% as Republican. If an analyst were to randomly pick one individual from this population the probability that the person would be a registered Democrat is 0.40—and Republican, 0.60. **Random selection** means that the respective probabilities remain constant. If the analyst were to pick a sample of individuals from the population, the probabilities of selecting a Democrat or a Republican would remain the same, 0.4 and 0.6 respectively, for each and every selection, just as the probability of heads coming up on a flip of a coin remains constant at 0.5 regardless of previous outcomes. The method used to pick an individual must favor neither Democrats nor Republicans. Random selection, like a coin toss, has no memory.

Now suppose that the analyst wants to form a large number of five-person committees comprised of people randomly selected from this population. What proportion of these committees would have no Democrats as members? one Democrat? two Democrats? three? four? five?

Exhibit 4–2 illustrates the selection of one such five-person committee. Imagine that the committee members will be selected one at a time. Each selection is a separate event. In the diagram each event is depicted by a ● symbol and the possible outcomes of each event are shown by lines. The first event can result in the selection of a Democrat (the probability of this outcome is 0.4) or a Republican (the probability of this happening is 0.6). Regardless of what happens, the second committee member is picked next. The same two alternative outcomes are present and because it's a very large population, the probabilities remain unchanged. The outcome of the second event is not affected in any way by whatever the outcome was of the first event—that is, the events are *independent*. The committee selection process continues until all five committee members are picked. The diagram shows all the different paths by which every possible combination of Democrats and Republicans can be selected for the committee. There are 32 possible resultant outcomes, each having a unique order for the selection of its Republican and Democrat members. The probability of each committee makeup can be calculated by multiplying the probabilities of the outcomes that occurred along the path. For example, the probability of a Republican *and* a Democrat *and* a Republican *and* a

## *Exhibit 4–2*

**Tree diagram illustrating the random selection of five people for a committee from a population that is divided into two groups, *D* and *R*, with $p_D = 0.4$ and $p_R = 0.6$**

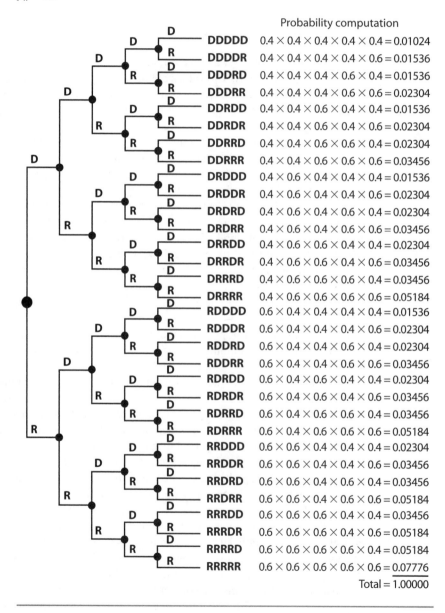

Probability computation

| | |
|---|---|
| **DDDDD** | $0.4 \times 0.4 \times 0.4 \times 0.4 \times 0.4 = 0.01024$ |
| **DDDDR** | $0.4 \times 0.4 \times 0.4 \times 0.4 \times 0.6 = 0.01536$ |
| **DDDRD** | $0.4 \times 0.4 \times 0.4 \times 0.6 \times 0.4 = 0.01536$ |
| **DDDRR** | $0.4 \times 0.4 \times 0.4 \times 0.6 \times 0.6 = 0.02304$ |
| **DDRDD** | $0.4 \times 0.4 \times 0.6 \times 0.4 \times 0.4 = 0.01536$ |
| **DDRDR** | $0.4 \times 0.4 \times 0.6 \times 0.4 \times 0.6 = 0.02304$ |
| **DDRRD** | $0.4 \times 0.4 \times 0.6 \times 0.6 \times 0.4 = 0.02304$ |
| **DDRRR** | $0.4 \times 0.4 \times 0.6 \times 0.6 \times 0.6 = 0.03456$ |
| **DRDDD** | $0.4 \times 0.6 \times 0.4 \times 0.4 \times 0.4 = 0.01536$ |
| **DRDDR** | $0.4 \times 0.6 \times 0.4 \times 0.4 \times 0.6 = 0.02304$ |
| **DRDRD** | $0.4 \times 0.6 \times 0.4 \times 0.6 \times 0.4 = 0.02304$ |
| **DRDRR** | $0.4 \times 0.6 \times 0.4 \times 0.6 \times 0.6 = 0.03456$ |
| **DRRDD** | $0.4 \times 0.6 \times 0.6 \times 0.4 \times 0.4 = 0.02304$ |
| **DRRDR** | $0.4 \times 0.6 \times 0.6 \times 0.4 \times 0.6 = 0.03456$ |
| **DRRRD** | $0.4 \times 0.6 \times 0.6 \times 0.6 \times 0.4 = 0.03456$ |
| **DRRRR** | $0.4 \times 0.6 \times 0.6 \times 0.6 \times 0.6 = 0.05184$ |
| **RDDDD** | $0.6 \times 0.4 \times 0.4 \times 0.4 \times 0.4 = 0.01536$ |
| **RDDDR** | $0.6 \times 0.4 \times 0.4 \times 0.4 \times 0.6 = 0.02304$ |
| **RDDRD** | $0.6 \times 0.4 \times 0.4 \times 0.6 \times 0.4 = 0.02304$ |
| **RDDRR** | $0.6 \times 0.4 \times 0.4 \times 0.6 \times 0.6 = 0.03456$ |
| **RDRDD** | $0.6 \times 0.4 \times 0.6 \times 0.4 \times 0.4 = 0.02304$ |
| **RDRDR** | $0.6 \times 0.4 \times 0.6 \times 0.4 \times 0.6 = 0.03456$ |
| **RDRRD** | $0.6 \times 0.4 \times 0.6 \times 0.6 \times 0.4 = 0.03456$ |
| **RDRRR** | $0.6 \times 0.4 \times 0.6 \times 0.6 \times 0.6 = 0.05184$ |
| **RRDDD** | $0.6 \times 0.6 \times 0.4 \times 0.4 \times 0.4 = 0.02304$ |
| **RRDDR** | $0.6 \times 0.6 \times 0.4 \times 0.4 \times 0.6 = 0.03456$ |
| **RRDRD** | $0.6 \times 0.6 \times 0.4 \times 0.6 \times 0.4 = 0.03456$ |
| **RRDRR** | $0.6 \times 0.6 \times 0.4 \times 0.6 \times 0.6 = 0.05184$ |
| **RRRDD** | $0.6 \times 0.6 \times 0.6 \times 0.4 \times 0.4 = 0.03456$ |
| **RRRDR** | $0.6 \times 0.6 \times 0.6 \times 0.4 \times 0.6 = 0.05184$ |
| **RRRRD** | $0.6 \times 0.6 \times 0.6 \times 0.6 \times 0.4 = 0.05184$ |
| **RRRRR** | $0.6 \times 0.6 \times 0.6 \times 0.6 \times 0.6 = 0.07776$ |

Total $= \overline{1.00000}$

Democrat *and* a Republican being picked in that order is $0.6 \times 0.4 \times 0.6 \times 0.4 \times 0.6$, which equals 0.03456. It's certain (that is, the probability is 1.00) that 1 of these 32 committee permutations must occur, and this is verified by the sum of the 32 probabilities totaling 1.00.

Exhibit 4–3 summarizes the results obtained by our analysis of the *tree diagram*. There are six possible combinations of Democrats and Republicans for the committee, ranging from all five committee members being Democrats to all five being Republican. Some combinations can occur several different ways. For

## *Exhibit 4–3*

**Frequency distribution for the random selection of a five-person committee from a hypothetical population that is 40% Democrat and 60% Republican**

| *Variable x* $x_1 + x_2 = n$ | | | | |
| --- | --- | --- | --- | --- |
| *Number of Democrats* $x_1$ | *Number of Republicans* $x_2$ | **Permutations** | **Relative frequency** | **Cumulative frequency** |
| 0 | 5 | RRRRR | 0.07776 | 0.07776 |
| 1 | 4 | DRRRR<br>RDRRR<br>RRDRR<br>RRRDR<br>RRRRD | $5 \times 0.05184$ $= 0.2592$ | 0.33696 |
| 2 | 3 | DDRRR RDRDR<br>DRDRR RDRRD<br>DRRDR RRDDR<br>DRRRD RRDRD<br>RDDRR RRRDD | $10 \times 0.03456$ $= 0.3456$ | 0.6825 |
| 3 | 2 | DDDRR DRRDD<br>DDRDR RDDDR<br>DDRRD RDDRD<br>DRDDR RDRDD<br>DRDRD RRDDD | $10 \times 0.02304$ $= 0.2304$ | 0.91296 |
| 4 | 1 | DDDDR<br>DDDRD<br>DDRDD<br>DRDDD<br>RDDDD | $5 \times 0.01536$ $= 0.0768$ | 0.98976 |
| 5 | 0 | DDDDD | 0.01024 | 1.00000 |
| | | Total | 1.00000 | |

instance, there are 10 permutations that each result in a committee with two Democrats and three Republicans. Each of these permutations has a probability of 0.03456. The net probability of the resultant two-Democrat, three-Republican combination is found by totaling the probabilities associated with the 10 ways that this can occur—that is, $10 \times 0.03456 = 0.3456$.

Suppose that many five-person committees are being randomly selected from an infinitely large population that is 40% Democrat and 60% Republican. What proportion of these committees will have two Democrat and three Republican members? Exhibit 4–3 shows that this result will occur with a relative frequency of 0.3456 or 34.56%. What proportion will have three Democrat and two Republican members? Again, referring to Exhibit 4–3, the proportion will be 0.2304 or 23.04%. What proportion of the committees will have a Republican majority? This result will occur if either three *or* four *or* five members of the committee are Republican. The respective probabilities of these outcomes must be added in order to obtain the answer—$0.07776 + 0.2592 + 0.3456 = 0.68256 \approx 68.2\%$.

This is an example of an expected frequency distribution called a **binomial distribution**. There are only two possible outcomes to each event. One of these outcomes will be designated as the outcome of particular interest. The result of each event is that either this outcome of interest occurs or it does not occur. If the outcome of interest occurs, the observation will be designated by assigning the numeric score "1." If the outcome of interest does not occur, the observation will be scored by a "0." The outcome of one event does not affect the outcome of any subsequent event (the events are statistically independent). The probabilities of the respective outcomes remain constant for all the events.

The observed variable, called $x$, is number of outcomes of interest that occur in $n$ events. For each event, the probability, $p$, for the outcome of interest, and $1 - p$ for the opposite outcome, remain constant. In this example there are five events. The outcome of each event is either the selection of a Democrat or the selection of a Republican. One of these outcomes, the selection of a Democrat, is regarded as the outcome of interest. The opposite outcome is the selection of a Republican. The variable in the problem is the number of Democrats selected for the committee. The possible values that this variable can take on range from 0 (no Democrats selected) to 5 (all committee members are Democrats). Each time a committee member is selected the probability of picking a Democrat is 0.40 and the probability of a Republican is 0.60.

The probabilities of the binomial distribution can be calculated by the following equation for the probability, $P_x$.[1]

$$P_x = \frac{n!}{x!(n-x)!}\, p^x(1-p)^{n-x}$$

---

[1] The notation "!" means "factorial" and is defined as the multiplication of an integer by every successively lower positive integer. For example, $5! = 5 \times 4 \times 3 \times 2 \times 1 = 120$. To make everything work out mathematically, 1! is defined as equaling 1 and 0! is also defined as equaling 1. Spreadsheets and advanced calculators have this function built in.

where

$P_x$ = net probability that among $n$ events exactly $x$ outcomes of interest will occur

$x$ = the number of times an outcome of interest is observed in $n$ events

$n$ = number of opportunities, events

$p$ = the probability of an outcome of interest occurring for any one independent event

For example, the computation of the probability of a five-person committee having three Democrats and two Republicans if the proportion of Democrats in the population is 0.4 proceeds as follows:

$$P_x = \frac{n!}{x!(n-x)!} \, p^x(1-p)^{n-x}$$

$$n = 5, x = 3, p = 0.4$$

$$P_x = \frac{5!}{3!(5-3)!} \, (0.4)^3(1-0.4)^{5-3}$$

$$P_x = 0.2304$$

Appendix A lists binomial probabilities. The table was created by solving the binomial equation for every combination of $n$, and $x$ up to $n = 20$ with probabilities ranging from 0.01 to 0.50 at 0.01 increments.

In order to become familiar with this table, here are four brief numeric exercises:

1. When $n = 8$ and $p = 0.3$, what is the probability that $x$ is exactly equal to 5? Enter the table at $n = 8$, go across to the column headed $p = 0.3$, and down to the row marked $x = 5$. The number found here, 0.0467, is the probability that $x$ is equal to 5.

2. When $n = 10$ and $p = 0.2$, what is the probability that $x$ is less than or equal to 4 ($x \leq 4$)? Enter that table at $n = 10$, go across to the column headed $p = 0.2$, and down to the row marked $x = 4$. This probability is 0.0881. Now add to this probability the probabilities for $x = 0, 1, 2,$ or 3. The final result is 0.1074 + 0.2684 + 0.3020 + 0.2013 + 0.0881 = 0.9672.

3. When $n = 13$ and $p = 0.45$, what is the probability that $x$ will be greater than 7 ($x > 7$)? Enter the table at $n = 13$, go across to the column headed $p = 0.45$, and down to the rows marked $x = 8, 9, 10, 11, 12,$ and 13. The sum of the numbers found here, 0.1787, is the probability of $x > 7$.

4. When $n = 18$ and $p = 0.8$, what is the probability that $x$ will be less than or equal to 10 ($x \leq 10$)? It appears that the table does not cover this situation. However, this question is the same thing as asking, "When $n = 18$ and $p = 0.2$, what is the probability that $x$ will be greater or equal to 8 ($x \geq 8$)?" The answer is 0.0120 + 0.0033 + 0.0008 + 0.0001 = 0.0162.

Turning to a real evaluation example—agricultural inspectors in California have the authority to stop a produce truck on its way to market in order to inspect the contents. One time the inspectors stopped a truck carrying 20 tons of watermelons. According to state regulations 90% of a sample of watermelons must pass inspection in order for the shipment to be allowed to proceed to market. The inspectors picked 20 watermelons at random, lined them up by the side of the truck, and split them open—2 watermelons were deemed to be "bad," of unacceptable quality. This was exactly 90% of the sample so the shipment passed inspection and was allowed to proceed to market.

Examine what these agricultural inspectors were doing in more detail. Their job was to *evaluate* this shipment of watermelons. Evaluation requires that an observation be compared to an expectation. The inspectors expected that at least 90% of the watermelons in the shipment would be good quality. They observed that 2 out of a random sample of 20 watermelons from the shipment were bad. They had to ask themselves a question and make a judgment. Was the shipment *different* from what they expected? They judged that 2 substandard watermelons out of 20 was not different from expectation and passed the shipment. But suppose that they had found 3 or more bad watermelons in their sample. They would have rejected the shipment, turned the truck around, and sent all 20 tons back to the grower.

What is the probability of finding three or more bad watermelons in a random sample of 20 if, indeed, the proportion of acceptable watermelons in the shipment is 90%. Turn to the table of binomial probabilities. Let the outcome of interest be that a watermelon is unacceptable. Thus, $n = 20$, $p = 0.10$ (the *expected* incidence of unacceptable watermelons), and $x \geq 3$ (the *observed* number of unacceptable watermelons).

The problem is sketched in Exhibit 4–4. Notice that it is not enough just to determine the probability of exactly three deficient watermelons. The analyst must find the net cumulative probability of all outcomes at least that extreme.

Use Appendix A to find the binomial probabilities for $n = 20$ and $p = 0.10$.

| $x \leq 2$ | $x \geq 3$ |
|---|---|
| $P_{x=0} = 0.1216$ | $P_{x=3} = 0.1901$ |
| $P_{x=1} = 0.2702$ | $P_{x=4} = 0.0898$ |
| $P_{x=2} = 0.2852$ | $P_{x=5} = 0.0319$ |
| | $P_{x=6} = 0.0089$ |
| | $P_{x=7} = 0.0020$ |
| | $P_{x=8} = 0.0004$ |
| | $P_{x=9} = 0.0001$ |
| $P_{x \leq 2} = 0.6770$ | $P_{x \geq 3} = 0.3231$ |

So it appears that the trucker and grower were pretty lucky in this produce inspection. If 90% of the watermelons were okay, the shipment still had about a 1 in 3 chance of being rejected.

## *Exhibit 4–4*

**20 watermelons**

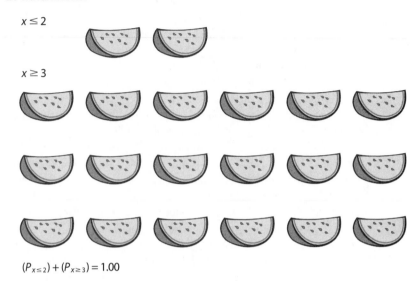

$x \leq 2$

$x \geq 3$

$(P_{x \leq 2}) + (P_{x \geq 3}) = 1.00$

# *Quick Concepts: Statistical Significance and Type I and Type II Errors*

If the agricultural inspectors had found three or more bad watermelons in the sample, they would have judged this observation to *significantly differ* from expectation. They would have rejected the notion that the proportion of good watermelons in the statistical population (the total shipment) was at least 90% and accepted the alternate conclusion that the true proportion of good watermelons in the shipment was less than 90%. The observation was judged to be unusual, different, not consistent, not the same as the expectation. The **level of significance** is the probability at which the idea of no difference, sameness, consistency, or equality between observation and expectation is rejected. In this example the agricultural inspectors used a level of significance of 0.32 or 32%. But they could be wrong. Although the sample data indicate that observation differs from expectation, maybe in truth there really is no difference. The con-

*(continued)*

cept is the same as erroneously convicting a defendant who is truly innocent. This is called a *Type I error*. It is also called a "false positive" result. The level of significance is the chance the analyst chooses to take of making a Type I error. What do you think of the level of significance used by the agricultural inspectors? Why did the agricultural inspectors use a level of significance of 32% rather than 5%? Discuss this question with your colleagues. Consider both the interests of the grower and the consumer.

*The level of significance is the defining threshold probability used by an evaluator for judging whether the difference between observation and expectation is unusual.* Imagine flipping a penny 20 times.* Suppose that the net result is 8 heads and 12 tails. The probability of 8 or fewer heads in 20 flips of a fair coin is 0.2517 or about 25%—1 chance in 4. This is called a ***p*-value**, the probability of obtaining an outcome at least as extreme as the one observed, given that the null hypothesis is true. Would you reject the idea that the coin was fair? How low a probability must an outcome have in order for you to judge the observation of that outcome as unusual? Is an outcome that has 1 chance in 5 (20%) of occurring unusual? Is 1 chance in 10 (10%) unusual? How about 1 chance in 20 (5%), or 1 chance in 100 (1%)? Most statisticians agree that if, based on initial expectation, an outcome has *a probability of 5% or less of occurring* by chance, and that outcome is indeed observed, the result is so unusual that it should lead us to question the truthfulness or accuracy of our initial expectation. An outcome that has a low probability, but nevertheless occurs, leads analysts to reject the null hypothesis of no difference and decide instead that observations (sample data) are unusually different from expectation—beyond a reasonable doubt—**statistically significant**. Analysts would like to set the possibility of a Type I error low so that the "burden of proof," so to speak, is on the data and the "benefit of the doubt" is given to the null hypothesis.

An analyst can also make another mistake: failing to reject a null hypothesis when in truth it is really false—like exonerating a defendant who is really guilty. This is called a *Type II error*. As the probability of a Type I error is decreased, the probability of a Type II error increases. (However, the two probabilities do not add to 1.0 so that specifying the level of significance does not allow immediate computation of the chance of a Type II error.) See Exhibit 4–5.

The "power" of a statistical test is equivalent to the probability of correctly rejecting a false null hypothesis (finding a truly guilty defendant guilty despite a plea of innocence.) (An equivalent definition is that the "power" of a test equals 1 minus the probability of a Type II error.) The power of a test is also

*(continued)*

---

*The null hypothesis is that the coin is fair—yielding about as many heads as tails in the long run.

influenced by the nature of the alternate hypothesis (one-tailed tests are more powerful than two-tailed tests) and by sample size (increasing the sample size will increase the power of a test). Sometimes one statistical test is preferred over another because it is regarded as more powerful. However, it is more important for the analyst to pay attention to the respective assumptions inherent in different statistical tests than to worry about relative power.

## *Exhibit 4–5*

**Type I and Type II Errors**

| | **"True reality" (unknown to the analyst)** | |
| --- | --- | --- |
| | *Null hypothesis true* | *Null hypothesis false* |
| **Analyst's decision based on sample data** | No difference between observation and expectation | Difference between observation and expectation |
| *The null hypothesis is "innocent!"* | *Not guilty* | *Guilty* |
| Reject null hypothesis Decide: *guilty* | Type I error The probability of this outcome is the "level of significance." | Correct! No error. The probability of this outcome is the "power" of a statistical test. |
| Do not reject null hypothesis Decide: *not guilty* | Correct! No error. | Type II error |

### 4.1.2 Normal Approximation to the Binomial

The table of cumulative binomial probabilities (Appendix A) only goes up to $n = 20$. What happens when $n$ is more than 20? Exhibits 4–6 and 4–7 show histograms of binomial probabilities for two situations: $n = 12$, $p = 0.791$; and $n = 20$, $p = 0.791$. In each diagram a curve is superimposed on the distribution. As the sample size, $n$, increases the probabilities of the binomial distribution approach ever closer to the probabilities shown by the curve.

The curve shown in these figures, called a *normal distribution*, is very special and important in the field of statistics.[2]

---

[2] The probability (relative frequency) for the normal distribution is defined by the equation

$$f(x) = \frac{1}{\sqrt{2\pi} \cdot \sigma} e^{-0.5[\frac{(x-\mu)}{\sigma}]^2}$$

## Exhibit 4–6

**Normal Approximation to the Binomial ($n = 12, p = 0.791$)**

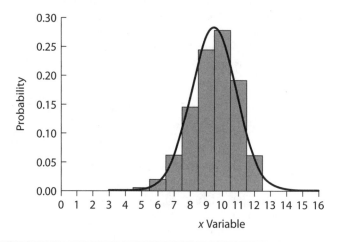

## Exhibit 4–7

**Normal Approximation to the Binomial ($n = 20, p = 0.791$)**

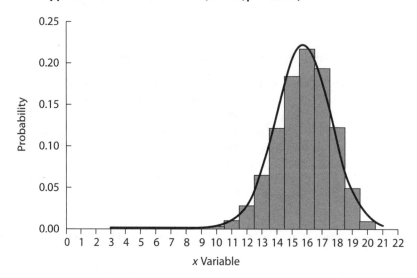

As $n$ becomes larger the values of a binomial distribution approach those of a normal distribution having a mean, $\mu$, equal to $n \cdot p$ and a variance, $\sigma^2$, equal to $n \cdot p \cdot (1 - p)$. This is called the *normal approximation to the binomial*.[3]

### 4.1.3  Mean and Standard Deviation of the Normal Approximation to the Binomial

$$\mu = n \cdot p$$
$$\sigma = \sqrt{n \cdot p \cdot (1 - p)}$$

The normal distribution has three special characteristics:

1. A normal distribution is symmetrical about its mean. If the distribution is separated into two parts by drawing a vertical line through the mean, the two halves of the curve are exact mirror images of each other.
2. The area under the normal curve, like the area under all relative frequency distributions, is equal to 1.00.
3. All normal distributions are fundamentally alike. Exhibit 4–8 shows three normal distributions. The value of the variable $x$ is shown on the horizontal axis and the corresponding probability of $x$ taking on any value is shown on the vertical axis. The three normal curves have the same mean, $\mu = 50$, but different standard deviations, $\sigma = 5, 10,$ and $20$. The larger the value of standard deviation, the more spread out is the shape of the distribution. In the second part of Exhibit 4–8, the three normal distributions are redrawn. First, the value of the mean is subtracted from every value of $x$. This, in effect, moves the zero point of the horizontal axis to the middle of the distributions. Values of $x$ greater than the mean have positive values of $x - \mu$ and values of $x$ less than the mean have negative values of $x - \mu$. The next step is to divide the values of $x - \mu$ for each distribution by the respective values of the standard deviation. Instead of values of $x$ the horizontal axis is now scaled in units of standard deviation above and below the mean. With a mean value of 50, an $x$ value of 60 is 2 units of standard deviation above the mean if $\sigma = 5$; 1 standard deviation above the

---

[3]The normal approximation to the binomial is recommended when $n$ is greater than 20. How well the approximation works depends on the sizes of $n$ and $p$. As a rule of thumb, both $n \cdot p$ and $n \cdot (1 - p)$ should equal at least 9. Situations may arise in which $n$ exceeds 20, yet the rule of thumb is violated because $p$ approaches 0 or 1. In these situations the analyst should either use the binomial equation (however, the numbers obtained by the expressions $n!$ or $(1 - p)^{n-x}$ may be too large or too small for many calculators or computer programs) or use the Poisson distribution approximation to the binomial. In the Poisson distribution, the probability of a specific value for the variable $x$ is defined by

$$f(x) = \frac{(n \cdot p)^x \cdot e^{-n \cdot p}}{x!}$$

## Exhibit 4–8

**(a) Normal Distributions (mean = 50, standard deviations (SD) = 1, 10, 20)**
**(b) Standardized Normal Distributions (standard deviations = 5, 10, 20)**

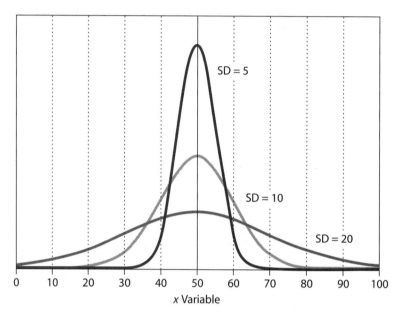

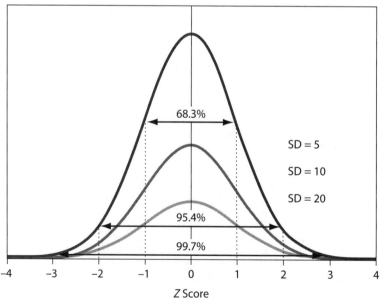

mean if $\sigma = 10$, and 0.5 standard deviations above the mean if $\sigma = 20$. The process is analogous to changing from representing your "height" as the distance from your feet to your head using the floor as the zero reference point and measuring with a ruler marked in inches to representing your "height" as the distance from your waistline to your feet in one direction and from your waistline to your head in the other using a yardstick. The computation $(x - \mu)/\sigma$ is called the **Z statistic** or *Z score*. Representing a distribution by computing the Z statistic is called *standardizing* the distribution. All normal distributions are fundamentally alike once they are represented in terms of the Z statistic. The proportion of the area under a normal curve within a specified Z statistic range is the same for every normal distribution. The proportionate areas are shown in Exhibits 4–8 and 4–9.

$$Z = \frac{x - \mu}{\sigma}$$

Areas under a relative frequency distribution describe probability. The probability of a normally distributed random variable, $x$, having a value within one standard deviation of the mean is 68.26%. All these values would be within a Z statistic range of $\pm 1$. What would be the range of the Z statistic such that the value of a normally distributed variable would have less than a 5% chance of occurring at random? As shown in Exhibit 4–10, if data are normally distributed, 95% of all observed values fall within the Z statistic range between $-1.96$ and $+1.96$. Therefore, any observed value of $x$ having a Z statistic outside of this range (that is, $Z < -1.96$ or $Z > +1.96$) has less than a 5% chance of occurring at random. The area describing this range is evenly split between the tails of the normal distribution (2.5% in each tail). Similarly, a value outside of the range $-2.57$ to $+2.57$ would have a probability of less than 1% of being observed at random.

If a value of a variable has less than a 5% chance of occurring at random, and nevertheless it is observed, it is a very unusual event. While unusual events can

## *Exhibit 4–9*

**Percentages of the Area under a Normal Curve**

| Z Statistic | Range | Percentage of the area |
|---|---|---|
| $\pm 1.00$ | $\mu \pm \sigma$ | 68.26% |
| $\pm 1.96$ | $\mu \pm 1.96\sigma$ | 95.00% |
| $\pm 2.00$ | $\mu \pm 2\sigma$ | 95.44% |
| $\pm 2.576$ | $\mu \pm 2.576\sigma$ | 99.00% |
| $\pm 3.00$ | $\mu \pm 3\sigma$ | 99.74% |

## *Exhibit 4–10*

**Areas Under a Normal Distribution**

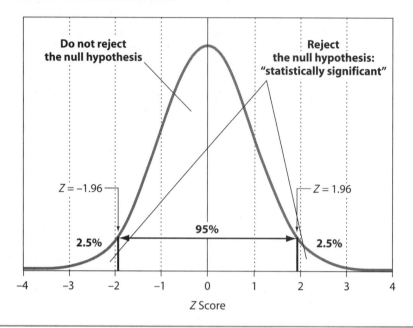

and sometimes do occur, their incidence is so rare that the observation of an event having such a low probability raises suspicions either about the reasonableness of our expectations regarding the characteristics of the population or about the randomness of the selection process.

### 4.1.4    Example: Jury Selection—A Landmark Case in the Definition of Discrimination

The United States Supreme Court has held that it is a denial of the equal protection of the laws guaranteed by the Fourteenth Amendment to the United States Constitution to try a defendant who has been indicted by a grand jury from which persons of his race or of an identifiable group to which he belongs have been purposefully excluded. Consider the situation of Rodrigo Partida, a Mexican–American, indicted in 1972 in Hidalgo County, Texas, for burglary of a private residence at night with intent to rape. He appealed his conviction—first in the state courts and then in the federal courts on a habeas corpus petition—alleging that the grand jury that indicted him had been selected in a discriminatory fashion. Part of the petitioner's proof involved comparing the observed number of Mexican–

## *Exhibit 4–11*

**Comparison of Hidalgo County, Texas, Grand Jury Sample and Countywide Adult Distributions by Ethnicity**

| Ethnicity | Observed distribution of grand jurors | | Expected distribution |
| | Number | Relative frequency | County population |
| --- | --- | --- | --- |
| Mexican–American | 339 | 39.0% | 79.1% |
| Other | 531 | 61.0% | 20.9% |
| Total | 870 | 100.0% | 100.0% |

Americans selected as grand jurors to an expected number. Over an 11-year period a total of 870 persons were summoned to serve on grand juries in Hidalgo County. The number of Mexican–Americans among this total was 339. This is the observation. The U.S. Bureau of the Census reports that in 1970 the percentage of the adult population in Hidalgo County classified as "Persons of Spanish Language or Spanish Surname" was about 79.1%.[4] This is the expectation. (See Exhibit 4–11.)

The expected number of Mexican–American grand jurors is

$$\mu = n \cdot p$$
$$\mu = 870 \cdot 0.791$$
$$\mu = 688$$

The standard deviation for the binomial distribution associated with $n$ and $p$ is

$$\sigma = \sqrt{n \cdot p \cdot (1 - p)}$$
$$\sigma = \sqrt{870 \cdot 0.791 \cdot (1 - 0.791)}$$
$$\sigma = 11.99$$

[4]The court examined questions about "Persons of Spanish Language or Spanish Surname" as an adequate operational definition of Mexican–Americans eligible to serve on a grand jury (for example, the possibility of counting illegal aliens who have Spanish surnames) but concluded that any adjustments to the assumption that all the persons of Spanish language or Spanish surname were Mexican–American were negligible.

The associated $Z$ statistic is

$$Z = \frac{\begin{bmatrix} \text{observed number of} & \_ & \text{expected number of} \\ \text{events of interest} & & \text{events of interest} \end{bmatrix}}{\begin{array}{c}\text{standard deviation of the number of events} \\ \text{of interest assuming the hypothesized value of } p\end{array}}$$

$$Z = \frac{x - \mu}{\sigma}$$

where

$x$ = observed number of events of interest

$\mu$ = expected number of events of interest

$\sigma$ = standard deviation of the expected number of events of interest

$n$ = sample size, that is, total number of observations (the number of opportunities for an event of interest to occur)

In this case,

$$Z = \frac{x - \mu}{\sigma}$$

$$Z = \frac{339 - 688}{11.99}$$

$$Z = -29.1$$

The difference between the observed and expected values is indeed statistically significant since the calculated value of $-29.1$ for the $Z$ statistic is less than the critical value of $-1.96$ at the 0.05 level of significance.[5]

This was an actual case argued before the United States Supreme Court.[6] In this case the Court "for the first time used formal statistical methods to determine whether data showing an underrepresentation of a particular ethnic group among persons selected to serve on grand juries supported an inference of discrimination against that group in violation of the equal protection clause of the fourteenth amendment to the Constitution."[7] The Court stated, "As a general rule for such

---

[5]The probability of obtaining a calculated value for $Z$ of $-29.1$ by chance is less than 1 in $10^{140}$.
[6]*Castaneda v. Partida* 430 U.S. 482 (1977).
[7]Thomas J. Sugrue and William B. Fairley, "A Case of Unexamined Assumptions: The Use and Misuse of the Statistical Analysis of *Castaneda/Hazelwood* in Discrimination Litigation," *Boston College Law Review*, 24 (July 1983): pp. 925–960.

large samples, if the difference between the expected value and observed number is greater than two or three standard deviations, then the hypothesis that the jury drawing was random would be suspect to a social scientist."[8] The Court concluded that the difference between observation and expectation could not be attributed to chance and constituted a prima facie case of intentional discrimination against Mexican–Americans in the grand jury selection process.

We can also use proportions in the computation of the $Z$ statistic. Dividing both the numerator and denominator by $n$, the equation for $Z$ becomes

$$Z = \frac{\dfrac{x}{n} - \dfrac{\mu}{n}}{\dfrac{\sigma}{n}}$$

The quantity $x/n$ is the observed incidence of the events of interest. It is expressed as $p_O$, the observed proportion of the total number of events in the sample.

The expected incidence of the event of interest, $p_E$, is derived from the relationship $\mu = np$. It is also expressed as a proportion of the sample size:

$$p_E = \frac{\mu}{n}$$

Recognizing that $\sigma = \sqrt{n \cdot p_E \cdot (1 - p_E)}$, the denominator becomes

$$\frac{\sigma}{n} = \frac{\sqrt{n \cdot p_E \cdot (1 - p_E)}}{n} = \sqrt{\frac{p_E(1 - p_E)}{n}}$$

and the equation for $Z$ is

$$Z = \frac{p_O - p_E}{\sqrt{\dfrac{p_E(1 - p_E)}{n}}}$$

Work the same example again using the formula for proportions:

$$Z = \frac{0.390 - 0.791}{\sqrt{\dfrac{0.791 \cdot (1 - 0.791)}{870}}}$$

$$Z = -29.1$$

---

[8]Sugrue and Fairley: "Grand jurors were not in fact selected by random drawing, but rather, under the Texas 'key man' system, on the personal judgment of jury commissioners." p. 928.

## 4.2    More Than Two Categories

### 4.2.1    Chi-Square Goodness-of-Fit Test

Evaluation as a process of comparing observation against expectation becomes clearer when the problem involves more than two categories of a single, nominally measured variable. The statistical test that applies in this situation is called the *chi-square* or *goodness-of-fit test*.

Suppose that an organization specializing in survey research contacts a random sample of voters within a state asking their opinion on a policy issue such as health care. The survey shows the following distribution of respondents by party registration: 51% Democratic, 39% Republican, and 10% other. These were the observations. The expectations come from the actual statewide distribution of party registration known by the state agency that supervises voter registration and elections—say it is 53% Democratic, 36% Republican, and 11% other affiliations.

Is there a statistically significant difference between the survey respondents and the population of registered voters with respect to party registration?

Exhibits 4–12 and 4–13 present the observed and expected frequency distributions.

The observed and expected absolute frequencies for each category are the product of the respective cell relative frequency and the sample size, as shown in Exhibit 4–14. Let "$f_{Oi}$" symbolize the observed frequency and "$f_{Ei}$" symbolize the expected frequency of the number of voters in each party category. The $\chi^2$ statistic (chi-square) is calculated by first squaring the difference between each ob-

## *Exhibit 4–12*

**Observed Distribution—Political Registration Reported in a Public Opinion Survey**

| Political registration | Observed distribution | |
| --- | --- | --- |
| | *Number* | *Relative frequency* |
| Democrat | Cell 1 471 | 51% |
| Republican | Cell 2 360 | 39% |
| Other | Cell 3 92 | 10% |
| Total | 923 | 100% |

## Exhibit 4-13

**Expected Distribution—Known Distribution of Political Registration**

| Political registration | Expected distribution Relative frequency |
|---|---|
| Democrat | Cell 1 53% |
| Republican | Cell 2 36% |
| Other | Cell 3 11% |
| Total | 100% |

served and expected frequency; then dividing by each expected frequency, respectively; and, finally, summing the results.

$$\chi^2 = \sum \frac{(f_{Oi} - f_{Ei})^2}{f_{Ei}}$$

Here are the computations, carried out cell by cell:

$$\text{Partial } \chi^2 \text{ for cell 1} = \frac{(471 - 489.19)^2}{489.19} = \frac{(-18.19)^2}{489.19} = \frac{330.88}{489.19} = 0.68$$

$$\text{Partial } \chi^2 \text{ for cell 2} = \frac{(360 - 332.28)^2}{332.28} = \frac{(27.72)^2}{332.28} = \frac{768.40}{332.28} = 2.32$$

$$\text{Partial } \chi^2 \text{ for cell 3} = \frac{(92 - 101.53)^2}{101.53} = \frac{(-9.53)^2}{101.53} = \frac{90.82}{101.53} = 0.89$$

$$\text{Total } \chi^2_{\text{calculated}} = 0.68 + 2.32 + 0.89 = 3.89$$

How unusual is a $\chi^2_{\text{calculated}}$ value of 3.89? Is the probability more than 5% (not statistically significant) or less than 5% (statistically significant)? To answer these questions we need to *compare* the *calculated* value of the $\chi^2$ statistic against a *critical* value of the $\chi^2$ statistic. The critical value marks the region of statistical significance for the $\chi^2$ distribution. Any calculated value of $\chi^2$ that exceeds the critical value has less than a 5% chance of occurring by random chance.

However, unlike the standard normal distribution, there are many $\chi^2$ distributions (Exhibit 4–15). The analyst selects the $\chi^2$ distribution applicable to the

## *Exhibit 4–14*

**Computation of the Expected Political Registration Frequency Among the Respondents to the Survey**

| Political registration | Number of voters |
|---|---|
| Democrat | Cell $i = 1$ <br> Observed frequency $= 0.51 \cdot 923 = 471$ <br> Expected frequency $= 0.53 \cdot 923 = 489.19$ |
| Republican | Cell $i = 2$ <br> Observed frequency $= 0.39 \cdot 923 = 360$ <br> Expected frequency $= 0.36 \cdot 923 = 332.28$ |
| Other | Cell $i = 3$ <br> Observed frequency $= 0.10 \cdot 923 = 92$ <br> Expected frequency $= 0.11 \cdot 923 = 101.53$ |

problem in order to determine the appropriate $\chi^2$ reference value. The distributions differ on the basis of *degrees of freedom*. For a one-variable problem, the number of degrees of freedom, *df*, equals the number of cells minus 1.

In this problem, there are three categories: Democratic, with a frequency of 471; Republican, with a frequency of 360; and Other, with a frequency of 92. The

## *Exhibit 4–15*

**Chi-Square Distributions (Degrees of Freedom = 1, 2, 3, 4, and 5)**

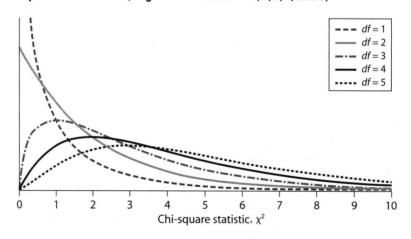

Chi-square statistic, $\chi^2$

categories are "linked" by the computation of the total frequency, 923. Knowing the total frequency, the analyst needs to know the frequency of only two of the three categories in order to fill in all the information about the observations.

$$\text{Degrees of freedom, } df = \text{number of cells} - 1$$
$$df = (3 - 1)$$
$$df = 2$$

Appendix D shows critical values for the chi-square statistic. The table is used by specifying the number of degrees of freedom for the problem and the desired level of significance. Using the table for 2 degrees of freedom and 0.05 (5%) level of significance, the $\chi^2$ critical value is 5.99. The calculated $\chi^2$ value of 3.89 is less than the critical $\chi^2$ value of 5.99. Therefore, the analyst concludes that there is no significant difference between the distribution of political affiliation among the survey respondents and the known distribution of political affiliation in the population from which the survey sample was drawn.[9]

## 4.3 Assumptions

Every statistical analysis involves assumptions. Assumptions mean "Watch out!" Assumptions are conditions that must be met before a statistical procedure can be applied. These prerequisite conditions may not be taken for granted. Each and every time you must stop, and think, and check whether or not they exist in the current problem that you are studying. If the conditions are not met, then the results of the statistical procedure, including any inferences or conclusions drawn from the results, are invalid—wrong. Do not assume! Verify!

A test of significance answers the question, "Is the difference between expectation and observation due to chance?"

Unless there is a clearly defined chance model, a test of significance makes no sense.

---

[9]The chi-square goodness-of-fit statistic is an approximation of the log-likelihood ratio. *G*-tests are coming into increasing use for goodness-of-fit problems. The equation for the *G* statistic is

$$G = 2 \cdot \sum \left[ f_{Oi} \cdot \ln \frac{f_{Oi}}{f_{Ei}} \right]$$

where ln denotes the natural logarithm (log to the base *e*), and the sum is taken over all cells. Degrees of freedom equal the number of cells minus 1 and the chi-squared table of critical values is used. In this example $G = 3.86$.

The binomial and chi-square tests have the tacit assumptions that

■ The observed events in the sample are all part of a stable, homogeneous statistical population in which all events (units of analysis) are alike except for the one characteristic (variable) by which we can logically classify the events into one or another categories.

■ Each unit of analysis is separate, unique, and independent. Whether or not a particular event is included in the observed sample has no effect upon whether any other event is included.

■ The probability that an observed unit of analysis will be of one type or another equals the respective proportion that the nominal categories make up in the statistical population.

■ Each of the events in the sample was selected in a manner tantamount to a random draw from the statistical population. For the chi-square test, the sample size must be large enough so that each of the expected frequencies is at least 5.

If these assumptions are false, the statistical methods do not apply, and if used may give erroneous results.

For instance, suppose that a program is supposed to be funded equally from federal, state, and local government agencies yet an audit shows the following record of actual expenditures depicted in Exhibit 4–16.

There is nothing to prevent the analyst from mathematically charging ahead and computing a test statistic such as $\chi^2$. However, an independent random selection model is assumed—consisting of 1,822,678 separate events. The assumption is not justified. The $1,822,678 cost of the program was not funded by randomly dipping into a vault filled with a mixture of federal, state, and local dollar bills. It is not a constant probability model. Rather, the monies were separate appropriations through planned budgetary processes. After appropriation, the dollars are not randomly selected for expenditure but are spent on various program functions influenced in part by the source of the funds. The table by itself does not say whether this program is properly administering the monies, and a simple test based only on summary proportions is the wrong way to find out.

## Exhibit 4–16

**Funding for a Hypothetical Program**

| Source of funding | Amount | Percentage |
|---|---|---|
| Federal | $599,427 | 32.9% |
| State | $613,388 | 33.6 |
| Local | $609,863 | 33.4 |
| Total | $1,822,678 | 99.9% |

# Homework Exercises

**4-1** Public health officials, conducting an immunization survey, found that in a sample of 537 people under the age of 15, a total of 460 had had the usual sequence of diptheria-pertussis-tetanus (DPT) vaccinations. Suppose that any community having fewer than 90% of their under-15 population vaccinated with the DPT series should be the target of an intensive immunization program. Should this particular community be included? Why?

---

For each of the 537 medical records reviewed in the survey the question was, Has this person received the usual sequence of DPT vaccinations? The possible values for this variable are Yes and No. The variable has a nominal level of measurement with two categories. The question involves a comparison of observation against an expectation (evaluation)—90% of the under-15 population should have the complete DPT series. For one-variable evaluation, nominal level of measurement, two categories, the appropriate statistical method is a binomial test. If the sample size is small (under 20), the binomial tables can be used. If the sample size is large, as in this problem, the normal approximation to the binomial can be used. The analyst wants to determine whether the observed number of people with the complete vaccination series, 460, is statistically significantly different from the criterion (expectation) of 90%—or $(0.90)(537) = 483.3$. The standard deviation is $\sigma = \sqrt{np(1 - p)} = \sqrt{537 \cdot 0.9(1.0 - 0.9)} = 6.95$.

$$Z_{calculated} = (x - \mu)/\sigma = (460 - 483.3)/6.95 = -3.35$$

The critical value for the $Z$ statistic at the 0.05 level of significance is $-1.64$ for a one-tailed test. Thus the proportion of people in Atlanta with the complete DPT series vaccinations is significantly lower than the 90% goal and the area qualifies for the intensive immunization program.

---

**4-2** Consider again the case of the agricultural inspection of the watermelon shipment. Remember that 90% of a sample must be acceptable in order to approve the shipment.

**a.** What is the probability of finding five or more unacceptable watermelons?

**b.** What would the proportion of acceptable watermelons in the shipment have to be in order for the probability of observing 2 or more unacceptable watermelons in a sample of 20 to be less than or equal to 5% (0.05)?

**c.** Find the probability of finding 2 or fewer unacceptable watermelons in a sample of 20 if only 80% of the watermelon shipment was of acceptable quality.

---

**a.** Let $n = 20$, $p = 0.1$, and $x \geq 5$. The probability of this happening is 0.0433.

**b.** Usually the analyst looks for $n$, $p$, and $x$ in the problem and solves for the binomial probability $P$. However, the problem can be solved if we know any three of the four factors. This question provides information about $n = 20$, $x \geq 2$, and $P = 0.05$. The analyst must find $p$. Transforming the binomial equation to solve for $p$ is not easy, but the analyst can use a computer to home in on a solution by trial and error. First, look at the binomial distribution for $n = 20$ and $p = 0.10$ (the proportion of acceptable watermelons in the shipment is 90%). The probability of finding 2 or more unacceptable watermelons in a sample of 20 is $P = 0.6081$. This is not the solution because the problem asked for $p$ such that $p \leq 0.05$. Next look at the binomial distribution for $n = 20$ and $p = 0.05$ (the proportion of acceptable watermelons is 95%). Now the probability of finding two or more unacceptable watermelons is $P = 0.2639$. This is still not the answer. Look at other binomial distributions with $n = 20$ and $p$ less than 0.05. Finally, examine the distribution for $n = 20$ and $p = 0.018$ (the proportion of acceptable watermelons is 98.2%). For this situation $P = 0.0495$. Here is the answer. In order for the probability to be less than 0.05 for finding 2 or more unacceptable watermelons out of a random sample of 20, the proportion of acceptable watermelons in the population (shipment) would have to be at least 98.2%. See Exhibit HW4–2A.

**c.** Let $n = 20$, $p = 0.2$, and $x \leq 2$. The probability is probability is 0.206.

## Exhibit HW4–2A

**Binomial Distributions for $n = 20$ and $p = 0.10, 0.05$, and $0.018$**

| $x$ | $p = 0.10$ Binomial probability | $p = 0.10$ Cumulative binomial probability | $p = 0.05$ Cumulative binomial probability | $p = 0.05$ Binomial probability | $p = 0.018$ Cumulative binomial probability | $p = 0.018$ Binomial probability |
|---|---|---|---|---|---|---|
| 0 | 0.1216 | 0.1216 | 0.3585 | 0.3585 | 0.6954 | 0.6954 |
| 1 | 0.2704 | 0.3919 | 0.3776 | 0.7361 | 0.2551 | 0.9505 |
| $\geq 2$ | 0.6081 | 1.0000 | 0.2639 | 1.0000 | 0.0495 | 1.0000 |

**4-3** Consider again the case of Mexican–American representation on the grand juries in Hidalgo County, Texas.

**a.** Suppose that the number of Mexican–Americans picked for grand jury service during the 11-year period in question was 675. Is this statistically significantly different from what was expected?

**b.** Return to the problem as it was first stated—339 Mexican–Americans out of a total of 870 serving on grand juries over an 11-year period. Now suppose that Mexican–Americans comprised 50% of the county's population instead of 79.1%. Is the observed grand jury call still statistically significantly different from expectation?

**a.**

$$Z = \frac{p_O - p_E}{\sqrt{\dfrac{p_E(1 - p_E)}{n}}}$$

$$Z = \frac{\dfrac{675}{870} - 0.791}{\sqrt{\dfrac{0.791 \cdot (1 - 0.791)}{870}}}$$

$$Z = -1.1$$

The difference between observation and expectation is not statistically significant.

**b.**

$$Z = \frac{p_O - p_E}{\sqrt{\dfrac{p_E(1 - p_E)}{n}}}$$

$$Z = \frac{0.390 - 0.500}{\sqrt{\dfrac{0.500 \cdot (1 - 0.500)}{870}}}$$

$$Z = -6.5$$

The difference between observation and expectation is statistically significant.

---

**4-4** Sort out the relevant data from the following description. Is there a prima facie case of a pattern or practice of racial discrimination? Why?

The Hazelwood School District covers 78 square miles in the northern part of St. Louis County, Missouri. By the 1967–1968 school year, 17,550 students were enrolled in the district, of whom only 59 were African–American; the number of African–American pupils increased to 576 of 25,166 in 1972–1973, a total of just over 2%. Hazelwood hired its first African–American teacher in 1969. The number of African–American faculty members gradually increased in successive years: 6 of 957 in the 1970 school year; 16 of 1,107 by the end of the 1972 school year; 22 of 1,231 in the 1973 school year. By comparison, according to the 1970 census figures, of more than 19,000 teachers employed in that year in the St. Louis area, 15.4% were African–American. That percentage figure included the St. Louis School District, which in recent years followed a policy of attempting to maintain a 50% African–American teaching staff. Apart from that school district, 5.7% of the teachers in the county were African–American in 1970. For the

1972–1973 school year, there were 2,373 applications for 282 vacancies and 10 African–American teachers were hired. The following year the District hired 123 new teachers, 5 of whom were African–Americans.[1]

## Exhibit HW4–4A

**Employment Disparities in the Hazelwood School District Computations for the Normal Approximation to the Binomial**

| Observation $x$ | Expected number of events $n$ | Relative frequency $p$ | Expectation $\mu = n \cdot p$ | Standard deviation $\sigma = \sqrt{n \cdot p \cdot (1 - p)}$ |
|---|---|---|---|---|
| 1969–70 | | | | |
| 6 | 957 | 15.4% | $957(0.154) = 147$ | $\sqrt{957(0.154)(1 - 0.154)} = 11$ |
| | | or | | |
| | | 5.7% | $957(0.057) = 54$ | $\sqrt{957(0.057)(1 - 0.057)} = 7$ |

$$Z = \frac{x - \mu}{\sigma}$$

$$Z = \frac{6 - 147}{11} = -12.8 \text{ or } Z = \frac{6 - 54}{7} = -6.8$$

| 1971–72 | | | | |
|---|---|---|---|---|
| 16 | 1,107 | 15.4% | $1,107(0.154) = 170$ | $\sqrt{1,107(0.154)(1 - 0.154)} = 12$ |
| | | or | | |
| | | 5.7% | $1,107(0.057) = 63$ | $\sqrt{1,107(0.057)(1 - 0.057)} = 7.7$ |

$$Z = \frac{x - \mu}{\sigma}$$

$$Z = \frac{16 - 170}{12} = -12.8 \text{ or } Z = \frac{16 - 63}{7.7} = -6.1$$

| 1972–73 | | | | |
|---|---|---|---|---|
| 22 | 1,231 | 15.4% | $1,231(0.154) = 190$ | $\sqrt{1,231(0.154)(1 - 0.154)} = 12.7$ |
| | | or | | |
| | | 5.7% | $1,231(0.057) = 70$ | $\sqrt{1,231(0.057)(1 - 0.057)} = 8.1$ |

$$Z = \frac{x - \mu}{\sigma}$$

$$Z = \frac{22 - 190}{12.7} = -13.2 \text{ or } Z = \frac{22 - 70}{8.1} = -5.9$$

[1]*Hazelwood School District v. United States*, 433 U.S. 299 (1977).

This is an actual case that came before the U.S. Supreme Court, *Hazelwood School District v. United States,* 433 U.S. 299 (1977). Three observations were made. Six African–American teachers comprised 0.63% of the Hazelwood School District's staff of 957 in 1969–1970. Sixteen, 1.44%, of the 1,107 teachers in 1971–1972 and 22, 1.79%, of 1,231 in 1972–1973 were African–American. Title VII of the Civil Rights Act of 1964 prohibits discrimination by employers on the basis of race. Therefore, "absent explanation, it is ordinarily to be expected that nondiscriminatory hiring practices will in time result in a work force more or less representative of the racial and ethnic composition of the population in the community from which employees are hired." The relevant expectation then is either 15.4% African–American teachers based on the known proportion of African–American school teachers in the St. Louis area, or 5.7% based on the known proportion of African–American teachers in the county outside of the St. Louis School District. Using the normal approximation to the binomial, the calculations proceed as shown in Exhibit HW4–4A.

There is nothing to prevent an analyst from mathematically charging ahead and computing a test statistic such as Z. However, there are two sources of variation; first, in recruiting the applicants, and second, in deciding which applicants to hire. It is almost impossible to define the pool of potential applicants, and even if you could, the actual applicants were not drawn from this pool by any constant probability (random) method; so there is no way to calculate chances. Therefore, the first source of variability cannot be dealt with. Neither can the second source—the selection procedure itself. Employers do not hire people by randomly drawing names from a hat; they use their judgment. The table by itself does not say whether this employer discriminates on the basis of race, and making a simple test based only on demographic proportions is the wrong way to find out.

**4-5** Consider the results of a survey of 330 city, 133 county, and 51 combined city–county planning commissions. In Exhibit HW4–5A the planning commissioners are categorized by race and population of the place where they serve.[2] The table also provides the relative frequency distribution for race in the U.S. population at the time.

**a.** Does the total distribution of planning commissioners by race differ significantly from the makeup of the U.S. population? Is the makeup of the U.S. population a relevant basis for comparison?

**b.** Divide all the absolute numbers in the table by 10 in order to simulate a smaller sample, but maintain the same relative frequencies. How does the comparison with respect to the racial distribution of the U.S. population change?

[2]Carolyn Browne, The Planning Commission: Its Composition and Function, 1979, American Planning Association, Planning Advisory Service, Chicago, IL 60637, Report No. 348, March 1980.

## Exhibit HW4–5A

**Composition of Planning Commissions, by Race/Ethnicity**

| Population | White | African–American | Latino | Other | Total |
|---|---|---|---|---|---|
| | | **Ethnicity** | | | |
| Under 25,000 | 384 | 8 | 10 | 1 | 403 |
| 25,000–50,000 | 735 | 29 | 11 | 2 | 777 |
| 50,001–100,000 | 643 | 27 | 10 | 4 | 684 |
| 100,001–250,000 | 347 | 33 | 13 | 1 | 394 |
| 250,001–500,000 | 106 | 19 | 4 | 4 | 133 |
| Over 500,000 | 52 | 12 | 7 | 1 | 72 |
| Total | 2,267 | 128 | 55 | 13 | 2,463 |
| Percentage | 92.04% | 5.20% | 2.23% | 0.53% | 100% |
| U.S. population percentage | 80.9% | 11.6% | 5.6% | 1.9% | 100.0% |

**c.** Multiply all the absolute numbers in the table by 10 in order to simulate a larger sample, but maintain the same relative frequencies. How does the comparison with respect to the racial distribution of the U.S. population change?

**d.** Is the summary conclusion for this evaluation the same regardless of population category?

**a.** See Exhibit HW4–5B.

## Exhibit HW4–5B

**Computation of the Chi-square Statistic**

| | | | | |
|---|---|---|---|---|
| Observed number | 2,267 | 128 | 55 | 13 |
| Expected number | 1,992.567 | 285.708 | 137.928 | 46.797 |
| $f_O - f_E$ | 274.433 | −157.708 | −82.928 | −33.797 |
| $(f_O - f_E)^2$ | 75,313.47 | 24,871.81 | 6,877.053 | 1,142.237 |
| $\dfrac{(f_O - f_E)^2}{f_E}$ | 37.8 | 87.1 | 49.8 | 24.4 |

$\chi^2_{\text{calculated}} = 199.1$

$df = 3$    $\chi^2_{\text{critical}} = 7.815$

**b.** See Exhibit HW4–5C.

## Exhibit HW4–5C

**Computation of the Chi-Square Statistic for a Simulated Smaller Sample**

| Population | White | African–American | Latino | Other | Total |
|---|---|---|---|---|---|
| Under 25,000 | 38 | 1 | 1 | 0 | 40 |
| 25,000–50,000 | 74 | 3 | 1 | 0 | 78 |
| 50,001–100,000 | 64 | 3 | 1 | 0 | 68 |
| 100,001–250,000 | 35 | 3 | 1 | 0 | 39 |
| 250,001–500,000 | 11 | 2 | 0 | 0 | 13 |
| Over 500,000 | 5 | 1 | 1 | 0 | 7 |
| Total | 227 | 13 | 5 | 0 | 245 |
| Percentages | 92.65% | 5.31% | 2.04% | 0.00% | 100.00% |
| U.S. population percentage | 80.9% | 11.6% | 5.6% | 1.9% | 100.0% |
| Expected number | 198.205 | 28.42 | 13.72 | 4.655 | |
| $f_O - f_E$ | 28.795 | −15.42 | −8.72 | −4.655 | |
| $(f_O - f_E)^2$ | 829.152 | 237.776 | 76.038 | 21.669 | |
| $\dfrac{(f_O - f_E)^2}{f_E}$ | 4.2 | 8.4 | 5.5 | 4.6 | |

$$\chi^2_{\text{calculated}} = 22.75$$
$$df = 3 \quad \chi^2_{\text{critical}} = 7.815$$

**c.** See Exhibit HW4–5D.

Parts a, b, and c of this problem illustrate that the $\chi^2$ statistic can be inflated by sample size even though the relative frequency distribution remains unchanged. A 10-fold increase in sample size with the same relative frequencies increases the chi-square statistic by a factor of 10. Similarly, a decrease in sample size decreases the value of the chi-square statistic by the same fraction.

**d.** No. For example, examine the population category shown in Exhibit HW4–5E.

# Exhibit HW4–5D

**Computation of the Chi-Square Statistic for a Simulated Larger Sample**

| Population | White | African–American | Latino | Other | Total |
|---|---|---|---|---|---|
| Under 25,000 | 3,840 | 80 | 100 | 10 | 4,030 |
| 25,000–50,000 | 7,350 | 290 | 110 | 20 | 7,770 |
| 50,001–100,000 | 6,430 | 270 | 100 | 40 | 6,840 |
| 100,001–250,000 | 3,470 | 330 | 130 | 10 | 3,940 |
| 250,001–500,000 | 1,060 | 190 | 40 | 40 | 1,330 |
| Over 500,000 | 520 | 120 | 70 | 10 | 720 |
| Total | 22,670 | 1,280 | 550 | 130 | 24,630 |
| Percentages | 92.65% | 5.31% | 2.04% | 0.00% | 100.00% |
| U.S. population percentage | 80.9% | 11.6% | 5.6% | 1.9% | 100.0% |
| Expected number | 19,925 | 2,857 | 1,379 | 468 | |
| $f_O - f_E$ | 2,745 | −1,577 | −829 | −338 | |
| $(f_O - f_E)^2$ | 7,535,025 | 2,486,929 | 687,241 | 114,244 | |
| $\dfrac{(f_O - f_E)^2}{f_E}$ | 378 | 870 | 498 | 244 | |

$\chi^2_{\text{calculated}} = 1{,}990$

$df = 3 \quad \chi^2_{\text{critical}} = 7.815$

# Exhibit HW4–5E

**Computation of the Chi-Square Statistic for the 250,001–500,000 Population Category**

| Population | White | African–American | Latino | Other | Total |
|---|---|---|---|---|---|
| 250,001–500,000 | 106 | 19 | 4 | 4 | 133 |
| Percentages | 79.70% | 14.29% | 3.01% | 3.01% | 100.00% |
| U.S. population percentage | 80.9% | 11.6% | 5.6% | 1.9% | 100.0% |
| Expected number | 107.597 | 15.428 | 7.448 | 2.527 | |
| $f_O - f_E$ | −1.597 | 3.572 | −3.448 | 1.473 | |
| $(f_O - f_E)^2$ | 2.55 | 12.76 | 11.89 | 2.17 | |
| $\dfrac{(f_O - f_E)^2}{f_E}$ | 0.02 | 0.83 | 1.60 | 0.86 | |

$\chi^2_{\text{calculated}} = 3.31$

$df = 3 \quad \chi^2_{\text{critical}} = 7.815$

**4-6** Suppose that a pollster issued a report that described the opinions of 273 parents of elementary school children in one school district on the question of "year-round school." There are seven schools in the district. The survey showed the distribution of respondents by school attendance area is shown in Exhibit HW4–6A. Is there a statistically significant difference between the distribution of survey respondents and the enrollment of elementary school children by school attendance area within the district?

## *Exhibit HW4–6A*

**Distribution of Respondents by School**

| School | Survey respondents | Actual student enrollment |
|---|---|---|
| 1 | 4.8% | 6.0% |
| 2 | 14.6 | 16.8 |
| 3 | 22.3 | 19.7 |
| 4 | 10.2 | 11.0 |
| 5 | 28.2 | 20.8 |
| 6 | 8.8 | 11.8 |
| 7 | 11.0 | 13.8 |

See Exhibit HW4–6B

$$\chi^2_{\text{calculated}} = 13.4 \quad \text{degrees of freedom} = (7 - 1) = 6$$

$$\chi^2_{\text{critical}} = 12.59 \quad 0.05 \text{ level of significance}$$

## *Exhibit HW4–6B*

**Survey of Parents of Elementary School Children**

| School | Relative frequency | | Absolute frequency ($n = 273$) | |
|---|---|---|---|---|
| | *Observed respondents* | *Expected respondents* | *Observed respondents* | *Expected respondents* |
| 1 | 4.8% | 6.0% | 13.1 | 16.4 |
| 2 | 14.6% | 16.8% | 39.9 | 45.9 |
| 3 | 22.3% | 19.7% | 60.9 | 53.8 |
| 4 | 10.2% | 11.0% | 27.8 | 30.0 |
| 5 | 28.2% | 20.8% | 77.0 | 56.8 |
| 6 | 8.8% | 11.8% | 24.0 | 32.2 |
| 7 | 11.0% | 13.8% | 30.0 | 37.7 |
| Total | 99.9% | 99.9% | 272.73 | 272.73 |

The difference between the distribution of survey respondents and the enrollment of elementary school children by school attendance area is statistically significant.

---

**4-7** Exhibit HW4–7A shows the probability of defendants making bail before and after the passage of a new law called the Bail Reform Act.[3]

**a.** What is the matter with the following display of results? Can you reproduce the analysis?

**b.** What are the "$N$"s listed in the table? The total number charged with an offense? The total number not making bail after being charged with an offense?

## Exhibit HW4–7A

**Probability of Defendants Not Making Bail, by Type of Offense: before and after the Law**

| Offense | $N$ | % | $Z$ | $p$ |
|---------|-----|-----|------|------|
| Illegal alien | 188 | | | |
| prelaw | | 95.7 | | |
| postlaw | | 100.0 | −2.46 | < 0.01 |
| White collar | 97 | | | |
| prelaw | | 25.0 | | |
| postlaw | | 11.5 | 1.73 | < 0.084 |
| Drug | 179 | | | |
| prelaw | | 39.1 | | |
| postlaw | | 51.3 | −1.56 | < 0.12 |
| Personal | 105 | | | |
| prelaw | | 83.7 | | |
| postlaw | | 72.6 | 1.34 | < 0.18 |

**a.** We cannot reproduce the computation of the $Z$ statistic from the data given.

**b.** It is not clear whether the "$N$"s in the table are the total number of people charged with an offense or the total number not making bail after being charged with an offense.

---

[3]Camille Nicholas, "Impact of the Bail Reform Act on Bail and Detention: Controlling for Type of Offense," unpublished manuscript, Department of Sociology, California State University, Sacramento, April 1987.

**4-8** Suppose that an agency is making a hiring decision. The general practice at this agency is to identify five finalists on the basis of evaluating each applicant's résumé and letters of recommendation. The five finalists are invited for a personal interview, after which a hiring decision is made.

**a.** For one job opening two of the finalists were female and three were male. One of the male applicants was hired. Do these observations support a prima facie charge of sex discrimination?

**b.** Two more job openings occur. Again there were two females and three males among each group of finalists. Each time one of the male finalists was hired. Do these observations (three hiring decisions) support a prima facie charge of sex discrimination?

**c.** Over the course of the next three years this agency had 16 more job openings in which there were two females and three males in the finalist group. Each time one of the male finalists was hired. Do these observations (19 hiring decisions) support a prima facie charge of sex discrimination? [4]

---

**a.** Assuming that the final hiring decision can be approximated by a random selection model—i.e., each of the five finalists has an equal probability of being hired—the probability of hiring a male is 3 out of 5, or 60%. This is not unusual and does not support a prima facie charge of sex discrimination.

**b.** Now there are three observations, each of which has a 60% probability that a male will be hired. The net probability that the three independent hiring decisions result in three male hires is $0.60 \cdot 0.60 \cdot 0.60 = 0.216$, or about 22%. Again, this is not unusual and does not support a prima facie charge of sex discrimination.

**c.** Now there are 19 observations, each of which has a 60% probability that a male will be hired. The net probability that the three independent hiring decisions result in three male hires is $(0.60)^{19} = 0.000061$. Another way to find the answer is to use the table for the binomial distribution where $p = 0.40$ (the probability that a female will be selected in any one hiring decision), $n = 19$ (the number of hiring decisions), and $x = 0$ (the number of females hired). The result is statistically significant. Indeed, it is nearly impossible that these outcomes could have occurred by chance. A prima facie charge of sex discrimination is supported.

The point is that although the outcome of any one event is not judged unusual, the net outcomes of a set of similar events may be unusual. The data in this problem are a simplified representation of a court case in which the erroneous

---

[4]A.J. Jaffe and Herbert F. Spirer, *Misused Statistics: Straight Talk for Twisted Numbers*, (New York: Marcel Dekker, Inc., 1987) p. 176, after Charles R. Mann, "Abuses of Statistics in Civil Rights Legislation," 1980 Annual Meeting, The American Statistical Association, Houston, 1980.

conclusion was, "Since no individual case allows a conclusion of disparity (at the 0.05 level), it is concluded that there is no reason to believe that [the jobs] were disproportionately awarded to males."

---

**4-9**  Suppose that an agency has an office in each of the 20 counties in a state. A serious budget crunch requires a significant reduction in force. Allegations of age discrimination are made, and a statistical test at each site (at the 0.05 level of significance) shows a relationship between age and layoff at 2 of the 20 sites. Does the agency have an inherent practice of age discrimination?

   **a.** At each site the statistical test has a 0.05 probability of indicating statistical significance when there is really no relationship between the age of the employee and the layoff decision. What is the probability of finding two sites with a statistically significant relationship in the application of the statistical test to 20 different samples?

   **b.** What is the probability of finding two or more sites with a statistically significant relationship in the application of the statistical test to 20 different samples?

   **c.** How many sites need to show a statistically significant relationship between the age of the employee and the layoff decision in order to conclude that the agency has an inherent practice of age discrimination?

---

Use Appendix A, Binomial Probability Distribution.

   **a.** $x = 2$
   $p = 0.05$
   $n = 20$
   $P = 0.1887$

   **b.** $x \geq 2$
   $p = 0.05$
   $n = 20$
   $P = 0.2641$

   **c.** $P \leq 0.05$
   $p = 0.05$
   $n = 20$
   $x \geq 4 ; P = 0.0158$

---

**4-10**  In court cases dealing with divorce, most of the time it is the male former spouse who is ordered to pay child support. However, in one county, in 3.4% of the cases, females must pay support. In recent years, the family support division of the district attorney's office prosecuted 310 cases for failure to pay support. Five of these cases had female defendants. The county public defender's office alleges that the district attorney's family support division selectively enforces the law and discriminates against men in prosecuting child support cases.

**a.** What is the probability that *x* (the number of cases with female defendants) is five or fewer?

**b.** Examine the assumptions in this problem. Is the public defender's allegation of discrimination supported by the statistical analysis? How could a statistical analysis study be designed in order to check the charge of sex discrimination in deciding which cases to prosecute?

---

**a.** The expected number of cases involving female defendants is 10.54. $(n)(p) = (310)(0.034) = 10.54$. The probability of selecting a sample of 310 cases, five or fewer cases having female defendants, out of a larger statistical population comprised of 3.4% potential female defendants and 96.6% potential male defendants is 0.0465, using the binomial distribution. (Using the normal approximation to the binomial: mean = 10.54; standard deviation = 3.19; $Z = -1.74$; $P_{x \leq 5} = 0.0409$. Using the Poisson approximation to the binomial: mean = 10.54; $P_{x \leq 5} = 0.0492$.)

**b.** The binomial distribution is a mathematical (statistical) model. All statistical models have assumptions. The usefulness of a statistical model to explain a management or policy problem depends on the extent to which the assumptions are verified, that is, reasonably describe the situation. The inferences from a statistical model are useful only to the extent that the assumptions make sense. The inherent assumptions in the use of the binomial distribution in this situation are (1) There is a large population of potential prosecutions (many more than 310); (2) Women comprise 3.4% of this population because (a) women who are ordered to pay child support are as likely to renege on their obligation as men, (b) women who renege on their child support obligations have the same potential ability to pay as men, and (c) no other variables are relevant to the district attorney's office in deciding which cases to prosecute; and (3) Otherwise, the district attorney's office uses a decision-making process tantamount to random selection in determining which cases to prosecute.

An analyst, designing an evaluation study, should determine the proportion of all complaints of nonpayment that involve potential female defendants, the proportion of all potential cases in which female defendants have about the same ability to pay as male defendants, and compare these proportions to the proportion of female defendants among the cases actually prosecuted.

---

**4-11** Two inmates at San Quentin Prison were charged with possession of a weapon as a prisoner. One is Latino; the other African–American. They filed motions in superior court to dismiss the charges alleging discriminatory enforcement of the law by the Marin County district attorney. In one year, 16 out of 23 defendants (69.5%) referred to the public defender on weapons offenses from San Quentin were nonwhite. The racial/ethnic makeup of San Quentin's inmates at the time was 36% white, 21% African–American, 19% Mexican–American, and 24% "other." A total of 541 reports of weapons offenses were filed with the district attorney during this same period. Is the allegation of selective prosecution supported by the evidence at hand?[5]

---

Using the binomial distribution, the probability that 16 or more of the 23 weapons cases referred to the public defender would involve nonwhite inmates, if the nonwhite proportion in the population is 0.64, is 0.3748. This assumes that the proportion of nonwhite inmates charged with weapons offenses is the same as the proportion of nonwhite inmates in San Quentin. It does not seem that there is a prima facie showing of discriminatory enforcement.

---

**4-12**  Exhibit HW4–12A presents data regarding the African–American population and percent of traffic stops in which the driver was African–American for the 10 police districts in San Francisco.[6] Do these data support an allegation of "racial profiling?

## *Exhibit HW4–12A*

**African–Americans as Percentage of Population and Traffic Stops by Police District, San Francisco**

| District | Percent of population | Stop rate |
|---|---|---|
| A Central | 2.2 | 10.3 |
| B Southern | 11.9 | 15.3 |
| C Bayview | 38.8 | 52.1 |
| D Mission | 2.9 | 14.6 |
| E Northern | 8.8 | 15.3 |
| F Park | 10.4 | 13.5 |
| G Richmond | 2.7 | 4.6 |
| H Ingleside | 6.6 | 14.0 |
| I Taraval | 5.3 | 7.7 |
| J Tenderloin | 11.7 | 21.2 |

---

[5]*People v. Ochoa et al.*, 165 Cal.App.3d 885, 212 Cal. Rptr. 4.
[6]Mark Schlosberg, "A Department In Denial: The San Francisco Police Department's Failure To Address Racial Profiling," American Civil Liberties Union of Northern California, October 7, 2002. http://www.aclunc.org/police/021007-report.pdf

Yes. Calculated chi-square $\approx 107$

---

**4-13** "Scanning the crowded courtroom of 60 prospective jurors, Stockton defense attorney Patrick Piggott saw not one African–American face. He protested, and the judge dismissed the panel, bringing in 45 more would-be jurors. Again, not a single African–American was in the crowd."[7] Piggott filed a motion challenging the county's jury system. The county counsel stated, "Our system meets all the constitutional requirements. You don't have a right to select the specific jurors you want to hear your case. What the law says is you can't exclude specific people and that's not what's happening here." The jury commissioner randomly draws prospective jurors from the lists of registered voters and licensed drivers in the county. The ethnic makeup of the county is Anglo 56%, Latino 25%, Asian/Pacific Islander 14%, Black 5%, and Native American 1%. Assume that the adult population from which jury pools are drawn has the same ethnic distribution. How likely is it that a randomly drawn jury pool of 105 people will have no African–Americans?

Binomial test or $Z$ test (normal approximation to the binomial), $n = 105$

$$P_x = \frac{n!}{x!(n-x)!} \; p^x(1-p)^{n-x}$$

$$P_x = \frac{105!}{0!(105-0)!} \; (0.05)^0(1-0.05)^{105-0}$$

$$P_x = 0.0046$$

$$\mu = np$$

$$\mu = 105 \cdot 0.05$$

$$\mu = 5.25$$

$$\sigma = \sqrt{np(1-p)}$$

$$\sigma = \sqrt{105 \cdot 0.05 \cdot (1-0.05)}$$

$$\sigma = 2.23$$

---

[7]Elizabeth Bell, "Lawyer: Too Few Blacks on S.J. Juries" *The Record* (Stockton, CA), 9 November 1998.

$$Z = \frac{x - \mu}{\sigma}$$

$$Z = \frac{0 - 5.25}{2.23}$$

$$Z = -2.35$$

The difference between the observed and expected number of African–Americans in the 105-person jury pool is statistically significant.

# CHAPTER 5

# Ranks and Scales: One-Variable Evaluation—Ordinal and Interval Measures

| Kind of problem | *Evaluation* |
|---|---|
| Number of variables | *One* |
| Level of measurement | *Ordinal or interval* |

T his chapter continues the study of evaluation problems that involve only one variable. The preceding chapter focused on problems in which the variable had a nominal level of measurement. This chapter looks at situations in which the variable has an ordinal or an interval level of measurement. As before, the essence of evaluation is a comparison of observation against expectation.

First addressed are one-variable evaluation problems in which the variable has an ordinal level of measurement. The Kolmogorov–Smirnov one-variable test, which is appropriate for any sample size, compares an observed cumulative frequency distribution against an expected "population" cumulative frequency distribution. The evaluation question at hand is whether the observations included in the sample were drawn from the expected frequency distribution or, alternatively, are these observations so different (unusual) that an analyst should conclude that they are not representative of the expected distribution.

Next, one-variable evaluation problems in which the variable has an interval level of measurement are considered. The methods for this situation are the $Z$ test and $t$-test. These methods compare an observed frequency distribution against an expected frequency distribution using what is known about the central tendency (mean) and dispersion (standard deviation) of the observed and expected distributions (see Exhibit 5–1).

**107**

## Exhibit 5–1

**One-Variable Evaluation—Ordinal or Interval Level of Measurement**

| Sample size $n$ | Level of measurement | |
| | Ordinal | Interval |
| --- | --- | --- |
| $n \leq 30$ | | $t$-test |
| | Kolmogorov– Smirnov one-variable test | |
| | | $t$-test |
| $n > 30$ | | $Z$-test |

## 5.1 Ordinal Level of Measurement

### 5.1.1 Kolmogorov–Smirnov Test

The Kolmogorov–Smirnov one-variable test compares the observed cumulative frequency distribution against an expected cumulative frequency distribution. The greatest difference between observed values and expected values is determined. The test checks the probability of obtaining a maximum difference of this magnitude if the observations were really randomly selected from the population described by the expected distribution.

A study of traffic accident causes by the University of North Carolina Highway Safety Research Center for the AAA Foundation for Traffic Safety examined approximately 5,000 crashes. One variable considered was the age of the driver. The data are summarized in Exhibit 5–2. The variable *age* has been grouped into five categories. Therefore, it has an ordinal level of measurement. The age distribution of all drivers, as known by the Federal Highway Administration, is also shown.

## Exhibit 5–2

**Age Distributions of Drivers Involved in Crashes and All Drivers**

| Age group | Relative frequency | |
| | Involved in crashes | All drivers |
| --- | --- | --- |
| < 20 | 16.9% | 4.7% |
| 20–29 | 29.9 | 17.2 |
| 30–49 | 35.4 | 40.3 |
| 50–64 | 9.9 | 23.2 |
| 65+ | 7.8 | 14.5 |
| Total | 99.9% | 99.9% |

The frequency distribution is recast in Exhibit 5–3 to show *observed cumulative proportions* and *expected cumulative proportions*.

The differences, *d*, between the observed and expected cumulative proportions are listed in the last column for each ordinal category. The largest value of *d*, regardless of whether it is positive or negative, is the calculated value of the Kolmogorov–Smirnov *D* statistic. In this example, *D* = 0.249.

How likely is it that an analyst will observe a value for *D* of 0.249 if traffic accidents are random events occurring with about equal likelihood among all age groups? The criterion for "unusualness" is a probability of 0.05 (5%). This probability value is called the *level of significance*. The calculated value of the *D* statistic must be compared against the critical value of the *D* statistic at the specified level of significance. If the calculated value is greater than the critical value, the observed frequency distribution is dubbed unusual or "statistically significant" since it would have less than a 5% probability of occurring given the assumption that the specified expected distribution truly depicts the population.

Appendix E lists critical values of the Kolmogorov–Smirnov *D* statistic for different sample sizes and level of significance. The sample size in this example exceeds 100, so the critical value of the *D* statistic is determined by the following computation:

$$D_{\text{critical } n > 100} = \frac{1.358}{\sqrt{n + \Delta n}}$$

$$\text{where } \Delta n = \frac{\sqrt{n + 4}}{3.5} = \frac{\sqrt{5004}}{3.5} = 20.21$$

$$D_{\text{critical } n > 100} = \frac{1.358}{\sqrt{5000 + 20.21}} = 0.019$$

The calculated value for the *D* statistic of 0.249 is greater than the critical value of 0.019. Therefore the difference between the observed age distribution of drivers and the expected age distribution is statistically significant. An analyst can

## Exhibit 5–3

**Age Distributions of Drivers Involved in Crashes—Showing Computations for the Kolmogorov–Smirnov One-Variable Test**

| Age group | Observed cumulative proportion | Expected cumulative proportion | Difference *d* |
|---|---|---|---|
| < 20 | 0.169 | 0.047 | 0.122 |
| 20–29 | 0.468 | 0.219 | **0.249 = *D*** |
| 30–49 | 0.822 | 0.622 | 0.200 |
| 50–64 | 0.921 | 0.854 | 0.067 |
| 65+ | 0.999 | 0.999 | 0.000 |

conclude that in terms of age the drivers involved in crashes are not representative of the total population of drivers. It is reasonable to infer that age is associated with accident risk. It is up to policy makers and public administrators to develop appropriate rules for driver licensing and vehicle operation.

## 5.2   One Variable, Interval Level of Measurement (n > 30)

### 5.2.1   The Z Test

This section addresses the problem of comparing the observation against expectation for a variable having an interval or ratio level of measurement. The discussion starts with a hypothetical consumer protection case.

Suppose a consumer buys a bag of potato chips at a local store. The wrapper of the bag states, "Net weight 8 ounces." The consumer decides to check this information—opens the bag and dumps the contents onto a scale. The scale indicates that the weight is 7.8 oz. Was the consumer gypped? Should the consumer file a complaint? The observed weight is 0.2 oz less than expected. The difference could be due to chance—a random occurrence—or it could have been due to some systematic process that results in underfilled bags of potato chips. To decide which, the consumer–analyst needs some more information. How are potato chips made? More precisely, how do potato chips come to be placed in bags labeled "Net weight 8 ounces"? Imagine that at the end of the assembly line there is a potato chip bagging machine with a big dial on it set to 8 oz. Loose potato chips and empty bags come in at one end and filled bags come out the other. The potato chip bagging machine is set so that the mean weight of the contents will be 8 oz. However, the machine is not perfect (and potato chips after all are supposed to be chips, not crumbs), so that some bags have slightly less than 8 oz and some bags have slightly more than 8 oz. The extent to which the potato chip bagging machine turns out underweight and overweight bags is described by the standard deviation. The standard deviation is not printed on the bag so the consumer–analyst consults the operating manual for the machine. Suppose the manual says that the potato chip bagging machine operates in such a fashion that the distribution of the net weight of the contents is a normal distribution with a mean of 8 oz and a standard deviation of 0.2 oz.

Did the consumer purchase an unusually underweight bag of potato chips? Compare observation to expectation, using the Z statistic.

$$Z = \frac{x - \mu}{\sigma}$$

$$Z = \frac{7.8 - 8.0}{0.2}$$

$$Z = -1.0$$

For an observation to be unusual, it must meet the accepted criterion of statistical significance. That is, the probability of the observation occurring by random chance must be less than 5%. For a normal distribution the 5% region is defined by a $Z$ statistic value of $\pm 1.96$. Since the calculated $Z$ statistic value of $-1.00$ is not less than $-1.96$, the one bag of potato chips cannot be deemed unusually underweight.

Now suppose that the consumer–analyst still questions whether 8-oz bags of potato chips are being systematically underfilled by the potato chip bagging machine. Checking the weight of one bag after another—one at a time—will get nowhere. In addition, there are two other problems with this procedure. First, there is no basis to assume that the frequency distribution of the weight approaches a normal curve. Maybe it does. Maybe it doesn't. Second, the consumer–analyst had to rely on the statement in the instruction manual (or some other source) about the standard deviation of the statistical population.

There is a mathematical principle that will let the evaluation proceed. It's called the *central limit theorem*.

Continuing the hypothetical potato chip example: after the filled bags of potato chips exit the potato chip bagging machine they are stored in the potato chip bag warehouse. Imagine opening the door and seeing millions upon billions of 8-oz bags of potato chips. Suppose somehow the consumer–analyst knew the frequency distribution of the net weight of this statistical population of bags of potato chips. It could look like the distribution shown in Exhibit 5–4. The distribution has

## *Exhibit 5–4*

**Hypothetical Population Frequency Distribution (mean = 8.0, standard deviation = 0.2)**

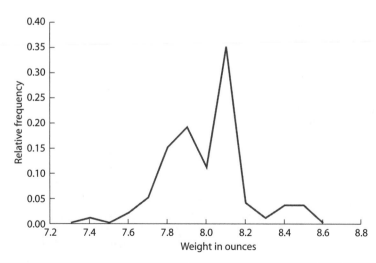

a mean of 8 oz and a standard deviation of 0.2 oz but it does not in the slightest re-semble a normal curve. Now suppose the consumer–analyst brings every friend and relative to the warehouse and each one randomly selects a sample of 100 bags, weighs the contents of each, and calculates the mean (arithmetic average) of the sample. Each person reports the mean weight of the sample and the consumer–analyst draws a frequency distribution of the sample means. This will approximate a normal distribution (see Exhibits 5–5 and 5–6)! Its mean will be the same as the population mean. Its standard deviation will be less than the population standard deviation by a factor based on the size of each sample. The standard deviation of the frequency distribution of sample means is $\sigma/\sqrt{n}$.

This is **the central limit theorem**: *Regardless of the population frequency distribution, the distribution of sample means, for large samples, approaches a normal distribution with a mean equal to the population mean, $\mu$, and a standard deviation of $\sigma/\sqrt{n}$, where $\sigma$ is the population standard deviation* (see Exhibit 5–7).

Actually, the consumer–analyst is going to obtain just one sample—randomly pick just 100 bags of potato chips out of the seemingly infinite population and find the mean weight of this one sample. Suppose that the mean weight is 7.8 oz. What does this say about the population of all bags of potato chips labeled "Net weight

## *Exhibit 5–5*

**Distribution of Sample Means (mean = 8 oz, standard deviation = $\dfrac{\sigma}{\sqrt{n}}$ = $\dfrac{0.2}{\sqrt{100}}$ = 0.02)**

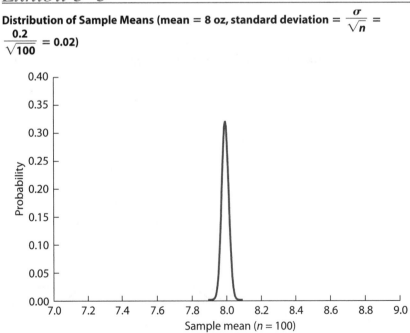

## *Exhibit 5–6*

**Distribution of Sample Means—enlarged (mean = 8 oz, standard deviation =**
$\frac{\sigma}{\sqrt{n}} = \frac{0.2}{\sqrt{100}} = 0.02$)

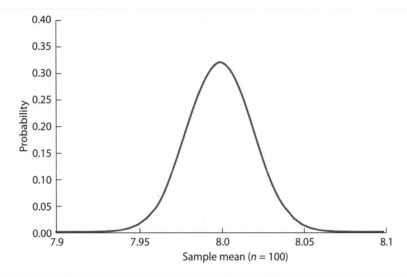

## *Exhibit 5–7*

**The Central Limit Theorem**

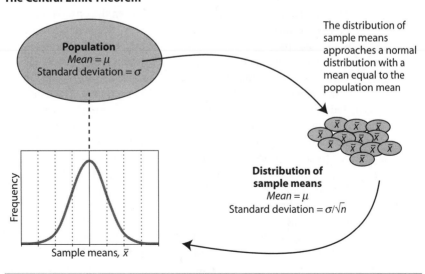

8 ounces"? In order to answer this evaluation question the consumer–analyst must compare the observed mean weight from the sample of 100 to an expected distribution of sample means. Because of the central limit theorem, the expected distribution of sample means is known to be closely approximated by a normal distribution with a mean of $\mu$, the population mean, and a standard deviation of $\sigma/\sqrt{n}$, where $\sigma$ is the population standard deviation. Using this information a $Z$ statistic is calculated representing a comparison of observation against expectation. The observed event outcome is no longer the weight of the contents of a single bag of potato chips, but the single mean weight from one sample of 100 bags of potato chips. Therefore, the observed value in the numerator is the sample mean, $\bar{x}$. The expected characteristics are the mean, $\mu$, and the standard deviation of the distribution of sample means, $\sigma/\sqrt{n}$.

$$Z = \frac{\bar{x} - \mu}{\dfrac{\sigma}{\sqrt{n}}}$$

$$Z = \frac{7.8 - 8.0}{\dfrac{0.2}{\sqrt{100}}}$$

$$Z = -10$$

Is a calculated value of $-10$ for the $Z$ statistic unusual? The critical value for the $Z$ statistic at the 0.05 level of significance is $\pm 1.96$. The calculated value of $Z$ greatly exceeds the critical value. Obtaining a sample of 100 bags that has an observed mean weight of 7.8 oz from a statistical population in which the expected true mean weight is really 8.0 oz has much less than a 5% chance of occurring by random happenstance. The difference between the observed central tendency and expected central tendency is statistically significant. The less than 5% probability is so small that the consumer–analyst rejects the notion that somehow a "rare" sample was obtained—instead, the consumer–analyst concludes that the characteristics of the sample are all too typical—therefore, it must be the expectation rather than the observation that is out of the ordinary. The consumer–analyst concludes that the potato chip bagging machine is putting less product in the bags than it is supposed to according to the package label. Whether intended or unintended the action is systematic and constitutes a prima facie case for investigation and action by the appropriate consumer protection agency.

As illustrated in Exhibits 5–8 and 5–9, hypothesis tests are designated as either *one-tailed* or *two-tailed*, referring to the end regions of the frequency distribution—where the probability values are small. A two-tailed test means that the analyst is interested in checking whether observations differ from expectation by *either* being too high *or* too low. A calculated value of the test statistic is significant at the 5% level if it is among than the top 2.5% of possible values or within the lowest 2.5% of possible values. For a normal distribution the top 2.5% region begins at $Z = 1.96$ and the bottom 2.5% region begins at $Z = -1.96$.

## Exhibit 5–8

**The Two-Tailed Test**

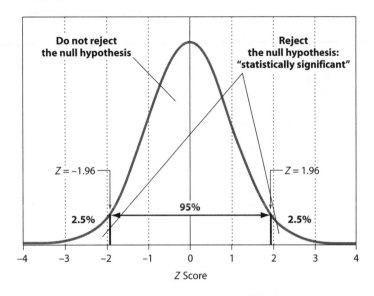

## Exhibit 5–9

**The One-Tailed Test**

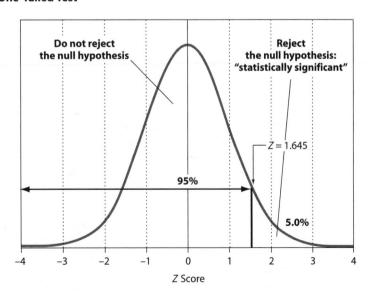

Sometimes the analyst is interested only in whether observations are higher than expectation—or, vice versa, whether they are lower than expectation. This is a one-tailed test. The calculated value of the test statistic is significant at the 5% level if it is among the most extreme (highest or lowest) 5% of possible values. For a normal distribution the top 5% region begins at $Z = 1.645$ and the bottom 5% region begins at $Z = -1.645$. In the potato chip example, the consumer–analyst probably doesn't mind if the contents are actually more than 8 oz—only if they are less. If so, then this is a one-tailed problem and the appropriate critical value for $Z$ at the 0.05 level of significance is $-1.645$.

### 5.2.2 The *t*-Test

Only one problem remains. The evaluation analysis depended upon knowledge of the standard deviation of the population, $\sigma$. In the preceding example the analyst somehow conveniently knew the answer. However, most of the time an analyst does not know anything about the statistical population—not the shape of its frequency distribution—not its central tendency—not its dispersion. The only information the analyst has is the central tendency and dispersion of the observations that obtained in the sample.

Fortunately, there is a way out of this dilemma. It is to use another statistic and another frequency distribution. The statistic is the $t$ statistic. The $t$ statistic compares an observed sample with a sample mean, $\bar{x}$, and sample standard deviation, $s$, against an expected distribution with a mean, $\mu$.

$$t = \frac{\bar{x} - \mu}{\frac{s}{\sqrt{n}}}$$

In 1995, a Manhattan-bound New York subway J train traveling at about 34 mph ran through a red signal on the Williamsburg Bridge. The emergency brakes were automatically activated but failed to stop the train before it crashed into another train 288 feet past the signal. The motorman was killed and 54 passengers were injured. The cars on the J train were the R-40 model, built between 1967 and 1969, and overhauled in 1988 and 1989. The rebuilding contract specified that trains should be able to come to an emergency stop from 30 mph on a level track in 220 to 250 feet. On reenacting the accident a few days later, experts observed that a test train needed about 350 feet to stop.[1] Suppose that braking tests were conducted on a sample of five randomly selected R-40 trains with the results shown Exhibit 5–10.

Is the average stopping distance in this sample statistically significantly different from the maximum expected distance specified in the rebuilding contract? In order to examine this question the analyst sets up a hypothesis test. The first

---

[1]Richard Pérez-Peña, "Brake Deterioration Is Tied to Brooklyn Subway Crash," *New York Times,* June 30, 1995: B3.

## Exhibit 5–10

**R-40 Trains: distance to stop from 30 mph (hypothetical data)**

| Observation number | Distance to stop from 30 mph (feet) |
| --- | --- |
| 1 | 240 |
| 2 | 275 |
| 3 | 316 |
| 4 | 250 |
| 5 | 299 |

step is to state a *null hypothesis*. This is a statement that there is *no difference* between observation and expectation. A null hypotheses is a "straw man." The analyst purposely sets up the null hypothesis to try to refute it using the observed data. If, given the null hypothesis, the probability of the analyst's observations is very small (say less than 5%), the analyst rejects the null hypothesis as untrue and is left with the *alternate hypothesis*—in this example that the actual braking distance for R-40 trains does not comply with the expected standard.

The next step is to calculate a value for the *t* statistic using the sample data and the null hypothesis that there is no difference between the observed mean and the expected mean for braking distance. The five observed braking distances have a mean of 276 feet and a standard deviation of 32.02 feet. Say that the average expected braking distance is 240 feet (within the range specified by the contract).

$$t = \frac{\bar{x} - \mu}{\frac{s}{\sqrt{n}}}$$

$$t = \frac{276 - 240}{\frac{32.02}{\sqrt{5}}}$$

$$t_{calculated} = 2.51$$

Unlike the standard normal distribution, the distribution of the *t* statistic depends on the sample size. For each value of *n*, there is a different *t* distribution. At large sample sizes the differences are minor and, in fact, the *t* distribution closely approximates the standard normal distribution. However, at small sample sizes ($n < 30$) the analyst needs to look up unique critical values of the given the sample size in the problem. The sample size comes into play in determining the *degrees of freedom*. For a one variable problem, in which we want to employ the *t*-test, the degrees of freedom, *df*, equal $n - 1$. There are 4 degrees of freedom in this problem example.

The critical values for the *t* statistic for one-tailed and two-tailed tests for various degrees of freedom and levels of significance are listed in Appendix F.

## *Exhibit 5–11*

**t Distributions**

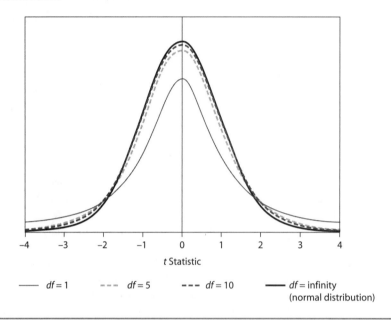

If the analyst is interested in the question of the braking distance being either more than or less than the expected average (a two-tailed test) at the 0.05 (5%) level of significance, the critical value of the *t* statistic is ±2.776. A two-tailed test at the 0.01 (1%) level of significance is ±4.604. If the analyst is interested only in the braking distance exceeding the standard (one-tailed test), *t* critical is ±2.132 at the 0.05 level of significance and ±3.747 at the 0.01 level of significance. The calculated value of *t*, $t_{calculated}$ = 2.51, does not exceed the critical value for a two-tailed test at the 0.05 level of significance, but it does exceed the critical value with a one-tailed test. Therefore, the central tendency of the observed braking distances significantly differs (exceeds) the expected average of 240 feet. The analyst rejects the null hypothesis that the mean braking distance is 240 feet—leaving the alternate hypothesis that the R-40s braking distance is more than it should be.

## *Homework Exercises*

**5-1** The "Great San Francisco Parking Meter Scandal." In 1972 a civil grand jury in San Francisco reported the information shown in Exhibit HW5–1A contrasting the average daily parking meter collections for a 120-day period on selected routes against the average collections on the same routes for a 5-day period during which collections were closely supervised.[1] Exhibit HW5–1B presents hypothetical data for this 5-day period. Examine these data and report your conclusions.

## Exhibit HW5–1A

**Parking Meter Collections**

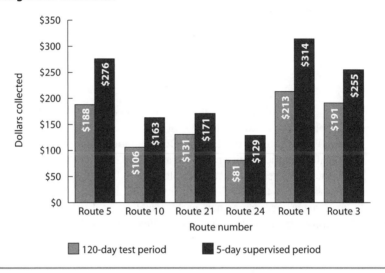

## Exhibit HW5–1B

**San Francisco Grand Jury Figures on Meter Money, 1972**

| Route | Average daily collections during 120-day test period | Daily collections during supervised 5-day period | | | | |
|---|---|---|---|---|---|---|
| | | Day 1 | Day 2 | Day 3 | Day 4 | Day 5 |
| FINANCIAL | | | | | | |
| Route 5 | $188 | $294 | $336 | $260 | $257 | $235 |
| Route 10 | 106 | 183 | 148 | 229 | 113 | 141 |
| MISSION | | | | | | |
| Route 21 | 131 | 207 | 197 | 143 | 129 | 180 |
| Route 24 | 81 | 153 | 105 | 78 | 103 | 204 |
| REST OF CITY | | | | | | |
| Route 1 | 213 | 261 | 296 | 343 | 314 | 358 |
| Route 3 | 191 | 258 | 243 | 278 | 233 | 262 |

[1]Russ Cone and Jim Wood, "Metergate: An Early Warning," *San Francisco Examiner*, 26 March 1978.

The average daily collections for the 5-day period are certainly different from the 120-day period. But is the difference great enough to warrant a call to the district attorney? Treat the average daily collection of the 120-day period as the population mean. Let the daily collections during the 5-day observed period be a five-case sample. The mean and standard deviation of these daily collections can be computed for each route. Because the sample size is small, use a one-sample (one-variable) *t*-test.

$$t = \frac{\bar{x} - \mu}{\frac{s}{\sqrt{n}}} \text{ where } n \text{ equals the sample size, } 5$$

The critical value for *t* for a one-tailed test at the 0.05 level of significance, 4 degrees of freedom, is 2.1—at the 0.01 level of significance it is 3.7. Exhibit HW5–1C shows results of the computations and indicates that there are statistically significant differences in average daily collections on all the routes at either the 0.05 level (*) or at the 0.01 level (**). The analysis needs to be qualified by the assumption that the 5-day supervised period is not unlike the 120-day test period (That is, there are no new parking meters, no differences in parking regulations or enforcement, and no seasonal traffic differences).

## *Exhibit HW5–1C*

**San Francisco Grand Jury Figures on Meter Money, 1972**

| Route | Average daily collections 120-day test period $\mu$ | Sample mean $\bar{x}$ | $\bar{x} - \mu$ | Sample standard deviation $s$ | Statistic $t$ |
|---|---|---|---|---|---|
| FINANCIAL | | | | | |
| Route 5 | $188 | $276 | $88 | 39.4 | 5.0** |
| Route 10 | 106 | 163 | 57 | 44.6 | 2.8* |
| MISSION | | | | | |
| Route 21 | 131 | 171 | 40 | 33.9 | 2.7* |
| Route 24 | 81 | 129 | 48 | 50.1 | 2.1* |
| REST OF CITY | | | | | |
| Route 1 | 213 | 314 | 101 | 38.4 | 5.9** |
| Route 3 | 191 | 255 | 64 | 17.4 | 8.2** |

*Significant at the 0.05 level.
**Significant at the 0.01 level.

**5-2** In 1980 a three-year study of cement kiln dust (CKD) was approved by Congress.

> Cement kiln dust is a waste product that accumulates at the rate of 4 to 12 million tons per year in the United States. This dust has considerable resource potential: It is already being used as a neutralizer for coal mine waste effluents, and the agricultural and construction industries are beginning to use it more extensively as a substitute for lime. . . . Part of the concern over the environmental effects of waste CKD resulted from a single study of the heavy metals content of a CKD sample [sic] from Blaubeuren, West Germany, showing lead content of 5,620 micrograms per gram. The only other analysis of CKD for heavy metals was a sample [sic] from Polk County, Georgia, showing 124 micrograms per gram for lead.[2]

A previous contracted Environmental Protection Agency study of the cement industry concluded:

> Waste kiln dust is probably the most serious pollution control problem facing the cement industry at this time. Relatively little is known about the dust, so environmentally adequate management techniques are difficult to specify.[3]

One hundred thirteen (113) one-gallon containers of CKD were obtained from 102 plants in the United States. The mean lead concentration of this sample was 253 micrograms per gram with a standard deviation of 303 micrograms per gram. Assume that these results are representative of CKD throughout the United States.

**a.** Is the mean lead content of CKD in the United States statistically significantly different from the reported lead content of CKD in Germany?

**b.** Is the mean lead content of CKD in the United States statistically significantly different from the reported lead content of CKD in Georgia?

---

**a.** Use a one-variable $t$-test with $\bar{x} = 253$, $\mu = 5{,}620$, $s = 303$, and $n = 113$. The mean lead concentration of the 113 one-gallon containers of CKD is significantly lower than the value reported in Germany.

**b.** Use a one-variable $t$-test with $\bar{x} = 253$, $\mu = 124$, $s = 303$, and $n = 113$. The mean lead concentration of the 113 one-gallon containers of CKD is significantly higher than the value reported in Georgia.

---

[2]Benjamin W. Haynes and Gary W. Kramer, *Characterization of U.S. Cement Kiln Dust*, Information Circular 8885, U.S. Department of the Interior, Bureau of Mines, Washington, DC, September 1982.

[3]As cited in Haynes and Kramer, A.T. Kearney, Inc., *Multimedia Assessment and Environmental Research Needs of the Cement Industry*, Contract 68-03-2586, U.S. Environmental Protection Agency, Report No. G-195 (1979).

**5-3** Student Evaluations of Teaching (SET) are very important in most colleges and universities. They are often referred to in making decisions regarding the retention, promotion, or tenure of faculty members. A typical SET method is to distribute a questionnaire, at the end of each semester, that contains a series of multiple-choice questions about the course and the instructor. The student is asked to respond to each question by checking one category on a five-point scale like this:

1 ❏ excellent or strongly agree    2 ❏ good or agree    3 ❏ neutral    4 ❏ poor or disagree    5 ❏ very poor or strongly disagree

Suppose that an instructor has 10 students in a seminar and in response to a question on an SET survey about providing a summary overall rating for the course the frequency distribution of their responses is as follows:

| | |
|---|---|
| Excellent | 3 |
| Good | 5 |
| Neutral | 0 |
| Poor | 0 |
| Very poor | 2 |

Suppose further that the overall university relative frequency distribution of SET responses to this question is as follows:

| | |
|---|---|
| Excellent | 27.6% |
| Good | 64.4 |
| Neutral | 4.9 |
| Poor | 2.1 |
| Very poor | 1.0 |

**a.** Is the SET rating of this course significantly different from other courses at this university?

**b.** Suppose that the SET survey for another seminar with ten students showed the following results:

| | |
|---|---|
| Excellent | 3 |
| Good | 0 |
| Neutral | 5 |
| Poor | 0 |
| Very poor | 2 |

Is the SET rating of this course significantly different from other courses at this university?

---

This problem involves one variable having an ordinal level of measurement. Therefore, use a Kolmogorov–Smirnov test for the evaluation.

**a.** Set the problem up as in Exhibit HW5–3A.

The observed value for the *D* statistic is 0.190. From Appendix E, Critical Values of *D* in the Kolmogorov–Smirnov One-Variable Test, with a sample size of 10, the critical value of *D* at the 0.05 level of significance is 0.410. Since the observed value of *D* is less than the critical value of *D*, the analyst concludes that the distribution of SET values for the seminar is not statistically significantly different from the overall university-wide distribution of SET scores on this variable.

**b.** Set the problem up as in Exhibit HW5–3B.

The observed value for the *D* statistic is 0.620. As before, the critical value for the *D* statistic for a sample size of 10 and 0.05 level of significance is 0.41. In this situation the observed value of *D* exceeds the critical value of *D*. Therefore, the distribution of SET scores for this seminar is statistically significantly different from the university-wide distribution for this variable.

## *Exhibit HW5–3A*

**Computations for the Kolmogorov–Smirnov One-Variable Test**

| Category | Observed absolute frequency | Observed cumulative frequency | Observed cumulative proportion | Expected relative frequency | Expected cumulative proportion | Difference *d* |
|---|---|---|---|---|---|---|
| 1 | 3 | 3 | 0.3 | 0.276 | 0.276 | 0.024 |
| 2 | 5 | 8 | 0.8 | 0.644 | 0.920 | 0.120 |
| 3 | 0 | 8 | 0.8 | 0.049 | 0.969 | 0.169 |
| 4 | 0 | 8 | 0.8 | 0.021 | 0.990 | **0.190 = D** |
| 5 | 2 | 10 | 1.0 | 0.010 | 1.000 | 0.000 |

## *Exhibit HW5–3B*

**Computations for the Kolmogorov–Smirnov One-Variable Test**

| Category | Observed absolute frequency | Observed cumulative frequency | Observed cumulative proportion | Expected relative frequency | Expected cumulative proportion | Difference *d* |
|---|---|---|---|---|---|---|
| 1 | 3 | 3 | 0.3 | 0.276 | 0.276 | 0.024 |
| 2 | 0 | 3 | 0.3 | 0.644 | 0.920 | **0.620 = D** |
| 3 | 5 | 8 | 0.8 | 0.049 | 0.969 | 0.169 |
| 4 | 0 | 8 | 0.8 | 0.021 | 0.990 | 0.190 |
| 5 | 2 | 10 | 1.0 | 0.010 | 1.000 | 0.000 |

**5-4** Does the distribution of Graduate Management Admission Test (GMAT) scores presented in Homework Exercise 3–1 differ significantly from a normal distribution? The GM Council reported that the mean GMAT score of 622,975 people taking the test between 2004 and 2006 was 526.6 with a standard deviation of 117.

## Exhibit HW5–4A

**Kolmogorov–Smirnov One-Variable Test Comparing the Distribution of a GMAT Scores against a Normal Distribution With Mean = 526.6 and Standard Deviation = 117**

| Total score | Proportion below | Z value of score | Expected cumulative proportion | d |
|---|---|---|---|---|
| 260 | 0.02 | −2.2786 | 0.0113 | 0.0087 |
| 280 | 0.02 | −2.1077 | 0.0175 | 0.0025 |
| 300 | 0.03 | −1.9368 | 0.0264 | 0.0036 |
| 320 | 0.04 | −1.7658 | 0.0387 | 0.0013 |
| 340 | 0.06 | −1.5949 | 0.0554 | 0.0046 |
| 360 | 0.08 | −1.4239 | 0.0772 | 0.0028 |
| 380 | 0.11 | −1.2530 | 0.1051 | 0.0049 |
| 400 | 0.14 | −1.0821 | 0.1396 | 0.0004 |
| 420 | 0.18 | −0.9111 | 0.1811 | −0.0011 |
| 440 | 0.22 | −0.7402 | 0.2296 | −0.0096 |
| 460 | 0.27 | −0.5692 | 0.2846 | −0.0146 |
| 480 | 0.33 | −0.3983 | 0.3452 | −0.0152 |
| 500 | 0.39 | −0.2274 | 0.4101 | −0.0201 |
| 520 | 0.45 | −0.0564 | 0.4775 | −0.0275 |
| 540 | 0.51 | 0.1145 | 0.5456 | −0.0356 |
| 560 | 0.58 | 0.2855 | 0.6124 | −0.0324 |
| 580 | 0.64 | 0.4564 | 0.6760 | **−0.0360 = D** |
| 600 | 0.70 | 0.6274 | 0.7348 | −0.0348 |
| 620 | 0.76 | 0.7983 | 0.7876 | −0.0276 |
| 640 | 0.80 | 0.9692 | 0.8338 | −0.0338 |
| 660 | 0.86 | 1.1402 | 0.8729 | −0.0129 |
| 680 | 0.89 | 1.3111 | 0.9051 | −0.0151 |
| 700 | 0.92 | 1.4821 | 0.9308 | −0.0108 |
| 720 | 0.96 | 1.6530 | 0.9508 | 0.0092 |
| 740 | 0.98 | 1.8239 | 0.9659 | 0.0141 |
| 760 | 0.99 | 1.9949 | 0.9770 | 0.0130 |

Exercise 3–1 presents an ordinal ranking of scores and a cumulative relative frequency distribution. Compute the Kolmogorov–Smirnov $D$ statistic, $D = -0.036$. The sample size, $n$, is 100 (that is, 100%). At the 0.05 level of significance the critical value of the $D$ statistic is 0.136. Therefore, the distribution of GMAT scores is not statistically significantly different from a normal distribution with the stated mean and standard deviation. See Exhibit HW5–4A.

**5-5** The preferred evaluation method for a problem with one variable having an ordinal level of measurement is the Kolmogorov–Smirnov one-variable test. However, sometimes the chi-square one-variable goodness-of-fit test is used. The chi-square test compares the number (frequency) of observations in each category to an expected number. Although the categories are ranked to form an ordinal level of measurement, unlike the Kolmogorov–Smirnov test the chi-square test does not use this additional information and treats the categories as a nominal level of measurement. If the differences between the observed and expected frequencies for each category are small, the calculated value for the $\chi^2$ statistic will also be small. However, as the magnitude of the differences increase it becomes less likely that the observations were drawn from the same population described by the expected frequency distribution. The chi-square test should only be employed for intermediate sample sizes ($30 < n < 250$).

Pertussis (whooping cough) is a highly contagious, vaccine-preventable bacterial illness. In the United States, most hospitalizations and nearly all deaths from pertussis are reported in infants aged less than 6 months. Infant/childhood vaccination has contributed to a reduction of more than 90% in pertussis-related morbidity and mortality since the early 1940s. Among 28,923 persons from the 50 states and the District of Columbia with pertussis for whom age was reported during 2001–2003, 6,608 (23%) were aged less than 1 year (including 5,872 aged under 6 months), 3,353 (12%) were aged 1–4 years, 2,553 (9%) were aged 5–9 years, 9,609 (33%) were aged 10–19 years, and 6,800 (23%) were aged 20 or over. Suppose that in a given year a state reports the distribution of pertussis cases by age group as shown in Exhibit HW5–5A.

## Exhibit HW5–5A

**Number of Pertussis Cases by Age Group**

| Age group | Number of cases |
|---|---|
| < 6 mo | 57 |
| 6–12 mo | 41 |
| 13–18 mo | 6 |
| 19–23 mo | 6 |
| 2–4 yr | 18 |
| 5–9 yr | 17 |
| ≥ 10 yr | 12 |

*Exhibit HW5–5B*

**Pertussis Cases by Age Group: Calculation of χ² and Kolmogorov–Smirnov D**

| Age group | Observed frequency | Observed relative frequency | Expected relative frequency | Cumulative observed frequency | Cumulative expected frequency | d | Expected frequency | Partial chi-squared |
|---|---|---|---|---|---|---|---|---|
| < 6 mo | 57 | 0.3631 | 0.2030 | 0.3631 | 0.2030 | 0.1600 | 31.8744 | 19.8057 |
| 6–12 mo | 41 | 0.2611 | 0.0254 | 0.6242 | 0.2285 | 0.3957 | 3.9952 | 342.7543 |
| 1–4 yr | 30 | 0.1911 | 0.1159 | 0.8153 | 0.3444 | 0.4709 | 18.2008 | 7.6492 |
| 5–9 yr | 17 | 0.1083 | 0.0883 | 0.9236 | 0.4327 | **0.4909** = D | 13.8582 | 0.7123 |
| 10 + | 12 | 0.0764 | 0.5673 | 1.0000 | 1.0000 | 0.0000 | 89.0714 | 66.6881 |
| Total | 157 | 1.0000 | 0.9999 | | | | 157 | 437.6 |

Does this distribution differ significantly from the nationwide data? Use a chi-squared goodness-of-fit test as well as a Kolmogorov–Smirnov one-variable test.

The observed state distribution of pertussis incidence by age differs significantly from the national distribution. The calculated value of Kolmogorov–Smirnov $D$ is 0.49 and calculated chi-square equals 437 (see Exhibit HW5–5B).

**5-6**  At one time, the court system in one New Jersey county had about 400 cases on its docket more than a year old. It hired a new court administrator who had a track record of success in reducing a large backlog of cases. The administrator set productivity goals for judges—three trials and 40 cases to be disposed of every month—and reorganized the court staff into teams—judges, attorneys, support staff, typists, and data entry clerks—to identify bottlenecks and keep cases moving.[4] Exhibit HW5–6A shows the backlog distribution of cases for two consecutive years.

**a.**  Was the case backlog in significantly reduced?

**b.**  Draw cumulative relative frequency bar charts.

## *Exhibit HW5–6A*

**Active Pending Criminal Cases**

| Time pending: More than | Percentage of cases | |
|---|---|---|
| | *Year 1* | *Year 2* |
| 0 months | 100% | 100% |
| 4 months | 68% | 62% |
| 12 months | 35% | 31% |
| 18 months | 22% | 18% |

**a.**

## *Exhibit HW5–6A-a*

**Results: Kolmogorov–Smirnov One-variable Test**

| Time pending: More than | Kolmogorov–Smirnov $d$ |
|---|---|
| 0 months | 0.00 |
| 4 months | **0.06 = D** |
| 12 months | 0.04 |
| 18 months | 0.04 |

[4]Rob Gurwitt, "Joseph A. Falcone: The Docketeer," *Governing*, 1996: 100.

About 400, or 35%, of the pending cases in Year 1 were more than 12 months old. Therefore

$$n \approx \frac{400}{0.35} \approx 1143$$

The critical value of the Kolmogorov–Smirnov $D$ statistic at the 0.05 level of significance is approximately

$$\frac{1.36}{\sqrt{n}} \approx \frac{1.36}{\sqrt{1143}} \approx 0.04$$

The observed value of the Kolmogorov–Smirnov $D$ statistic equals 0.06. This exceeds the critical value (0.04) at the 0.05 level of significance. Therefore, there is a statistically significant difference between the two backlog distributions.

**b.**

## *Exhibit HW5–6A-b*

**Cumulative Relative Frequency of Court Case Backlog: Passaic County, NJ 1995 and 1996**

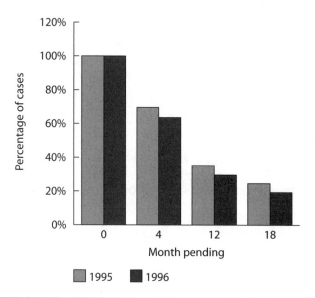

# CHAPTER 6

# Confidence: One-Variable Estimation

| | |
|---|---|
| Kind of problem | *Estimation* |
| Number of variables | *One* |
| Level of measurement | *Nominal or interval* |

This chapter addresses the problem of estimating the central tendency and dispersion of a variable without having to observe every unit of analysis in the statistical population.

Estimation problems determine "best estimate" values for the central tendency and dispersion of a variable. They also determine an error range, called a *confidence interval,* within which there is a high probability that the true central tendency of the statistical population, were it known, would fall. The estimation problems for one variable most often involve either (1) determining the proportion of event outcomes that are of one kind or another, the variable having a dichotomous nominal level of measurement, or (2) estimating the mean of a variable having an interval level of measurement. The estimate of a proportion is derived from the normal approximation to the binomial. The estimates for the mean and standard deviation of an intervally measured variable come from the known (due to the central limit theorem) characteristics of the distribution of sample means, that is, a normal distribution. Estimation equations for central tendency, dispersion, confidence intervals for a variable having either a dichotomous nominal or interval level of measurement are shown in Exhibit 6–1.

## 6.1 Confidence Intervals

The estimation of a population mean consists of two parts: (1) A "best estimate" of the value of the population mean and (2) a range of error called a *confidence interval.* The latter is a pair of values, greater than and less than the best estimate, specifying the upper and lower limits of a range such that there is a known degree

## *Exhibit 6–1*

**One-Variable Estimation**

| | Level of measurement | |
|---|---|---|
| **Population estimate** | *Nominal—Two categories* | *Interval* |
| Central tendency | $\mu \approx np_O$ | $\mu \approx \bar{x}$ |
| Dispersion | $p_E \approx p_O \pm Z\sqrt{\dfrac{0.25}{n}}$ | $\sigma \approx s\sqrt{n}$ |
| Confidence interval | $p_E \approx p_O \pm Z\sqrt{\dfrac{0.25}{n}}$ | $\mu \approx \bar{x} \pm t\dfrac{s}{\sqrt{n}}$ |

of certainty that the "true" value for the population mean lies within the error range.

The preceding chapter introduced the central limit theorem (the distribution of sample means, for large samples, approaches a normal distribution with a mean equal to the population mean, $\mu$, and a standard deviation equal to $\sigma/\sqrt{n}$) and the idea that the standard deviation of an observed sample, $s$, is the best estimate of the population standard deviation. These are the central concepts in defining the $t$ statistic.

$$t = \frac{\bar{x} - \mu}{\dfrac{s}{\sqrt{n}}}$$

The key to estimation is transforming this equation so that the central tendency of the statistical population is the unknown quantity on the left-hand side of the equation.

$$\mu = \bar{x} \pm t\frac{s}{\sqrt{n}}$$

The equation says that the unknown central tendency of the statistical population (the population mean) can be estimated from knowing the size, mean, and standard deviation of a random sample picked by the analyst. The right-hand side of the equation specifies that the best estimate for the population mean is the sample mean and the error range for a given confidence level is the product of critical value of $t$ and the sample's standard error, $s/\sqrt{n}$, where

- $n$ is the size of the random sample. Who determined how large the random sample should be? Who actually selected the sample? The analyst did.
- $\bar{x}$ is the central tendency, the mean, of the observations in the random sample. The very same random sample, of course, that was picked by the analyst.

- $s$ is the indicator of dispersion, the standard deviation of the random sample. Again, this is the same random sample that was picked by the analyst.
- $t$ is the critical value for the test statistic that defines the range of "unusual" observed values for the variable in question—the cumulative probability of observing any value in the "unusual" range is less than 5% (a more stringent criterion is 1%). This "level of significance" is also picked by the analyst.

The process is a lot like the dart game depicted in Exhibit 6–2. The dart represents the unknown population mean. The dartboard represents the right-hand side of the equation. The center of the dartboard is $\bar{x}$, and the expression $\pm t\, s/\sqrt{n}$ specifies the width (diameter) of the board—the confidence interval.

However, the game is not played in the usual way. The dart is not thrown at the dartboard. That is, population mean is not used to estimate the sample mean— just the other way around—the dart, the unknown population mean, is the target. The player–analyst, in effect, creates a dartboard (by picking the size of the random sample) and throws the dartboard at the dart! The objective of the game is to hit the dart—to estimate the population mean within a known range of error and with a known probability of success (represented by the width of the dartboard). The value of the sample statistic, $t$, indicates the degree of certainty the analyst

## *Exhibit 6–2*

**A Curious Game of Darts**

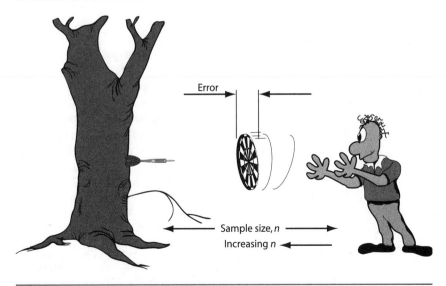

wants in hitting the target dart with the dartboard. If the analyst wants to be 95% sure of hitting the target, the dartboard will be a certain size—if the analyst wants to be 99% sure, the value of the $t$ statistic will be larger (increasing the size of the dartboard). The analyst can be almost certain of hitting the dart simply by increasing the width of the dartboard—but that increases the error associated with estimating the population mean. Alternatively, the analyst could move closer to the target dart. But moving closer comes at a price. The analyst has to increase the sample size, $n$. As the sample size is increased, the confidence of hitting the target dart (estimating the mean of the statistical population within a given error range) increases. As the sample size, $n$, is increased, the width of the dartboard (the error range) is reduced while keeping the same degree of assurance of hitting the target dart (the mean of the statistical population)—the analyst can use a smaller dartboard (reducing the error range) but still be just as sure of hitting the target dart as when standing farther away. The analyst can be as accurate as he/she wants to be and as confident as he/she wants to be in predicting the mean of the statistical population simply be increasing the sample size.[1]

An analyst can estimate the unknown mean of a statistical population and a confidence interval on the basis of the mean and standard error (SE), $s/\sqrt{n}$, of a sample. So the population estimate equals the sample mean plus or minus the confidence interval.

$$\mu = \bar{x} \pm t \frac{s}{\sqrt{n}}$$

Population estimate = sample mean ± confidence interval

Sometimes analysts report the *relative standard error* (coefficient of variation), $s/\bar{x}$, to indicate the dispersion of the data.

For example, in support of developing energy policy in the United States, the Energy Information Administration (EIA) of the Department of Energy conducts the Commercial Buildings Energy Consumption Survey (CBECS)—a national sample survey that collects information on the stock of U.S. commercial buildings, their energy-related building characteristics, and their energy consumption and expenditures. The 2006 CBECS report is based on a sample of 5,215 buildings in 2003.[2] The EIA analysts report that the average floorspace measured in the 2003 CBECS is 71,658 million square feet with a relative standard error, *RSE*, of 3.1%. The standard error, *SE*, can be obtained by dividing the *RSE* by 100 and multiplying by the survey estimate, $\bar{x}$—2,221 million square feet.

---

[1]One should really say "as the analyst can *afford* to be" rather than "as the analyst wants to be," since increasing the sample size requires increased effort and a larger budget.

[2]Commercial Buildings Energy Consumption Survey (CBECS) www.eia.doe.gov/emeu/cbecs/

$$SE = \frac{RSE}{100} \cdot \bar{x}$$

$$SE = \frac{3.1}{100} \cdot 71{,}658$$

$$SE = 2{,}221$$

For a "large" sample ($n > 30$), the value of $t$ would be 1.96. Therefore, the 95% confidence interval is $1.96 \times 2{,}221$ million square feet, or 4,354 million square feet. Therefore, with 95% confidence, the estimated "true" amount of floorspace in commercial buildings in the United States in 2003 was 71,658 plus or minus 4,354 million square feet, or, the range was from 67,304 to 76,012 million square feet.

$$\mu = \bar{x} \pm t \frac{s}{\sqrt{n}}$$

$$\mu = 71{,}658 \pm 1.96 \cdot 2{,}221$$

$$\mu = 71{,}658 \pm 4{,}354$$

If the EIA analysts had obtained a large number of samples, each having 5,215 units of analysis, and calculated a 95% confidence interval using each of these samples, then approximately 95% of these intervals would contain $\mu$, the population mean response to the question being asked.

However, the analysts obtained only the one sample with 5,215 observations. The 95% value indicates probability. Assuming that the observed sample is representative of the statistical population, the probability that the population mean falls somewhere within the range of the calculated confidence interval is 95%. The analysts estimate that there is no greater than 5% probability that they by chance obtained a sample for which the calculated range of the 95% confidence interval misses the "true" mean of the statistical population.

Notice that the size of the statistical population is irrelevant. A confidence interval for the mean of a statistical population is calculated from the observed sample mean, observed sample standard deviation, observed sample size, and the level of confidence selected by the analyst.

Analysts often want to estimate a confidence interval for the relative frequency (proportion) of a group in a statistical population. Survey research—in which an analyst asks a randomly selected sample of respondents to describe a recent event or experience or to express their opinion about a matter of public interest—is a common application. This estimate is derived using central limit theorem and normal distribution principles.

$$Z = \frac{\bar{x} - \mu}{\frac{\sigma}{\sqrt{n}}}$$

where

$n$ = observed sample size

$p_O = \dfrac{x}{n}$ = observed sample proportion

$p_E = \dfrac{\mu}{n}$ = expected sample proportion

$\sigma = \sqrt{n \cdot p_E \cdot (1 - p_E)}$ = standard deviation

$Z$ = the critical value for the desired level of confidence

$Z$ = 1.96 for large samples ($n > 30$), at the 95% confidence level

$$Z = \frac{p_O - p_E}{\sqrt{\dfrac{p_E \cdot (1 - p_E)}{n}}}$$

$$p_E = p_O \pm Z \cdot \sqrt{\dfrac{p_E \cdot (1 - p_E)}{n}}$$

There is an apparent dilemma—the expression $p_E$ appears on both sides of the equation. One cannot solve for $p_E$ without being required to use it on the right-hand side as part of the computation. However, examine the product $p_E \cdot (1 - p_E)$ more closely. The maximum value that it can take on is 0.25. Therefore, the equation defining the confidence interval for a proportion becomes

$$p_E \approx p_O \pm Z \cdot \sqrt{\dfrac{0.25}{n}}$$

In November 2006, as Massachusetts voters elected the state's first African–American governor, Deval Patrick, researchers at the University of Massachusetts Boston asked 749 randomly selected Massachusetts adults (including 433 whites, 113 Latinos, 103 Asian–Americans, and 100 African–Americans) about their confidence in government.

One question on the survey was, "How much confidence do you have in the local government in your city or town?" Twenty-four percent of all 749 respondents expressed "a great deal of confidence" in local government. Estimate the proportion (and 95% confidence interval) of Massachusetts adults who trust local government. In this example $p_O = 0.24$. This is the best estimate for $p_E$, the expected proportion in the statistical population. The confidence interval for this estimate is defined by the equation using the $Z$ statistic.

$$p_E \approx p_O \pm Z \cdot \sqrt{\frac{0.25}{n}}$$

$$p_E \approx 0.24 \pm \sqrt{\frac{0.25}{749}}$$

$$p_E \approx 0.24 \pm 0.02$$

Based on this sample, the analyst is 95% confident that between 22% and 26% of all Massachusetts adults—about 1 in 4—have high confidence in their local government.

## 6.2   *Estimation of Sample Size*

One of the first, and most important, questions asked by someone planning on acquiring data for a statistical analysis is, "What should the sample size be? How many units of analysis?" To answer this question an analyst turns once again to the defining equation for the $t$ statistic.

$$t = \frac{\bar{x} - \mu}{\dfrac{s}{\sqrt{n}}}$$

Now, instead of solving the equation for $\mu$ to determine a confidence interval, solve the equation for $n$, the sample size.

$$n = \frac{t^2 \cdot s^2}{(x - \mu)^2}$$

The difference between expectation and observation, $(x - \mu)$, in the denominator will be called *error*.

$$n = \frac{t^2 \cdot s^2}{(error)^2}$$

The defining equation for the $Z$ statistic in the normal approximation to the binomial distribution can be solved in a similar fashion in order to determine the sample size needed to estimate a population proportion.

$$Z = \frac{p_O - p_E}{\sqrt{\dfrac{p_E \cdot (1 - p_E)}{n}}}$$

$$n = \frac{Z^2 \cdot [p_E \cdot (1 - p_E)]}{(p_O - p_E)^2}$$

As before, the difference between expectation and observation, $(p_O - p_E)$, is called *error* and the maximum value of the product $p_E \cdot (1 - p_E)$ will be 0.25. So the necessary sample size for a desired error range and confidence level (specified by the value of $Z$) is given by

$$Z = \frac{0.25 \cdot Z^2}{(error)^2}$$

For large samples the reference value of the $Z$ statistic is 1.96, approximately 2.0, at the 95% confidence level. With this information it may be convenient to remember that the required sample size for estimating a proportion is approximately $1/(error)^2$.

$$n \approx \frac{0.25 \cdot 2^2}{(error)^2}$$

$$n \approx \frac{1}{(error)^2}$$

Suppose a media outlet wanted to estimate the proportion of potential voters who favor each of the candidates in a forthcoming presidential election. How many people in the country would have to be surveyed in order to be 95% confident that the "true" population proportions were within a ±3% error range of the proportions in the sample? Using the previous relationship:

$$n \approx \frac{1}{(error)^2}$$

$$n \approx \frac{1}{(0.03)^2}$$ Note that the error range is expressed in decimal form, not percentage.

$$n \approx 1,111$$

The next time you read about a national poll in a newspaper or hear the results reported on the evening news, pay attention to the reported sample size and error range. There will usually be about 1,200 to 1,500 respondents and a ±3% error. The polling organization, of course, does not know exactly how many people will actually respond to a survey, so they plan to randomly select and attempt to contact more people than are minimally required by the calculations.

Now suppose that the analyst wants to change the target statistical population from the country at large to just the state of New Jersey. How many respondents are needed for the same confidence level and error range? 1,111. Focus on Essex County, New Jersey. How many respondents are needed? 1,111. What if the analyst was interested just in the potential voters who live in East Orange, Essex County, New Jersey? How many respondents do we need? 1,111. The required sample size has absolutely nothing at all to do with the size of the target statistical population (provided that the statistical population is "large"—say at least 10 times greater—than the sample size). Since the cost of a survey is principally determined by sample size, the cost of focusing the survey on a specific city or state is about the same as looking at the whole country.

The error range and confidence level are picked by the analyst. The analyst can be as error-free and as confident as he/she wants to be that the "true" population mean or proportion is in the desired error range. Suppose the analyst wants 99% confidence level with only a $\pm 1\%$ error range.

$$n \approx \frac{0.25 \cdot Z^2}{(error)^2}$$

$$n \approx \frac{0.25 \cdot (2.57)^2}{(0.01)^2}$$

$$n \approx 16,512$$

The required sample size is 16,512. Given the costs of survey research we should amend the previous statement to say that the analyst can be as confident and error-free as he/she can *afford* to be.

## Quick Concepts: Sampling

The data are a sample, a subset, of a statistical population. However, an analyst is not interested in just any subset—but a sample that is representative of the intended target statistical population—a so-called cross section of the population. This is much easier said than done. The saying, "Garbage in! Garbage out!" applies. If the data are no good, the application of statistical analysis is not going to make the situation any better.

Basically, there are four requirements: (1) First, the sample must be drawn from the intended statistical population. (2) Second, an unbiased technique

*(continued)*

must be used to measure or observe the values of each variable. (3) Third, the variability of the sample (standard deviation, standard error, or confidence interval) must be reported. (4) Lastly, if overall characteristics of the target statistical population are known (perhaps by a pervious census) the makeup of the sample should be checked against the makeup of the population. Samples that meet these requirements are called *valid*.

Some states are considering ballot measures (propositions) to "end affirmative action programs." One such measure reads, "Neither the State nor any of its political subdivisions or agents shall use race, sex, color, ethnicity, or national origin as a criterion for either discriminating against, or granting preferential treatment to, any individual or group in the operation of the State's system of public employment, public education, or public contracting." Suppose an analyst wants to gauge the status of public opinion on this subject. One television station asks viewers to respond to the question, "Do you favor legislation to end affirmative action programs?" Viewers are asked to e-mail or text-message one number to respond Yes and another number to respond No. The totals are reported on the late evening news (with the disclaimer that this is a "nonscientific" survey). The public being sampled is that portion of the television audience that day who care enough about the matter to have formed a pro or con opinion and are motivated to contact the station. The respondents do not represent all viewers, much less all adults or all voters in the state. Many surveys, such as mailed questionnaires or ballots published in newspapers or on the Internet, rely on self-chosen respondents. They all suffer the same validity problem. To ensure that the sample is drawn from the intended target population, the decision of who (or what) will be selected for observation must be the analyst's, not the respondent's.

There are three principal techniques for avoiding bias in selecting a sample from a statistical population: (1) simple random sampling, (2) systematic sampling, and (3) stratified sampling.

Simple random sampling requires that all members of a statistical population be identified and listed. If each item or person in the statistical population is assigned a unique identification number, a table of random numbers (such as the table in Appendix N), or a computerized random number generator can be used to select those that will be included in the sample. For example, suppose that an analyst wanted to survey the opinion regarding affirmative action among the student body at your university. If the analyst had a complete student list and numbered the members consecutively, the analyst could just pick the identification numbers for the sample directly from the random number table.

*(continued)*

Or the analyst could use the random number table to move through the list. Using three-digit strings starting with the random numbers of the first row of the table (2262 6502 1796 . . .), the 226th student on the list is the first person selected for the sample. Then the analyst counts ahead 265 names to pick the second person, ahead another 21 names for the third, another 796 names forward identifies the fourth, and so on. Continue to rotate through the list until the desired sample size is obtained. Everyone has an equal chance of being picked.

An analyst often knows the approximate size of the statistical population. Say a university reports that it has about 10,000 full-time students. An analyst can obtain a systematic sample of 500 by randomly picking a starting point in the student list and then every 20th name thereafter.

If the analyst wanted the respondents to reflect the diversity of the student population, the analyst would specifically seek to include participants of various groups such as sex, ethnicity, or age, based on their proportion in the total population. If the analyst knew that 15% of the students were majoring in business, 50% in social studies, 20% in science, and 15% in other majors, the analyst could *stratify* the random sample to ensure that the makeup of the sample closely matched the known makeup of the population and thus claim that this stratified sample was more representative of the student population than a simple random sample or a systematic sample.

# Homework Exercises

**6-1** An analysis of the potatoes from 26 representative locations in New York State indicates a mean concentration of the heavy metal cadmium of 0.028 micrograms per gram wet weight with a relative standard deviation (coefficient of variation) of 52.1%.[1]

**a.** What is the 95% confidence interval for the concentration of cadmium in the potatoes grown in this state?

**b.** A sample of sweet corn from 32 locations in New York indicates a mean cadmium concentration of 0.004 micrograms per gram wet weight with a coefficient of variation of 82.7%. Can we compare potatoes with sweet corn? Gram for gram, which crop has the higher concentration of cadmium?

---

[1]Karen A. Wolnik, and others, "Elements in Major Raw Agricultural Crops in the United States: Cadmium and Lead in Lettuce, Peanuts, Potatoes, Soybeans, Sweet Corn, and Wheat," *Journal of Agricultural and Food Chemistry* 31 (1983): 1240–1244.

**c.** Potatoes from 26 locations in Idaho were determined to have a mean cadmium concentration of 0.038 micrograms per gram wet weight (coefficient of variation = 35.9%). Is the difference in cadmium concentration between New York and Idaho potatoes statistically significant?

---

**a.**

$$\mu \approx \bar{x} \pm t \cdot \frac{s}{\sqrt{n}}$$

coefficient of variation $= \dfrac{s}{\bar{x}}$ (see Chapter 3)

$s = (0.028)(0.521)$

$s = 0.0146$ micrograms Cd/gram

degrees of freedom $= (n - 1)$

$$df = 25$$

$t_{critical} = 2.06$

$$\mu \approx 0.028 \pm 2.06 \cdot \frac{0.0146}{\sqrt{26}}$$

$$\mu \approx 0.028 \pm 0.006 \text{ micrograms Cd/gram}$$

**b.** An analyst does not always have to strictly segregate "apples" from "oranges." If the analyst can regard potatoes and sweet corn as two foodstuffs that are roughly interchangeable in a diet, then their respective mean cadmium concentrations can be compared.

$$\mu \approx 0.004 \pm 0.001 \text{ micrograms Cd/gram for New York sweet corn}$$

Therefore, gram for gram potatoes have the higher concentration of cadmium.

**c.** $\mu \approx 0.038 \pm 0.006$ micrograms Cd/gram for Idaho potatoes

$\mu \approx 0.028 \pm 0.006$ micrograms Cd/gram for New York potatoes

The difference in cadmium concentration between the New York and Idaho crops is not statistically significant.

---

**6-2**  Fill in Exhibit HW6–2A.

## Exhibit HW6–2A

**Confidence Intervals by Sample Size**

| | Plus/minus percentage range of confidence interval | |
|---|---|---|
| **Sample size** | *95% confidence* | *99% confidence* |
| 30 | | |
| 50 | | |
| 100 | | |
| 200 | | |
| 300 | | |
| 400 | | |
| 600 | | |
| 800 | | |
| 1,000 | | |
| 1,100 | | |
| 1,200 | | |
| 1,500 | | |
| 2,000 | | |
| 2,500 | | |
| 3,000 | | |
| 5,000 | | |
| 10,000 | | |
| 15,000 | | |

See Exhibit HW6–2B.

$$\text{Confidence interval} = \pm Z \cdot \sqrt{\frac{0.25}{n}}$$

## *Exhibit HW6–2B*

**Confidence Intervals by Sample Size**

| Sample size | Plus/minus percentage range of confidence interval | |
|---|---|---|
| | *95% confidence*<br>*(Z = 1.96)* | *99% confidence*<br>*(Z = 2.57)* |
| 30 | 17.9% | 23.5% |
| 50 | 13.9 | 18.2 |
| 100 | 9.8 | 12.9 |
| 200 | 6.9 | 9.1 |
| 300 | 5.7 | 7.4 |
| 400 | 4.9 | 6.4 |
| 600 | 4.0 | 5.2 |
| 800 | 3.5 | 4.5 |
| 1,000 | 3.1 | 4.1 |
| 1,100 | 3.0 | 3.9 |
| 1,200 | 2.8 | 3.7 |
| 1,500 | 2.5 | 3.3 |
| 2,000 | 2.2 | 2.9 |
| 2,500 | 2.0 | 2.6 |
| 3,000 | 1.8 | 2.3 |
| 5,000 | 1.4 | 1.8 |
| 10,000 | 1.0 | 1.3 |
| 15,000 | 0.8 | 1.0 |

**6-3** Refer to Exercise 5–2. Compute a 95% confidence interval for the mean lead content of cement kiln dust in the United States.

$$\mu \approx \bar{x} \pm t \cdot \frac{s}{\sqrt{n}}$$

$\bar{x} = 253$ micrograms lead per gram of CKD

$s = 303$ micrograms lead per gram of CKD

$n = 113, df = (n - 1) = (113 - 1) = 112$

$$t_{\text{critical}} \approx 1.98 \ (\text{two-tailed test, } df = 112)$$

$$\mu \approx 253 \pm 1.98 \cdot \frac{303}{113}$$

$$\mu \approx 253 \pm 56 \text{ micrograms lead per gram of CKD}$$

**6-4** In a study of radon concentration within households in the Ventura County and northwestern Los Angeles County region, researchers identified three areas with seemingly "high," "medium," and "low" radon measurements, respectively.[2] Calculate the 95% confidence interval for the mean residential radon concentration in each area. See Exhibit HW6–4A.

## *Exhibit HW6–4A*

**Residential Radon Concentrations in the Ventura County and Northwestern Los Angeles County Region: 1989–1990**

| Area classification by apparent range of radon measurements | Sample size | Mean (pCi/l) | Standard deviation (pCi/l) |
|---|---|---|---|
| High | 71 | 2.51 | 1.67 |
| Medium | 169 | 2.01 | 1.44 |
| Low | 622 | 1.28 | 1.08 |

Note: pCi/l = picocuries per liter.

$$\mu \approx \bar{x} \pm t \cdot \frac{s}{\sqrt{n}}$$

High:   $\mu \approx 2.51 \pm 2.0 \cdot \dfrac{1.67}{\sqrt{71}} \approx 2.51 \pm 0.40 \text{ pCi/liter}$

Medium: $\mu \approx 2.01 \pm 1.96 \cdot \dfrac{1.44}{\sqrt{169}} \approx 2.01 \pm 0.22 \text{ pCi/liter}$

Low:   $\mu \approx 1.28 \pm 1.96 \cdot \dfrac{1.08}{\sqrt{622}} \approx 1.28 \pm 0.08 \text{ pCi/liter}$

[2]Kai-Shen Liu, Yu-Lin Chang, Steven B. Hayward, and Fan-Yen Huang, Survey of Residential Radon Levels in Ventura County and Northwestern Los Angeles County, Indoor Air Quality Program, Air and Industrial Hygiene Laboratory, California Department of Health Services, Berkeley, CA, September 1991.

**6-5** The county Department of Public Health sent 24 high school students to 114 tobacco vendors across the county to test the retailers' willingness to sell to people under 18. Under the supervision of undercover law enforcement officers, the teens reported that 26% of the vendors sold them cigarettes. But compared with a previous estimate that about one-third of stores sold to minors, it is an improvement. What is the 95% confidence interval for the estimate of the proportion of tobacco vendors selling to minors? Is the improvement statistically significant?

$$p_E = p_O \pm Z \sqrt{\frac{0.25}{n}}$$

$$p_E = 0.26 \pm 1.96 \sqrt{\frac{0.25}{114}} = 0.26 \pm 0.09$$

$$Z = \frac{p_O - p_E}{\sqrt{\frac{p_E(1 - p_E)}{n}}}$$

$$Z = \frac{0.26 - 0.33}{\sqrt{\frac{0.33(1 - 0.33)}{114}}} = -1.6$$

The 95% confidence interval is ± 9%. The improvement is not statistically significant.

---

**6-6** A telephone poll of 1,003 registered voters nationwide was conducted January 13–17, 2005, by Republican firm Bellwether Research and Democratic pollsters Lake, Snell, Perry and Associates for the Alaska Coalition, an alliance of national and local groups who favor protection for the Arctic National Wildlife Refuge. In response to the question, "Should oil drilling be allowed in America's Arctic National Wildlife Refuge?" 53% said, "Do Not Allow Oil Drilling," and 38% said, "Allow Oil Drilling."

**a.** What is the 95% confidence level margin of error for the reported percentages in this survey?

**b.** What would the 95% confidence level margin of error be if there were 436 respondents?

**c.** What would the sample size have to be in order to have a ±2% margin of error at the 99% confidence level?

**a.** 95% C.I. $= \pm Z \sqrt{\dfrac{0.25}{n}} = \pm 1.96 \sqrt{\dfrac{0.25}{1003}} = 0.031$, that is, $\pm 3.1\%$

**b.** 95% C.I. $= \pm Z \sqrt{\dfrac{0.25}{n}} = \pm 1.96 \sqrt{\dfrac{0.25}{436}} = 0.045$, that is, $\pm 4.5\%$

**c.** The number of respondents (sample size) needed is

$$n \approx \frac{1}{(error)^2} \approx \frac{1}{(0.02)^2} \approx 2{,}500$$

*Seven*

# Tables and Graphs: Two-Variable Description

| | |
|---|---|
| Kind of problem | *Description* |
| Number of variables | *Two* |
| Level of measurement | *Variable 1, nominal, ordinal, or interval* |
| | *Variable 2, nominal, ordinal, or interval* |

his chapter is about the construction of tables and graphs—sometimes called *presentation graphics*. A table or graph has two purposes: (1) to summarize a data file, and (2) to depict the way two variables may be related. The graphic techniques used depend upon the respective level of measurement of the two variables. Exhibit 7–1 shows that if either variable has a nominal or ordinal level of measurement, one of three kinds of tables is employed: a crosstabulation, a crosstabulation with grouped interval data, or a data table. A scatterplot is constructed if both variables have an interval level of measurement.

In a two-variable problem, one of the variables describes an initial condition (event outcome) that seems to set the units of analysis apart—that allows the analyst to distinguish among the units of analysis. The units of analysis might have a characteristic by which they can be classified in nominal categories like ethnicity or ordinal categories like age group. Or the units of analysis might have observed differences in a characteristic measured on an interval scale, like income. These initial conditions might be due to inherent "environmental" differences among the units of analysis or they might be imposed by management action. The variable that describes the initial observed condition is called the *independent variable*. Later, the analyst observes a second characteristic or attribute of the units of analysis (the outcome of another event). This variable might also have a nominal, ordinal, or interval level of measurement. The variable that describes the outcome of a subsequent event is called the *dependent variable*. The event described by the independent variable occurs before the event described by the dependent variable.

**147**

## *Exhibit 7–1*

**Two-Variable Description**

| | Independent variable | |
|---|---|---|
| **Dependent variable** | *Nominal or ordinal level of measurement* | *Interval level of measurement* |
| Nominal or ordinal level of measurement | Crosstabulation | Crosstabulation (group interval data) |
| Interval level of measurement | Table or chart | Scatterplot |

The measurement of the independent variable is conventionally symbolized by $x$, and the measurement of the dependent variable by $y$. The two observations for the first unit of analysis would be $(x_1, y_1)$; the observations for the second case $(x_2, y_2)$ ; and so on. The sample with $n$ units of analysis consists of the following data: $(x_1, y_1), (x_2, y_2), (x_3, y_3) \ldots (x_n, y_n)$.

Measures of resultant effects—efficiency, needs, or demands—are often used as dependent variables. Variables indicating environmental factors—resources consumed, and program operation characteristics (or personal attributes and characteristics)—are common kinds of independent variables. Sometimes, in one problem context a variable will be regarded as dependent, and in another, as independent. An analyst wants to know whether the observations of the dependent variable are associated with the earlier observed values of the initial condition described by the independent variable. If the initial condition was environmental, the analyst might be interested in an evaluation question such as, Did the starting condition influence the subsequent outcome? If the initial condition was established by management action, the evaluation questions might be, Did the program work? Was there any change? Did a program policy or management action affect the outcome measure? These questions suggest that differences in the initial influencing condition described by the independent variable "cause" the subsequent effect described by the dependent variable. The analyst needs to be very cautious about causal inference. There are three requirements for causality:

1. Changes in the program (independent variable) must correspond ("covary") with changes in the outcome measure (dependent variable).
2. Changes in the independent variable must precede changes in the dependent variable.
3. All alternative explanations of change in the dependent variable must be ruled out so that a change in the outcome measure can be attributed only to a change in the program rather than a change in another unanticipated variable.[1]

---

[1]Laura Irwin Langbein. 1980. *Discovering Whether Programs Work: A Guide to Statistical Methods for Program Evaluation,* Goodyear Publishing Company, p. 32.

However, statistical tests examine only the degree to which the observed relationship between the values for two variables could be ascribed to chance. If the probability is small enough (i.e., less than 5%), the analyst infers that the outcome (dependent variable) is related in some way to the initial condition (independent variable). This does not definitively "prove" causality. Causal statements (such as the Surgeon General's warning on cigarette packs: "Smoking causes lung cancer, heart disease, emphysema, and may complicate pregnancy.") regarding human behavior and social systems generally require a great many separate studies by independent analysts with consistent reinforcing findings.

## 7.1  The Data File

Analysis should start with examining the structure and contents of the data file. It is not always intuitively apparent how many variables a problem has, or how to distinguish between units of analysis, events, and variables. The data file explicitly lists the objects being observed, the two characteristics or attributes (independent and dependent) being measured for each object, and the respective levels of measurement. Exhibit 7–2 shows that the basic structure of a data file. Each row in the file specifies the identity and measurements for one unit of analysis. The columns contain the values for the independent and dependent variables.

## *Exhibit 7–2*

**Structure of a Data File**

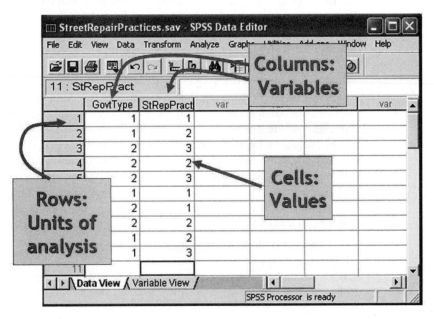

## 7.2   Crosstabulations

A crosstabulation (also called a *contingency table*) is a two-dimensional table that shows the conditional frequency distributions for two variables. Both variables are measured in terms of nominal or ordinal categories. The independent variable conventionally labels the columns of the table. Each value that the independent variable can take on defines a separate column. The dependent variable labels the rows of the table. Each category of the dependent variable designates a separate row in the table. The intersection of a row and a column is called a *cell*. The content of each cell is a frequency—the number of cases in the sample that are observed as having both the unique value of the independent variable specified by the column heading and the unique value of the dependent variable specified by the row heading. The several cells in a given row or column comprise a frequency distribution of the values taken on by one of the variables for the specified category, *condition,* of the other variable. Thus, the columns of a crosstabulation contain the conditional frequency distribution of the dependent variable for every independent variable category.

The frequencies in the crosstabulation should be totaled both by row and column. These figures are called the *marginal totals*. The total of all cell frequencies is the number of units of analysis. In addition to the absolute frequency, each cell may contain the relative frequency by column, the relative frequency by row, or the total relative frequency. Of these, the relative frequency by column is most important—percentages are computed for each cell as a proportion of the column total so that each column totals 100%.[2] These column relative frequencies indicate whether the distribution of the dependent variable changes (covaries) with different values of the independent variable. If the relative frequency distributions are the same for each column the variables are unrelated. Values of the dependent variable are associated with changes in the independent variable if the relative frequency distributions differ from column to column.

Exhibit 7–3 shows the schematic structure of a 2 × 3 crosstabulation (two columns by three rows). The values of the independent variable label the columns and the values of the dependent variable appear at the left of the table designating the rows. The contents of each cell show the frequency of cases with the respective values of the independent and dependent variables indicated by the column and row headings. Do not jump to the conclusion that every two-dimensional table is a crosstabulation. Sometimes the values of a third or fourth variable are reported either as cell contents or row–column labels. The crosstabulation should have row and marginal totals and it is also useful to compute column relative frequencies. However, relative frequencies should never be reported without the marginal absolute frequencies. The title of the crosstabulation provides important information

---

[2]The row relative frequencies show the distribution of the independent variable for each category of the dependent variable. The total relative frequencies show the cases in each cell as a proportion of all cases in the sample.

## Exhibit 7–3

**General Structure of a 2 × 3 Crosstabulation**

| Dependent variable (DV) nominal or ordinal level of measurement | Independent variable (IV) nominal or ordinal level of measurement | | Total |
|---|---|---|---|
| | *IV value 1* | *IV value 2* | **Total** |
| DV value 1 | $f_a$ | $f_b$ | $f_a + f_b$ |
| DV value 2 | $f_c$ | $f_d$ | $f_c + f_d$ |
| DV value 3 | $f_e$ | $f_f$ | $f_e + f_f$ |
| Total | $n_1 = f_a + f_c + f_e$ | $n_2 = f_b + f_d + f_f$ | $n = f_a + f_b + f_c + f_d + f_e + f_f$ |

and should be carefully constructed. Ideally, it should name the dependent variable, the independent variable, the units of analysis, and the statistical population, in that order.

Suppose an analyst is interested in the different street repair practices of local governments. Cities and counties can choose to handle street repairs by using their own public employees exclusively, by contracting out part of the work and using public employees for the remainder, or by contracting out all of the work. Consider the sample summarized in Exhibit 7–4. There are 1,639 units of analysis—

## Exhibit 7–4

**Street Repair Practices by Type of Local Government**

| Street repair practice | Type of local government | | Total |
|---|---|---|---|
| | *1 City* | *2 County* | **Total** |
| 1 Solely public | 966 69.1% | 172 71.4% | 1,138 |
| 2 Public employees and contracting out | 396 28.3% | 61 25.3% | 457 |
| 3 Solely contracting | 36 2.6% | 8 3.3% | 44 |
| Total | 1,398 100% | 241 100% | 1,639 |

*Source:* James Ferris and Elizabeth Graddy, "Contracting Out: For What? With Whom?", *Public Administration Review* (July/August 1986): 332–344. Reporting data from a survey by the International City/County Management Association.

local governments. Two variables were observed for each local government: the *type of government* and its *street repair practice*. There are two categories for type of local government (city or county) and three categories of street repair practice (solely public, a combination of using public employees and contracting, and solely contracting). *Type of local government* is the independent variable since it logically precedes the decision regarding performing street repairs with public employees or contractors. The first column shows the frequency distribution of street repair practices for the "city" subsample of cases and the second column shows another distribution for the "county" group. The column relative frequency distributions show that both cities and counties tend to rely heavily on public employees to perform street repairs (*cities:* 69.1% solely public; *counties:* 71.4% solely public). However, when counties do use contract services, they are somewhat more likely than cities to do all the street repair work via contract (*cities:* 2.6% solely contract; *counties:* 3.3% solely contract).

## 7.3   *Scatterplots*

A *scatterplot* (also sometimes called a *scatter diagram* or *scattergram*) is a graphic drawing in which the values of the independent variable, *x*, and the dependent variable, *y*, for each unit of analysis constitute the coordinates of a point. These points are plotted on a two-dimensional field defined by a horizontal axis for the independent variable and a vertical axis for the dependent variable. The scatterplot visually depicts the relationship between *x* and *y*.

Each axis contains a ruler-like scale marked in equal divisions that covers the range of possible values the variable can take on. The values and spacing of the divisions on the two axes may be different. Principal scale divisions are indicated by numeric values. Intermediate scale divisions are noted by small marks, called "ticks," on each axis. Each scale begins at the intersection of the perpendicular axes—called the "origin." At this point the value on each scale is 0. All scale divisions are multiples of 1 (0, 1, 2, 3, 4, . . .), 2 (0, 2, 4, 6, 8, . . .), or 5 (0, 5, 10, 15, 20, . . .). The scale values may be multiplied or divided by powers of 10 to obtain divisions as large or small as needed (for example, 0, 0.001, 0.002, 0.003, . . . or 0, 5,000, 10,000, 15,000, . . .). The scales should provide a well-proportioned display that neither deemphasizes nor exaggerates the variations between the data points. Sometimes, it may be necessary to "break" a scale in order to achieve desired overall proportions for the diagram. Full scale breaks are best—separating the diagram into distinct panels, each with its own range on the scale. The scale divisions remain constant.

Each data point (set of *x*, *y* coordinates) is indicated by a symbol (like a circle, square, or triangle) about 1/16 inch in diameter. The use of very visible symbols indicates that the coordinates are measurements and therefore subject to error. Sometimes, a line or curve is drawn connecting the data points or through a cluster of data points. This should be done only if the analyst is suggesting a continuous mathematical equation that "explains" the relationship between *y* and *x*.

The two axes are labeled with the name of the independent or dependent variable and the scale dimensions (for example, speed in miles per hour). The diagram is also given a title that, like the title for a crosstabulation, should name the dependent variable, the independent variable, the units of analysis, and statistical population, in that order.

Standardized tests are currently used as outcomes assessment in K–12 education and the results are publicly reported for each school. Many factors, including poverty, parental education, teacher certification, and class size, are thought to be associated with test scores. Exhibit 7–5 lists the percentage of students scoring at a proficiency level and the pupil–teacher ratio for 51 high schools in the Los Angeles Unified School District.

The data can be more clearly understood if they are shown on a scatterplot. Each data point is shown by a small symbol (indicating that it is an observation subject to measurement error). Now it can be seen that generally low language arts test scores merit public concern but do not seem to be associated with pupil–teacher ratio at the high schools.

## *Exhibit 7–5*

**Percent Testing as Proficient in Language Arts by Pupil–Teacher Ratio: High Schools in the Los Angeles Unified School District 2004–2005**

| School | Total tested (approximate enrollment) | Pupil– teacher ratio | Language arts (percent proficient and above) |
|---|---|---|---|
| Abraham Lincoln Senior High | 2,236 | 22.6 | 18% |
| Alain Leroy Locke Senior High | 2,260 | 24.6 | 8% |
| Alexander Hamilton Senior High | 2,450 | 24.8 | 39% |
| Bell Senior High | 3,810 | 26.5 | 17% |
| Belmont Senior High | 3,932 | 24.9 | 13% |
| Benjamin Franklin Senior High | 2,464 | 23.1 | 23% |
| Birmingham Senior High | 2,759 | 26.0 | 32% |
| Canoga Park Senior High | 1,725 | 24.2 | 22% |
| Carson Senior High | 2,643 | 27.1 | 23% |
| Chatsworth Senior High | 2,269 | 26.7 | 33% |
| Crenshaw Senior High | 2,153 | 25.2 | 13% |
| David Starr Jordan Senior High | 1,808 | 26.7 | 11% |
| Eagle Rock High | 2,446 | 25.2 | 41% |
| El Camino Real Senior High | 2,729 | 29.9 | 54% |
| Fairfax Senior High | 2,198 | 24.8 | 28% |
| Francisco Bravo Medical Magnet | 1,286 | 25.2 | 62% |
| Gardena Senior High | 2,533 | 25.1 | 16% |
| George Washington Preparatory | 2,073 | 22.2 | 10% |

*(continued)*

## *Exhibit 7–5*

**Percent Testing as Proficient in Language Arts by Pupil–Teacher Ratio: High Schools in the Los Angeles Unified School District 2004–2005** *(continued)*

| School | Total tested (approximate enrollment) | Pupil– teacher ratio | Language arts (percent proficient and above) |
|---|---|---|---|
| Granada Hills Charter High | 2,742 | 25.1 | 65% |
| Grover Cleveland High | 2,907 | 26.5 | 41% |
| Hollywood Senior High | 2,064 | 24.5 | 25% |
| Huntington Park Senior High | 3,646 | 25.3 | 15% |
| James A. Garfield Senior High | 3,485 | 24.9 | 15% |
| James Monroe High | 3,439 | 24.0 | 23% |
| John C. Fremont Senior High | 3,790 | 24.4 | 8% |
| John F. Kennedy High | 2,537 | 26.9 | 35% |
| John H. Francis Polytechnic | 3,414 | 27.1 | 20% |
| John Marshall Senior High | 3,527 | 24.9 | 29% |
| King/Drew Medical Magnet High | 1,238 | 25.5 | 42% |
| Los Angeles Senior High | 3,591 | 25.6 | 13% |
| Manual Arts Senior High | 2,960 | 24.4 | 11% |
| Nathaniel Narbonne Senior High | 2,510 | 25.5 | 27% |
| North Hollywood Senior High | 3,151 | 23.7 | 33% |
| Palisades Charter High | 2,042 | 27.3 | 56% |
| Phineas Banning Senior High | 2,542 | 26.1 | 18% |
| Reseda Senior High | 2,062 | 21.9 | 29% |
| San Fernando Senior High | 3,272 | 23.6 | 17% |
| San Pedro Senior High | 2,638 | 25.2 | 32% |
| South Gate Senior High | 3,880 | 26.6 | 17% |
| Susan Miller Dorsey Senior High | 1,462 | 22.9 | 11% |
| Sylmar Senior High | 2,711 | 25.8 | 22% |
| Theodore Roosevelt Senior High | 3,728 | 23.8 | 13% |
| Thomas Jefferson Senior High | 2,848 | 23.2 | 8% |
| Ulysses S. Grant Senior High | 2,207 | 24.8 | 27% |
| University Senior High | 1,724 | 23.5 | 30% |
| Van Nuys Senior High | 2,617 | 24.1 | 29% |
| Venice Senior High | 2,280 | 24.5 | 33% |
| Verdugo Hills Senior High | 1,742 | 27.0 | 33% |
| Westchester Senior High | 1,801 | 24.8 | 29% |
| William Howard Taft Senior High | 2,388 | 27.8 | 38% |
| Woodrow Wilson Senior High | 2,174 | 23.3 | 16% |

*Source:* California Department of Education, Educational Demographics Unit, *DataQuest,* dq.cde.ca.gov/dataquest/

## Exhibit 7–6

**Scatterplot—Percent Testing as Proficient in Language Arts by Pupil–Teacher Ratio: High Schools in the Los Angeles Unified School District 2004–2005**

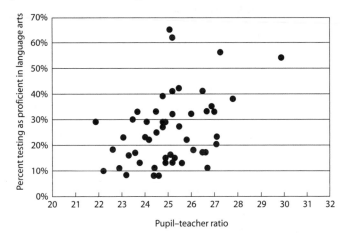

# Homework Exercises

**7-1**  What is the problem with the following chart describing United States postal rates? Redraw the graph.

## Exhibit HW7–1A

**U.S. Postal Rates**

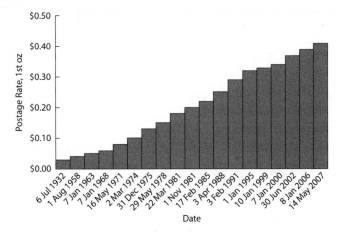

"Date" should not be treated as defining nominal categories. See Exhibit HW7–1B.

## *Exhibit HW7–1B*

**Line Graph-U.S. Postal Rates**

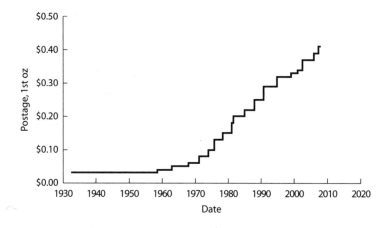

**7-2** Plot the relationship between the plus/minus percentage range of confidence intervals and sample size previously calculated in Homework Exercise 6–2.

## *Exhibit HW7–2A*

**Confidence Intervals by Sample Size**

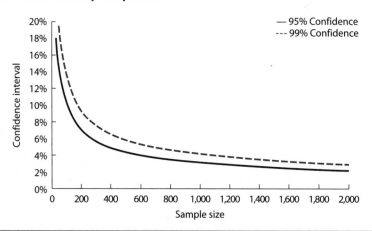

**7-3** The student absence rate at a high school may be associated the rate of progress toward graduation. The more days students miss, the less likely they are to earn a high school diploma. Describe the data in Exhibit HW7–3A in an appropriate graph.

## *Exhibit HW7–3A*

**Absence Data**

| High school | Average number of days absent per student per year | Percent not on track to graduate |
|---|---|---|
| A | 10 | 19% |
| B | 11 | 22% |
| C | 12 | 25% |
| D | 11 | 20% |
| E | 13 | 24% |

## *Exhibit HW7–3B*

**Progress Toward Graduation by Student Absenteeism: Five High Schools**

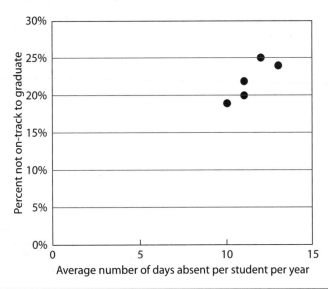

**7-4** Staff from the U.S. Probation Office and the Federal Bureau of Prisons (BOP) recommended that the Northern District of Ohio develop additional sentencing options that were more restrictive than a traditional halfway house but less restrictive than prison. As a result, the Comprehensive Sanctions Center (CSC) was created as a BOP community corrections contract facility. Operated from October 1, 1992, until April 28, 1994, the CSC was an "intensive, multidimensional halfway house program that incorporated several rehabilitative programs and varying levels of supervision." During this time 62 offenders were placed in the CSC as an intermediate sanction. (Seven were removed for various reasons. Thus, 55 were available for follow-up.) Twenty offenders were placed in the CSC for "drug use" related violations. Fourteen offenders (25%) violated the rules or committed a new offense within 6 months after release from the CSC. Construct a crosstabulation.

*Source:* Joseph V. Callahan and Keith A. Koenning, "The Comprehensive Sanctions Center in the Northern District of Ohio," *Federal Probation* 1995: 59, 52.

See Exhibit HW7–4A.

## Exhibit HW7-4A

**Recidivism by Type of Offense: Comprehensive Sanctions Center, Ohio, 1992–1994**

| Recidivism: Rule violation or new offense | Offense | | Total |
|---|---|---|---|
| | *Drug use* | *Other* | |
| No | 15 | 26 | 41 |
| Yes | 5 | 9 | 14 |
| Total | 20 | 35 | 55 |

**7-5** Violent crime affects African–Americans at about twice the rate of the white population. Analysts have pointed out that the unemployment rate among African–Americans is also higher. See Exhibit HW7–5A. Draw a scatterplot showing the incidence of violent crime versus unemployment among African–Americans for 1978–2005.

## Exhibit HW7–5A

**Incidence of Violent Crime and African–American Unemployment, 1978–2005**

| Year | Rate of violent crime victimization (reported incidents per 1,000 persons age 12+) | | African–American unemployment rate (percent among African–American labor force) |
|------|----------|----------|----------|
| | White | Black | |
| 1978 | 18.8 | 33.2 | 12.8 |
| 1979 | 19.6 | 33.2 | 12.3 |
| 1980 | 18.7 | 34.0 | 14.3 |
| 1981 | 19.7 | 40.4 | 15.6 |
| 1982 | 19.0 | 36.9 | 18.9 |
| 1983 | 16.3 | 33.1 | 19.5 |
| 1984 | 17.1 | 32.7 | 15.9 |
| 1985 | 15.6 | 28.9 | 15.1 |
| 1986 | 15.6 | 25.2 | 14.5 |
| 1987 | 15.0 | 33.8 | 13.0 |
| 1988 | 16.0 | 31.4 | 11.7 |
| 1989 | 16.1 | 29.5 | 11.4 |
| 1990 | 15.4 | 31.8 | 11.4 |
| 1991 | 16.2 | 31.3 | 12.5 |
| 1992 | 16.9 | 33.0 | 14.2 |
| 1993 | 17.8 | 34.3 | 13.0 |
| 1994 | 17.1 | 33.5 | 11.5 |
| 1995 | 13.5 | 26.4 | 10.4 |
| 1996 | 13.3 | 26.3 | 10.5 |
| 1997 | 12.9 | 20.7 | 10.0 |
| 1998 | 11.6 | 19.2 | 8.9 |
| 1999 | 10.2 | 19.5 | 8.0 |
| 2000 | 8.7 | 16.2 | 7.6 |
| 2001 | 8.4 | 12.7 | 8.6 |
| 2002 | 6.6 | 13.0 | 10.2 |
| 2003 | 6.5 | 12.8 | 10.8 |
| 2004 | 6.3 | 11.2 | 10.4 |
| 2005 | 6.5 | 13.6 | 10.0 |

*Sources:* National Crime Victimization Survey, Uniform Crime Reports, and Bureau of Labor Statistics

See Exhibit HW7–5B.

## *Exhibit HW7–5B*

**Violent Crime Victimization among African–Americans by African–American Unemployment Rate, 1978–2005**

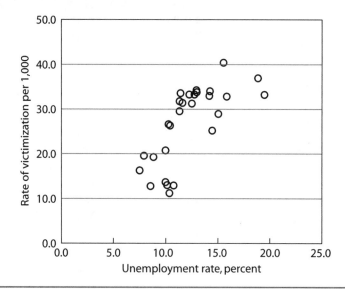

# CHAPTER 8

# Two by Two: Two-Variable Evaluation—Nominal–Nominal Measures

| | |
|---|---|
| Kind of problem | *Evaluation* |
| Number of variables | *Two* |
| Level of measurement | *Variable 1, nominal* |
| | *Variable 2, nominal* |

This chapter introduces evaluation problems that involve two variables with both the independent and dependent variables having a nominal level of measurement. Following chapters will gradually introduce methods that address other combinations of nominal, ordinal, and interval levels of measurement for the independent and dependent variables.

The analyst wants to know whether the observations of the dependent variable are associated with differences in the initial condition described by the independent variable. Did the starting condition influence the subsequent outcome? Did the program work? Was there any change? Did the policy have an effect?

There seems to be an implication that differences in the initial condition described by the independent variable "cause" the subsequent effect described by the dependent variable. However, statistical tests examine only the degree to which the observed values for two variables could be ascribed to chance rather than being the product of a systematic or purposeful process. If the probability of chance is small enough (that is, less than 5%), the analyst infers that the outcome (dependent variable) is related, or *associated,* in some way to the initial condition (independent variable). This does not definitively "prove" causality; we will discuss the problems of proving causality later.

Two questions must be asked of the relationship: (1) First, is the relationship statistically *significant?* Statistical tests that address this question examine

## Exhibit 8–1

**Two-Variable Evaluation—Nominal–Nominal Measures**

| | | Independent variable | | | |
| | | Nominal level of measurement | | | |
| | | Two categories | | More than two categories | |
| **Dependent variable** | | Unpaired units of analysis | Paired units of analysis | Unmatched units of analysis | Matched units of analysis |
| Nominal level of measurement | Two categories | | | | |
| | Strength of association | Odds ratio Relative risk ratio Somers' d Yule's Q Phi statistic | | Cramer's V Lambda, λ | |
| | Statistical significance | $n > 30$ Z test for the difference between two proportions<br><br>$26 < n \leq 250$ Chi-square test with Yates's correction<br><br>$n \leq 26$ Fisher's exact probability test | McNemar test for significance of changes | Chi-square test | Cochran's Q test |
| | More than two categories | | | | |
| | Strength of association | Cramer's V Lambda, λ | | Cramer's V Lambda, λ | |
| | Statistical significance | Chi-square test | | Chi-square test | |

the probability of observing particular combinations of the values of the independent and dependent variable. The possible answers to the statistical significance question are "yes" (the probability of the interaction pattern is less than 5% by random chance) or "no" (it isn't). (2) A test of statistical significance, however, does not indicate the degree to which the values of the dependent variable are accounted for by the values of the independent variable. An answer to this second question requires a separate statistic indicating *strength of association.* Think of statistical significance as telling us whether or not there is a fever and strength of association being a thermometer that measures the fever and tells us whether it is weak or strong. Usually (but not always) the strength-of-association thermometer is a statistic that takes on a value between 0.0 and 1.0, where 0.0 means no association and 1.0 means a perfect pattern between the values of the dependent and independent variables. Every evaluation problem must address both questions.

Units of analysis—the observations—can be *paired* or *unpaired*—*matched* or *unmatched.* Unpaired (unmatched) units of analysis are singular and independent. Paired units of analysis are encountered in problems where a unit of analysis—a person, object, or event—is observed twice. The units of analysis are observed as sets—either "before and after" situations straddling the implementation of a policy or program, or "twin" persons or objects identical in all respects (a pair) save for the one unique dichotomous characteristic or attribute, the independent variable, that sets them apart. The characteristic that uniquely separates the pair is the independent variable. Matched units of analysis extend the concept to sets having more than two components.

Exhibit 8–1 shows that for unpaired units of analysis, three tests of statistical significance are available: (1) the *Z* test for the difference between two proportions, (2) chi-square test, or (3) Fisher's exact probability test. The choice depends on sample size. If the units of analysis are paired, the McNemar test for significance of changes should be used. The strength-of-association statistics that are available for both unpaired and paired units of analysis are called the *phi statistic, odds ratio, relative risk ratio, Somers' d,* and *Yule's Q.*

If the nominally measured independent variable has more than two categories the analyst needs to determine whether the units of analysis are *unmatched* or *matched.* If the data are unmatched, the chi-square test for statistical significance should be used. If the data are matched, *Cochran's Q* test for statistical significance applies. The strength-of-association statistics that will be introduced are called *Cramer's V* and *lambda.* They are appropriate for either matched or unmatched data.

If the dependent variable has more than two categories in its nominal scale, the chi-square significance test should be applied regardless of whether the data are unpaired or paired. Cramer's *V* and lambda statistics indicate strength of association.

## 8.1   Both Variables Have Two Categories, Unpaired Data, n > 30

### 8.1.1   *Z* Test for the Difference between Two Proportions

Previously, the normal approximation to the binomial method was described for one-variable evaluation problems. Each unit of analysis had one of two possible values with respect to the variable of interest. Either the unit of analysis possessed a certain quality or it didn't. The object of the test was to compare the observed proportion of cases that possessed the quality of interest against a known expected proportion. This expected proportion characterized the population from which the observed sample was drawn. Whatever the size of the sample, it had to be small in comparison to the size of the population.

The two-variable evaluation problem is similar. It addresses situations in which either the analyst does not know an expected population proportion or the sample size is not small in comparison to the population (therefore the probability of selecting each case in the sample cannot be regarded as constant).

The sample is divided into two groups. Each case in the sample has the characteristic of being either in one group or the other. This is the independent variable—a dichotomous (two-category) nominal level of measurement. One of these groups will probably be of particular interest. In addition, each case will also be distinguished on the basis of either possessing or not possessing some other quality of interest. This is the dependent variable. The analyst examines the frequency distribution, the makeup, of each group with respect to the dependent variable. Instead of asking the one-variable evaluation question, "Is the makeup of the sample different from the expected makeup of the population?" the analyst asks, "Is the makeup of one group in the sample different from the makeup of the other group?" The respective proportions of both groups possessing the quality of interest comprise our observation. The expectation (the null hypothesis) is that both groups within the sample are drawn from one and the same population. Therefore, there should be no difference in the proportionate makeup of the two groups. If the observed difference is such that the likelihood of drawing such a sample from a single homogeneous population is less than 5%, the analyst infers that the sample was, indeed, not drawn from one population but, alternatively, that the group categories of the independent variable describe distinctly different populations (the alternate hypothesis).

Consider the evaluation problem depicted in Exhibit 8–2. In 1972–1973, 902 inmates were eligible for parole at the Nebraska Penal and Correctional Complex; 535 were paroled. By racial/ethnic group, 358 parolees are white, 148 are African–American, 24 are Native Americans, and 5 are Mexican–Americans. The following table summarizes the data as they were presented in an actual court case.[1]

---

[1]*Inmates of the Nebraska Penal and Correctional Complex v. Greenholtz,* 567 F.2d 1368 (8th Cir. 1977), cert. denied, 439 U.S. 841 (1978) as discussed in Thomas J. Sugrue and William B. Fairley, "A Case of Unexamined Assumptions: The Use and Misuse of the Statistical Analysis of Castaneda/Hazelwood in Discrimination Litigation," *Boston College Law Review,* 24 (July 1983): 925–960.

## Exhibit 8–2

**Discretionary Parole, Inmates of the Nebraska Penal and Correctional Complex, 1972–1973**

| Parole status | Race/ethnicity | | | | |
|---|---|---|---|---|---|
| | *White* | *Black* | *Native American* | *Mexican– American* | **Total** |
| Eligible for release by discretionary parole | 590 | 235 | 59 | 18 | 902 |
| Received discretionary parole | 358 | 148 | 24 | 5 | 235 |
| Percentage that received discretionary parole | 60.7% | 63.0% | 40.7% | 27.8% | 59.3% |

Did the proportion of Native Americans who are paroled differ significantly from the proportion of non–Native Americans paroled?

An analyst cannot compare the proportion of Native Americans paroled against the proportion of Native Americans among all those eligible for parole using the normal approximation to the binomial because the number of parolees is a large fraction of the population. The size of the population in this problem is the number of inmates eligible for parole—902. Of this population, 59% received parole. Of all Native Americans eligible, 40% were paroled.

Divide the parolees into two groups—Native Americans and non–Native Americans (comprised of white, black, and Mexican–American parolees) and compare the parole status between the two groups. The independent variable is racial/ethnic group. It has a dichotomous nominal level of measurement. The numeral 1 indicates the group of particular interest, Native American, and the numeral 0 indicates the non–Native American category. The dependent variable is the outcome of the parole decision. Each eligible inmate is either paroled (indicated by the numeral 1) or not paroled (indicated by the numeral 0).

Summarize the data in a 2 × 2 crosstabulation as shown in Exhibit 8–3. The cells are identified as $a$, $b$, $c$, and $d$.

Now compare observation against expectation and calculate a value for a test statistic based on this comparison. With large sample sizes the difference in the proportionate makeup between two groups in a population can be represented as a normal distribution. Compute a value for the $Z$ statistic using the following formula. The observed difference in proportions is $p_2 - p_1$. The expected difference is 0. Therefore the quantity in the numerator, observed minus expected, is $(p_2 - p_1) - 0 = (p_2 - p_1)$. In the denominator, the computation for the standard error uses $p_n$, the proportion of the total number of cases with the outcome of interest for the dependent variable.

$$Z = \frac{p_2 - p_1}{\sqrt{p_n \cdot (1 - p_n) \cdot \left[\dfrac{1}{n_1} + \dfrac{1}{n_2}\right]}}$$

where

$p_n$ = proportion of the total $n$ selected ($n = n_1 + n_2$)

$p_1$ = proportion of the first group selected

$p_2$ = proportion of the second group selected

$n_1$ = size of the first group

$n_2$ = size of the second group

Remember that one category of the dependent variable describes an outcome of particular interest. In this example the outcome of interest is a positive parole decision. The analyst is interested in the proportions of the first group (Native Americans) and second group (non–Native Americans) selected for this category of the dependent variable (parole). The calculations proceed as follows:

$$Z = \frac{p_2 - p_1}{\sqrt{p_n(1 - p_n) \cdot \left[\dfrac{1}{n_1} + \dfrac{1}{n_2}\right]}}$$

$$Z = \frac{0.6062 - 0.4068}{\sqrt{0.5931 \cdot (1 - 0.5931) \cdot \left[\dfrac{1}{59} + \dfrac{1}{843}\right]}}$$

$$Z_{\text{calculated}} \approx 3.01$$

## Exhibit 8–3

**Parole Status by Race/Ethnicity for Nebraska Inmates**

| Paroled | Race/ethnicity | | Total |
|---|---|---|---|
| | *Native American* | *Non–Native American* | |
| Yes | *a*   24 <br> 40.68% | *b*   511 <br> 60.62% | 535 <br> 59.31% |
| No | *c*   35 <br> 59.32% | *d*   332 <br> 39.38% | 367 <br> 40.69% |
| Total | 59 <br> 100.00% | 843 <br> 100.00% | 902 <br> 100.00% |

Thus, the observed difference between the proportion of Native Americans paroled and the proportion of non–Native Americans paroled diverges from the expected difference by approximately three standard deviations. This calculated value for the $Z$ statistic needs to be compared against a "critical" value at a designated level of significance. The level of significance is the probability of observing a difference between the proportions of the two groups in the sample if there is no difference between the two groups. The minimum level of significance criterion is 0.05 (5%). If an observed difference in proportions has this probability, or less, of occurring—and, nevertheless, occurs—the analyst rejects the idea (hypothesis) that there is no difference between the two groups in the sample and adopts the alternative idea that there is a difference. The analyst infers that the sample was not obtained from one homogeneous population, in which all the cases were treated identically, but from at least two populations, where the cases in one population were treated differently from the cases in the others.

The critical value for the $Z$ statistic is obtained from Appendix C, Percentage of the Area Under the Standard Normal Curve. Find the value of $Z$ corresponding to the combined area in the tails of the normal distribution being 0.05. The critical value of the $Z$ statistic is 1.96. Since the calculated $Z$ statistic value of 3.01 is greater than the critical value of 1.96, the analyst should conclude that the difference between the proportions is statistically significant. Repeat this calculation for Mexican–Americans. The calculated $Z$ statistic is 2.75. This value is also statistically significant.[2]

Observation differs from expectation. It should alert public officials to examine the policies and administrative procedures associated with parole decisions. Is there a reasonable basis for treating parole eligible inmates differently by racial/ethnic group? Decision-making practices should assure fairness and equity (that is, no statistically significant difference between racial/ethnic groups) in the award of parole to eligible inmates.

## 8.1.2 Odds Ratio and Relative Risk Ratio

Evaluation problems do not end with a determination about statistical significance. A second part of the problem is to examine the strength of association between the independent and dependent variables.

The odds ratio and relative risk ratio compare the likelihood of an event between two groups. The odds ratio compares the odds—how often an event occurs divided by how often it does not occur. Using the Nebraska inmate parole example, the odds for Native Americans receiving parole were 2 to 3 against parole (24/35 = 0.68). For non–Native Americans, the odds were 3 to 2 in favor of parole

---

[2]Nevertheless, the court held in favor of the State of Nebraska. Citing the precedent *Castaneda v. Partida* 430 U.S. 482 (1972), but misunderstanding the criteria and meaning of statistical significance, the court noted that the calculated value of the test statistic in *Nebraska* was less than the value calculated in *Castaneda*. In effect, rather than applying a level of significance of 0.05 or 0.01 to reject the null hypothesis of no discrimination in parole decisions, it used a standard of less than one in a trillion.

(511/332 = 1.5). The odds ratio is 2.2 (1.5/0.68). The odds of parole for non–Native Americans is more than double the odds for Native Americans.

The relative risk ratio compares the probability—how often an event occurs divided by the total number of opportunities for that event to occur. For Native American inmates the probability of parole is 41% (24/59). For non–Native Americans, the probability is 61% (511/843). There is a 1.5 (0.61/0.41) greater probability of non–Native Americans being paroled than Native Americans. Both statistics indicate that administrators should examine how an inmate's race/ethnicity influences parole decisions.[3]

### 8.1.3 Somers' *d* Statistic

Somers' *d* statistic for strength-of-association is usually employed with variables having an ordinal level of measurement (it will be seen again in the next two chapters). However, it can also be applied to a problem comparing two groups. In a 2 × 2 crosstabulation, Somers' *d* is simply the difference between the respective probabilities—the columns relative frequencies. On a scale of 0 to 100%, the value for the Somers' *d* statistic indicates the effect of the independent variable on the dependent variable. In the Nebraska inmate parole example 40.68% of the eligible Native American inmates were paroled while 60.62% of the eligible non–Native American inmates were paroled. The difference between these relative frequencies is the value for Somers' *d*, 19.94%. The parole "rate" for Native American inmates is about 20% less than that for non–Native American inmates. This is a "moderate" difference on the strength-of-association thermometer depicted in Appendix H. Assuming that there are no other explanatory variables, an analyst should infer that an inmate's race has a substantial determining influence on the parole decision.

### 8.1.4 Yule's *Q*

Yule's *Q* is another easy-to-calculate strength-of-association statistic for a 2 × 2 crosstabulation. First, multiply the absolute frequencies of the diagonal cells in the crosstabulation (that is, find the product of the absolute frequencies for $a \times d$ and $b \times c$). Then divide the difference between the products by the sum of the products.

$$Q = \frac{a \cdot d - b \cdot c}{a \cdot d + b \cdot c}$$

$$Q = \frac{24 \cdot 332 - 511 \cdot 35}{24 \cdot 332 + 511 \cdot 35}$$

$$Q = 0.38$$

---

[3]To convert a probability into odds, take the probability and divide it by one minus the probability: *odds = probability/(1 − probability)*. Knowing the odds in favor of an event, the probability is the odds divided by one plus the odds: *probability = odds/(1 + odds)*.

In the Nebraska inmate example, Yule's $Q$ equals 0.38. Again referring to the strength-of-association thermometer in Appendix H, this result indicates a substantial association between Native American ethnicity and parole status.

## 8.2    *Unpaired Data, 26 < n ≤ 250*

### 8.2.1    Chi-Square Test with Yates's Correction

The relationship between two nominal variables can be examined by constructing a crosstabulation with the values of the dependent variable in the rows and the values of the independent variable in the columns. The absolute frequencies in each cell are called "conditional" frequencies. They are the frequency with which values of the dependent variable are observed given preceding outcomes of the event described by the independent variable. In addition to the absolute frequencies, the conditional relative frequencies can also be shown. These are the distribution of proportions by column (each column being a value of the independent variable) with each column totaling 100%. If the relative frequency distributions differ from one column to another, the values of the dependent variable are contingent to some extent upon the values of the independent variable. If the variables are not related, the relative frequency distribution in each column will be the same as the overall relative frequency distribution of the dependent variable presented in the right-hand margin of the crosstabulation.

The chi-square statistic compares observed frequencies in each cell of a crosstabulation against a computation of the cell frequencies that are expected under the null hypothesis that there is no association between the dependent and independent variables. The expected frequencies are derived by applying the proportion of cases in each dependent category (row total divided by sample size) to the number of cases in each group (column total). The chi-square statistic is calculated as the sum over all cells of the squared difference between the observed and expected frequencies divided by the expected frequency. If the observed conditional frequency in each cell is the same as the expected frequency of the dependent variable, the value of the chi-square statistic will be 0. Differences between observed and expected frequencies will increase the calculated value of the chi-square statistic. If the chi-square calculated value becomes so large that it has less than a 5% probability of occurring by chance, the relationship between the two variables is judged to be statistically significant.

$$\chi^2 = \sum \left[ \frac{(\text{Observed frequencies} - \text{Expected frequencies})^2}{\text{Expected frequencies}} \right]$$

$$\chi^2 = \sum \left[ \frac{(f_{Oi} - f_{Ei})^2}{f_{Ei}} \right]$$

Many communities have implemented mobile crisis programs to assist the police in responding to psychiatric emergencies. In DeKalb County, Georgia, a team comprised of a psychiatric nurse and two officers is on call for 911 psychiatric emergency situations. One goal of such programs is to reduce criminalization of mentally ill persons by diverting them from jail to treatment. Because the DeKalb County team cannot respond to every psychiatric emergency call, some psychiatric emergencies are handled by a regular police response. An evaluation study examined 131 psychiatric emergency incidents during a three-month period in 1995—73 handled by a mobile crisis team and 58 handled by regular police intervention—comparing the frequency of psychiatric hospitalizations. (Other outcomes include arrest or on-site counseling and referral.) The crosstabulation in Exhibit 8–4 shows the outcomes.

First, find an expected frequency for each cell. The null-hypothesis expectation is that the psychiatric hospitalization rate is the same for both the mobile crisis team and regular police response (see Exhibit 8–5). There were 33 psychiatric hospitalizations among the 73 mobile crisis team cases compared to 42 hospitalizations among the 58 regular police response cases. With the null hypothesis of no difference, an analyst would expect a psychiatric hospitalization outcome in 57.5% (44.79) of the mobile crisis team responses and (44.79) and 57.25% (33.21) of the police responses. (The discrete—whole number—frequency counts in the cells are being treated as if they were measurements on a continuous scale so the computations of expected frequencies are carried to two decimal places rather than rounded off to integers.)

Treating the observed frequencies in $2 \times 2$ crosstabulations as if they were measurements on a continuous scale biases the chi-square computation toward slightly increased values. (As sample sizes increase the effect is less noticeable.)

## *Exhibit 8–4*

**Observed Frequency: Disposition of Psychiatric Emergencies Handled by a Mobile Crisis Team and by Regular Police Intervention: DeKalb County, GA, October–December 1995**

| | Responder | | |
| | *Mobile Crisis Team* | *Police* | |
| **Incident outcome** | | | **Total** |
|---|---|---|---|
| *a* | | *b* | |
| Psychiatric hospitalization | 33 | 42 | 75 |
| *c* | | *d* | |
| Other (including arrest or on-site counseling and referral) | 40 | 16 | 56 |
| Total | 73 | 58 | 131 |

*Source:* Roger L. Scott. "Evaluation of a Mobile Crisis Program: Effectiveness, Efficiency, and Consumer Satisfaction," *Psychiatric Services.* v. 51 n. 9, September 2000, pp. 1153–1156.

## Exhibit 8–5

**Computation of Expected Frequency**

| | Responder | | |
| --- | --- | --- | --- |
| **Incident outcome** | *Mobile Crisis Team* | *Police* | **Total** |
| | *a* | *b* | |
| Psychiatric hospitalization | $\frac{75}{131} \cdot 73 = 41.79$ | $\frac{75}{131} \cdot 58 = 33.21$ | 75 |
| | *c* | *d* | |
| Other (including arrest or on-site counseling and referral) | $\frac{56}{131} \cdot 73 = 31.21$ | $\frac{56}{131} \cdot 58 = 24.79$ | 56 |
| Total | 73 | 58 | 131 |

The bias is corrected by subtracting 0.5 from the absolute difference between the observed and expected frequency in each cell. This is called "Yates's correction for continuity." It applies only to 2 × 2 crosstabulations. The quantity $|f_O - f_{Ei}|$ means that the expected frequency is subtracted from the observed frequency for each cell and that the difference is represented as a non-negative "absolute" value. Exhibit 8–6 shows that the computation uses the observed and expected frequency counts, not percentages. Finally, the individual cell computations are added up over all four combinations of row and column locations. To indicate that the chi-square computation applies to a 2 × 2 crosstabulation and includes Yates's correction, the symbol for the statistic is $\chi^2_Y$.

$$\chi^2_Y = \sum \left[ \frac{(|\text{Observed frequencies} - \text{Expected frequencies}| - 0.5)^2}{\text{Expected frequencies}} \right]$$

$$\chi^2_Y = \sum \left[ \frac{(|f_O - f_{Ei}| - 0.5)^2}{f_{Ei}} \right]$$

The next step is to compare the calculated value for the chi-square statistic against a "critical" value at a designated level of significance. The level of significance is the probability of observing a difference between the observed and expected frequency distributions of the two groups in the sample if there "really" is no difference between the two groups. The minimum level of significance standard is 0.05 (5%). If an observed difference between observations and expectations has this probability, or less, of occurring—and, nevertheless, is, indeed, observed in the crosstabulation—the analyst rejects the null hypothesis—the idea that there is "really" no difference between the two groups—and adopts the alternative idea that there "really" is a difference. The analyst infers that our sample

## *Exhibit 8–6*

**Computation of Chi-Square**

| Cell | Chi-Square $\dfrac{(f_{Oi} - f_{Ei})^2}{f_{Ei}}$ | Yates's Correction $\dfrac{(\lvert f_{Oi} - f_{Ei}\rvert - 0.5)^2}{f_{Ei}}$ |
|------|------|------|
| $a$ | $(33 - 41.79)^2/41.79 = 1.85$ | $(\lvert 33 - 41.79 \rvert - 0.5)^2/41.79 = 1.64$ |
| $b$ | $(42 - 33.21)^2/33.21 = 2.33$ | $(\lvert 42 - 33.21 \rvert - 0.5)^2/33.21 = 2.07$ |
| $c$ | $(40 - 24.79)^2/24.79 = 2.48$ | $(\lvert 40 - 24.79 \rvert - 0.5)^2/24.79 = 2.20$ |
| $d$ | $(16 - 31.21)^2/31.21 = 3.12$ | $(\lvert 16 - 31.21 \rvert - 0.5)^2/31.21 = 2.77$ |
| Total | 9.78 | 8.70 |

was not obtained from one homogeneous population, in which all the cases are treated identically, but from at least two populations, where the cases in one population are treated differently from the cases in the others.

The critical values for the chi-square statistic are listed in Appendix D. To use the table the analyst needs to specify the appropriate level of significance and the number of degrees of freedom in the problem. The computation of the number of degrees of freedom for a chi-square distribution depends upon the number of cells in the crosstabulation as shown in the following equation. This problem has 1 degree of freedom.

Degrees of freedom
for the $\chi^2$ distribution, $df = $ [number of rows $-$ 1] $\cdot$ [number of columns $-$ 1]

$$df = (2 - 1) \cdot (2 - 1)$$

$$df = 1$$

The critical value of the chi-square statistic for a problem with 1 degree of freedom, at the 0.05 level of significance, is 3.84. Since the calculated value of the corrected chi-square statistic, 8.70, exceeds the critical value, the analyst concludes that outcome differs significantly between a mobile crisis team and regular police response to psychiatric emergency incidents.

### 8.2.2 Phi Statistic

The chi-square test indicates only whether the two variables in the problem are related. The magnitude of the calculated value can be compared to critical values of the statistic in order to determine the probability (level of significance) that the observed frequencies would occur by chance. However, level of significance is not the same as strength of association. The chi-square statistic can be used as a basis for estimating strength of association if it is corrected for the fact that the value of chi-square increases as the sample size increases. This is done by dividing the calculated value of chi-square by the sample size. The square root of this quotient is called the phi statistic, symbolized by $\phi$. Phi has a value of 0.0 when there is no relationship between the independent and dependent variables, and has a maximum value of $+1.0$ if the variables were perfectly related (a situation in which all of the cases would be classified in the diagonal cells, $a$ and $d$, or $b$ and $c$). The calculated uncorrected chi-square statistic for the DeKalb County example is 9.78.

$$\phi = \sqrt{\frac{\chi^2}{n}}$$

$$\phi = \sqrt{\frac{9.78}{113}}$$

$$\phi = 0.27$$

The phi statistic is 0.27. Generally speaking, on a 0 to 1 scale for strength of association: 0 to 0.2 is described as "weak"; 0.2 to 0.5 as "moderate"; and 0.5 to 1.0 as "strong."

## 8.3   *Unpaired Data, n ≤ 26*

### 8.3.1   **Fisher's Exact Probability Test**

Fisher's exact probability test is a useful technique for analyzing $2 \times 2$ crosstabulations that have small sample sizes. It does just what its title says—find the exact probability of a $2 \times 2$ crosstabulation having the observed frequencies, or any more extreme set of frequencies, in its four cells. Fisher's exact test computes the probability, given the observed marginal frequencies, of obtaining exactly the frequencies observed and any configuration more extreme.

$$P = \frac{\dfrac{(a+c)!}{a!c!} \cdot \dfrac{(b+d)!}{b!d!}}{\dfrac{n!}{(a+b)! \cdot (c+d)!}}$$

$$P = \frac{(a+b)! \cdot (c+d)! \cdot (a+c)! \cdot (b+d)!}{n!a!b!c!d!}$$

Consider this example of alleged age discrimination. A company laid off two employees, both 56 years of age. Seventeen other employees, ranging in age from 28 to 61, were retained.

Laid Off:       56, 56
Not Laid Off:   61, 56, 54, 54, 52, 48, 47, 47, 43, 40, 39, 37, 33, 33, 39, 28

Divide the employees into two groups—those over 55 years of age and those less than or equal to 55. The dividing line seems somewhat arbitrary—but it might be based on some policy or "rule" that would logically separate the two groups. Perhaps it is the minimum age for qualifying for partial retirement benefits or it is an age specified in a law prohibiting age discrimination. The groups are defined by the two categories of the independent variable, age. The outcome described by the dependent variable is whether or not a foreman was laid off. The crosstabulation is shown in Exhibit 8–7.

To use Appendix I, the crosstabulation should be set up so that $(a + b)$ is greater than or equal to $(c + d)$ and $a$ is greater than or equal to $b$. The crosstabulation can be rearranged to meet these requirements by interchanging the rows as shown in Exhibit 8–8. Each variable has a nominal level of measurement so that the order in which the values of the variables are placed in the crosstabulation does not matter.

Once the crosstabulation table has been arranged properly, no further calculations are necessary and Appendix I may be consulted directly. The frequency in cell $c$ is the value of the test statistic. In this example, $C_{calculated} = 0$. Find the appropriate line in the reference table for the values of $n$, $(a + b)$, $a$, and $b$. The reference table gives critical values for $C$. The observed value of the frequency in cell $c$ must be *less than or equal to* the value listed in the table in order for the relationship to be statistically significant.

In this example, $n = 19$, $(a + b) = 17$, $a = 15$, and $b = 2$. The critical value of $C$ for a one-tailed test at the 0.05 level of significance is 0. A one-tailed test is appropriate because the analyst wants to know whether there are disproportionately more layoffs among the older group than among the younger group. An inquiry as to whether the layoffs among the older group were either more or less than those among the younger group would call for a two-tailed test. The observed value of $C$ is 0. Since the observed value of $C$ is less than or equal to the critical

## Exhibit 8–7

**Layoff Status by Age Group**

| Laid off | Age group | | Total |
|---|---|---|---|
| | ≤ 55 | > 55 | |
| Yes | *a*<br>0 | *b*<br>2 | 2 |
| No | *c*<br>15 | *d*<br>2 | 17 |
| Total | 15 | 4 | 19 |

*Source: Mastie v. Great Lakes Steel Corporation*, 424 F. Supp. 1299 as described in Gregory L. Harper, "Statistics as Evidence of Age Discrimination," *Hastings Law Journal*, May 1981, pp. 1347–1375.

## Exhibit 8–8

**Layoff Status by Age Group**

| Laid off | Age group | | Total |
|----------|-----------|--------|-------|
|          | $\leq 55$ | $> 55$ |       |
| No       | *a* 15    | *b* 2  | 17    |
| Yes      | *c* 0     | *d* 2  | 2     |
| Total    | 15        | 4      | 19    |

*Source: Mastie v. Great Lakes Steel Corporation*, 424 F. Supp. 1299 as described in Gregory L. Harper, "Statistics as Evidence of Age Discrimination," *Hastings Law Journal*, May 1981, pp. 1347–1375.

value, the analyst concludes that the observed frequency of layoffs among the over-55 group is statistically significantly different from the distribution of layoffs among the younger group.

## 8.4 Paired Data

### 8.4.1 McNemar Test for Significance of Changes

In the paired (matched) situations each unit of analysis is observed two or more times. The independent variable identifies either the time when each observation was made or a unique environmental condition, a "state," that existed when each observation was made. Two (a pair) or more (matched) successive observations are made—the same unit of analysis is observed repeatedly with respect to the same dependent variable. The records in the resultant data file show the change in the dependent variable over time for each unit of analysis. The only thing that sets the observations apart is time. Perhaps something in the environment has changed. If everything remains identical in all respects (including, of course, the units of analysis themselves) except for one known change in the environment, then any difference in the values of the dependent variable is inferred to be an effect of this change.

If the respective categories of both the independent and dependent variables are designated "0" and "1," the McNemar test examines the frequency with which a "0" value for the independent variable is associated with a value of "1" for the dependent variable, and vice versa.[4]

The Evaluation Division in the Office of Policy Development and Research of the U.S. Department of Housing and Urban Development (HUD) attempted to

---

[4]The Cochran $Q$ test, introduced later in this chapter, can also be applied to this problem.

assess the extent of racial discrimination in American housing markets. In a report published in 1979 the public administration researchers present their method and findings. They set up an experiment in which black and white researchers simulated the behavior of actual housing seekers.

The simulated housing search experiment, known as an audit, is a procedure whereby a white individual and a black individual successively visit a given real estate or rental agency in search of housing. Two individuals of the same sex are matched as closely as possible in terms of age, general appearance, income, and family size—that is, in every relevant way except skin color. The two individuals request identical housing and carefully record their respective experiences on standardized reporting forms. The quantity and quality of information and service provided to each are then compared, and any systematic difference in treatment accorded black auditors and white auditors is presumed to be because of race.[5]

Each team of auditors is a matched pair. For all intents and purposes they are identical except for skin color.

Audits were conducted on a sample of rental agencies and real estate offices in 40 different Standard Metropolitan Statistical Areas (SMSAs). One of these was Akron, Ohio, where 26 were conducted. The reported results were that the white rental housing seeker was favored in 13 of the audits, the black housing seeker was favored 6 times, and there was no racial difference in the remaining 7 audits. Suppose that the results of each visit by a black or white researcher could be summarized as either *not favorable* or *favorable*.

Note that each pair is treated as one observation (case). These data can be summarized in the 2 × 2 crosstabulation shown in Exhibit 8–9.

The McNemar test for significance of changes focuses on the two cells on the diagonal that describe different outcomes between the paired observations—cell *c* (white auditor not favored and black auditor favored) and cell *b* (white auditor favored and black auditor not favored). The McNemar test proceeds by calculating a value for the chi-square statistic using the following formula:

$$\chi^2_M = \frac{(|c - b| - 1)^2}{c + b}$$

where

$$c = \text{frequency in cell } c$$

$$b = \text{frequency in cell } b$$

$$c + b = \text{number of pairs showing changes}$$

$$|c - b| = \text{absolute value of the difference between the frequencies in cell } c \text{ and cell } b$$

---

[5]U.S. Department of Housing and Urban Development, *Measuring Racial Discrimination in American Housing Markets*, April 1979.

## Exhibit 8–9

**Rental Housing Audit, Akron, Ohio SMSA, 1979**

| Black auditor | White auditor | | Total |
|---|---|---|---|
| | *Not favorable* | *Favorable* | |
| Not favorable | *a*<br>2 | *b*<br>13 | 15 |
| Favorable | *c*<br>6 | *d*<br>5 | 11 |
| Total | 8 | 18 | 26 |

and

Degrees of freedom, $df = $ [number of rows $-$ 1] $\cdot$ [number of columns $-$ 1]

$$\chi^2_{M} = \frac{(|6 - 13| - 1)^2}{6 + 13}$$

$\chi^2_{M \text{ calculated}} = 1.89 \quad df = 1$

$\chi^2_{\text{critical}} = 3.84$ at the 0.05 level of significance

Therefore, the observed differences between the frequency of audits deemed "white favored" versus audits that were "black favored" is not statistically significant for the sample obtained in the Akron, Ohio SMSA.

## 8.5 *More than Two Categories*

### 8.5.1 Chi-Square Test

A chi-square test can also be employed if the problem involves the association between two variables, either or both of which are described by more than two categories. The computational method has been described earlier. The analyst wants to determine whether there is a relationship between the variables, that is, whether being a member of one or the other group is associated with certain outcomes. This type of problem is often encountered in public opinion surveys.

Acquired Immune Deficiency Syndrome (AIDS) is caused by the transmission of the Human Immunosuppressant Virus (HIV) from one person to another via blood or semen. This principally occurs in the United States by the sharing of contaminated hypodermic syringes among drug users, engaging in unprotected sexual intercourse, inadvertent transfusions of infected blood or blood products, and transmission of the disease to unborn infants by mothers who are HIV positive. The disease is not spread by environmental conditions, casual contact, or by donating blood to a blood bank. Some opinion surveys have reported that non-white respondents exhibit less knowledge about the transmission of AIDS, suggesting that AIDS education and prevention programs might be targeted toward African–Americans, Hispanics, or other racial and ethnic groups.

A public opinion survey regarding AIDS was conducted by the Field Institute in late 1985.[6] The survey included nine questions about the transmission of AIDS:

Do you think that a person can get AIDS

By kissing a person who has AIDS?
By working in the same office with someone who has AIDS?
By using unclean public toilets?
By shaking hands with a person who has AIDS?
By drinking from a glass used by a person who has AIDS?
By being nearby when someone who has AIDS has just sneezed?
By giving blood to a blood bank or a hospital?
By eating food that has been handled by a person who has AIDS?
By being exposed to the saliva of a person who has AIDS?

The response to each question was coded: 1 = "very likely," 2 = "somewhat likely," 3 = "not too likely," 4 = "not at all likely." By adding the scores on these nine questions an analyst can develop a rough indicator of a respondent's AIDS "knowledge" on a scale ranging from a minimum of 9 points (incorrect) to a maximum of 36 points (correct).

Exhibit 8–10 is a 3 × 3 crosstabulation summarizing the survey results. It shows three categories of "accuracy" among the cumulative nine question responses, and three categories of ethnicity for 341 randomly selected adult respondents in California. The potential effect of differing educational backgrounds is "controlled" (that is, kept constant) by including in the crosstabulation only those respondents who have some college education (graduated high school but have not yet completed a four-year undergraduate degree). The two variables in the crosstabulation are treated has having a nominal level of measurement.

_____

[6]California Poll: November–December, 1985, *The Field Institute,* San Francisco. Misunderstandings persist. "In 2006, more than one-third of the public (37%) thinks HIV might be transmitted through kissing, 22% think it might be transmitted through sharing a drinking glass, and one in six (16%) think it might be transmitted through touching a toilet seat. More than four in ten adults (43%) hold at least one of these misconceptions. Misconceptions about HIV transmission are found in all segments of the population. For instance, while education does increase people's level of knowledge about transmission somewhat, still 32% of college graduates held at least one misconception about [how] HIV is transmitted." Kaiser Family Foundation, Kaiser Public Opinion Spotlight, The Public's Knowledge and Perceptions About HIV/AIDS, August 2006.

## Exhibit 8–10

**Distribution of Opinion by Ethnicity, Cumulative Response to Nine Questions About the Transmission of AIDS, California Field Poll, 1985, All Respondents Having Some College Education**

| Cumulative response to 9 opinion questions about the transmission of HIV (minimum score = 9, maximum score = 36) | Ethnicity | | | |
| --- | --- | --- | --- | --- |
| | *White, Non-Hispanic* | *Black* | *Hispanic* | **Total** |
| Category 1 | 45 | 14 | 8 | 67 |
| Less accurate responses | 67.16% | 20.90% | 11.94% | 100.00% |
| 9 ≤ score ≤ 20 | 16.30% | 38.89% | 27.59% | 19.65% |
| | (54.23) | (7.07) | (5.70) | |
| Category 2 | 136 | 13 | 15 | 164 |
| Somewhat accurate responses | 82.93% | 7.93% | 9.15% | 100.00% |
| 21 ≤ score ≤ 30 | 49.28% | 36.11% | 51.72% | 48.09% |
| | (132.73) | (17.31) | (13.95) | |
| Category 3 | 95 | 9 | 6 | 110 |
| More accurate responses | 86.36% | 8.18% | 5.45% | 100.00% |
| 31 ≤ score ≤ 36 | 34.42% | 25.00% | 20.69% | 32.26% |
| | (89.04) | (11.61) | (9.36) | |
| Total | 276 | 36 | 29 | 341 |
| | 80.94% | 10.56% | 8.50% | 100.00% |
| | 100.00% | 100.00% | 100.00% | 100.00% |

Cell contents: observed frequency, row percent, column percent (expected frequency)

The chi-square statistic is calculated by the following equation.

$$\chi^2 = \sum \left[ \frac{(f_{Oi} - f_{Ei})^2}{f_{Ei}} \right]$$

$$\chi^2_{\text{calculated}} = 12.72 \quad df = 4$$

The critical value of chi-square is 9.49 at the 0.05 level of significance. The relationship between ethnicity and cumulative opinion score is statistically significant.

### 8.5.2 Cramer's *V* Statistic

The chi-square statistic indicates the likelihood of the independent and dependent variables being related. It does not indicate the strength of the relationship. The determination of statistical significance is affected by both sample size (the value of the chi-square statistic increases with sample size) and number of cells in the crosstabulation (the critical value of chi-square increases with degrees of freedom). The Cramer's $V$ statistic for strength of association corrects for these effects by dividing the calculated value of chi-square by a product including the sample size and the minimum dimension of the crosstabulation.

Cramer's $V$ provides us a "thermometer" reading on a scale of 0 to $+1$ for the strength-of-association between the independent and dependent variables. A large value of Cramer's $V$ indicates that units of analysis that fall in independent variable categories designated by higher numbers also tend to fall in the categories of the dependent variable designated by higher numbers. It sheds no light on how this association occurs.

From Exhibit 8–10:

$$\text{Cramer's } V = \sqrt{\dfrac{\chi^2}{n \cdot \text{minimum} \begin{cases} (\text{number of rows} - 1) \\ \text{or} \\ (\text{number of columns} - 1) \end{cases}}}$$

$$\text{Cramer's } V = \sqrt{\dfrac{12.71}{341 \cdot \text{minimum} \begin{cases} (3 - 1) \\ \text{or} \\ (3 - 1) \end{cases}}}$$

$$\text{Cramer's } V = 0.137$$

The results show a statistically significant, but weak, association between ethnicity and the cumulative score of responses to the nine-question survey. A word of caution now needs to be sounded about the interpretation of these results. This example, used to illustrate the application of the chi-square test, is the most rudimentary form of social science analysis. In and of itself, such variables as skin color or parental origin are dubious explanations of behaviors or reactions to serious social issues. At best the implied explanations are simplistic, at worst racist.

### 8.5.3 Lambda Statistic

The extent to which the value of the independent variable helps an analyst anticipate the value of the dependent variable is another indicator of the strength of association between the two variables. Greater accuracy means fewer errors—so a statistic that examines predictive association between variables with a nominal level of measurement (and, as we will see later, ordinal level of measurement) is called a *proportionate reduction in error*, PRE, statistic. The lambda statistic, $\lambda$, is such a measure.

The lambda statistic compares the number of predictive errors in the crosstabulation of two nominal variables against the number of errors that would have been made if only the dependent variable had been observed.

$$\lambda = 1 - \frac{\begin{bmatrix} \text{Number of errors in prediction} \\ \text{knowing value of independent variable} \end{bmatrix}}{\begin{bmatrix} \text{Number of errors in prediction} \\ \text{not knowing value of independent variable} \end{bmatrix}}$$

Suppose an analyst examined the data file of 341 respondents to the questions about the transmission of HIV as shown in Exhibit 8–11. Without knowledge of ethnicity, what would be the best guess as to the accuracy score of each respondent? The best guess would be the modal category of the dependent variable—the most frequently occurring outcome. The best estimate of the most frequently occurring accuracy score is "Category 2: Somewhat accurate responses." Among the 341 cases in the sample, the best guess would be correct 164 times and in error $67 + 110 = 177$ times.

Does knowledge of ethnicity reduce the error? Among the 276 white non-Hispanics in the sample the most frequent outcome was "Category 2." This would be the correct prediction for 136 cases, but in error for $45 + 95 = 145$. Among the 36 black respondents in the sample, the most frequent outcome is "Category 1." This is the correct prediction for 14 cases, but it is incorrect for $13 + 9 = 22$ cases. In a similar fashion there are 14 errors using "Category 2" as the outcome prediction for Hispanic respondents.

## Exhibit 8-11

**Distribution of Opinion by Ethnicity, Cumulative Response to Nine Questions About the Transmission of HIV/AIDS**

| Cumulative response to 9 opinion questions about the transmission of HIV (minimum score = 9, maximum score = 36) | Ethnicity | | | **Total** |
|---|---|---|---|---|
| | *White, Non-Hispanic* | *Black* | *Hispanic* | |
| Category 1 Less accurate responses 9 ≤ score ≤ 20 | 45 | 14← | 8 | 67 |
| Category 2 Somewhat accurate responses 21 ≤ score ≤ 30 | 136← | 13 | 15← | 164← |
| Category 3 More accurate responses 31 ≤ score ≤ 36 | 95 | 9 | 6 | 110 |
| Total | 276 | 36 | 29 | 341 |

Errors: knowing value of independent variable = $(45 + 95) + (13 + 9) + (8 + 6) = 176$
Errors: not knowing value of independent variable = $67 + 110 = 177$

Therefore, there are 177 predictive errors in the sample without reference to the independent variable and $(45 + 95) + (13 + 9) + (8 + 6) = 176$ predictive errors when the value of the independent variable is known for each case. The result is that we made 0.6% fewer errors. This is the value for the lambda statistic in this example.

$$\lambda = 1 - \frac{\begin{bmatrix} \text{Number of errors in prediction} \\ \text{knowing value of independent variable} \end{bmatrix}}{\begin{bmatrix} \text{Number of errors in prediction} \\ \text{not knowing value of independent variable} \end{bmatrix}}$$

$$\lambda = 1 - \frac{(45 + 95) + (13 + 9) + (8 + 6)}{67 + 110}$$

$$\lambda = 0.006$$

The lambda statistic has a value between 0 and $+1.0$. The higher the value, the greater the proportionate reduction in error in the sample—an indicator of the strength of association between the independent and dependent variables. In this example, ethnicity is a very poor predictor of responses to questions about contracting HIV.

## 8.6 *Matched Data*

### 8.6.1 Cochran Q Test

Matched units of analysis occur if the same person or object is observed repeatedly or if sets of two or more persons or objects are identified as alike in all respects except for the nominal characteristic or attribute defined by the independent variable. A dichotomous nominal resultant outcome is defined by the dependent variable.

In the Cochran $Q$ test, each value of the independent variable identifies a "group." The question at hand is whether the observed outcomes significantly differ between the groups.[7]

For example, Longview State Hospital (Ohio) developed a program called "Training in Independent Living" to ". . . teach institutionalized (psychiatric) patients the resocialization and living skills felt necessary for successful community living."[8]

---

[7]The Cochran Q test is also an alternative to the McNemar test for significance of changes introduced earlier in this chapter.

[8]Kayla J. Springer and Steven Beck, "Evaluation of 'Training in Independent Living' Treatment Effectiveness in Longview State Hospital," in U.S. Department of Health, Education, and Welfare, National Institute of Mental Health, *Evaluation in Practice* (Washington, DC: U.S. Superintendent of Documents, 1979).

A follow-up check of the status of each TIL participant was conducted at 3-month, 6-month, and 15-month intervals after completing the program. Exhibit 8–12 presents hypothetical results for 15 patients. A 0 indicates that the patient was hospitalized at the time, whereas a 1 indicates that the patient was in the community.

The Cochran $Q$ statistic is defined by the following formula. Some intermediate computational results are shown in Exhibit 8–12.

$$Q = \frac{(k-1) \cdot [k \cdot \Sigma C_j^2 - (\Sigma C_j)^2]}{k \cdot \Sigma C_j - \Sigma_i R_i^2} \text{ with } k - 1 \text{ degrees of freedom}$$

## *Exhibit 8–12*

**Results of Treatment in Independent Living Program (Hypothetical Data)**

| Patient *i* | Status (0 = hospitalized) (1 = in the community) | | | $R_i$ | $R_i^2$ |
|---|---|---|---|---|---|
| | *3 months* $j = 1$ | *6 months* $j = 2$ | *15 months* $j = 3$ | | |
| 1 | 1 | 0 | 1 | 2 | 4 |
| 2 | 0 | 1 | 1 | 2 | 4 |
| 3 | 0 | 1 | 1 | 2 | 4 |
| 4 | 0 | 1 | 0 | 1 | 1 |
| 5 | 0 | 0 | 1 | 1 | 1 |
| 6 | 1 | 1 | 1 | 3 | 9 |
| 7 | 0 | 0 | 0 | 0 | 0 |
| 8 | 1 | 1 | 1 | 3 | 9 |
| 9 | 0 | 0 | 0 | 0 | 0 |
| 10 | 0 | 1 | 1 | 2 | 4 |
| 11 | 1 | 1 | 1 | 3 | 9 |
| 12 | 0 | 0 | 1 | 1 | 1 |
| 13 | 0 | 0 | 0 | 0 | 0 |
| 14 | 0 | 0 | 1 | 1 | 1 |
| 15 | 0 | 1 | 1 | 2 | 4 |
| Total | 4 | 8 | 11 | 23 | 51 |

where

$i$ = case number: $i = 1, 2, 3, \ldots, n$

$j$ = index of independent variable

$k$ = number of values for the independent variable

$C_j$ = sum of the values (that is, number of favorable responses) for each value of the independent variable (column)

$R_i$ = sum of the values (that is, number of favorable responses) for each case (row)

$$Q = \frac{(3 - 1) \cdot [3 \cdot (4^2 + 8^2 + 11^2) - (4 + 8 + 11)^2]}{3 \cdot (4 + 8 + 11) - 51}$$

$Q_{\text{calculated}} = 8.22$

The distribution of the $Q$ statistic is closely approximated by the chi-square distribution. Refer to Appendix I for critical values of $Q$. Thus, at 2 degrees of freedom, 0.05 level of significance, $Q_{\text{critical}} = 5.99$. $Q_{\text{calculated}}$ exceeds $Q_{\text{critical}}$, so the outcomes between the three follow-up time periods are statistically significant. Since the chi-square test is one-tailed, besides $Q$ the analyst also needs to examine whether the $R$ values increase or decrease over time to determine the nature of the changes. In this example the sum of the $R$ values tends to increase. The results indicate that the patients who have completed the TIL program tend to be in the community rather than in the hospital.

## *Homework Exercises*

**8-1** What conditions affect sentencing of persons charged with the commission of property crime? Exhibit HW8–1A summarizes the disposition of nonresidential burglary and other property crime cases come from a study conducted in one year. Is the existence of a prior criminal record or the nature of the offense charged associated with the chance of receiving a prison sentence? Show your work and write a conclusion. Hint: Careful—there are three variables in this table. Redisplay these data in two separate crosstabulations.

## *Exhibit HW8–1A*

**Disposition of Nonresidential Burglary and Property Crime Cases by Prior Arrest Record and Type of Offense**

| | Type of offense | | | |
| | Nonresidential burglary | | Other property | |
| | Prior arrests | | Prior arrests | |
| **Disposition** | *None* | *Some* | *None* | *Some* |
| --- | --- | --- | --- | --- |
| No prison | 38 | 67 | 244 | 302 |
| Prison | 17 | 42 | 21 | 67 |

## *Exhibit HW8–1B*

**Disposition of Nonresidential Burglary and Property Crime Cases by Prior Arrest Record**

| | Prior arrests | | |
| **Disposition** | *None* | *Some* | **Total** |
| --- | --- | --- | --- |
| No prison | 282 | 369 | 651 |
| | 88.1% | 77.2% | 81.6% |
| Prison | 38 | 109 | 147 |
| | 11.9% | 22.8% | 18.4% |
| Total | 320 | 478 | 798 |
| | 100.0% | 100.0% | 100.0% |

$$Z = \frac{p_2 - p_1}{\sqrt{p_n(1 - p_n) \cdot \left[\dfrac{1}{n_1} + \dfrac{1}{n_2}\right]}}$$

$$Z = \frac{0.881 - 0.772}{\sqrt{0.816\,(1 - 0.816) \cdot \left[\dfrac{1}{320} + \dfrac{1}{478}\right]}}$$

$$Z = 3.89$$

## Exhibit HW8–1C

**Disposition of Nonresidential Burglary and Property Crime Cases by Type of Offense**

| | Type of offense | | |
| | *Nonresidential* | *Other* | |
| **Disposition** | *burglary* | *property* | **Total** |
| No prison | 105 | 546 | 651 |
| | 64.0% | 86.1% | 81.6% |
| Prison | 59 | 88 | 147 |
| | 36.0% | 13.9% | 18.4% |
| Total | 164 | 634 | 798 |
| | 100.0% | 100.0% | 100.0% |

$$Z = \frac{0.640 - 0.861}{\sqrt{0.816\,(1 - 0.816) \cdot \left[\dfrac{1}{164} + \dfrac{1}{634}\right]}} = -6.51$$

**8-2**  Analyze the differences between cities and counties with respect to the functional responsibilities assigned risk managers, given the data shown in Exhibit HW8–2A.

## Exhibit HW8–2A

**Functional Responsibilities of Full-Time Risk Managers in Cities and Counties**

| | Cities | | Counties | |
| **Responsibility** | *Number* | *%* | *Number* | *%* |
| Insurance procurement | 95 | 89.6 | 53 | 98.1 |
| Workers' compensation | 88 | 83.0 | 49 | 90.7 |
| Group health and life insurance | 56 | 52.8 | 33 | 61.1 |
| Safety, accident prevention, and loss control | 88 | 83.0 | 50 | 92.6 |
| Claims handling | 89 | 84.0 | 49 | 90.7 |
| Self-insurance programs | 91 | 85.8 | 50 | 92.6 |
| Other | 25 | 23.6 | 20 | 37.0 |
| Total | 106 | | 54 | |

Set up a 2 × 2 table like Exhibit HW8–2B. Compute $\alpha$.

## Exhibit HW8–2B

**Insurance Procurement Responsibilities of City and County Risk Managers**

| Responsibility | Cities | Counties | Total |
|---|---|---|---|
| Responsible for insurance procurement | $a$<br>95 | $b$<br>53 | 148 |
| Not responsible for insurance procurement | $c$<br>11 | $d$<br>1 | 12 |
| Total | 106 | 54 | 160 |

$$\alpha = \frac{\dfrac{a}{c}}{\dfrac{b}{d}} = \frac{\dfrac{95}{11}}{\dfrac{53}{1}} = 0.163$$

$\alpha$, the odds ratio, ranges from 0 to $\infty$ with 1.0 indicating no association—statistical independence. 0.163 indicates that the odds of cities assigning insurance procurement to their risk manager tends to be about 6 times less than the odds of counties assigning the task to the risk manager.

---

**8-3**  Employees of the Department of Income Maintenance in one state were required to achieve a passing score on a written examination in order to qualify for promotion to permanent status as Welfare Eligibility Supervisors.[1] The passing score was set at 65. Exhibit HW8–3A shows the passing rates of 329 candidates who took the test by racial/ethnic group.

**a.** Is the difference in the passing rates for this examination between African–American and white candidates statistically significant?

**b.** What is the strength of association?

---

[1]*Connecticut v. Teal*, 457 U.S. 440–464 (1982).

## Exhibit HW8–3A

**Test Results of Applicants for Welfare Eligibility Supervisor**

| Group | Number | Number receiving passing score | Passing rate (%) |
|---|---|---|---|
| African–American | 48 | 26 | 54.2 |
| Hispanic | 4 | 3 | 75.0 |
| Native American | 3 | 2 | 66.7 |
| White | 259 | 206 | 79.5 |
| Unidentified | 15 | 9 | 60.0 |
| Total | 329 | 246 | 74.8 |

## Exhibit HW8–3B

**Test Results of Applicants for Welfare Eligibility Supervisor**

| | Group | | |
|---|---|---|---|
| Test outcome | African–American | White | Total |
| Pass | 26<br>54.2% | 206<br>79.5% | 232<br>75.6% |
| Not pass | 22<br>45.8% | 53<br>20.5% | 75<br>24.4% |
| Total | 48 | 259 | 307 |

**a.** $Z$ test for the difference between two proportions

$$Z = \frac{p_2 - p_1}{\sqrt{p_n \cdot (1 - p_n) \cdot \left[\frac{1}{n_1} + -\frac{1}{n_2}\right]}}$$

$$Z = \frac{0.795 - 0.542}{\sqrt{0.756 \cdot (1 - 0.756) \cdot \left[\frac{1}{48} + \frac{1}{259}\right]}}$$

$$Z = 3.75$$

The difference in the passing rates is statistically significant at the 95% confidence level.

**b.** Somers' $d = p_2 - p_1 = 0.795 - 0.542 = 0.25$

The strength-of-association statistic indicates a moderate association.

**8-4** One of the most well known and influential legal decisions in the United States of the twentieth century was the U.S. Supreme Court case *Miranda v. Arizona.*[2] Made famous by television and movie dramas, the decision requires investigators and prosecutors to inform the criminally accused of their constitutional right to have appointed counsel before any custodial questioning can legally begin. Some have criticized the *Miranda* ruling as unnecessarily hindering crime investigation and prosecution by thwarting the obtaining and use of confessions to convict suspects. One analyst investigated this question by observing police interrogations in three California cities.[3,4] Exhibit HW8–4A shows the fate of "in-custody" suspects who were "*Mirandized.*" Analyze these results. Does it seem that *Miranda* has hindered criminal prosecution?

## Exhibit HW8-4A

**Suspect's Response to *Miranda* Warning by In-custody Suspect's Prior Criminal Record**

| Response to *Miranda* warning | Suspect's prior record | | | Total |
|---|---|---|---|---|
| | *None* | *Misdemeanor* | *Felony* | |
| Waived | 22 | 42 | 72 | 136 |
| | 91.7% | 89.4% | 69.9% | 78.2% |
| Invoked | 2 | 5 | 31 | 38 |
| | 8.3% | 10.6% | 30.1% | 21.8% |
| Total | 24 | 47 | 103 | 174 |
| | 100% | 100% | 100% | 100% |

Chi-square $= 10.134$, Cramer's $V = 0.241$, $P = 0.006$. A suspect with a felony record was almost four times as likely to invoke his *Miranda* rights as a suspect with no prior record and almost three times as likely to invoke as a suspect with a misdemeanor record.

[2]*Miranda v Arizona*, 384 U.S. 436 (1966).
[3]Richard A. Leo, "Inside the Interrogation Room," *The Journal of Criminal Law & Criminology,* 86, Winter 1996, 266.
[4]Richard A. Leo, "The Impact of *Miranda* Revisited" *The Journal of Criminal Law & Criminology,* 86, n. 3, Spring 1996, 621–692.

## Exhibit HW8–4B

**Case Outcome by In-Custody Suspect's Response to *Miranda* Warning**

| Case outcome | Response to *Miranda* warning | | Total |
| --- | --- | --- | --- |
| | *Waived* | *Invoked* | |
| Not convicted | 48 | 15 | 63 |
| | 37.2% | 46.9% | 39.1% |
| Convicted | 81 | 17 | 98 |
| | 62.8% | 53.1% | 60.9% |
| Total | 129 | 32 | 161 |
| | 100.0% | 100.0% | 100.0% |

$\chi_Y^2 = 0.641$, Somers' $d = -0.097$, $\phi = -0.079$, $P = 0.316$. Although in-custody suspects who waived *Miranda* rights were more likely to be convicted, this difference is not statistically significant.

## Exhibit HW8–4C

**Case Outcome by Charged Suspect's Response to *Miranda* Warning**

| Case outcome | Response to *Miranda* warning | | Total |
| --- | --- | --- | --- |
| | *Waived* | *Invoked* | |
| Not convicted | 3 | 5 | 8 |
| | 3.6% | 22.7% | 7.5% |
| Convicted | 81 | 17 | 98 |
| | 96.4% | 77.3% | 92.5% |
| Total | 84 | 22 | 106 |
| | 100.0% | 100.0% | 100.0% |

$\chi_Y^2 = 6.629$, Somers' $d = -0.192$, $\phi = -0.294$, $P = 0.01$. Among those suspects charged, the relationship between conviction and response to the *Miranda* warning is statistically significant. This needs to be interpreted cautiously because the number of suspects not convicted is low—one cell is less than 5. These data show that suspects who had invoked their *Miranda* rights and had subsequently been charged had about a 20% lower conviction rate.

# Exhibit HW8–4D

**Severity of Sentence by Convicted Suspect's Response to *Miranda* Warning**

| | Response to *Miranda* warning | | |
| Severity of sentence | *Waived* | *Invoked* | **Total** |
|---|---|---|---|
| Low | 46<br>60.5% | 9<br>52.9% | 55<br>59.1% |
| Medium | 15<br>19.7% | 2<br>11.8% | 17<br>18.3% |
| High | 15<br>19.7% | 6<br>35.3% | 21<br>22.6% |
| Total | 76<br>100.0% | 17<br>100.0% | 93<br>100.0% |

Kolmogorov–Smirnov $D = 0.156$, $P = 0.89$, Somers' $d = 0.122$. The analysis shows no significant relationship between waiving or invoking *Miranda* rights and sentence upon conviction.

**8-5** Exhibit HW8–5A shows additional results from the audits conducted by the U.S. Department of Housing and Urban Development in which black and white individuals successively visited real estate agencies and rental offices in search of housing. In which SMSAs is the difference between "white favored" and "African–American favored" statistically significant?

# Exhibit HW8–5A

**Rental Market Index of Housing Availability**

| | | | Result of audit | |
| SMSA | *n* | *No difference* | *White favored* | *African–American favored* |
|---|---|---|---|---|
| Greenville, SC | 30 | 40% | 37% | 23% |
| Los Angeles–Long Beach, CA | 30 | 20% | 63% | 17% |
| Tulsa, OK | 30 | 47% | 47% | 7% |
| Stockton, CA | 28 | 32% | 46% | 21% |
| Savannah, GA | 15 | 27% | 47% | 27% |
| Springfield–Chicopee–Holyoke, MA–CT | 29 | 35% | 59% | 7% |
| York, PA | 29 | 31% | 52% | 17% |

*Source:* Ronald E. Wienk, and others, *Measuring Racial Discrimination in American Housing Markets: The Housing Market Practices Survey,* U.S. Department of Housing and Urban Development, April 1979.

Use the McNemar test for significance of changes.

## Exhibit HW8–5B

**Calculations: Rental Market Index of Housing Availability**

| SMSA | $n$ | Result of audit | | | $\chi^2_M$ |
|---|---|---|---|---|---|
| | | *No difference* | *White favored* | *African–American favored* | |
| Greenville, SC | 30 | 12 | 11 | 7 | 0.5 |
| Los Angeles–Long Beach, CA | 30 | 6 | 19 | 5 | 7.0** |
| Tulsa, OK | 30 | 14 | 14 | 2 | 7.6** |
| Stockton, CA | 28 | 9 | 13 | 6 | 1.9 |
| Savannah, GA | 15 | 4 | 7 | 4 | 0.4 |
| Springfield–Chicopee–Holyoke, MA–CT | 29 | 10 | 17 | 2 | 10.3** |
| York, PA | 29 | 9 | 15 | 5 | 4.1* |

degrees of freedom = 1
*significant at the 0.05 level
**significant at the 0.01 level

**8-6** Do women who are exposed to radiation from video display terminals (VDTs) have a higher risk of miscarriages? A seven-year study compared the pregnancies of 323 telephone operators who worked with VDTs and 407 who worked in similar jobs without VDTs. The women, all between the ages of 18 and 33, were employees of Bell South and American Telephone and Telegraph in eight Southeastern states. The two groups were similar with respect to race, educational background, and socioeconomic status. The study found that 14.8% of pregnant women who worked with VDTs reported miscarriages, compared to 15.9% for women who did not work with VDTs,[5] as shown in Exhibit HW8–6A.

The difference in the rate of miscarriages between the women who worked with VDTs and those who did not is statistically insignificant.

---

[5]Bob Baker, "7-Year U.S. Study Finds No VDT Link to Miscarriages," *Los Angeles Times,* 14 March 1991.

## Exhibit HW8–6A

**Miscarriages by Women Working with Video Display Terminals**

| Pregnancy outcome | Radiation exposure | | Total |
| --- | --- | --- | --- |
| | *Working with VDTs* | *Not working with VDTs* | |
| Miscarriage | *a*<br>49<br>(14.8%) | *b*<br>65<br>(15.9%) | 114 |
| No miscarriage | *c*<br>274 | *d*<br>342 | 616 |
| Total | 323 | 407 | 730 |

$$Z = \frac{p_2 - p_1}{\sqrt{p_n(1 - p_n) \cdot \left[\frac{1}{n_1} + \frac{1}{n_2}\right]}}$$

$$Z = \frac{0.148 - 0.159}{\sqrt{0.156\,(1 - 0.156) \cdot \left[\frac{1}{323} + \frac{1}{407}\right]}} = -0.41$$

$$Q = \frac{bc - ad}{bc + ad} = \frac{65(274) - 49(342)}{65(274) + 49(342)} = 0.03$$

**8-7** The Kentucky Injury Prevention and Research Center of the University of Kentucky looked at the risk factors with respect to traumatic brain injury (TBI) in motorcycle accidents within the state over the period 1995–2000.[6] Exhibit HW8–7A presents their observations. Analyze each potential risk factor to determine if it is statistically significantly related to the outcome (TBI or no TBI) of a motorcycle crash. Report strength-of-association for any relationships that are significant.

[6]W. Jay Christian. *Motorcycle Helmets and Traumatic Brain Injury in Kentucky, 1995–2000,* Kentucky Injury Prevention and Research Center, University of Kentucky, 2003.

## Exhibit HW8–7A

**Frequency of Traumatic Brain Injury in Motorcycle Accidents by Risk Factor, Kentucky 1995–2000 (dependent variable presented in columns to conserve space)**

| Risk factor | Value | Traumatic brain injury | |
|---|---|---|---|
| | | *Yes* | *No* |
| Age | 0–20 | 15 | 13 |
| | 21–40 | 67 | 126 |
| | 41–60 | 41 | 61 |
| | 61+ | 2 | 11 |
| Gender | Male | 112 | 181 |
| | Female | 13 | 30 |
| Season | Jan–Mar | 15 | 24 |
| | Apr–Jun | 41 | 69 |
| | Jul–Sep | 51 | 93 |
| | Oct–Dec | 18 | 25 |
| Type of accident | Traffic | 117 | 203 |
| | Non-traffic | 8 | 8 |
| Time of accident | Night (8 P.M.–5 A.M.) | 54 | 95 |
| | Day (5 A.M.–8 P.M.) | 71 | 116 |
| Drug Screen | Positive | 34 | 53 |
| | Negative | 91 | 158 |
| Race | Black | 7 | 18 |
| | White | 118 | 193 |
| Blood alcohol content | > 0.08 | 40 | 35 |
| | < 0.08 | 85 | 176 |
| Helmet use | Yes | 39 | 131 |
| | No | 86 | 80 |

Age group $\times$ TBI          $\chi^2 = 6.8$, $df = 3$, $V = 0.14$

Gender $\times$ TBI          $\chi^2_Y = 0.71$, $df = 1$

Season $\times$ TBI          $\chi^2 = 0.62$, $df = 3$

Type of accident $\times$ TBI          $\chi^2_Y = 0.67$, $df = 1$

Time of accident $\times$ TBI          $\chi^2_Y = 0.04$, $df = 1$

Drug screen $\times$ TBI          $\chi^2_Y = 0.08$, $df = 1$

Race $\times$ TBI          $\chi^2_Y = 0.60$, $df = 1$

BAC $\times$ TBI          $\chi^2_Y = 9.88$, $df = 1$, $\phi = 0.18$

Helmet use $\times$ TBI          $\chi^2_Y = 28.73$, $df = 1$, $\phi = 0.30$

# CHAPTER 9

# Order Within Groups: Two-Variable Evaluation— Nominal–Ordinal Measures

| | |
|---|---|
| Kind of problem | *Evaluation* |
| Number of variables | *Two* |
| Level of measurement | *Variable 1, nominal* |
| | *Variable 2, ordinal* |

his chapter continues two-variable evaluation problems. One variable, having a nominal level of measurement, divides the units of analysis into two or more groups. Another variable, having an ordinal level of measurement, describes a second characteristic or attribute of each event. Several tests for statistical significance and strength-of-association are available, as shown in Exhibit 9–1. Usually the nominal variable is the independent variable while the ordinal variable is dependent. However, the same statistical methods apply if it is the ordinal variable that is independent and the nominal variable dependent, so Exhibit 9–1 uses the terms *first variable* and *second variable*. The choice initially depends upon the number of categories that the nominal variable has and the paired–unpaired nature of the cases. The classifications are dichotomous, with unpaired units of analysis; dichotomous, with paired units of analysis; or nondichotomous—having more than two categories. Other considerations for utilizing each method will be pointed out in the discussion.

## 9.1 *The Nominally Measured Variable Has Two Categories, Unpaired Data*

### 9.1.1 Mann–Whitney *U* Test

The Mann–Whitney *U* test can be used to evaluate the difference between two groups with respect to some ordinal characteristic or attribute. It is the test of

# *Exhibit 9–1*

**Two-Variable Evaluation—Nominal–Ordinal Measures**

| Second variable | | First variable: Nominal level of measurement | | |
| --- | --- | --- | --- | --- |
| | | **Two categories** | | **More than two categories** |
| | | *Unpaired units of analysis* | *Paired units of analysis* | |
| Ordinal level of measurement | Strength of association | Somers' *d* | | * |
| | Statistical significance | Mann–Whitney *U* Test | Wilcoxon matched pairs signed-ranks test | Kruskal–Wallis test |
| | | Kolmogorov–Smirnov two-variable test | | |

*Note: Not covered in this text. L.C. Freeman developed a strength-of-association statistic for the situation in which the ordinal variable is dependent. See L.C. Freeman. 1965. *Elementary Applied Statistics for Students in Behavioral Science.* New York: Wiley.

choice in this problem situation because it is better at distinguishing, and rejecting, null hypotheses (statements of no difference between observation and expectation) when they are indeed false.

In the previous chapter we addressed the problem of potential age discrimination. The analyst split the workers into two groups—those over 55 years of age and those under. Thus the variable *age* was treated as a dichotomous nominal level of measurement. By doing this the analyst lost information—the ordinal rankings of age among the workers. Reanalyze the problem treating age as an ordinal level of measurement (see Exhibit 9–2).

The first step is to arrange the cases in order (either ascending or descending). Then a rank is assigned to each case in the data set. If two or more cases have identical values of the ordinal variable, the rank given to each case is the mean of the ranks that would have been assigned if there had been no ties. For example, after arranging the foremen in descending order of their age, notice that three workers, the second, third, and fourth cases in the data set, are each 56 years old. They are each assigned a numeric rank of 3 which is the mean of 2, 3, and 4.

Next, the cases are separated according to the value of the nominal variable and the ranks of the cases in each group are totaled. In this example, two workers were laid off. The sum of their ranks on the ordinal variable *age* is 6. The sum of the ranks assigned to the 17 other workers is 184. The analyst can check whether the computations are correct to this point with the following equation, called an *identity*. The value for each symbol is known. If the total on the left-hand side of

## Exhibit 9–2

**Computations for Mann–Whitney *U* Test: Age Discrimination**

| Rank | Age | Laid off? | Rank adjusted for ties | Ranks: Laid off | Ranks: Not laid off |
|------|-----|-----------|------------------------|-----------------|---------------------|
| 1 | 61 | No | 1 | — | 1 |
| 2 | 56 | Yes | 3 | 3 | — |
| 3 | 56 | No | 3 | — | 3 |
| 4 | 56 | Yes | 3 | 3 | — |
| 5 | 54 | No | 5.5 | — | 5.5 |
| 6 | 54 | No | 5.5 | — | 5.5 |
| 7 | 52 | No | 7 | — | 7 |
| 8 | 48 | No | 8 | — | 8 |
| 9 | 47 | No | 9.5 | — | 9.5 |
| 10 | 47 | No | 9.5 | — | 9.5 |
| 11 | 43 | No | 11.5 | — | 11.5 |
| 12 | 43 | No | 11.5 | — | 11.5 |
| 13 | 40 | No | 13 | — | 13 |
| 14 | 39 | No | 14 | — | 14 |
| 15 | 37 | No | 15 | — | 15 |
| 16 | 33 | No | 16.5 | — | 16.5 |
| 17 | 33 | No | 16.5 | — | 16.5 |
| 18 | 29 | No | 18 | — | 18 |
| 19 | 28 | No | 19 | — | 19 |
| Total | | | | $R_1 = 6$ | $R_2 = 184$ |
| | | | | $n_1 = 2$ | $n_2 = 17$ |

the equation equals the total on the right-hand side of the equation the ranks of the cases have been properly assigned.

$$R_1 + R_2 = \frac{(n_1 + n_2)}{2} \cdot (n_1 + n_2 + 1)$$

$$6 + 184 = \frac{(2 + 17)}{2} \cdot (2 + 17 + 1)$$

$$190 = 190$$

Having checked that the rankings are correct, the analyst can now calculate a value for the Mann–Whitney $U$ statistic.

$$U = n_1 \cdot n_2 + \frac{n_1 \cdot (n_1 + 1)}{2} - R_1$$

$$U = 2 \cdot 17 + \frac{2 \cdot (2 + 1)}{2} - 6$$

$$U_{\text{calculated}} = 31$$

The null hypothesis expectation is that there is no difference in the age distribution between the group laid off and the group not laid off. In order to test whether observation differs from expectation the analyst needs to compare the calculated value of the $U$ statistic against a critical value. Refer to Appendix J (critical values of $U$ in the Mann–Whitney test). Critical values for $U$ are listed for each combination of level of significance and $n_1$ and $n_2$. To be statistically significant, the calculated value of $U$ must be less than or equal to this critical value, $U_{\text{L critical}}$ or greater than or equal to a higher critical value, $n_1 n_2 - U_{\text{L critical}}$. Using a two-tailed test at the 0.05 level of significance for $n_1 = 2$ and $n_2 = 17$, the lower critical value is 2 and the higher critical value is 32. A two-tailed test says, in effect, that the workers who were laid off have either higher or lower age than those not laid off. Since the calculated value, $U = 31$, is not less than the lower critical value critical value of 2, or greater than the higher critical value of 32, the analyst concludes that there is not a statistically significant difference between the ages of the workers laid off and those not laid off.[1]

This result apparently contradicts the conclusion we reached using Fisher's exact probability test at the same (0.05) level of significance.[2] However, Fisher's exact probability test is one-tailed. This, in effect, says that the workers who were laid off have a higher age (not either higher or lower) than those not laid off. The one-tailed test also makes sense conceptually since potential age discrimination would adversely affect older workers. For a one-tailed Mann–Whitney $U$ test at

---

[1]As a double check, a second $U$ statistic, called $U'$ ($U$ prime) can be calculated. The conclusion regarding statistical significance should be the same whether $U$ or $U'$ is used as the calculated value of the test statistic.

$$U' = n_1 \cdot n_2 - U$$
$$U' = 2 \cdot 17 - 31$$
$$U' = 3$$

[2]This sometimes can happen. In this situation the Mann–Whitney $U$ test uses more of the available information about age, by treating age as an ordinal level of measurement, than does Fisher's exact probability test in which age was measured on a dichotomous nominal scale.

the 0.05 level of significance with $n_1 = 2$ and $n_2 = 17$, the lower critical value is 6 and the higher critical value is 28. Now the calculated value, $U = 31$, exceeds the higher critical value and the analyst concludes that the difference between the ages of the workers laid off and those who were kept on is statistically significant. The choice of a one-tailed or two-tailed test is important in problems where the calculated test statistics lead to borderline judgments about statistical significance.

If either $n_1$ or $n_2$ exceeds 25, the limit of the tables of critical values, the distribution of the $U$ statistic can be approximated by a normal distribution with the following mean and standard deviation:

$$\mu_U = \frac{n_1 \cdot n_2}{2}$$

$$\sigma_U = \sqrt{\frac{n_1 \cdot n_2 \cdot (n_1 + n_2 + 1)}{12}}$$

The $Z$ statistic can be calculated and compared to reference values obtained from the standard normal distribution.

$$Z = \frac{U - \mu_U}{\sigma_U}$$

The Mann–Whitney $U$ test has two basic assumptions: (1) The first assumption is that each case is independent and has an equal probability of being drawn from a target statistical population. (2) The second assumption is that the ordinal scale for one of the variables describes a characteristic that has underlying continuity—that is, would be an interval level of measurement if only the observations were precise enough. Because of this last assumption, when cases have tied ordinal values, the analyst gives each of these cases the average of the ranks that would have been assigned had there been no tie. However, if a problem occurred in which most of the cases were tied with other cases or if many cases had exactly the same ordinal value, it would be better to apply the Kolmogorov–Smirnov two-variable test.

## 9.1.2   Kolmogorov–Smirnov Two-Variable Test

The Kolmogorov–Smirnov two-variable test is similar to the Kolmogorov–Smirnov one-variable test. The one-variable test evaluated the difference between an observed and an expected cumulative frequency distribution. The two-variable test evaluates the difference between two frequency distributions, one for each value of the nominal variable. The greatest difference between the cumulative relative frequency distributions is the basis for the significance test.

Many important problems in public works administration involve protection of public health by properly engineered and managed water and sewage systems. Here is a problem that affected the municipal water system of Greenville, a small

## Exhibit 9–3

**Water Consumption and Illness—Greenville, FL, 1983**

| Illness | Average number of 8-oz glasses of water drunk per day | | | | | Total |
|---|---|---|---|---|---|---|
| | *0* | *1* | *2* | *3* | *≥ 4* | |
| Not ill | 72 | 12 | 8 | 4 | 15 | 111 |
| Ill | 4 | 1 | 9 | 13 | 49 | 76 |
| Total | 76 | 13 | 17 | 17 | 64 | 187 |

city in northern Florida with a 1980 census population of 1,096 (65% Black, 35% White; 42% male, 58% female). In May 1983, an estimated 865 cases of epidemic gastrointestinal disease occurred. Inquiries about pharmacy sales of antidiarrheal medicine suggested that the outbreak was confined to Greenville and its immediate vicinity. Bacteria that cause gastroenteritis can be transmitted by person-to-person contact, contact with animals, handling raw chicken, or consumption of contaminated food, raw milk, and water. Two days after the initial reports of illness were received by the county public health unit, tests of the water supply showed 45–47 total coliform counts (the general standard is zero) and a boil-water notice was issued. So the public water system was immediately suspect. This was unusual because the municipal water was supplied by a chlorinated deep-well system. The question at hand was whether a more direct "dose-response" relationship could be established between water consumption and illness.[3]

The crosstabulation in Exhibit 9–3 summarizes the survey data regarding water consumption and illness among 187 randomly surveyed Greenville residents. Analysts wanted to evaluate the possible relationship between these variables. The expectation is that water consumption (an ordinal level of measurement) should not be associated with illness (a dichotomous nominal level of measurement).

Exhibit 9–4 repeats the crosstabulation and goes on to present the cumulative relative frequency distributions of water consumption for persons who were classified as ill and not ill. The last column shows the absolute differences, $d$, between the cumulative distributions for each ordinal value of water consumption. The largest value of $d$ is the calculated value of the Kolmogorov–Smirnov $D$ statistic. In this example, $D = 0.6909$.

Critical values of $D$ in the Kolmogorov–Smirnov two-variable test are provided in Appendix K. For sample sizes greater than 30 the critical value for $D$ is

---

[3]Jeffrey J. Sacks, et al., "Epidemic Campylobacteriosis Associated with a Community Water Supply," *American Journal of Public Health,* 76 n. 4 (April 1986): 424–429.

## Exhibit 9–4

**Computations for the Kolmogorov–Smirnov Two-Variable Test**

| Average number of 8-oz glasses of water drunk per day | Absolute and relative frequencies | | Cumulative relative frequencies | | Absolute difference |
|---|---|---|---|---|---|
| | *Ill* | *Not ill* | *Ill* | *Not ill* | *d* |
| 0 | 4 | 72 | 0.0526 | 0.6486 | 0.5960 |
| | 0.0526 | 0.6486 | | | |
| 1 | 1 | 12 | 0.0658 | 0.7567 | **0.6909** = *D* |
| | 0.0132 | 0.1081 | | | |
| 2 | 9 | 8 | 0.1842 | 0.8288 | 0.6446 |
| | 0.1184 | 0.0721 | | | |
| 3 | 13 | 4 | 0.3553 | 0.8648 | 0.5095 |
| | 0.1711 | 0.0360 | | | |
| ≥ 4 | 49 | 15 | 1.0000 | 0.9999 | 0.0000 |
| | 0.6447 | 0.1351 | | | |
| Total | 76 | 111 | | | |
| | 1.000 | 1.000 | | | |

computed from an equation. For a two-tailed test at the 0.05 level of significance, the equation is

$$D_{\text{critical}} = 1.36 \cdot \sqrt{\frac{n_1 + n_2}{n_1 \cdot n_2}}$$

$$D_{\text{critical}} = 1.36 \cdot \sqrt{\frac{76 + 111}{76 \cdot 111}}$$

$$D_{\text{critical}} = 0.2025$$

Since $D_{\text{calculated}} = 0.6909$ exceeds $D_{\text{critical}} = 0.2025$ the appropriate conclusion is that the relationship between consumption of city water and onset of illness is statistically significant. The more city water that respondents reported consuming, the more likely they were to have been ill. An examination of the municipal water system revealed the likely source of the problem. The well water was chlorinated, aerated over an open-top settling tank, passed through two open-top sand filters, and chlorinated again before entering an underground cistern. Birds were observed roosting on the aerator and droppings carrying potentially harmful bacteria were found on the grillwork.

The Kolmogorov–Smirnov two-variable test is useful for comparing the distributions of two groups of cases with respect to some ordinal variable. The data are distributed in a crosstabulation with two nominal categories and $k$ ordinal categories. The Kolmogorov–Smirnov two-variable test is less powerful than the Mann–Whitney test in rejecting false indications of no difference between observation and expectation but the scale of the ordinal variable need not have underlying continuity as in the Mann–Whitney test. The Kolmogorov–Smirnov test allows a lot of tied values (ties occur in every cell having a frequency count greater than one).

# *Quick Concepts: Concordant and Discordant Pairs*

Several strength-of-association statistics have been developed for problems involving ordinal data (the other statistics will be introduced in the next chapter for evaluation problems in which both variables have an ordinal level of measurement). The statistics compare the ordinal ranking of each case against that of every other case in the sample. For a sample having $n$ units of analysis, $n(n-1)/2$ comparisons are possible. Each comparison pair can be classified as "concordant," "discordant," or "tied." A pair of cases is concordant if, for each variable, the ordinal rank (the value) for the first case is less than the respective rank values taken on by the second case. For example, using Exhibit 9–5, compare a case from cell $a$ against a case from cell $d$. The case from cell $a$ has a value of 1 for the independent variable and a value of 1 for the dependent variable while the case from cell $d$ has a value of 2 for each variable. Each pair of cases between cells $a$ and $d$ is concordant. The total number of these pairs is the product of the absolute frequency in cell $a$ times the absolute frequency in cell $d$. The total number of concordant pairs in the whole crosstabulation is sum of the products of the frequency in each cell multiplied by the

*(continued)*

## *Exhibit 9–5*

**Schematic Structure of the Crosstabulation**

| Dependent variable | Independent variable | |
|---|---|---|
| | *Rank 1 (low)* | *Rank 2 (high)* |
| Rank 1 (low) | $a$ | $b$ |
| Rank 2 | $c$ | $d$ |
| Rank 3 (high) | $e$ | $f$ |

frequencies in the cells located below and to the right—that is, the number of concordant pairs in the table equals $ad + af + cf$. A pair of cases is discordant if each value describing the first case is higher than the respective values for the second case. The total number of discordant pairs in the whole crosstabulation is the sum of the products of the frequency in each cell multiplied by the frequencies in the cells located below and to the left—that is, the number of discordant pairs in the table equals $bc + be + de$. A pair of cases may be classified as tied by having either the same rank values for the independent variable, the same rank values for the dependent variable, or the same rank values for both variables. The number of pairs tied on the independent variable is the sum of the products of the frequency in each cell times the frequencies in the cells located below it in the same column—that is, $a(c + e) + ce + b(d + f) + df$. The number of pairs tied on the dependent variable is the sum of the products of the frequency in each cell times the frequencies in the cell(s) located to the right of it in each row—that is, $ab + cd + ef$. The number of pairs tied on both variables is determined by finding the number of ways pairs can be formed between cases in the same cell. For this example, the number of pairs tied on both variables equals

$$\frac{a(a-1)}{2} + \frac{b(b-1)}{2} + \frac{c(c-1)}{2} + \frac{d(d-1)}{2} + \frac{e(e-1)}{2} + \frac{f(f-1)}{2}$$

The analyst can carry out these computations using the previous example about the water supply in Greenville, Florida.

Number of concordant pairs of cases:

$72 \cdot (1 + 9 + 13 + 49) + 12 \cdot (9 + 13 + 49) + 8 \cdot (13 + 49) + 4 \cdot (49) + 15 \cdot (0) = 6{,}728$

Number of discordant pairs of cases:

$72 \cdot (0) + 12 \cdot (4) + 8 \cdot (4 + 1) + 4 \cdot (4 + 1 + 9) + 15 \cdot (4 + 1 + 9 + 13) = 549$

Number of pairs tied on dependent variable:

$72 \cdot (12 + 8 + 4 + 15) + 12 \cdot (8 + 4 + 15) + 8 \cdot (4 + 15) + 4 \cdot (15)$
$+ 4 \cdot (1 + 9 + 13 + 49) + 1 \cdot (9 + 13 + 49)$
$+ 9 \cdot (13 + 49) + 13 \cdot (49) = 4{,}898$

*(continued)*

Number of pairs tied on independent variable:

$$72 \cdot (4) + 12 \cdot (1) + 8 \cdot (9) + 4 \cdot (13) + 15 \cdot (49) = 1{,}159$$

Number of pairs tied on both variables:

$$\frac{72 \cdot (72 - 1)}{2} + \frac{4 \cdot (4 - 1)}{2} + \frac{12 \cdot (12 - 1)}{2} + \frac{1 \cdot (1 - 1)}{2}$$

$$+ \frac{8 \cdot (8 - 1)}{2} + \frac{9 \cdot (9 - 1)}{2} + \frac{4 \cdot (4 - 1)}{2}$$

$$+ \frac{13 \cdot (13 - 1)}{2} + \frac{15 \cdot (15 - 1)}{2} + \frac{49 \cdot (49 - 1)}{2} = 4{,}057$$

The computations can be checked by the following identity:

$$\begin{pmatrix} \text{Concordant} \\ \text{pairs} \end{pmatrix} + \begin{pmatrix} \text{Discordant} \\ \text{pairs} \end{pmatrix} + \begin{pmatrix} \text{Pairs on} \\ \text{dependent} \\ \text{variable} \end{pmatrix} + \begin{pmatrix} \text{Pairs on} \\ \text{independent} \\ \text{variable} \end{pmatrix} + \begin{pmatrix} \text{Pairs on} \\ \text{both} \\ \text{variables} \end{pmatrix} = \frac{n \cdot (n - 1)}{2}$$

$$6{,}728 + 549 + 4{,}898 + 1{,}159 + 4{,}057 = \frac{187 \cdot (187 - 1)}{2}$$

$$17{,}391 = 17{,}391$$

### 9.1.3  Somers' $d$ Statistic

Somers' $d$ is defined by the following equation:

$$\text{Somers' } d = \frac{\begin{bmatrix} \text{number of} & & \text{number of} \\ \text{concordant} & - & \text{discordant} \\ \text{pairs} & & \text{pairs} \end{bmatrix}}{\begin{bmatrix} \text{number of} & & \text{number of} & & \text{number of ties} \\ \text{concordant} & + & \text{discordant} & + & \text{on dependent} \\ \text{pairs} & & \text{pairs} & & \text{variable} \end{bmatrix}}$$

$$\text{Somers' } d = \frac{6{,}728 - 549}{6{,}728 + 549 + 4{,}898}$$

$$\text{Somers' } d = 0.508$$

Somers' *d* can take on a value between 0, meaning no association, and +1, strongest association. In general, the value of Somers' *d* can be interpreted using the strength of association "thermometer" in Appendix H. In this example, the results indicate that there is a strong association between water consumption and onset of illness.

## 9.2 The Nominally Measured Variable Has Two Categories, Paired Data

### 9.2.1 Wilcoxon's Matched Pairs Signed-Ranks Test

In this type of problem the dichotomous nominal variable defines two groups: the two respective components of each pair. The paired components are assumed to be exactly alike except for the dichotomy described by the nominal (independent) variable. A unit of analysis, for example, could be two people who have exactly the same attributes and characteristics except for their race. Another example could be a "before–after" situation where a person or object is observed at two points in time. The dependent variable measures the rank of each member of each pair on an ordinal scale. In the Wilcoxon test, the analyst first finds the difference between the members of each pair. Then the couples are ranked by the magnitude of the difference. The sum of these ranks, a statistic designated *W*, has a known probability distribution, the critical values of which are listed in Appendix L, "Critical Values of *W* in the Wilcoxon Test."

The question at hand is whether the differences in the distribution of ranks between the two groups are random or systematic. If they are systematic, the analyst infers that the changes are either associated with some environmental condition that affected one component of the pair differently than the other or, in the "before–after" situation, the unit of analysis fundamentally changed during the interim period.

The previous chapter contained an example in which pairs of auditors, paired African–American to white, visited real estate offices and housing rental agencies in an attempt to assess the extent of race discrimination in the housing market. Suppose that each auditor assessed the treatment they received on a scale ranging from 1 to 5, where 1 indicated "very favorable" treatment and 5, at the other extreme, indicated "very unfavorable" treatment. A hypothetical data file of 26 such visits is shown in Exhibit 9–6.

The appropriate statistic to test for differences between the matched pairs of auditors is the Wilcoxon matched pairs signed-ranks test. The computation is shown in Exhibit 9–7. The first step is to determine the difference between the values of the ordinal variable for each pair. For pair 3, the white auditor assigned a ranking of 5. The African–American auditor ranked the treatment as 1. The difference, *d*, in rankings between the two auditors was 4.

Next, the cases are sorted in ascending order on the basis of the difference between the paired auditor rankings, regardless of sign. If two or more cases have

## Exhibit 9–6

**Hypothetical Data File: Results of Rental Housing Audits for Matched Pairs of African–American and White Applicants**

| | Independent variable | |
| | Race/ethnicity of the auditor | |
| | White | African–American |
| | Dependent variable | |
| Pair number | Rating | |
|---|---|---|
| 1 | 3 | 3 |
| 2 | 3 | 3 |
| 3 | 5 | 1 |
| 4 | 1 | 3 |
| 5 | 3 | 3 |
| 6 | 1 | 5 |
| 7 | 2 | 3 |
| 8 | 1 | 4 |
| 9 | 3 | 1 |
| 10 | 1 | 2 |
| 11 | 1 | 4 |
| 12 | 4 | 5 |
| 13 | 1 | 1 |
| 14 | 1 | 5 |
| 15 | 1 | 2 |
| 16 | 5 | 4 |
| 17 | 1 | 4 |
| 18 | 3 | 2 |
| 19 | 1 | 5 |
| 20 | 1 | 1 |
| 21 | 1 | 1 |
| 22 | 4 | 1 |
| 23 | 2 | 5 |
| 24 | 1 | 4 |
| 25 | 4 | 1 |
| 26 | 2 | 1 |

## Exhibit 9–7

**Computations for Wilcoxon's Matched Pairs Signed-Ranks Test, Differences in Auditor Ratings by Race/Ethnicity**

| Pair number | Independent variable<br>*Race/ethnicity of the auditor*<br>White<br>**Dependent variable**<br>*Rating* | African–American<br><br><br> | **Difference**<br>*d* | **Absolute difference** | **Rank** | **Rank of absolute difference adjusted for ties** | **Signed rank** |
|---|---|---|---|---|---|---|---|
| 5 | 3 | 3 | 0 | 0 | — | — | — |
| 13 | 1 | 1 | 0 | 0 | — | — | — |
| 20 | 1 | 1 | 0 | 0 | — | — | — |
| 2 | 3 | 3 | 0 | 0 | — | — | — |
| 1 | 3 | 3 | 0 | 0 | — | — | — |
| 21 | 1 | 1 | 0 | 0 | — | — | — |
| 15 | 1 | 2 | −1 | 1 | 1 | 4 | −4 |
| 12 | 4 | 5 | −1 | 1 | 2 | 4 | −4 |
| 18 | 3 | 2 | 1 | 1 | 3 | 4 | +4 |
| 16 | 5 | 4 | 1 | 1 | 4 | 4 | +4 |
| 26 | 2 | 1 | 1 | 1 | 5 | 4 | +4 |
| 7 | 2 | 3 | −1 | 1 | 6 | 4 | −4 |
| 10 | 1 | 2 | −1 | 1 | 7 | 4 | −4 |
| 4 | 1 | 3 | −2 | 2 | 8 | 8.5 | −8.5 |
| 9 | 3 | 1 | 2 | 2 | 9 | 8.5 | +8.5 |
| 25 | 4 | 1 | 3 | 3 | 10 | 13 | +13 |
| 23 | 2 | 5 | −3 | 3 | 11 | 13 | −13 |
| 11 | 1 | 4 | −3 | 3 | 12 | 13 | −13 |
| 8 | 1 | 4 | −3 | 3 | 13 | 13 | −13 |
| 17 | 1 | 4 | −3 | 3 | 14 | 13 | −13 |
| 24 | 1 | 4 | −3 | 3 | 15 | 13 | −13 |
| 22 | 4 | 1 | 3 | 3 | 16 | 13 | +13 |
| 6 | 1 | 5 | −4 | 4 | 17 | 18.5 | −18.5 |
| 14 | 1 | 5 | −4 | 4 | 18 | 18.5 | −18.5 |
| 3 | 5 | 1 | 4 | 4 | 19 | 18.5 | +18.5 |
| 19 | 1 | 5 | −4 | 4 | 20 | 18.5 | −18.5 |
| Absolute sum | | | | | | | $W = 80$ |

identical values of the ordinal variable, the rank given to each case is the mean of the ranks that would have been assigned if there had been no ties. (Cases 4 and 9 each have a *d* value of 2. They are the eighth and ninth cases listed when the pairs are sorted by *d* value. The adjusted rank for each case is 8.5.) For some case pairs the African–American auditor assigned a higher numeric ("worse") rating than did the white auditor and the resulting *d* value was a negative number (for example, cases 4, 6, 8, and 10). This situation is called a "negative difference" and the negative sign is attached to the adjusted rank for those cases. Similarly, for other case pairs the African–American auditor assigned a lower numeric ("better") rating than did the white auditor (for example, cases 3, 9, and 16). This situation is called a "positive difference" and, again, the positive sign is attached to the adjusted rank.

The calculated value of the Wilcoxon test statistic *W* is the absolute sum of the signed ranks. In this example, *W* is 80.

Appendix L lists the critical values of *W*. The sample size, *n*, is the number of pairs; $n_1$ is the number of signed ranks; $n_2$ is the number of unsigned ranks (that is the number of ties or pairs having zero differences). In this example, $n_1 = 20$ (six cases have a zero difference). Referring to the table, the critical value of *W* at the 0.05 level of significance for a two-tailed test is 48. The calculated value of *W* must be less than or equal to the critical value in order to demonstrate statistical significance. The calculated value of 80 is not less than the critical value of 48. The difference in ranks between the paired observations is not statistically significant.

For samples that exceed the range of the table the following formula can be used to compute a *Z* statistic:[4]

$$Z = \frac{0.5 \cdot n_1(n + 1)}{\sqrt{\dfrac{n_1 n_2 (n + 1)}{12}}}$$

The basic assumptions of the Wilcoxon test are (1) random selection of the cases from a target population, (2) paired units of analysis, and (3) the assumption that the ordinal scale describes a characteristic that has underlying continuity (would be an interval level of measurement if only the observations were precise enough).

---

[4]L. R. Verdooren, "Extended Tables of Critical Values for Wilcoxon's Test Statistic," *Biometrika,* 50. 1 and 2, 1963.

## 9.3    *The Nominally Measured Variable Has More Than Two Categories*

### 9.3.1    Kruskal–Wallis Test

The Kruskal–Wallis test is useful for deciding whether more than two groups, identified by a variable having a nominal level of measurement, are from the same statistical population or are from different statistical populations. The question is whether the observed differences among the groups indicate genuine population differences or whether they represent chance variations that might be expected in any set of random observations of the same population.

The variable describing the key characteristic or attribute for the units of analysis in each group should have an ordinal (or interval) level of measurement with an underlying continuous scale.

A consulting organization studying the distribution of disease and acute health problems in California classified the occurrence of heart failure, stroke, and lung cancer by the patient's zip code. This allowed a detailed geographic breakdown of the incidence of these health problems. Exhibit 9–8 lists the rate of hospital admission for heart failure, stroke, and lung cancer in the communities that

## *Exhibit 9–8*

**Hospital Admissions per 1,000 People in the San Francisco Bay Area (geographic zones determined by zip code)**

| | | Reason for hospitalization | | |
|---|---|---|---|---|
| **Community** | **Location** | *Heart failure* | *Stroke* | *Lung cancer* |
| Pittsburg | EB | 3.94 | 1.98 | 0.82 |
| San Pablo | EB | 3.09 | 1.98 | 0.50 |
| San Jose East | SB | 3.11 | 1.85 | 0.50 |
| San Jose Center | SB | 2.99 | 1.91 | 0.45 |
| San Francisco—Ingleside | SF | 2.60 | 2.00 | 0.62 |
| San Francisco—Potrero, Mission, Hunters Point | SF | 2.58 | 1.89 | 0.72 |
| San Francisco—Marina Pacific Heights | SF | 2.29 | 1.90 | 0.88 |
| Antioch | EB | 2.64 | 1.92 | 0.47 |
| Oakland | EB | 2.54 | 1.88 | 0.60 |
| Petaluma | NB | 2.35 | 1.72 | 0.67 |
| Pinole | EB | 2.12 | 1.98 | 0.64 |

*(continued)*

## *Exhibit 9–8*

**Hospital Admissions per 1,000 People in the San Francisco Bay Area (geographic zones determined by zip code)** *(continued)*

| Community | Location | Reason for hospitalization | | |
|---|---|---|---|---|
| | | *Heart failure* | *Stroke* | *Lung cancer* |
| San Francisco—Civic Center Tenderloin | SF | 2.28 | 1.55 | 0.81 |
| Daly City | SB | 2.27 | 1.67 | 0.61 |
| San Francisco—Russian Hill, Chinatown, North Beach | SF | 1.93 | 2.04 | 0.44 |
| Alameda | EB | 2.01 | 1.70 | 0.69 |
| Hayward | EB | 2.21 | 1.73 | 0.41 |
| Fremont | EB | 2.36 | 1.25 | 0.66 |
| San Francisco—Haight, Noe Valley, Diamond Heights | SF | 1.85 | 1.74 | 0.65 |
| Novato | NB | 2.04 | 1.72 | 0.39 |
| Vallejo | NB | 2.08 | 1.54 | 0.50 |
| San Bruno | SB | 1.95 | 1.59 | 0.48 |
| Berkeley | EB | 1.91 | 1.54 | 0.53 |
| Livermore | EB | 2.08 | 1.37 | 0.52 |
| Concord | EB | 1.95 | 1.441 | 0.51 |
| Santa Rosa West | NB | 1.93 | 1.33 | 0.58 |
| San Francisco—Richmond District | SF | 1.74 | 1.67 | 0.36 |
| Napa | NB | 1.82 | 1.25 | 0.57 |
| San Leandro | EB | 1.73 | 1.47 | 0.34 |
| San Francisco—Sunset | SF | 1.55 | 1.47 | 0.43 |
| San Jose Northwest | SB | 1.79 | 1.29 | 0.31 |
| San Rafael | NB | 1.32 | 1.52 | 0.41 |
| Redwood City | SB | 1.46 | 1.22 | 0.54 |
| Fairfield | NB | 1.52 | 1.31 | 0.35 |
| Santa Rosa East | NB | 1.60 | 0.99 | 0.55 |
| San Mateo | SB | 1.31 | 1.39 | 0.42 |
| San Jose Southwest | SB | 1.49 | 1.29 | 0.25 |
| Mountain View | SB | 1.24 | 1.07 | 0.28 |
| Walnut Creek | EB | 0.98 | 0.95 | 0.35 |
| Palo Alto | SB | 1.07 | 0.95 | 0.26 |

*Location:*  SF = San Francisco; EB = East Bay; NB = North Bay; SB = South Bay

make up the San Francisco Bay area. Each community in the region is identified as either in the City of San Francisco, or the East Bay, North Bay, or South Bay area. Is the principal reason for hospital admission for heart failure the same throughout the San Francisco Bay area?

The first step is to rank the communities in descending order on the basis of the rate of hospital admission for heart failure. The ranks of ties are averaged. Then a table, like Exhibit 9–9, is formed listing the communities by region, the nominal variable. The sum of the ranks of the cases in each group is found and then squared.

Next, a value for the Kruskal–Wallis $K$ statistic is computed by dividing the squared sum-of-ranks by the number of cases respectively in each group and summing over all groups.

$$K = \sum \left[ \frac{(\text{Sum of ranks})_j^2}{n_j} \right]$$

where

$$K = \text{Kruskal–Wallis } K \text{ statistic}$$

$$(\text{Sum of ranks})_j^2 = \text{square of the sum of the ranks for the } j\text{th group}$$

$$n_j = \text{number of cases in the } j\text{th group}$$

$$K = \frac{20,306.25}{8} + \frac{41,209}{13} + \frac{59,780.25}{10} + \frac{36,100}{8}$$

$$K = 16,198.72$$

The final step is to compute a value for a chi-square statistic using the following formula:

$$\chi^2_{KW} = \frac{12 \cdot K}{n \cdot (n + 1)} - 3 \cdot (n + 1)$$

with

$$\text{degrees of freedom, } df = (\text{number of columns} - 1)$$

$$\chi^2_{KW} = \text{chi-square statistic for the Kruskal–Wallis test}$$

$$K = \text{Kruskal–Wallis } K \text{ statistic}$$

$$n = \text{total number of cases in the sample}$$

$$\chi^2_{KW} = \frac{12 \cdot (16,198.72)}{39 \cdot (39 + 1)} - 3 \cdot (39 + 1)$$

$$\chi^2_{KW} = 4.61$$

$$df = (4 - 1) = 3$$

## Exhibit 9–9

**Hospital Admissions Due to Heart Failure by Region in the San Francisco Bay Area**

| San Francisco | | | East Bay | | | South Bay | | | North Bay | | |
|---|---|---|---|---|---|---|---|---|---|---|---|
| Location | Admissions for heart failure per 1,000 pop. | Rank | Location | Admissions for heart failure per 1,000 pop. | Rank | Location | Admissions for heart failure per 1,000 pop. | Rank | Location | Admissions for heart failure per 1,000 pop. | Rank |
| S.F.- I | 2.60 | 6 | Pittsburg | 3.94 | 1 | San Jose East | 3.11 | 2 | Petaluma | 2.35 | 10 |
| S.F.- P | 2.58 | 7 | San Pablo | 3.09 | 3 | San Jose Ctr | 2.99 | 4 | Novato | 2.04 | 18 |
| S.F.- M | 2.29 | 11 | Antioch | 2.64 | 5 | Daly City | 2.27 | 13 | Vallejo | 2.08 | 16.5 |
| S.F.- C | 2.28 | 12 | Oakland | 2.54 | 8 | San Bruno | 1.95 | 20.5 | Santa Rosa W | 1.93 | 22.5 |
| S.F.- Ru | 1.93 | 22.5 | Pinole | 2.12 | 15 | San Jose NW | 1.79 | 27 | Napa | 1.82 | 26 |
| S.F.- H | 1.85 | 25 | Alameda | 2.01 | 19 | Redwood City | 1.46 | 34 | San Rafael | 1.32 | 35 |
| S.F.- Ri | 1.74 | 28 | Hayward | 2.21 | 14 | San Mateo | 1.31 | 36 | Fairfield | 1.52 | 32 |
| S.F.- S | 1.55 | 31 | Fremont | 2.36 | 9 | San Jose SW | 1.49 | 33 | Santa Rosa E | 1.60 | 30 |
| | | | Berkeley | 1.91 | 24 | Mountain View | 1.24 | 37 | | | |
| | | | Livermore | 2.08 | 16.5 | Palo Alto | 1.07 | 38 | | | |
| | | | Concord | 1.95 | 20.5 | | | | | | |
| | | | San Leandro | 1.73 | 29 | | | | | | |
| | | | Walnut Creek | 0.98 | 39 | | | | | | |
| $n_j$ | | 8 | | | 13 | | | 10 | | | 8 |
| Sum of ranks | | 142.5 | | | 203 | | | 244.5 | | | 190 |
| (Sum of ranks)$^2$ | | 20,306.25 | | | 41,209 | | | 59,780.25 | | | 36,100 |
| (Sum of ranks)$^2/n_j$ | | 2,538.28 | | | 3,169.92 | | | 5,978.02 | | | 4,512.5 |

This calculated value can be compared against a critical value obtained from Appendix D. For 3 degrees of freedom at the 0.05 level of significance, $\chi^2_{KW\ critical} = 7.82$. The calculated value does not exceed the critical value. Therefore the observed differences between different regions in the San Francisco Bay area in hospital admissions because of heart failure are not statistically significant.

## Homework Exercises

**9-1** Do states in which the governor has line-item budget veto power tend to spend less per capita than states in which the governor does not have this power? Examine the data in Exhibit HW9–1A. Use per capita spending rank and apply the Mann–Whitney test.

## Exhibit HW9–1A

**State Spending Per Capita and Gubernatorial Line Item Veto Power**

| State | Spending per capita | Rank | Line item veto |
|---|---|---|---|
| Alabama | $6,910 | 30 | 1 |
| Alaska | $15,227 | 1 | 1 |
| Arizona | $6,284 | 45 | 1 |
| Arkansas | $5,936 | 49 | 1 |
| California | $9,057 | 5 | 1 |
| Colorado | $7,473 | 22 | 1 |
| Connecticut | $8,241 | 11 | 1 |
| Delaware | $8,339 | 8 | 1 |
| Florida | $6,646 | 37 | 1 |
| Georgia | $6,552 | 39 | 1 |
| Hawaii | $7,820 | 15 | 1 |
| Idaho | $6,040 | 47 | 1 |
| Illinois | $7,506 | 21 | 1 |
| Indiana | $6,317 | 44 | 0 |
| Iowa | $6,971 | 27 | 1 |
| Kansas | $6,715 | 34 | 1 |
| Kentucky | $6,487 | 40 | 1 |
| Louisiana | $6,898 | 32 | 1 |

*(continued)*

# Exhibit HW9–1A

**State Spending Per Capita and Gubernatorial Line Item Veto Power** *(continued)*

| State | Spending per capita | Rank | Line item veto |
|---|---|---|---|
| Maine | $7,625 | 19 | 1 |
| Maryland | $6,930 | 29 | 0 |
| Massachusetts | $9,057 | 4 | 1 |
| Michigan | $7,676 | 18 | 1 |
| Minnesota | $8,268 | 9 | 1 |
| Mississippi | $6,705 | 35 | 1 |
| Missouri | $6,175 | 46 | 1 |
| Montana | $6,687 | 36 | 1 |
| Nebraska | $8,042 | 12 | 1 |
| Nevada | $6,936 | 28 | 0 |
| New Hampshire | $6,425 | 42 | 0 |
| New Jersey | $8,356 | 7 | 1 |
| New Mexico | $7,393 | 23 | 1 |
| New York | $11,344 | 2 | 1 |
| North Carolina | $6,621 | 38 | 0 |
| North Dakota | $7,054 | 26 | 1 |
| Ohio | $7,825 | 14 | 1 |
| Oklahoma | $5,913 | 50 | 1 |
| Oregon | $7,857 | 13 | 1 |
| Pennsylvania | $7,618 | 20 | 1 |
| Rhode Island | $8,250 | 10 | 0 |
| South Carolina | $7,254 | 24 | 1 |
| South Dakota | $5,982 | 48 | 1 |
| Tennessee | $7,086 | 25 | 1 |
| Texas | $6,447 | 41 | 1 |
| Utah | $6,901 | 31 | 1 |
| Vermont | $7,748 | 16 | 0 |
| Virginia | $6,389 | 43 | 1 |
| Washington | $8,749 | 6 | 1 |
| West Virginia | $6,724 | 33 | 1 |
| Wisconsin | $7,705 | 17 | 1 |
| Wyoming | $10,040 | 3 | 1 |
| U.S. average | $7,712 | — | — |

$$\sum R_{\text{YES } n=43} = 1,068$$

$$\sum R_{\text{NO } n=7} = 207$$

$$U = 179$$

$$U' = 122$$

$$\mu_U = 150.5$$

$$\sigma_U = 35.77$$

$$Z_{\text{calculated}} = 0.80$$

Difference in per capita spending is not statistically significant.

**9-2** Refer to the hospital admission data for the San Francisco Bay Area, shown in Exhibit 9–8.

**a.** Are hospital admissions for stroke significantly different within the region?

**b.** Are hospital admissions for lung cancer significantly different within the region?

**a.** See Exhibit HW9–2A.

$$K = \sum \frac{R_k^2}{n_k} = \frac{R_1^2}{n_1} + \frac{R_2^2}{n_2} + \cdots + \frac{R_k^2}{n_k} = 16,741.14$$

$$\chi_{\text{KW}}^2 = \frac{12K}{n \cdot (n + 1)} - 3 \cdot (n + 1)$$

$$\chi_{\text{KW}}^2 = 8.78$$

Degrees of freedom $= (k - 1) = 3$

$$\chi_{\text{KW critical}}^2 = 7.82 \text{ at the } 0.05 \text{ level of significance}$$

Therefore, the observed disparity between different Bay Area regions with respect to hospital admissions because of stroke is statistically significant.

## Exhibit HW9–2A

**Hospital Admissions Due to Stroke: San Francisco Bay Area Region**

| San Francisco | | | East Bay | | | South Bay | | | North Bay | | |
|---|---|---|---|---|---|---|---|---|---|---|---|
| Location | Admissions for stroke per 1,000 pop. | Rank | Location | Admissions for stroke per 1,000 pop. | Rank | Location | Admissions for stroke per 1,000 pop. | Rank | Location | Admissions for stroke per 1,000 pop. | Rank |
| S.F.- I | 2.00 | 2 | Pittsburg | 1.98 | 4 | San Jose East | 1.85 | 11 | Petaluma | 1.72 | 14.5 |
| S.F.- P | 1.89 | 9 | San Pablo | 1.98 | 4 | San Jose Ctr | 1.91 | 7 | Novato | 1.72 | 14.5 |
| S.F.- M | 1.90 | 8 | Antioch | 1.92 | 6 | Daly City | 1.67 | 17.5 | Vallejo | 1.54 | 21.5 |
| S.F.- C | 1.55 | 20 | Oakland | 1.88 | 10 | San Bruno | 1.59 | 19 | Santa Rosa W | 1.33 | 29 |
| S.F.- Ru | 2.04 | 1 | Pinole | 1.98 | 4 | San Jose NW | 1.29 | 31.5 | Napa | 1.25 | 33.5 |
| S.F.- H | 1.74 | 12 | Alameda | 1.70 | 16 | Redwood City | 1.22 | 35 | San Rafael | 1.52 | 23 |
| S.F.- Ri | 1.67 | 17.5 | Hayward | 1.73 | 13 | San Mateo | 1.39 | 27 | Fairfield | 1.31 | 30 |
| S.F.- S | 1.47 | 24.5 | Fremont | 1.25 | 33.5 | San Jose SW | 1.29 | 31.5 | Santa Rosa E | 0.99 | 37 |
| | | | Berkeley | 1.54 | 21.5 | Mountain View | 1.07 | 36 | | | |
| | | | Livermore | 1.37 | 28 | Palo Alto | 0.95 | 38.5 | | | |
| | | | Concord | 1.41 | 26 | | | | | | |
| | | | San Leandro | 1.47 | 24.5 | | | | | | |
| | | | Walnut Creek | 0.95 | 38.5 | | | | | | |
| $n$ | 8 | | | 13 | | | 10 | | | 8 | |
| Sum of ranks | 94 | | | 229 | | | 254 | | | 203 | |
| (Sum of ranks)$^2$/$n$ | 1,104.5 | | | 4,033.92 | | | 6,451.6 | | | 5,151.12 | |

## Exhibit HW9–2B

**Hospital Admissions Due to Lung Cancer: San Francisco Bay Area Region**

| San Francisco | | | East Bay | | | South Bay | | | North Bay | | |
|---|---|---|---|---|---|---|---|---|---|---|---|
| Location | Admissions for lung cancer per 1,000 pop. | Rank | Location | Admissions for lung cancer per 1,000 pop. | Rank | Location | Admissions for lung cancer per 1,000 pop. | Rank | Location | Admissions for lung cancer per 1,000 pop. | Rank |
| S.F.- I | 0.62 | 10 | Pittsburg | 0.82 | 2 | San Jose East | 0.50 | 21 | Petaluma | 0.67 | 6 |
| S.F.- P | 0.72 | 4 | San Pablo | 0.50 | 21 | San Jose Ctr | 0.45 | 25 | Novato | 0.39 | 31 |
| S.F.- M | 0.88 | 1 | Antioch | 0.47 | 24 | Daly City | 0.61 | 11 | Vallejo | 0.50 | 21 |
| S.F.- C | 0.81 | 3 | Oakland | 0.60 | 12 | San Bruno | 0.48 | 23 | Santa Rosa W | 0.58 | 13 |
| S.F.- Ru | 0.44 | 26 | Pinole | 0.64 | 9 | San Jose NW | 0.31 | 36 | Napa | 0.57 | 14 |
| S.F.- H | 0.65 | 8 | Alameda | 0.69 | 5 | Redwood City | 0.54 | 16 | San Rafael | 0.41 | 29.5 |
| S.F.- Ri | 0.36 | 32 | Hayward | 0.41 | 29.5 | San Mateo | 0.42 | 28 | Fairfield | 0.35 | 33.5 |
| S.F.- S | 0.43 | 27 | Fremont | 0.66 | 7 | San Jose SW | 0.25 | 39 | Santa Rosa E | 0.55 | 15 |
| | | | Berkeley | 0.53 | 17 | Mountain View | 0.28 | 37 | | | |
| | | | Livermore | 0.52 | 18 | Palo Alto | 0.26 | 38 | | | |
| | | | Concord | 0.51 | 19 | | | | | | |
| | | | San Leandro | 0.34 | 35 | | | | | | |
| | | | Walnut Creek | 0.35 | 33.5 | | | | | | |
| $n$ | 8 | | | 13 | | | 10 | | | 8 | |
| Sum of ranks | 111 | | | 232 | | | 274 | | | 163 | |
| (Sum of ranks)$^2$/$n$ | 1,540.12 | | | 4,140.31 | | | 7,507.6 | | | 3,321.12 | |

**b.** See Exhibit HW9–2B.

$$K = 16,509.15$$

$$\chi^2_{KW\ calculated} = 6.99$$

$$\chi^2_{KW\ critical} = 7.82 \text{ at the } 0.05 \text{ level of significance}$$

Therefore, the observed differences between different Bay Area regions with respect to hospital admissions because of lung cancer are not statistically significant.

**9-3** Consider Exhibit HW9–3A describing layoffs at a manufacturing plant. Do these data support a prima facie charge of age discrimination? Treat the variable *age* as having an ordinal level of measurement.

## Exhibit HW9–3A

**Layoff Status at a Manufacturing Company**

| Age | Layoff status<br>*0 = not laid off*<br>*1 = laid off* |
| --- | --- |
| 51 | 0 |
| 58 | 0 |
| 48 | 1 |
| 53 | 1 |
| 45 | 1 |
| 43 | 0 |
| 49 | 0 |
| 59 | 1 |
| 56 | 1 |
| 56 | 0 |
| 54 | 1 |
| 55 | 0 |
| 54 | 0 |
| 48 | 0 |
| 39 | 0 |
| 47 | 1 |
| 59 | 0 |
| 58 | 1 |
| 55 | 1 |
| 57 | 1 |
| 57 | 0 |
| 53 | 0 |

$$U = n_1 \cdot n_2 + \frac{n_1 \cdot (n_1 + 1)}{2} - R_1$$

$$U = 10 \cdot 12 + \frac{10(10 + 1)}{2} - 101$$

$$U = 74$$

The critical values of $U$ at the 0.05 level of significance for $n_1 = 10$ and $n_2 = 12$ are 29 and 91. The calculated value of $U$ must fall outside of this range in order to

## Exhibit HW9–3B

**Computations for Mann–Whitney *U* Test**

| Layoff status | Age | Age rank | Age rank adjusted for ties | Ranks: laid off | Ranks: not laid off |
|---|---|---|---|---|---|
| 1 | 59 | 1 | 1.5 | 1.5 | |
| 0 | 59 | 2 | 1.5 | | 1.5 |
| 0 | 58 | 3 | 3.5 | | 3.5 |
| 0 | 58 | 4 | 3.5 | | 3.5 |
| 1 | 57 | 5 | 5.5 | 5.5 | |
| 1 | 57 | 6 | 5.5 | 5.5 | |
| 1 | 56 | 7 | 7.5 | 7.5 | |
| 1 | 56 | 8 | 7.5 | 7.5 | |
| 1 | 55 | 9 | 9.5 | 9.5 | |
| 1 | 55 | 10 | 9.5 | 9.5 | |
| 0 | 54 | 11 | 11.5 | | 11.5 |
| 0 | 54 | 12 | 11.5 | | 11.5 |
| 1 | 53 | 13 | 13.5 | 13.5 | |
| 0 | 53 | 14 | 13.5 | | 13.5 |
| 0 | 51 | 15 | 15 | | 15 |
| 0 | 49 | 16 | 16 | | 16 |
| 0 | 48 | 17 | 17.5 | | 17.5 |
| 0 | 48 | 18 | 17.5 | | 17.5 |
| 0 | 47 | 19 | 19 | | 19 |
| 1 | 45 | 20 | 20 | 20 | |
| 1 | 43 | 21 | 21 | 21 | |
| 0 | 39 | 22 | 22 | | 22 |
| | | | | $R_1 = 101$ | $R_2 = 152$ |
| | | | | $n_1 = 10$ | $n_2 = 12$ |

be judged statistically significant. Therefore, the observations do not support a prima facie charge of age discrimination.

9-4    A survey of human services provided by cities identified nine types of services that could be provided to aid the elderly: nutrition centers, "meals on wheels," homemaker services, day care/respite care, special transportation, recreation programs, job placement, volunteer opportunities, and counseling.[1] The analysts classified the provision of one to three programs from this list as a low level of service, four to six programs as medium, and seven to nine programs as high. The crosstabulation in Exhibit HW9–4A summarizes level of service to the elderly by the city's form of government. Is the relationship statistically significant?

## Exhibit HW9–4A

**Level of Direct Service Delivery to the Elderly by Form of Government for Cities Over 10,000 Population**

|  | Form of government | | |
|---|---|---|---|
| **Level of service** | *Mayor-council* | *Council-manager* | **Total** |
| None | 104 | 211 | 315 |
| Low | 82 | 246 | 328 |
| Medium | 15 | 50 | 65 |
| High | 6 | 8 | 14 |
| Total | 207 | 515 | 722 |

$$D_{\text{critical}} = 1.36 \sqrt{\frac{n_1 + n_2}{n_1 \cdot n_2}}$$

$D_{\text{critical}} = 0.11$

$D_{\text{observed}} = 0.092$ not statistically significant at the 0.05 level of significance

---

[1]Robert Agranoff and Alex N. Pattakos, "Local Government Human Services," *Baseline Data Report,* v. 17 n. 4, 1985.

## Exhibit HW9–4B

**Absolute, Relative, and Cumulative Relative Frequencies: Level of Direct Service Delivery to the Elderly by Form of Government for Cities Over 10,000 Population**

| Level of service | Form of government | | |
| --- | --- | --- | --- |
| | *Mayor-council* | *Council-manager* | *d* |
| None | 104 | 211 | |
| | 0.502 | 0.410 | |
| | 0.502 | 0.410 | 0.092 |
| Low | 82 | 246 | |
| | 0.396 | 0.478 | |
| | 0.898 | 0.888 | 0.010 |
| Medium | 15 | 50 | |
| | 0.072 | 0.097 | |
| | 0.970 | 0.985 | 0.015 |
| High | 6 | 8 | |
| | 0.029 | 0.015 | |
| | 0.999 | 1.000 | 0.000 |
| Total | 207 | 515 | |

**9-5** The crosstabulation in Exhibit HW9–5A summarizes the responses received to an inquiry directed to business firms about their preference for being located near a university.[2] Assess the significance of the suggested relationship between firm type and location preference using the Kruskal–Wallis text.

## Exhibit HW9–5A

**Preference for Proximity to Universities by Firm Type**

| Prefer location near university | Information processing firms | Heavy manufacturing firms | Light manufacturing firms | Primary industry firms |
| --- | --- | --- | --- | --- |
| Yes | 10 | 5 | 2 | 0 |
| Sometimes | 6 | 9 | 6 | 6 |
| No | 2 | 6 | 3 | 7 |

[2]William L. Waugh, Jr. and Deborah M. Waugh, "Baiting the Hook: Targeting Economic Development Monies More Effectively," *Public Administration Quarterly,* Summer 1988, pp. 216-234.

## *Exhibit HW9–5B*

**Calculations for the *K* Statistic**

| Prefer location near university | Row count | Ranks | Mean rank | Cell count × Mean rank | | | |
|---|---|---|---|---|---|---|---|
| | | | | *Information processing* | *Heavy manufacturing* | *Light manufacturing* | *Primary industry* |
| Yes | 17 | 1 through 17 | 9 | 90 | 45 | 18 | 0 |
| Sometimes | 27 | 18 through 44 | 31 | 186 | 279 | 186 | 186 |
| No | 18 | 45 through 62 | 53.5 | 107 | 321 | 160.5 | 374.5 |
| $R$ | | | | 383 | 645 | 364.5 | 560.5 |
| $R^2/n$ | | | | 8,149.39 | 20,801.25 | 12,078.20 | 24,166.17 |

$$K = \sum R^2/n = 65,195$$

$$\chi^2_{KW \text{ calculated}} = 11.29$$

$$\chi^2_{KW \text{ critical 3df}} = 7.82$$

# A Tale of Two Ranks: Two-Variable Evaluation—Ordinal–Ordinal and Ordinal–Interval Measures

| | |
|---|---|
| Kind of problem | *Evaluation* |
| Number of variables | *Two* |
| Level of measurement | *Variable 1, ordinal* |
| | *Variable 2, ordinal or interval* |

Τ his chapter continues the study of evaluation problems that involve two variables—situations in which the dependent variable has an ordinal level of measurement and the independent variable can have either an ordinal or an interval level of measurement. The null hypothesis is that there is no relationship between the two variables.

As shown in Exhibit 10–1, the principal method for both the ordinal–ordinal problem and the ordinal–interval problem is calculation of the Spearman's rank correlation coefficient statistic for strength-of-association. This statistic can also be used in a test for statistical significance. For the ordinal–ordinal problem, strength-of-association is also indicated by the Goodman and Kruskal's gamma, Kendall's tau, and Somers' *d* statistics.

## *10.1 Spearman's Rank Correlation Coefficient*

Spearman's rank correlation coefficient, rho ($\rho$), is a strength-of-association statistic for a problem in which two variables are observed for each unit of analysis. Both variables have an ordinal level of measurement.[1]

---

[1]A variable having an interval level of measurement can also be regarded as having an ordinal level of measurement.

## *Exhibit 10–1*

**Two-Variable Evaluation: Ordinal–Ordinal and Ordinal–Interval Measures**

| Dependent variable | | Independent variable | |
|---|---|---|---|
| | | *Ordinal level of measurement* | *Interval level of measurement* |
| Ordinal level of measurement | Strength of association | Spearman's rank correlation coefficient, $\rho$ | |
| | | Goodman and Kruskal's gamma, $\gamma$ | Spearman's rank correlation coefficient, $\rho$ |
| | | Somers' $d$ | |
| | | Kendall's tau, $\tau$ | |
| | Statistical significance | Spearman's rank correlation coefficient, $\rho$ | |
| | | Goodman and Kruskal's gamma, $\gamma$ | |
| | | Kendall's tau, $\tau$ | |

There are many problems with illicit injection drug use in a community including crime, disease transmission, and unsafe disposal of drug paraphernalia. Many cities have programs for the distribution and safe return of syringes. Sydney, Australia, Vancouver, Canada, and more than two dozen European cities have opened facilities where drug users can safely inject previously obtained illegal drugs and receive medical care and social services. One indicator of whether such facilities increase public order is the amount of injection-related litter such as syringe wrappers, syringe caps, sterile water containers, and "cookers," discarded in the immediate neighborhood. For the first 12 weeks after opening a safer injecting facility, Vancouver analysts used mean daily visits and the amount of injection-related material collected in the surrounding area as ordinal indicators of measures of use and public drug use.[2]

The analysts determined the degree of association between the use of the facility and injection-related litter by computing Spearman's rank correlation coefficient. As shown in Exhibit 10–2, the statistic is calculated by first finding the numeric ordinal rank that each unit of analysis (in this example, week) has for each variable. Then for each city the difference between the respective ranks is found and squared—and the squared differences are totaled for the sample. This result is divided by the quantity $n(n^2 - 1)/6$ (which is the "average" or "expected" value of the sum of the squared differences for two sets of completely unrelated

[2]Evan Wood, and others, "Changes in public order after the opening of a medically supervised safer injecting facility for illicit injection drug users," *Canadian Medical Association Journal*, 7 28 September 2004: 731–734.

## *Exhibit 10–2*

**Computations for Spearman's Rank Correlation Coefficient: Vancouver Injection Drug User Facility (data estimated from published report)**

| | | | Rankings | | Difference | |
|---|---|---|---|---|---|---|
| **Week** | **Mean daily use of facility** | **IDU litter (number of items)** | *Mean daily use of facility* | *IDU litter (number of items)* | $\|d\|$ | $d^2$ |
| 1 | 160 | 380 | 1 | 9 | 8 | 64 |
| 2 | 220 | 460 | 2 | 12 | 10 | 100 |
| 3 | 325 | 410 | 3 | 11 | 8 | 64 |
| 4 | 385 | 390 | 4 | 10 | 6 | 36 |
| 5 | 405 | 290 | 5 | 7 | 2 | 4 |
| 6 | 470 | 270 | 8 | 5 | 3 | 9 |
| 7 | 495 | 260 | 11 | 4 | 7 | 49 |
| 8 | 480 | 300 | 9 | 8 | 1 | 1 |
| 9 | 520 | 280 | 12 | 6 | 6 | 36 |
| 10 | 490 | 230 | 10 | 3 | 7 | 49 |
| 11 | 425 | 210 | 6 | 2 | 4 | 16 |
| 12 | 450 | 175 | 7 | 1 | 6 | 36 |
| Total | | | | | | 464 |

values) and subtracted from 1 to produce the calculated value of the Spearman's rho ($\rho$) statistic.

$$\rho = 1 - \frac{6\sum d^2}{n(n^2 - 1)}$$

where

$\sum d^2$ = the sum of the squared difference between the repective rankings

$n$ = the number of cases in the sample

$$\rho = 1 - \frac{6 \cdot 464}{12(12^2 - 1)}$$

$$\rho = -0.62$$

The range of values for Spearman's rho statistic is between $+1$ and $-1$. If the relative rankings for each unit of analysis are the same for both variables, the sum of $d^2$ will be zero and $\rho$ will equal $+1$. For no association, $\rho$ will equal 0, and for perfect inverse association $\rho$ will equal $-1$.

The magnitude of the calculated value for Spearman's $\rho$, $\rho = -0.62$, indicates a strong association between use of the facility and less injection-related litter in the community.

This example has no ties in the rankings of either variable. If there are tied ranks, the computational formula (used in most statistical calculators and programs) is

$$\rho = \frac{\left[\dfrac{n(n^2-1)}{12} - \sum T_X\right] + \left[\dfrac{n(n^2-1)}{12} - \sum T_Y\right] - \sum d^2}{2\sqrt{\left[\dfrac{n(n^2-1)}{12} - \sum T_X\right] \cdot \left[\dfrac{n(n^2-1)}{12} - \sum T_Y\right]}}$$

where

$$\sum T_X = 0.5x_2 + 2x_3 + 5x_4 + 10x_5 + 17.5x_6 + 28x_7 + \cdots + \left[\frac{n(n^2-1)}{12}\right]x_n$$

$$\sum T_Y = 0.5y_2 + 2y_3 + 5y_4 + 10y_5 + 17.5y_6 + 28y_7 + \cdots + \left[\frac{n(n^2-1)}{12}\right]y_n$$

and

$x_2$ = number of ties involving 2 cases for $x$ variable rankings

$x_3$ = number of ties involving 3 cases for $x$ variable rankings

$x_4$ = number of ties involving 4 cases for $x$ variable rankings

$\cdots$

$y_2$ = number of ties involving 2 cases for $y$ variable rankings

$y_3$ = number of ties involving 3 cases for $y$ variable rankings

$y_4$ = number of ties involving 4 cases for $y$ variable rankings

When $n$ is less than 100, the statistical significance of $\rho$ can be determined by comparing the computed value for $\rho$ against the appropriate critical value from Appendix M, "Critical Values of the Spearman Rank Correlation Coefficient." With a sample size of 12, the critical value of $\rho$ for a two-tailed test at the 0.05 level of significance is 0.587. Since the calculated value of $\rho$ in this example ($\rho = 0.62$) exceeds the critical value, the analyst concludes that there is a statistically significant correlation between the facility use and reduced injection-related litter during the opening 12-week period.

If *n* is greater than 100, a value for the *t* statistic can be computed using the following formula. The calculated value can be checked against a critical *t* value for (*n* − 2) degrees of freedom obtained from the table of critical values of the *t* statistic, Appendix F.

$$t = \rho \sqrt{\frac{n - 2}{1 - \rho^2}}$$

## 10.2  *Goodman and Kruskal's Gamma Statistic*

If two variables are observed and the cases arranged in ascending order of the values taken on by the independent variable, the extent to which the corresponding values of the dependent variable also appear to be arrayed in increasing order indicates the strength-of-association between the variables. Goodman and Kruskal's gamma ($\gamma$) statistic, like the Somers' *d* statistic introduced in the preceding chapter, compares the number of concordant pairs in the crosstabulation to the number of discordant pairs. The statistic is calculated by dividing the difference between the number of concordant and discordant pairs by the sum of the concordant and discordant pairs. It represents the extent to which pairs of cases (having no tied values) tend to have a uniform order. If there is no consistency between the respective values of the two variables, the number of concordant pairs should be about the same as the number of discordant pairs, and the statistic will have a value close to zero. If the ordinal ranking of the dependent variable tends to increase as the value of the independent variable increases, the statistic will have a positive value approaching 1.0. On the other hand, if the ordinal ranking of the dependent variable tends to be lower as cases take on higher independent variable values, the gamma will have a negative value approaching −1.0.

$$\gamma = \frac{\begin{bmatrix} \text{number of} & \text{number of} \\ \text{concordant} - \text{discordant} \\ \text{pairs} & \text{pairs} \end{bmatrix}}{\begin{bmatrix} \text{number of} & \text{number of} \\ \text{concordant} + \text{discordant} \\ \text{pairs} & \text{pairs} \end{bmatrix}}$$

As part of an ongoing effort to monitor the role of American local governments in providing services to children and youth, analysts surveyed several hundred U.S. municipalities with populations of 10,000 or more. Eight types of direct service were identified: day care centers, counseling, job placement, nutrition, adoption services, foster homes, protective services/shelter, and youth recreation. The analysts assigned an ordinal level of involvement "score" to each municipality based on the variety of services it provides: the provision of only one program was classified as a "low" level of service; two or three programs was "medium"; and four or more programs was regarded as "high." Exhibit 10–3 summarizes the level of direct service involvement by population size for the 749 U.S. cities that responded to the survey. It seems by looking at the column relative frequencies that larger cities tend to provide more types of services than smaller cities. An analyst can use the gamma statistic to examine the strength of this relationship.

Calculating the number of concordant and discordant pairs in order to compute a value for the gamma statistic is a tedious process—subject to error if one is using only a pocket calculator. The analyst will save a great deal of time by using a statistical program on a computer for the calculations. Some computer programs will allow the analyst to enter the respective cell frequencies exactly as they are provided in the structure of the crosstabulation. Other computer programs will require that the respective ordinal values taken on by the two variables be entered along with frequency for each cell. The computer program, in effect, constructs the crosstabulation by "weighting" each cell by the given frequency. Exhibit 10–4 shows this form of data entry.

## Exhibit 10–3

**Level of Service to Children and Youth by Population**

| Level of service | | City population category | | | | Total |
|---|---|---|---|---|---|---|
| | | *1*<br>*10,000 up to 25,000* | *2*<br>*25,000 up to 50,000* | *3*<br>*50,000 up to 100,000* | *4*<br>*100,000 up to 250,000* | |
| None | 1 | 197<br>47.8% | 61<br>31.9% | 26<br>26.3% | 9<br>19.1% | 293<br>39.1% |
| Low | 2 | 171<br>41.5% | 83<br>43.5% | 45<br>45.4% | 21<br>44.7% | 320<br>42.7% |
| Medium | 3 | 40<br>9.7% | 39<br>20.4% | 22<br>22.2% | 13<br>27.7% | 114<br>15.2% |
| High | 4 | 4<br>1.0% | 8<br>4.2% | 6<br>6.1% | 4<br>8.5% | 22<br>2.9% |
| Total | | 412<br>100.0% | 191<br>100.0% | 99<br>100.0% | 47<br>100.0% | 749<br>99.9% |

*Source:* Robert Agranoff and Alex N. Pattakos, "Local Government Human Services," *Baseline Data Report,* vol. 17, no. 4 (Washington, DC: International City/County Management Association, 1985), p. 10.

## Exhibit 10–4

**Format for Data Entry: Level of Service to Children and Youth by Population**

| City population category | Level of service category | Frequency |
|:---:|:---:|:---:|
| 1 | 0 | 197 |
| 1 | 1 | 171 |
| 1 | 2 | 40 |
| 1 | 3 | 4 |
| 2 | 0 | 61 |
| 2 | 1 | 83 |
| 2 | 2 | 39 |
| 2 | 3 | 8 |
| 3 | 0 | 26 |
| 3 | 1 | 45 |
| 3 | 2 | 22 |
| 3 | 3 | 6 |
| 4 | 0 | 9 |
| 4 | 1 | 21 |
| 4 | 2 | 13 |
| 4 | 3 | 4 |

Using the method presented in Chapter 9, the number of concordant, discordant, and tied pairs for the 4 × 4 crosstabulation of level of service to children and youth against city population are

| | |
|---|---|
| Number of concordant pairs: | 76,666 |
| Number of discordant pairs: | 36,747 |
| Number of pairs tied | |
|     On independent variable: | 66,223 |
|     On dependent variable: | 57,970 |
|     On both variables: | 42,520 |
| Sum | 280,126 |

The calculated value of gamma ($\gamma = 0.352$) indicates that cities with larger populations have a moderate tendency to provide a higher level of services to children.

For problems where the sample size exceeds 40, statistical significance can be tested using the $Z$ statistic:

$$Z = \gamma \cdot \sqrt{\frac{\begin{array}{cc}\text{Number of} & \text{Number of} \\ \text{concordant} - \text{discordant} \\ \text{pairs} & \text{pairs}\end{array}}{n(1 - \gamma^2)}}$$

$$Z = 0.352 \cdot \sqrt{\frac{76,666 - 36,747}{749(1 - 0.352^2)}}$$

$$Z = 2.74$$

Using a two-tailed test at the 0.05 level of significance, the critical value of $Z$ is 1.96. Since the calculated value of $Z$ in this example exceeds the critical value, the analyst concludes that the association between city population and level of service to children is statistically significant.

The gamma statistic has a proportionate-reduction-in-error interpretation. It indicates the consistency of the rank ordering in the crosstabulation. The gamma statistic is the number of consistent rank orderings minus the number of inconsistent rank orderings, expressed as a proportion of all possible rank orderings (excluding ties). It is the probability that any two cases in the sample (a pair) will have the same relative rank order on both of the observed variables. Gamma will have a value of $+1$ if all the cases are arrayed on the descending left-to-right diagonal of a crosstabulation (and a value of $-1$ if the cases fall on the ascending left-to-right diagonal). However, because gamma does not recognize ties, Exhibit 10–5 shows other "consistent" rank order patterns, besides the diagonal, for which gamma will also achieve a value of $+1$. Because the gamma statistic tends to yield relatively high values for strength of association (since it ignores ties) for many patterns in the crosstabulation that appear "consistent," it is referred to as an "undisciplined" measure.

## *Exhibit 10–5*

**Hypothetical Crosstabulations for Which $\gamma = +1$**

| 4 | 0 | 0 | 0 |
|---|---|---|---|
| 0 | 3 | 0 | 0 |
| 0 | 0 | 3 | 0 |
| 0 | 0 | 0 | 4 |

| 4 | 0 | 0 | 0 |
|---|---|---|---|
| 0 | 3 | 0 | 0 |
| 0 | 3 | 0 | 0 |
| 0 | 0 | 3 | 4 |

| 4 | 3 | 3 | 4 |
|---|---|---|---|
| 0 | 0 | 0 | 3 |
| 0 | 0 | 0 | 3 |
| 0 | 0 | 0 | 4 |

## 10.3 Somers' d Statistic

Somers' *d* statistic modifies gamma by discounting for pairs of cases with tied values on the dependent variable. This provides a more stringent criterion for strength of association. Somers' *d* will equal 1.0 only when all of the cases have values that lie along the diagonal of the crosstabulation.

The value of Somers' *d* for the level of service versus population crosstabulation is 0.23—a moderate degree of association.

$$\text{Somers' } d = \frac{\left[\begin{array}{c}\text{Number of} \\ \text{concordant} \\ \text{pairs}\end{array} - \begin{array}{c}\text{Number of} \\ \text{discordant} \\ \text{pairs}\end{array}\right]}{\left[\begin{array}{c}\text{Number of} \\ \text{concordant} \\ \text{pairs}\end{array} + \begin{array}{c}\text{Number of} \\ \text{discordant} \\ \text{pairs}\end{array} + \begin{array}{c}\text{Number of ties} \\ \text{on dependent} \\ \text{variable}\end{array}\right]}$$

$$\text{Somers' } d = \frac{76{,}666 - 36{,}747}{76{,}666 + 36{,}747 + 57{,}970}$$

$$\text{Somers' } d = 0.233$$

## 10.4 Kendall's Tau Statistics

There are three Kendall's tau statistics, designated $\tau_a$, $\tau_b$, and $\tau_c$. Basically, these statistics assess the degree of consistency in the crosstabulation. If the analyst observes two variables for each unit of analysis, and arranges the data in ascending order of the values taken on by the independent variable, the extent to which the corresponding values of the dependent variable are also arrayed in increasing order indicates the strength of association between the independent and dependent variables. The Kendall's tau statistics, like gamma and Somers' *d*, compare the number of concordant pairs in the crosstabulation to the number of discordant pairs. If there is no consistency between the respective values of the two variables, the number of concordant pairs should be about the same as the number of discordant pairs, and the statistic will have a value close to zero. If the ordinal ranking of the dependent variable tends to increase as the value of the independent variable increases, the statistic will have a positive value approaching 1.0. On the other hand, if the ordinal ranking of the dependent variable tends to be lower as cases take on higher independent variable values, the statistic will have a negative value approaching $-1.0$.

The $\tau_a$ statistic compares the difference between the number of concordant and discordant pairs to the maximum case pairs that are possible given the number of units of analysis in the sample. It emphasizes the concordant–discordant difference by not correcting for any tied values on either the independent or the dependent variable, so it should be used only in that situation—no ties, that is, the frequency in each cell of the crosstabulation should either be 0 or 1. These are the same conditions under which Spearman's rank correlation coefficient is applicable and Spearman's rho statistic seems to be the one that is most commonly employed.

$$
\tau_a = \frac{\begin{bmatrix} \text{Number of} & & \text{Number of} \\ \text{concordant} & - & \text{discordant} \\ \text{pairs} & & \text{pairs} \end{bmatrix}}{\dfrac{n(n-1)}{2}}
$$

The $\tau_b$ statistic allows for a large number of ties. It is suited for the analysis of crosstabulations with many cases in each cell (and in this situation is preferred over Spearman's rho). However, it can attain its greatest value of 1.0 or $-1.0$ only for "square" crosstabulations where the number of rows equals the number of columns, so its use should be restricted to this type of problem.

$$
\tau_b = \frac{\begin{bmatrix} \text{Number of} & & \text{Number of} \\ \text{concordant} & - & \text{discordant} \\ \text{pairs} & & \text{pairs} \end{bmatrix}}{\sqrt{\begin{matrix} \text{Number of} & + & \text{Number of} & + & \text{Number of ties} \\ \text{concordant} & & \text{discordant} & & \text{on independent} \\ \text{pairs} & & \text{pairs} & & \text{variable} \end{matrix}} \cdot \sqrt{\begin{matrix} \text{Number of} & + & \text{Number of} & + & \text{Number of ties} \\ \text{concordant} & & \text{discordant} & & \text{on dependent} \\ \text{pairs} & & \text{pairs} & & \text{variable} \end{matrix}}}
$$

$$
\tau_b = \frac{76{,}666 - 36{,}747}{\sqrt{76{,}666 + 36{,}747 + 66{,}223} \cdot \sqrt{76{,}666 + 36{,}747 + 57{,}970}}
$$

$$
\tau_b = 0.228
$$

The $\tau_c$ statistic should be used for "rectangular" crosstabulations, where there are many cases in each cell and the number of rows does not equal the number of columns. This statistic compares the concordant–discordant difference to an approximation of the total number of pairs in the crosstabulation using either the number of rows or the number of columns, whichever is least.

$$
\tau_c = \frac{\begin{bmatrix} \text{Number of} & & \text{Number of} \\ \text{concordant} & - & \text{discordant} \\ \text{pairs} & & \text{pairs} \end{bmatrix}}{\dfrac{n^2 \cdot (m-1)}{2m}}
$$

where

$$m = \text{minimum} \left\{ \begin{array}{c} \text{number of rows} \\ \text{or} \\ \text{number of columns} \end{array} \right\}$$

Kendall's $\tau_b$ and $\tau_c$ statistics will provide lower, more "conservative," values for strength of association than either Goodman and Kruskal's gamma or Somers' $d$. Although the value of gamma will always be higher than either Somers' $d$ or the tau statistics, it has the simplest proportionate-reduction-in-error interpretation.

If the sample size is greater than 10, the distribution of $\tau_a$ (and the tau statistics corrected for ties, $\tau_b$, and $\tau_c$) can be approximated by a normal distribution. The expected value of tau is 0. The analyst can use the following equation for the $Z$ statistic to check whether the calculated value of tau differs significantly from this expectation for the crosstabulation in Exhibit 10–3:

$$Z = \frac{\tau}{\sqrt{\frac{2 \cdot (2n + 5)}{9n \cdot (n - 1)}}}$$

$$Z = \frac{0.228}{\sqrt{\frac{2 \cdot (2 \cdot 749 + 5)}{9 \cdot 749 \cdot (749 - 1)}}}$$

$$Z = 9.3$$

The $Z$ test (two-tailed test at the 0.05 level of significance) using the $\tau_b$ statistic shows a statistically significant relationship between city population and the level of service to children and youth.

# Homework Exercises

**10-1** A survey of local governments inquired about public officials "errors and omissions" liabilities claims. The analysts wondered whether larger local government jurisdictions tended to have larger public officials liability claims filed against them. Consider the data in Exhibit HW10–1A.

## Exhibit HW10–1A

**Monetary Damages Sought for Public Officials Liability Claims (1985)**

| Population | Number of reported claims | Percentage of claims with demand in excess of: | | | | | |
|---|---|---|---|---|---|---|---|
| | | *$100,000* | *$250,000* | *$500,000* | *$1 million* | *$5 million* | *$20 million* |
| 10,000–24,999 | 169 | 39.1% | 30.2% | 25.4% | 17.8% | 8.9% | 2.4% |
| 25,000–49,999 | 128 | 48.4 | 33.6 | 28.9 | 18.0 | 9.4 | 1.6 |
| 50,000–99,999 | 169 | 45.0 | 36.1 | 30.8 | 17.2 | 5.9 | 2.4 |
| 100,000–250,000 | 120 | 37.5 | 29.2 | 20.0 | 9.2 | 3.3 | 0.8 |

Exhibit HW10–1A is not a crosstabulation. Within each population category, it provides a cumulative frequency distribution of the monetary damages sought. A crosstabulation needs to be constructed with the amount of the claim (the dependent variable) shown as ordinal categories, as presented in Exhibit HW10–1B.

$$\text{Goodman–Kruskal Gamma} = -0.0278$$
$$\text{Somers' } d = -0.0176$$
$$\text{Kendall } \tau_c = -0.0175$$

The results do not support the statement that larger claims tend to be filed against governmental jurisdictions having larger populations.

## Exhibit HW10–1B

**Monetary Damages Sought by Claimants by Population**

| Claims | Population | | | | Total |
|---|---|---|---|---|---|
| | *10,000–24,999* | *25,000–49,999* | *50,000–99,999* | *100,000–250,000* | |
| Less than $100,000 | 103 | 66 | 93 | 75 | 337 |
| $100,000-$249,999 | 15 | 19 | 15 | 10 | 59 |
| $250,000-$499,999 | 8 | 6 | 9 | 11 | 34 |
| $500,000-$999,999 | 13 | 14 | 23 | 13 | 63 |
| $1-$5 million | 15 | 11 | 19 | 7 | 52 |
| $5-$20 million | 11 | 10 | 6 | 3 | 30 |
| Over $20 million | 4 | 2 | 4 | 1 | 11 |
| Total | 169 | 128 | 169 | 120 | 586 |

**10-2** Alcohol availability and consumption are related to many public problems ranging from complaints about litter and noise to sales to minors, drunk driving, public inebriation, violence, and drug sales. Local governments, through planning and zoning ordinances, can regulate the placement, hours, and conditions for the retail

sale of alcohol. California cities can use conditional-use permits (CUPs) to establish such requirements as minimum distances between alcohol outlets and between
alcohol outlets and residences; to prohibit the sale of alcohol and gasoline at the
same location; to mandate special security measures for alcohol outlets; or to limit
the hours of operation of alcohol outlets. The adoption of CUP regulations may be
related to the perceived importance of alcohol-related problems. Exhibits
HW10–2A and HW10–2B compare CUP regulatory activity with a subjective rat-

## Exhibit HW10–2A

**Importance of Alcohol-Related Problems Compared with Other Planning Issues**

| Conditional-use permit regulatory activity | Much more important | Somewhat more important | Somewhat less important | Much less important | Total |
|---|---|---|---|---|---|
| Highly active | 1 | 19 | 19 | 43 | 82 |
| | 33.3% | 46.3% | 27.9% | 38.4% | 36.6% |
| Moderately active | 2 | 9 | 22 | 34 | 67 |
| | 66.7% | 22.0% | 32.4% | 30.4% | 29.9% |
| Inactive | 0 | 13 | 27 | 35 | 75 |
| | 0.0% | 31.7% | 39.7% | 31.3% | 33.5% |
| Total | 3 | 41 | 68 | 112 | 224 |
| | 100.0% | 100.0% | 100.0% | 100.0% | 100.0% |

## Exhibit HW10–2B

**Conditional-Use Permit Regulatory Activity by Number of Kinds of Problems with Alcohol Outlets\***

| Conditional-use permit regulatory activity | None | 1 or 2 | 3 to 5 | 6 or more | Total |
|---|---|---|---|---|---|
| Highly active | 15 | 20 | 34 | 27 | 96 |
| | 17.4% | 29.4% | 37.8% | 41.5% | 31.1% |
| Moderately active | 21 | 21 | 27 | 21 | 90 |
| | 24.4% | 30.9% | 30.0% | 32.3% | 29.1% |
| Inactive | 50 | 27 | 29 | 17 | 123 |
| | 58.1% | 39.7% | 32.2% | 27.2% | 39.8% |
| Total | 86 | 68 | 90 | 65 | 309 |
| | 100.0% | 100.0% | 100.0% | 100.0% | 100.0% |

\*Kinds of problems: loitering, sales to minors, litter, selling alcohol and gasoline at the same
location, drunk driving, noise, drinking at public places, large numbers of outlets concentrated in a
particular area, appearance of chronic inebriates in public places, drug sales, violence, vice activities
such as prostitution and gambling.

ing of the importance of alcohol-related problems against other planning issues and the number of different kinds of problems reportedly occurring at alcohol outlets.[1] Determine the statistical significance, strength of association, and direction of the relationships.

Conditional-use permit regulatory activity by perceived importance of alcohol-related problems

Goodman–Kruskal Gamma $= -0.0103$
Somers' $d = -0.0069$
Kendall $\tau_c = -0.0065$

The relationship between CUP activity and reported importance of alcohol-related problems is weak and not statistically significant.

CUP regulatory activity by the perceived number of kinds of problems with alcohol outlets

Goodman–Kruskal Gamma $= -0.3061$
Somers' $d = -0.2048$
Kendall $\tau_c = -0.2289$

The relationship between CUP activity and perceived number of problems is moderate and statistically significant.

**10-3** Citizen participation in community planning often involves a relatively small group of self-selected active participants. In order to check how well planning activists reflected the viewpoints of the general population, one community contacted a random sample of the general population by means of a mailed questionnaire. Respondents were asked to identify the issue of "highest importance" to the community. Exhibit HW10–3A shows the ranking assigned to 21 growth and development issues by the active-participant and general population groups respectively.

  **a.** Is there a statistically significant difference between the rankings assigned by the active participants and the general population groups?

  **b.** What is the strength of association of the relationship between the rankings?

  **c.** Is the difference between the two groups with respect to the importance of the "water quality" issue statistically significant?

---

[1]Friedner D. Wittman and Michael E. Hilton, "Uses of Planning and Zoning Ordinances to Regulate Alcohol Outlets in California Cities," in H. Holder, ed., *Advances in Substance Abuse: Behavioral and Biological Research,* Supplement 1 (Greenwich, CT: Jai Press, 1987), 337–365.

## Exhibit HW10–3A

**Ranking of Most Important Growth and Development Issues Facing the Community Comparison of Active Participants and General Population (number of respondents ranking the issue of "highest importance")**

| Issues | Active participants ($n = 149$) | | General population respondents ($n = 250$) | |
|---|---|---|---|---|
| | *Frequency* | *Rank* | *Frequency* | *Rank* |
| Water quality | 98 | 1 | 171 | 2 |
| Traffic congestion | 88 | 2 | 192 | 1 |
| Loss of important natural areas | 88 | 3 | 148 | 3 |
| Attracting new industry and commerce | 82 | 4 | 103 | 6 |
| Sewer and water facilities | 72 | 5 | 144 | 4 |
| High cost of city service | 61 | 6 | 98 | 7 |
| Need to increase city's tax base | 61 | 7 | 45 | 17 |
| Housing affordability | 58 | 8 | 69 | 10 |
| Air pollution | 56 | 9 | 130 | 5 |
| Loss of open space | 51 | 10 | 97 | 8 |
| Mass/public transit | 44 | 11 | 61 | 13 |
| Inappropriate scale and intensity of new development | 42 | 12 | 75 | 9 |
| Improvement/revitalization of downtown | 38 | 13 | 39 | 18 |
| Reduction of flood hazards | 28 | 14 | 67 | 11 |
| Substandard housing | 27 | 15 | 46 | 16 |
| Historic preservation | 24 | 16 | 58 | 14 |
| Medical/health facilities | 23 | 17 | 64 | 12 |
| Regulation/control of signs and billboards | 22 | 18 | 49 | 15 |
| Need for tennis courts, golf courses, other recreational facilities | 17 | 19 | 33 | 20 |
| Need for pedestrian and bike routes/facilities | 11 | 20 | 37 | 19 |
| Ugly/aesthetically displeasing architecture | 8 | 21 | 31 | 21 |

**d.** Is the difference between the two groups with respect to the importance of the "housing affordability" issue statistically significant?

**a. and b.** Calculate Spearman's rank correlation coefficient. See Exhibit HW10–3B.

Spearman's $\rho_{\text{calculated}} = 0.85$

$\rho_{\text{critical}} = 0.556$ (two-tailed test at the 0.01 level of significance)

## *Exhibit HW10–3B*

**Ranking of Most Important Growth and Development Issues Facing the Community: Comparison of Active Participants and General Population (number of respondents ranking the issue of "highest importance")**

| Issues | Active participants ($n = 149$) | | General population respondents ($n = 250$) | | Difference (after correcting for ties | $d^2$ |
|---|---|---|---|---|---|---|
| | *Frequency* | *Rank* | *Frequency* | *Rank* | | |
| Water quality | 98 | 1 | 171 | 2 | $-1$ | 1 |
| Traffic congestion | 88 | 2 | 192 | 1 | 1.5 | 2.25 |
| Loss of important natural areas | 88 | 3 | 148 | 3 | $-0.5$ | 0.25 |
| Attracting new industry and commerce | 82 | 4 | 103 | 6 | $-2$ | 4 |
| Sewer and water facilities | 72 | 5 | 144 | 4 | 1 | 1 |
| High cost of city service | 61 | 6 | 98 | 7 | $-0.5$ | 0.25 |
| Need to increase city's tax base | 61 | 7 | 45 | 17 | $-10.5$ | 110.25 |
| Housing affordability | 58 | 8 | 69 | 10 | $-2$ | 4 |
| Air pollution | 56 | 9 | 130 | 5 | 4 | 16 |
| Loss of open space | 51 | 10 | 97 | 8 | 2 | 4 |
| Mass/public transit | 44 | 11 | 61 | 13 | $-2$ | 4 |
| Inappropriate scale and intensity of new development | 42 | 12 | 75 | 9 | 3 | 9 |
| Improvement/revitalization of downtown | 38 | 13 | 39 | 18 | $-5$ | 25 |
| Reduction of flood hazards | 28 | 14 | 67 | 11 | 3 | 9 |
| Substandard housing | 27 | 15 | 46 | 16 | $-1$ | 1 |
| Historic preservation | 24 | 16 | 58 | 14 | 2 | 4 |
| Medical/health facilities | 23 | 17 | 64 | 12 | 5 | 25 |
| Regulation/control of signs and billboards | 22 | 18 | 49 | 15 | 3 | 9 |
| Need for tennis courts, golf courses, other recreational facilities | 17 | 19 | 33 | 20 | $-1$ | 1 |
| Need for pedestrian and bike routes/facilities | 11 | 20 | 37 | 19 | 1 | 1 |
| Ugly/aesthetically displeasing architecture | 8 | 21 | 31 | 21 | 0 | 0 |
| Total | | | | | | 231 |

There is a strong statistically significant relationship between the active participants and the general population in their respective rankings of the importance of issues facing the community.

c. Use a $Z$ test for the difference between two proportions:
$Z_{calculated} = -0.54$ not statistically significant

d. Use a $Z$ test for the difference between two proportions:
$Z_{calculated} = 2.35$ statistically significant difference at the 0.05 level of significance

# *t* Time with a Bit of ANOVA: Two-Variable Evaluation— Nominal–Interval Measures

| | |
|---|---|
| Kind of problem | *Evaluation* |
| Number of variables | *Two* |
| Level of measurement | *Variable 1, nominal* |
| | *Variable 2, interval* |

This chapter addresses two-variable evaluation problems in which one variable (usually the independent variable) has a nominal level of measurement and the second variable (dependent variable) has an interval level of measurement. Exhibit 11–1 outlines available statistical methods. The most important methods are the *t* tests for unpaired and paired units of analysis. The use of randomization tests will be discussed for problems that have very few cases. The analysis-of-variance *F* test and the strength-of-association statistic eta-squared ($\eta^2$) are introduced both for their utility in addressing problems encountered in public administration and to lay necessary groundwork for regression analysis in the next chapter.

## 11.1 The Independent Variable Has Two Categories

### 11.1.1 Two-Variable *t*-Test for Unpaired Data

Many evaluation problems involve the comparison of two groups. Perhaps one group has been subject to a new policy or program while the other group has not. The two groups are defined by the independent variable, *x*, a dichotomous

## *Exhibit 11–1*

**Two-Variable Evaluation—Nominal–Interval Measures**

| Dependent variable | | Independent variable | | |
| --- | --- | --- | --- | --- |
| | | *Nominal level of measurement* | | |
| | | Two categories | | |
| | | *Unpaired units of analysis* | *Paired units of analysis* | More than two categories |
| Interval level of measurement | Strength of association | Eta-squared, $\eta^2$ | | Eta-squared, $\eta^2$ |
| | Statistical significance | $n > 12$[a] Two-variable *t* test for unpaired data | $n > 12$ Two-variable *t* test for paired data | Analysis-of-variance *F* test[b] |
| | | $n \leq 12$ Randomization test for unpaired data | $n \leq 12$ Randomization test for paired data | |

[a]The Mann–Whitney *U* test is an alternative.
[b]The Kruskal–Wallis test is an alternative.

nominal level of measurement. Analysts are interested in whether a particular characteristic or attribute (the dependent variable, *y*) differs "on the average" between the two groups. Having divided the units of analysis into two groups, the analyst will calculate the mean value of the dependent variable for each group. The observed difference between the mean values can be tested using a modification to the *t* statistic that will be designated $t_C$. The expectation (null hypothesis) is that there is no relationship between group identification and the values taken on by the dependent variable—both groups were selected from the same statistical population and any difference between the means can be attributed to random error. The alternative hypothesis is that the dichotomous independent variable identifies units of analysis that were selected from two distinct statistical populations with different mean values for the dependent variable. The $t_C$ statistic is used to assess the likelihood of the observed difference between the respective group means. We conclude that the difference is statistically significant, and reject the hypothesis of no difference, if the probability indicated by the $t_C$ statistic is less than the specified "level of significance" (usually 0.05 or 0.01).

$$t_C = \frac{\bar{y}_1 - \bar{y}_2}{\sqrt{\dfrac{s_1^2}{n_1} + \dfrac{s_2^2}{n_2}}}$$

$\bar{y}_1$ = mean of group 1

$\bar{y}_2$ = mean of group 2

$s_1^2$ = variance of group 1

$s_2^2$ = variable of group 2

$n_1$ = number of observations in group 1

$n_2$ = number of observations in group 2

The Environmental Protection Agency requires owners and operators of solid waste management units (landfills) to periodically monitor the groundwater for potential releases of hazardous elements such as arsenic, barium, cadmium, chromium, lead, mercury, selenium, and silver, as well as certain pesticide and herbicide compounds. Some measurements provide an indication of background groundwater quality that is representative of the area. Other measurements are obtained at compliance-monitoring wells "located at the hydraulically downgradient limit of the waste management area that extends down into the uppermost aquifer underlying the regulated units."[1] The owner or operator must compare data collected at the compliance point to the background groundwater quality data. A statistically significant difference triggers notification of the EPA regional administrator, further monitoring, and corrective action if warranted. Consider the data in Exhibit 11–2 in which the owner or operator obtains 16 measurements of background chromium concentration from one well and 12 measurements from a second compliance–monitoring well. (The maximum contaminant level for chromium in groundwater is 50 micrograms per liter, 0.05 parts per million.)

The calculated value of the $t_C$ statistic is $-2.75$.

$$t_C = \frac{\bar{y}_1 - \bar{y}_2}{\sqrt{\dfrac{s_1^2}{n_1} + \dfrac{s_2^2}{n_2}}}$$

$$t_C = \frac{18.875 - 37.83}{\sqrt{\dfrac{13.95^2}{16} + \dfrac{20.74^2}{12}}}$$

$$t_C = -2.75$$

---

[1] 40 Code of Federal Regulations 264

## Exhibit 11–2

**Concentration of Chromium at a Landfill (hypothetical data)**

| Observation number | Background concentration (micrograms/liter) | Monitoring well (micrograms/liter) |
|---|---|---|
| 1 | 35 | 19 |
| 2 | 15 | 56 |
| 3 | 2 | 23 |
| 4 | 40 | 46 |
| 5 | 4 | 59 |
| 6 | 16 | 21 |
| 7 | 4 | 26 |
| 8 | 37 | 44 |
| 9 | 6 | 34 |
| 10 | 10 | 33 |
| 11 | 4 | 83 |
| 12 | 11 | 10 |
| 13 | 24 | |
| 14 | 40 | |
| 15 | 30 | |
| 16 | 22 | |
| Mean | 18.75 | 37.83 |
| Standard deviation | 13.95 | 20.74 |
| *n* | 16 | 12 |

The analyst can compare this against a critical value of the $t_C$ statistic at a specified level of significance. However, the distribution of $t_C$ does not precisely follow that of the *t* distribution introduced earlier. The following rules should be applied in determining a critical value for $t_C$.[2]

1. If $n_1 = n_2$, obtain the critical value for $t_C$ from the table of critical values for the *t* statistic using $(n_1 - 1)$ degrees of freedom.

---

[2]George W. Snedecor and William G. Cochran. 1967. *Statistical Methods,* Sixth edition (Ames, IA: Iowa State University Press).

**2.** If $n_1 \neq n_2$, look up critical values of $t$ for $(n_1 - 1)$ and $(n_2 - 1)$ degrees of freedom. These values will be designated $t_1$ and $t_2$, respectively. Then calculate a critical value for $t_C$ using the following approximation:

$$t_{C \text{ critical}} = \frac{w_1 t_1 + w_2 t_2}{w_1 + w_2}$$

where

$$w_1 = \frac{s_1^2}{n_1} \quad \text{and} \quad w_2 = \frac{s_2^2}{n_2}$$

In this example, using a two-tailed test at the 0.05 level of significance, we have

$$w_1 = \frac{13.95^2}{16} = 12.16 \quad \text{and} \quad w_2 = \frac{20.74^2}{12} = 35.86$$

$$t_{C \text{ critical}} = \frac{12.16 \cdot 2.131 + 35.86 \cdot 2.201}{12.16 + 35.86} = 2.18$$

The calculated value of $t_C$ (2.75) exceeds the critical value. The analyst concludes that the difference in chromium concentration between the background and monitoring wells is statistically significant.

If the assumptions are met, this is the best test for determining the statistical significance of the differences between two groups. There are three important assumptions. (1) The observations of each unit of analysis are assumed to be independent (not affecting and not affected by the characteristics or attributes of any other unit of analysis). (2) Each unit of analysis is assumed to be randomly selected from the statistical population. (3) The frequency distribution of the dependent variable in the statistical population is assumed to be a normal distribution. If the normality assumption is not met, analysts usually treat the dependent variable as having an ordinal level of measurement and apply the tests discussed in the preceding chapter.

## 11.1.2   Randomization Test for Unpaired Data

The randomization test for unpaired data is a useful alternative to the $t$ test because the analyst is not required to assume normal distributions or constant variance in the statistical populations. However, computational difficulty limits its application to small sample sizes ($n_1 + n_2 \leq 12$).

Consider a situation with a small sample size. The dichotomous independent variable separates the cases into two groups. The analyst wants to determine whether the cases were drawn from the same statistical population or from

## Exhibit 11–3

**Traffic Speeds on Plaza Terrace**

| | | | | |
|---|---|---|---|---|
| **Independent variable: Direction of traffic** | | | | |
| *Group 1* *Eastbound* | | | *Group 2* *Westbound* | |
| **Time** | Dependent variable: *Mean speed (mph)* | | **Time** | Dependent variable: *Mean speed (mph)* |
| 9 A.M. | 32.2 | | 9 A.M. | 32.1 |
| 1 P.M. | 33.0 | | 1 P.M. | 32.6 |
| 8 P.M. | 33.5 | | 8 P.M. | 31.2 |

different statistical populations. If all $n_1 + n_2$ cases were drawn from one and the same statistical population, then it is merely a matter of arbitrary coincidence that some observations were classified as being in group 1 and others in group 2. Given the null hypothesis of no difference between the mean of the observations in group 1 and the mean of the observations in group 2, the number of ways $n_1 + n_2$ observations could have been randomly assigned to the two groups is specified by the following equation:

$$\text{Number of possible outcomes} = \frac{(n_1 + n_2)!}{n_1! \cdot n_2!}$$

where

$$n_1 = \text{number of observations in group 1}$$

$$n_2 = \text{number of observations in group 2}$$

The data file in Exhibit 11–3 lists the average speed of highway traffic three times a day in each of two directions, eastbound and westbound.[3] There are three observations in group 1 and three observations in group 2. There are a total of 20 ways of listing these six observations in two groups.

$$\text{Number of possible outcomes} = \frac{(3 + 3)!}{3! \cdot 3!} = 20$$

---

[3]Harry S. Lum, "The Use of Road Markings to Narrow Lanes for Controlling Speed in Residential Areas," *Public Roads* (September 1983): 56–60.

The most extreme possible outcome is that the highest speeds would be in one group and the lowest speeds would be in the other. The analyst could list all 20 arrangements of three speeds in one group and three in the other. Each arrangement has a probability of one divided by the number of possible outcomes or 1/20. This is a probability distribution and the analyst can examine the "tails" of the distribution—the extreme outcome arrangements—to test the null hypothesis. The analyst will focus on those arrangements that constitute the most extreme 5% (the level of significance—a more stringent criterion would be 1%) of all possible outcomes. Thus, the number of outcome arrangements of interest is the product of the level of significance times the number of possible outcomes. (In this example, this is $0.05 \times 20 = 1$ outcome.) If the observed arrangement of measurements is one of the 5% most extreme outcomes, the analyst rejects the null hypothesis of no difference between the two groups and adopts the alternate hypothesis that the observed cases were drawn from two different statistical populations.

$$\begin{matrix} \text{Number of possible} \\ \text{outcomes in the} \\ \text{critical region} \end{matrix} = \begin{matrix} \text{Level} \\ \text{of} \\ \text{significance} \end{matrix} \times \begin{matrix} \text{Number of} \\ \text{possible} \\ \text{outcomes} \end{matrix}$$

$$\begin{matrix} \text{Number of possible} \\ \text{outcomes in the} \\ \text{critical region} \end{matrix} = 0.05 \times 20 = 1$$

Exhibit 11–4 lists the most extreme arrangements of outcome measurements for this example. The actual arrangement of speeds does not fall in the critical region (above the dashed line). Therefore, the analyst cannot reject the null hypothesis that there is no difference in the mean speed of traffic in each direction.

## *Exhibit 11–4*

**The Most Extreme Possible Outcomes for Vehicle Speeds (mph)**

| | Greatest $n_1 = 3$ values among all cases | | | Lowest $n_2 = 3$ values among all cases | | | Sum | |
|---|---|---|---|---|---|---|---|---|
| (1) | 33.5 | 33.0 | 32.6 | 31.2 | 32.1 | 32.2 | $99.1 - 95.5 = 3.6$ | Critical region |
| (2)[a] | 33.5 | 33.0 | 32.2 | 31.2 | 32.1 | 32.6 | $98.7 - 95.9 = 2.8$ | |
| (3) | 33.5 | 33.0 | 32.1 | 31.2 | 32.2 | 32.6 | $98.6 - 96.0 = 2.6$ | |

[a]The sample observed

### 11.1.3    Two-Variable *t*-Test for Paired Data

If the units of analysis are pairs, a *t*-test very similar to the one-variable test can be applied. A pair can be an object or event observed twice—at two points in time—a before–after or pre–post condition during which there was some policy change or management intervention. A pair can also be "twins"—two objects or events identical in every material respect save for the one supposedly incidental characteristic or attribute—the dichotomous independent variable—that sets them apart. The dependent variable is the measured difference between the components of each pair. The problem calls for comparing the mean of the observed differences against the expectation (null hypothesis) that the average difference in the statistical population is zero.

$$t = \frac{\bar{d} - 0}{\frac{s_d}{\sqrt{n}}} = \frac{\bar{d}}{\frac{s_d}{\sqrt{n}}}$$

where

$n$ = number of pairs in the sample

Degrees of freedom, $df = n - 1$

$$\bar{d} = \frac{\sum d}{n}$$

and

$$s_d = \sqrt{\frac{\sum(d_i - \bar{d})^2}{n - 1}} \text{ or, in another form } s_d = \sqrt{\frac{\sum d^2}{n - 1} - \frac{(\sum d)^2}{n(n - 1)}}$$

The Space Shuttle was developed in the 1970s using electromechanical gauges and multiple Cathode Ray Tube (CRT) displays in the cockpit—technology that was advanced for its time, but soon became dated. No major upgrades were made to the cockpit for two decades. The Multifunction Electronic Display System (MEDS) introduced in 2000 remedied some of the display problems. NASA later developed a Cockpit Avionics Upgrade (CAU) system. The two systems were compared by 18 shuttle crews (comprised of a commander, pilot, and mission specialist) in flight simulator runs. The MEDS-CAU runs were separated by several months and there was no preparatory CAU training. After each run, the shuttle crew answered a series of technical "situation awareness" questions. Therefore, the dichotomous independent variable was the type of cockpit display system—MEDS or CAU—and the dependent variable was the difference between the situation awareness scores.[4] Exhibit 11–5 shows simulated data for the NASA evaluation including mean and standard deviation of the MEDS-CAU differences.

---

[4]Jeffrey W. McCandless et al., "Evaluation of the Space Shuttle Cockpit Avionics Upgrade (CAU) Displays," *Proceedings of the Human Factors and Ergonomics Society,* 2005.

## Exhibit 11–5

**Evaluation of Space Shuttle Cockpit Systems: Multifunction Electronic Display System (MEDS) v. Cockpit Avionics Upgrade (CAU)**
(hypothetical data)

| Shuttle crew number | Difference between situation awareness test scores: MEDS vs. CAU Systems |
|---|---|
| 1 | 60 |
| 2 | 70 |
| 3 | 80 |
| 4 | 120 |
| 5 | 170 |
| 6 | −20 |
| 7 | −25 |
| 8 | −30 |
| 9 | 25 |
| 10 | 60 |
| 11 | 70 |
| 12 | 100 |
| 13 | −30 |
| 14 | 60 |
| 15 | 120 |
| 16 | 80 |
| 17 | 70 |
| 18 | 10 |
| Mean | 55 |
| Standard deviation | 57 |

The two-variable $t$ statistic for paired data can be calculated:

$$t = \frac{\bar{d}}{\frac{s_d}{\sqrt{n}}}$$

$$t = \frac{55}{\frac{57}{\sqrt{18}}}$$

$$t_{\text{calculated}} = 4.1$$

The significance of the calculated *t* statistic is determined by comparing it to a critical value of the *t* statistic at a specified level of significance. This problem has $n - 1 = 17$ degrees of freedom. Using a two-tailed test indicates that the analyst is interested in the mean change in scores being either greater than or less than zero. At the 0.05 level of significance (two-tailed test, 17 degrees of freedom) the critical value for the *t* statistic is 2.1. The calculated value of *t* (4.1) exceeds the critical value. The analyst rejects the null hypothesis of no difference between the MEDS and CAU systems and concludes alternatively that "the CAU is an improvement over MEDS in the tested environment."

If the assumptions are met, the *t*-test should be used to determine the statistical significance of the differences between paired units of analysis. There are four important assumptions. (1) Each component of a pair is assumed to be like its mate in all respects except for the characteristics or attributes measured by the independent and dependent variables. (2) Each pair is assumed to be independent (that is, not affecting and not affected by the characteristics or attributes of any other pair). (3) Each pair is assumed to be randomly selected from the statistical population. (4) The frequency distribution of the dependent variable (the paired differences) in the statistical population is assumed to be a normal distribution. These assumptions should be verified by the analyst. If the assumptions are not met, analysts usually treat the dependent variable as having an ordinal level of measurement and apply the tests discussed in the preceding chapter.

### 11.1.4   Randomization Test for Paired Data

The randomization test can also be applied to paired data. Again, it is a useful alternative to the *t*-test because the analyst is not required to assume normal distributions or constant variance in the statistical populations. However, computational difficulty limits its application to small sample sizes (*n*, the number of pairs $\leq 12$).

Consider the following problem in which there were only a few observations. One very common complaint reported to local government officials is speeding on residential streets. Traffic experts know that speeding ". . . generally occurs on wide streets that have little or no horizontal or vertical curvature so drivers have a long sight distance." Previous literature in the traffic engineering field suggests that narrowing the street width or creating the impression of a narrow street helps reduce traffic speeds. This idea was tested at one site in Orlando, Florida—chosen because of citizen complaints about traffic speed. The road was modified to create the perception of a narrow street. The principal modification was to change the road markings (lanes) to reduce the width of the traffic lanes to 9 feet. Exhibit 11–6 presents before and after data. Is there a statistically significant difference between the mean speeds before and after the treatments?

The dichotomous independent variable separates the cases into two groups—observations made before and observations made after the road narrowing treatment. We want to determine whether the cases were drawn from the same statistical population or from different statistical populations. If all the observa-

## *Exhibit 11–6*

**Traffic Speeds Before and Immediately After Road Modification**

| Unit of analysis: Site | Independent variable: Before and after treatment | |  |
|---|---|---|---|
| | *Before treatment* | *Immediately after treatment* | |
| | Dependent variable: Mean speed (mph) | Dependent variable: Mean speed (mph) | **Difference** |
| 9 A.M. Westbound | 32.1 | 33.0 | +0.9 |
| 9 A.M. Eastbound | 32.2 | 32.9 | +0.7 |
| 1 P.M. Westbound | 32.6 | 32.4 | −0.2 |
| 1 P.M. Eastbound | 33.0 | 31.0 | −2.0 |
| 8 P.M. Westbound | 31.2 | 31.4 | +0.2 |
| 8 P.M. Eastbound | 33.5 | 31.6 | −1.9 |
| | | | Total −2.3 |

tions, whether before or after, were drawn from the same statistical population, then it is merely a matter of chance that some observations were classified as being "before" and others "after." Given the null hypothesis that the net difference between the mean speeds "before" and the mean speeds "after" is 0, the total number of differences that could be obtained by an arrangement of $n$ "before" observations and $n$ "after" observations is $2^n$. With six pairs, there are $2^6 = 64$ possible arrangements.

The analyst could list all 64 arrangements—each arrangement giving rise to a net speed difference. Each arrangement has a probability of one divided by the number of possible outcomes or 1/64. This is a probability distribution and the analyst can examine the "tails" of the distribution—the extreme outcome arrangements—to test the null hypothesis. The analyst will focus on the arrangements that constitute the most extreme 5% (the level of significance—a more stringent criterion would be 1%) of all possible outcomes. The number of outcome arrangements of interest is the product of the level of significance times the number of possible outcomes. (In this example, this is $0.05 \times 64 \approx 3$ outcomes.) If the observed arrangement of measurements is one of the 5% most extreme outcomes, the analyst rejects the null hypothesis of no before–after difference and adopts the alternate hypothesis that the observed cases were drawn from two different statistical populations.

Exhibit 11–7 lists the most extreme arrangements of net differences for this example. The observed net difference in before–after speed of −2.3 mph from Exhibit 11–6 does not fall within the critical region. Therefore, the mean speeds did not differ significantly from what they were before treatment.

## *Exhibit 11–7*

**The Most Extreme Possible Outcomes of Change in Mean Speed**

(1)   $-0.9 - 0.7 - 0.2 - 2.0 - 0.2 - 1.9 = -5.9$

(2)   $-0.9 - 0.7 + 0.2 - 2.0 - 0.2 - 1.9 = -5.5$

   $-0.9 - 0.7 - 0.2 - 2.0 + 0.2 - 1.9 = -5.5$    $\bigg\}$ Critical region

(3)   $-0.9 - 0.7 + 0.2 - 2.0 + 0.2 - 1.9 = -5.1$

(4)   $-0.9 + 0.7 - 0.2 - 2.0 - 0.2 - 1.9 = -4.5$

(5)   $+0.9 - 0.7 - 0.2 - 2.0 - 0.2 - 1.9 = -4.1$

   $-0.9 + 0.7 + 0.2 - 2.0 - 0.2 - 1.9 = -4.1$

   $-0.9 + 0.7 - 0.2 - 2.0 + 0.2 - 1.9 = -4.1$

## 11.2    *The Independent Variable Has More than Two Categories*

### 11.2.1    **Analysis-of-Variance *F* Test**

The *F* test for analysis of variance (ANOVA) is a procedure that tests whether more than two groups differ significantly from one another with respect to some intervally measured dependent characteristic or attribute. The independent variable measures how the units of analysis differ with respect to type, kind, place, or time. Each nominal category is a group. The analyst wishes to determine whether the values of the intervally measured dependent variable are associated with the units of analysis being classified into the identified groups.

Consider the problem of monitoring potential contaminants of ground water in compliance with the Resource Conservation and Recovery Act. Exhibit 11–8 presents hypothetical data for two background wells and one downgradient monitoring well checking for chromium contamination.

The mean chromium concentrations observed in each well were 24.25, 30.88, and 52.50 parts per billion, respectively. The evaluation question at hand is whether these three observation groups could be considered as having been drawn from the same statistical population (the differences between the respective means for the three groups being attributable to random sampling error) or whether there are two or three statistical populations, defined by the well location, and having different chromium concentrations. The null hypothesis is that there is no difference in the average chromium concentration between the three wells. The alternate hypothesis is that the average chromium concentration for at least one of the wells differs significantly from the other two.

The analysis proceeds by calculating two indices of variation—in effect, variance. The term *variation* refers to the numerator of the variance computation—the sum of the squared deviations about the mean (sum of squares). The variance

## Exhibit 11–8

**Chromium Concentration in Groundwater Monitoring Wells**
(hypothetical data)

| Row number | Concentration (parts per billion) | | |
|---|---|---|---|
| | *Background well 1* <br> *j = 1* | *Background well 2* <br> *j = 2* | *Monitoring well* <br> *j = 3* |
| *i* = 1 | 33 | 62 | 60 |
| *i* = 2 | 46 | 35 | 80 |
| *i* = 3 | 22 | 40 | 49 |
| *i* = 4 | 20 | 47 | 70 |
| *i* = 5 | 46 | 8 | 25 |
| *i* = 6 | 15 | 14 | 31 |
| *i* = 7 | 30 | 16 | |
| *i* = 8 | 4 | 25 | |
| *i* = 9 | 13 | | |
| *i* = 10 | 31 | | |
| *i* = 11 | 5 | | |
| *i* = 12 | 26 | | |
| Count | 12 | 8 | 6 |
| Mean | 24.25 | 30.88 | 52.50 |

would be computed by dividing the sum of squares by degrees of freedom. This will be called *mean square*. A within-column variation is obtained by comparing the dependent values in each column to the respective column mean. Then a between-column variation is obtained by comparing the mean of each column to the overall mean—the *grand mean*—of all the data. The within-column variation is principally due to random observation error. The between-column variation is principally due to differences between the identified groups. If the between-column variation is about the same as the within-column variation, the analyst does not reject the null hypothesis that all the units of analysis, regardless of group, were drawn from one statistical population. However, if the between-column variation greatly exceeds the within-column variation—such that the probability of observing the magnitude of the difference by random chance is less than 5%—the analyst rejects the null hypothesis and accepts the alternate conclusion that at least one of the groups has a population mean different from the others—hence, at least one of the groups indicated by the independent variable represents a unique statistical population.

The within-column variation is computed as the sum of the squared devia-tions of each unit of analysis from the mean of its respective group. The result is called the *within-column sum-of-squares* or *error sum-of-squares* (see Exhibit 11–9).

$$\text{Within-column sum-of-squares} = \sum_j \sum_i (y_{ij} - \bar{y}_j)^2$$

where

$y_{ij}$ = value of the observation in the *i*th row and *j*th column.

$\bar{y}_j$ = mean of the *j*th column

$\sum_j \sum_i$ = sum the squared deviations for all observations within a column, then sum over all columns

## Exhibit 11–9

**Computation of Within-Column Sum-of-Squares**

| Row number | Concentration (parts per billion) | | |
|---|---|---|---|
| | Background well 1 *j = 1* | Background well 2 *j = 2* | Monitoring well *j = 3* |
| i = 1 | $(33 - 24.25)^2 = 76.5625$ | $(62 - 30.875)^2 = 968.7656$ | $(60 - 52.50)^2 = 56.2500$ |
| i = 2 | $(46 - 24.25)^2 = 473.0625$ | $(35 - 30.875)^2 = 17.0156$ | $(80 - 52.50)^2 = 756.2500$ |
| i = 3 | $(22 - 24.25)^2 = 5.0625$ | $(40 - 30.875)^2 = 83.2656$ | $(49 - 52.50)^2 = 12.2500$ |
| i = 4 | $(20 - 24.25)^2 = 18.0625$ | $(47 - 30.875)^2 = 260.0156$ | $(70 - 52.50)^2 = 306.2500$ |
| i = 5 | $(46 - 24.25)^2 = 473.0625$ | $(8 - 30.875)^2 = 523.2656$ | $(25 - 52.50)^2 = 756.2500$ |
| i = 6 | $(15 - 24.25)^2 = 85.5625$ | $(14 - 30.875)^2 = 284.7656$ | $(31 - 52.50)^2 = 462.2500$ |
| i = 7 | $(30 - 24.25)^2 = 33.0625$ | $(16 - 30.875)^2 = 221.2656$ | |
| i = 8 | $(4 - 24.25)^2 = 410.0625$ | $(25 - 30.875)^2 = 34.5156$ | |
| i = 9 | $(13 - 24.25)^2 = 126.5625$ | | |
| i = 10 | $(31 - 24.25)^2 = 45.5625$ | | |
| i = 11 | $(5 - 24.25)^2 = 370.5625$ | | |
| i = 12 | $(26 - 24.25)^2 = 3.0625$ | | |
| Total | 2,120.25 | 2,392.88 | 2,349.50 |

$$\text{Within-column sum-of-squares} = \sum_j \sum_i (y_{ij} - \bar{y}_j)^2$$
$$= 2,120.25 + 2,392.88 + 2,349.50$$
$$= 6,862.62$$
$$df = (n = \text{number of columns}) = 26 - 3 = 23$$

The between-column variation is computed as the sum of the squared deviations between the mean of each group and the mean of all observations regardless of group, the grand mean. In the summation the squared deviation for each group is weighted by the number of units of analysis in that group. The result is called the *between-column sum-of-squares* or *factor sum-of-squares* (see Exhibit 11–10).

$$\text{Between-column sum-of-squares} = \sum_j [n_j(\bar{y}_j - \bar{Y})^2]$$

where

$n_j$ = number of rows (sample size in the calculation of each column mean)

$\bar{y}_j$ = mean of the $j$th column

$\bar{Y}$ = grand mean of the dependent variable

$\sum_j$ = sum over all columns

The next step is to create a table summarizing the calculations (see Exhibit 11–11). For each source of variation (between or within columns), the analyst lists the degrees of freedom and the sum of squares. Then the analyst computes the between-columns and within-columns mean squares by dividing the respective sum of squares by the degrees of freedom. The within-column mean square is the variance associated with chance observational error. The between-column mean square is the variance potentially due to differences between the groups defined by the independent variable.

## *Exhibit 11–10*

**Computation of Between-Columns Sum-of-Squares**

| Concentration (parts per billion) | | |
|---|---|---|
| $j = 1$ <br> $n_1(\bar{y}_1 - \bar{Y})^2$ | $j = 2$ <br> $n_2(\bar{y}_2 - \bar{Y})^2$ | $j = 3$ <br> $n_3(\bar{y}_3 - \bar{Y})^2$ |
| $12(24.25 - 32.81)^2 = 878.81$ | $8(30.88 - 32.81)^2 = 29.88$ | $6(52.50 - 32.81)^2 = 2{,}326.72$ |

$$\text{Between-column sum-of-squares} = \sum_j [n_j(\bar{y}_j - \bar{Y})^2]$$
$$= 878.81 + 29.88 + 2{,}326.72$$
$$= 3{,}235.41$$
$$df = (\text{number of columns} - 1) = 3 - 1 = 2$$

## Exhibit 11–11

**Analysis of Variance Summary of Results for Well Contamination**

| Source of variation | Degrees of freedom df | Sum of squares SS | Mean square MS | F Statistic |
|---|---|---|---|---|
| Factor (between columns) | 2 | 3,235.41 | 1,617.71 | 5.42 |
| Error (within columns) | 23 | 6,862.62 | 298.38 | |
| Total | 25 | 10,098.04 | | |

$$\text{Mean square between columns} = \frac{\text{Between column sum-of-squares}}{\text{Between column degrees of freedom}} = \frac{3,235.41}{2} = 1,617.71$$

$$\text{Mean square within columns} = \frac{\text{Within columns sum-of-squares}}{\text{Within columns degrees of freedom}} = \frac{6,862.62}{23} = 298.38$$

Then the test statistic, $F$, is calculated as the ratio of the between-columns mean square to the within-columns mean square.

$$F = \frac{\text{Mean square between columns}}{\text{Mean square within columns}} = \frac{1,617.71}{298.38} = 5.42$$

Use the $F$ statistic to determine whether the between-columns variance is significantly greater than the within-columns variance. The $F$ statistic has a unique distribution for each combination of between-columns degrees of freedom and within-columns degrees of freedom (see Exhibit 11–12). (The between-columns degrees of freedom is sometimes referred to as "degrees of freedom numerator" and the within-columns degrees of freedom is called "degrees of freedom denominator.") A table of critical values for the $F$ statistic is presented as Appendix G. The calculated value of the $F$ statistic for this example is 5.42. From the table, the critical value of $F$ for a problem with 2 degrees-of-freedom numerator and 23 degrees-of-freedom denominator is approximately 3.42 at the 0.05 level of significance. Since the calculated value exceeds the critical value, the analyst rejects the null hypothesis and concludes that there is a statistically significant difference among the three wells in terms of chromium concentration.

## Exhibit 11–12

**F Distributions**

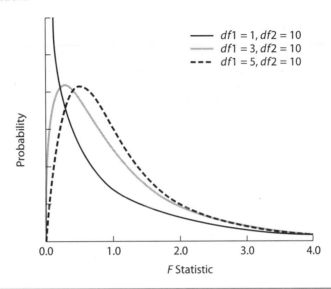

The analysis-of-variance $F$ test indicates whether or not there is a statistically significant difference among the nominal groups. It does not indicate the *manner* in which the groups are related to the dependent variable—only that they are related. Further, the test does not indicate which groups are statistically significantly different from the others. The analyst could repeatedly apply the two-variable $t$ test to compare each group mean with every other group mean or could employ another set of statistical procedures (sometimes called "postmortem tests" because they are used after an $F$ test has shown statistical significance to systematically assess the differences between each group mean.

The analysis-of-variance $F$ test is the most powerful test of the differences between groups. However, it has several important assumptions that need to be checked and verified by the analyst for each problem in which ANOVA is employed. The dependent variable must have an interval level of measurement. The units of analysis must have been randomly selected so that the value of the dependent variable for any one unit of analysis is not contingent upon the value for any other unit of analysis. There are two more difficult assumptions. For each group, the values of the dependent variable must approximate a normal distribution and the variances for the respective distributions within each group must be approximately the same. (This condition—constant variance—is called *homoscedasticity*.) Small departures from strictly meeting these latter assumptions will have a negligible effect on the value of $F$, particularly if the sample size is large. However, clear violations of the assumptions should lead the analyst to employ alternative techniques or acquire more data. One useful alternative method is the Kruskal–Wallis test introduced in Chapter 9.

## 11.2.2    Eta-Squared Statistic

The appropriate indicator for strength-of-association for the interval-nominal (dependent-independent) problem is the eta-squared, $\eta^2$, statistic. Eta-squared is easy to calculate if an ANOVA summary table has been obtained. It is the ratio of the between-column sum of squares to the total (between + within) sum of squares. Thus, eta-squared is the proportion of the total variance of the dependent variable that is accounted for by the nominal groups defined by the independent variable.[5]

$$\eta^2 = \frac{\text{Between-column sum-of-squares}}{\text{Between-column sum-of-squares} + \text{Within-column sum-of-squares}}$$

$$\eta^2 = \frac{\text{Between-column sum-of-squares}}{\text{Total sum-of-squares}}$$

$$\eta^2 = \frac{3235.41}{10098.04}$$

$$\eta^2 = 0.32$$

The eta-squared statistic for the well-monitoring example indicates that 32% of the variance in the 26 measurements is explained by the three well locations.

---

[5]The following equation is an alternative means of calculating $\eta^2$ for *j* groups:

$$\eta^2 = 1 - \frac{(\sum y^2) - [n_1(\bar{y}_1)^2 + n_2(\bar{y}_2)^2 + n_3(\bar{y}_3)^2 + \cdots + n_j(\bar{y}_j)^2]}{(\sum y^2) - n(\bar{Y})^2}$$

where

$\sum y^2$ = sum of the squared values of the dependent variable for the whole sample

$n_j$ = number of observations in the *j*th group

$n$ = sample size

$\bar{y}_j$ = mean value of the dependent variable in the *j*th group

$\bar{Y}$ = grand mean of the dependent variable

# Homework Exercises

**11-1** Do states in which the governor has line-item budget veto power tend to spend less per capita than states in which the governor does not have this power? Examine the data in Exhibit HW9–1A. Use the two-variable *t*-test.

$t_{C \text{ calculated}} = 1.49$   $t_{C \text{ critical two-tail}} = 2.25$

Difference in per capita spending is not statistically significant

**11-2** Exhibit HW11–2A summarizes some results of a survey of public employees regarding their feelings that pay may be a function of gender in the federal public service.[1] Opinion is measured on a five-point scale: 1 = "agree," 2 = "somewhat agree," 3 = "neutral," 4 = "somewhat disagree," 5 = "disagree." The analysts treated the variables as having an interval level of measurement. Do men and women express the same attitudes in response to the survey questions?

## Exhibit HW11–2A

**Public Employee Attitudes toward Pay as a Function of Gender in the Federal Public Service**

| Attitude indicators | Men | Women |
|---|---|---|
| 1. "All-in-all, I'm satisfied with my pay." [1 = disagree, 5 = agree] | $\bar{y} = 3.09$ $\sigma = 1.32$ $n = 8,206$ | $\bar{y} = 3.52$ $\sigma = 1.22$ $n = 854$ |
| 2. "Considering the skills and effort I put into my work, I'm satisfied with my pay." [1 = disagree, 5 = agree] | $\bar{y} = 2.86$ $\sigma = 1.29$ $n = 8,212$ | $\bar{y} = 3.21$ $\sigma = 1.26$ $n = 855$ |

Indicator 1: $t_C = 9.7$   Indicator 2: $t_C = 7.7$

There is a statistically significant difference between the attitudes expressed by men and women.

---

[1] Brent S. Steel and Nicholas P. Lovrich, Jr., "Comparable Worth: The Problematic Politicization of a Public Personnel Issue," *Public Personnel Management* 16, no. 1, (Spring 1987): 23–46.

**11-3** Exhibit HW11–3A presents additional data about the road-narrowing experiment described in this chapter.[2]

   **a.** Is there a statistically significant difference in the mean speeds before and after the treatments?

   **b.** On the basis of these results, write a summary conclusion and recommendation for this project.

## *Exhibit HW11–3A*

**Traffic Speeds: Road-Narrowing Experiment, Orlando, Florida**

| Site | Before treatment | Mean Speeds (miles per hour) | |
| --- | --- | --- | --- |
| | | *Immediately after treatment* | *Approximately 2 weeks after treatment* |
| Plaza Terrace | | | |
| 9 A.M. westbound | 32.1 | 33.0 | 33.0 |
| 9 A.M. eastbound | 32.2 | 32.9 | 33.6 |
| 1 P.M. westbound | 32.6 | 32.4 | 32.6 |
| 1 P.M. eastbound | 33.0 | 31.0 | 34.2 |
| 8 P.M. westbound | 31.2 | 31.4 | 31.5 |
| 8 P.M. eastbound | 33.5 | 31.6 | 33.1 |
| South Lake Orlando Parkway | | | |
| 7 A.M. westbound | 32.5 | 35.2 | 33.8 |
| 7 A.M. eastbound | 35.1 | 35.4 | 35.6 |
| 3 P.M. westbound | 35.9 | 36.9 | 36.1 |
| 3 P.M. eastbound | 33.6 | 35.1 | 34.0 |
| 6 P.M. westbound | 37.7 | 36.8 | 35.6 |
| 6 P.M. eastbound | 33.9 | 33.4 | 34.4 |

   **a.** See Exhibit HW11–3B.

The number of possible outcomes in the critical region is 3 (following the same computation as in the chapter example). Using a one-tailed test for a decrease in speed, the most extreme possible outcomes are

-------

[2]Lum, "Use of Road Markings."

(1) $-0.9 -1.4 -0.0 -1.2 -0.3 -0.4 = -4.2$

(2) $-0.9 -1.4 +0.0 -1.2 +0.3 -0.4 = -3.6$

(3) $-0.9 -1.4 +0.0 -1.2 -0.3 +0.4 = -3.4$

There is no statistically significant decrease in speed between the before– and 2 weeks after–observations. Actually, if we had turned this problem around, a one-tailed test shows a statistically significant *increase* in the observed average traffic speed on Plaza Terrace.

## Exhibit HW11–3B

**Traffic Speeds before and 2 Weeks after Road Modification**

| | Independent Variable: Before or after treatment | | |
| --- | --- | --- | --- |
| | *Dependent variable mean speed (mph)* | | |
| **Unit of analysis site** | Before treatment | 2 Weeks after treatment | Difference |
| Plaza Terrace | | | |
| 9 A.M. westbound | 32.1 | 33.0 | +0.9 |
| 9 A.M. eastbound | 32.2 | 33.6 | +1.4 |
| 1 P.M. westbound | 32.6 | 32.6 | 0.0 |
| 1 P.M. eastbound | 33.0 | 34.2 | +1.2 |
| 8 P.M. westbound | 31.2 | 31.5 | +0.3 |
| 8 P.M. eastbound | 33.5 | 33.1 | −0.4 |
| | | | Total: +3.4 |

b.  Attempts to reduce average traffic speeds by road-narrowing designs were unsuccessful. The marked lanes may have aided the driver's perception of the road and contributed to increase in speed over the two-week period of the experiment. Traditional speed control methods (enforcement and appropriate speed zoning) are recommended.

**11-4**  Proponents of the death penalty for criminal punishment have sometimes argued that it would help reduce the crime rate. Exhibits HW11–4A, HW11–4B, and HW11–4C present data regarding the crime rates in 14 countries one year before, one year after, and five years after the abolition of the death penalty.[3] Is there a statistically significant change in the crime rate?

---

[3]Dane Archer and Rosemary Gartner, *Violence and Crime in Cross-National Perspective* (New Haven, CT: Yale University Press, 1984), pp. 133–135.

# Exhibit HW11–4A

**Crime Rates One Year before Abolition of the Death Penalty**

| Jurisdiction (date of abolition, indicator) | Crimes per 100,000 population one-year pre-abolition | | | | | |
|---|---|---|---|---|---|---|
| | *H* | *M* | *R* | *A* | *Ro* | *T* |
| Austria (1968, e) | 0.72 | 0.33 | 7.96 | 40.36 | 8.16 | 762.85 |
| England and Wales (1965, a) | 0.36 | 0.23 | 1.09 | 46.19 | 6.48 | 1,487.36 |
| Finland (1949, a) | 1.05 | 3.66 | 2.02 | 26.53 | 11.99 | 244.63 |
| Israel (1954, a) | 4.00 | — | — | 156.61 | 7.58 | 883.09 |
| Italy (1890, a) | 13.30 | — | — | — | — | — |
| Sweden (1921, b) | 0.43 | — | 0.31 | 44.03 | 43.72 | — |
| Switzerland (1942, d) | 45.25 | — | 25.99 | 45.25 | — | 207.75 |
| Canada (1967, a) | 1.10 | 0.71 | — | 25.42 | 39.73 | 102.14 |
| Denmark (1930, c) | 33.89 | — | 45.69 | 33.89 | — | 1,388.68 |
| Netherlands Antilles (1957, a) | 13.19 | — | 112.09 | — | 152.75 | 402.20 |
| New Zealand (1961, b) | 0.04 | — | 0.72 | 42.29 | 1.77 | 166.65 |
| Norway (1905, b) | 0.35 | — | 0.22 | 14.61 | — | 77.86 |

*Notes:* H = homicide; M = manslaughter; R = rape; A = assault; Ro = robbery; T = theft.
a = homicide offenses known; b = murder, manslaughter, or homicide convictions; c = violent offenses known; d = violent offenses convictions; e = criminal statistics.

# Exhibit HW11–4B

**Crime Rates One Year after Abolition of the Death Penalty**

| Jurisdiction (date of abolition, indicator) | Crimes per 100,000 population one-year pre-abolition | | | | | |
|---|---|---|---|---|---|---|
| | *H* | *M* | *R* | *A* | *Ro* | *T* |
| Austria (1968, e) | 0.71 | 0.41 | 8.94 | 39.66 | 7.46 | 888.68 |
| England and Wales (1965, a) | 0.35 | 0.36 | 1.34 | 52.15 | 9.32 | 1,616.98 |
| Finland (1949, a) | 0.72 | 2.69 | 3.94 | 23.85 | 6.46 | 140.43 |
| Israel (1954, a) | 1.72 | — | — | 218.94 | 3.43 | 827.35 |
| Italy (1890, a) | 12.94 | — | — | — | — | — |
| Sweden (1921, b) | 0.15 | — | 0.13 | 29.49 | 28.03 | — |
| Switzerland (1942, d) | 35.65 | — | 29.01 | 35.65 | — | 221.19 |
| Canada (1967, a) | 1.52 | — | — | — | — | — |
| Denmark (1930, c) | 35.68 | — | 45.76 | 35.68 | — | 1,504.70 |
| Netherlands Antilles (1957, a) | 20.32 | — | 56.15 | — | 231.02 | 456.15 |
| New Zealand (1961, b)* | 0.08 | — | 0.80 | 53.80 | 1.01 | 159.80 |
| Norway (1905, b) | 0.39 | — | 0.30 | 12.70 | 0.77 | 67.25 |

*Notes:* H = homicide; M = manslaughter; R = rape; A = assault; Ro = robbery; T = theft.
a = homicide offenses known; b = murder, manslaughter, or homicide convictions; c = violent offenses known; d = violent offenses convictions; e = criminal statistics; * = this 100% increase reflects a change from 1 to 2 cases.

## Exhibit HW11–4C

**Crime Rates Five Years after Abolition of the Death Penalty**

| Jurisdiction (date of abolition, indicator) | Crimes per 100,000 population five years post-abolition | | | | | |
|---|---|---|---|---|---|---|
| | *H* | *M* | *R* | *A* | *Ro* | *T* |
| Austria (1968, e) | 0.93 | 0.45 | 8.38 | 41.64 | 10.97 | 1,085.97 |
| England and Wales (1965, a) | 0.38 | 0.37 | 1.80 | 80.15 | 12.80 | 1,867.16 |
| Finland (1949, a) | 0.95 | 1.81 | 3.75 | 18.52 | 5.27 | 111.00 |
| Israel (1954, a) | 1.65 | — | — | 432.12 | 2.67 | 940.85 |
| Italy (1890, a) | — | — | — | — | — | — |
| Sweden (1921, b) | 0.20 | — | 0.21 | 35.14 | 33.04 | — |
| Switzerland (1942, d) | — | — | 34.59 | 43.10 | — | 202.43 |
| Canada (1967, a) | 2.19 | — | — | — | — | — |
| Denmark (1930, c) | — | — | 23.84 | 37.62 | 1.30 | 1,602.03 |
| Netherlands Antilles (1957, a) | 17.17 | — | 80.81 | — | 276.26 | 394.44 |
| New Zealand (1961, b) | 0.22 | — | 1.12 | 69.81 | 0.90 | 193.81 |
| Norway (1905, b) | 0.59 | — | 0.21 | 11.71 | 0.59 | 65.05 |

*Notes:* H = homicide; M = manslaughter; R = rape; A = assault; Ro = robbery; T = theft.
a = homicide offenses known; b = murder, manslaughter, or homicide convictions;
c = violent offenses known; d = violent offenses convictions; e = criminal statistics

The comarison of homicide rates before and after abolition is shown in Exhibit HW11–4D.

Homicide rates: one year pre-abolition versus one year post-abolition

$$t = \frac{\bar{x} - \mu}{\frac{s}{\sqrt{n}}}$$

$$\bar{x} = \bar{d} = 0.287$$

$$s = 3.70$$

$$\mu = 0$$

$$t_{calculated} = -0.27$$

$$df = 11$$

$$t_{critical\ 0.05} = -2.2$$

## Exhibit HW11–4D

**Homicide Rates before and after Abolition of the Death Penalty**

| Jurisdiction | Homicides per 100,000 pop. | | | Difference One year pre- to one year post-abolition | Difference One year pre- to five years post-abolition |
|---|---|---|---|---|---|
| | One year pre-abolition | One year post-abolition | Five years post-abolition | | |
| Austria | 0.72 | 0.71 | 0.93 | −0.01 | 0.21 |
| England and Wales | 0.36 | 0.35 | 0.38 | −0.01 | 0.02 |
| Finland | 1.05 | 0.72 | 0.95 | −0.33 | −0.10 |
| Israel | 4.00 | 1.72 | 1.65 | −2.28 | −2.35 |
| Italy | 13.30 | 12.94 | — | −0.36 | — |
| Sweden | 0.43 | 0.15 | 0.20 | −0.28 | −0.23 |
| Switzerland | 45.25 | 35.65 | — | −9.60 | — |
| Canada | 1.10 | 1.52 | 2.19 | 0.42 | 1.09 |
| Denmark | 33.89 | 35.68 | — | 1.79 | — |
| Netherlands Antilles | 13.19 | 20.32 | 17.17 | 7.13 | 3.98 |
| New Zealand | 0.04 | 0.08 | 0.22 | 0.04 | 0.18 |
| Norway | 0.35 | 0.39 | 0.59 | 0.04 | 0.24 |
| Mean | | | | −0.287 | 0.338 |
| Standard deviation | | | | 3.70 | 1.65 |

Homicide rates: one year pre-abolition versus five years post-abolition

$$t_{calculated} = 0.61$$

$$df = 8$$

$$t_{critical\ 0.05} = 2.3$$

**11-5**  Consider, again, the situation describing layoffs at a manufacturing plant (Exhibit HW9–3A). Do these data support a prima facie charge of age discrimination? Treat the variable "age" as having an interval level of measurement.

$$t_{C\ calculated} = -0.89$$

$$t_{C\ critical} = -2.23$$

The mean age of the employees laid off does not differ significantly from the mean age of the employees not laid off. Therefore, the data do not support a prima facie charge of age discrimination.

**11-6** "San Francisco's public transit system raises only 22 percent of its operating expenses at the fare box—a rate that falls short of the national average—in part due to broken fare boxes and riders who cheat the system, city officials acknowledge.... Last year, [Muni's 28] fare inspectors issued about 9,500 citations, mainly for fare evasion.... A survey conducted in 2005 on the 30-Stockton, one of the busiest routes in the system, found that the average bus collected $376.27 a day when fare inspectors weren't present and $436 a day when they were."[4] Exhibit HW11–6A shows hypothetical data for one month during which fare inspectors were supervised for 10 days and were unsupervised for 20 days.

## Exhibit HW11–6A

**Fare Collections**

| Supervised | Unsupervised |
|---|---|
| $490.87 | $379.29 |
| $519.36 | $378.12 |
| $478.55 | $410.08 |
| $433.09 | $274.59 |
| $456.82 | $370.22 |
| $413.94 | $332.80 |
| $432.09 | $412.56 |
| $355.31 | $322.62 |
| $383.65 | $339.19 |
| $396.29 | $343.99 |
| | $436.42 |
| | $372.07 |
| | $384.33 |
| | $341.63 |
| | $405.16 |
| | $415.89 |
| | $407.09 |
| | $298.23 |
| | $456.28 |
| | $444.88 |

$$t_{C\ calculated} = 3.06$$
$$t_{C\ critical} = 2.2$$

The fare collections differ significantly.

[4]Rachel Gordon, "No Fare: Cheats on Muni," *San Francisco Chronicle*, 27 February 2007.

# CHAPTER 12

# Going Straight: Two-Variable Evaluation—Interval–Interval Measures

| | |
|---|---|
| Kind of problem | *Evaluation* |
| Number of variables | *Two* |
| Level of measurement | *Variable 1, interval* |
| | *Variable 2, interval* |

This chapter continues the study of evaluation problems involving two variables. Now situations in which both the dependent variable and the independent variable have an interval level of measurement will be examined. The interval–interval situation is very important. As listed in Exhibit 12–1, regression analysis will be used to evaluate the nature of the relationship between the independent and dependent variables. Correlation analysis evaluates the *strength of association* and *direction of association* between the variables.

"Direction of association" is a new concept. A positive direction of association means that the value of the dependent variable increases as the value of the independent variable increases. If the value of the dependent variable decreases with an increase in the independent variable, the direction of association is negative. Direction of association is indicated by the sign of the *b* statistic.

The evaluation problem for two interval variables—an independent variable, *x*, and a dependent variable, *y*—occurs frequently in public administration. A few examples are listed in Exhibit 12–2. The analysis centers on estimating the nature of the relationship between the variables. If there is an association between the two variables, *y* will tend to change as *x* changes and the value of *y* will be associated in a regular, consistent way with the value of *x*. Regression analysis is the process of explaining the association by determining the mathematical equation of a curve (in the simplest case—a straight line) that best approximates the regular change in *y* as a function of *x* (fits the data). The regression equation models the

**269**

## Exhibit 12–1

**Two-Variable Evaluation—Interval–Interval Measures**

| Dependent variable | | Independent variable: Interval level of measurement |
|---|---|---|
| Interval level of measurement | Strength of association | Coefficient of determination $r^2$ |
| | Statistical significance | Linear regression $t$-test on the $b$ statistic |
| | Direction of association | Sign of the $b$ statistic |

relationship. It shows how $y$ tends to change as $x$ changes. Correlation analysis is the process of determining the degree to which values of the dependent variable are accounted for (explained) by values of the independent variable. If the regression relationship is a good fit to the data, the correlation is strong. If the differences between the regression and the data are large, the correlation is weak.

## 12.1 Regression Analysis

Although many kinds of mathematical equations could potentially be used to model the relationship between two variables, the simplest and most useful equation will be that of a straight line. A straight-line model is used for several

## Exhibit 12–2

**Possible Relationships between Two Interval Variables**

Income varies with education

Nitrous oxide atmospheric pollution varies with number of automobiles

Number of alcohol related accidents varies with the legal drinking age in the state

Nursing hours in a hospital varies with patient census

School funds vary with number of students

Reservoir depth varies with rainfall in watershed

Salary varies with seniority

Peak yearly electrical demand varies with population

Peak daily electrical demand varies with temperature

Cost varies with number of employees

Sales tax revenue varies with sales tax rate

Blood alcohol level varies with alcohol consumption

reasons: (1) Many relationships between two variables have been observed to be essentially linear. (2) A linear model tends to provide a conservative description of an association between two variables (reduce the chances of falsely concluding that there is a relationship when, in fact, the variables are not related). (3) Theoretical models in politics and public administration are often so general that the analyst does not know the nature of a possible nonlinear specification. (4) When viewing a scatterplot, sometimes either there are so few observations or the spread of the data is so large that no alternative to a straight-line model is readily apparent.

The analyst derives a straight-line mathematical model that best fits the observed data. The characteristics of the model will be compared against the expectation (null hypothesis) that there is no relationship between the two variables. If there were indeed no relationship between the variables, the straight line that would best account for the values of the dependent variable would be a horizontal line through $\bar{y}$, the mean of the values of the dependent variable. Any other fitted line will be compared against this horizontal line to test for a statistically significant relationship.

## *Quick Concepts: Linear Models*

A straight line, showing the relationship between two variables, is drawn in two dimensions. The values of the dependent variable, $y$, are arrayed vertically and the values of the independent variable, $x$, are arrayed horizontally. A straight line is specified by two parameters: its $y$-intercept (also called the "constant") and its slope. The $y$-intercept, designated by the symbol $a$, is the value of $y$ where the line crosses the $y$-axis (the vertical line through the origin where $x = 0$ and $y = 0$). The slope of a line, designated by the symbol $b$, is the amount of change in $y$ per unit change in $x$: a slope of $+1.0$ means that $y$ increases one unit for each one-unit increase in the value of $x$; a slope of $+0.33$ means that $y$ increases 0.33 units with a one-unit increase in $x$; and a slope of $-1.5$ means that the value of $y$ decreases by 1.5 units for each one-unit increase in $x$. An equivalent definition of the slope of a line is to define it as the ratio of the rise of the line to the run of the line—the ratio of the vertical change to the horizontal change. When drawing a straight line, the run is always to the right. Therefore, the rise will be up if the slope is a positive number and down if the slope is a negative number.

$$y\text{-intercept: } a = \text{the value of } y \text{ when } x = 0$$

$$\text{Slope: } b = \frac{\text{change in } y}{\text{one-unit increase in } x} = \frac{\text{rise}}{\text{run}}$$

*(continued)*

The equation of a straight line is

$$y = a + bx$$

where

$y$ = value of the dependent variable

$x$ = value of the independent variable

$a$ = the $y$-intercept

$b$ = the slope: the change in the value of the dependent variable with a one-unit increase in the value of the independent variable, also called linear regression coefficient

Exhibit 12–3 shows three straight lines. The $x$ and $y$ scales indicate both positive and negative values. The graph is divided into four quadrants with the

*(continued)*

## *Exhibit 12–3*

**Three Lines**

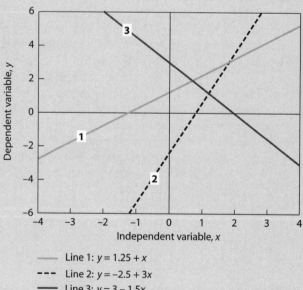

Line 1: $y = 1.25 + x$

Line 2: $y = -2.5 + 3x$

Line 3: $y = 3 - 1.5x$

origin ($x = 0$, $y = 0$) in the center. Line 1, $y = 1.25 + x$, intercepts the $y$-axis at $y = 1.25$. Its slope is $+1.0$, so the line rises to the right. At $x = 1$, the value of $y$ is 2.25. At $x = 4$, the value of $y$ is 5.25. Going in the other direction, Line 1 crosses the $x$-axis (the value of $y$ is 0 at this point) at $x = -1.25$. Line 2, $y = -2.5 + 3x$, intercepts the $y$-axis below the origin at $y = -2.5$. The value of its slope, $+3.0$, is greater than that of Line 1 so it rises at a steeper angle to the right. Line 3, $y = 3 - 1.5x$, has a negative slope, $b = -1.5$. The $y$-intercept, $a$, is $+3.0$. The value of $y$ decreases 1.5 units with each one-unit increase in the value of $x$. Thus, at $x = 2$ the value of $y$ is 0 and this is the point where the line crosses the $x$-axis. Mathematically, straight lines are infinitely long and $x$ and $y$ can take on positive or negative values. However, in most cases of interest to us, $x$ and $y$ have only positive values. Therefore, the origin is usually placed in the lower left-hand corner and the upper right-hand quadrant is used.

American economist Arthur Okun (1928–1980) advised several presidential administrations, and served as chairman of the President's Council of Economic Advisers in 1968. His name is associated with a "law" (a rule-of-thumb economic principle) he propounded in 1962. Okun's Law states that to avoid the waste of unemployment, an economy must continually expand and that economic growth and unemployment are related such that decreases in unemployment are associated with increased productivity, and increasing unemployment with declining productivity. Is GDP change associated with the unemployment rate? Consider the data in Exhibit 12–4 listing the annual change in the U.S. gross domestic product as a dependent variable versus the annual change in the U.S. unemployment rate, as an independent variable, for the years 1990 to 2004.

Exhibit 12–5 shows a scatterplot. It looks like there's an inverse relationship. If unemployment increases, GDP decreases.

The next step is to determine a "best fit" straight-line model for the data. The scatter of the data is such that no straight line will fit all the data points. The observed values of the dependent variable, $y$, and estimated values of $y$ provided by a straight-line model will differ. These differences (sometimes called "errors") are called *residuals*. Out of an infinite number of straight lines that could be drawn through the data, the best fit straight line will be defined as the one line that minimizes the sum of the squared residuals. This is the *least-squares regression line*.

The slope of the least-squares regression line, $b$, is a statistic called the linear regression coefficient. It is specified by the following formula in which the numerator represents the covariance of $x$ and $y$ and the denominator is the variance of $x$:

$$b = \frac{\sum[(x_i - \bar{x})(y_i - \bar{y})]}{\sum[(x_i - \bar{x})^2]}$$

## Exhibit 12–4

**GDP v. Unemployment**

| Year | Independent variable<br>x<br>*Change in unemployment rate<br>from the previous year<br>(percentage points)* | Dependent variable<br>y<br>*Change in gross domestic product<br>from the previous year<br>(percentage points)* |
|---|---|---|
| 1990 | 0.36 | 1.9 |
| 1991 | 1.23 | −0.2 |
| 1992 | 0.64 | 3.3 |
| 1993 | −0.58 | 2.7 |
| 1994 | −0.81 | 4.0 |
| 1995 | −0.51 | 2.5 |
| 1996 | −0.18 | 3.7 |
| 1997 | −0.47 | 4.5 |
| 1998 | −0.43 | 4.2 |
| 1999 | −0.28 | 4.4 |
| 2000 | −0.21 | 3.7 |
| 2001 | 0.78 | 0.8 |
| 2002 | 0.99 | 1.9 |
| 2003 | 0.20 | 3.0 |
| 2004 | −0.50 | 4.4 |

## Exhibit 12–5

**Scatterplot: GDP v. Unemployment**

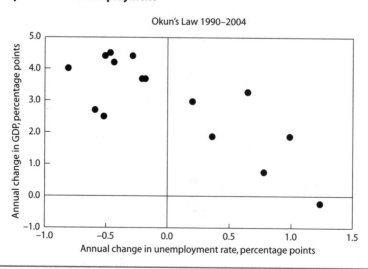

An equivalent computational formula for the linear regression coefficient is

$$b = \frac{n\sum(x_i \cdot y_i) - \sum x_i \cdot \sum y_i}{n\sum(x_i)^2 - (\sum x_i)^2}$$

Exhibit 12–6 shows the intermediate calculations.

$$b = \frac{15 \cdot (-9.2) - 0.23 \cdot 44.8}{15 \cdot 5.8 - (0.23)^2}$$

$$b = -1.72$$

# *Exhibit 12–6*

**Computations of $x \cdot y$, $x^2$, and $y^2$**

| Year | Independent variable<br>$x$<br>*Change in unemployment rate from the previous year (percentage points)* | Dependent variable<br>$y$<br>*Change in gross domestic product from the previous year (percentage points)* | $x \cdot y$ | $x^2$ | $y^2$ |
|---|---|---|---|---|---|
| 1990 | 0.36 | 1.9 | 0.681 | 0.128 | 3.610 |
| 1991 | 1.23 | −0.2 | −0.247 | 1.521 | 0.040 |
| 1992 | 0.64 | 3.3 | 2.118 | 0.412 | 10.890 |
| 1993 | −0.58 | 2.7 | −1.575 | 0.340 | 7.290 |
| 1994 | −0.81 | 4.0 | −3.233 | 0.653 | 16.000 |
| 1995 | −0.51 | 2.5 | −1.271 | 0.258 | 6.250 |
| 1996 | −0.18 | 3.7 | −0.678 | 0.034 | 13.690 |
| 1997 | −0.47 | 4.5 | −2.100 | 0.218 | 20.250 |
| 1998 | −0.43 | 4.2 | −1.820 | 0.188 | 17.640 |
| 1999 | −0.28 | 4.4 | −1.247 | 0.080 | 19.360 |
| 2000 | −0.21 | 3.7 | −0.771 | 0.043 | 13.690 |
| 2001 | 0.78 | 0.8 | 0.620 | 0.601 | 0.640 |
| 2002 | 0.99 | 1.9 | 1.884 | 0.983 | 3.610 |
| 2003 | 0.20 | 3.0 | 0.600 | 0.040 | 9.000 |
| 2004 | −0.50 | 4.4 | −2.200 | 0.250 | 19.360 |
| Total | 0.23 | 44.8 | −9.2 | 5.8 | 161.3 |
| Mean | 0.02 | 2.99 | | | |

The calculated value of the $b$ statistic, the slope, is $-1.72$. This means that a one percentage point increase in the unemployment rate was typically accompanied by a decrease of 1.72 percentage points in the gross domestic product.

One of the important characteristics of the least-squares regression line is that it passes through the point described by the mean of the $x$ variable, $\bar{x}$, and the mean of the $y$ variable, $\bar{y}$. Knowing this, and having calculated a value for the slope, the value of the $y$-intercept, $a$, can be calculated.

Thus:

$$\bar{y} = a + b\bar{x}$$

and

$$a = \frac{\sum y_i - b\sum x_i}{n}$$

Using the previously calculated value of the slope, $b = -1.72$, and the values of $\bar{x}$ and $\bar{y}$ for this example, the constant in the regression equation, $a$, the $y$-intercept, is calculated as 3.01.

$$a = \frac{\sum y_i - b\sum x_i}{n}$$

$$a = \frac{44.8 - (-1.72) \cdot (0.23)}{13}$$

$$a = 3.01$$

Having calculated values for the $a$ and $b$ statistics, the equation for the least-squares regression can be written as

$$y = 3.01 - 1.72x$$

It is common practice to superimpose the least-squares regression line on the data scatterplot. When graphing the regression line, first locate the $y$-intercept, $a$. Then recognize that the slope, $b$, is the amount of change in the value of the $y$ variable for a unit change in the value of the $x$ variable.

$$b = \frac{\Delta y}{\Delta x}$$

where

$$\Delta x = 1$$

In the case of the regression line $y = 3.01 - 1.72x$, the line will go through the $y$-intercept point $(0, 3.01)$, through the point defined by the mean of $x$ and the mean of $y$, $\bar{x}$, $\bar{y}$ (0.02, 2.99), through (1.0, 1.29), and through (−0.5, 3.87). The regression line can be drawn on the scatterplot once any two convenient points are located, shown in Exhibits 12–7 and 12–8.

If there is no relationship between the two variables, then the least-squares regression line will be no better at estimating a value for $y$ given a value of $x$ than simply using the mean of the values of the dependent variable. On a scatterplot this would appear as a horizontal straight line through $\bar{y}$. The analyst wants to test whether the least-squares regression line is statistically significantly different from a horizontal line through $\bar{y}$. This can be done by examining the slope. The observed slope is the regression coefficient, $b$, a statistic that describes the average change in the value of $y$ for a unit change in the value of $x$. The slope of a horizontal straight line is 0. The analyst can compare these two values with a one-variable $t$-test.

$$t = \frac{b_{observed} - b_{expected}}{s_b}$$

where

$$b_{expected} = 0$$

## Exhibit 12–7

**Scatterplot With Least-Squares Regression Line: Okun's Law 1990–2004**

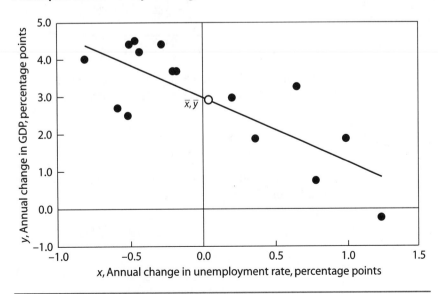

## *Exhibit 12–8*

**Scatterplot Detail**

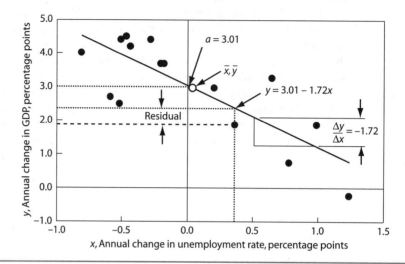

The numerator of the $t$ statistic is the difference in the values of the slope. Since the null hypothesis is a horizontal line, $b_{expected}$ is zero. The term in the denominator, $s_b$, is the standard error of the regression coefficient—is the standard deviation of $y$ about the regression line divided by the variation of $x$.

$$s_b = \frac{\sqrt{\dfrac{\sum[(y_i - y_{i\,\text{estimated}})^2]}{n-2}}}{\sqrt{\sum[(x_i - \overline{x})^2]}}$$

The numerator of this formula, the standard deviation of $y$ about the regression line, is called the *standard error of the estimate*, $s_{y \cdot x}$.

$$s_{y \cdot x} = \sqrt{\frac{\sum[(y_i - y_{i\,\text{estimated}})^2]}{n-2}}$$

Equivalent computational formulas for the standard error of the estimate and the standard error of the regression coefficient are

$$s_{y \cdot x} = \sqrt{\frac{\sum(y_i^2) - a\sum y_i - b\sum(x_i \cdot y_i)}{n-2}}$$

$$s_b = \frac{s_{y \cdot x}}{\sqrt{\sum(x_i^2) - n \cdot \overline{x}^2}}$$

Using these formulas, the standard error of the estimate is 0.895 and the standard error of the regression coefficient is 0.374.

The analyst calculates the $t$ statistic in order to test for the statistical significance of the regression coefficient.

$$t = \frac{b_{observed} - b_{expected}}{s_b}$$

$$t = \frac{-1.72 - 0}{0.374}$$

$$t = -4.62$$

For this example, $t$ is calculated as $-4.62$. There are $n - 2$ degrees of freedom, since there are two estimated regression coefficients ($a$ and $b$) in the problem. The critical value of $t$ for $15 - 2 = 13$ degrees of freedom, two-tailed test, at the 0.05 level of significance is 2.16. Therefore, the least-squares linear regression relationship is statistically significantly different from using the horizontal line through $\bar{y}$ as an estimate of the values of the dependent variable.

Another test of significance can be done by examining the variance of the dependent variable. The variance of $y$ is based upon the sum of the squared dispersions of the observed values of $y$ about their mean. This total variation will be abbreviated as SST, sum-of-squares total. Fitting a regression line to the data separates the total variation into two components. One component, explained variation, is the sum of the squared differences between the estimated values of $y$ (the regression line) and $\bar{y}$. This component is abbreviated SSR, sum-of-squares regression. The other component, unexplained variation, is the sum of the squared residuals between the observed $y$ values and the estimated $y$ values on the regression line. It is abbreviated SSE, sum-of-squares error. The computational results are shown in Exhibit 12–9.

$$\frac{\text{Total}}{\text{variation}} = \frac{\text{Explained}}{\text{variation}} + \frac{\text{Unexplained}}{\text{variation}}$$

$$SST = SSR + SSE$$

$$SST = \sum(y_i - \bar{y})^2$$

$$SSR = \sum(y_{estimated} - \bar{y})^2$$

$$SSE = \sum(y_i - y_{estimated})^2$$

Now we can construct an analysis of variance table and compute a value for the $F$ statistic. The critical value of $F$ for 1 degree of freedom, numerator, and 13 degrees of freedom, denominator, at the 0.05 level of significance is 4.67. Since the calculated value of $F$, 21.3, exceeds the critical value, the analysis indicates that the relationship between the change in the unemployment rate and change in

# *Exhibit 12–9*

**Computation of the Sum-of-Squares**

| Year | Independent variable $x$ Change in unemployment rate from the previous year (percentage points) | Dependent variable $y$ Change in gross domestic product from the previous year (percentage points) | Estimated $y$ $3.01 - 1.72x$ | Residual about regression $y - y_{est}$ | Residual about $y$-bar $y - \bar{y}$ | Difference between $y$-estimated and $y$-bar $y_{est} - \bar{y}$ | Squared residual about regression $(y - y_{est})^2$ | Squared residual about $y$-bar $(y - \bar{y})^2$ | Squared difference between $y$-estimated and $y$-bar $(y_{est} - \bar{y})^2$ |
|------|------|------|------|------|------|------|------|------|------|
| 1990 | 0.36 | 1.9 | 2.395 | −0.495 | −1.087 | −0.592 | 0.245 | 1.181 | 0.351 |
| 1991 | 1.23 | −0.2 | 0.886 | −1.086 | −3.187 | −2.101 | 1.178 | 10.155 | 4.415 |
| 1992 | 0.64 | 3.3 | 1.906 | 1.394 | 0.313 | −1.081 | 1.944 | 0.098 | 1.168 |
| 1993 | −0.58 | 2.7 | 4.019 | −1.319 | −0.287 | 1.032 | 1.739 | 0.082 | 1.065 |
| 1994 | −0.81 | 4.0 | 4.407 | −0.407 | 1.013 | 1.420 | 0.165 | 1.027 | 2.016 |
| 1995 | −0.51 | 2.5 | 3.889 | −1.389 | −0.487 | 0.903 | 1.930 | 0.237 | 0.815 |
| 1996 | −0.18 | 3.7 | 3.329 | 0.371 | 0.713 | 0.342 | 0.138 | 0.509 | 0.117 |
| 1997 | −0.47 | 4.5 | 3.817 | 0.683 | 1.513 | 0.831 | 0.466 | 2.290 | 0.690 |
| 1998 | −0.43 | 4.2 | 3.760 | 0.440 | 1.213 | 0.773 | 0.194 | 1.472 | 0.598 |
| 1999 | −0.28 | 4.4 | 3.501 | 0.899 | 1.413 | 0.514 | 0.808 | 1.998 | 0.265 |
| 2000 | −0.21 | 3.7 | 3.372 | 0.328 | 0.713 | 0.385 | 0.108 | 0.509 | 0.148 |
| 2001 | 0.78 | 0.8 | 1.676 | −0.876 | −2.187 | −1.311 | 0.767 | 4.782 | 1.718 |
| 2002 | 0.99 | 1.9 | 1.302 | 0.598 | −1.087 | −1.684 | 0.357 | 1.181 | 2.837 |
| 2003 | 0.20 | 3.0 | 2.668 | 0.332 | 0.013 | −0.319 | 0.110 | 0.000 | 0.102 |
| 2004 | −0.50 | 4.4 | 3.875 | 0.525 | 1.413 | 0.888 | 0.276 | 1.998 | 0.789 |
| Total | 0.23 | 44.8 | | 0.0 | 0.0 | | 10.4 | 27.5 | 17.1 |
| Mean | 0.02 | 2.99 | | | | | | | |

## Exhibit 12–10

**Analysis of Variance Summary**

| Source of variation | Sum of squares | Degrees of freedom | Mean square | *F* statistic |
|---|---|---|---|---|
| Regression | 17.1 | 1 | 17.1 | 21.3 |
| Residual | 10.4 | $(n-2) = 13$ | 0.802 | |
| Total | 27.5 | $(n-1) = 14$ | | |

gross domestic product as estimated by the least-squares regression equation is statistically significant.

The analysis of variance for two-variable linear regression provides essentially the same result as the *t*-test on the regression coefficient (see Exhibit 12–10). Note that $F = t^2$ for the two-variable problem. Analysis of variance is presented here in order to review the *F* statistic and introduce its use in regression analysis. The analysis of variance summary will be more important in a later discussion of multiple regression—involving more than one independent variable.

## 12.2 *Strength of Association—Correlation Analysis*

Without a linear regression model, the best estimate of the value of the dependent variable is provided by $\bar{y}$. In a graph this is represented by a horizontal straight line drawn through $\bar{y}$. If the regression model is any good, the regression line should fit the data better than the $\bar{y}$ line. The residuals between the observed data and the regression line should be less than the residuals with respect to $\bar{y}$. The regression relationship is calculated so as to minimize the variance of the observed data about the regression line. The degree to which the variance about the regression line differs from the variance about is a measure of strength of association. To do this the analyst will compare the sum of the squared residuals with respect to the regression line against the sum of the squared residuals about $\bar{y}$. If there is no relationship between the variables, the sum of the squared residuals with respect to the regression line will be about the same as the sum of the squared residuals with respect to $\bar{y}$ (the ratio of the two terms will approach 1.0). If, on the other hand, the regression relationship provides a better estimate for *y* than $\bar{y}$ over the range of values taken on by *x*, the sum of the squared residuals about the regression line will approach zero, and the ratio of the two terms will also approach zero. Subtracting the ratio of residuals from 1.0 gives a strength-of-association statistic on a continuous scale from 0 to 1.0, where 0 indicates no association and 1.0 represents perfect association. Intermediate values from 0 to 0.2 are interpreted as weak association, 0.2 to 0.5 as moderate association, and over 0.5 as strong association. This statistic is $r^2$ (*r*-squared), the *coefficient of determination.* It is the proportion of the variance of the dependent variable that is explained by the regression equation.

$$r^2 = 1 - \frac{\text{Sum of squared residuals about regression line}}{\text{Sum of squared residuals about } y}$$

$$r^2 = 1 - \frac{\sum[(y_i - y_{i\text{ estimated}})^2]}{\sum[(y_i - \bar{y})^2]}$$

An equivalent computational formula for $r^2$ is

$$r^2 = \left[ \frac{n\sum(x \cdot y) - \sum x \cdot \sum y}{\sqrt{n\sum(x^2) - (\sum x)^2} \cdot \sqrt{n\sum(y^2) - (\sum y)^2}} \right]$$

The coefficient of determination can be computed for our example using the calculations for the variation of $y$ about the regression line and about $\bar{y}$ shown in Exhibit 12–10. The value of $r^2 = 0.62$ means that 62% of the variance in the year-to-year change in GDP for this 15-year period is explained by the least-squares regression equation with the corresponding year-to-year change in unemployment rate as the independent variable.

$$r^2 = 1 - \frac{\sum[(y_i - y_{i\text{ estimated}})^2]}{\sum[(y_i - \bar{y})^2]}$$

$$r^2 = 1 - \frac{10.4}{27.5}$$

$$r^2 = 0.62$$

A related indicator of strength of association is the *correlation coefficient, r.* This statistic is the square root of the coefficient of determination. It can take on values between $-1$ and $+1$. The $+$ or $-$ sign that is assigned is the same as that for the regression coefficient, $b$ (if $b$ is positive, $r$ also has a positive sign, and if $b$ is negative, $r$ is negative). Values of $r$ close to zero indicate no association. Values close to $+1$ indicate strong positive association and values close to $-1$ indicate strong inverse association. In this example, the correlation coefficient, $r$, equals $-0.79$, a strong negative association.

So far, the analyst has found a least-squares regression line that has a slope statistically significantly different from zero (using a $t$-test on the $b$ statistic). This linear model, using the annual change in unemployment rate, provides a better explanation of the change in gross domestic product on an annual basis than simply using the mean value of GDP (analysis-of-variance $F$ test). The analyst also found (using the $r^2$ statistic) that the least-squares regression model explains 62% of the variance in annual GDP change. The analyst can compute a value for the $t$ statistic using only $r^2$ and $n$ in order to test the significance of $r^2$. This calculation, essentially the same as an analysis-of-variance $F$ test, is useful when the analyst does not have the sum-of-squares computations and the ANOVA table. The question at hand is, How likely is it that we would obtain an $r^2$ of 0.62 or larger if there were actually no linear association in the statistical population?

$$t = \sqrt{\frac{r^2(n-2)}{1-r^2}}$$

$$t = \sqrt{\frac{0.62 \cdot (15-2)}{1-0.62}}$$

$$t = 4.6$$

The critical value of $t$ for $n - 2 = 13$ degrees of freedom, one-tailed test, at the 0.05 level of significance is 2.16. The calculated value, $t = 4.6$, exceeds the critical value. Therefore, the probability of obtaining a value for $r^2$ of 0.62 or higher is less than 5% if there were indeed no association between the change in unemployment rate and change in GDP data. The relationship is statistically significant.

## 12.3    *Correlation is Not Causality*

Correlation indicates consistency. The coefficient of determination and the correlation coefficient represent the extent to which higher values of the dependent variable are associated with higher values of the independent variable (or, for an inverse relationship, higher dependent values with lower independent values). However, consistency, while a necessary symptom of a cause-and-effect relationship between variables, is not sufficient proof of such a relationship.

There are only two ways to establish such proof. One is to observe units of analysis in a "laboratory"—a completely controlled environment that is totally isolated from the real world. The other is to establish a causal argument based upon circumstantial evidence—repeated evaluation studies done by different analysts—all coming to essentially the same conclusion.

Regression analysis is concerned with describing the nature and significance of the pattern of values taken on by two intervally measured variables. As far as the technique (or computer) is concerned, it does not matter which variable is independent and which dependent. For instance, if an analyst observed both an increase in education expenditures and higher standardized test scores, did the increase in expenditures lead to the higher test scores or was it the other way around? Further, the computations are insensitive to the qualitative meaning of the variables and the logic of the model. If an analyst observed an increase in both the number of people who own computers and the number of people who are homeless, this may suggest that there are sharp socioeconomic disparities in the society but hardly supports the notion that a change in one variable causes a commensurate change in the other.

## 12.4  *Assumptions*

Regression analysis is a very powerful method for evaluation studies. However, there are several important assumptions. This section addresses these assumptions, reviews how they can be checked, and suggests measures that might be taken by the researcher to ensure compliance.

(1) Some data sets have outlying data points—*outliers*. The first assumption of regression analysis is that all of the units of analysis are fundamentally alike except for the independent variable. In other words, it is assumed that all units of analysis have been drawn from the same statistical population and are identical except for the characteristic measured by the independent variable. However, this may not be the case—and if it isn't, the results of a regression analysis will be wrong and misleading. Except for the independent variable, all of the units of analysis included in a regression analysis should be alike in every respect.

Outliers can be identified graphically by examining either the scatterplot of $x$ and $y$ variables, or a plot of the residuals about the regression line against either the estimated $y$ values or the independent variable $x$. (Outliers tend to be more apparent in a plot of residuals.) The usual remedy to meet this assumption is to examine the scatterplot and throw all outlying data points out of the analysis.

Outlying data points suggest that the assumption of one statistical population may be invalid. However, it is only a suggestion. Once identified, outlying units of analysis need to be examined by the analyst. An outlier may be due to an observation being made at a different time or place, or environmental conditions that affect that unit of analysis differently. These would lead the analyst to judge that the outlying observation is from a different statistical population (possibly explained by another "third" variable) and should be excluded from the analysis. On the other hand, an outlier may be a random measurement anomaly or a real, albeit unusual, occurrence following a change in the independent variable. So the issue is not clear cut and requires experience, judgment, and caution on the part of the analyst.

(2) Another assumption for regression analysis is that both the independent and dependent variables have an interval level of measurement. One of the most important aspects of regression analysis—one that makes the method so useful for problems encountered in public administration is that there are two loopholes that relax this assumption.

**a.** A variable that has a dichotomous nominal level of measurement can be treated mathematically as if it were an interval level of measurement.

**b.** A variable that has an ordinal level of measurement, in which the ordinal values comprise a uniform scale, can be treated mathematically as if it were an interval level of measurement.

These qualifications allow variables having a nominal or ordinal level of measurement to be used in regression analysis. A nominal or ordinal variable can be recoded to create a dichotomous nominal variable. For example, the nominal variable "geographic region" having the categories 1 = North, 2 = East, 3 = South, 4 = West could be recoded to two categories such as 0 = non-East, 1 = East. Once the variable has been recoded to two categories—where the two categories together include the entire statistical population (every unit of analysis is in either one category or the other) and are mutually exclusive (no unit of analysis falls into both categories) the variable can be used as either an independent or dependent variable in a regression analysis. A variable that has been recoded in this manner is called a *dummy variable*.

(3) A third assumption is that the value of the dependent variable, *y*, for each unit of analysis is not influenced by the *y* value of any other unit of analysis—the *y* values are independent of one another. Note that this assumption pertains only to the *y* values, not the *x* values. Sometimes, the analyst picks certain values of *x* for which measurements of *y* will be obtained. This assumption is usually met by ensuring proper data measurement methods. One method is random selection. The situation in which the value of *y* for one unit of analysis affects the *y* values of succeeding units of analysis is called "autocorrelation." One technique to check for autocorrelation is to number the units of analysis in the order in which the measurements are obtained and then plot the regression residuals versus this sequential identification number. A random scattering of the plot indicates no autocorrelation whereas a pattern of generally increasing or decreasing residual values suggests autocorrelation.

(4) A fourth assumption is that each unit of analysis can be considered as having been drawn from the same statistical population. This means that the units of analysis are assumed to be alike in all relevant respects except for the characteristics or attributes described by the variables included in the regression analysis. This condition can be checked by examining a plot of the residuals against the value of *y*-estimated by the regression equation (sometimes the *x* value is used). Any data points that seem to stand out by themselves, called "outliers," suggest that those units of analysis may not be part of the same statistical population as the remainder of the observations. The presence of outliers can seriously affect regression results—indicating statistically significant relationships that might not otherwise exist—or stronger relationships than might exist but for the outlying units of analysis. We should check each outlying unit of analysis to examine whether it is indeed similar in all respects, except the *x* and *y* values, to the other observations. If it is, leave the observation in the data set. If there is some question, remove the unit of analysis from the data set and re-run the regression and correlation analysis.

(5) A fifth assumption is that a linear model is a reasonable approximation of the relationship between the variables. Alternatively, a nonlinear model, such as a curve with steadily increasing or decreasing slope, might provide a better fit. This type of model may be more appropriate if the underlying relationship between the

variables is a process of growth or decay. In addition to examining the pattern of data points in the scatterplot, the linear assumption can be examined using a plot of the residuals about the regression line against the values of $y$-estimated by the regression equation. A linear model is indicated if the residuals points appear to be randomly scattered, with both positive and negative values, throughout the range of $y$-estimated. A distinct pattern in the residual plot suggests a nonlinear equation may be a better model for the relationship. Sometimes, rather than use a more complex equation to model the relationship, the data are transformed mathematically in order to more closely approximate a straight-line model. When an ascending or a descending curve is apparent in the scatterplot, a common data transformation technique is to take the natural logarithm (this is the logarithm to the base $e$, abbreviated ln) of either the dependent variable or both the dependent and independent variables. Upon redrawing the scatterplot ($\ln y$ versus $x$; or $\ln y$ versus $\ln x$) the analyst would see that the data have been "pulled" more closely into a straight line. The analyst can now fit a least-squares straight-line model such as $\ln y = a + b \ln x$.

(6) Sixth, it is assumed that the variance in $y$ about the regression line, throughout the range of the independent variable, should be approximately constant. This condition is called *homoscedasticity*. This assumption can be checked by examining the residuals about the regression line across the range of $x$. An apparent narrowing or widening of the residuals across the range of $x$ suggests that this assumption is not being met. Data transformations using natural logarithms or logarithm to the base 10 ($\log_{10} y$) may remedy the problem.

(7) The seventh assumption is that the values of $y$ are normally distributed about the regression line at each value of $x$. This assumption is sometimes hard to check because the values of $x$ are not being picked by the analyst and the sample size may be relatively small. With large sample sizes a plot of the residuals will help in examining this assumption. At each value of $x$ there should be positive and negative residuals with most of the residuals being within the standard error of the estimate of the regression line.

# *Homework Exercises*

**12-1**  Do states in which the governor has line-item budget veto power tend to spend less per capita than states in which the governor does not have this power? Examine the data in Exhibit HW9–1A. Treat *line item veto* as an interval variable and apply a linear regression analysis.

---

$a = 7{,}032.4 \quad b = 548.4 \quad t_{b\ \text{statistic}} = 0.87 \quad r^2 = 0.02$

Relationship is not statistically significant

---

**12-2** Keynesian economic theory postulates a direct, positive relationship between increases in government spending and growth in the real economy. Test this theory for the United States. Operationally define "government spending" as the total outlays of federal, state, and local governments as a percentage of the gross domestic product (GDP) and "economic growth" as the subsequent annual percentage change in real gross domestic product. (For example, total government expenditures in 1980 of 30.9% of GDP are associated with about a 2.5% change in GDP from 1980 to 1981.) Data for the period 1980–2003 are listed in Exhibit HW12–2A.

## Exhibit HW12–2A

**Government Spending and Economic Growth**

| Fiscal year | Total government expenditures (percent of GDP) | Annual growth in real GDP (percent) |
|---|---|---|
| 1980 | 30.9 | 2.52 |
| 1981 | 31.4 | −1.94 |
| 1982 | 32.9 | 4.52 |
| 1983 | 33.5 | 7.19 |
| 1984 | 31.8 | 4.13 |
| 1985 | 32.6 | 3.47 |
| 1986 | 32.5 | 3.38 |
| 1987 | 32.0 | 4.13 |
| 1988 | 31.6 | 3.54 |
| 1989 | 31.5 | 1.88 |
| 1990 | 32.4 | −0.17 |
| 1991 | 33.3 | 3.32 |
| 1992 | 33.2 | 2.67 |
| 1993 | 32.3 | 4.02 |
| 1994 | 31.7 | 2.50 |
| 1995 | 31.4 | 3.70 |
| 1996 | 30.9 | 4.50 |
| 1997 | 30.0 | 4.18 |
| 1998 | 29.4 | 4.45 |
| 1999 | 28.9 | 3.66 |
| 2000 | 28.8 | 0.75 |
| 2001 | 29.3 | 1.60 |
| 2002 | 30.1 | 2.51 |
| 2003 | 30.6 | 3.91 |

See Exhibit HW12–2B. Although annual growth in GDP apparently increases as total government spending increases, the relationship is not statistically significant ($a = -5.9$; $b = 0.29$; $t_{b\,\text{statistic}} = 1.07$; $r^2 = 0.05$). The Keynesian model is not supported by these data.

## *Exhibit HW12–2B*

**Scatterplot: Annual Growth in GDP by Total Government Expenditures, 1983–2003**

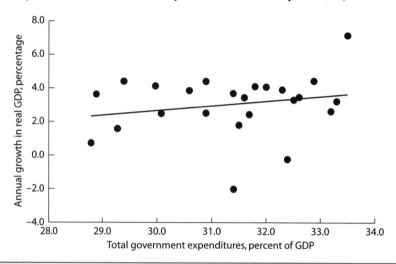

12-3   Identifying the dose–response relationship between exposure to lead in the work environment and lead concentration in workers' blood is important for possible regulatory action. Examine the scatterplot in Exhibit HW12–3A and the following regression results relating the average blood lead level to the average air lead exposure for 56 workers at a battery plant.[1]

| Regression results: | |
| --- | --- |
| Constant, $a$ | 38.0 |
| Std Err of $y$ Est | 7.72 |
| $r$-Squared | 0.037 |
| No. of Observations | 56 |
| Degrees of Freedom | 54 |
| $x$ Coefficient | 0.035 |
| Std Err of Coef. | 0.024 |
| $t$ | 1.44 |

---

[1]Lane Bishop and William J. Hill, "A Study of the Relationship Between Blood Lead Levels and Occupational Air Lead Levels," *The American Statistician* 37, no. 4 (November 1983): 471–475.

## Exhibit HW12–3A

**Blood Lead Level by Air Lead Level**

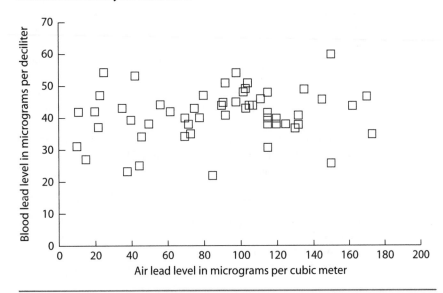

**a.** What is the equation that describes the dose–response relationship between exposure to lead in the work environment and lead concentration in worker's blood?

**b.** Is the relationship statistically significant at the 0.10 level of significance?

---

**a.** Regression equation: (blood lead level) = 38.0 + 0.035(air lead level)

**b.** $t = b/s_b$

The "$x$ coefficient" is the $b$ statistic.

$t = 1.44$

$t_{\text{critical } 0.10} \approx 1.67$ two-tailed test, $df = 54$

The relationship is not significant at the 0.10 level of significance.

---

**12-4** Selenium is an element that occurs naturally in various soils. In minute quantities it is essential to human nutrition. However, in slightly larger doses it is toxic to humans. Selenium toxicity has been associated with cancer, infant death, genetic malformation, and dental caries. The U.S. drinking water limit for selenium is 10 parts per billion (equivalent to10 micrograms per liter).

In the San Joaquin Valley of central California, irrigation water is drained into a 1,200-acre chain of evaporation ponds established by the U.S. Bureau of Reclamation. The ponds also serve as wildlife refuges. The used irrigation water, however, carries high concentrations of salts and minerals leached from the soil. In 1983, the U.S. Fish and Wildlife Service observed an extraordinary number of deaths and deformities among birds at a wildlife refuge near Los Banos, CA. There were high levels of selenium in the birds and in the drainage water. In 1986 it was reported that "levels of [selenium] contamination, 30 to 50 times higher than what the government says is safe in drinking water, have penetrated from 300 to 500 feet and are now separated from drinking water supplies only be a single layer of clay."[2]

Suppose analysts suspect that selenium has indeed contaminated drinking water supplies. How should individuals be tested for exposure to selenium via drinking water? What should be sent to the laboratory—blood samples, hair samples, or urine samples? In the late 1970s a team of researchers studied some residents from a small community in New Mexico in which home water wells contained concentrations of selenium ranging from 10 to 3,900 micrograms per liter—probably contaminated by a nearby uranium mill tailing pond. Blood, hair, and urine specimens were obtained from the residents. The original data are not available, but simulated data approximating the results are presented in Exhibit HW12–4A.[3]

**a.** Plot the urinary concentration of selenium as a function of selenium concentration in the well water.

**b.** Plot the hair concentration of selenium as a function of selenium concentration in the well water.

**c.** Plot the blood concentration of selenium as a function of selenium concentration in the well water.

Examine these plots in light of the assumptions required in order to use linear regression analysis. Now transform the data by finding the base 10 logarithm of each value in the data table and multiplying each logarithmic value by 100 as shown in Exhibit HW12–4B.

**d.** Plot $100 \times \log$ (urinary concentration of selenium) as a function of $100 \times \log$ (selenium concentration in well water). Find the linear regression equation and $R^2$.

**e.** Plot $100 \times \log$ (hair concentration of selenium) as a function of $100 \times \log$ (selenium concentration in well water). Find the linear regression equation and $R^2$.

**f.** Plot $100 \times \log$ (blood concentration of selenium) as a function of $100 \times \log$ (selenium concentration in well water). Find the linear regression equation and $R^2$.

---

[2] Tom Harris, "Selenium a Threat to Water," *Modesto Bee,* December 10, 1986, p. A16.
[3] Simulated data based on the results reported in Jane L. Valentine, Han K. Kang, and Gary H. Spivey, "Selenium Levels in Human Blood, Urine, and Hair in Response to Exposure via Drinking Water," *Environmental Research,* 17 (1978): 347–355.

## Exhibit HW12–4A

**Selenium Concentrations in Well Water and in Human Urine, Hair, and Blood for 44 Individuals**

| Well Water Se concentration (micro-grams/liter) | Urine Se (micro-grams/day) | Hair Se (micro-grams/gram) | Blood Se (micro-grams/100 ml) |
|---|---|---|---|
| 25 | 14.0 | 0.4 | 15.1 |
| 25 | 52.5 | — | 20.4 |
| 30 | 44.7 | 0.5 | 17.6 |
| 30 | — | 0.6 | 21.4 |
| 30 | 70.8 | 0.2 | 13.8 |
| 30 | 100.0 | 0.9 | 16.6 |
| 40 | 35.5 | 0.3 | 15.7 |
| 40 | 44.7 | 0.4 | 18.8 |
| 40 | 47.9 | 0.2 | 17.0 |
| 40 | 67.6 | 0.2 | 13.3 |
| 55 | 22.0 | 0.3 | 14.0 |
| 55 | 35.5 | 0.4 | 14.8 |
| 55 | 39.8 | 0.1 | 17.4 |
| 55 | 79.4 | 0.2 | 17.8 |
| 60 | 158.5 | 0.4 | 16.4 |
| 60 | — | 0.4 | 15.1 |
| 70 | 70.8 | 0.1 | 24.8 |
| 80 | — | 0.7 | 16.2 |
| 80 | — | 0.0 | 14.5 |
| 90 | — | 0.3 | 19.1 |
| 100 | 56.2 | 0.5 | 16.2 |
| 100 | 89.1 | 0.1 | 16.4 |
| 100 | 95.5 | 0.1 | 16.6 |
| 100 | 123.0 | 0.2 | 17.0 |
| 100 | 126.0 | 0.5 | 18.6 |
| 200 | 56.2 | 0.3 | 19.5 |
| 200 | 131.8 | 1.3 | 15.8 |
| 320 | 56.2 | 0.4 | 17.2 |
| 320 | 66.1 | 0.1 | 14.3 |

*(continued)*

# Exhibit HW12–4A

**Selenium Concentrations in Well Water and in Human Urine, Hair, and Blood for 44 Individuals** *(continued)*

| Well Water Se concentration (micrograms/liter) | Urine Se (micrograms/day) | Hair Se (micrograms/gram) | Blood Se (micrograms/100 ml) |
|---|---|---|---|
| 320 | 63.0 | 0.6 | 18.0 |
| 320 | 70.8 | 0.4 | 15.8 |
| 700 | 95.5 | 0.5 | 16.2 |
| 700 | 158.5 | — | 19.1 |
| 1200 | — | 0.2 | 15.7 |
| 1200 | — | 0.5 | 18.6 |
| 1400 | 112.2 | 0.7 | — |
| 1400 | 316.0 | — | 19.1 |
| 1600 | 89.1 | 0.4 | 17.2 |
| 1600 | 100.0 | 0.6 | 15.7 |
| 1600 | 250.0 | 1.5 | 23.4 |
| 1600 | 63.1 | 0.7 | 17.0 |
| 1800 | — | 2.0 | 18.6 |
| 1800 | — | 0.4 | 16.6 |
| 1800 | 125.9 | — | 15.1 |

# Exhibit HW12–4B

**Selenium Concentrations in Well Water and in Human Urine, Hair, and Blood for 44 Individuals—Data Transformation**

| 100 × Log (Well Water Se Concentration) (micrograms/liter) | 100 × Log (Urine Se) (micrograms/day) | 100 × Log (Hair Se) (micrograms/gram) | 100 × Log (Blood Se) (micrograms/100 ml) |
|---|---|---|---|
| 140 | 115 | −40 | 118 |
| 140 | 172 | — | 131 |
| 148 | 165 | −32 | 125 |
| 148 | — | −25 | 133 |
| 148 | 185 | −66 | 114 |
| 148 | 200 | −7 | 122 |
| 160 | 155 | −47 | 120 |
| 160 | 165 | −38 | 127 |
| 160 | 168 | −72 | 123 |

*(continued)*

**Selenium Concentrations in Well Water and in Human Urine, Hair, and Blood for 44 Individuals—Data Transformation** *(continued)*

| 100 × Log (Well Water Se Concentration) (micrograms/liter) | 100 × Log (Urine Se) (micrograms/day) | 100 × Log (Hair Se) (micrograms/gram) | 100 × Log (Blood Se) (micrograms/100 ml) |
|---|---|---|---|
| 160 | 183 | −77 | 112 |
| 174 | 134 | −60 | 115 |
| 174 | 155 | −46 | 117 |
| 174 | 160 | −110 | 124 |
| 174 | 190 | −66 | 125 |
| 178 | 220 | −38 | 121 |
| 178 | — | −46 | 118 |
| 185 | 185 | −105 | 139 |
| 190 | — | −15 | 121 |
| 190 | — | −170 | 116 |
| 195 | — | −55 | 128 |
| 200 | 175 | −32 | 121 |
| 200 | 195 | −122 | 121 |
| 200 | 198 | −89 | 122 |
| 200 | 209 | −68 | 123 |
| 200 | 210 | −35 | 127 |
| 230 | 175 | −59 | 129 |
| 230 | 212 | 12 | 120 |
| 251 | 175 | −40 | 124 |
| 251 | 182 | −105 | 116 |
| 251 | 180 | −25 | 126 |
| 251 | 185 | −46 | 120 |
| 285 | 198 | −32 | 121 |
| 285 | 220 | — | 128 |
| 308 | — | −74 | 120 |
| 308 | — | −32 | 127 |
| 315 | 205 | −15 | — |
| 315 | 250 | — | 128 |
| 320 | 195 | −40 | 124 |
| 320 | 200 | −20 | 120 |
| 320 | 240 | 17 | 137 |
| 320 | 180 | −18 | 123 |
| 326 | — | 30 | 127 |
| 326 | — | −46 | 122 |
| 326 | 210 | — | 118 |

Now compare the biological data.

**g.** Find the linear regression equation and $R^2$ for the hair concentration of selenium as a function of selenium concentration in urine

**h.** Find the linear regression equation and $R^2$ for the blood concentration of selenium as a function of selenium concentration in urine.

**i.** Find the linear regression equation and $R^2$ for the hair concentration of selenium as a function of selenium concentration in blood

**j.** Write a conclusion.

---

**a.** Exhibit HW12–4C: urinary concentration of selenium as a function of selenium concentration in the well water.

## *Exhibit HW12–4C*

**Individual Urine Selenium Concentration by Selenium Concentration in Well Water**

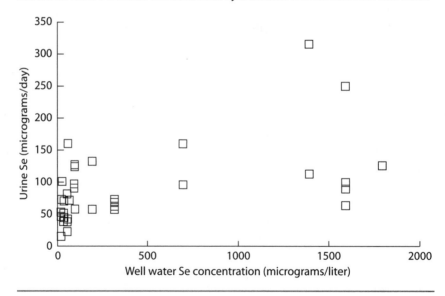

**b.** Exhibit HW12–4D: hair concentration of selenium as a function of selenium concentration in the well water.

## *Exhibit HW12–4D*

**Individual Hair Selenium Concentration by Selenium Concentration in Well Water**

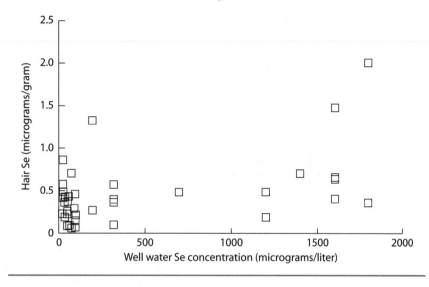

**c.** Exhibit HW12–4E: blood concentration of selenium as a function of selenium concentration in the well water.

## *Exhibit HW12–4E*

**Individual Blood Selenium Concentration v. Selenium Concentration in Well Water**

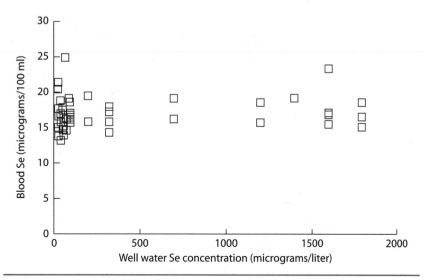

**d.** Exhibit HW12–4F: 100 log Urine Se by 100 log well water Se regression results

| | |
|---|---|
| Constant, $a$ | 133.4 |
| Std Err of $y$ Est | 22.2 |
| $r$-Squared | 0.34 |
| No. of Observations | 35 |
| Degrees of Freedom | 33 |
| $x$ Coefficient(s) | 0.24 |
| Std Err of Coef. | 0.06 |
| $t$ | 4.09 |

## *Exhibit HW12–4F*

**Log–Log Scatterplot: Individual Urinary Selenium Concentration v. Selenium Concentration in Well Water**

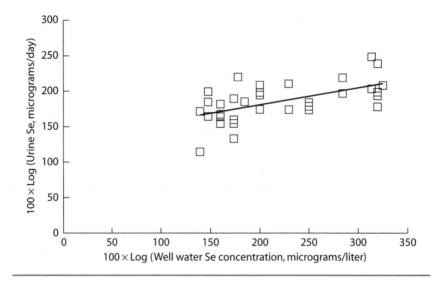

**e.** Exhibit HW12–4G: 100 log (Hair Se) by 100 log (well water Se) regression results

| | |
|---|---|
| Constant, $a$ | −94.3 |
| Std Err of $y$ Est | 36.4 |
| $r$-Squared | 0.12 |
| No. of Observations | 40 |
| Degrees of Freedom | 38 |
| $x$ Coefficient(s) | 0.21 |
| Std Err of Coef. | 0.09 |
| $t$ | 2.23 |

## Exhibit HW12–4G

**Log–Log Scatterplot: Individual Hair Selenium Concentration v. Selenium Concentration in Well Water**

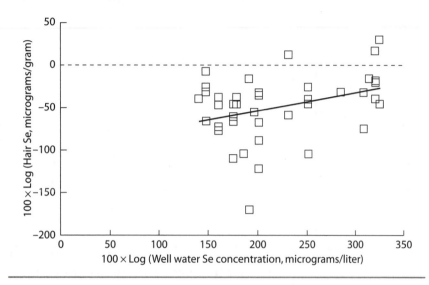

**f.** Exhibit HW12–4H: 100 log (Blood Se) by 100 log (well water Se) regression results

| | |
|---|---|
| Constant, $a$ | 120.55 |
| Std Err of $y$ Est | 5.74 |
| $r$-Squared | 0.02 |
| No. of Observations | 43 |
| Degrees of Freedom | 41 |
| $x$ Coefficient(s) | 0.0113 |
| Std Err of Coef. | 0.0137 |
| $t$ | 0.826 |

**g.** Hair Se v. Urine Se regression results:

| | |
|---|---|
| Constant, $a$ | 0.07 |
| Std Err of $y$ Est | 0.26 |
| $r$-Squared | 0.39 |
| No. of Observations | 31 |
| Degrees of Freedom | 29 |
| $x$ Coefficient(s) | 0.004 |
| Std Err of Coef. | 0.001 |
| $t$ | 4.27 |

## *Exhibit HW12–4H*

**Log–Log Scatterplot: Individual Blood Selenium Concentration v. Selenium Concentration in Well Water**

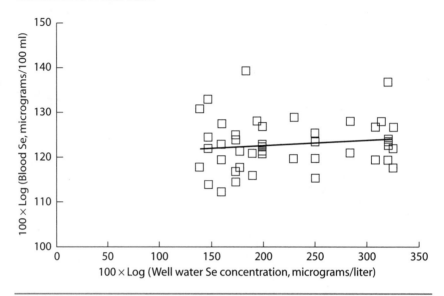

**h.** Blood Se v. Urine Se regression results:

| | |
|---|---|
| Constant, $a$ | 15.84 |
| Std Err of $y$ Est | 2.31 |
| $r$-Squared | 0.13 |
| No. of Observations | 34 |
| Degrees of Freedom | 32 |
| $x$ Coefficient(s) | 0.014 |
| Std Err of Coef. | 0.006 |
| $t$ | 2.18 |

**i.** Hair Se v. Blood Se regression results:

| | |
|---|---|
| Constant, $a$ | −0.34 |
| Std Err of $y$ Est | 0.38 |
| $r$-Squared | 0.08 |
| No. of Observations | 39 |
| Degrees of Freedom | 37 |
| $x$ Coefficient(s) | 0.046 |
| Std Err of Coef. | 0.026 |
| $t$ | 1.77 |

**j.** From the Valentine report:

> In assessing the selenium disease relationship, blood and urine seem to be the most common fluids examined; levels in hair or nails are rarely measured. This rare use of hair and nails is surprising in view of their usefulness in assessing the body burden of other trace elements. Since there are many body tissues and fluids that could be used as monitors of selenium status, it is important to determine which one or which combination would be best or most appropriate. . . . The nonsignificance of the correlations of blood selenium with water selenium and of blood selenium with hair selenium is of importance since blood is used quite often to assess the degree of exposure and to assess the selenium–disease relationship in humans. Our findings suggest that in such assessments it is not sufficient to use only blood as an indication of selenium status. Urine selenium comparisons with hair selenium and with water selenium gave significant positive correlations and suggest that urine or hair measurements would be more likely to give valid results. Thus if blood is to be used, another biological specimen, e.g., hair or urine, should be monitored simultaneously.[4]

---

[4]Valentine, Kang, and Spivey.

# CHAPTER 13

# Line-Up: Two-Variable Estimation—Interval–Interval Measures

| | |
|---|---|
| Kind of problem | *Estimation* |
| Number of variables | *Two* |
| Level of measurement | *Variable 1, interval* |
| | *Variable 2, interval* |

egression analysis can be used to obtain estimates of population characteristics from sample data. The analyst is interested in four types of estimates: (1) The "true" regression coefficient and (2) the coefficient of
determination for the variables in the statistical population, (3) a *mean* value and
(4) a *specific* value of the dependent variable in the statistical population for a
given value of the independent variable.

Estimated values for the statistical *population* are indicated by uppercase
symbols. Lowercase symbols refer to *sample* observations and estimates. The confidence intervals for estimating the mean, $\overline{Y}_x$, and an individual value, $Y_x$, vary with
the value of the independent variable. Exhibit 13–1 shows exact equations for the
confidence intervals, which should be used with sample sizes less than 30, and approximate equations, which are satisfactory for samples larger than 30.

## 13.1  *Regression Analysis—Example*

Consider this statement by a government scientist:

> Climate warming is projected to cause vegetation shifts because rising
> temperatures favor taller, denser vegetation, and will thus promote the

## *Exhibit 13–1*

**Two-Variable Estimation: Interval–Interval Measures**

| Population estimate | Sample size | Estimation equation |
|---|---|---|
| Regression coefficient | | $\beta = b \pm t_{\text{critical}} \cdot s_b$ |
| Coefficient of determination | | $r^2_{\text{adjusted}} = 1 - \left[ \dfrac{n-1}{n-k-1} \right] \cdot (1 - r^2)$ |
| Confidence interval for an individual value of $Y$ | $n < 30$ | $Y_x = y_{\text{estimated}} \pm t_{\text{critical}} \cdot s_{y.x} \cdot \sqrt{1 + \dfrac{1}{n} + \dfrac{(x - \bar{x})^2}{\sum[(x - \bar{x})^2]}}$ |
| | $n \geq 30$ | $Y_x \approx y_{\text{estimated}} \pm t_{\text{critical}} \cdot s_{y.x}$ |
| Confidence interval for the mean of $Y$ | $n < 30$ | $\bar{Y}_x = \bar{y}_{\text{estimated}} \pm t_{\text{critical}} \cdot s_{y.x} \cdot \sqrt{\dfrac{1}{n} + \dfrac{(x - \bar{x})^2}{\sum[(x - \bar{x})^2]}}$ |
| | $n \geq 30$ | $\bar{Y}_x \approx \bar{y}_{\text{estimated}} \pm t_{\text{critical}} \cdot \dfrac{s_{y.x}}{\sqrt{n}}$ |

expansion of forests into the Arctic tundra, and tundra into the polar deserts. . . . Half the current tundra area is projected to disappear in this century.

> —Dr. Robert W. Corell, testifying before the U.S. Senate Committee on Commerce, Science and Transportation, March 3, 2004.

Environmental analysts are concerned about a self-reinforcing feedback loop—increasing temperatures enhancing more vegetation in arctic regions, darkening the land, leading to further temperature increases. Exhibit 13–2 shows the observations of one science group of vegetation and temperature in an arctic region over the summer months in three successive years.[1] Exhibit 13–3 presents the least-squares regression results showing a statistically significant, strong association between NDVI and Temperature. Exhibit 13–4 is a scatterplot of the data with the least-squares regression line for the Normalized Difference Vegetation Index, NDVI = 0.16 + 0.10(Temp), superimposed.

---

[1] Arctic Transitions in the Land-Atmosphere System (ATLAS), Alaska Geobotany Center, University of Alaska, Fairbanks www.geobotany.uaf.edu/atlas/atlas_summary_conclusions.html

## Exhibit 13–2

**Vegetation and Temperature in an Arctic Region**

| Observation number | Average monthly summer temperature (°C), Temp | Normalized difference vegetation index, NDVI |
|---|---|---|
| 1 | 14 | 0.28 |
| 2 | 19 | 0.39 |
| 3 | 21 | 0.33 |
| 4 | 27 | 0.45 |
| 5 | 28 | 0.46 |
| 6 | 29 | 0.37 |
| 7 | 31 | 0.48 |
| Mean | 24.1428 | 0.3943 |
| Standard deviation | 6.2297 | 0.0737 |

## Exhibit 13–3

**Least-Squares Regression: Vegetation and Temperature in an Arctic Region**

Regression statistics

| | |
|---|---|
| $r$-Squared | 0.6768 |
| Standard error of the estimate | 0.0459 |

ANOVA

| | df | SS | MS | F |
|---|---|---|---|---|
| Regression | 1 | 0.022 | 0.022 | 10.47 |
| Residual | 5 | 0.011 | 0.002 | |
| Total | 6 | 0.033 | | |

| | Coefficients | Standard Error | t |
|---|---|---|---|
| Intercept | 0.16 | 0.075 | 2.135 |
| Temperature | 0.01 | 0.003 | 3.236 |

*Exhibit 13–4*

**Scatterplot: Vegetation and Temperature in an Arctic Region**

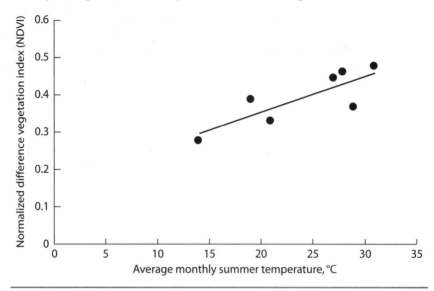

## 13.2  *Population Regression Coefficient*

Usually, an analyst's data comprise a sample drawn from a target statistical population. One of the goals is to learn about the "true" characteristics and attributes of the statistical population with a known degree of error and a known degree of confidence that the estimated population characteristics are within the error range. The best estimates of the true population parameters are the regression and correlation statistics calculated from the observed data.

If a least-squares regression equation were fitted for a statistical population in which the values of the *x* and *y* variables were known for every unit of analysis, the calculated slope would be the true regression coefficient, $\beta$. If our data are a sample, we want to find a best estimate and confidence interval for the population regression coefficient. The best estimate of the population regression coefficient is the *b* statistic, the calculated value of the slope. The confidence interval is specified by the product of two terms: the critical value of the *t* statistic and the calculated standard error of the regression coefficient, $s_b$. The critical value of the *t* statistic is found from Appendix F for a two-tailed test and $n - 2$ degrees of freedom, at either the 95% or 99% confidence level (0.05 or 0.01 level of significance). Thus

$$\beta = b \pm t_{\text{critical}} \cdot s_b$$

where

$$b = \text{the regression coefficient}$$

$$s_b = \text{standard error of the regression coefficient}$$

$$\beta = 0.01 \pm 2.571 \cdot 0.003$$

$$\beta = 0.01 \pm 0.008$$

## 13.3 Population Coefficient of Determination and Correlation Coefficient

If a significant association between $x$ and $y$ has been found, the analyst may wish to estimate the strength of association between the variables in the statistical population. The population coefficient of determination, $\rho^2$, is estimated by the ratio of the variance of $y$ about the regression line (the square of the standard error of the estimate, $s_{y.x}$) divided by the total variance of $y$ (the square of $s_y$). $\rho^2$ indicates the proportion of the total variance in the statistical population of a dependent variable $Y$ that can be explained by the least-squares regression relationship having an independent variable $X$.

$$\rho^2 \approx 1 - \frac{s_{y.x}^2}{s_y^2}$$

$$\rho^2 \approx 1 - \frac{(0.0459)^2}{(0.0737)^2}$$

$$\rho^2 \approx 0.61$$

The sample coefficient of determination, $r^2$, is a "biased" predictor of $\rho^2$. The estimate needs to be adjusted for the number of independent variables, $k$, and number of cases, particularly when the sample size is small. This is often designated as $r_{\text{adjusted}}^2$.

$$r_{\text{adjusted}}^2 = 1 - \left[ \frac{n-1}{n-k-1} \right] \cdot (1 - r^2)$$

$$r_{\text{adjusted}}^2 = 1 - \left[ \frac{7-1}{7-1-1} \right] \cdot (1 - 0.677)$$

$$r_{\text{adjusted}}^2 = 0.61$$

## 13.4  Confidence Interval for Estimating an Individual Value of Y

The least-squares regression equation can be used to obtain a specific estimate for the value of $Y$ for any value of $x$ within the data range.

$$Y_x = y_{\text{estimated}} \pm t_{\text{critical}} \cdot s_{y \cdot x} \cdot \sqrt{1 + \frac{1}{n} + \frac{(x - \overline{x})^2}{\sum(x - \overline{x})^2}}$$

where

$$y_{\text{estimated}} = a + bx$$

If the sample size is large ($n \geq 30$), the confidence interval is specified by the product of $t_{\text{critical}}$ and the standard error of the estimate.

$$Y_x \approx y_{\text{estimated}} \pm t_{\text{critical}} \cdot s_{y \cdot x}$$

Suppose the analyst is interested in estimating the vegetation index in the region during a summer month when the average temperature is 25°C. Using the least-squares regression equation, the best estimate of $y$ is 0.403. The 95% two-tailed confidence interval is 0.40 ± 0.13 as shown by the following calculation and Exhibit 13–5. Note how the confidence interval varies with $x$, narrowing in

## Exhibit 13–5

**95% Confidence Limits for an Individual Value of NDVI**

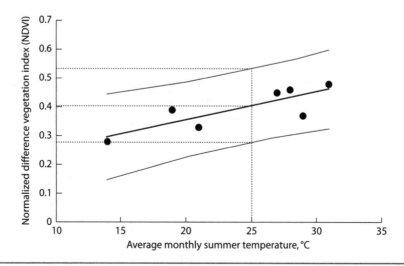

the center of the data field and expanding toward the independent variable's observed minimum and maximum values.

$$Y_x = 0.403 \pm 2.571 \cdot 0.0459 \cdot \sqrt{1 + \frac{1}{7} + \frac{(25 - 24.143)^2}{232.857}}$$

$$Y_x = 0.403 \pm 0.126$$

## 13.5  *Confidence Interval for Estimating* $\overline{Y}_x$

One of the assumptions of least-squares regression analysis is that the population of all $Y$ values at each value of $X$ is normally distributed. The following equation defines the estimated confidence interval for the mean value of $Y$ in the statistical population given a value of the independent variable, $x$. Estimating a specific value has greater error than estimating a mean value. The confidence interval for the mean of $Y$, $\overline{Y}_x$, is substantially less than that calculated for $Y_x$, and also varies with $x$, increasing in width as the values of $x$ approach the minimum and maximum values of the data range. On a scatterplot, this confidence interval appears as a band of varying width centered about the regression line. The confidence interval narrows when the difference between $x$ and $\overline{x}$ (the mean of the observed values of the independent variable, $x$) is small. The confidence interval widens for values of $x$ that are farther from $\overline{x}$.

$$\overline{Y}_x = \overline{y}_{estimated} \pm t_{critical} \cdot s_{y \cdot x} \cdot \sqrt{\frac{1}{n} + \frac{(x - \overline{x})^2}{\Sigma(x - \overline{x})^2}}$$

where

$$\overline{y}_{estimated} = a + bx$$

If the sample size is large ($n \geq 30$), the equation for the estimated confidence interval can be simplified:

$$\overline{Y}_x \approx \overline{y}_{estimated} \pm t_{critical} \cdot \frac{s_{y \cdot x}}{\sqrt{n}}$$

Suppose the analyst is interested in estimating the vegetation index throughout the Arctic during a summer month when the average temperature is 25°C. As before, using the least-squares regression equation, the best estimate of $y$ is 0.403.

## Exhibit 13–6

**95% Confidence Limits for Mean NDVI**

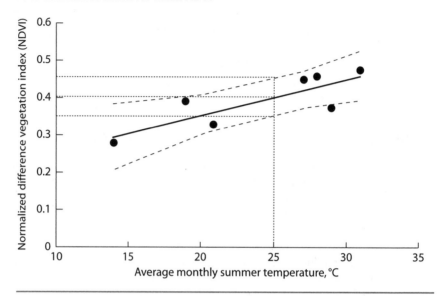

The 95% two-tailed confidence interval for $\bar{y}_x$ is 0.40 ± 0.045 as shown by the following calculation and Exhibit 13–6.

$$\bar{Y}_x = 0.403 \pm 2.571 \cdot 0.0459 \cdot \sqrt{1 + \frac{1}{7} + \frac{(25 - 24.143)^2}{232.857}}$$

$$\bar{Y}_x = 0.403 \pm 0.045$$

# Homework Exercises

**13-1** Exhibit HW13–1A shows enrollment by grade in a school district over a 34-year period. The junior high school (JHS) includes the seventh and eighth grades. The current enrollment (year 34) of the JHS is 939. The principal thinks that the JHS enrollment next year (year 35) will exceed 1,000. Estimate next year's JHS enrollment.

# *Exhibit HW 13–1A*

**School District Enrollment by Grade**

| | Grade | | | | | | | | | |
| | Elementary | | | | | | | JHS | | |
| Year | K | 1 | 2 | 3 | 4 | 5 | 6 | 7 | 8 | Total |
|---|---|---|---|---|---|---|---|---|---|---|
| 1 | 279 | 261 | 249 | 227 | 194 | 199 | 164 | 202 | 184 | 1,959 |
| 2 | 211 | 267 | 260 | 241 | 245 | 202 | 201 | 284 | 208 | 2,119 |
| 3 | 232 | 298 | 256 | 265 | 251 | 236 | 194 | 210 | 192 | 2,134 |
| 4 | 267 | 310 | 274 | 249 | 269 | 251 | 228 | 206 | 228 | 2,282 |
| 5 | 235 | 304 | 251 | 227 | 211 | 247 | 254 | 241 | 197 | 2,167 |
| 6 | 231 | 249 | 283 | 246 | 237 | 209 | 248 | 252 | 243 | 2,198 |
| 7 | 236 | 266 | 276 | 303 | 257 | 250 | 230 | 261 | 255 | 2,334 |
| 8 | 270 | 309 | 251 | 270 | 292 | 267 | 250 | 245 | 253 | 2,407 |
| 9 | 266 | 301 | 277 | 234 | 253 | 283 | 269 | 252 | 236 | 2,371 |
| 10 | 257 | 309 | 272 | 232 | 245 | 270 | 266 | 251 | 234 | 2,336 |
| 11 | 312 | 332 | 304 | 282 | 281 | 251 | 271 | 293 | 291 | 2,617 |
| 12 | 324 | 329 | 297 | 296 | 292 | 264 | 256 | 291 | 282 | 2,631 |
| 13 | 311 | 300 | 289 | 272 | 284 | 296 | 278 | 261 | 296 | 2,587 |
| 14 | 307 | 310 | 296 | 297 | 290 | 287 | 307 | 292 | 266 | 2,652 |
| 15 | 296 | 315 | 288 | 297 | 293 | 312 | 307 | 307 | 293 | 2,708 |
| 16 | 322 | 353 | 315 | 295 | 320 | 300 | 331 | 314 | 312 | 2,862 |
| 17 | 334 | 363 | 338 | 328 | 309 | 343 | 329 | 353 | 351 | 3,048 |
| 18 | 367 | 360 | 352 | 325 | 330 | 317 | 348 | 322 | 357 | 3,078 |
| 19 | 340 | 366 | 349 | 355 | 330 | 347 | 335 | 363 | 348 | 3,133 |
| 20 | 345 | 348 | 354 | 334 | 346 | 326 | 355 | 330 | 368 | 3,106 |
| 21 | 324 | 332 | 340 | 342 | 314 | 340 | 334 | 358 | 325 | 3,009 |
| 22 | 318 | 297 | 323 | 337 | 326 | 334 | 359 | 350 | 363 | 3,007 |
| 23 | 307 | 300 | 289 | 327 | 344 | 330 | 332 | 353 | 351 | 2,933 |
| 24 | 327 | 317 | 295 | 298 | 326 | 349 | 329 | 332 | 361 | 2,934 |
| 25 | 361 | 300 | 323 | 287 | 309 | 368 | 372 | 358 | 345 | 3,023 |
| 26 | 364 | 333 | 340 | 321 | 307 | 320 | 402 | 377 | 375 | 3,139 |
| 27 | 361 | 331 | 343 | 336 | 350 | 313 | 331 | 437 | 373 | 3,175 |
| 28 | 381 | 374 | 370 | 331 | 339 | 346 | 322 | 334 | 432 | 3,229 |
| 29 | 418 | 385 | 359 | 394 | 343 | 352 | 356 | 351 | 337 | 3,295 |
| 30 | 468 | 445 | 416 | 429 | 385 | 366 | 401 | 382 | 367 | 3,659 |
| 31 | 471 | 467 | 429 | 398 | 450 | 398 | 375 | 406 | 414 | 3,808 |
| 32 | 485 | 506 | 449 | 420 | 427 | 435 | 440 | 379 | 404 | 3,945 |
| 33 | 524 | 506 | 491 | 449 | 441 | 443 | 442 | 434 | 409 | 4,139 |
| 34 | 547 | 547 | 476 | 454 | 432 | 435 | 426 | 478 | 461 | 4,256 |

Some analysts might use "year" as an independent variable to predict enrollment. However, the mere passage of time is not the best predictor of enrollment. Most of next year's seventh- and eighth-graders are already currently enrolled as sixth- and seventh-graders. Sixth-grade enrollment over time can be used as a predictor of the following year's seventh-grade enrollment and, similarly, seventh-grade enrollment over time can be correlated with next year's eighth-grade enrollment. Over the 34-year period shown, the following regression relationships can be obtained:

(seventh-grade enrollment, year $t$) = 41.0 + 0.91 × (sixth-grade enrollment, year $t - 1$) $r$-squared = 0.88

(eighth-grade enrollment, year $t$) = −18.2 + 1.07 × (seventh-grade enrollment, year $t - 1$) $r$-squared = 0.91

(seventh-grade enrollment, year 35) = 41.0 + 0.91 × (sixth-grade enrollment, year 34)
(seventh-grade enrollment, year 35) = 41.0 + 0.91 × (426)
(seventh-grade enrollment, year 35) = 428.7

(eighth-grade enrollment, year 35) = −18.2 + 1.07 × (seventh-grade enrollment, year 34)
(eighth-grade enrollment, year 35) = −18.2 + 1.07 × (478)
(eighth-grade enrollment, year 35) = 493.3

Total JHS estimated enrollment, year 35 = 922

# CHAPTER 14

# The Flat Earth Society:
# More than Two Variables

---

| Kind of problem | *Evaluation or estimation* |
| --- | --- |
| Number of variables | *More than two* |
| Level of measurement | *Interval* |

This last chapter addresses problems that involve three or more variables. One of these variables, and only one, is a dependent variable—the resultant effect—whose values we are seeking to explain or change. Two or more independent variables (also called *predictor* or *explanatory* variables) describe the different characteristics and attributes of the observed units of analysis. Some of these variables may be environmental in nature—describing the different circumstances and conditions in which our observations take place. Other variables may describe differences brought about by policy or program action. The preceding chapters addressed problems with one or two variables and many specialized statistical techniques had to be introduced based on such considerations as level of measurement and sample size. Now, as the number of variables increases, a powerful general purpose method—multiple regression analysis—is introduced, in which variables with any level of measurement (with certain cautions) can be included.

All the statistical techniques introduced so far have assumed either that all the observations were obtained in a stable and unchanging environment or that whatever environmental changes did occur affected every unit of analysis equally. A laboratory-like setting was envisioned in which every unit of analysis was essentially identical, and remained so except for the changes that were observed in the independent and dependent variables. Thus, any observed change in the dependent variable was associated with a change in the independent variable. If the analyst could guarantee that the environment was constant, this would have been called an *experimental design* and an analyst could infer that any change in $x$ "caused" the subsequent change in $y$. Theoretically the variance in the dependent variable could have been completely accounted for by the values of the independent variable. Some evaluation problems employed matched comparison groups to

**311**

## *Exhibit 14–1*

**An Unknown Variable**

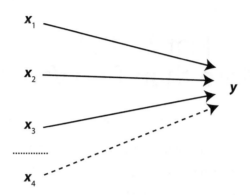

ensure that the units of analysis would be as similar as possible but for the group categories identified by the independent variable. With this *quasi-experimental design* an analyst could infer that any observed differences between the groups were related to the different values taken on by the independent variable.

Policy and program effects in the real world cannot be simply associated with a single independent variable. Observations are more likely to be the result of complex interactions involving possibly scores of independent variables. There are essentially three kinds of interactions in a multivariate problem: (1) independent–dependent relationships, (2) confounding relationships, and (3) spurious relationships. Exhibit 14–1 schematically represents a problem in which the variables $x_1$, $x_2$, and $x_3$ are known and observed independent variables; $x_4$ is another independent variable, unknown and unobserved by the analyst. Each separately influences the value of $y$, the dependent variable. The variance in $y$ cannot

## *Exhibit 14–2*

**A Confounding Relationship**

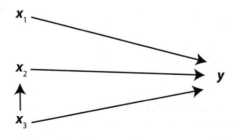

be completely explained because not every independent variable was measured and because of random error in the measurements.

In Exhibit 14–1 each independent variable separately and directly influences the dependent variable. However, it is possible that the independent variables can influence one another as well as influencing the dependent variable. If the analyst is unaware of or ignores the relationships between the independent variables, the apparent value of the dependent variable would be increased or decreased to an unknown extent. In Exhibit 14–2, $x_3$ influences $x_2$ as well as $y$—artificially magnifying the strength of the relationship between $x_2$ and $y$. The situation in which independent variables are related is called a *confounding* relationship.

Another complication is that there may be no relationship between a dependent variable and an independent variable yet both may be influenced by another third variable. In Exhibit 14–3, $x_3$ influences $x_2$ as well as $y$—but there is no relationship between $x_2$ and $y$. The analyst, who is unaware of variable $x_3$, would see only that the value of $y$ change as the value of $x_2$ changes and be fooled into thinking that $x_2$ and $y$ were related when the values of both were really driven by changes in $x_3$. The situation in which a third variable creates a false appearance of a relationship between an independent and dependent variable is called a *spurious* relationship.

To determine the nature of the relationship between any independent variable and the dependent variable the analyst needs to account for, explain, or remove the effects of other independent–dependent relationships, confounding relationships, and spurious relationships. Multivariate statistical procedures, chiefly multiple regression analysis, help the analyst isolate the effects of a particular policy or program from the outcomes of other environmental factors. Rather than trying to establish a controlled environment, multiple regression analysis lets the analyst measure many potentially influential independent variables and mathematically account for the effect of each one on the variation of the dependent variable. This type of evaluation is called a *non-experimental design.*

## *Exhibit 14–3*

**A Spurious Relationship**

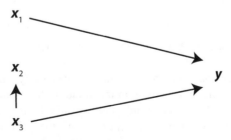

## *14.1  Multiple Regression Analysis*

Multiple regression analysis requires that each variable have an interval or ratio level of measurement. However, two significant loopholes allow the use of variables with nominal or ordinal levels of measurement. (1) A variable having a dichotomous (two-category) nominal level of measurement can be treated mathematically as if it has an interval level of measurement. Any nominally measured variable having $k$ categories can be recoded into $k - 1$ variables, each having two mutually exclusive categories. For example, the variable "region" having the values "North," "East," "South," and "West" can be recoded into three dichotomous variables describing regional location:

$$\text{North:}  \quad 0 = \text{No,} \quad 1 = \text{Yes}$$

$$\text{East:}  \quad 0 = \text{No,} \quad 1 = \text{Yes}$$

$$\text{South:}  \quad 0 = \text{No,} \quad 1 = \text{Yes}$$

There is no fourth variable, "West." That regional location is defined by the values of each of the other three variables being 0.

(2) A variable having an ordinal level of measurement with an implicit underlying scale can be treated mathematically as if it has an interval level of measurement.

The general form of a multiple regression equation is an extension of the $y = a + bx$ structure of the two-variable linear relationship. The so-called *ordinary least squares* (OLS) equation includes a numeric constant, $a$, and a "partial" regression coefficient, $b_i$, for each independent variable.

$$y = a + b_1 x_1 + b_2 x_2 + \cdots + b_i x_i$$

where

$y$ = the value of the dependent variable

$x_i$ = the value of the $i$th independent variable

$a$ = a numeric constant

$b_i$ = the partial regression coefficient ("slope") for the $i$th independent variable

$k$ = the number of independent variables

The partial regression coefficients specify what will happen to the value of $y$ with a one-unit increase in the value of that $x$ variable—provided the respective values of all the other independent variables remain unchanged. If the sign of the partial regression coefficient is positive ($+$) the value of $y$ will increase as $x$ increases. If the sign is negative ($-$) an increase in the value of $x$ has the effect of decreasing the value of $y$.

Consider the following multiple regression equation evaluating the K–12 education systems in the 50 states. The dependent variable is the adequacy of preparation for post-secondary education (PREP)—an indicator based on high school completion, curriculum, and student achievement. The independent (explanatory) variables are per-capita personal income (PCPI), percent of population that is non-white (PCMINST), and income inequality (GINI).[1,2]

$$PREP = 96.092 + 0.001 \cdot PCPI - 17.362 \cdot PCMINST - 125.863 \cdot GINI$$
$$\phantom{PREP = 96.092 + } (5.45)^* \phantom{xxxxxx} (2.07)^* \phantom{xxxxxxxxx} (2.25)^*$$

* significant at the 0.05 level of significance

A one-dollar increase in PCPI is associated with an increase of 0.001 in the PREP score while a 1 percent demographic increase in state nonwhite population corresponds with a 17.362 PREP score decrease. Similarly, as income inequality increases PREP score decreases. A +0.10 change in the Gini ratio, say from 0.40 to 0.50, is related to a 12.586 PREP score reduction. The number in parentheses below each partial regression coefficient is the value of the $t$ statistic for that coefficient obtained by dividing the value of $b$ by its standard error. The significance of each independent–dependent partial relationship can be checked by comparing the respective $t$ value against a critical value obtained from Appendix F. (For a linear regression model having a non-zero $a$ statistic—that is a $y$-intercept—the number of degrees of freedom equals $n - k - 1$, where $n$ is the sample size and $k$ is the number of independent variables. When standardized regression coefficients are used, the constant term vanishes and the number of degrees of freedom is $n - k$.)

Because the independent variables have different measurement scales, it is difficult to assess the relative influence of each independent variable on the dependent variable. The variable with the largest $b$ coefficient is not necessarily the most influential variable since the sizes of the $b$ coefficients depend on the dimensions in which the respective variables were measured. The effects of changing per-capita income, measured in dollars, cannot be compared to the index income inequality, measured in on a continuous scale ranging from 0 to 1—the old "apples and oranges" dilemma.

Calculating a regression equation with "standardized regression coefficients" allows the analyst to compare the relative weights of each independent variable upon the values of the dependent variable. Imagine that instead of using the actual observed values of the independent variables, $x$, and the dependent variable, $y$, the

---

[1]The Gini ratio (or index of income concentration) is a numeric indicator of income equality ranging from 0 to 1. A value of 1 indicates perfect inequality (one person has all the income and the rest have none). A value of 0 indicates perfect equality (everyone has the same income).

[2]After Alisa F. Cunningham and Jane V. Wellman. *Beneath the Surface: A Statistical Analysis of the Major Variables Associated with State Grades in 'Measuring Up 2000.'* National Center for Public Policy and Higher Education, November 2001. www.highereducation.org/reports/wellman/wellman.shtml and *Measuring Up 2000* measuringup.highereducation.org/2000/

analyst converted every value to a dimensionless value of the $Z$ statistic (a "standardized value") obtained by dividing the difference between each value and the mean by the variable's standard deviation.

$$Z_{xi} = \frac{x_i - \mu_{xi}}{\sigma_x}$$

and

$$Z_y = \frac{y_i - \mu_y}{\sigma_y}$$

If the multiple regression were now computed using the standardized values, $Z_x$ and $Z_y$, the analyst would obtain another regression equation with a standardized regression coefficient—designated as "beta" ($\beta$)—for each independent variable. The constant, $a$, of the standardized regression equation is zero. The standardized regression coefficient for each independent variable can also be calculated as the product of the unstandardized regression coefficient, $b$, times the ratio between the standard deviations of the independent variable to the dependent variable.

$$\beta = b\frac{\sigma_x}{\sigma_y}$$

The standardized regression coefficient for each independent variable specifies what will happen to the value of $y$ (expressed in units of standard deviation) with a one standard deviation increase in the value of that independent variable alone.

Which has the greatest association with PREP score—per-capita income, income inequality, or demography? The standardized regression coefficients indicate that the Gini ratio has the greatest association with the K–12 preparation index PREP, having more than twice the weight as percent nonwhite in the population (see Exhibit 14–4).

The degree of association of the dependent variable with the independent variables is indicated by the $R$-squared ($R^2$) statistic—the *coefficient of multiple determination*. $R$-squared is a proportionate-reduction-in-error statistic. It shows the proportion of the variance in the values of the dependent variable accounted for by the regression equation involving the independent variables. The $R$-squared statistic for the K–12 preparation example is 0.54—54% of the variance in the K–12 preparation index among the states was explained by the regression equation involving the two income variables and one demographic variable.

Now turn to a more complete example, starting with a data set, and review the output results from a typical computer program for statistical analysis.

## Exhibit 14–4

**Regression Analysis of K–12 Preparation Index for 50 States, 2000**

| Variable | b | t | Mean | Standard deviation | Beta |
|---|---|---|---|---|---|
| PCPI | +0.001 | 5.45 | $28,224 | $4,306 | +0.002 |
| PCMINST | −17.362 | 2.07 | 0.212 | 0.143 | −29.782 |
| GINI | −125.863 | 2.25 | 0.428 | 0.022 | +72.568 |
| PREP | | | 78 | 11 | |

In a study of the effectiveness of local government operations, Malcolm Getz focused on the urban fire department.[3] His data set, presented in Exhibit 14–5, for 187 cities includes variables that describe fire incidence and fire loss, fire department personnel, stations, equipment, and tactics. An analyst can use these data to frame an evaluation problem that relates fire incidence as an outcome indicator to several input measures.

The observations for some of the cities (cases) in the data set are incomplete. These missing values are indicated by blank spaces in the data table. However, when the data are analyzed with a computer program, the missing values should be designated by a unique symbol or numeric code. Commonly used symbols are a period (.) or distinct numeric code (such as −99). Nine variables were identified for the multiple regression computation. A computer program will ignore cases having a missing value for any variable to be included in the analysis. Forty-seven of the 187 cases in the data set had a missing value for one or more variables. Therefore, the regression computations were based only on the data for the remaining 140 cases with complete observations. Exhibit 14–6 lists the mean and standard deviation for the nine variables in the regression analysis calculated over the 140 cases.

The multiple-regression results provided by a computer program basically consist of three tables: the regression equation results (Exhibit 14–7), an analysis-of-variance summary (Exhibit 14–8), and correlation results (Exhibit 14–9). Exhibit 14–7 lists the b coefficient and standard error for each independent variable. The ratio of a variable's b coefficient to the standard error yields a t statistic for that coefficient. This tests whether the calculated partial regression coefficient is statistically significantly different from 0. In this example, two independent variables are found to have statistically significant b coefficients. The partial regression coefficient for STN indicates that, among the surveyed cities, each additional

---

[3]Malcolm Getz. 1979. *The Economics of the Urban Fire Department.* Nashville, TN: Vanderbilt University Press. 172–177.

*Exhibit 14–5*

**Urban Fire Department Survey**

| Observation number | City | LABOR | EQUIP | STN | INSP | HYD | FIRES | LCOST | LLCOST | RESINS | REPORT |
|---|---|---|---|---|---|---|---|---|---|---|---|
| 1 | Abilene, TX | 5.33 | 1.43 | 0.11 | 74.59 | 30.77 | 46.44 | 39,843 | 10.59 | 0 | 0 |
| 2 | Akron, OH | 6.81 | 1.36 | 0.26 | 28.92 | 131.19 | 34.89 | 54,327 | 10.90 | 0 | 0 |
| 3 | Albany, GA | 5.63 | 1.13 | 0.02 | 189.97 | 6.13 | 78.92 | 42,880 | 10.67 | 0 | 0 |
| 4 | Schenectady, NY | 6.19 | 1.29 | 0.64 | 58.79 | 255.27 | 101.01 | 84,758 | 11.35 | 0 | 1 |
| 5 | Troy, NY | 6.94 | 1.50 | 0.60 | 5.37 | 180.00 | 123.37 | 47,662 | 10.77 | 0 | 1 |
| 6 | Allentown, PA | 5.25 | 2.00 | 0.39 | — | 94.17 | 44.41 | 55,194 | 10.92 | 0 | 1 |
| 7 | Bethlehem, PA | 4.67 | 1.67 | 0.30 | — | 61.75 | 2.65 | 57,597 | 10.96 | 1 | 1 |
| 8 | Amarillo, TX | 5.93 | 1.40 | 0.56 | 65.82 | 104.33 | 24.90 | 48,704 | 10.79 | 0 | 0 |
| 9 | Anaheim, CA | 6.31 | 1.56 | 0.22 | 25.52 | 105.13 | 13.00 | 55,627 | 10.93 | 0 | 0 |
| 10 | Santa Ana, CA | 6.77 | 1.50 | 0.36 | 61.95 | 116.07 | 38.74 | 55,924 | 10.93 | 1 | 1 |
| 11 | Anderson, IN | 5.25 | 1.38 | 0.22 | 28.52 | 28.68 | — | 34,566 | 10.45 | 0 | 0 |
| 12 | Atlanta, GA | 9.10 | 1.89 | 0.26 | 56.59 | 132.35 | 32.27 | 48,652 | 10.79 | 0 | 1 |
| 13 | Atlantic City, NJ | 7.19 | 1.33 | 0.56 | 12.45 | 91.56 | 81.77 | 48,837 | 10.80 | 0 | 1 |
| 14 | Augusta, GA | 5.97 | 1.43 | 0.44 | 29.30 | 112.50 | 76.63 | 29,795 | 10.30 | 0 | 1 |
| 15 | Austin, TX | 6.47 | 1.25 | 0.19 | 104.65 | 61.52 | 16.24 | 38,121 | 10.55 | 0 | 1 |
| 16 | Baltimore, MD | 9.53 | 1.40 | 0.65 | 9.49 | 112.58 | 24.66 | 57,233 | 10.95 | 0 | 1 |
| 17 | Baton Rouge, LA | 7.86 | 1.71 | 0.28 | 76.00 | 78.48 | 26.69 | 36,610 | 10.51 | 0 | 1 |
| 18 | Beaumont, TX | 5.97 | 1.64 | 0.15 | 16.11 | 31.51 | 54.02 | 41,811 | 10.64 | 0 | 1 |
| 19 | Billings, MT | 4.90 | 1.80 | 0.28 | 49.11 | 96.11 | 33.99 | 59,543 | 10.99 | 1 | 1 |
| 20 | Birmingham, AL | 6.78 | 1.29 | 0.34 | 19.58 | 54.20 | — | 55,840 | 10.93 | 1 | 1 |
| 21 | Boise City, ID | 6.29 | 1.63 | 0.25 | 60.54 | 41.53 | 30.93 | 44,660 | 10.71 | 0 | 1 |
| 22 | Boston, MA | 11.63 | 2.20 | 0.85 | 32.23 | 302.08 | 80.47 | 80,333 | 11.29 | 0 | 0 |

| | | | | | | | | | | | |
|---|---|---|---|---|---|---|---|---|---|---|---|
| 23 | Bridgeport, CT | 8.04 | 2.15 | 0.72 | 25.81 | 113.06 | 331.47 | 54,854 | 10.91 | 0 | 1 |
| 24 | Brockton, MA | 9.13 | 1.33 | 0.29 | 32.64 | 114.29 | 60.88 | 65,132 | 11.08 | 0 | 1 |
| 25 | Buffalo, NY | 7.52 | 1.45 | 0.75 | 9.84 | 176.36 | 139.25 | 78,471 | 11.27 | 0 | 0 |
| 26 | Canton, OH | 5.89 | 1.44 | 0.45 | 16.58 | — | 15.38 | 43,782 | 10.69 | 0 | 1 |
| 27 | Cedar Rapids, IA | 3.13 | 0.90 | 0.18 | 1.71 | 12.38 | 13.62 | 49,947 | 10.82 | 0 | 1 |
| 28 | Charleston, SC | 4.64 | 1.00 | 0.76 | 91.57 | 76.12 | — | 34,395 | 10.45 | 0 | 1 |
| 29 | Charlotte, NC | 8.09 | 1.55 | 0.19 | 47.30 | 39.73 | 26.85 | 53,355 | 10.88 | 0 | 1 |
| 30 | Chattanooga, TN | 6.14 | 1.15 | 0.17 | 106.24 | 18.03 | 102.68 | 42,114 | 10.65 | 0 | 1 |
| 31 | Chicago, IL | 9.77 | 1.43 | 0.51 | 52.04 | 202.81 | 24.29 | 78,508 | 11.27 | 0 | 1 |
| 32 | Cincinnati, OH | 10.22 | 1.50 | 0.38 | 367.39 | 14.03 | 47.87 | 43,710 | 10.69 | 1 | 1 |
| 33 | Cleveland, OH | 8.40 | 1.51 | 0.46 | 5.45 | 240.79 | 91.98 | 56,867 | 10.95 | 0 | 1 |
| 34 | Columbia, MO | 4.94 | 1.33 | 0.14 | 26.85 | 31.57 | 54.15 | 51,574 | 10.85 | 0 | 0 |
| 35 | Columbia, SC | 10.58 | 1.75 | 0.08 | 144.09 | 12.46 | 92.82 | 44,470 | 10.70 | 0 | 0 |
| 36 | Columbus, OH | 8.87 | 1.44 | 0.16 | 5.63 | 86.64 | 60.00 | 52,139 | 10.86 | 0 | 1 |
| 37 | Dallas, TX | 8.81 | 1.38 | 0.13 | 353.11 | 47.62 | — | 58,175 | 10.97 | 0 | 0 |
| 38 | Davenport, IA | 6.50 | 1.67 | 0.10 | 46.94 | 47.97 | 51.38 | 57,259 | 10.96 | 0 | 1 |
| 39 | Rock Island, IL | 4.53 | 1.20 | 0.36 | 94.01 | 128.57 | — | 54,243 | 10.90 | 0 | 1 |
| 40 | Dayton,OH | 7.00 | 1.40 | 0.36 | 30.28 | 90.88 | — | 58,120 | 10.97 | 0 | 0 |
| 41 | Decatur, IL | 4.86 | 0.86 | 0.17 | 5.67 | 67.82 | 65.91 | 52,534 | 10.87 | 0 | 1 |
| 42 | Dubuque, IA | 4.67 | 1.33 | 0.33 | 69.28 | 88.89 | 17.86 | 51,905 | 10.86 | 1 | 1 |
| 43 | Duluth, MN | 4.56 | 1.44 | 0.13 | 5.17 | 25.99 | 34.98 | 55,223 | 10.92 | 0 | 1 |
| 44 | Superior, WI | 4.75 | 1.25 | 0.10 | 177.26 | 29.94 | 53.96 | 40,083 | 10.60 | 0 | 1 |
| 45 | El Paso, TX | 6.23 | 1.43 | 0.13 | 54.24 | 23.40 | 20.97 | 57,241 | 10.96 | 1 | 0 |
| 46 | Erie, PA | 5.50 | 1.33 | 0.43 | 20.36 | — | 58.05 | 55,698 | 10.93 | 0 | 0 |
| 47 | Eugene, OR | 6.04 | 1.75 | 0.09 | 112.80 | 20.55 | 44.69 | 44,819 | 10.71 | 0 | 1 |
| 48 | Fall River, MA | 9.11 | 1.86 | 0.21 | 12.09 | 69.70 | 37.04 | 61,500 | 11.03 | 0 | 1 |

*(continued)*

## *Exhibit 14–5*

**Urban Fire Department Survey (continued)**

| Observation number | City | LABOR | EQUIP | STN | INSP | HYD | FIRES | LCOST | LLCOST | RESINS | REPORT |
|---|---|---|---|---|---|---|---|---|---|---|---|
| 49 | Fargo, ND | 6.00 | 1.25 | 0.22 | 61.96 | 107.67 | 22.88 | 54,059 | 10.90 | 1 | 0 |
| 50 | Fayetteville, NC | 7.73 | 1.80 | 0.17 | 63.97 | 67.24 | 54.63 | 46,835 | 10.75 | 0 | 1 |
| 51 | Flint, MI | 9.49 | 2.13 | 0.23 | 13.08 | 128.57 | 47.68 | 68,305 | 11.13 | 0 | 0 |
| 52 | Hollywood, FL | 5.50 | 2.00 | 0.11 | 90.98 | 41.86 | 11.48 | 64,779 | 11.08 | 0 | 1 |
| 53 | Fort Worth, TX | 7.31 | 1.50 | 0.08 | 21.17 | 22.45 | 45.13 | 47,328 | 10.76 | 1 | 1 |
| 54 | Gainesville, FL | 7.39 | 1.67 | 0.05 | 54.39 | 14.13 | 68.80 | 51,210 | 10.84 | 0 | 1 |
| 55 | Gary, IN | 6.56 | 1.50 | 0.27 | 17.87 | 38.49 | 38.21 | 42,807 | 10.66 | 0 | 1 |
| 56 | Hammond, IN | 7.52 | 1.71 | 0.26 | 62.11 | 60.22 | 30.78 | 41,953 | 10.64 | 0 | 1 |
| 57 | East Chicago. IN | 5.72 | 1.71 | 0.50 | 8.26 | 45.42 | 76.76 | 48,656 | 10.79 | 1 | 0 |
| 58 | Grand Rapids, MI | 6.43 | 1.36 | 0.23 | 6.96 | 88.83 | 40.79 | 64,804 | 11.08 | 0 | 1 |
| 59 | Great Falls, MT | 4.63 | 1.75 | 0.24 | 57.13 | 117.65 | 23.12 | 68,686 | 11.14 | 0 | 1 |
| 60 | Green Bay, WI | 7.83 | 1.50 | 0.13 | 33.54 | 53.89 | 29.35 | 46,684 | 10.75 | 0 | 1 |
| 61 | Greensboro, NC | 7.53 | 1.58 | 0.20 | 91.80 | 108.03 | 16.83 | 59,406 | 10.99 | 0 | 1 |
| 62 | High Point, NC | 6.16 | 1.38 | 0.25 | 276.63 | 96.88 | 52.14 | 42,623 | 10.66 | 1 | 1 |
| 63 | Greenville, SC | 8.21 | 2.40 | 0.22 | 239.94 | 59.48 | 66.67 | 43,435 | 10.68 | 0 | 1 |
| 64 | Hamilton, OH | 6.00 | 1.60 | 0.29 | 73.78 | 93.76 | 25.19 | 50,363 | 10.83 | 0 | 0 |
| 65 | Middletown, OH | 4.20 | 1.40 | 0.25 | 68.91 | 64.90 | — | 46,280 | 10.74 | 0 | 1 |
| 66 | Harrisburg, PA | 3.32 | 1.25 | 0.67 | 11.51 | 125.00 | — | 56,915 | 10.95 | 0 | 1 |
| 67 | Honolulu, HI | 7.54 | 1.24 | 0.06 | 11.16 | 19.71 | 19.09 | 65,122 | 11.08 | 1 | 1 |
| 68 | Houston, TX | 9.07 | 1.54 | 0.13 | 16.85 | 47.91 | 26.05 | 63,754 | 11.06 | 0 | 1 |
| 69 | Huntington, WV | 5.46 | 1.88 | 0.47 | 65.04 | 70.59 | 10.46 | 39,768 | 10.59 | 0 | 0 |
| 70 | Ashland, KY | 6.33 | 1.67 | 0.33 | 28.14 | 111.33 | 48.86 | 30,084 | 10.31 | 0 | 0 |

| | | | | | | | | | | |
|---|---|---|---|---|---|---|---|---|---|---|
| 71 | Indianapolis, IN | 7.84 | 1.30 | 0.41 | 28.77 | 124.80 | 30.92 | 43,905 | 10.69 | 1 | 1 |
| 72 | Jackson, MS | 6.50 | 1.16 | 0.32 | 206.47 | 64.00 | 164.88 | 33,782 | 10.43 | 0 | 1 |
| 73 | Jacksonville, FL | 5.10 | 1.21 | 0.05 | 41.49 | 6.64 | 29.88 | 48,288 | 10.78 | 0 | 0 |
| 74 | Kansas City, MO | 5.76 | 1.34 | 0.14 | 20.64 | 48.05 | 39.62 | 55,665 | 10.93 | 0 | 1 |
| 75 | Kenosha, WI | 8.75 | 2.25 | 0.29 | 15.73 | 143.43 | 24.13 | 47,780 | 10.77 | 0 | 1 |
| 76 | Knoxville, TN | 7.12 | 1.42 | 0.24 | 44.61 | 63.41 | 32.24 | 37,995 | 10.55 | 0 | 1 |
| 77 | La Crosse, WI | 8.00 | 2.00 | 0.22 | 19.69 | 78.61 | — | 44,730 | 10.71 | 0 | 1 |
| 78 | Lafayette, LA | 5.43 | 1.43 | 0.20 | 6.80 | 70.60 | 73.82 | 39,566 | 10.59 | 0 | 1 |
| 79 | Lancaster, PA | 6.64 | 1.50 | 0.57 | 104.93 | 144.43 | 30.46 | 51,689 | 10.85 | 1 | 1 |
| 80 | Lansing, MI | 7.40 | 1.50 | 0.29 | 22.74 | 85.82 | 41.03 | 56,278 | 10.94 | 0 | 1 |
| 81 | Lawrence, MA | 6.32 | 1.43 | 1.00 | 27.08 | 154.86 | 78.91 | 56,112 | 10.94 | 0 | 1 |
| 82 | Haverhill, MA | 4.54 | 1.29 | 0.19 | 146.30 | 25.00 | 31.23 | 51,469 | 10.85 | 0 | 0 |
| 83 | Lawton, OK | 5.33 | 1.50 | 0.19 | 4.82 | 78.13 | 75.68 | 32,734 | 10.40 | 0 | 1 |
| 84 | Lexington, KY | 8.38 | 1.71 | 0.07 | 435.25 | 18.72 | 52.19 | 33,934 | 10.43 | 0 | 0 |
| 85 | Little Rock, AR | 5.51 | 1.24 | 0.28 | 47.76 | 66.38 | 96.40 | 38,924 | 10.57 | 0 | 1 |
| 86 | Lorain, OH | 4.95 | 1.40 | 0.19 | 16.18 | 79.04 | 18.14 | 41,910 | 10.64 | 0 | 1 |
| 87 | Elyria, OH | 6.17 | 1.50 | 0.18 | 7.05 | 78.14 | 25.25 | 43,594 | 10.68 | 0 | 1 |
| 88 | Los Angeles, CA | 8.79 | 1.87 | 0.22 | 21.54 | 105.42 | 52.60 | 57,286 | 10.96 | 0 | 1 |
| 89 | Los Angeles County. CA | 4.78 | 1.29 | 0.06 | 344.27 | 18.83 | — | 67,800 | 11.12 | 0 | 1 |
| 90 | Long Beach, CA | 6.48 | 1.14 | 0.38 | 22.30 | 91.71 | 42.91 | 63,823 | 11.06 | 0 | 1 |
| 91 | Louisville, KY | 8.41 | 1.24 | 0.36 | 48.40 | 85.33 | 31.64 | 41,514 | 10.63 | 1 | 1 |
| 92 | Lubbock, TX | 6.91 | 1.45 | 0.13 | 10.74 | 27.91 | 49.95 | 47,225 | 10.76 | 0 | 1 |
| 93 | Macon, GA | 8.04 | 1.33 | 0.18 | 75.65 | 32.69 | 13.42 | 41,804 | 10.64 | 0 | 0 |
| 94 | Madison, WI | 6.03 | 1.50 | 0.20 | 92.50 | 89.54 | 17.12 | 77,162 | 11.25 | 0 | 0 |
| 95 | Memphis, TN | 6.93 | 1.43 | 0.17 | 17.86 | 56.45 | 40.42 | 67,591 | 11.12 | 0 | 0 |
| 96 | Meriden, CT | 5.05 | 1.40 | 0.21 | 46.46 | 45.83 | 50.74 | 65,294 | 11.09 | 0 | 1 |

*(continued)*

## Exhibit 14–5

**Urban Fire Department Survey (continued)**

| Observation number | City | LABOR | EQUIP | STN | INSP | HYD | FIRES | LCOST | LLCOST | RESINS | REPORT |
|---|---|---|---|---|---|---|---|---|---|---|---|
| 97 | Milwaukee, WI | 9.57 | 1.59 | 0.35 | 1009.26 | 165.25 | 49.27 | 61,050 | 11.02 | 0 | 0 |
| 98 | Minneapolis, MN | 8.42 | 1.55 | 0.34 | 46.62 | 136.00 | 99.82 | 71,306 | 11.17 | 0 | 0 |
| 99 | St. Paul, MN | 8.96 | 1.65 | 0.31 | 21.98 | 127.27 | 32.75 | 55,471 | 10.92 | 1 | 0 |
| 100 | Mobile, AL | 7.70 | 1.11 | 0.09 | 49.11 | 32.24 | — | 43,930 | 10.69 | 0 | 1 |
| 101 | Montgomery, AL | 7.69 | 1.46 | 0.25 | 101.46 | 84.27 | — | 47,662 | 10.77 | 0 | 1 |
| 102 | Nashville, TN | 7.13 | 1.46 | 0.39 | 33.75 | 109.05 | 12.63 | 43,993 | 10.69 | 0 | 0 |
| 103 | Newark, NJ | 8.84 | 1.26 | 1.15 | 88.78 | 212.77 | 74.90 | 63,709 | 11.06 | 1 | 1 |
| 104 | New Bedford, MA | 7.17 | 1.40 | 0.38 | — | 87.65 | 113.16 | 62,750 | 11.05 | 0 | 1 |
| 105 | New Orleans, LA | 7.73 | 1.38 | 0.21 | 29.43 | 73.71 | 37.20 | 49,700 | 10.81 | 0 | 1 |
| 106 | Newport News, VA | 5.67 | 1.67 | 0.14 | 6.28 | 46.88 | 42.65 | 54,329 | 10.90 | 0 | 1 |
| 107 | Hampton, VA | 4.70 | 2.00 | 0.16 | 9.99 | 29.96 | — | 39,451 | 10.58 | 0 | 0 |
| 108 | Ogden, UT | 7.27 | 1.60 | 0.24 | 315.74 | 78.57 | 23.91 | 51,043 | 10.84 | 1 | 1 |
| 109 | Omaha, NE | 9.31 | 1.53 | 0.20 | 128.05 | 150.49 | 30.01 | 52,580 | 10.87 | 0 | 1 |
| 110 | Owensboro, KY | 7.25 | 1.75 | 0.36 | 66.04 | 145.45 | 46.47 | 33,452 | 10.42 | 0 | 1 |
| 111 | Oxnard, CA | 5.71 | 1.20 | 0.22 | 279.62 | 91.30 | 35.73 | 51,758 | 10.85 | 1 | 1 |
| 112 | Ventura, CA | 5.36 | 1.75 | 0.24 | 21.65 | 138.24 | 43.14 | 50,419 | 10.83 | 0 | 1 |
| 113 | Paterson, NJ | 7.55 | 1.50 | 1.20 | — | 228.90 | 213.33 | 62,225 | 11.04 | 0 | 0 |
| 114 | Peoria, IL | 4.86 | 1.50 | 0.24 | 21.26 | 68.46 | 39.56 | 69,642 | 11.15 | 0 | 0 |
| 115 | Phoenix, AZ | 6.92 | 1.26 | 0.12 | 22.26 | 63.94 | 42.56 | 53,514 | 10.89 | 0 | 1 |
| 116 | Pine Bluff, AR | 3.89 | 1.17 | 0.35 | 34.23 | 88.24 | 37.93 | 32,326 | 10.38 | 0 | 1 |
| 117 | Pittsburgh, PA | 6.24 | 1.51 | 0.77 | 11.64 | 158.93 | 56.23 | 51,755 | 10.85 | 0 | 1 |
| 118 | Pittsfield, MA | 6.70 | 1.80 | 0.12 | 54.93 | 34.52 | — | 62,799 | 11.05 | 0 | 1 |

| | | | | | | | | | | | |
|---|---|---|---|---|---|---|---|---|---|---|---|
| 119 | Portland, ME | 6.35 | 1.30 | 0.37 | 337.90 | 44.78 | 74.69 | 51,724 | 10.85 | 1 | 1 |
| 120 | Portland, OR | 6.64 | 1.20 | 0.33 | 3.03 | 96.67 | 25.73 | 61,127 | 11.02 | 0 | 1 |
| 121 | Pawtucket, RI | 5.38 | 1.50 | 0.67 | 2.84 | 157.22 | — | 61,719 | 11.03 | 0 | 1 |
| 122 | Warwick. RI | 5.00 | 1.38 | 0.22 | 36.15 | 45.06 | 25.18 | 62,802 | 11.05 | 0 | 1 |
| 123 | Provo, UT | 5.67 | 2.50 | 0.07 | 64.25 | 30.34 | 17.31 | 48,588 | 10.79 | 0 | 1 |
| 124 | Pueblo, CO | 5.22 | 1.22 | 0.27 | 77.73 | 75.76 | 34.91 | 38,507 | 10.56 | 0 | 0 |
| 125 | Racine, WI | 6.57 | 1.57 | 0.50 | 10.66 | 160.57 | 12.01 | 45,010 | 10.71 | 0 | 1 |
| 126 | Raleigh, NC | 6.48 | 1.43 | 0.30 | 42.60 | 71.20 | 82.08 | 49,173 | 10.80 | 0 | 1 |
| 127 | Richmond, VA | 8.84 | 2.05 | 0.33 | 102.15 | 84.29 | 62.04 | 53,400 | 10.89 | 0 | 1 |
| 128 | Rochester, MN | 6.92 | 1.75 | 0.25 | 46.05 | 108.00 | 29.57 | 44,995 | 10.71 | 1 | 1 |
| 129 | Rockford, IL | 7.61 | 1.36 | 0.26 | 12.39 | 78.07 | 42.02 | 56,824 | 10.95 | 1 | 1 |
| 130 | Sacramento, CA | 7.53 | 1.43 | 0.22 | 28.93 | 62.28 | 34.60 | 49,962 | 10.82 | 0 | 1 |
| 131 | Salem, OR | 6.14 | 1.57 | 0.13 | 37.39 | 25.00 | 30.05 | 49,286 | 10.81 | 0 | 1 |
| 132 | Salt Lake City, UT | 7.50 | 1.43 | 0.24 | 34.59 | 131.24 | 42.20 | 47,734 | 10.77 | 0 | 0 |
| 133 | San Angelo, TX | 5.05 | 1.29 | 0.19 | 21.70 | 17.50 | 43.37 | 33,132 | 10.41 | 0 | 1 |
| 134 | San Antonio, TX | 7.57 | 1.19 | 0.14 | 29.70 | 37.21 | 24.62 | 60,727 | 11.01 | 1 | 1 |
| 135 | San Bernardino, CA | 5.32 | 1.36 | 0.22 | 103.82 | 56.92 | — | 57,782 | 10.96 | 1 | 1 |
| 136 | Riverside, CA | 6.60 | 1.56 | 0.12 | 10.77 | 50.32 | — | 54,337 | 10.90 | 0 | 1 |
| 137 | Ontario, CA | 4.36 | 1.20 | 0.16 | 17.38 | 125.00 | — | 46,727 | 10.75 | 0 | 1 |
| 138 | San Francisco, CA | 11.01 | 1.45 | 1.00 | 23.96 | 211.70 | 52.10 | 64,751 | 11.08 | 1 | 0 |
| 139 | Oakland, CA | 7.36 | 1.33 | 0.51 | 4.02 | 113.19 | 55.47 | 55,844 | 10.93 | 0 | 0 |
| 140 | San Jose, CA | 6.89 | 1.84 | 0.17 | 22.98 | 66.54 | 35.50 | 61,579 | 11.03 | 0 | 0 |
| 141 | San Barbara, CA | 4.52 | 1.14 | 0.39 | 184.59 | 104.22 | 29.07 | 58,126 | 10.97 | 1 | 1 |
| 142 | Santa Rosa, CA | 4.40 | 1.20 | 0.20 | 33.89 | 76.00 | 21.59 | 57,386 | 10.96 | 0 | 1 |
| 143 | Savannah, GA | 7.41 | 1.67 | 0.24 | 22.76 | 81.22 | 54.21 | 52,060 | 10.86 | 0 | 1 |
| 144 | Scranton, PA | 5.07 | 1.33 | 0.48 | 10.20 | — | 20.23 | 46,649 | 10.75 | 0 | 0 |

*(continued)*

*Exhibit 14–5*

**Urban Fire Department Survey *(continued)***

| Observation number | City | LABOR | EQUIP | STN | INSP | HYD | FIRES | LCOST | LLCOST | RESINS | REPORT |
|---|---|---|---|---|---|---|---|---|---|---|---|
| 145 | Seattle, WA | 7.19 | 1.31 | 0.39 | 46.27 | 122.22 | 21.14 | 64,800 | 11.08 | 0 | 1 |
| 146 | Everett, WA | 5.80 | 1.40 | 0.22 | 40.66 | 53.26 | 42.56 | 68,026 | 11.13 | 0 | 0 |
| 147 | Sioux Falls, SD | 5.61 | 1.17 | 0.18 | 6.79 | 51.91 | 12.30 | 50,153 | 10.82 | 0 | 1 |
| 148 | South Bend, IN | 6.58 | 1.64 | 0.32 | 33.08 | 93.24 | — | 36,772 | 10.51 | 0 | 1 |
| 149 | Spokane, WA | 5.65 | 1.29 | 0.33 | 31.91 | 92.16 | 61.98 | 49,685 | 10.81 | 0 | 1 |
| 150 | Springfield, MO | 6.44 | 1.33 | 0.14 | 8.84 | 55.90 | 36.75 | 42,761 | 10.66 | 0 | 1 |
| 151 | Springfield, OH | 5.43 | 1.43 | 0.41 | 36.77 | 110.29 | 30.85 | 51,270 | 10.84 | 0 | 1 |
| 152 | Holyoke, MA | 6.63 | 1.50 | 0.26 | 45.97 | 52.17 | — | 48,509 | 10.79 | 0 | 0 |
| 153 | Steubenville, OH | 3.87 | 1.40 | 0.63 | 19.16 | 125.00 | 22.60 | 39,029 | 10.57 | 0 | 1 |
| 154 | Weirton, WV | 4.00 | 4.00 | 0.08 | — | 43.69 | 28.65 | 48,821 | 10.80 | 0 | 1 |
| 155 | Stockton, CA | 5.78 | 1.33 | 0.26 | 26.11 | 68.71 | 45.01 | 56,188 | 10.94 | 1 | 0 |
| 156 | Syracuse, NY | 9.17 | 1.58 | 0.46 | — | 207.69 | 141.30 | 75,382 | 11.23 | 0 | 1 |
| 157 | Tacoma, WA | 5.13 | 1.13 | 0.33 | 21.62 | 82.58 | 40.66 | 51,463 | 10.85 | 0 | 1 |
| 158 | Tampa, FL | 9.46 | 1.26 | 0.23 | 85.10 | 59.52 | — | 55,198 | 10.92 | 0 | 1 |
| 159 | St. Petersburg, FL | 8.12 | 1.73 | 0.19 | 10.10 | 63.76 | 30.14 | 51,465 | 10.85 | 0 | 1 |
| 160 | Topeka, KS | 6.03 | 1.25 | 0.24 | 42.69 | 56.10 | 35.66 | 40,959 | 10.62 | 0 | 1 |
| 161 | Tucson, AZ | 10.07 | 1.50 | 0.15 | 6.18 | 72.65 | 33.72 | 44,348 | 10.70 | 1 | 1 |
| 162 | Tulsa, OK | 6.38 | 1.47 | 0.18 | 10.75 | 48.94 | 41.18 | 42,107 | 10.65 | 0 | 1 |
| 163 | Vallejo, CA | 4.61 | 1.33 | 0.22 | 9.14 | 61.63 | — | 54,374 | 10.90 | 1 | 0 |
| 164 | Vineland, NJ | 1.20 | 1.20 | 0.07 | — | 17.38 | 47.92 | 42,694 | 10.66 | 0 | 1 |
| 165 | Washington, DC | 10.87 | 2.45 | 0.48 | 35.50 | 130.04 | 35.24 | 119,446 | 11.69 | 0 | 1 |
| 166 | West Palm Beach, FL | 7.20 | 1.80 | 0.12 | 39.20 | 24.29 | 57.00 | 53,032 | 10.88 | 0 | 1 |

| # | City | LABOR | INSP | STN | EQUIP | FIRES | HYD | LCOST | LLCOST | RESINS | REPORT |
|---|------|-------|------|-----|-------|-------|-----|-------|--------|--------|--------|
| 167 | Wheeling, | 4.57 | 1.29 | 0.54 | 23.90 | 82.15 | 34.80 | 40,474 | 10.61 | 0 | 1 |
| 168 | Wichita, KS | 8.49 | 1.80 | 0.16 | 64.11 | 46.44 | 25.34 | 49,650 | 10.81 | 1 | 1 |
| 169 | Wichita Falls, TX | 6.24 | 1.71 | 0.14 | 26.94 | 35.61 | 41.06 | 37,579 | 10.53 | 0 | 1 |
| 170 | Wilkes Barre, PA | 4.03 | 2.00 | 1.00 | 2.09 | 75.00 | 67.30 | 57,425 | 10.96 | 0 | 1 |
| 171 | Worcester, MA | 9.05 | 1.64 | 0.37 | 37.98 | 124.16 | 69.07 | 61,076 | 11.02 | 0 | 0 |
| 172 | Youngstown, OH | 6.28 | 1.23 | 0.37 | 51.17 | 124.29 | 29.99 | 44,247 | 10.70 | 0 | 0 |
| 173 | Burlington, NC | 7.00 | 1.67 | 0.19 | 36.37 | 87.50 | — | 48,786 | 10.80 | 1 | 1 |
| 174 | Casper, WY | 4.67 | 1.25 | 0.36 | 9.23 | 84.09 | — | 54,083 | 10.90 | 0 | 0 |
| 175 | Springdale, AR | 2.22 | 1.33 | 0.19 | 0.35 | — | — | 27,095 | 10.21 | 0 | 1 |
| 176 | Florence, AL | 3.93 | 1.40 | 0.24 | 14.45 | 30.71 | — | 35,536 | 10.48 | 0 | 1 |
| 177 | Killeen, TX | 2.80 | 1.40 | 0.19 | 38.18 | 25.00 | — | 36,667 | 10.51 | 0 | 1 |
| 178 | Bristol, VA | 6.33 | 2.67 | 0.25 | — | 34.92 | — | 28,741 | 10.27 | 0 | 1 |
| 179 | New Brunswick, NJ | 6.00 | 1.25 | 0.80 | — | — | — | 56,967 | 10.95 | 0 | 0 |
| 180 | Plainfield, NJ | 8.92 | 2.00 | 0.50 | 26.35 | 113.33 | — | 67,493 | 11.12 | 0 | 0 |
| 181 | Kennewick, WA | 3.50 | 1.50 | 0.18 | 7.22 | 37.09 | — | 39,431 | 10.58 | 0 | 1 |
| 182 | Boca Raton, FL | 4.43 | 2.00 | 0.10 | 12.28 | 26.74 | — | 66,867 | 11.11 | 0 | 0 |
| 183 | Boulder, CO | 6.11 | 1.67 | 0.21 | 24.24 | 128.57 | — | 49,423 | 10.81 | 0 | 1 |
| 184 | Cedar Falls, IA | 7.67 | 6.00 | 0.02 | 1.89 | 12.38 | — | 51,196 | 10.84 | 0 | 1 |
| 185 | Fairfield, CA | 5.67 | 5.00 | 0.04 | 11.59 | 44.00 | — | 63,384 | 11.06 | 0 | 0 |
| 186 | Seaside, CA | 6.00 | 2.00 | 0.33 | 14.55 | 86.67 | — | 45,557 | 10.73 | 0 | 1 |
| 187 | Virginia Beach, VA | 2.53 | 2.40 | 0.05 | 85.80 | 8.06 | — | 49,085 | 10.80 | 0 | 1 |

LABOR = suppression labor on duty per station; EQUIP = active first-line equipment per station; INSP = Inspections per 1,000 people; STN = Stations per square mile; FIRES = fires per square mile; HYD = hydrants per square mile; LCOST = labor cost per single-family housing unit; LCOST = labor cost per duty post base salary × number of shifts × (1 + fringe benefits rate), where base salary is a weighted average of captain and first-class firefighter salaries; LLCOST = natural logarithm of the labor cost per duty shift; RESINS 1 = a regular residential inspection program; REPORT 1 = fires only reported when losses occurred; used with permission, Malcolm Getz. 1979. *The Economics of the Urban Fire Department.* Nashville, TN: Vanderbilt University Press, 172–177.

# Exhibit 14–6

**Descriptive Statistics for the Variables in the Regression Analysis: Urban Fire Departments**

| Variable | Mean | Standard deviation | Number of cases |
|----------|------|--------------------|-----------------|
| LABOR | 6.8229 | 1.6276 | 140 |
| EQUIP | 1.5074 | 0.2827 | 140 |
| STN | 0.2976 | 0.2030 | 140 |
| INSP | 64.1101 | 108.9176 | 140 |
| HYD | 84.4772 | 52.0482 | 140 |
| FIRES | 46.6964 | 35.1904 | 140 |
| LLCOST* | 10.8356 | 0.2189 | 140 |
| RESINS | 0.1786 | 0.3844 | 140 |
| REPORT | 0.7429 | 0.4386 | 140 |

*The mean labor cost per duty post is $52,050 with a standard deviation of $12,078.

# Exhibit 14–7

**Regression Equation Results: Urban Fire Departments**
Dependent Variable: FIRES $n = 140$

| Variable | $b$ coefficient | Standard error of $b$ | Standardized coefficient $\beta$ | $t$ Statistic |
|----------|-----------------|-----------------------|----------------------------------|---------------|
| CONSTANT | 124.686 | 151.110 | 0.000 | 0.825 |
| LABOR | 2.993 | 2.117 | 0.138 | 1.414 |
| EQUIP | 4.561 | 11.105 | 0.037 | 0.411 |
| STN | 79.126 | 20.124 | 0.457 | 3.932* |
| INSP | 0.020 | 0.027 | 0.062 | 0.743 |
| HYD | −0.114 | 0.085 | −0.169 | −1.348 |
| LLCOST | −11.030 | 14.205 | −0.069 | −0.776 |
| RESINS | −15.483 | 7.674 | −0.169 | −2.017* |
| REPORT | 2.457 | 6.544 | 0.031 | 0.376 |

*statistically significant (two-tailed test at the 0.05 level of significance)

# Exhibit 14–8

**Analysis-of-Variance Results: Urban Fire Departments**

| Source | Sum-of-squares | df | Mean square | F |
|--------|----------------|-----|-------------|------|
| Regression | 27,916.516 | 8 | 3,489.564 | 3.170 |
| Residual | 144,215.973 | 131 | 1,100.885 | |
| Total | 172,132.489 | 139 | | |

## Exhibit 14–9

**Correlation Results: Urban Fire Departments**

Dependent variable = FIRES

$n = 140$

47 cases deleted due to missing data

$R = 0.403$

$R^2 = 0.162$

$R^2$ adjusted $= 0.111$

Standard error of estimate $= 33.180$

---

fire station per square mile is associated with an increase in the fire incidence rate of 79 fires per 1,000 single family residences. The partial regression coefficient for RESINS indicates that the fire incidence rate is 15.5 fires per 1,000 single family units lower in cities with a residential inspection program than in cities without such a program. The standardized regression coefficients indicate that equipment per station, inspections per 1,000 population, labor cost, and fire reporting method are weakly related to fire incidence in contrast to the number of firefighters per station, stations per square mile, hydrants per square mile, and having a residential inspection program.

The association between fire stations and fire incidence is an example of a spurious relationship. Fire stations do not "cause" fires (although maybe fires inspire building stations). Rather, some other characteristic, such as a city's population density, is possibly affecting both the rate of fire occurrence and the city government's response to the perceived danger in terms of building more fire stations.

An analysis-of-variance computation provides an overall test of significance for the relationship specified by the regression equation. Each variable, including the dependent variable, defines a distinct group consisting of the values that that variable takes on over the 140 cities included in the analysis. The analysis of variance table compares the between-group variance (called the "regression" variation) to the within-group variance (called the "residual" variation). The ratio yields an $F$ statistic that may be checked for statistical significance with a reference table using the degrees of freedom specified in the problem. In this example the calculated $F$ value of 3.17 exceeds the critical value of $F$ of approximately 2.1 at the 0.05 level of significance. Therefore, there are statistically significant differences between the variables in the regression relationship and the probability of obtaining a relationship such as that specified by the regression equation by chance is less than 5%.

The results of a multiple regression analysis will also include summary correlation statistics including Pearson's correlation coefficient, *R,* the coefficient of multiple determination, $R^2$, an adjusted $R^2$, and the standard error of the estimate.

$R^2$, the coefficient of multiple determination, indicates the proportion of the variance of the dependent variable that is explained by the regression equation. In this example, 16.2% of the variance in the number of fires per 1,000 single family residences among the 140 cities is explained by the regression relationship including the eight independent variables. The analyst can check the computation of $R^2$ with the results summarized in the analysis-of-variance table. $R^2$ equals the ratio of the between-groups sum of squares (sum-of-squares regression) to the total sum of squares (regression + residual).

$$R^2 = \frac{\text{SSR}}{\text{SST}} = 1 - \frac{\text{SSE}}{\text{SST}}$$

where

SSE = sum-of-squares error (residual)

SSR = sum-of-squares regression

SST = sum-of-squares total (residual + regression)

The value of $R^2$ tends to increase with the number of independent variables in the regression equation. If the analyst uses $R^2$ as an estimate of the population coefficient of determination (say to use the multiple-regression equation to predict a fire incidence, given values for each of the independent variables), the strength-of-association should be corrected—taking into account the number of degrees of freedom in the problem. The resultant, somewhat smaller value for the coefficient of multiple determination is called $R^2_{\text{adjusted}}$.

$$R^2_{\text{adjusted}} = 1 - \frac{\text{SSE}}{\text{SST}} - \frac{n-1}{n-k-1}$$

where

$n$ = sample size—number of units of analysis included in the regression analysis

$k$ = number of independent variables

Multiple-regression analysis is a versatile technique for multivariate analysis. However, as with linear-regression analysis, there are several important prerequisite conditions and assumptions that the analyst must consciously examine and verify.

(1) The first requirement is that the analyst should formulate a sensible theoretical model. Each multiple regression problem should tell a story about why the dependent variable is potentially affected by the independent variables. Some-

times analysts are tempted to include every variable they can measure in the analysis and omit variables that are too much work to measure—hoping that the mathematical computations will explain what is happening. However, to the computer these data are merely numbers and the results may indicate nonsensical and spurious relationships in which the analyst is hard pressed to find any meaning, while the influence of other variables, potentially providing a better explanation, is not addressed. Also, analysts sometimes include many variables in a search for a high $R^2$. But an explanatory equation with 25 to 50 independent variables is not as useful in a management or policy sense as an equation with only one, two, or three key variables.

(2) Another requirement is that the sample size must be large enough to support statistical analysis. The number of independent variables should not outstrip the units of analysis. In general, there should be at least 10 or 20 times as many units of analysis included in the analysis as there are independent variables. Further, the analyst should assure that no systematic errors were introduced in obtaining the observations.

(3) A third assumption is that each unit of analysis can be considered as having been drawn from the same statistical population. This means that the units of analysis are assumed to be alike in all relevant respects except for the characteristics or attributes described by the variables included in the regression analysis. Sometimes analysts inadvertently merge different groups into the same data set, include observations from a time when different policies were in effect, or include places or objects with different environmental conditions among the observed units of analysis. Some computer programs will help the analyst identify outliers—cases with large residuals. The residual is the difference between the observed value of the dependent variable and the value "predicted" by the regression equation. Standardized residuals are obtained by dividing each residual by the standard deviation of residual values for every case in the sample. For large sample sizes the standardized residual for about 95% of the cases should be between $-2$ and $+2$. Cases with larger standardized residuals should be examined to check why they might differ from other cases in the sample. The remedy, if this assumption is not verified, is to eliminate certain cases from the analysis, or return to the units of analysis, observe additional variables that describe the possible differences, and include these variables in the multiple-regression analysis.

(4) Every variable is assumed to have an interval level of measurement. Variables having a nominal level of measurement can be introduced if they are recoded as dummy variables with dichotomous categories. Variables having an ordinal level of measurement also can be introduced if the ordinal categories represent the regular grouping of values on an underlying interval scale (for example, age groups or level-of-education groups).

(5) A fifth assumption is that the data are not "autocorrelated." Autocorrelation exists if the units of analysis somehow interact so that the observed values for one unit of analysis are influenced by the observations of other units of analysis. Analysts need to be sensitive to the possibility of autocorrelation if the units of

analysis are successive points in time—that is, if repeated observations, daily, weekly, monthly, or yearly, are made of the same object or at the same site. Plotting the standardized regression residuals in the order that each case was observed or computation of the Durbin–Watson statistic can assist the analyst in verifying that autocorrelation is not a problem.

(6) A sixth assumption is the absence of a condition called "multicollinearity." Basically, the independent variables need to be independent of each other. If the values of two or more independent variables are correlated with one another, "intercorrelated," the analyst cannot isolate the effects of each variable on the dependent variable. The standardized partial regression coefficients will not accurately represent the relative importance of the variables. The partial regression coefficients will tend to take on a wide range of values (that is, have large standard errors) and the total $R^2$ will also be artificially high. One way to check for multicollinearity is to compute Pearson's correlation coefficient, $r$, for each two-variable relationship in the problem. The results are usually presented in a correlation matrix showing the $r$ statistic obtained upon correlating every variable with every other variable. If the sample size exceeds 50, an approximate test for the significance of each $r$ can be conducted with the following relationship:

$$r_{critical} = \frac{Z_{critical}}{n - 1} = \frac{1.96}{n - 1}$$

The analyst should scan the correlation matrix. The only significant relationships should involve the dependent variable. Exhibit 14–10 shows the correlation matrix for the variables in the urban fire department example. The variables describing the characteristics of the fire departments are intercorrelated (LABOR with EQUIP, LABOR with HYD, STN with HYD). Possible remedies to multicollinearity include eliminating one or more of the involved independent variables from the analysis or creating a new independent variable by dividing one of the intercorrelated independent variables by another (for example, if LABOR were divided by STN the analyst would have a new independent variable—firefighters per square mile—that would replace both LABOR and STN in the analysis).

(7) The variance in the dependent variable, $y$, throughout the range of each independent variable, should be approximately constant. This condition is called "homoscedasticity." This assumption can be checked by examining scatterplots of the standardized regression residuals against the predicted values of the dependent variable or against the observed values of each independent variable. An apparent narrowing or widening of the residuals across the range of the data suggests that this assumption is not being met. Data transformations using natural logarithms (designated ln $x$) or logarithm to the base 10 (designated $\log_{10}x$) may remedy the problem.

(8) It is assumed that a linear model is a reasonable approximation of the relationship between the dependent variable and each independent variable. The linear assumption can also be examined using a scatterplot of the standardized

# Exhibit 14–10

**Correlation Matrix: Urban Fire Departments**

|          | LABOR  | EQUIP  | STN    | INSP   | HYD    | FIRES  | LLCOST | RESINS | REPORT |
|----------|--------|--------|--------|--------|--------|--------|--------|--------|--------|
| LABOR    | 1.000  |        |        |        |        |        |        |        |        |
| EQUIP    | 0.404  | 1.000  |        |        |        |        |        |        |        |
| STN      | 0.171  | 0.052  | 1.000  |        |        |        |        |        |        |
| INSP     | 0.152  | 0.025  | −0.061 | 1.000  |        |        |        |        |        |
| HYD      | 0.360  | 0.130  | 0.711  | −0.023 | 1.000  |        |        |        |        |
| FIRES    | 0.134  | 0.103  | 0.326  | 0.038  | 0.179  | 1.000  |        |        |        |
| LLCOST   | 0.283  | 0.161  | 0.225  | −0.076 | 0.358  | 0.001  | 1.000  |        |        |
| RESINS   | 0.143  | −0.107 | 0.092  | 0.140  | 0.018  | −0.109 | 0.055  | 1.000  |        |
| REPORT   | −0.072 | −0.006 | −0.028 | −0.129 | −0.077 | 0.018  | −0.121 | 0.018  | 1.000  |

regression residuals against the predicted values of the dependent variable or against the observed values of each independent variable. A linear model is indicated if the residuals points appear to be randomly scattered, with both positive and negative values, throughout the range of y-estimated. A convex, concave, slanted, or other distinct pattern in the residual plot suggests that the regression equation should be nonlinear and the analyst should simplify the regression model by eliminating some independent variables or carefully understand the nature of the relationship between the dependent variable and each independent variable. Logarithmic data transformations may also help here.

(9) Lastly, it is assumed that the values of the dependent variable are normally distributed for each independent variable. Plotting a histogram of the regression residuals will help in examining this assumption. Its shape should approximate that of a normal distribution. The analyst should combine an examination of this assumption with a review of the assumptions for constant variance and linearity. Sometimes data transformations will provide a more normal distribution of residuals; another possible remedy is to increase the sample size.

# Homework Exercises

**14-1** Some policy analysts have reported a positive relationship between mortality and income inequality. Consider the data in Exhibit HW14–1A presenting mortality, high school education, and income inequality variables for the 25 most populous states. The "Gini ratio" econometric indicator of income inequality rages from 0 to 1. A value of 0 indicates perfect income equality. A value of 1 indicates perfect inequality—one individual has all the income while the rest have none. Examine the relationship between MORTALITY as the dependent variable and PCTLTHS (percent of state population having less than a high school education) and GINI.

## Exhibit HW14–1A

**Measures of Mortality, Education, and Income Inequality in the 25 Most Populous States**

| State | Mortality: Age-adjusted deaths per 100,000 (2003) MORTALITY | Percent less than high school (2003) PCTLTHS | Gini ratio (1999) GINI |
|---|---|---|---|
| Alabama | 1,001.7 | 20.5% | 0.475 |
| Arizona | 787.1 | 17.0% | 0.450 |
| California | 754.3 | 19.2% | 0.475 |
| Colorado | 784.3 | 12.8% | 0.438 |
| Florida | 776.0 | 16.4% | 0.470 |
| Georgia | 946.4 | 16.5% | 0.461 |
| Illinois | 834.5 | 15.1% | 0.456 |
| Indiana | 894.5 | 15.1% | 0.424 |
| Kentucky | 977.7 | 17.9% | 0.468 |
| Louisiana | 1,004.6 | 20.7% | 0.483 |
| Maryland | 852.9 | 12.9% | 0.434 |
| Massachusetts | 778.7 | 13.5% | 0.463 |
| Michigan | 850.5 | 13.5% | 0.440 |
| Minnesota | 713.0 | 9.7% | 0.426 |
| Missouri | 902.6 | 12.5% | 0.449 |
| New Jersey | 794.8 | 14.2% | 0.460 |
| New York | 760.1 | 16.5% | 0.499 |
| North Carolina | 905.8 | 19.2% | 0.452 |
| Ohio | 889.8 | 14.0% | 0.441 |
| Pennsylvania | 849.2 | 15.4% | 0.452 |
| Tennessee | 982.2 | 19.3% | 0.465 |
| Texas | 855.7 | 23.5% | 0.470 |
| Virginia | 850.9 | 13.4% | 0.449 |
| Washington | 775.9 | 13.3% | 0.436 |
| Wisconsin | 772.5 | 12.4% | 0.413 |

The results presented in Exhibit 14–1B show that the relationship between income inequality and mortality is weak and not statistically significant. Lack of high school education is associated with both mortality and income inequality.

## *Exhibit HW14–1B*

**Multiple Regression Results: Mortality Versus Income Inequality and Education in 25 States**

Regression statistics

| | |
|---|---|
| Multiple *R* | 0.54 |
| *R*-square | 0.29 |
| Adjusted *R*-square | 0.23 |
| Standard error | 73.66 |
| Observations | 25 |

ANOVA

| | *df* | SS | MS | *F* |
|---|---|---|---|---|
| Regression | 2 | 49,646.39 | 24,823.19 | 4.57 |
| Residual | 22 | 119,374.94 | 5,426.13 | |
| Total | 24 | 169,021.33 | | |

| | Coefficients | Standard error | *t* Stat | *P*-value |
|---|---|---|---|---|
| Intercept | 928.94 | 410.11 | 2.27 | 0.03 |
| Gini ratio 1999 | −751.42 | 1,041.00 | −0.72 | 0.48 |
| Pct less than high school 2003 | 1,673.01 | 637.00 | 2.63 | 0.02 |

Correlation Matrix

| | MORTALITY | PCTLTHS | GINI |
|---|---|---|---|
| MORTALITY | 1 | | |
| PCTLTHS | 0.53 | 1 | |
| GINI | 0.27 | 0.69 | 1 |

**14-2** Natural gas distribution companies must keep records of leak surveys, incidents, repairs, and other maintenance operations, but they lack a practical means of using these data on a systemwide basis to reduce their operational costs and to improve safety. If statistical models can be developed with existing or readily available data, then distribution companies could predict the likelihood of leak occurrence for individual gas mains and services or for larger portions of their distribution system. Such models would assist in establishing cost-effective inspection, repair, and replacement schedules, and would help to minimize potentially hazardous conditions.

The following regression model was developed for a Midwestern system based upon a random sample of the repair records of 1,360 pipe sections.[1]

$$Y = 0.532 - 0.500 \text{ CO} + 0.142 \text{ G1} + 0.103 \text{ COUPLED} \\ + 0.001 \text{ LENGTH} + 0.311 \text{ C4} - 1.131 \text{ WALL} - 0.244 \text{ C1} \\ - 0.119 \text{ SILT} - 0.089 \text{ GRAVEL} + 0.061 \text{ ARTST} + 0.003 \text{ AGE}$$

where

$$Y = \text{repair record—repaired} = 1 \text{ nonrepaired} = 0$$
$$\text{CO} = \text{pipe condition—no pits} = 1 \text{ pits} = 0$$
$$\text{C1} = \text{pipe condition—isolated light pits} = 1 \text{ otherwise} = 0$$
$$\text{C4} = \text{pipe condition—frequent deep pits} = 1 \text{ otherwise} = 0$$
$$\text{G1} = \text{geographical area—central city} = 1 \text{ otherwise} = 0$$
$$\text{COUPLED} = \text{coupled joints} = 1; \text{ weld or screw joints} = 0$$
$$\text{LENGTH} = \text{length of pipe}$$
$$\text{WALL} = \text{wall thickness of pipe}$$
$$\text{SILT} = \text{soil type—silts and fine soils} = 1 \text{ otherwise} = 0$$
$$\text{GRAVEL} = \text{soil type—gravelly soils} = 1 \text{ otherwise} = 0$$
$$\text{ARTST} = \text{type of street—arterial street} = 1 \text{ local street} = 0$$
$$\text{AGE} = \text{age of pipe}$$

The analyst's report states that the coefficients are all statistically significant. The $R^2$ value for the model is 0.21.

Examine the sign and value of the partial regression coefficients and answer the following questions:

**a.** Which variable is the most important predictor of repair?

**b.** The coefficient of COUPLED is positive. What does this mean?

**c.** What does the $R^2$ value mean?

**d.** In a written statement describe the characteristics of a pipe that is likely to need repair.

**e.** What should be done about a pipe in a residential area that is fairly new, with welded joints, and is lightly pitted?

---

[1]D.W. Harwood, A.D. St. John, and K.M. Bauer, *Application of Statistical Techniques to Gas Operations* (Midwest Research Institute, Kansas City, Missouri for Gas Research Institute, Chicago, Illinois, July 1982).

**f.** Exhibit HW14–2A compares repair estimates from the preceding model and actual repair records. Provide a specific numeric indicator for the usefulness of the regression model.

## Exhibit HW14–2A

**Actual Versus Estimated Repair Records**

|  | Number of main pipe sections | |
|---|---|---|
| **Repair record** | *Actual* | *Estimated* |
| Repaired | 246 | 176 |
| Not repaired | 1,114 | 803 |

**a.** The most important indicator is whether or not the pipe is pitted.

**b.** The positive coefficient of COUPLED means that pipes with screw couplings rather than welded joints are more likely to have been repaired.

**c.** A pipe that is likely to need repair is an older pipe that is pitted, tends to be longer and have a thinner wall thickness, has coupled rather than welded joints, and is located beneath an arterial street in a central city in soil that is neither silt nor gravel composition.

**d.** The meaning of $R^2$, the coefficient of multiple determination, is that 21% of the variance of the dependent variable, repair record, is explained by the regression equation containing the 11 independent variables.

**e.** A fairly new pipe, with welded joints, located in a residential area is not likely to have been repaired, even if it is lightly pitted.

**f.** There is no statistically significant difference between the observed proportion of pipes that needed repair and the proportion estimated from the regression equation. The strength of association can be represented by the odds ratio: $\alpha = 0.99$

**14-3** What variables help explain postsecondary education performance? Analysts at the National Center for Public Policy and Higher Education examined an indicator of success, PREP, in relation to several economic and demographic variables measured state by state.[2] The data are listed in Exhibit HW14–3A. However, many of these variables are correlated with one another as shown in Exhibit HW14–3B. Explore possible multiple regression relationships using no more than

[2]Alisa F. Cunningham and Jane V. Wellman, "Beneath the Surface: A Statistical Analysis of the Major Variables Associated with State Grades in *Measuring Up 2000*," National Center for Public Policy and Higher Education, San Jose, CA, November 2001
www.highereducation.org/reports/wellman/wellman.shtml

three independent variables at a time. Avoid using two highly correlated variables together.

where

|  |  |
|---|---|
| PREP | = Indicator on scale of 0 to 100 representing adequacy of state preparation for postsecondary education and training. Components include high school completion (20%), appropriate K–12 college prep courses (40%), K–12 student achievement (40%) |
| PCPI | = Per capita personal income, 2000 |
| POP | = State population, 1998–1999 |
| CHGGRADS | = Projected percentage change in the number of all high school graduates 1999–2010 |
| LESSHS | = Percentage of state population with less than high school diploma, 1998 |
| PCMINST | = Percentage of state population that is nonwhite, 1998–1999 |
| PCMETRO | = Percentage of households in the state living in metropolitan areas, 1998 |
| PERPOV | = Percentage of children living in poverty, 1997 |
| GINI | = Gini ratio. An indicator of income inequality, 1998 |
| EXPGSP | = Education spending per $1,000 gross state product, 1998 |
| EXPSTUD | = Elementary and secondary public education spending per student, 1990 |

The results shown in Exhibit HW14–3C indicate PREP score decreases as both income inequality (GINI) and the anticipated rate of high school graduates (CHGGRADS) increase—or, perhaps more sensibly, PREP score tends to increase with greater income equality and lessened anticipated pace of high school graduation.

# Exhibit HW14-3A

**Variables Associated with Educational Peformance**

| State | PREP | PCPI | POP | CHGGRADS | LESSHS | PCMINST | PCMETRO | PERPOV | GINI | EXPGSP | EXPSTUD |
|---|---|---|---|---|---|---|---|---|---|---|---|
| AL | 56 | $23,471 | 4,369,862 | 11% | 21% | 28% | 70% | 24% | 0.458 | $36 | $5,022 |
| AK | 90 | $30,064 | 619,500 | 21% | 9% | 28% | 42% | 16% | 0.397 | $44 | $8,543 |
| AZ | 67 | $25,578 | 4,778,332 | 21% | 18% | 32% | 88% | 23% | 0.439 | $35 | $4,643 |
| AR | 64 | $22,257 | 2,551,373 | 11% | 23% | 19% | 49% | 25% | 0.450 | $40 | $4,876 |
| CA | 70 | $32,275 | 33,145,121 | 27% | 20% | 49% | 97% | 25% | 0.441 | $34 | $5,845 |
| CO | 86 | $32,949 | 4,056,133 | 16% | 10% | 21% | 84% | 15% | 0.426 | $33 | $5,749 |
| CT | 97 | $40,640 | 3,282,031 | 7% | 16% | 19% | 96% | 15% | 0.434 | $37 | $9,321 |
| DE | 77 | $31,255 | 753,538 | 8% | 15% | 25% | 82% | 15% | 0.411 | $27 | $7,684 |
| FL | 74 | $28,145 | 15,111,244 | 21% | 18% | 31% | 93% | 22% | 0.450 | $36 | $5,750 |
| GA | 68 | $27,940 | 7,788,240 | 17% | 20% | 33% | 69% | 23% | 0.446 | $37 | $5,848 |
| HI | 73 | $28,221 | 1,185,497 | 24% | 15% | 71% | 73% | 16% | 0.408 | $31 | $6,003 |
| ID | 68 | $24,180 | 1,251,700 | 20% | 17% | 10% | 38% | 17% | 0.421 | $42 | $4,889 |
| IL | 93 | $32,259 | 12,128,370 | 6% | 16% | 28% | 85% | 18% | 0.440 | $34 | $5,968 |
| IN | 70 | $27,011 | 5,942,901 | 6% | 17% | 12% | 72% | 15% | 0.411 | $44 | $6,689 |
| IA | 84 | $26,723 | 2,869,413 | 3% | 12% | 5% | 45% | 14% | 0.412 | $39 | $6,286 |
| KS | 83 | $27,816 | 2,654,052 | 10% | 11% | 13% | 56% | 15% | 0.428 | $41 | $5,938 |
| KY | 74 | $24,294 | 3,960,825 | 6% | 22% | 9% | 48% | 23% | 0.456 | $36 | $5,970 |
| LA | 56 | $23,334 | 4,372,035 | 9% | 21% | 36% | 75% | 26% | 0.476 | $32 | $5,408 |
| ME | 88 | $25,623 | 1,253,040 | 8% | 13% | 2% | 36% | 15% | 0.414 | $49 | $6,881 |
| MD | 88 | $33,872 | 5,171,634 | 11% | 15% | 35% | 93% | 15% | 0.410 | $40 | $6,935 |
| MA | 99 | $37,992 | 6,175,169 | 6% | 14% | 15% | 96% | 17% | 0.428 | $34 | $7,910 |
| MI | 85 | $29,612 | 9,863,775 | 3% | 15% | 19% | 83% | 18% | 0.429 | $49 | $7,106 |
| MN | 78 | $32,101 | 4,775,508 | 9% | 11% | 8% | 70% | 13% | 0.418 | $42 | $7,240 |
| MS | 66 | $20,993 | 2,768,619 | 8% | 23% | 38% | 36% | 25% | 0.475 | $35 | $4,570 |
| MO | 77 | $27,445 | 5,468,338 | 8% | 17% | 14% | 68% | 18% | 0.438 | $37 | $5,387 |

## Exhibit HW14–3A

**Variables Associated with Educational Peformance (continued)**

| State | PREP | PCPI | POP | CHGGRADS | LESSHS | PCMINST | PCMETRO | PERPOV | GINI | EXPGSP | EXPSTUD |
|---|---|---|---|---|---|---|---|---|---|---|---|
| MT | 86 | $22,569 | 882,779 | 13% | 11% | 9% | 33% | 21% | 0.421 | $48 | $5,953 |
| NE | 90 | $27,829 | 1,666,028 | 9% | 12% | 10% | 52% | 13% | 0.414 | $38 | $6,170 |
| NV | 67 | $30,529 | 1,809,253 | 17% | 11% | 29% | 86% | 15% | 0.420 | $32 | $5,447 |
| NH | 86 | $33,332 | 1,201,134 | 12% | 16% | 3% | 60% | 10% | 0.387 | $34 | $6,746 |
| NJ | 97 | $36,983 | 8,143,412 | 9% | 14% | 31% | 100% | 15% | 0.431 | $43 | $9,986 |
| NM | 62 | $22,203 | 1,739,844 | 24% | 20% | 52% | 57% | 28% | 0.448 | $37 | $5,450 |
| NY | 83 | $34,547 | 18,196,601 | 4% | 19% | 35% | 92% | 25% | 0.467 | $40 | $9,167 |
| NC | 84 | $27,194 | 7,650,789 | 14% | 19% | 27% | 67% | 19% | 0.430 | $30 | $5,444 |
| ND | 83 | $25,068 | 633,666 | 6% | 16% | 7% | 43% | 17% | 0.409 | $38 | $5,531 |
| OH | 79 | $28,400 | 11,256,654 | 2% | 14% | 14% | 81% | 16% | 0.427 | $40 | $6,221 |
| OK | 69 | $23,517 | 3,358,044 | 12% | 15% | 20% | 61% | 24% | 0.445 | $41 | $5,518 |
| OR | 71 | $28,350 | 3,316,154 | 18% | 15% | 12% | 73% | 16% | 0.421 | $37 | $6,361 |
| PA | 78 | $29,539 | 11,994,016 | 2% | 16% | 14% | 85% | 17% | 0.435 | $43 | $7,599 |
| RI | 76 | $29,685 | 990,819 | 7% | 19% | 13% | 94% | 17% | 0.420 | $43 | $7,929 |
| SC | 70 | $24,321 | 3,885,736 | 13% | 21% | 32% | 70% | 23% | 0.428 | $40 | $5,594 |
| SD | 76 | $26,115 | 733,133 | 8% | 14% | 10% | 34% | 19% | 0.394 | $35 | $5,271 |
| TN | 71 | $26,239 | 5,483,535 | 13% | 23% | 19% | 68% | 19% | 0.451 | $30 | $5,026 |
| TX | 74 | $27,871 | 20,044,141 | 21% | 22% | 44% | 85% | 24% | 0.457 | $37 | $5,688 |
| UT | 100 | $23,907 | 2,129,836 | 21% | 11% | 11% | 77% | 13% | 0.395 | $39 | $3,866 |
| VT | 80 | $26,901 | 593,740 | 7% | 13% | 2% | 28% | 13% | 0.385 | $54 | $7,326 |
| VA | 84 | $31,162 | 6,872,912 | 13% | 17% | 27% | 78% | 17% | 0.425 | $35 | $6,850 |
| WA | 79 | $31,528 | 5,756,361 | 21% | 8% | 17% | 83% | 15% | 0.414 | $37 | $6,049 |
| WV | 68 | $21,915 | 1,806,928 | 1% | 24% | 4% | 42% | 25% | 0.448 | $53 | $7,456 |
| WI | 90 | $28,232 | 5,250,446 | 7% | 12% | 10% | 68% | 14% | 0.402 | $46 | $7,505 |
| WY | 72 | $27,230 | 479,602 | 22% | 10% | 9% | 30% | 15% | 0.395 | $37 | $7,192 |

# Exhibit HW14–3B

**Correlation Matrix**

| | PCPI | POP | CHGGRADS | LESSHS | PCMINST | PCMETRO | PERPOV | GINI | EXPGSP | EXPSTUD |
|---|---|---|---|---|---|---|---|---|---|---|
| PCPI | 1.000 | | | | | | | | | |
| POP | 0.309 | 1.000 | | | | | | | | |
| CHGGRADS | −0.087 | 0.143 | 1.000 | | | | | | | |
| LESSHS | −0.351 | 0.281 | −0.084 | 1.000 | | | | | | |
| PCMINST | 0.072 | 0.409 | 0.512 | 0.342 | 1.000 | | | | | |
| PCMETRO | 0.648 | 0.553 | 0.072 | 0.069 | 0.430 | 1.000 | | | | |
| PERPOV | −0.472 | 0.341 | 0.142 | 0.749 | 0.489 | −0.005 | 1.000 | | | |
| GINI | −0.209 | 0.415 | −0.073 | 0.724 | 0.429 | 0.253 | 0.815 | 1.000 | | |
| EXPGSP | −0.177 | −0.208 | −0.162 | −0.140 | −0.340 | −0.366 | −0.056 | −0.216 | 1.000 | |
| EXPSTUD | 0.685 | 0.073 | −0.375 | −0.245 | −0.123 | 0.257 | −0.325 | −0.197 | 0.201 | 1.000 |

## Exhibit HW14–3C

**Correlation Matrix**

Regression statistics

| Multiple $R$ | 0.55 |
|---|---|
| $R$-square | 0.31 |
| Adjusted $R$-square | 0.28 |
| Standard error | 9.04 |
| Observations | 50 |

ANOVA

|  | df | SS | MS | F |
|---|---|---|---|---|
| Regression | 2 | 1688.30 | 844.15 | 10.33 |
| Residual | 47 | 3840.98 | 81.72 | |
| Total | 49 | 5529.28 | | |

|  | Coefficients | Standard error | $t$ Stat | $P$-value |
|---|---|---|---|---|
| Intercept | 186.78 | 25.59 | 7.30 | 0.00 |
| CHGGRADS | −43.75 | 19.23 | −2.28 | 0.03 |
| GINI | −241.92 | 59.14 | −4.09 | 0.00 |

Correlation Matrix

|  | CHGGRADS | GINI |
|---|---|---|
| CHGGRADS | 1 | |
| GINI | −0.07 | 1 |

**14-4** Two ordinary least squares (OLS) multiple regression models are presented using budgeted expenditures and property tax revenues of San Joaquin County as dependent variables and per capita income, employment, urban area, population density, and the existence of Proposition 13 as independent variables for a 22-year period, 1971–1972 to 1992–1993 (Exhibit HW14–4A).[3]

Using San Joaquin County general government expenditures (ggovtexp) as the dependent variable, the ordinary least-squares regression results shown in Exhibit HW14–4B were obtained.

Note that the $R$-square value is very high, 0.97 on a scale of 0 to 1, but that none of the coefficients of the independent variables is statistically significant ($P > |t|$ is not less than 0.05).

A correlation matrix shown in Exhibit HW14–4C was obtained.

Using San Joaquin County property tax revenues as the dependent variable, the ordinary least-squares regression results shown in Exhibit HW14–4D were obtained.

[3]Phillip H. Allman, *An Econometric Model of the Fiscal Impact of Urbanization on Stockton and San Joaquin County,* San Joaquin County Land Utilization Trust, July 1994, 21 pp.

## Exhibit HW14–4A

**San Joaquin County Budgeted Expenditures, Property Tax Revenues, Per Capita Income, Employment, Urban Area, Population Density, and the Existence of Proposition 13: 1971–1972 through 1992–1993 Fiscal Years**

| Obs. no. | Fiscal year | General government expenditures | Property tax revenues | Per capita income | Employment | Urban area | Population density | Before/After Proposition 13 |
|---|---|---|---|---|---|---|---|---|
| | *Year* | *Ggovtexp* | *Proptax* | *Income* | *Emp* | *Urbarea* | *Popacre* | *Prop13* |
| 1. | 1971–72 | 6799 | 29773 | 4.441 | 108.8 | 43789 | 0.330 | 0 |
| 2. | 1972–73 | 6816 | 31090 | 4.798 | 108.3 | 44050 | 0.331 | 0 |
| 3. | 1973–74 | 7151 | 31730 | 5.319 | 114.0 | 45248 | 0.331 | 0 |
| 4. | 1974–75 | 8817 | 34477 | 6.028 | 118.7 | 45323 | 0.328 | 0 |
| 5. | 1975–76 | 12893 | 38745 | 6.524 | 121.1 | 45651 | 0.333 | 0 |
| 6. | 1976–77 | 15289 | 42491 | 6.087 | 123.0 | 45767 | 0.338 | 0 |
| 7. | 1977–78 | 18123 | 47420 | 7.653 | 125.2 | 50212 | 0.344 | 0 |
| 8. | 1978–79 | 20289 | 21961 | 8.357 | 130.2 | 50242 | 0.352 | 1 |
| 9. | 1979–80 | 25333 | 29356 | 9.357 | 136.8 | 49893 | 0.361 | 1 |
| 10. | 1980–81 | 21368 | 32838 | 10.325 | 137.1 | 49926 | 0.394 | 1 |
| 11. | 1981–82 | 23431 | 35800 | 10.982 | 139.9 | 49939 | 0.409 | 1 |
| 12. | 1982–83 | 23935 | 37300 | 11.252 | 136.0 | 50217 | 0.420 | 1 |
| 13. | 1983–84 | 21155 | 38500 | 11.359 | 133.2 | 50474 | 0.434 | 1 |
| 14. | 1984–85 | 33013 | 39583 | 12.398 | 141.0 | 51855 | 0.452 | 1 |
| 15. | 1985–86 | 37435 | 43658 | 12.984 | 144.5 | 52668 | 0.467 | 1 |
| 16. | 1986–87 | 42785 | 46188 | 13.544 | 148.5 | 53265 | 0.483 | 1 |
| 17. | 1987–88 | 44101 | 49652 | 14.148 | 157.3 | 53912 | 0.500 | 1 |
| 18. | 1988–89 | 47028 | 53259 | 14.745 | 182.6 | 60873 | 0.510 | 1 |
| 19. | 1989–90 | 54249 | 61722 | 15.549 | 164.4 | 63031 | 0.530 | 1 |
| 20. | 1990–91 | 52889 | 68798 | 16.183 | 168.3 | 63760 | 0.543 | 1 |
| 21. | 1991–92 | 50484 | 75641 | 16.374 | 170.8 | 65029 | 0.558 | 1 |
| 22. | 1992–93 | 56102 | 71136 | 16.942 | 170.0 | 66297 | 0.571 | 1 |

year = Fiscal year; ggovtexp = San Joaquin Co General Government Expenditures in $Thousands; proptax = San Joaquin Co Property Tax Revenues in $Thousands; income = San Joaquin Co Per Capita Income in $Thousands; emp = San Joaquin Co Total Employment in Thousands; urbarea = San Joaquin Co Estimated Urban Area in Acres; popacre = San Joaquin Co Population Density (Persons/Acre); prop13 = Proposition 13 Dummy Variable (0 prior to 1978–79, otherwise 1)

## Exhibit HW14–4B

**Dependent Variable: ggovtexp**

| Source | SS | df | MS | |
|---|---|---|---|---|
| Model | 5.7331e+09 | 5 | 1.1466e+09 | Number of obs = 22 |
| Residual | 199509408 | 16 | 12469338.0 | $F(5, 16) = 91.95$ |
| Total | 5.9326e+09 | 21 | 282503828 | Prob $> F = 0.0000$ |
| | | | | $R$-square = 0.9664 |
| | | | | Adj $R$-square = 0.9559 |
| | | | | Root MSE = 3531.2 |

| ggovtexp | Coef. | Std. Error | $t$ | $P > |t|$ | [95% Conf. Interval] | |
|---|---|---|---|---|---|---|
| income | 2232.73 | 1725.25 | 1.294 | 0.214 | −1424.6 | 5890.1 |
| emp | 176.26 | 143.20 | 1.231 | 0.236 | −127.3 | 479.8 |
| urbarea | 0.34 | 0.40 | 0.851 | 0.407 | −0.5 | 1.2 |
| popacre | 32571.53 | 58487.68 | 0.557 | 0.585 | −91416.8 | 56559.9 |
| prop13 | −3438.21 | 4257.12 | −0.808 | 0.431 | −12462.9 | 5586.5 |
| constant | −49427.44 | 17479.58 | −2.828 | 0.012 | −86482.5 | −12372.4 |

## Exhibit HW14–4C

**Correlation Matrix**

| | ggovtexp | income | emp | urbarea | popacre | prop13 |
|---|---|---|---|---|---|---|
| ggovtexp | 1.0000 | | | | | |
| income | 0.9704 | 1.0000 | | | | |
| emp | 0.9594 | 0.9540 | 1.0000 | | | |
| urbarea | 0.9499 | 0.9279 | 0.9436 | 1.0000 | | |
| popacre | 0.9693 | 0.9783 | 0.9381 | 0.9386 | 1.0000 | |
| prop13 | 0.7393 | 0.8324 | 0.7511 | 0.6572 | 0.7397 | 1.0000 |

Note that the $R$-square value is very high, 0.97 on a scale of 0 to 1. The coefficients of per capita income, urban area, and Proposition 13 are statistically significant in relation to property tax revenue.

A correlation matrix shown in Exhibit HW14–4E was obtained.

Are these OLS models explaining county revenues and expenditures valid?

Examine and discuss the assumptions inherent in these OLS regression analyses.

## Exhibit HW14–4D

**Dependent Variable: proptax**

| Source | SS | df | MS | |
|---|---|---|---|---|
| Model | 4.2923e+09 | 5 | 858452770 | Number of obs = 22 |
| Residual | 133236249 | 16 | 8327265.55 | $F(5, 16) = 103.09$ |
| Total | 4.4255e+09 | 21 | 210738100 | Prob > $F$ = 0.0000 |
| | | | | $R$-square = 0.9699 |
| | | | | Adj $R$-square = 0.9605 |
| | | | | Root MSE = 2885.7 |

| proptax | Coef. | Std. Error | t | $P > |t|$ | [95% Conf. Interval] | |
|---|---|---|---|---|---|---|
| income | 4441.98 | 1409.87 | 3.151 | 0.006 | 1453.2 | 7430.8 |
| emp | −148.84 | 117.02 | −1.272 | 0.222 | −396.9 | 99.2 |
| urbarea | 1.08 | 0.33 | 3.280 | 0.005 | 0.4 | 1.8 |
| popacre | −3246.96 | 47796.26 | −0.068 | 0.947 | −104570.5 | 98076.6 |
| prop13 | −26262.10 | 3478.92 | −7.549 | 0.000 | −33637.1 | −18887.1 |
| constant | −20467.29 | 14284.35 | −1.433 | 0.171 | −50748.8 | 9814.2 |

## Exhibit HW14–4E

**Correlation Matrix**

| | proptax | income | emp | urbarea | popacre | prop13 |
|---|---|---|---|---|---|---|
| proptax | 1.0000 | | | | | |
| income | 0.7918 | 1.0000 | | | | |
| emp | 0.8034 | 0.9540 | 1.0000 | | | |
| urbarea | 0.8938 | 0.9279 | 0.9436 | 1.0000 | | |
| popacre | 0.8534 | 0.9783 | 0.9381 | 0.9386 | 1.0000 | |
| prop13 | 0.3446 | 0.8324 | 0.7511 | 0.6572 | 0.7397 | 1.0000 |

OLS regression results in which a high $R$-square value is obtained, yet few, if any, of the coefficients of the independent variables are statistically significant suggests the possibility of multicollinearity in the regression model. Multicollinearity is a situation in which the values of the independent variables are interrelated making it impossible to separate the effects of the independent variables on the dependent variable.

Multicollinearity is confirmed by the correlation matrices and matrix graphs. The correlation coefficients are very high, most exceeding 0.9. The matrix graphs show that as the value of any one independent variable increases so does the value of every other independent variable.

The data were also examined for autocorrelation. Autocorrelation, a situation in which the values of the same variable are interrelated from one case to the next (that is, from one fiscal year to the next), is a potential problem with time series data. Rather than separate observations as required for OLS regression models, the data describe sequences. Given the known nature of budgeting decision-making—incremental adjustments to a budgetary base from year to year rather than zero-base budgeting—the data, at least for governmental expenditures, should be considered autocorrelated.

The Bottom Line: When extreme multicollinearity exists, as it does in this OLS regression model, there is no acceptable way to perform regression analysis using the given set of independent variables. The model is invalid, and any inferential statements based on the model are invalid.

**14-5**  Many cities control the number of taxicabs by law or regulation. Too many or too few taxicabs can seriously affect both the economic viability of the taxicab business and the quality of service to the public. Bruce Shaller developed a multiple regression model shown in Exhibit HW14–5A for the number of taxicabs in U.S. cities.[4]

## Exhibit HW14–5A

**Shaller's Model for the Number of Taxicabs in U.S. Cities (in thousands)**

| Variable | Coefficient | St. Error | $t$-statistic |
|---|---|---|---|
| Subway commuters | 21.81 | 1.72 | 12.7 |
| No-vehicle households | 5.14 | 1.29 | 4.0 |
| Airport taxi trips | 0.64 | 0.09 | 7.2 |
| Dummy for no-vehicle households greater than 19,000 | 129.95 | 92.02 | 1.4 |
| Constant | 31.42 | 48.84 | 0.6 |
| Observations | 118 | | |
| Adj. $R^2$ | 0.989 | | |
| $F$ statistic | 2,568.9 | | |

[4]Bruce Schaller, "A Regression Model of the Number of Taxicabs in U.S. Cities," National Center for Transit Research, University of South Florida, *Journal of Public Transportation*, v. 8 n. 5, 2005. www.nctr.usf.edu/jpt/pdf/JPT%208-5%20Schaller.pdf

**a.** Explain each of the coefficients.

**b.** Estimate the number of taxicabs for a metropolitan area with about 60,000 subway commuters per day, 110,000 no-vehicle households, and 2,850 airport taxi trips per day (similar to Miami–Dade County, Florida).

**a.** Shaller concludes.

> The coefficient for no-car households is 5.1, indicating that a change of 1,000 no-car households is associated with a change of 5 taxicabs in the observed cities and counties, other factors being held constant. The coefficient for subway commuters is 21.8, indicating that a change of 1,000 subway commuters is associated with a change of 22 taxicabs. For airport taxi trips, the coefficient is 0.64, indicating that each 1,000 annual airport taxi trips accounts for 0.64 taxicabs. These results indicate that an increment of 1,000 subway commuters is associated with four times more additional taxicabs as compared with an increment of 1,000 no-car households. The subway commuter variable is most likely playing a strong proxy role for parking costs and availability and, more generally, the degree of density and urbanization of cities with large subway systems, as well as direct demand from subway commuters' use of cabs.[5]

b. Number of taxicabs $\approx 2,037$.

----

[5]Shaller.

# Procedures

## One-Variable Description

| Description | Level of measurement | | |
|---|---|---|---|
| | *Nominal* | *Ordinal* | *Interval* |
| Summary of observations | Frequency table | Frequency table | Grouped frequency table |
| | Bar chart | Bar chart | Histogram |
| | Dot chart | Dot chart | Box plot |
| | Pie chart | | One-way scatterplot |
| Central tendency | Mode | Median | Mean |
| | | | Median |
| Dispersion | Relative frequency of the mode | Interquartile range | Standard deviation |

## One-Variable Evaluation, Nominal Measure

| Sample size $n$ | Two categories | More than two categories |
|---|---|---|
| Small $n \leq 20$ | Binomial test | * |
| Large $n > 20$ | Binomial test<br>Normal approximation to the binomial—$Z$ test | Chi-square goodness-of-fit test |

*Either combine categories in order to use the binomial test, or increase the sample size.

### One-Variable Evaluation, Ordinal or Interval Level of Measurement

| Sample size $n$ | Level of measurement | |
| --- | --- | --- |
| | *Ordinal* | *Interval* |
| $n \leq 30$ | Kolmogorov–Smirnov one-variable test | $t$-test |
| $n > 30$ | | $t$-test |
| | | $Z$-test |

### One-Variable Estimation

| Population estimate | Level of measurement | |
| --- | --- | --- |
| | *Nominal—Two categories* | *Interval* |
| Central tendency | $\mu \approx np_O$ | $\mu \approx \bar{x}$ |
| Dispersion | $p_E \approx p_O \pm Z\sqrt{\dfrac{0.25}{n}}$ | $\sigma \approx s\sqrt{n}$ |
| Confidence interval | $p_E \approx p_O \pm Z\sqrt{\dfrac{0.25}{n}}$ | $\mu \approx \bar{x} \pm t\,\dfrac{s}{\sqrt{n}}$ |

### Two-Variable Description

| Dependent variable | Independent variable | |
| --- | --- | --- |
| | *Nominal or ordinal level of measurement* | *Interval level of measurement* |
| Nominal or ordinal level of measurement | Crosstabulation | Crosstabulation (group interval data) |
| Interval level of measurement | Table or chart | Scatterplot |

**Two-Variable Evaluation—Nominal–Nominal Measures**

| Dependent variable | | Independent variable — Nominal level of measurement | | | |
|---|---|---|---|---|---|
| | | Two categories | | More than two categories | |
| | | *Unpaired units of analysis* | *Paired units of analysis* | *Unmatched units of analysis* | *Matched units of analysis* |
| Nominal level of measurement — Two categories | Strength of association | Odds ratio Relative risk ratio Somers' $d$ Yule's $Q$ Phi statistic | | Cramer's $V$ Lambda, $\lambda$ | |
| | Statistical significance | $n > 30$ $Z$ test for the difference between two proportions  $26 < n \leq 250$ Chi-square test with Yates's correction  $n \leq 26$ Fisher's exact probability test | McNemar test for significance of changes | Chi-square test | Cochran's $Q$ test |
| More than two categories | Strength of association | Cramer's $V$ Lambda, $\lambda$ | | Cramer's $V$ Lambda, $\lambda$ | |
| | Statistical significance | Chi-square test | | Chi-square test | |

**Two-Variable Evaluation—Nominal–Ordinal Measures**

| Second variable | | First variable: Nominal level of measurement | | |
| | | Two categories | | More than two categories |
| | | Unpaired units of analysis | Paired units of analysis | |
| Ordinal level of measurement | Strength of association | Somers' d | | * |
| | Statistical significance | Mann–Whitney U Test  Kolmogorov–Smirnov two-variable test | Wilcoxon matched pairs signed-rank test | Kruskal–Wallis test |

*Note: Not covered in this text. L.C. Freeman developed a strength-of-association statistic for the situation in which the ordinal variable is dependent. See L.C. Freeman. 1965. *Elementary Applied Statistics for Students in Behavioral Science.* New York: Wiley.

**Two-Variable Evaluation—Ordinal–Ordinal and Ordinal–Interval Measures**

| Dependent variable | | Independent variable | |
| | | Ordinal level of measurement | Interval level of measurement |
| Ordinal level of measurement | Strength of association | Spearman's rank correlation coefficient, $\rho$  Goodman and Kruskal's gamma, $\gamma$  Somers' d  Kendall's tau, $\tau$ | Spearman's rank correlation coefficient, $\rho$ |
| | Statistical significance | Spearman's rank correlation coefficient, $\rho$  Goodman and Kruskal's gamma, $\gamma$  Kendall's tau, $\tau$ | |

**Two-Variable Evaluation—Nominal–Interval Measures**

| Dependent variable | | Independent variable | | |
| --- | --- | --- | --- | --- |
| | | *Nominal level of measurement* | | |
| | | Two categories | | More than two categories |
| | | *Unpaired units of analysis* | *Paired units of analysis* | |
| Interval level of measurement | Strength of association | Eta-squared, $\eta^2$ | | Eta-squared, $\eta^2$ |
| | Statistical significance | $n > 12$[a] <br> Two-variable $t$ test for unpaired data <br><br> $n \leq 12$ <br> Randomization test for unpaired data | $n > 12$ <br> Two-variable $t$ test for paired data <br><br> $n \leq 12$ <br> Randomization test for paired data | Analysis-of-variance $F$ test[b] |

[a] The Mann–Whitney $U$ test is an alternative.
[b] The Kruskal–Wallis test is an alternative.

**Two-Variable Evaluation—Interval–Interval Measures**

| Dependent variable | | Independent variable |
| --- | --- | --- |
| | | *Interval level of measurement* |
| Interval level of measurement | Strength of association | Coefficient of determination $r^2$ |
| | Statistical significance | Linear regression $t$-test on the $b$ statistic |
| | Direction of association | Sign of the $b$ statistic |

**Two-Variable Estimation—Interval–Interval Measures**

| Population estimate | Sample size | Estimation equation |
| --- | --- | --- |
| Regression coefficient | | $\beta = b \pm t_{\text{critical}} \cdot s_b$ |
| Coefficient of determination | | $r_{\text{adjusted}}^2 = 1 - \left[ \dfrac{n-1}{n-k-1} \right] \cdot (1 - r^2)$ |
| Confidence interval for an individual value of $Y$ | $n < 30$ | $Y_x = y_{\text{estimated}} \pm t_{\text{critical}} \cdot s_{y \cdot x} \cdot \sqrt{1 + \dfrac{1}{n} + \dfrac{(x - \bar{x})^2}{\sum (x - \bar{x})^2}}$ |
| | $n \geq 30$ | $Y_x \approx y_{\text{estimated}} \pm t_{\text{critical}} \cdot s_{y \cdot x}$ |
| Confidence interval for the mean of $Y$ | $n < 30$ | $\bar{Y}_x = \bar{y}_{\text{estimated}} \pm t_{\text{critical}} \cdot s_{y \cdot x} \cdot \sqrt{\dfrac{1}{n} + \dfrac{(x - \bar{x})^2}{\sum (x - \bar{x})^2}}$ |
| | $n \geq 30$ | $\bar{Y}_x \approx \bar{y}_{\text{estimated}} \pm t_{\text{critical}} \cdot \dfrac{s_{y \cdot x}}{\sqrt{n}}$ |

# Glossary of Terms

**alternate hypothesis**   A proposition that the analyst is compelled to adopt if the "null hypothesis" is rejected.

**average**   A point of central tendency among observed values. The "mode," "median," or "mean" value.

**binomial distribution**   A frequency distribution in which the variable can have only two possible values.

**case**   See "record" and "unit of analysis."

**categorical variable**   A variable measured by a limited number of mutually exclusive nominal values.

**coefficient of variation**   The ratio of the standard deviation to the mean

**continuous variables**   Variables that have an infinite number of fractional values.

**data**   The recorded observations of event outcomes or conditions.

**data file**   A list of the measured, recorded observations of a set of related events or conditions.

**dependent variable**   The variable that describes the outcome of a following event. See "independent variable."

**description**   The process of summarizing data in the form of a frequency distribution, table, or graph and calculating statistics that indicate a variable's central tendency and dispersion.

**dichotomous**   Having two possible values.

**discrete variables**   Variables that have a finite number of values.

**dispersion**   The extent to which data are spread out from the point of central tendency.

**estimation**   The process of forecasting a particular value for a variable or predicting the variable's central tendency and dispersion in the statistical population.

**evaluation**   The process of comparing observation against expectation and reaching a normative judgment about the result.

**event**   An action—an occurrence—an opportunity for physical or social change or action. A happening.

**frequency distribution**    A count of the number of times each value of a nominally or ordinally measured variable occurs in a data set.

**independent variable**    The variable that describes an initial observed condition. See "dependent variable."

**interval (level of measurement)**    Measurement by classifying each event outcome on a scale in which there is a fixed difference between each consecutive measurement unit. The scale has an arbitrary reference (zero) point.

**level of measurement**    The complete set of all related events which are of interest and observable.

**level of significance**    The probability at which the idea of no difference, sameness, consistency, or equality between observation and expectation is rejected. See "statistically significant."

**mean**    The average—point of central tendency—for a variable having an interval or ratio level of measurement. The value of the mean is computed by dividing the sum of the values for all the cases in the data set by the number of cases.

**measurement**    The process of obtaining a value for a variable; observation.

**median**    The value of a case at the middle position of a frequency distribution. Half of the units of analysis will have values greater than the median—and the other half will have values less than the median.

**mode**    The most frequently occurring value in a distribution.

**net outcome**    A result that is a combination of several concurrent or consecutive event outcomes.

**nominal (level of measurement)**    Measurement by classifying each event outcome into a unique category.

**null hypothesis**    A proposition that there is no difference between observation and expectation. Everything is equal, the same, balanced, and fair. See "alternate hypothesis."

**observation**    Measurement. See "record."

**operational definition**    The specific, detailed step-by-step procedure by which values are obtained and recorded for a variable

**ordinal (level of measurement)**    Measurement by classifying each event outcome into a unique ranked category. The cases in one category possess more or less of some implicit quality associated with the variable being observed than the cases in another category.

**outcome**    One of the possible results of an event. The resultant change or occurrence.

*p*-**value**    The probability of obtaining an outcome at least as extreme as the one observed, given that the null hypothesis is true.

**population**    All of the related items or events for which observations (measurements) could possibly be obtained. (Also called a statistical population, target population, event population, or universe).

**probability**    An expression of how likely it is that a particular event will occur by comparing the number of times that an event occurred (or might occur) to the number of opportunities there have been (are or will be) for that event to occur.

**random selection**   Each unit of analysis in a statistical population has an equal probability of being observed or picked for inclusion in a sample.

**ratio (level of measurement)**   Measurement by classifying event outcomes on a scale in which there is a fixed difference between each consecutive measurement unit and a natural zero origin.

**record**   A set of observations (values for different variables) about the event outcomes involving or affecting one unit of analysis.

**relative frequency**   The prevalence of each value in a data set expressed as a proportion of the total number of observations.

**standard error**   The ratio of a sample standard deviation to the square root of the sample size.

**statistically significant**   A difference between observation and expectation so large and having such a low probability of occurring by chance that the result is judged to be out of the ordinary—beyond a reasonable doubt. The null hypothesis is rejected.

**unit of analysis**   The object of observation.

**value**   A specific observed outcome of an event. The measurement of a variable.

**variable**   A general characteristic or attribute that can be observed and recorded about the outcomes of a set of related events.

# Rules for Rounding Off

To round a number to $n$ significant figures, inspect the $(n + 1)$th digit:

|  |  |  | **Examples** |
|---|---|---|---|
| If | 0 | Round to the $n$th digit | $5.00 \cong 5.0$ <br> $5.30 \cong 5.3$ <br> $5.80 \cong 5.8$ <br> $5.50 \cong 5.5$ |
| If | 1 <br> 2 <br> 3 <br> 4 | Round down | $5.01 \cong 5.0$ <br> $5.53 \cong 5.5$ <br> $5.24 \cong 5.2$ <br> $5.72 \cong 5.7$ |
| If | 5 | Round to the even value* | $5.55 \cong 5.6$ <br> $5.25 \cong 5.2$ <br> $5.05 \cong 5.0$ <br> $5.15 \cong 5.2$ <br> $5.85 \cong 5.8$ <br> $5.75 \cong 5.8$ <br> $5.95 \cong 6.0$ |
| If | 6 <br> 7 <br> 8 <br> 9 | Round up | $5.36 \cong 5.4$ <br> $5.98 \cong 6.0$ <br> $5.59 \cong 5.6$ <br> $5.07 \cong 5.1$ |

---

*The odds, then, on rounding down versus rounding up are 50:50.

# Glossary of Symbols

| | |
|---|---|
| $a$ | $y$-intercept of the sample least-squares regression line |
| $b$ | Regression coefficient—the slope of the sample least-squares regression line |
| $C$ | $C$ statistic in Fisher's exact probability test; total of all frequencies in a column of a crosstabulation |
| $d$ | The difference between an observed value and an expected value; Somers' $d$ statistic |
| $df$ | Degrees of freedom |
| $D$ | $D$ statistic in the Kolmogorov–Smirnov test |
| $e$ | The constant 2.71828 . . . ; the base of natural logarithms |
| $f$ | Cell frequency; absolute frequency |
| $f_E$ | Expected frequency |
| $f_O$ | Observed frequency |
| $f(x)$ | Function of $x$ |
| $F$ | $F$ statistic |
| $k$ | The number of independent variables |
| $K$ | $K$ statistic in Kruskal–Wallis test |
| $m$ | Group midpoint |
| $n$ | Sample size—number of units of analysis (cases) in the sample |
| $N$ | Size of the statistical population |
| $p$ | Probability of an outcome of interest occurring for any one independent event; proportion |
| $P_x$ | Net probability that exactly $x$ outcomes of interest will occur in $n$ events |
| $Q$ | Yule's $Q$ statistic; Cochran's $Q$ statisitic |
| $Q_1$ | Lower limit of interquartile range (25th percentile) |
| $Q_3$ | Upper limit of interquartile range (75th percentile) |

| | |
|---|---|
| $r$ | Sample correlation coefficient |
| $r^2$ | Sample coefficient of determination |
| $R$ | Total of all frequencies in a row of a crosstabulation |
| $R^2$ | Sample coefficient of multiple determination |
| $s$ | Sample standard deviation |
| $s^2$ | Sample variance |
| $s_b$ | Standard error of the regression coefficient |
| $s_{y.x}$ | Standard error of the estimate |
| SSE | Sum-of-squares error |
| SSR | Sum-of-squares regression |
| SST | Sum-of-squares total |
| $t$ | $t$ statistic |
| $U$ | $U$ statistic in the Mann–Whitney test |
| $V$ | Cramer's $V$ statistic |
| $W$ | $W$ statistic in the Wilcoxon test |
| x | An observed value of an independent variable; number of times an outcome of interest is observed in a binomial test |
| $\bar{x}$ | Mean of the observed values of an independent variable; sample mean |
| $y$ | An observed value of a dependent variable |
| $\bar{y}$ | Mean of the observed values of a dependent variable |
| $Y$ | A value of a dependent variable that can be taken on by any unit in a statistical population |
| $Y_x$ | Estimated value of a dependent variable given a specified value of an independent variable |
| $\bar{Y}_x$ | Estimated mean of a dependent variable for all units of analysis in the statistical population having a specified value of an independent variable |
| $Z$ | $Z$ statistic; standard score |
| $\alpha$ | Odds ratio |
| $\beta$ | Estimated population regression coefficient |
| $\chi^2$ | Chi-squared statistic |
| $\gamma$ | Gamma statistic |
| $\eta^2$ | Eta-squared statistic |
| $\Delta$ | Change in . . . |
| $\lambda$ | Lambda statistic |
| $\mu$ | Population mean |

| | |
|---|---|
| $\pi$ | Pi; the constant $3.14159\ldots$ |
| $\rho$ | Spearman's rank correlation coefficient; estimated population correlation coefficient |
| $\rho^2$ | Estimated population coefficient of determination |
| $\sigma$ | Population standard deviation |
| $\sigma^2$ | Population variance |
| $\sum$ | Sum of . . . |
| $\tau$ | Kendall's tau statistic |
| $\phi$ | Phi statistic |

# Appendix A

**The Binomial Probability Distribution**

$n = 1$

| | $p =$ | 0.01 | 0.02 | 0.03 | 0.04 | 0.05 | 0.06 | 0.07 | 0.08 | 0.09 | 0.10 |
|---|---|---|---|---|---|---|---|---|---|---|---|
| $x =$ | 0 | 0.9900 | 0.9800 | 0.9700 | 0.9600 | 0.9500 | 0.9400 | 0.9300 | 0.9200 | 0.9100 | 0.9000 |
| | 1 | 0.0100 | 0.0200 | 0.0300 | 0.0400 | 0.0500 | 0.0600 | 0.0700 | 0.0800 | 0.0900 | 0.1000 |
| | $p =$ | 0.11 | 0.12 | 0.13 | 0.14 | 0.15 | 0.16 | 0.17 | 0.18 | 0.19 | 0.20 |
| $x =$ | 0 | 0.8900 | 0.8800 | 0.8700 | 0.8600 | 0.8500 | 0.8400 | 0.8300 | 0.8200 | 0.8100 | 0.8000 |
| | 1 | 0.1100 | 0.1200 | 0.1300 | 0.1400 | 0.1500 | 0.1600 | 0.1700 | 0.1800 | 0.1900 | 0.2000 |
| | $p =$ | 0.21 | 0.22 | 0.23 | 0.24 | 0.25 | 0.26 | 0.27 | 0.28 | 0.29 | 0.30 |
| $x =$ | 0 | 0.7900 | 0.7800 | 0.7700 | 0.7600 | 0.7500 | 0.7400 | 0.7300 | 0.7200 | 0.7100 | 0.7000 |
| | 1 | 0.2100 | 0.2200 | 0.2300 | 0.2400 | 0.2500 | 0.2600 | 0.2700 | 0.2800 | 0.2900 | 0.3000 |
| | $p =$ | 0.31 | 0.32 | 0.33 | 0.34 | 0.35 | 0.36 | 0.37 | 0.38 | 0.39 | 0.40 |
| $x =$ | 0 | 0.6900 | 0.6800 | 0.6700 | 0.6600 | 0.6500 | 0.6400 | 0.6300 | 0.6200 | 0.6100 | 0.6000 |
| | 1 | 0.3100 | 0.3200 | 0.3300 | 0.3400 | 0.3500 | 0.3600 | 0.3700 | 0.3800 | 0.3900 | 0.4000 |
| | $p =$ | 0.41 | 0.42 | 0.43 | 0.44 | 0.45 | 0.46 | 0.47 | 0.48 | 0.49 | 0.50 |
| $x =$ | 0 | 0.5900 | 0.5800 | 0.5700 | 0.5600 | 0.5500 | 0.5400 | 0.5300 | 0.5200 | 0.5100 | 0.5000 |
| | 1 | 0.4100 | 0.4200 | 0.4300 | 0.4400 | 0.4500 | 0.4600 | 0.4700 | 0.4800 | 0.4900 | 0.5000 |

*(continued)*

## The Binomial Probability Distribution *(continued)*

### *n* = 2

| | *p* = | *0.01* | *0.02* | *0.03* | *0.04* | *0.05* | *0.06* | *0.07* | *0.08* | *0.09* | *0.10* |
|---|---|---|---|---|---|---|---|---|---|---|---|
| *x* = | 0 | 0.9801 | 0.9604 | 0.9409 | 0.9216 | 0.9025 | 0.8836 | 0.8649 | 0.8464 | 0.8281 | 0.8100 |
| | 1 | 0.0198 | 0.0392 | 0.0582 | 0.0768 | 0.0950 | 0.1128 | 0.1302 | 0.1472 | 0.1638 | 0.1800 |
| | 2 | 0.0001 | 0.0004 | 0.0009 | 0.0016 | 0.0025 | 0.0036 | 0.0049 | 0.0064 | 0.0081 | 0.0100 |

| | *p* = | *0.11* | *0.12* | *0.13* | *0.14* | *0.15* | *0.16* | *0.17* | *0.18* | *0.19* | *0.20* |
|---|---|---|---|---|---|---|---|---|---|---|---|
| *x* = | 0 | 0.7921 | 0.7744 | 0.7569 | 0.7396 | 0.7225 | 0.7056 | 0.6889 | 0.6724 | 0.6561 | 0.6400 |
| | 1 | 0.1958 | 0.2112 | 0.2262 | 0.2408 | 0.2550 | 0.2688 | 0.2822 | 0.2952 | 0.3078 | 0.3200 |
| | 2 | 0.0121 | 0.0144 | 0.0169 | 0.0196 | 0.0225 | 0.0256 | 0.0289 | 0.0324 | 0.0361 | 0.0400 |

| | *p* = | *0.21* | *0.22* | *0.23* | *0.24* | *0.25* | *0.26* | *0.27* | *0.28* | *0.29* | *0.30* |
|---|---|---|---|---|---|---|---|---|---|---|---|
| *x* = | 0 | 0.6241 | 0.6084 | 0.5929 | 0.5776 | 0.5625 | 0.5476 | 0.5329 | 0.5184 | 0.5041 | 0.4900 |
| | 1 | 0.3318 | 0.3432 | 0.3542 | 0.3648 | 0.3750 | 0.3848 | 0.3942 | 0.4032 | 0.4118 | 0.4200 |
| | 2 | 0.0441 | 0.0484 | 0.0529 | 0.0576 | 0.0625 | 0.0676 | 0.0729 | 0.0784 | 0.0841 | 0.0900 |

| | *p* = | *0.31* | *0.32* | *0.33* | *0.34* | *0.35* | *0.36* | *0.37* | *0.38* | *0.39* | *0.40* |
|---|---|---|---|---|---|---|---|---|---|---|---|
| *x* = | 0 | 0.4761 | 0.4624 | 0.4489 | 0.4356 | 0.4225 | 0.4096 | 0.3969 | 0.3844 | 0.3721 | 0.3600 |
| | 1 | 0.4278 | 0.4352 | 0.4422 | 0.4488 | 0.4550 | 0.4608 | 0.4662 | 0.4712 | 0.4758 | 0.4800 |
| | 2 | 0.0961 | 0.1024 | 0.1089 | 0.1156 | 0.1225 | 0.1296 | 0.1369 | 0.1444 | 0.1521 | 0.1600 |

| | *p* = | *0.41* | *0.42* | *0.43* | *0.44* | *0.45* | *0.46* | *0.47* | *0.48* | *0.49* | *0.50* |
|---|---|---|---|---|---|---|---|---|---|---|---|
| *x* = | 0 | 0.3481 | 0.3364 | 0.3249 | 0.3136 | 0.3025 | 0.2916 | 0.2809 | 0.2704 | 0.2601 | 0.2500 |
| | 1 | 0.4838 | 0.4872 | 0.4902 | 0.4928 | 0.4950 | 0.4968 | 0.4982 | 0.4992 | 0.4998 | 0.5000 |
| | 2 | 0.1681 | 0.1764 | 0.1849 | 0.1936 | 0.2025 | 0.2116 | 0.2209 | 0.2304 | 0.2401 | 0.2500 |

### *n* = 3

| | *p* = | *0.01* | *0.02* | *0.03* | *0.04* | *0.05* | *0.06* | *0.07* | *0.08* | *0.09* | *0.10* |
|---|---|---|---|---|---|---|---|---|---|---|---|
| *x* = | 0 | 0.9703 | 0.9412 | 0.9127 | 0.8847 | 0.8574 | 0.8306 | 0.8044 | 0.7787 | 0.7536 | 0.7290 |
| | 1 | 0.0294 | 0.0576 | 0.0847 | 0.1106 | 0.1354 | 0.1590 | 0.1816 | 0.2031 | 0.2236 | 0.2430 |
| | 2 | 0.0003 | 0.0012 | 0.0026 | 0.0046 | 0.0071 | 0.0102 | 0.0137 | 0.0177 | 0.0221 | 0.0270 |
| | 3 | 0.0000 | 0.0000 | 0.0000 | 0.0001 | 0.0001 | 0.0002 | 0.0003 | 0.0005 | 0.0007 | 0.0010 |

| | *p* = | *0.11* | *0.12* | *0.13* | *0.14* | *0.15* | *0.16* | *0.17* | *0.18* | *0.19* | *0.20* |
|---|---|---|---|---|---|---|---|---|---|---|---|
| *x* = | 0 | 0.7050 | 0.6815 | 0.6585 | 0.6361 | 0.6141 | 0.5927 | 0.5718 | 0.5514 | 0.5314 | 0.5120 |
| | 1 | 0.2614 | 0.2788 | 0.2952 | 0.3106 | 0.3251 | 0.3387 | 0.3513 | 0.3631 | 0.3740 | 0.3840 |
| | 2 | 0.0323 | 0.0380 | 0.0441 | 0.0506 | 0.0574 | 0.0645 | 0.0720 | 0.0797 | 0.0877 | 0.0960 |
| | 3 | 0.0013 | 0.0017 | 0.0022 | 0.0027 | 0.0034 | 0.0041 | 0.0049 | 0.0058 | 0.0069 | 0.0080 |

*(continued)*

**The Binomial Probability Distribution** *(continued)*

| | $p =$ | 0.21 | 0.22 | 0.23 | 0.24 | 0.25 | 0.26 | 0.27 | 0.28 | 0.29 | 0.30 |
|---|---|---|---|---|---|---|---|---|---|---|---|
| $x =$ | 0 | 0.4930 | 0.4746 | 0.4565 | 0.4390 | 0.4219 | 0.4052 | 0.3890 | 0.3732 | 0.3579 | 0.3430 |
| | 1 | 0.3932 | 0.4015 | 0.4091 | 0.4159 | 0.4219 | 0.4271 | 0.4316 | 0.4355 | 0.4386 | 0.4410 |
| | 2 | 0.1045 | 0.1133 | 0.1222 | 0.1313 | 0.1406 | 0.1501 | 0.1597 | 0.1693 | 0.1791 | 0.1890 |
| | 3 | 0.0093 | 0.0106 | 0.0122 | 0.0138 | 0.0156 | 0.0176 | 0.0197 | 0.0220 | 0.0244 | 0.0270 |

| | $p =$ | 0.31 | 0.32 | 0.33 | 0.34 | 0.35 | 0.36 | 0.37 | 0.38 | 0.39 | 0.40 |
|---|---|---|---|---|---|---|---|---|---|---|---|
| $x =$ | 0 | 0.3285 | 0.3144 | 0.3008 | 0.2875 | 0.2746 | 0.2621 | 0.2500 | 0.2383 | 0.2270 | 0.2160 |
| | 1 | 0.4428 | 0.4439 | 0.4444 | 0.4443 | 0.4436 | 0.4424 | 0.4406 | 0.4382 | 0.4354 | 0.4320 |
| | 2 | 0.1989 | 0.2089 | 0.2189 | 0.2289 | 0.2389 | 0.2488 | 0.2587 | 0.2686 | 0.2783 | 0.2880 |
| | 3 | 0.0298 | 0.0328 | 0.0359 | 0.0393 | 0.0429 | 0.0467 | 0.0507 | 0.0549 | 0.0593 | 0.0640 |

| | $p =$ | 0.41 | 0.42 | 0.43 | 0.44 | 0.45 | 0.46 | 0.47 | 0.48 | 0.49 | 0.50 |
|---|---|---|---|---|---|---|---|---|---|---|---|
| $x =$ | 0 | 0.2054 | 0.1951 | 0.1852 | 0.1756 | 0.1664 | 0.1575 | 0.1489 | 0.1406 | 0.1327 | 0.1250 |
| | 1 | 0.4282 | 0.4239 | 0.4191 | 0.4140 | 0.4084 | 0.4024 | 0.3961 | 0.3894 | 0.3823 | 0.3750 |
| | 2 | 0.2975 | 0.3069 | 0.3162 | 0.3252 | 0.3341 | 0.3428 | 0.3512 | 0.3594 | 0.3674 | 0.3750 |
| | 3 | 0.0689 | 0.0741 | 0.0795 | 0.0852 | 0.0911 | 0.0973 | 0.1038 | 0.1106 | 0.1176 | 0.1250 |

$n = 4$

| | $p =$ | 0.01 | 0.02 | 0.03 | 0.04 | 0.05 | 0.06 | 0.07 | 0.08 | 0.09 | 0.10 |
|---|---|---|---|---|---|---|---|---|---|---|---|
| $x =$ | 0 | 0.9606 | 0.9224 | 0.8853 | 0.8493 | 0.8145 | 0.7807 | 0.7481 | 0.7164 | 0.6857 | 0.6561 |
| | 1 | 0.0388 | 0.0753 | 0.1095 | 0.1416 | 0.1715 | 0.1993 | 0.2252 | 0.2492 | 0.2713 | 0.2916 |
| | 2 | 0.0006 | 0.0023 | 0.0051 | 0.0088 | 0.0135 | 0.0191 | 0.0254 | 0.0325 | 0.0402 | 0.0486 |
| | 3 | 0.0000 | 0.0000 | 0.0001 | 0.0002 | 0.0005 | 0.0008 | 0.0013 | 0.0019 | 0.0027 | 0.0036 |
| | 4 | 0.0000 | 0.0000 | 0.0000 | 0.0000 | 0.0000 | 0.0000 | 0.0000 | 0.0000 | 0.0001 | 0.0001 |

| | $p =$ | 0.11 | 0.12 | 0.13 | 0.14 | 0.15 | 0.16 | 0.17 | 0.18 | 0.19 | 0.20 |
|---|---|---|---|---|---|---|---|---|---|---|---|
| $x =$ | 0 | 0.6274 | 0.5997 | 0.5729 | 0.5470 | 0.5220 | 0.4979 | 0.4746 | 0.4521 | 0.4305 | 0.4096 |
| | 1 | 0.3102 | 0.3271 | 0.3424 | 0.3562 | 0.3685 | 0.3793 | 0.3888 | 0.3970 | 0.4039 | 0.4096 |
| | 2 | 0.0575 | 0.0669 | 0.0767 | 0.0870 | 0.0975 | 0.1084 | 0.1195 | 0.1307 | 0.1421 | 0.1536 |
| | 3 | 0.0047 | 0.0061 | 0.0076 | 0.0094 | 0.0115 | 0.0138 | 0.0163 | 0.0191 | 0.0222 | 0.0256 |
| | 4 | 0.0001 | 0.0002 | 0.0003 | 0.0004 | 0.0005 | 0.0007 | 0.0008 | 0.0010 | 0.0013 | 0.0016 |

| | $p =$ | 0.21 | 0.22 | 0.23 | 0.24 | 0.25 | 0.26 | 0.27 | 0.28 | 0.29 | 0.30 |
|---|---|---|---|---|---|---|---|---|---|---|---|
| $x =$ | 0 | 0.3895 | 0.3702 | 0.3515 | 0.3336 | 0.3164 | 0.2999 | 0.2840 | 0.2687 | 0.2541 | 0.2401 |
| | 1 | 0.4142 | 0.4176 | 0.4200 | 0.4214 | 0.4219 | 0.4214 | 0.4201 | 0.4180 | 0.4152 | 0.4116 |
| | 2 | 0.1651 | 0.1767 | 0.1882 | 0.1996 | 0.2109 | 0.2221 | 0.2331 | 0.2439 | 0.2544 | 0.2646 |
| | 3 | 0.0293 | 0.0332 | 0.0375 | 0.0420 | 0.0469 | 0.0520 | 0.0575 | 0.0632 | 0.0693 | 0.0756 |
| | 4 | 0.0019 | 0.0023 | 0.0028 | 0.0033 | 0.0039 | 0.0046 | 0.0053 | 0.0061 | 0.0071 | 0.0081 |

*(continued)*

**The Binomial Probability Distribution** *(continued)*

| | $p =$ | 0.31 | 0.32 | 0.33 | 0.34 | 0.35 | 0.36 | 0.37 | 0.38 | 0.39 | 0.40 |
|---|---|---|---|---|---|---|---|---|---|---|---|
| $x =$ | 0 | 0.2267 | 0.2138 | 0.2015 | 0.1897 | 0.1785 | 0.1678 | 0.1575 | 0.1478 | 0.1385 | 0.1296 |
| | 1 | 0.4074 | 0.4025 | 0.3970 | 0.3910 | 0.3845 | 0.3775 | 0.3701 | 0.3623 | 0.3541 | 0.3456 |
| | 2 | 0.2745 | 0.2841 | 0.2933 | 0.3021 | 0.3105 | 0.3185 | 0.3260 | 0.3330 | 0.3396 | 0.3456 |
| | 3 | 0.0822 | 0.0891 | 0.0963 | 0.1038 | 0.1115 | 0.1194 | 0.1276 | 0.1361 | 0.1447 | 0.1536 |
| | 4 | 0.0092 | 0.0105 | 0.0119 | 0.0134 | 0.0150 | 0.0168 | 0.0187 | 0.0209 | 0.0231 | 0.0256 |

| | $p =$ | 0.41 | 0.42 | 0.43 | 0.44 | 0.45 | 0.46 | 0.47 | 0.48 | 0.49 | 0.50 |
|---|---|---|---|---|---|---|---|---|---|---|---|
| $x =$ | 0 | 0.1212 | 0.1132 | 0.1056 | 0.0983 | 0.0915 | 0.0850 | 0.0789 | 0.0731 | 0.0677 | 0.0625 |
| | 1 | 0.3368 | 0.3278 | 0.3185 | 0.3091 | 0.2995 | 0.2897 | 0.2799 | 0.2700 | 0.2600 | 0.2500 |
| | 2 | 0.3511 | 0.3560 | 0.3604 | 0.3643 | 0.3675 | 0.3702 | 0.3723 | 0.3738 | 0.3747 | 0.3750 |
| | 3 | 0.1627 | 0.1719 | 0.1813 | 0.1908 | 0.2005 | 0.2102 | 0.2201 | 0.2300 | 0.2400 | 0.2500 |
| | 4 | 0.0283 | 0.0311 | 0.0342 | 0.0375 | 0.0410 | 0.0448 | 0.0488 | 0.0531 | 0.0576 | 0.0625 |

$$n = 5$$

| | $p =$ | .01 | 0.02 | 0.03 | 0.04 | 0.05 | 0.06 | 0.07 | 0.08 | 0.09 | 0.10 |
|---|---|---|---|---|---|---|---|---|---|---|---|
| $x =$ | 0 | 0.9510 | 0.9039 | 0.8587 | 0.8154 | 0.7738 | 0.7339 | 0.6957 | 0.6591 | 0.6240 | 0.5905 |
| | 1 | 0.0480 | 0.0922 | 0.1328 | 0.1699 | 0.2036 | 0.2342 | 0.2618 | 0.2866 | 0.3086 | 0.3281 |
| | 2 | 0.0010 | 0.0038 | 0.0082 | 0.0142 | 0.0214 | 0.0299 | 0.0394 | 0.0498 | 0.0610 | 0.0729 |
| | 3 | 0.0000 | 0.0001 | 0.0003 | 0.0006 | 0.0011 | 0.0019 | 0.0030 | 0.0043 | 0.0060 | 0.0081 |
| | 4 | 0.0000 | 0.0000 | 0.0000 | 0.0000 | 0.0000 | 0.0001 | 0.0001 | 0.0002 | 0.0003 | 0.0005 |

| | $p =$ | 0.11 | 0.12 | 0.13 | 0.14 | 0.15 | 0.16 | 0.17 | 0.18 | 0.19 | 0.20 |
|---|---|---|---|---|---|---|---|---|---|---|---|
| $x =$ | 0 | 0.5584 | 0.5277 | 0.4984 | 0.4704 | 0.4437 | 0.4182 | 0.3939 | 0.3707 | 0.3487 | 0.3277 |
| | 1 | 0.3451 | 0.3598 | 0.3724 | 0.3829 | 0.3915 | 0.3983 | 0.4034 | 0.4069 | 0.4089 | 0.4096 |
| | 2 | 0.0853 | 0.0981 | 0.1113 | 0.1247 | 0.1382 | 0.1517 | 0.1652 | 0.1786 | 0.1919 | 0.2048 |
| | 3 | 0.0105 | 0.0134 | 0.0166 | 0.0203 | 0.0244 | 0.0289 | 0.0338 | 0.0392 | 0.0450 | 0.0512 |
| | 4 | 0.0007 | 0.0009 | 0.0012 | 0.0017 | 0.0022 | 0.0028 | 0.0035 | 0.0043 | 0.0053 | 0.0064 |
| | 5 | 0.0000 | 0.0000 | 0.0000 | 0.0001 | 0.0001 | 0.0001 | 0.0001 | 0.0002 | 0.0002 | 0.0003 |

| | $p =$ | 0.21 | 0.22 | 0.23 | 0.24 | 0.25 | 0.26 | 0.27 | 0.28 | 0.29 | 0.30 |
|---|---|---|---|---|---|---|---|---|---|---|---|
| $x =$ | 0 | 0.3077 | 0.2887 | 0.2707 | 0.2536 | 0.2373 | 0.2219 | 0.2073 | 0.1935 | 0.1804 | 0.1681 |
| | 1 | 0.4090 | 0.4072 | 0.4043 | 0.4003 | 0.3955 | 0.3898 | 0.3834 | 0.3762 | 0.3685 | 0.3602 |
| | 2 | 0.2174 | 0.2297 | 0.2415 | 0.2529 | 0.2637 | 0.2739 | 0.2836 | 0.2926 | 0.3010 | 0.3087 |
| | 3 | 0.0578 | 0.0648 | 0.0721 | 0.0798 | 0.0879 | 0.0962 | 0.1049 | 0.1138 | 0.1229 | 0.1323 |
| | 4 | 0.0077 | 0.0091 | 0.0108 | 0.0126 | 0.0146 | 0.0169 | 0.0194 | 0.0221 | 0.0251 | 0.0284 |
| | 5 | 0.0004 | 0.0005 | 0.0006 | 0.0008 | 0.0010 | 0.0012 | 0.0014 | 0.0017 | 0.0021 | 0.0024 |

*(continued)*

## The Binomial Probability Distribution *(continued)*

| p = | 0.31 | 0.32 | 0.33 | 0.34 | 0.35 | 0.36 | 0.37 | 0.38 | 0.39 | 0.40 |
|---|---|---|---|---|---|---|---|---|---|---|
| x = 0 | 0.1564 | 0.1454 | 0.1350 | 0.1252 | 0.1160 | 0.1074 | 0.0992 | 0.0916 | 0.0845 | 0.0778 |
| 1 | 0.3513 | 0.3421 | 0.3325 | 0.3226 | 0.3124 | 0.3020 | 0.2914 | 0.2808 | 0.2700 | 0.2592 |
| 2 | 0.3157 | 0.3220 | 0.3275 | 0.3323 | 0.3364 | 0.3397 | 0.3423 | 0.3441 | 0.3452 | 0.3456 |
| 3 | 0.1418 | 0.1515 | 0.1613 | 0.1712 | 0.1811 | 0.1911 | 0.2010 | 0.2109 | 0.2207 | 0.2304 |
| 4 | 0.0319 | 0.0357 | 0.0397 | 0.0441 | 0.0488 | 0.0537 | 0.0590 | 0.0646 | 0.0706 | 0.0768 |
| 5 | 0.0029 | 0.0034 | 0.0039 | 0.0045 | 0.0053 | 0.0060 | 0.0069 | 0.0079 | 0.0090 | 0.0102 |

| p = | 0.41 | 0.42 | 0.43 | 0.44 | 0.45 | 0.46 | 0.47 | 0.48 | 0.49 | 0.50 |
|---|---|---|---|---|---|---|---|---|---|---|
| x = 0 | 0.0715 | 0.0656 | 0.0602 | 0.0551 | 0.0503 | 0.0459 | 0.0418 | 0.0380 | 0.0345 | 0.0313 |
| 1 | 0.2484 | 0.2376 | 0.2270 | 0.2164 | 0.2059 | 0.1956 | 0.1854 | 0.1755 | 0.1657 | 0.1563 |
| 2 | 0.3452 | 0.3442 | 0.3424 | 0.3400 | 0.3369 | 0.3332 | 0.3289 | 0.3240 | 0.3185 | 0.3125 |
| 3 | 0.2399 | 0.2492 | 0.2583 | 0.2671 | 0.2757 | 0.2838 | 0.2916 | 0.2990 | 0.3060 | 0.3125 |
| 4 | 0.0834 | 0.0902 | 0.0974 | 0.1049 | 0.1128 | 0.1209 | 0.1293 | 0.1380 | 0.1470 | 0.1563 |
| 5 | 0.0116 | 0.0131 | 0.0147 | 0.0165 | 0.0185 | 0.0206 | 0.0229 | 0.0255 | 0.0282 | 0.0313 |

### n = 6

| p = | 0.01 | 0.02 | 0.03 | 0.04 | 0.05 | 0.06 | 0.07 | 0.08 | 0.09 | 0.10 |
|---|---|---|---|---|---|---|---|---|---|---|
| x = 0 | 0.9415 | 0.8858 | 0.8330 | 0.7828 | 0.7351 | 0.6899 | 0.6470 | 0.6064 | 0.5679 | 0.5314 |
| 1 | 0.0571 | 0.1085 | 0.1546 | 0.1957 | 0.2321 | 0.2642 | 0.2922 | 0.3164 | 0.3370 | 0.3543 |
| 2 | 0.0014 | 0.0055 | 0.0120 | 0.0204 | 0.0305 | 0.0422 | 0.0550 | 0.0688 | 0.0833 | 0.0984 |
| 3 | 0.0000 | 0.0002 | 0.0005 | 0.0011 | 0.0021 | 0.0036 | 0.0055 | 0.0080 | 0.0110 | 0.0146 |
| 4 | 0.0000 | 0.0000 | 0.0000 | 0.0000 | 0.0001 | 0.0002 | 0.0003 | 0.0005 | 0.0008 | 0.0012 |
| 5 | 0.0000 | 0.0000 | 0.0000 | 0.0000 | 0.0000 | 0.0000 | 0.0000 | 0.0000 | 0.0000 | 0.0001 |

| p = | 0.11 | 0.12 | 0.13 | 0.14 | 0.15 | 0.16 | 0.17 | 0.18 | 0.19 | 0.20 |
|---|---|---|---|---|---|---|---|---|---|---|
| x = 0 | 0.4970 | 0.4644 | 0.4336 | 0.4046 | 0.3771 | 0.3513 | 0.3269 | 0.3040 | 0.2824 | 0.2621 |
| 1 | 0.3685 | 0.3800 | 0.3888 | 0.3952 | 0.3993 | 0.4015 | 0.4018 | 0.4004 | 0.3975 | 0.3932 |
| 2 | 0.1139 | 0.1295 | 0.1452 | 0.1608 | 0.1762 | 0.1912 | 0.2057 | 0.2197 | 0.2331 | 0.2458 |
| 3 | 0.0188 | 0.0236 | 0.0289 | 0.0349 | 0.0415 | 0.0486 | 0.0562 | 0.0643 | 0.0729 | 0.0819 |
| 4 | 0.0017 | 0.0024 | 0.0032 | 0.0043 | 0.0055 | 0.0069 | 0.0086 | 0.0106 | 0.0128 | 0.0154 |
| 5 | 0.0001 | 0.0001 | 0.0002 | 0.0003 | 0.0004 | 0.0005 | 0.0007 | 0.0009 | 0.0012 | 0.0015 |
| 6 | 0.0000 | 0.0000 | 0.0000 | 0.0000 | 0.0000 | 0.0000 | 0.0000 | 0.0000 | 0.0000 | 0.0001 |

*(continued)*

**The Binomial Probability Distribution** *(continued)*

| | p = | 0.21 | 0.22 | 0.23 | 0.24 | 0.25 | 0.26 | 0.27 | 0.28 | 0.29 | 0.30 |
|---|---|---|---|---|---|---|---|---|---|---|---|
| x = | 0 | 0.2431 | 0.2252 | 0.2084 | 0.1927 | 0.1780 | 0.1642 | 0.1513 | 0.1393 | 0.1281 | 0.1176 |
| | 1 | 0.3877 | 0.3811 | 0.3735 | 0.3651 | 0.3560 | 0.3462 | 0.3358 | 0.3251 | 0.3139 | 0.3025 |
| | 2 | 0.2577 | 0.2687 | 0.2789 | 0.2882 | 0.2966 | 0.3041 | 0.3105 | 0.3160 | 0.3206 | 0.3241 |
| | 3 | 0.0913 | 0.1011 | 0.1111 | 0.1214 | 0.1318 | 0.1424 | 0.1531 | 0.1639 | 0.1746 | 0.1852 |
| | 4 | 0.0182 | 0.0214 | 0.0249 | 0.0287 | 0.0330 | 0.0375 | 0.0425 | 0.0478 | 0.0535 | 0.0595 |
| | 5 | 0.0019 | 0.0024 | 0.0030 | 0.0036 | 0.0044 | 0.0053 | 0.0063 | 0.0074 | 0.0087 | 0.0102 |
| | 6 | 0.0001 | 0.0001 | 0.0001 | 0.0002 | 0.0002 | 0.0003 | 0.0004 | 0.0005 | 0.0006 | 0.0007 |

| | p = | 0.31 | 0.32 | 0.33 | 0.34 | 0.35 | 0.36 | 0.37 | 0.38 | 0.39 | 0.40 |
|---|---|---|---|---|---|---|---|---|---|---|---|
| x = | 0 | 0.1079 | 0.0989 | 0.0905 | 0.0827 | 0.0754 | 0.0687 | 0.0625 | 0.0568 | 0.0515 | 0.0467 |
| | 1 | 0.2909 | 0.2792 | 0.2673 | 0.2555 | 0.2437 | 0.2319 | 0.2203 | 0.2089 | 0.1976 | 0.1866 |
| | 2 | 0.3267 | 0.3284 | 0.3292 | 0.3290 | 0.3280 | 0.3261 | 0.3235 | 0.3201 | 0.3159 | 0.3110 |
| | 3 | 0.1957 | 0.2061 | 0.2162 | 0.2260 | 0.2355 | 0.2446 | 0.2533 | 0.2616 | 0.2693 | 0.2765 |
| | 4 | 0.0660 | 0.0727 | 0.0799 | 0.0873 | 0.0951 | 0.1032 | 0.1116 | 0.1202 | 0.1291 | 0.1382 |
| | 5 | 0.0119 | 0.0137 | 0.0157 | 0.0180 | 0.0205 | 0.0232 | 0.0262 | 0.0295 | 0.0330 | 0.0369 |
| | 6 | 0.0009 | 0.0011 | 0.0013 | 0.0015 | 0.0018 | 0.0022 | 0.0026 | 0.0030 | 0.0035 | 0.0041 |

| | p = | 0.41 | 0.42 | 0.43 | 0.44 | 0.45 | 0.46 | 0.47 | 0.48 | 0.49 | 0.50 |
|---|---|---|---|---|---|---|---|---|---|---|---|
| x = | 0 | 0.0422 | 0.0381 | 0.0343 | 0.0308 | 0.0277 | 0.0248 | 0.0222 | 0.0198 | 0.0176 | 0.0156 |
| | 1 | 0.1759 | 0.1654 | 0.1552 | 0.1454 | 0.1359 | 0.1267 | 0.1179 | 0.1095 | 0.1014 | 0.0938 |
| | 2 | 0.3055 | 0.2994 | 0.2928 | 0.2856 | 0.2780 | 0.2699 | 0.2615 | 0.2527 | 0.2436 | 0.2344 |
| | 3 | 0.2831 | 0.2891 | 0.2945 | 0.2992 | 0.3032 | 0.3065 | 0.3091 | 0.3110 | 0.3121 | 0.3125 |
| | 4 | 0.1475 | 0.1570 | 0.1666 | 0.1763 | 0.1861 | 0.1958 | 0.2056 | 0.2153 | 0.2249 | 0.2344 |
| | 5 | 0.0410 | 0.0455 | 0.0503 | 0.0554 | 0.0609 | 0.0667 | 0.0729 | 0.0795 | 0.0864 | 0.0938 |
| | 6 | 0.0048 | 0.0055 | 0.0063 | 0.0073 | 0.0083 | 0.0095 | 0.0108 | 0.0122 | 0.0138 | 0.0156 |

**n = 7**

| | p = | 0.01 | 0.02 | 0.03 | 0.04 | 0.05 | 0.06 | 0.07 | 0.08 | 0.09 | 0.10 |
|---|---|---|---|---|---|---|---|---|---|---|---|
| x = | 0 | 0.9321 | 0.8681 | 0.8080 | 0.7514 | 0.6983 | 0.6485 | 0.6017 | 0.5578 | 0.5168 | 0.4783 |
| | 1 | 0.0659 | 0.1240 | 0.1749 | 0.2192 | 0.2573 | 0.2897 | 0.3170 | 0.3396 | 0.3578 | 0.3720 |
| | 2 | 0.0020 | 0.0076 | 0.0162 | 0.0274 | 0.0406 | 0.0555 | 0.0716 | 0.0886 | 0.1061 | 0.1240 |
| | 3 | 0.0000 | 0.0003 | 0.0008 | 0.0019 | 0.0036 | 0.0059 | 0.0090 | 0.0128 | 0.0175 | 0.0230 |
| | 4 | 0.0000 | 0.0000 | 0.0000 | 0.0001 | 0.0002 | 0.0004 | 0.0007 | 0.0011 | 0.0017 | 0.0026 |
| | 5 | 0.0000 | 0.0000 | 0.0000 | 0.0000 | 0.0000 | 0.0000 | 0.0000 | 0.0001 | 0.0001 | 0.0002 |

*(continued)*

## The Binomial Probability Distribution *(continued)*

| | $p =$ | 0.11 | 0.12 | 0.13 | 0.14 | 0.15 | 0.16 | 0.17 | 0.18 | 0.19 | 0.20 |
|---|---|---|---|---|---|---|---|---|---|---|---|
| $x =$ | 0 | 0.4423 | 0.4087 | 0.3773 | 0.3479 | 0.3206 | 0.2951 | 0.2714 | 0.2493 | 0.2288 | 0.2097 |
| | 1 | 0.3827 | 0.3901 | 0.3946 | 0.3965 | 0.3960 | 0.3935 | 0.3891 | 0.3830 | 0.3756 | 0.3670 |
| | 2 | 0.1419 | 0.1596 | 0.1769 | 0.1936 | 0.2097 | 0.2248 | 0.2391 | 0.2523 | 0.2643 | 0.2753 |
| | 3 | 0.0292 | 0.0363 | 0.0441 | 0.0525 | 0.0617 | 0.0714 | 0.0816 | 0.0923 | 0.1033 | 0.1147 |
| | 4 | 0.0036 | 0.0049 | 0.0066 | 0.0086 | 0.0109 | 0.0136 | 0.0167 | 0.0203 | 0.0242 | 0.0287 |
| | 5 | 0.0003 | 0.0004 | 0.0006 | 0.0008 | 0.0012 | 0.0016 | 0.0021 | 0.0027 | 0.0034 | 0.0043 |
| | 6 | 0.0000 | 0.0000 | 0.0000 | 0.0000 | 0.0001 | 0.0001 | 0.0001 | 0.0002 | 0.0003 | 0.0004 |

| | $p =$ | 0.21 | 0.22 | 0.23 | 0.24 | 0.25 | 0.26 | 0.27 | 0.28 | 0.29 | 0.30 |
|---|---|---|---|---|---|---|---|---|---|---|---|
| $x =$ | 0 | 0.1920 | 0.1757 | 0.1605 | 0.1465 | 0.1335 | 0.1215 | 0.1105 | 0.1003 | 0.0910 | 0.0824 |
| | 1 | 0.3573 | 0.3468 | 0.3356 | 0.3237 | 0.3115 | 0.2989 | 0.2860 | 0.2731 | 0.2600 | 0.2471 |
| | 2 | 0.2850 | 0.2935 | 0.3007 | 0.3067 | 0.3115 | 0.3150 | 0.3174 | 0.3186 | 0.3186 | 0.3177 |
| | 3 | 0.1263 | 0.1379 | 0.1497 | 0.1614 | 0.1730 | 0.1845 | 0.1956 | 0.2065 | 0.2169 | 0.2269 |
| | 4 | 0.0336 | 0.0389 | 0.0447 | 0.0510 | 0.0577 | 0.0648 | 0.0724 | 0.0803 | 0.0886 | 0.0972 |
| | 5 | 0.0054 | 0.0066 | 0.0080 | 0.0097 | 0.0115 | 0.0137 | 0.0161 | 0.0187 | 0.0217 | 0.0250 |
| | 6 | 0.0005 | 0.0006 | 0.0008 | 0.0010 | 0.0013 | 0.0016 | 0.0020 | 0.0024 | 0.0030 | 0.0036 |
| | 7 | 0.0000 | 0.0000 | 0.0000 | 0.0000 | 0.0001 | 0.0001 | 0.0001 | 0.0001 | 0.0002 | 0.0002 |

| | $p =$ | 0.31 | 0.32 | 0.33 | 0.34 | 0.35 | 0.36 | 0.37 | 0.38 | 0.39 | 0.40 |
|---|---|---|---|---|---|---|---|---|---|---|---|
| $x =$ | 0 | 0.0745 | 0.0672 | 0.0606 | 0.0546 | 0.0490 | 0.0440 | 0.0394 | 0.0352 | 0.0314 | 0.0280 |
| | 1 | 0.2342 | 0.2215 | 0.2090 | 0.1967 | 0.1848 | 0.1732 | 0.1619 | 0.1511 | 0.1407 | 0.1306 |
| | 2 | 0.3156 | 0.3127 | 0.3088 | 0.3040 | 0.2985 | 0.2922 | 0.2853 | 0.2778 | 0.2698 | 0.2613 |
| | 3 | 0.2363 | 0.2452 | 0.2535 | 0.2610 | 0.2679 | 0.2740 | 0.2793 | 0.2838 | 0.2875 | 0.2903 |
| | 4 | 0.1062 | 0.1154 | 0.1248 | 0.1345 | 0.1442 | 0.1541 | 0.1640 | 0.1739 | 0.1838 | 0.1935 |
| | 5 | 0.0286 | 0.0326 | 0.0369 | 0.0416 | 0.0466 | 0.0520 | 0.0578 | 0.0640 | 0.0705 | 0.0774 |
| | 6 | 0.0043 | 0.0051 | 0.0061 | 0.0071 | 0.0084 | 0.0098 | 0.0113 | 0.0131 | 0.0150 | 0.0172 |
| | 7 | 0.0003 | 0.0003 | 0.0004 | 0.0005 | 0.0006 | 0.0008 | 0.0009 | 0.0011 | 0.0014 | 0.0016 |

| | $p =$ | 0.41 | 0.42 | 0.43 | 0.44 | 0.45 | 0.46 | 0.47 | 0.48 | 0.49 | 0.50 |
|---|---|---|---|---|---|---|---|---|---|---|---|
| $x =$ | 0 | 0.0249 | 0.0221 | 0.0195 | 0.0173 | 0.0152 | 0.0134 | 0.0117 | 0.0103 | 0.0090 | 0.0078 |
| | 1 | 0.1211 | 0.1119 | 0.1032 | 0.0950 | 0.0872 | 0.0798 | 0.0729 | 0.0664 | 0.0604 | 0.0547 |
| | 2 | 0.2524 | 0.2431 | 0.2336 | 0.2239 | 0.2140 | 0.2040 | 0.1940 | 0.1840 | 0.1740 | 0.1641 |
| | 3 | 0.2923 | 0.2934 | 0.2937 | 0.2932 | 0.2918 | 0.2897 | 0.2867 | 0.2830 | 0.2786 | 0.2734 |
| | 4 | 0.2031 | 0.2125 | 0.2216 | 0.2304 | 0.2388 | 0.2468 | 0.2543 | 0.2612 | 0.2676 | 0.2734 |
| | 5 | 0.0847 | 0.0923 | 0.1003 | 0.1086 | 0.1172 | 0.1261 | 0.1353 | 0.1447 | 0.1543 | 0.1641 |
| | 6 | 0.0196 | 0.0223 | 0.0252 | 0.0284 | 0.0320 | 0.0358 | 0.0400 | 0.0445 | 0.0494 | 0.0547 |
| | 7 | 0.0019 | 0.0023 | 0.0027 | 0.0032 | 0.0037 | 0.0044 | 0.0051 | 0.0059 | 0.0068 | 0.0078 |

*(continued)*

## The Binomial Probability Distribution *(continued)*

### *n = 8*

| | $p =$ | 0.01 | 0.02 | 0.03 | 0.04 | 0.05 | 0.06 | 0.07 | 0.08 | 0.09 | 0.10 |
|---|---|---|---|---|---|---|---|---|---|---|---|
| $x =$ | 0 | 0.9227 | 0.8508 | 0.7837 | 0.7214 | 0.6634 | 0.6096 | 0.5596 | 0.5132 | 0.4703 | 0.4305 |
| | 1 | 0.0746 | 0.1389 | 0.1939 | 0.2405 | 0.2793 | 0.3113 | 0.3370 | 0.3570 | 0.3721 | 0.3826 |
| | 2 | 0.0026 | 0.0099 | 0.0210 | 0.0351 | 0.0515 | 0.0695 | 0.0888 | 0.1087 | 0.1288 | 0.1488 |
| | 3 | 0.0001 | 0.0004 | 0.0013 | 0.0029 | 0.0054 | 0.0089 | 0.0134 | 0.0189 | 0.0255 | 0.0331 |
| | 4 | 0.0000 | 0.0000 | 0.0001 | 0.0002 | 0.0004 | 0.0007 | 0.0013 | 0.0021 | 0.0031 | 0.0046 |
| | 5 | 0.0000 | 0.0000 | 0.0000 | 0.0000 | 0.0000 | 0.0000 | 0.0001 | 0.0001 | 0.0002 | 0.0004 |

| | $p =$ | 0.11 | 0.12 | 0.13 | 0.14 | 0.15 | 0.16 | 0.17 | 0.18 | 0.19 | 0.20 |
|---|---|---|---|---|---|---|---|---|---|---|---|
| $x =$ | 0 | 0.3937 | 0.3596 | 0.3282 | 0.2992 | 0.2725 | 0.2479 | 0.2252 | 0.2044 | 0.1853 | 0.1678 |
| | 1 | 0.3892 | 0.3923 | 0.3923 | 0.3897 | 0.3847 | 0.3777 | 0.3691 | 0.3590 | 0.3477 | 0.3355 |
| | 2 | 0.1684 | 0.1872 | 0.2052 | 0.2220 | 0.2376 | 0.2518 | 0.2646 | 0.2758 | 0.2855 | 0.2936 |
| | 3 | 0.0416 | 0.0511 | 0.0613 | 0.0723 | 0.0839 | 0.0959 | 0.1084 | 0.1211 | 0.1339 | 0.1468 |
| | 4 | 0.0064 | 0.0087 | 0.0115 | 0.0147 | 0.0185 | 0.0228 | 0.0277 | 0.0332 | 0.0393 | 0.0459 |
| | 5 | 0.0006 | 0.0009 | 0.0014 | 0.0019 | 0.0026 | 0.0035 | 0.0045 | 0.0058 | 0.0074 | 0.0092 |
| | 6 | 0.0000 | 0.0001 | 0.0001 | 0.0002 | 0.0002 | 0.0003 | 0.0005 | 0.0006 | 0.0009 | 0.0011 |
| | 7 | 0.0000 | 0.0000 | 0.0000 | 0.0000 | 0.0000 | 0.0000 | 0.0000 | 0.0000 | 0.0001 | 0.0001 |

| | $p =$ | 0.21 | 0.22 | 0.23 | 0.24 | 0.25 | 0.26 | 0.27 | 0.28 | 0.29 | 0.30 |
|---|---|---|---|---|---|---|---|---|---|---|---|
| $x =$ | 0 | 0.1517 | 0.1370 | 0.1236 | 0.1113 | 0.1001 | 0.0899 | 0.0806 | 0.0722 | 0.0646 | 0.0576 |
| | 1 | 0.3226 | 0.3092 | 0.2953 | 0.2812 | 0.2670 | 0.2527 | 0.2386 | 0.2247 | 0.2110 | 0.1977 |
| | 2 | 0.3002 | 0.3052 | 0.3087 | 0.3108 | 0.3115 | 0.3108 | 0.3089 | 0.3058 | 0.3017 | 0.2965 |
| | 3 | 0.1596 | 0.1722 | 0.1844 | 0.1963 | 0.2076 | 0.2184 | 0.2285 | 0.2379 | 0.2464 | 0.2541 |
| | 4 | 0.0530 | 0.0607 | 0.0689 | 0.0775 | 0.0865 | 0.0959 | 0.1056 | 0.1156 | 0.1258 | 0.1361 |
| | 5 | 0.0113 | 0.0137 | 0.0165 | 0.0196 | 0.0231 | 0.0270 | 0.0313 | 0.0360 | 0.0411 | 0.0467 |
| | 6 | 0.0015 | 0.0019 | 0.0025 | 0.0031 | 0.0038 | 0.0047 | 0.0058 | 0.0070 | 0.0084 | 0.0100 |
| | 7 | 0.0001 | 0.0002 | 0.0002 | 0.0003 | 0.0004 | 0.0005 | 0.0006 | 0.0008 | 0.0010 | 0.0012 |
| | 8 | 0.0000 | 0.0000 | 0.0000 | 0.0000 | 0.0000 | 0.0000 | 0.0000 | 0.0000 | 0.0001 | 0.0001 |

| | $p =$ | 0.31 | 0.32 | 0.33 | 0.34 | 0.35 | 0.36 | 0.37 | 0.38 | 0.39 | 0.40 |
|---|---|---|---|---|---|---|---|---|---|---|---|
| $x =$ | 0 | 0.0514 | 0.0457 | 0.0406 | 0.0360 | 0.0319 | 0.0281 | 0.0248 | 0.0218 | 0.0192 | 0.0168 |
| | 1 | 0.1847 | 0.1721 | 0.1600 | 0.1484 | 0.1373 | 0.1267 | 0.1166 | 0.1071 | 0.0981 | 0.0896 |
| | 2 | 0.2904 | 0.2835 | 0.2758 | 0.2675 | 0.2587 | 0.2494 | 0.2397 | 0.2297 | 0.2194 | 0.2090 |
| | 3 | 0.2609 | 0.2668 | 0.2717 | 0.2756 | 0.2786 | 0.2805 | 0.2815 | 0.2815 | 0.2806 | 0.2787 |
| | 4 | 0.1465 | 0.1569 | 0.1673 | 0.1775 | 0.1875 | 0.1973 | 0.2067 | 0.2157 | 0.2242 | 0.2322 |
| | 5 | 0.0527 | 0.0591 | 0.0659 | 0.0732 | 0.0808 | 0.0888 | 0.0971 | 0.1058 | 0.1147 | 0.1239 |
| | 6 | 0.0118 | 0.0139 | 0.0162 | 0.0188 | 0.0217 | 0.0250 | 0.0285 | 0.0324 | 0.0367 | 0.0413 |
| | 7 | 0.0015 | 0.0019 | 0.0023 | 0.0028 | 0.0033 | 0.0040 | 0.0048 | 0.0057 | 0.0067 | 0.0079 |
| | 8 | 0.0001 | 0.0001 | 0.0001 | 0.0002 | 0.0002 | 0.0003 | 0.0004 | 0.0004 | 0.0005 | 0.0007 |

*(continued)*

## The Binomial Probability Distribution *(continued)*

| | $p =$ | 0.41 | 0.42 | 0.43 | 0.44 | 0.45 | 0.46 | 0.47 | 0.48 | 0.49 | 0.50 |
|---|---|---|---|---|---|---|---|---|---|---|---|
| $x =$ | 0 | 0.0147 | 0.0128 | 0.0111 | 0.0097 | 0.0084 | 0.0072 | 0.0062 | 0.0053 | 0.0046 | 0.0039 |
| | 1 | 0.0816 | 0.0742 | 0.0672 | 0.0608 | 0.0548 | 0.0493 | 0.0442 | 0.0395 | 0.0352 | 0.0313 |
| | 2 | 0.1985 | 0.1880 | 0.1776 | 0.1672 | 0.1569 | 0.1469 | 0.1371 | 0.1275 | 0.1183 | 0.1094 |
| | 3 | 0.2759 | 0.2723 | 0.2679 | 0.2627 | 0.2568 | 0.2503 | 0.2431 | 0.2355 | 0.2273 | 0.2188 |
| | 4 | 0.2397 | 0.2465 | 0.2526 | 0.2580 | 0.2627 | 0.2665 | 0.2695 | 0.2717 | 0.2730 | 0.2734 |
| | 5 | 0.1332 | 0.1428 | 0.1525 | 0.1622 | 0.1719 | 0.1816 | 0.1912 | 0.2006 | 0.2098 | 0.2188 |
| | 6 | 0.0463 | 0.0517 | 0.0575 | 0.0637 | 0.0703 | 0.0774 | 0.0848 | 0.0926 | 0.1008 | 0.1094 |
| | 7 | 0.0092 | 0.0107 | 0.0124 | 0.0143 | 0.0164 | 0.0188 | 0.0215 | 0.0244 | 0.0277 | 0.0313 |
| | 8 | 0.0008 | 0.0010 | 0.0012 | 0.0014 | 0.0017 | 0.0020 | 0.0024 | 0.0028 | 0.0033 | 0.0039 |

### $n = 9$

| | $p =$ | 0.01 | 0.02 | 0.03 | 0.04 | 0.05 | 0.06 | 0.07 | 0.08 | 0.09 | 0.10 |
|---|---|---|---|---|---|---|---|---|---|---|---|
| $x =$ | 0 | 0.9135 | 0.8337 | 0.7602 | 0.6925 | 0.6302 | 0.5730 | 0.5204 | 0.4722 | 0.4279 | 0.3874 |
| | 1 | 0.0830 | 0.1531 | 0.2116 | 0.2597 | 0.2985 | 0.3292 | 0.3525 | 0.3695 | 0.3809 | 0.3874 |
| | 2 | 0.0034 | 0.0125 | 0.0262 | 0.0433 | 0.0629 | 0.0840 | 0.1061 | 0.1285 | 0.1507 | 0.1722 |
| | 3 | 0.0001 | 0.0006 | 0.0019 | 0.0042 | 0.0077 | 0.0125 | 0.0186 | 0.0261 | 0.0348 | 0.0446 |
| | 4 | 0.0000 | 0.0000 | 0.0001 | 0.0003 | 0.0006 | 0.0012 | 0.0021 | 0.0034 | 0.0052 | 0.0074 |
| | 5 | 0.0000 | 0.0000 | 0.0000 | 0.0000 | 0.0000 | 0.0001 | 0.0002 | 0.0003 | 0.0005 | 0.0008 |
| | 6 | 0.0000 | 0.0000 | 0.0000 | 0.0000 | 0.0000 | 0.0000 | 0.0000 | 0.0000 | 0.0000 | 0.0001 |

| | $p =$ | 0.11 | 0.12 | 0.13 | 0.14 | 0.15 | 0.16 | 0.17 | 0.18 | 0.19 | 0.20 |
|---|---|---|---|---|---|---|---|---|---|---|---|
| $x =$ | 0 | 0.3504 | 0.3165 | 0.2855 | 0.2573 | 0.2316 | 0.2082 | 0.1869 | 0.1676 | 0.1501 | 0.1342 |
| | 1 | 0.3897 | 0.3884 | 0.3840 | 0.3770 | 0.3679 | 0.3569 | 0.3446 | 0.3312 | 0.3169 | 0.3020 |
| | 2 | 0.1927 | 0.2119 | 0.2295 | 0.2455 | 0.2597 | 0.2720 | 0.2823 | 0.2908 | 0.2973 | 0.3020 |
| | 3 | 0.0556 | 0.0674 | 0.0800 | 0.0933 | 0.1069 | 0.1209 | 0.1349 | 0.1489 | 0.1627 | 0.1762 |
| | 4 | 0.0103 | 0.0138 | 0.0179 | 0.0228 | 0.0283 | 0.0345 | 0.0415 | 0.0490 | 0.0573 | 0.0661 |
| | 5 | 0.0013 | 0.0019 | 0.0027 | 0.0037 | 0.0050 | 0.0066 | 0.0085 | 0.0108 | 0.0134 | 0.0165 |
| | 6 | 0.0001 | 0.0002 | 0.0003 | 0.0004 | 0.0006 | 0.0008 | 0.0012 | 0.0016 | 0.0021 | 0.0028 |
| | 7 | 0.0000 | 0.0000 | 0.0000 | 0.0000 | 0.0000 | 0.0001 | 0.0001 | 0.0001 | 0.0002 | 0.0003 |
| | 8 | 0.0000 | 0.0000 | 0.0000 | 0.0000 | 0.0000 | 0.0000 | 0.0000 | 0.0000 | 0.0000 | 0.0000 |

*(continued)*

## The Binomial Probability Distribution *(continued)*

| | p = | 0.21 | 0.22 | 0.23 | 0.24 | 0.25 | 0.26 | 0.27 | 0.28 | 0.29 | 0.30 |
|---|---|---|---|---|---|---|---|---|---|---|---|
| x = | 0 | 0.1199 | 0.1069 | 0.0952 | 0.0846 | 0.0751 | 0.0665 | 0.0589 | 0.0520 | 0.0458 | 0.0404 |
| | 1 | 0.2867 | 0.2713 | 0.2558 | 0.2404 | 0.2253 | 0.2104 | 0.1960 | 0.1820 | 0.1685 | 0.1556 |
| | 2 | 0.3049 | 0.3061 | 0.3056 | 0.3037 | 0.3003 | 0.2957 | 0.2899 | 0.2831 | 0.2754 | 0.2668 |
| | 3 | 0.1891 | 0.2014 | 0.2130 | 0.2238 | 0.2336 | 0.2424 | 0.2502 | 0.2569 | 0.2624 | 0.2668 |
| | 4 | 0.0754 | 0.0852 | 0.0954 | 0.1060 | 0.1168 | 0.1278 | 0.1388 | 0.1499 | 0.1608 | 0.1715 |
| | 5 | 0.0200 | 0.0240 | 0.0285 | 0.0335 | 0.0389 | 0.0449 | 0.0513 | 0.0583 | 0.0657 | 0.0735 |
| | 6 | 0.0036 | 0.0045 | 0.0057 | 0.0070 | 0.0087 | 0.0105 | 0.0127 | 0.0151 | 0.0179 | 0.0210 |
| | 7 | 0.0004 | 0.0005 | 0.0007 | 0.0010 | 0.0012 | 0.0016 | 0.0020 | 0.0025 | 0.0031 | 0.0039 |
| | 8 | 0.0000 | 0.0000 | 0.0001 | 0.0001 | 0.0001 | 0.0001 | 0.0002 | 0.0002 | 0.0003 | 0.0004 |

| | p = | 0.31 | 0.32 | 0.33 | 0.34 | 0.35 | 0.36 | 0.37 | 0.38 | 0.39 | 0.40 |
|---|---|---|---|---|---|---|---|---|---|---|---|
| x = | 0 | 0.0355 | 0.0311 | 0.0272 | 0.0238 | 0.0207 | 0.0180 | 0.0156 | 0.0135 | 0.0117 | 0.0101 |
| | 1 | 0.1433 | 0.1317 | 0.1206 | 0.1102 | 0.1004 | 0.0912 | 0.0826 | 0.0747 | 0.0673 | 0.0605 |
| | 2 | 0.2576 | 0.2478 | 0.2376 | 0.2270 | 0.2162 | 0.2052 | 0.1941 | 0.1831 | 0.1721 | 0.1612 |
| | 3 | 0.2701 | 0.2721 | 0.2731 | 0.2729 | 0.2716 | 0.2693 | 0.2660 | 0.2618 | 0.2567 | 0.2508 |
| | 4 | 0.1820 | 0.1921 | 0.2017 | 0.2109 | 0.2194 | 0.2272 | 0.2344 | 0.2407 | 0.2462 | 0.2508 |
| | 5 | 0.0818 | 0.0904 | 0.0994 | 0.1086 | 0.1181 | 0.1278 | 0.1376 | 0.1475 | 0.1574 | 0.1672 |
| | 6 | 0.0245 | 0.0284 | 0.0326 | 0.0373 | 0.0424 | 0.0479 | 0.0539 | 0.0603 | 0.0671 | 0.0743 |
| | 7 | 0.0047 | 0.0057 | 0.0069 | 0.0082 | 0.0098 | 0.0116 | 0.0136 | 0.0158 | 0.0184 | 0.0212 |
| | 8 | 0.0005 | 0.0007 | 0.0008 | 0.0011 | 0.0013 | 0.0016 | 0.0020 | 0.0024 | 0.0029 | 0.0035 |
| | 9 | 0.0000 | 0.0000 | 0.0000 | 0.0001 | 0.0001 | 0.0001 | 0.0001 | 0.0002 | 0.0002 | 0.0003 |

| | p = | 0.41 | 0.42 | 0.43 | 0.44 | 0.45 | 0.46 | 0.47 | 0.48 | 0.49 | 0.50 |
|---|---|---|---|---|---|---|---|---|---|---|---|
| x = | 0 | 0.0087 | 0.0074 | 0.0064 | 0.0054 | 0.0046 | 0.0039 | 0.0033 | 0.0028 | 0.0023 | 0.0020 |
| | 1 | 0.0542 | 0.0484 | 0.0431 | 0.0383 | 0.0339 | 0.0299 | 0.0263 | 0.0231 | 0.0202 | 0.0176 |
| | 2 | 0.1506 | 0.1402 | 0.1301 | 0.1204 | 0.1110 | 0.1020 | 0.0934 | 0.0853 | 0.0776 | 0.0703 |
| | 3 | 0.2442 | 0.2369 | 0.2291 | 0.2207 | 0.2119 | 0.2027 | 0.1933 | 0.1837 | 0.1739 | 0.1641 |
| | 4 | 0.2545 | 0.2573 | 0.2592 | 0.2601 | 0.2600 | 0.2590 | 0.2571 | 0.2543 | 0.2506 | 0.2461 |
| | 5 | 0.1769 | 0.1863 | 0.1955 | 0.2044 | 0.2128 | 0.2207 | 0.2280 | 0.2347 | 0.2408 | 0.2461 |
| | 6 | 0.0819 | 0.0900 | 0.0983 | 0.1070 | 0.1160 | 0.1253 | 0.1348 | 0.1445 | 0.1542 | 0.1641 |
| | 7 | 0.0244 | 0.0279 | 0.0318 | 0.0360 | 0.0407 | 0.0458 | 0.0512 | 0.0571 | 0.0635 | 0.0703 |
| | 8 | 0.0042 | 0.0051 | 0.0060 | 0.0071 | 0.0083 | 0.0097 | 0.0114 | 0.0132 | 0.0153 | 0.0176 |
| | 9 | 0.0003 | 0.0004 | 0.0005 | 0.0006 | 0.0008 | 0.0009 | 0.0011 | 0.0014 | 0.0016 | 0.0020 |

*(continued)*

## The Binomial Probability Distribution *(continued)*

$$n = 10$$

| $p =$ | 0.01 | 0.02 | 0.03 | 0.04 | 0.05 | 0.06 | 0.07 | 0.08 | 0.09 | 0.10 |
|---|---|---|---|---|---|---|---|---|---|---|
| $x = 0$ | 0.9044 | 0.8171 | 0.7374 | 0.6648 | 0.5987 | 0.5386 | 0.4840 | 0.4344 | 0.3894 | 0.3487 |
| 1 | 0.0914 | 0.1667 | 0.2281 | 0.2770 | 0.3151 | 0.3438 | 0.3643 | 0.3777 | 0.3851 | 0.3874 |
| 2 | 0.0042 | 0.0153 | 0.0317 | 0.0519 | 0.0746 | 0.0988 | 0.1234 | 0.1478 | 0.1714 | 0.1937 |
| 3 | 0.0001 | 0.0008 | 0.0026 | 0.0058 | 0.0105 | 0.0168 | 0.0248 | 0.0343 | 0.0452 | 0.0574 |
| 4 | 0.0000 | 0.0000 | 0.0001 | 0.0004 | 0.0010 | 0.0019 | 0.0033 | 0.0052 | 0.0078 | 0.0112 |
| 5 | 0.0000 | 0.0000 | 0.0000 | 0.0000 | 0.0001 | 0.0001 | 0.0003 | 0.0005 | 0.0009 | 0.0015 |
| 6 | 0.0000 | 0.0000 | 0.0000 | 0.0000 | 0.0000 | 0.0000 | 0.0000 | 0.0000 | 0.0001 | 0.0001 |

| $p =$ | 0.11 | 0.12 | 0.13 | 0.14 | 0.15 | 0.16 | 0.17 | 0.18 | 0.19 | 0.20 |
|---|---|---|---|---|---|---|---|---|---|---|
| $x = 0$ | 0.3118 | 0.2785 | 0.2484 | 0.2213 | 0.1969 | 0.1749 | 0.1552 | 0.1374 | 0.1216 | 0.1074 |
| 1 | 0.3854 | 0.3798 | 0.3712 | 0.3603 | 0.3474 | 0.3331 | 0.3178 | 0.3017 | 0.2852 | 0.2684 |
| 2 | 0.2143 | 0.2330 | 0.2496 | 0.2639 | 0.2759 | 0.2856 | 0.2929 | 0.2980 | 0.3010 | 0.3020 |
| 3 | 0.0706 | 0.0847 | 0.0995 | 0.1146 | 0.1298 | 0.1450 | 0.1600 | 0.1745 | 0.1883 | 0.2013 |
| 4 | 0.0153 | 0.0202 | 0.0260 | 0.0326 | 0.0401 | 0.0483 | 0.0573 | 0.0670 | 0.0773 | 0.0881 |
| 5 | 0.0023 | 0.0033 | 0.0047 | 0.0064 | 0.0085 | 0.0111 | 0.0141 | 0.0177 | 0.0218 | 0.0264 |
| 6 | 0.0002 | 0.0004 | 0.0006 | 0.0009 | 0.0012 | 0.0018 | 0.0024 | 0.0032 | 0.0043 | 0.0055 |
| 7 | 0.0000 | 0.0000 | 0.0000 | 0.0001 | 0.0001 | 0.0002 | 0.0003 | 0.0004 | 0.0006 | 0.0008 |
| 8 | 0.0000 | 0.0000 | 0.0000 | 0.0000 | 0.0000 | 0.0000 | 0.0000 | 0.0000 | 0.0001 | 0.0001 |

| $p =$ | 0.21 | 0.22 | 0.23 | 0.24 | 0.25 | 0.26 | 0.27 | 0.28 | 0.29 | 0.30 |
|---|---|---|---|---|---|---|---|---|---|---|
| $x = 0$ | 0.0947 | 0.0834 | 0.0733 | 0.0643 | 0.0563 | 0.0492 | 0.0430 | 0.0374 | 0.0326 | 0.0282 |
| 1 | 0.2517 | 0.2351 | 0.2188 | 0.2030 | 0.1877 | 0.1730 | 0.1590 | 0.1456 | 0.1330 | 0.1211 |
| 2 | 0.3011 | 0.2984 | 0.2942 | 0.2885 | 0.2816 | 0.2735 | 0.2646 | 0.2548 | 0.2444 | 0.2335 |
| 3 | 0.2134 | 0.2244 | 0.2343 | 0.2429 | 0.2503 | 0.2563 | 0.2609 | 0.2642 | 0.2662 | 0.2668 |
| 4 | 0.0993 | 0.1108 | 0.1225 | 0.1343 | 0.1460 | 0.1576 | 0.1689 | 0.1798 | 0.1903 | 0.2001 |
| 5 | 0.0317 | 0.0375 | 0.0439 | 0.0509 | 0.0584 | 0.0664 | 0.0750 | 0.0839 | 0.0933 | 0.1029 |
| 6 | 0.0070 | 0.0088 | 0.0109 | 0.0134 | 0.0162 | 0.0195 | 0.0231 | 0.0272 | 0.0317 | 0.0368 |
| 7 | 0.0011 | 0.0014 | 0.0019 | 0.0024 | 0.0031 | 0.0039 | 0.0049 | 0.0060 | 0.0074 | 0.0090 |
| 8 | 0.0001 | 0.0002 | 0.0002 | 0.0003 | 0.0004 | 0.0005 | 0.0007 | 0.0009 | 0.0011 | 0.0014 |
| 9 | 0.0000 | 0.0000 | 0.0000 | 0.0000 | 0.0000 | 0.0000 | 0.0001 | 0.0001 | 0.0001 | 0.0001 |

*(continued)*

## The Binomial Probability Distribution *(continued)*

| | p = | 0.31 | 0.32 | 0.33 | 0.34 | 0.35 | 0.36 | 0.37 | 0.38 | 0.39 | 0.40 |
|---|---|---|---|---|---|---|---|---|---|---|---|
| x = | 0 | 0.0245 | 0.0211 | 0.0182 | 0.0157 | 0.0135 | 0.0115 | 0.0098 | 0.0084 | 0.0071 | 0.0060 |
| | 1 | 0.1099 | 0.0995 | 0.0898 | 0.0808 | 0.0725 | 0.0649 | 0.0578 | 0.0514 | 0.0456 | 0.0403 |
| | 2 | 0.2222 | 0.2107 | 0.1990 | 0.1873 | 0.1757 | 0.1642 | 0.1529 | 0.1419 | 0.1312 | 0.1209 |
| | 3 | 0.2662 | 0.2644 | 0.2614 | 0.2573 | 0.2522 | 0.2462 | 0.2394 | 0.2319 | 0.2237 | 0.2150 |
| | 4 | 0.2093 | 0.2177 | 0.2253 | 0.2320 | 0.2377 | 0.2424 | 0.2461 | 0.2487 | 0.2503 | 0.2508 |
| | 5 | 0.1128 | 0.1229 | 0.1332 | 0.1434 | 0.1536 | 0.1636 | 0.1734 | 0.1829 | 0.1920 | 0.2007 |
| | 6 | 0.0422 | 0.0482 | 0.0547 | 0.0616 | 0.0689 | 0.0767 | 0.0849 | 0.0934 | 0.1023 | 0.1115 |
| | 7 | 0.0108 | 0.0130 | 0.0154 | 0.0181 | 0.0212 | 0.0247 | 0.0285 | 0.0327 | 0.0374 | 0.0425 |
| | 8 | 0.0018 | 0.0023 | 0.0028 | 0.0035 | 0.0043 | 0.0052 | 0.0063 | 0.0075 | 0.0090 | 0.0106 |
| | 9 | 0.0002 | 0.0002 | 0.0003 | 0.0004 | 0.0005 | 0.0006 | 0.0008 | 0.0010 | 0.0013 | 0.0016 |
| | 10 | 0.0000 | 0.0000 | 0.0000 | 0.0000 | 0.0000 | 0.0000 | 0.0000 | 0.0001 | 0.0001 | 0.0001 |

| | p = | 0.41 | 0.42 | 0.43 | 0.44 | 0.45 | 0.46 | 0.47 | 0.48 | 0.49 | 0.50 |
|---|---|---|---|---|---|---|---|---|---|---|---|
| x = | 0 | 0.0051 | 0.0043 | 0.0036 | 0.0030 | 0.0025 | 0.0021 | 0.0017 | 0.0014 | 0.0012 | 0.0010 |
| | 1 | 0.0355 | 0.0312 | 0.0273 | 0.0238 | 0.0207 | 0.0180 | 0.0155 | 0.0133 | 0.0114 | 0.0098 |
| | 2 | 0.1111 | 0.1017 | 0.0927 | 0.0843 | 0.0763 | 0.0688 | 0.0619 | 0.0554 | 0.0494 | 0.0439 |
| | 3 | 0.2058 | 0.1963 | 0.1865 | 0.1765 | 0.1665 | 0.1564 | 0.1464 | 0.1364 | 0.1267 | 0.1172 |
| | 4 | 0.2503 | 0.2488 | 0.2462 | 0.2427 | 0.2384 | 0.2331 | 0.2271 | 0.2204 | 0.2130 | 0.2051 |
| | 5 | 0.2087 | 0.2162 | 0.2229 | 0.2289 | 0.2340 | 0.2383 | 0.2417 | 0.2441 | 0.2456 | 0.2461 |
| | 6 | 0.1209 | 0.1304 | 0.1401 | 0.1499 | 0.1596 | 0.1692 | 0.1786 | 0.1878 | 0.1966 | 0.2051 |
| | 7 | 0.0480 | 0.0540 | 0.0604 | 0.0673 | 0.0746 | 0.0824 | 0.0905 | 0.0991 | 0.1080 | 0.1172 |
| | 8 | 0.0125 | 0.0147 | 0.0171 | 0.0198 | 0.0229 | 0.0263 | 0.0301 | 0.0343 | 0.0389 | 0.0439 |
| | 9 | 0.0019 | 0.0024 | 0.0029 | 0.0035 | 0.0042 | 0.0050 | 0.0059 | 0.0070 | 0.0083 | 0.0098 |
| | 10 | 0.0001 | 0.0002 | 0.0002 | 0.0003 | 0.0003 | 0.0004 | 0.0005 | 0.0006 | 0.0008 | 0.0010 |

### $n = 11$

| | p = | 0.01 | 0.02 | 0.03 | 0.04 | 0.05 | 0.06 | 0.07 | 0.08 | 0.09 | 0.10 |
|---|---|---|---|---|---|---|---|---|---|---|---|
| x = | 0 | 0.8953 | 0.8007 | 0.7153 | 0.6382 | 0.5688 | 0.5063 | 0.4501 | 0.3996 | 0.3544 | 0.3138 |
| | 1 | 0.0995 | 0.1798 | 0.2433 | 0.2925 | 0.3293 | 0.3555 | 0.3727 | 0.3823 | 0.3855 | 0.3835 |
| | 2 | 0.0050 | 0.0183 | 0.0376 | 0.0609 | 0.0867 | 0.1135 | 0.1403 | 0.1662 | 0.1906 | 0.2131 |
| | 3 | 0.0002 | 0.0011 | 0.0035 | 0.0076 | 0.0137 | 0.0217 | 0.0317 | 0.0434 | 0.0566 | 0.0710 |
| | 4 | 0.0000 | 0.0000 | 0.0002 | 0.0006 | 0.0014 | 0.0028 | 0.0048 | 0.0075 | 0.0112 | 0.0158 |
| | 5 | 0.0000 | 0.0000 | 0.0000 | 0.0000 | 0.0001 | 0.0002 | 0.0005 | 0.0009 | 0.0015 | 0.0025 |
| | 6 | 0.0000 | 0.0000 | 0.0000 | 0.0000 | 0.0000 | 0.0000 | 0.0000 | 0.0001 | 0.0002 | 0.0003 |

*(continued)*

## The Binomial Probability Distribution *(continued)*

| | p = | 0.11 | 0.12 | 0.13 | 0.14 | 0.15 | 0.16 | 0.17 | 0.18 | 0.19 | 0.20 |
|---|---|---|---|---|---|---|---|---|---|---|---|
| x = | 0 | 0.2775 | 0.2451 | 0.2161 | 0.1903 | 0.1673 | 0.1469 | 0.1288 | 0.1127 | 0.0985 | 0.0859 |
| | 1 | 0.3773 | 0.3676 | 0.3552 | 0.3408 | 0.3248 | 0.3078 | 0.2901 | 0.2721 | 0.2541 | 0.2362 |
| | 2 | 0.2332 | 0.2507 | 0.2654 | 0.2774 | 0.2866 | 0.2932 | 0.2971 | 0.2987 | 0.2980 | 0.2953 |
| | 3 | 0.0865 | 0.1025 | 0.1190 | 0.1355 | 0.1517 | 0.1675 | 0.1826 | 0.1967 | 0.2097 | 0.2215 |
| | 4 | 0.0214 | 0.0280 | 0.0356 | 0.0441 | 0.0536 | 0.0638 | 0.0748 | 0.0864 | 0.0984 | 0.1107 |
| | 5 | 0.0037 | 0.0053 | 0.0074 | 0.0101 | 0.0132 | 0.0170 | 0.0214 | 0.0265 | 0.0323 | 0.0388 |
| | 6 | 0.0005 | 0.0007 | 0.0011 | 0.0016 | 0.0023 | 0.0032 | 0.0044 | 0.0058 | 0.0076 | 0.0097 |
| | 7 | 0.0000 | 0.0001 | 0.0001 | 0.0002 | 0.0003 | 0.0004 | 0.0006 | 0.0009 | 0.0013 | 0.0017 |
| | 8 | 0.0000 | 0.0000 | 0.0000 | 0.0000 | 0.0000 | 0.0000 | 0.0001 | 0.0001 | 0.0001 | 0.0002 |

| | p = | 0.21 | 0.22 | 0.23 | 0.24 | 0.25 | 0.26 | 0.27 | 0.28 | 0.29 | 0.30 |
|---|---|---|---|---|---|---|---|---|---|---|---|
| x = | 0 | 0.0748 | 0.0650 | 0.0564 | 0.0489 | 0.0422 | 0.0364 | 0.0314 | 0.0270 | 0.0231 | 0.0198 |
| | 1 | 0.2187 | 0.2017 | 0.1854 | 0.1697 | 0.1549 | 0.1408 | 0.1276 | 0.1153 | 0.1038 | 0.0932 |
| | 2 | 0.2907 | 0.2845 | 0.2768 | 0.2680 | 0.2581 | 0.2474 | 0.2360 | 0.2242 | 0.2121 | 0.1998 |
| | 3 | 0.2318 | 0.2407 | 0.2481 | 0.2539 | 0.2581 | 0.2608 | 0.2619 | 0.2616 | 0.2599 | 0.2568 |
| | 4 | 0.1232 | 0.1358 | 0.1482 | 0.1603 | 0.1721 | 0.1832 | 0.1937 | 0.2035 | 0.2123 | 0.2201 |
| | 5 | 0.0459 | 0.0536 | 0.0620 | 0.0709 | 0.0803 | 0.0901 | 0.1003 | 0.1108 | 0.1214 | 0.1321 |
| | 6 | 0.0122 | 0.0151 | 0.0185 | 0.0224 | 0.0268 | 0.0317 | 0.0371 | 0.0431 | 0.0496 | 0.0566 |
| | 7 | 0.0023 | 0.0030 | 0.0039 | 0.0050 | 0.0064 | 0.0079 | 0.0098 | 0.0120 | 0.0145 | 0.0173 |
| | 8 | 0.0003 | 0.0004 | 0.0006 | 0.0008 | 0.0011 | 0.0014 | 0.0018 | 0.0023 | 0.0030 | 0.0037 |
| | 9 | 0.0000 | 0.0000 | 0.0001 | 0.0001 | 0.0001 | 0.0002 | 0.0002 | 0.0003 | 0.0004 | 0.0005 |

| | p = | 0.31 | 0.32 | 0.33 | 0.34 | 0.35 | 0.36 | 0.37 | 0.38 | 0.39 | 0.40 |
|---|---|---|---|---|---|---|---|---|---|---|---|
| x = | 0 | 0.0169 | 0.0144 | 0.0122 | 0.0104 | 0.0088 | 0.0074 | 0.0062 | 0.0052 | 0.0044 | 0.0036 |
| | 1 | 0.0834 | 0.0744 | 0.0662 | 0.0587 | 0.0518 | 0.0457 | 0.0401 | 0.0351 | 0.0306 | 0.0266 |
| | 2 | 0.1874 | 0.1751 | 0.1630 | 0.1511 | 0.1395 | 0.1284 | 0.1177 | 0.1075 | 0.0978 | 0.0887 |
| | 3 | 0.2526 | 0.2472 | 0.2408 | 0.2335 | 0.2254 | 0.2167 | 0.2074 | 0.1977 | 0.1876 | 0.1774 |
| | 4 | 0.2269 | 0.2326 | 0.2372 | 0.2406 | 0.2428 | 0.2438 | 0.2436 | 0.2423 | 0.2399 | 0.2365 |
| | 5 | 0.1427 | 0.1533 | 0.1636 | 0.1735 | 0.1830 | 0.1920 | 0.2003 | 0.2079 | 0.2148 | 0.2207 |
| | 6 | 0.0641 | 0.0721 | 0.0806 | 0.0894 | 0.0985 | 0.1080 | 0.1176 | 0.1274 | 0.1373 | 0.1471 |
| | 7 | 0.0206 | 0.0242 | 0.0283 | 0.0329 | 0.0379 | 0.0434 | 0.0494 | 0.0558 | 0.0627 | 0.0701 |
| | 8 | 0.0046 | 0.0057 | 0.0070 | 0.0085 | 0.0102 | 0.0122 | 0.0145 | 0.0171 | 0.0200 | 0.0234 |
| | 9 | 0.0007 | 0.0009 | 0.0011 | 0.0015 | 0.0018 | 0.0023 | 0.0028 | 0.0035 | 0.0043 | 0.0052 |
| | 10 | 0.0001 | 0.0001 | 0.0001 | 0.0001 | 0.0002 | 0.0003 | 0.0003 | 0.0004 | 0.0005 | 0.0007 |

*(continued)*

## The Binomial Probability Distribution *(continued)*

| | $p =$ | 0.41 | 0.42 | 0.43 | 0.44 | 0.45 | 0.46 | 0.47 | 0.48 | 0.49 | 0.50 |
|---|---|---|---|---|---|---|---|---|---|---|---|
| $x =$ | 0 | 0.0030 | 0.0025 | 0.0021 | 0.0017 | 0.0014 | 0.0011 | 0.0009 | 0.0008 | 0.0006 | 0.0005 |
| | 1 | 0.0231 | 0.0199 | 0.0171 | 0.0147 | 0.0125 | 0.0107 | 0.0090 | 0.0076 | 0.0064 | 0.0054 |
| | 2 | 0.0801 | 0.0721 | 0.0646 | 0.0577 | 0.0513 | 0.0454 | 0.0401 | 0.0352 | 0.0308 | 0.0269 |
| | 3 | 0.1670 | 0.1566 | 0.1462 | 0.1359 | 0.1259 | 0.1161 | 0.1067 | 0.0976 | 0.0888 | 0.0806 |
| | 4 | 0.2321 | 0.2267 | 0.2206 | 0.2136 | 0.2060 | 0.1978 | 0.1892 | 0.1801 | 0.1707 | 0.1611 |
| | 5 | 0.2258 | 0.2299 | 0.2329 | 0.2350 | 0.2360 | 0.2359 | 0.2348 | 0.2327 | 0.2296 | 0.2256 |
| | 6 | 0.1569 | 0.1664 | 0.1757 | 0.1846 | 0.1931 | 0.2010 | 0.2083 | 0.2148 | 0.2206 | 0.2256 |
| | 7 | 0.0779 | 0.0861 | 0.0947 | 0.1036 | 0.1128 | 0.1223 | 0.1319 | 0.1416 | 0.1514 | 0.1611 |
| | 8 | 0.0271 | 0.0312 | 0.0357 | 0.0407 | 0.0462 | 0.0521 | 0.0585 | 0.0654 | 0.0727 | 0.0806 |
| | 9 | 0.0063 | 0.0075 | 0.0090 | 0.0107 | 0.0126 | 0.0148 | 0.0173 | 0.0201 | 0.0233 | 0.0269 |
| | 10 | 0.0009 | 0.0011 | 0.0014 | 0.0017 | 0.0021 | 0.0025 | 0.0031 | 0.0037 | 0.0045 | 0.0054 |
| | 11 | 0.0001 | 0.0001 | 0.0001 | 0.0001 | 0.0002 | 0.0002 | 0.0002 | 0.0003 | 0.0004 | 0.0005 |

### $n = 12$

| | $p =$ | 0.01 | 0.02 | 0.03 | 0.04 | 0.05 | 0.06 | 0.07 | 0.08 | 0.09 | 0.10 |
|---|---|---|---|---|---|---|---|---|---|---|---|
| $x =$ | 0 | 0.8864 | 0.7847 | 0.6938 | 0.6127 | 0.5404 | 0.4759 | 0.4186 | 0.3677 | 0.3225 | 0.2824 |
| | 1 | 0.1074 | 0.1922 | 0.2575 | 0.3064 | 0.3413 | 0.3645 | 0.3781 | 0.3837 | 0.3827 | 0.3766 |
| | 2 | 0.0060 | 0.0216 | 0.0438 | 0.0702 | 0.0988 | 0.1280 | 0.1565 | 0.1835 | 0.2082 | 0.2301 |
| | 3 | 0.0002 | 0.0015 | 0.0045 | 0.0098 | 0.0173 | 0.0272 | 0.0393 | 0.0532 | 0.0686 | 0.0852 |
| | 4 | 0.0000 | 0.0001 | 0.0003 | 0.0009 | 0.0021 | 0.0039 | 0.0067 | 0.0104 | 0.0153 | 0.0213 |
| | 5 | 0.0000 | 0.0000 | 0.0000 | 0.0001 | 0.0002 | 0.0004 | 0.0008 | 0.0014 | 0.0024 | 0.0038 |
| | 6 | 0.0000 | 0.0000 | 0.0000 | 0.0000 | 0.0000 | 0.0000 | 0.0001 | 0.0001 | 0.0003 | 0.0005 |

| | $p =$ | 0.11 | 0.12 | 0.13 | 0.14 | 0.15 | 0.16 | 0.17 | 0.18 | 0.19 | 0.20 |
|---|---|---|---|---|---|---|---|---|---|---|---|
| $x =$ | 0 | 0.2470 | 0.2157 | 0.1880 | 0.1637 | 0.1422 | 0.1234 | 0.1069 | 0.0924 | 0.0798 | 0.0687 |
| | 1 | 0.3663 | 0.3529 | 0.3372 | 0.3197 | 0.3012 | 0.2821 | 0.2627 | 0.2434 | 0.2245 | 0.2062 |
| | 2 | 0.2490 | 0.2647 | 0.2771 | 0.2863 | 0.2924 | 0.2955 | 0.2960 | 0.2939 | 0.2897 | 0.2835 |
| | 3 | 0.1026 | 0.1203 | 0.1380 | 0.1553 | 0.1720 | 0.1876 | 0.2021 | 0.2151 | 0.2265 | 0.2362 |
| | 4 | 0.0285 | 0.0369 | 0.0464 | 0.0569 | 0.0683 | 0.0804 | 0.0931 | 0.1062 | 0.1195 | 0.1329 |
| | 5 | 0.0056 | 0.0081 | 0.0111 | 0.0148 | 0.0193 | 0.0245 | 0.0305 | 0.0373 | 0.0449 | 0.0532 |
| | 6 | 0.0008 | 0.0013 | 0.0019 | 0.0028 | 0.0040 | 0.0054 | 0.0073 | 0.0096 | 0.0123 | 0.0155 |
| | 7 | 0.0001 | 0.0001 | 0.0002 | 0.0004 | 0.0006 | 0.0009 | 0.0013 | 0.0018 | 0.0025 | 0.0033 |
| | 8 | 0.0000 | 0.0000 | 0.0000 | 0.0000 | 0.0001 | 0.0001 | 0.0002 | 0.0002 | 0.0004 | 0.0005 |
| | 9 | 0.0000 | 0.0000 | 0.0000 | 0.0000 | 0.0000 | 0.0000 | 0.0000 | 0.0000 | 0.0000 | 0.0001 |

*(continued)*

## The Binomial Probability Distribution *(continued)*

| | p = | 0.21 | 0.22 | 0.23 | 0.24 | 0.25 | 0.26 | 0.27 | 0.28 | 0.29 | 0.30 |
|---|---|---|---|---|---|---|---|---|---|---|---|
| x = | 0 | 0.0591 | 0.0507 | 0.0434 | 0.0371 | 0.0317 | 0.0270 | 0.0229 | 0.0194 | 0.0164 | 0.0138 |
| | 1 | 0.1885 | 0.1717 | 0.1557 | 0.1407 | 0.1267 | 0.1137 | 0.1016 | 0.0906 | 0.0804 | 0.0712 |
| | 2 | 0.2756 | 0.2663 | 0.2558 | 0.2444 | 0.2323 | 0.2197 | 0.2068 | 0.1937 | 0.1807 | 0.1678 |
| | 3 | 0.2442 | 0.2503 | 0.2547 | 0.2573 | 0.2581 | 0.2573 | 0.2549 | 0.2511 | 0.2460 | 0.2397 |
| | 4 | 0.1460 | 0.1589 | 0.1712 | 0.1828 | 0.1936 | 0.2034 | 0.2122 | 0.2197 | 0.2261 | 0.2311 |
| | 5 | 0.0621 | 0.0717 | 0.0818 | 0.0924 | 0.1032 | 0.1143 | 0.1255 | 0.1367 | 0.1477 | 0.1585 |
| | 6 | 0.0193 | 0.0236 | 0.0285 | 0.0340 | 0.0401 | 0.0469 | 0.0542 | 0.0620 | 0.0704 | 0.0792 |
| | 7 | 0.0044 | 0.0057 | 0.0073 | 0.0092 | 0.0115 | 0.0141 | 0.0172 | 0.0207 | 0.0246 | 0.0291 |
| | 8 | 0.0007 | 0.0010 | 0.0014 | 0.0018 | 0.0024 | 0.0031 | 0.0040 | 0.0050 | 0.0063 | 0.0078 |
| | 9 | 0.0001 | 0.0001 | 0.0002 | 0.0003 | 0.0004 | 0.0005 | 0.0007 | 0.0009 | 0.0011 | 0.0015 |
| | 10 | 0.0000 | 0.0000 | 0.0000 | 0.0000 | 0.0000 | 0.0001 | 0.0001 | 0.0001 | 0.0001 | 0.0002 |

| | p = | 0.31 | 0.32 | 0.33 | 0.34 | 0.35 | 0.36 | 0.37 | 0.38 | 0.39 | 0.40 |
|---|---|---|---|---|---|---|---|---|---|---|---|
| x = | 0 | 0.0116 | 0.0098 | 0.0082 | 0.0068 | 0.0057 | 0.0047 | 0.0039 | 0.0032 | 0.0027 | 0.0022 |
| | 1 | 0.0628 | 0.0552 | 0.0484 | 0.0422 | 0.0368 | 0.0319 | 0.0276 | 0.0237 | 0.0204 | 0.0174 |
| | 2 | 0.1552 | 0.1429 | 0.1310 | 0.1197 | 0.1088 | 0.0986 | 0.0890 | 0.0800 | 0.0716 | 0.0639 |
| | 3 | 0.2324 | 0.2241 | 0.2151 | 0.2055 | 0.1954 | 0.1849 | 0.1742 | 0.1634 | 0.1526 | 0.1419 |
| | 4 | 0.2349 | 0.2373 | 0.2384 | 0.2382 | 0.2367 | 0.2340 | 0.2302 | 0.2254 | 0.2195 | 0.2128 |
| | 5 | 0.1688 | 0.1787 | 0.1879 | 0.1963 | 0.2039 | 0.2106 | 0.2163 | 0.2210 | 0.2246 | 0.2270 |
| | 6 | 0.0885 | 0.0981 | 0.1079 | 0.1180 | 0.1281 | 0.1382 | 0.1482 | 0.1580 | 0.1675 | 0.1766 |
| | 7 | 0.0341 | 0.0396 | 0.0456 | 0.0521 | 0.0591 | 0.0666 | 0.0746 | 0.0830 | 0.0918 | 0.1009 |
| | 8 | 0.0096 | 0.0116 | 0.0140 | 0.0168 | 0.0199 | 0.0234 | 0.0274 | 0.0318 | 0.0367 | 0.0420 |
| | 9 | 0.0019 | 0.0024 | 0.0031 | 0.0038 | 0.0048 | 0.0059 | 0.0071 | 0.0087 | 0.0104 | 0.0125 |
| | 10 | 0.0003 | 0.0003 | 0.0005 | 0.0006 | 0.0008 | 0.0010 | 0.0013 | 0.0016 | 0.0020 | 0.0025 |
| | 11 | 0.0000 | 0.0000 | 0.0000 | 0.0001 | 0.0001 | 0.0001 | 0.0001 | 0.0002 | 0.0002 | 0.0003 |

| | p = | 0.41 | 0.42 | 0.43 | 0.44 | 0.45 | 0.46 | 0.47 | 0.48 | 0.49 | 0.50 |
|---|---|---|---|---|---|---|---|---|---|---|---|
| x = | 0 | 0.0018 | 0.0014 | 0.0012 | 0.0010 | 0.0008 | 0.0006 | 0.0005 | 0.0004 | 0.0003 | 0.0002 |
| | 1 | 0.0148 | 0.0126 | 0.0106 | 0.0090 | 0.0075 | 0.0063 | 0.0052 | 0.0043 | 0.0036 | 0.0029 |
| | 2 | 0.0567 | 0.0502 | 0.0442 | 0.0388 | 0.0339 | 0.0294 | 0.0255 | 0.0220 | 0.0189 | 0.0161 |
| | 3 | 0.1314 | 0.1211 | 0.1111 | 0.1015 | 0.0923 | 0.0836 | 0.0754 | 0.0676 | 0.0604 | 0.0537 |
| | 4 | 0.2054 | 0.1973 | 0.1886 | 0.1794 | 0.1700 | 0.1602 | 0.1504 | 0.1405 | 0.1306 | 0.1208 |
| | 5 | 0.2284 | 0.2285 | 0.2276 | 0.2256 | 0.2225 | 0.2184 | 0.2134 | 0.2075 | 0.2008 | 0.1934 |
| | 6 | 0.1851 | 0.1931 | 0.2003 | 0.2068 | 0.2124 | 0.2171 | 0.2208 | 0.2234 | 0.2250 | 0.2256 |
| | 7 | 0.1103 | 0.1198 | 0.1295 | 0.1393 | 0.1489 | 0.1585 | 0.1678 | 0.1768 | 0.1853 | 0.1934 |
| | 8 | 0.0479 | 0.0542 | 0.0611 | 0.0684 | 0.0762 | 0.0844 | 0.0930 | 0.1020 | 0.1113 | 0.1208 |
| | 9 | 0.0148 | 0.0175 | 0.0205 | 0.0239 | 0.0277 | 0.0319 | 0.0367 | 0.0418 | 0.0475 | 0.0537 |
| | 10 | 0.0031 | 0.0038 | 0.0046 | 0.0056 | 0.0068 | 0.0082 | 0.0098 | 0.0116 | 0.0137 | 0.0161 |
| | 11 | 0.0004 | 0.0005 | 0.0006 | 0.0008 | 0.0010 | 0.0013 | 0.0016 | 0.0019 | 0.0024 | 0.0029 |
| | 12 | 0.0000 | 0.0000 | 0.0000 | 0.0001 | 0.0001 | 0.0001 | 0.0001 | 0.0001 | 0.0002 | 0.0002 |

*(continued)*

## The Binomial Probability Distribution *(continued)*

### $n = 13$

| $p =$ | 0.01 | 0.02 | 0.03 | 0.04 | 0.05 | 0.06 | 0.07 | 0.08 | 0.09 | 0.10 |
|---|---|---|---|---|---|---|---|---|---|---|
| $x =$ 0 | 0.8775 | 0.7690 | 0.6730 | 0.5882 | 0.5133 | 0.4474 | 0.3893 | 0.3383 | 0.2935 | 0.2542 |
| 1 | 0.1152 | 0.2040 | 0.2706 | 0.3186 | 0.3512 | 0.3712 | 0.3809 | 0.3824 | 0.3773 | 0.3672 |
| 2 | 0.0070 | 0.0250 | 0.0502 | 0.0797 | 0.1109 | 0.1422 | 0.1720 | 0.1995 | 0.2239 | 0.2448 |
| 3 | 0.0003 | 0.0019 | 0.0057 | 0.0122 | 0.0214 | 0.0333 | 0.0475 | 0.0636 | 0.0812 | 0.0997 |
| 4 | 0.0000 | 0.0001 | 0.0004 | 0.0013 | 0.0028 | 0.0053 | 0.0089 | 0.0138 | 0.0201 | 0.0277 |
| 5 | 0.0000 | 0.0000 | 0.0000 | 0.0001 | 0.0003 | 0.0006 | 0.0012 | 0.0022 | 0.0036 | 0.0055 |
| 6 | 0.0000 | 0.0000 | 0.0000 | 0.0000 | 0.0000 | 0.0001 | 0.0001 | 0.0003 | 0.0005 | 0.0008 |
| 7 | 0.0000 | 0.0000 | 0.0000 | 0.0000 | 0.0000 | 0.0000 | 0.0000 | 0.0000 | 0.0000 | 0.0001 |

| $p =$ | 0.11 | 0.12 | 0.13 | 0.14 | 0.15 | 0.16 | 0.17 | 0.18 | 0.19 | 0.20 |
|---|---|---|---|---|---|---|---|---|---|---|
| $x =$ 0 | 0.2198 | 0.1898 | 0.1636 | 0.1408 | 0.1209 | 0.1037 | 0.0887 | 0.0758 | 0.0646 | 0.0550 |
| 1 | 0.3532 | 0.3364 | 0.3178 | 0.2979 | 0.2774 | 0.2567 | 0.2362 | 0.2163 | 0.1970 | 0.1787 |
| 2 | 0.2619 | 0.2753 | 0.2849 | 0.2910 | 0.2937 | 0.2934 | 0.2903 | 0.2848 | 0.2773 | 0.2680 |
| 3 | 0.1187 | 0.1376 | 0.1561 | 0.1737 | 0.1900 | 0.2049 | 0.2180 | 0.2293 | 0.2385 | 0.2457 |
| 4 | 0.0367 | 0.0469 | 0.0583 | 0.0707 | 0.0838 | 0.0976 | 0.1116 | 0.1258 | 0.1399 | 0.1535 |
| 5 | 0.0082 | 0.0115 | 0.0157 | 0.0207 | 0.0266 | 0.0335 | 0.0412 | 0.0497 | 0.0591 | 0.0691 |
| 6 | 0.0013 | 0.0021 | 0.0031 | 0.0045 | 0.0063 | 0.0085 | 0.0112 | 0.0145 | 0.0185 | 0.0230 |
| 7 | 0.0002 | 0.0003 | 0.0005 | 0.0007 | 0.0011 | 0.0016 | 0.0023 | 0.0032 | 0.0043 | 0.0058 |
| 8 | 0.0000 | 0.0000 | 0.0001 | 0.0001 | 0.0001 | 0.0002 | 0.0004 | 0.0005 | 0.0008 | 0.0011 |
| 9 | 0.0000 | 0.0000 | 0.0000 | 0.0000 | 0.0000 | 0.0000 | 0.0000 | 0.0001 | 0.0001 | 0.0001 |

| $p =$ | 0.21 | 0.22 | 0.23 | 0.24 | 0.25 | 0.26 | 0.27 | 0.28 | 0.29 | 0.30 |
|---|---|---|---|---|---|---|---|---|---|---|
| $x =$ 0 | 0.0467 | 0.0396 | 0.0334 | 0.0282 | 0.0238 | 0.0200 | 0.0167 | 0.0140 | 0.0117 | 0.0097 |
| 1 | 0.1613 | 0.1450 | 0.1299 | 0.1159 | 0.1029 | 0.0911 | 0.0804 | 0.0706 | 0.0619 | 0.0540 |
| 2 | 0.2573 | 0.2455 | 0.2328 | 0.2195 | 0.2059 | 0.1921 | 0.1784 | 0.1648 | 0.1516 | 0.1388 |
| 3 | 0.2508 | 0.2539 | 0.2550 | 0.2542 | 0.2517 | 0.2475 | 0.2419 | 0.2351 | 0.2271 | 0.2181 |
| 4 | 0.1667 | 0.1790 | 0.1904 | 0.2007 | 0.2097 | 0.2174 | 0.2237 | 0.2285 | 0.2319 | 0.2337 |
| 5 | 0.0797 | 0.0909 | 0.1024 | 0.1141 | 0.1258 | 0.1375 | 0.1489 | 0.1600 | 0.1705 | 0.1803 |
| 6 | 0.0283 | 0.0342 | 0.0408 | 0.0480 | 0.0559 | 0.0644 | 0.0734 | 0.0829 | 0.0928 | 0.1030 |
| 7 | 0.0075 | 0.0096 | 0.0122 | 0.0152 | 0.0186 | 0.0226 | 0.0272 | 0.0323 | 0.0379 | 0.0442 |
| 8 | 0.0015 | 0.0020 | 0.0027 | 0.0036 | 0.0047 | 0.0060 | 0.0075 | 0.0094 | 0.0116 | 0.0142 |
| 9 | 0.0002 | 0.0003 | 0.0005 | 0.0006 | 0.0009 | 0.0012 | 0.0015 | 0.0020 | 0.0026 | 0.0034 |
| 10 | 0.0000 | 0.0000 | 0.0001 | 0.0001 | 0.0001 | 0.0002 | 0.0002 | 0.0003 | 0.0004 | 0.0006 |
| 11 | 0.0000 | 0.0000 | 0.0000 | 0.0000 | 0.0000 | 0.0000 | 0.0000 | 0.0000 | 0.0000 | 0.0001 |

*(continued)*

## The Binomial Probability Distribution *(continued)*

| $p =$ | 0.31 | 0.32 | 0.33 | 0.34 | 0.35 | 0.36 | 0.37 | 0.38 | 0.39 | 0.40 |
|---|---|---|---|---|---|---|---|---|---|---|
| $x = 0$ | 0.0080 | 0.0066 | 0.0055 | 0.0045 | 0.0037 | 0.0030 | 0.0025 | 0.0020 | 0.0016 | 0.0013 |
| 1 | 0.0469 | 0.0407 | 0.0351 | 0.0302 | 0.0259 | 0.0221 | 0.0188 | 0.0159 | 0.0135 | 0.0113 |
| 2 | 0.1265 | 0.1148 | 0.1037 | 0.0933 | 0.0836 | 0.0746 | 0.0663 | 0.0586 | 0.0516 | 0.0453 |
| 3 | 0.2084 | 0.1981 | 0.1874 | 0.1763 | 0.1651 | 0.1538 | 0.1427 | 0.1317 | 0.1210 | 0.1107 |
| 4 | 0.2341 | 0.2331 | 0.2307 | 0.2270 | 0.2222 | 0.2163 | 0.2095 | 0.2018 | 0.1934 | 0.1845 |
| 5 | 0.1893 | 0.1974 | 0.2045 | 0.2105 | 0.2154 | 0.2190 | 0.2215 | 0.2227 | 0.2226 | 0.2214 |
| 6 | 0.1134 | 0.1239 | 0.1343 | 0.1446 | 0.1546 | 0.1643 | 0.1734 | 0.1820 | 0.1898 | 0.1968 |
| 7 | 0.0509 | 0.0583 | 0.0662 | 0.0745 | 0.0833 | 0.0924 | 0.1019 | 0.1115 | 0.1213 | 0.1312 |
| 8 | 0.0172 | 0.0206 | 0.0244 | 0.0288 | 0.0336 | 0.0390 | 0.0449 | 0.0513 | 0.0582 | 0.0656 |
| 9 | 0.0043 | 0.0054 | 0.0067 | 0.0082 | 0.0101 | 0.0122 | 0.0146 | 0.0175 | 0.0207 | 0.0243 |
| 10 | 0.0008 | 0.0010 | 0.0013 | 0.0017 | 0.0022 | 0.0027 | 0.0034 | 0.0043 | 0.0053 | 0.0065 |
| 11 | 0.0001 | 0.0001 | 0.0002 | 0.0002 | 0.0003 | 0.0004 | 0.0006 | 0.0007 | 0.0009 | 0.0012 |
| 12 | 0.0000 | 0.0000 | 0.0000 | 0.0000 | 0.0000 | 0.0000 | 0.0001 | 0.0001 | 0.0001 | 0.0001 |

| $p =$ | 0.41 | 0.42 | 0.43 | 0.44 | 0.45 | 0.46 | 0.47 | 0.48 | 0.49 | 0.50 |
|---|---|---|---|---|---|---|---|---|---|---|
| $x = 0$ | 0.0010 | 0.0008 | 0.0007 | 0.0005 | 0.0004 | 0.0003 | 0.0003 | 0.0002 | 0.0002 | 0.0001 |
| 1 | 0.0095 | 0.0079 | 0.0066 | 0.0054 | 0.0045 | 0.0037 | 0.0030 | 0.0024 | 0.0020 | 0.0016 |
| 2 | 0.0395 | 0.0344 | 0.0298 | 0.0256 | 0.0220 | 0.0188 | 0.0160 | 0.0135 | 0.0114 | 0.0095 |
| 3 | 0.1007 | 0.0913 | 0.0823 | 0.0739 | 0.0660 | 0.0587 | 0.0519 | 0.0457 | 0.0401 | 0.0349 |
| 4 | 0.1750 | 0.1653 | 0.1553 | 0.1451 | 0.1350 | 0.1250 | 0.1151 | 0.1055 | 0.0962 | 0.0873 |
| 5 | 0.2189 | 0.2154 | 0.2108 | 0.2053 | 0.1989 | 0.1917 | 0.1838 | 0.1753 | 0.1664 | 0.1571 |
| 6 | 0.2029 | 0.2080 | 0.2121 | 0.2151 | 0.2169 | 0.2177 | 0.2173 | 0.2158 | 0.2131 | 0.2095 |
| 7 | 0.1410 | 0.1506 | 0.1600 | 0.1690 | 0.1775 | 0.1854 | 0.1927 | 0.1992 | 0.2048 | 0.2095 |
| 8 | 0.0735 | 0.0818 | 0.0905 | 0.0996 | 0.1089 | 0.1185 | 0.1282 | 0.1379 | 0.1476 | 0.1571 |
| 9 | 0.0284 | 0.0329 | 0.0379 | 0.0435 | 0.0495 | 0.0561 | 0.0631 | 0.0707 | 0.0788 | 0.0873 |
| 10 | 0.0079 | 0.0095 | 0.0114 | 0.0137 | 0.0162 | 0.0191 | 0.0224 | 0.0261 | 0.0303 | 0.0349 |
| 11 | 0.0015 | 0.0019 | 0.0024 | 0.0029 | 0.0036 | 0.0044 | 0.0054 | 0.0066 | 0.0079 | 0.0095 |
| 12 | 0.0002 | 0.0002 | 0.0003 | 0.0004 | 0.0005 | 0.0006 | 0.0008 | 0.0010 | 0.0013 | 0.0016 |
| 13 | 0.0000 | 0.0000 | 0.0000 | 0.0000 | 0.0000 | 0.0000 | 0.0001 | 0.0001 | 0.0001 | 0.0001 |

### $n = 14$

| $p =$ | 0.01 | 0.02 | 0.03 | 0.04 | 0.05 | 0.06 | 0.07 | 0.08 | 0.09 | 0.10 |
|---|---|---|---|---|---|---|---|---|---|---|
| $x = 0$ | 0.8687 | 0.7536 | 0.6528 | 0.5647 | 0.4877 | 0.4205 | 0.3620 | 0.3112 | 0.2670 | 0.2288 |
| 1 | 0.1229 | 0.2153 | 0.2827 | 0.3294 | 0.3593 | 0.3758 | 0.3815 | 0.3788 | 0.3698 | 0.3559 |
| 2 | 0.0081 | 0.0286 | 0.0568 | 0.0892 | 0.1229 | 0.1559 | 0.1867 | 0.2141 | 0.2377 | 0.2570 |
| 3 | 0.0003 | 0.0023 | 0.0070 | 0.0149 | 0.0259 | 0.0398 | 0.0562 | 0.0745 | 0.0940 | 0.1142 |
| 4 | 0.0000 | 0.0001 | 0.0006 | 0.0017 | 0.0037 | 0.0070 | 0.0116 | 0.0178 | 0.0256 | 0.0349 |
| 5 | 0.0000 | 0.0000 | 0.0000 | 0.0001 | 0.0004 | 0.0009 | 0.0018 | 0.0031 | 0.0051 | 0.0078 |
| 6 | 0.0000 | 0.0000 | 0.0000 | 0.0000 | 0.0000 | 0.0001 | 0.0002 | 0.0004 | 0.0008 | 0.0013 |
| 7 | 0.0000 | 0.0000 | 0.0000 | 0.0000 | 0.0000 | 0.0000 | 0.0000 | 0.0000 | 0.0001 | 0.0002 |

*(continued)*

**The Binomial Probability Distribution** *(continued)*

| | p = | 0.11 | 0.12 | 0.13 | 0.14 | 0.15 | 0.16 | 0.17 | 0.18 | 0.19 | 0.20 |
|---|---|---|---|---|---|---|---|---|---|---|---|
| x = | 0 | 0.1956 | 0.1670 | 0.1423 | 0.1211 | 0.1028 | 0.0871 | 0.0736 | 0.0621 | 0.0523 | 0.0440 |
| | 1 | 0.3385 | 0.3188 | 0.2977 | 0.2759 | 0.2539 | 0.2322 | 0.2112 | 0.1910 | 0.1719 | 0.1539 |
| | 2 | 0.2720 | 0.2826 | 0.2892 | 0.2919 | 0.2912 | 0.2875 | 0.2811 | 0.2725 | 0.2620 | 0.2501 |
| | 3 | 0.1345 | 0.1542 | 0.1728 | 0.1901 | 0.2056 | 0.2190 | 0.2303 | 0.2393 | 0.2459 | 0.2501 |
| | 4 | 0.0457 | 0.0578 | 0.0710 | 0.0851 | 0.0998 | 0.1147 | 0.1297 | 0.1444 | 0.1586 | 0.1720 |
| | 5 | 0.0113 | 0.0158 | 0.0212 | 0.0277 | 0.0352 | 0.0437 | 0.0531 | 0.0634 | 0.0744 | 0.0860 |
| | 6 | 0.0021 | 0.0032 | 0.0048 | 0.0068 | 0.0093 | 0.0125 | 0.0163 | 0.0209 | 0.0262 | 0.0322 |
| | 7 | 0.0003 | 0.0005 | 0.0008 | 0.0013 | 0.0019 | 0.0027 | 0.0038 | 0.0052 | 0.0070 | 0.0092 |
| | 8 | 0.0000 | 0.0001 | 0.0001 | 0.0002 | 0.0003 | 0.0005 | 0.0007 | 0.0010 | 0.0014 | 0.0020 |
| | 9 | 0.0000 | 0.0000 | 0.0000 | 0.0000 | 0.0000 | 0.0001 | 0.0001 | 0.0001 | 0.0002 | 0.0003 |

| | p = | 0.21 | 0.22 | 0.23 | 0.24 | 0.25 | 0.26 | 0.27 | 0.28 | 0.29 | 0.30 |
|---|---|---|---|---|---|---|---|---|---|---|---|
| x = | 0 | 0.0369 | 0.0309 | 0.0258 | 0.0214 | 0.0178 | 0.0148 | 0.0122 | 0.0101 | 0.0083 | 0.0068 |
| | 1 | 0.1372 | 0.1218 | 0.1077 | 0.0948 | 0.0832 | 0.0726 | 0.0632 | 0.0548 | 0.0473 | 0.0407 |
| | 2 | 0.2371 | 0.2234 | 0.2091 | 0.1946 | 0.1802 | 0.1659 | 0.1519 | 0.1385 | 0.1256 | 0.1134 |
| | 3 | 0.2521 | 0.2520 | 0.2499 | 0.2459 | 0.2402 | 0.2331 | 0.2248 | 0.2154 | 0.2052 | 0.1943 |
| | 4 | 0.1843 | 0.1955 | 0.2052 | 0.2135 | 0.2202 | 0.2252 | 0.2286 | 0.2304 | 0.2305 | 0.2290 |
| | 5 | 0.0980 | 0.1103 | 0.1226 | 0.1348 | 0.1468 | 0.1583 | 0.1691 | 0.1792 | 0.1883 | 0.1963 |
| | 6 | 0.0391 | 0.0466 | 0.0549 | 0.0639 | 0.0734 | 0.0834 | 0.0938 | 0.1045 | 0.1153 | 0.1262 |
| | 7 | 0.0119 | 0.0150 | 0.0188 | 0.0231 | 0.0280 | 0.0335 | 0.0397 | 0.0464 | 0.0538 | 0.0618 |
| | 8 | 0.0028 | 0.0037 | 0.0049 | 0.0064 | 0.0082 | 0.0103 | 0.0128 | 0.0158 | 0.0192 | 0.0232 |
| | 9 | 0.0005 | 0.0007 | 0.0010 | 0.0013 | 0.0018 | 0.0024 | 0.0032 | 0.0041 | 0.0052 | 0.0066 |
| | 10 | 0.0001 | 0.0001 | 0.0001 | 0.0002 | 0.0003 | 0.0004 | 0.0006 | 0.0008 | 0.0011 | 0.0014 |
| | 11 | 0.0000 | 0.0000 | 0.0000 | 0.0000 | 0.0000 | 0.0001 | 0.0001 | 0.0001 | 0.0002 | 0.0002 |

| | p = | 0.31 | 0.32 | 0.33 | 0.34 | 0.35 | 0.36 | 0.37 | 0.38 | 0.39 | 0.40 |
|---|---|---|---|---|---|---|---|---|---|---|---|
| x = | 0 | 0.0055 | 0.0045 | 0.0037 | 0.0030 | 0.0024 | 0.0019 | 0.0016 | 0.0012 | 0.0010 | 0.0008 |
| | 1 | 0.0349 | 0.0298 | 0.0253 | 0.0215 | 0.0181 | 0.0152 | 0.0128 | 0.0106 | 0.0088 | 0.0073 |
| | 2 | 0.1018 | 0.0911 | 0.0811 | 0.0719 | 0.0634 | 0.0557 | 0.0487 | 0.0424 | 0.0367 | 0.0317 |
| | 3 | 0.1830 | 0.1715 | 0.1598 | 0.1481 | 0.1366 | 0.1253 | 0.1144 | 0.1039 | 0.0940 | 0.0845 |
| | 4 | 0.2261 | 0.2219 | 0.2164 | 0.2098 | 0.2022 | 0.1938 | 0.1848 | 0.1752 | 0.1652 | 0.1549 |
| | 5 | 0.2032 | 0.2088 | 0.2132 | 0.2161 | 0.2178 | 0.2181 | 0.2170 | 0.2147 | 0.2112 | 0.2066 |
| | 6 | 0.1369 | 0.1474 | 0.1575 | 0.1670 | 0.1759 | 0.1840 | 0.1912 | 0.1974 | 0.2026 | 0.2066 |
| | 7 | 0.0703 | 0.0793 | 0.0886 | 0.0983 | 0.1082 | 0.1183 | 0.1283 | 0.1383 | 0.1480 | 0.1574 |
| | 8 | 0.0276 | 0.0326 | 0.0382 | 0.0443 | 0.0510 | 0.0582 | 0.0659 | 0.0742 | 0.0828 | 0.0918 |
| | 9 | 0.0083 | 0.0102 | 0.0125 | 0.0152 | 0.0183 | 0.0218 | 0.0258 | 0.0303 | 0.0353 | 0.0408 |
| | 10 | 0.0019 | 0.0024 | 0.0031 | 0.0039 | 0.0049 | 0.0061 | 0.0076 | 0.0093 | 0.0113 | 0.0136 |
| | 11 | 0.0003 | 0.0004 | 0.0006 | 0.0007 | 0.0010 | 0.0013 | 0.0016 | 0.0021 | 0.0026 | 0.0033 |
| | 12 | 0.0000 | 0.0000 | 0.0001 | 0.0001 | 0.0001 | 0.0002 | 0.0002 | 0.0003 | 0.0004 | 0.0005 |
| | 13 | 0.0000 | 0.0000 | 0.0000 | 0.0000 | 0.0000 | 0.0000 | 0.0000 | 0.0000 | 0.0000 | 0.0001 |

*(continued)*

**The Binomial Probability Distribution** *(continued)*

| p = | 0.41 | 0.42 | 0.43 | 0.44 | 0.45 | 0.46 | 0.47 | 0.48 | 0.49 | 0.50 |
|---|---|---|---|---|---|---|---|---|---|---|
| x = 0 | 0.0006 | 0.0005 | 0.0004 | 0.0003 | 0.0002 | 0.0002 | 0.0001 | 0.0001 | 0.0001 | 0.0001 |
| 1 | 0.0060 | 0.0049 | 0.0040 | 0.0033 | 0.0027 | 0.0021 | 0.0017 | 0.0014 | 0.0011 | 0.0009 |
| 2 | 0.0272 | 0.0233 | 0.0198 | 0.0168 | 0.0141 | 0.0118 | 0.0099 | 0.0082 | 0.0068 | 0.0056 |
| 3 | 0.0757 | 0.0674 | 0.0597 | 0.0527 | 0.0462 | 0.0403 | 0.0350 | 0.0303 | 0.0260 | 0.0222 |
| 4 | 0.1446 | 0.1342 | 0.1239 | 0.1138 | 0.1040 | 0.0945 | 0.0854 | 0.0768 | 0.0687 | 0.0611 |
| 5 | 0.2009 | 0.1943 | 0.1869 | 0.1788 | 0.1701 | 0.1610 | 0.1515 | 0.1418 | 0.1320 | 0.1222 |
| 6 | 0.2094 | 0.2111 | 0.2115 | 0.2108 | 0.2088 | 0.2057 | 0.2015 | 0.1963 | 0.1902 | 0.1833 |
| 7 | 0.1663 | 0.1747 | 0.1824 | 0.1892 | 0.1952 | 0.2003 | 0.2043 | 0.2071 | 0.2089 | 0.2095 |
| 8 | 0.1011 | 0.1107 | 0.1204 | 0.1301 | 0.1398 | 0.1493 | 0.1585 | 0.1673 | 0.1756 | 0.1833 |
| 9 | 0.0469 | 0.0534 | 0.0605 | 0.0682 | 0.0762 | 0.0848 | 0.0937 | 0.1030 | 0.1125 | 0.1222 |
| 10 | 0.0163 | 0.0193 | 0.0228 | 0.0268 | 0.0312 | 0.0361 | 0.0415 | 0.0475 | 0.0540 | 0.0611 |
| 11 | 0.0041 | 0.0051 | 0.0063 | 0.0076 | 0.0093 | 0.0112 | 0.0134 | 0.0160 | 0.0189 | 0.0222 |
| 12 | 0.0007 | 0.0009 | 0.0012 | 0.0015 | 0.0019 | 0.0024 | 0.0030 | 0.0037 | 0.0045 | 0.0056 |
| 13 | 0.0001 | 0.0001 | 0.0001 | 0.0002 | 0.0002 | 0.0003 | 0.0004 | 0.0005 | 0.0007 | 0.0009 |
| 14 | 0.0000 | 0.0000 | 0.0000 | 0.0000 | 0.0000 | 0.0000 | 0.0000 | 0.0000 | 0.0000 | 0.0001 |

**n = 15**

| p = | 0.01 | 0.02 | 0.03 | 0.04 | 0.05 | 0.06 | 0.07 | 0.08 | 0.09 | 0.10 |
|---|---|---|---|---|---|---|---|---|---|---|
| x = 0 | 0.8601 | 0.7386 | 0.6333 | 0.5421 | 0.4633 | 0.3953 | 0.3367 | 0.2863 | 0.2430 | 0.2059 |
| 1 | 0.1303 | 0.2261 | 0.2938 | 0.3388 | 0.3658 | 0.3785 | 0.3801 | 0.3734 | 0.3605 | 0.3432 |
| 2 | 0.0092 | 0.0323 | 0.0636 | 0.0988 | 0.1348 | 0.1691 | 0.2003 | 0.2273 | 0.2496 | 0.2669 |
| 3 | 0.0004 | 0.0029 | 0.0085 | 0.0178 | 0.0307 | 0.0468 | 0.0653 | 0.0857 | 0.1070 | 0.1285 |
| 4 | 0.0000 | 0.0002 | 0.0008 | 0.0022 | 0.0049 | 0.0090 | 0.0148 | 0.0223 | 0.0317 | 0.0428 |
| 5 | 0.0000 | 0.0000 | 0.0001 | 0.0002 | 0.0006 | 0.0013 | 0.0024 | 0.0043 | 0.0069 | 0.0105 |
| 6 | 0.0000 | 0.0000 | 0.0000 | 0.0000 | 0.0000 | 0.0001 | 0.0003 | 0.0006 | 0.0011 | 0.0019 |
| 7 | 0.0000 | 0.0000 | 0.0000 | 0.0000 | 0.0000 | 0.0000 | 0.0000 | 0.0001 | 0.0001 | 0.0003 |

| p = | 0.11 | 0.12 | 0.13 | 0.14 | 0.15 | 0.16 | 0.17 | 0.18 | 0.19 | 0.20 |
|---|---|---|---|---|---|---|---|---|---|---|
| x = 0 | 0.1741 | 0.1470 | 0.1238 | 0.1041 | 0.0874 | 0.0731 | 0.0611 | 0.0510 | 0.0424 | 0.0352 |
| 1 | 0.3228 | 0.3006 | 0.2775 | 0.2542 | 0.2312 | 0.2090 | 0.1878 | 0.1678 | 0.1492 | 0.1319 |
| 2 | 0.2793 | 0.2870 | 0.2903 | 0.2897 | 0.2856 | 0.2787 | 0.2692 | 0.2578 | 0.2449 | 0.2309 |
| 3 | 0.1496 | 0.1696 | 0.1880 | 0.2044 | 0.2184 | 0.2300 | 0.2389 | 0.2452 | 0.2489 | 0.2501 |
| 4 | 0.0555 | 0.0694 | 0.0843 | 0.0998 | 0.1156 | 0.1314 | 0.1468 | 0.1615 | 0.1752 | 0.1876 |
| 5 | 0.0151 | 0.0208 | 0.0277 | 0.0357 | 0.0449 | 0.0551 | 0.0662 | 0.0780 | 0.0904 | 0.1032 |
| 6 | 0.0031 | 0.0047 | 0.0069 | 0.0097 | 0.0132 | 0.0175 | 0.0226 | 0.0285 | 0.0353 | 0.0430 |
| 7 | 0.0005 | 0.0008 | 0.0013 | 0.0020 | 0.0030 | 0.0043 | 0.0059 | 0.0081 | 0.0107 | 0.0138 |
| 8 | 0.0001 | 0.0001 | 0.0002 | 0.0003 | 0.0005 | 0.0008 | 0.0012 | 0.0018 | 0.0025 | 0.0035 |
| 9 | 0.0000 | 0.0000 | 0.0000 | 0.0000 | 0.0001 | 0.0001 | 0.0002 | 0.0003 | 0.0005 | 0.0007 |
| 10 | 0.0000 | 0.0000 | 0.0000 | 0.0000 | 0.0000 | 0.0000 | 0.0000 | 0.0000 | 0.0001 | 0.0001 |

*(continued)*

## The Binomial Probability Distribution *(continued)*

| $p =$ | 0.21 | 0.22 | 0.23 | 0.24 | 0.25 | 0.26 | 0.27 | 0.28 | 0.29 | 0.30 |
|---|---|---|---|---|---|---|---|---|---|---|
| $x = 0$ | 0.0291 | 0.0241 | 0.0198 | 0.0163 | 0.0134 | 0.0109 | 0.0089 | 0.0072 | 0.0059 | 0.0047 |
| 1 | 0.1162 | 0.1018 | 0.0889 | 0.0772 | 0.0668 | 0.0576 | 0.0494 | 0.0423 | 0.0360 | 0.0305 |
| 2 | 0.2162 | 0.2010 | 0.1858 | 0.1707 | 0.1559 | 0.1416 | 0.1280 | 0.1150 | 0.1029 | 0.0916 |
| 3 | 0.2490 | 0.2457 | 0.2405 | 0.2336 | 0.2252 | 0.2156 | 0.2051 | 0.1939 | 0.1821 | 0.1700 |
| 4 | 0.1986 | 0.2079 | 0.2155 | 0.2213 | 0.2252 | 0.2273 | 0.2276 | 0.2262 | 0.2231 | 0.2186 |
| 5 | 0.1161 | 0.1290 | 0.1416 | 0.1537 | 0.1651 | 0.1757 | 0.1852 | 0.1935 | 0.2005 | 0.2061 |
| 6 | 0.0514 | 0.0606 | 0.0705 | 0.0809 | 0.0917 | 0.1029 | 0.1142 | 0.1254 | 0.1365 | 0.1472 |
| 7 | 0.0176 | 0.0220 | 0.0271 | 0.0329 | 0.0393 | 0.0465 | 0.0543 | 0.0627 | 0.0717 | 0.0811 |
| 8 | 0.0047 | 0.0062 | 0.0081 | 0.0104 | 0.0131 | 0.0163 | 0.0201 | 0.0244 | 0.0293 | 0.0348 |
| 9 | 0.0010 | 0.0014 | 0.0019 | 0.0025 | 0.0034 | 0.0045 | 0.0058 | 0.0074 | 0.0093 | 0.0116 |
| 10 | 0.0002 | 0.0002 | 0.0003 | 0.0005 | 0.0007 | 0.0009 | 0.0013 | 0.0017 | 0.0023 | 0.0030 |
| 11 | 0.0000 | 0.0000 | 0.0000 | 0.0001 | 0.0001 | 0.0002 | 0.0002 | 0.0003 | 0.0004 | 0.0006 |
| 12 | 0.0000 | 0.0000 | 0.0000 | 0.0000 | 0.0000 | 0.0000 | 0.0000 | 0.0000 | 0.0001 | 0.0001 |

| $p =$ | 0.31 | 0.32 | 0.33 | 0.34 | 0.35 | 0.36 | 0.37 | 0.38 | 0.39 | 0.40 |
|---|---|---|---|---|---|---|---|---|---|---|
| $x = 0$ | 0.0038 | 0.0031 | 0.0025 | 0.0020 | 0.0016 | 0.0012 | 0.0010 | 0.0008 | 0.0006 | 0.0005 |
| 1 | 0.0258 | 0.0217 | 0.0182 | 0.0152 | 0.0126 | 0.0104 | 0.0086 | 0.0071 | 0.0058 | 0.0047 |
| 2 | 0.0811 | 0.0715 | 0.0627 | 0.0547 | 0.0476 | 0.0411 | 0.0354 | 0.0303 | 0.0259 | 0.0219 |
| 3 | 0.1579 | 0.1457 | 0.1338 | 0.1222 | 0.1110 | 0.1002 | 0.0901 | 0.0805 | 0.0716 | 0.0634 |
| 4 | 0.2128 | 0.2057 | 0.1977 | 0.1888 | 0.1792 | 0.1692 | 0.1587 | 0.1481 | 0.1374 | 0.1268 |
| 5 | 0.2103 | 0.2130 | 0.2142 | 0.2140 | 0.2123 | 0.2093 | 0.2051 | 0.1997 | 0.1933 | 0.1859 |
| 6 | 0.1575 | 0.1671 | 0.1759 | 0.1837 | 0.1906 | 0.1963 | 0.2008 | 0.2040 | 0.2059 | 0.2066 |
| 7 | 0.0910 | 0.1011 | 0.1114 | 0.1217 | 0.1319 | 0.1419 | 0.1516 | 0.1608 | 0.1693 | 0.1771 |
| 8 | 0.0409 | 0.0476 | 0.0549 | 0.0627 | 0.0710 | 0.0798 | 0.0890 | 0.0985 | 0.1082 | 0.1181 |
| 9 | 0.0143 | 0.0174 | 0.0210 | 0.0251 | 0.0298 | 0.0349 | 0.0407 | 0.0470 | 0.0538 | 0.0612 |
| 10 | 0.0038 | 0.0049 | 0.0062 | 0.0078 | 0.0096 | 0.0118 | 0.0143 | 0.0173 | 0.0206 | 0.0245 |
| 11 | 0.0008 | 0.0011 | 0.0014 | 0.0018 | 0.0024 | 0.0030 | 0.0038 | 0.0048 | 0.0060 | 0.0074 |
| 12 | 0.0001 | 0.0002 | 0.0002 | 0.0003 | 0.0004 | 0.0006 | 0.0007 | 0.0010 | 0.0013 | 0.0016 |
| 13 | 0.0000 | 0.0000 | 0.0000 | 0.0000 | 0.0001 | 0.0001 | 0.0001 | 0.0001 | 0.0002 | 0.0003 |

*(continued)*

**The Binomial Probability Distribution** *(continued)*

| | $p =$ | 0.41 | 0.42 | 0.43 | 0.44 | 0.45 | 0.46 | 0.47 | 0.48 | 0.49 | 0.50 |
|---|---|---|---|---|---|---|---|---|---|---|---|
| $x =$ | 0 | 0.0004 | 0.0003 | 0.0002 | 0.0002 | 0.0001 | 0.0001 | 0.0001 | 0.0001 | 0.0000 | 0.0000 |
| | 1 | 0.0038 | 0.0031 | 0.0025 | 0.0020 | 0.0016 | 0.0012 | 0.0010 | 0.0008 | 0.0006 | 0.0005 |
| | 2 | 0.0185 | 0.0156 | 0.0130 | 0.0108 | 0.0090 | 0.0074 | 0.0060 | 0.0049 | 0.0040 | 0.0032 |
| | 3 | 0.0558 | 0.0489 | 0.0426 | 0.0369 | 0.0318 | 0.0272 | 0.0232 | 0.0197 | 0.0166 | 0.0139 |
| | 4 | 0.1163 | 0.1061 | 0.0963 | 0.0869 | 0.0780 | 0.0696 | 0.0617 | 0.0545 | 0.0478 | 0.0417 |
| | 5 | 0.1778 | 0.1691 | 0.1598 | 0.1502 | 0.1404 | 0.1304 | 0.1204 | 0.1106 | 0.1010 | 0.0916 |
| | 6 | 0.2060 | 0.2041 | 0.2010 | 0.1967 | 0.1914 | 0.1851 | 0.1780 | 0.1702 | 0.1617 | 0.1527 |
| | 7 | 0.1840 | 0.1900 | 0.1949 | 0.1987 | 0.2013 | 0.2028 | 0.2030 | 0.2020 | 0.1997 | 0.1964 |
| | 8 | 0.1279 | 0.1376 | 0.1470 | 0.1561 | 0.1647 | 0.1727 | 0.1800 | 0.1864 | 0.1919 | 0.1964 |
| | 9 | 0.0691 | 0.0775 | 0.0863 | 0.0954 | 0.1048 | 0.1144 | 0.1241 | 0.1338 | 0.1434 | 0.1527 |
| | 10 | 0.0288 | 0.0337 | 0.0390 | 0.0450 | 0.0515 | 0.0585 | 0.0661 | 0.0741 | 0.0827 | 0.0916 |
| | 11 | 0.0091 | 0.0111 | 0.0134 | 0.0161 | 0.0191 | 0.0226 | 0.0266 | 0.0311 | 0.0361 | 0.0417 |
| | 12 | 0.0021 | 0.0027 | 0.0034 | 0.0042 | 0.0052 | 0.0064 | 0.0079 | 0.0096 | 0.0116 | 0.0139 |
| | 13 | 0.0003 | 0.0004 | 0.0006 | 0.0008 | 0.0010 | 0.0013 | 0.0016 | 0.0020 | 0.0026 | 0.0032 |
| | 14 | 0.0000 | 0.0000 | 0.0001 | 0.0001 | 0.0001 | 0.0002 | 0.0002 | 0.0003 | 0.0004 | 0.0005 |

$$n = 16$$

| | $p =$ | 0.01 | 0.02 | 0.03 | 0.04 | 0.05 | 0.06 | 0.07 | 0.08 | 0.09 | 0.10 |
|---|---|---|---|---|---|---|---|---|---|---|---|
| $x =$ | 0 | 0.8515 | 0.7238 | 0.6143 | 0.5204 | 0.4401 | 0.3716 | 0.3131 | 0.2634 | 0.2211 | 0.1853 |
| | 1 | 0.1376 | 0.2363 | 0.3040 | 0.3469 | 0.3706 | 0.3795 | 0.3771 | 0.3665 | 0.3499 | 0.3294 |
| | 2 | 0.0104 | 0.0362 | 0.0705 | 0.1084 | 0.1463 | 0.1817 | 0.2129 | 0.2390 | 0.2596 | 0.2745 |
| | 3 | 0.0005 | 0.0034 | 0.0102 | 0.0211 | 0.0359 | 0.0541 | 0.0748 | 0.0970 | 0.1198 | 0.1423 |
| | 4 | 0.0000 | 0.0002 | 0.0010 | 0.0029 | 0.0061 | 0.0112 | 0.0183 | 0.0274 | 0.0385 | 0.0514 |
| | 5 | 0.0000 | 0.0000 | 0.0001 | 0.0003 | 0.0008 | 0.0017 | 0.0033 | 0.0057 | 0.0091 | 0.0137 |
| | 6 | 0.0000 | 0.0000 | 0.0000 | 0.0000 | 0.0001 | 0.0002 | 0.0005 | 0.0009 | 0.0017 | 0.0028 |
| | 7 | 0.0000 | 0.0000 | 0.0000 | 0.0000 | 0.0000 | 0.0000 | 0.0000 | 0.0001 | 0.0002 | 0.0004 |
| | 8 | 0.0000 | 0.0000 | 0.0000 | 0.0000 | 0.0000 | 0.0000 | 0.0000 | 0.0000 | 0.0000 | 0.0001 |

| | $p =$ | 0.11 | 0.12 | 0.13 | 0.14 | 0.15 | 0.16 | 0.17 | 0.18 | 0.19 | 0.20 |
|---|---|---|---|---|---|---|---|---|---|---|---|
| $x =$ | 0 | 0.1550 | 0.1293 | 0.1077 | 0.0895 | 0.0743 | 0.0614 | 0.0507 | 0.0418 | 0.0343 | 0.0281 |
| | 1 | 0.3065 | 0.2822 | 0.2575 | 0.2332 | 0.2097 | 0.1873 | 0.1662 | 0.1468 | 0.1289 | 0.1126 |
| | 2 | 0.2841 | 0.2886 | 0.2886 | 0.2847 | 0.2775 | 0.2675 | 0.2554 | 0.2416 | 0.2267 | 0.2111 |
| | 3 | 0.1638 | 0.1837 | 0.2013 | 0.2163 | 0.2285 | 0.2378 | 0.2441 | 0.2475 | 0.2482 | 0.2463 |
| | 4 | 0.0658 | 0.0814 | 0.0977 | 0.1144 | 0.1311 | 0.1472 | 0.1625 | 0.1766 | 0.1892 | 0.2001 |
| | 5 | 0.0195 | 0.0266 | 0.0351 | 0.0447 | 0.0555 | 0.0673 | 0.0799 | 0.0930 | 0.1065 | 0.1201 |
| | 6 | 0.0044 | 0.0067 | 0.0096 | 0.0133 | 0.0180 | 0.0235 | 0.0300 | 0.0374 | 0.0458 | 0.0550 |
| | 7 | 0.0008 | 0.0013 | 0.0020 | 0.0031 | 0.0045 | 0.0064 | 0.0088 | 0.0117 | 0.0153 | 0.0197 |
| | 8 | 0.0001 | 0.0002 | 0.0003 | 0.0006 | 0.0009 | 0.0014 | 0.0020 | 0.0029 | 0.0041 | 0.0055 |
| | 9 | 0.0000 | 0.0000 | 0.0000 | 0.0001 | 0.0001 | 0.0002 | 0.0004 | 0.0006 | 0.0008 | 0.0012 |
| | 10 | 0.0000 | 0.0000 | 0.0000 | 0.0000 | 0.0000 | 0.0000 | 0.0001 | 0.0001 | 0.0001 | 0.0002 |

*(continued)*

**The Binomial Probability Distribution** *(continued)*

| | p = | 0.21 | 0.22 | 0.23 | 0.24 | 0.25 | 0.26 | 0.27 | 0.28 | 0.29 | 0.30 |
|---|---|---|---|---|---|---|---|---|---|---|---|
| x = | 0 | 0.0230 | 0.0188 | 0.0153 | 0.0124 | 0.0100 | 0.0081 | 0.0065 | 0.0052 | 0.0042 | 0.0033 |
| | 1 | 0.0979 | 0.0847 | 0.0730 | 0.0626 | 0.0535 | 0.0455 | 0.0385 | 0.0325 | 0.0273 | 0.0228 |
| | 2 | 0.1952 | 0.1792 | 0.1635 | 0.1482 | 0.1336 | 0.1198 | 0.1068 | 0.0947 | 0.0835 | 0.0732 |
| | 3 | 0.2421 | 0.2359 | 0.2279 | 0.2185 | 0.2079 | 0.1964 | 0.1843 | 0.1718 | 0.1591 | 0.1465 |
| | 4 | 0.2092 | 0.2162 | 0.2212 | 0.2242 | 0.2252 | 0.2243 | 0.2215 | 0.2171 | 0.2112 | 0.2040 |
| | 5 | 0.1334 | 0.1464 | 0.1586 | 0.1699 | 0.1802 | 0.1891 | 0.1966 | 0.2026 | 0.2071 | 0.2099 |
| | 6 | 0.0650 | 0.0757 | 0.0869 | 0.0984 | 0.1101 | 0.1218 | 0.1333 | 0.1445 | 0.1551 | 0.1649 |
| | 7 | 0.0247 | 0.0305 | 0.0371 | 0.0444 | 0.0524 | 0.0611 | 0.0704 | 0.0803 | 0.0905 | 0.1010 |
| | 8 | 0.0074 | 0.0097 | 0.0125 | 0.0158 | 0.0197 | 0.0242 | 0.0293 | 0.0351 | 0.0416 | 0.0487 |
| | 9 | 0.0017 | 0.0024 | 0.0033 | 0.0044 | 0.0058 | 0.0075 | 0.0096 | 0.0121 | 0.0151 | 0.0185 |
| | 10 | 0.0003 | 0.0005 | 0.0007 | 0.0010 | 0.0014 | 0.0019 | 0.0025 | 0.0033 | 0.0043 | 0.0056 |
| | 11 | 0.0000 | 0.0001 | 0.0001 | 0.0002 | 0.0002 | 0.0004 | 0.0005 | 0.0007 | 0.0010 | 0.0013 |
| | 12 | 0.0000 | 0.0000 | 0.0000 | 0.0000 | 0.0000 | 0.0001 | 0.0001 | 0.0001 | 0.0002 | 0.0002 |

| | p = | 0.31 | 0.32 | 0.33 | 0.34 | 0.35 | 0.36 | 0.37 | 0.38 | 0.39 | 0.40 |
|---|---|---|---|---|---|---|---|---|---|---|---|
| x = | 0 | 0.0026 | 0.0021 | 0.0016 | 0.0013 | 0.0010 | 0.0008 | 0.0006 | 0.0005 | 0.0004 | 0.0003 |
| | 1 | 0.0190 | 0.0157 | 0.0130 | 0.0107 | 0.0087 | 0.0071 | 0.0058 | 0.0047 | 0.0038 | 0.0030 |
| | 2 | 0.0639 | 0.0555 | 0.0480 | 0.0413 | 0.0353 | 0.0301 | 0.0255 | 0.0215 | 0.0180 | 0.0150 |
| | 3 | 0.1341 | 0.1220 | 0.1103 | 0.0992 | 0.0888 | 0.0790 | 0.0699 | 0.0615 | 0.0538 | 0.0468 |
| | 4 | 0.1958 | 0.1865 | 0.1766 | 0.1662 | 0.1553 | 0.1444 | 0.1333 | 0.1224 | 0.1118 | 0.1014 |
| | 5 | 0.2111 | 0.2107 | 0.2088 | 0.2054 | 0.2008 | 0.1949 | 0.1879 | 0.1801 | 0.1715 | 0.1623 |
| | 6 | 0.1739 | 0.1818 | 0.1885 | 0.1940 | 0.1982 | 0.2010 | 0.2024 | 0.2024 | 0.2010 | 0.1983 |
| | 7 | 0.1116 | 0.1222 | 0.1326 | 0.1428 | 0.1524 | 0.1615 | 0.1698 | 0.1772 | 0.1836 | 0.1889 |
| | 8 | 0.0564 | 0.0647 | 0.0735 | 0.0827 | 0.0923 | 0.1022 | 0.1122 | 0.1222 | 0.1320 | 0.1417 |
| | 9 | 0.0225 | 0.0271 | 0.0322 | 0.0379 | 0.0442 | 0.0511 | 0.0586 | 0.0666 | 0.0750 | 0.0840 |
| | 10 | 0.0071 | 0.0089 | 0.0111 | 0.0137 | 0.0167 | 0.0201 | 0.0241 | 0.0286 | 0.0336 | 0.0392 |
| | 11 | 0.0017 | 0.0023 | 0.0030 | 0.0038 | 0.0049 | 0.0062 | 0.0077 | 0.0095 | 0.0117 | 0.0142 |
| | 12 | 0.0003 | 0.0004 | 0.0006 | 0.0008 | 0.0011 | 0.0014 | 0.0019 | 0.0024 | 0.0031 | 0.0040 |
| | 13 | 0.0000 | 0.0001 | 0.0001 | 0.0001 | 0.0002 | 0.0003 | 0.0003 | 0.0005 | 0.0006 | 0.0008 |
| | 14 | 0.0000 | 0.0000 | 0.0000 | 0.0000 | 0.0000 | 0.0000 | 0.0000 | 0.0001 | 0.0001 | 0.0001 |

*(continued)*

## The Binomial Probability Distribution *(continued)*

| | *p =* | *0.41* | *0.42* | *0.43* | *0.44* | *0.45* | *0.46* | *0.47* | *0.48* | *0.49* | *0.50* |
|---|---|---|---|---|---|---|---|---|---|---|---|
| *x =* | 0 | 0.0002 | 0.0002 | 0.0001 | 0.0001 | 0.0001 | 0.0001 | 0.0000 | 0.0000 | 0.0000 | 0.0000 |
| | 1 | 0.0024 | 0.0019 | 0.0015 | 0.0012 | 0.0009 | 0.0007 | 0.0005 | 0.0004 | 0.0003 | 0.0002 |
| | 2 | 0.0125 | 0.0103 | 0.0085 | 0.0069 | 0.0056 | 0.0046 | 0.0037 | 0.0029 | 0.0023 | 0.0018 |
| | 3 | 0.0405 | 0.0349 | 0.0299 | 0.0254 | 0.0215 | 0.0181 | 0.0151 | 0.0126 | 0.0104 | 0.0085 |
| | 4 | 0.0915 | 0.0821 | 0.0732 | 0.0649 | 0.0572 | 0.0501 | 0.0436 | 0.0378 | 0.0325 | 0.0278 |
| | 5 | 0.1526 | 0.1426 | 0.1325 | 0.1224 | 0.1123 | 0.1024 | 0.0929 | 0.0837 | 0.0749 | 0.0667 |
| | 6 | 0.1944 | 0.1894 | 0.1833 | 0.1762 | 0.1684 | 0.1600 | 0.1510 | 0.1416 | 0.1319 | 0.1222 |
| | 7 | 0.1930 | 0.1959 | 0.1975 | 0.1978 | 0.1969 | 0.1947 | 0.1912 | 0.1867 | 0.1811 | 0.1746 |
| | 8 | 0.1509 | 0.1596 | 0.1676 | 0.1749 | 0.1812 | 0.1865 | 0.1908 | 0.1939 | 0.1958 | 0.1964 |
| | 9 | 0.0932 | 0.1027 | 0.1124 | 0.1221 | 0.1318 | 0.1413 | 0.1504 | 0.1591 | 0.1672 | 0.1746 |
| | 10 | 0.0453 | 0.0521 | 0.0594 | 0.0672 | 0.0755 | 0.0842 | 0.0934 | 0.1028 | 0.1124 | 0.1222 |
| | 11 | 0.0172 | 0.0206 | 0.0244 | 0.0288 | 0.0337 | 0.0391 | 0.0452 | 0.0518 | 0.0589 | 0.0667 |
| | 12 | 0.0050 | 0.0062 | 0.0077 | 0.0094 | 0.0115 | 0.0139 | 0.0167 | 0.0199 | 0.0236 | 0.0278 |
| | 13 | 0.0011 | 0.0014 | 0.0018 | 0.0023 | 0.0029 | 0.0036 | 0.0046 | 0.0057 | 0.0070 | 0.0085 |
| | 14 | 0.0002 | 0.0002 | 0.0003 | 0.0004 | 0.0005 | 0.0007 | 0.0009 | 0.0011 | 0.0014 | 0.0018 |
| | 15 | 0.0000 | 0.0000 | 0.0000 | 0.0000 | 0.0001 | 0.0001 | 0.0001 | 0.0001 | 0.0002 | 0.0002 |

### *n* = 17

| | *p =* | *0.01* | *0.02* | *0.03* | *0.04* | *0.05* | *0.06* | *0.07* | *0.08* | *0.09* | *0.10* |
|---|---|---|---|---|---|---|---|---|---|---|---|
| *x =* | 0 | 0.8429 | 0.7093 | 0.5958 | 0.4996 | 0.4181 | 0.3493 | 0.2912 | 0.2423 | 0.2012 | 0.1668 |
| | 1 | 0.1447 | 0.2461 | 0.3133 | 0.3539 | 0.3741 | 0.3790 | 0.3726 | 0.3582 | 0.3383 | 0.3150 |
| | 2 | 0.0117 | 0.0402 | 0.0775 | 0.1180 | 0.1575 | 0.1935 | 0.2244 | 0.2492 | 0.2677 | 0.2800 |
| | 3 | 0.0006 | 0.0041 | 0.0120 | 0.0246 | 0.0415 | 0.0618 | 0.0844 | 0.1083 | 0.1324 | 0.1556 |
| | 4 | 0.0000 | 0.0003 | 0.0013 | 0.0036 | 0.0076 | 0.0138 | 0.0222 | 0.0330 | 0.0458 | 0.0605 |
| | 5 | 0.0000 | 0.0000 | 0.0001 | 0.0004 | 0.0010 | 0.0023 | 0.0044 | 0.0075 | 0.0118 | 0.0175 |
| | 6 | 0.0000 | 0.0000 | 0.0000 | 0.0000 | 0.0001 | 0.0003 | 0.0007 | 0.0013 | 0.0023 | 0.0039 |
| | 7 | 0.0000 | 0.0000 | 0.0000 | 0.0000 | 0.0000 | 0.0000 | 0.0001 | 0.0002 | 0.0004 | 0.0007 |
| | 8 | 0.0000 | 0.0000 | 0.0000 | 0.0000 | 0.0000 | 0.0000 | 0.0000 | 0.0000 | 0.0000 | 0.0001 |

*(continued)*

**The Binomial Probability Distribution** *(continued)*

| | $p =$ | 0.11 | 0.12 | 0.13 | 0.14 | 0.15 | 0.16 | 0.17 | 0.18 | 0.19 | 0.20 |
|---|---|---|---|---|---|---|---|---|---|---|---|
| $x =$ | 0 | 0.1379 | 0.1138 | 0.0937 | 0.0770 | 0.0631 | 0.0516 | 0.0421 | 0.0343 | 0.0278 | 0.0225 |
| | 1 | 0.2898 | 0.2638 | 0.2381 | 0.2131 | 0.1893 | 0.1671 | 0.1466 | 0.1279 | 0.1109 | 0.0957 |
| | 2 | 0.2865 | 0.2878 | 0.2846 | 0.2775 | 0.2673 | 0.2547 | 0.2402 | 0.2245 | 0.2081 | 0.1914 |
| | 3 | 0.1771 | 0.1963 | 0.2126 | 0.2259 | 0.2359 | 0.2425 | 0.2460 | 0.2464 | 0.2441 | 0.2393 |
| | 4 | 0.0766 | 0.0937 | 0.1112 | 0.1287 | 0.1457 | 0.1617 | 0.1764 | 0.1893 | 0.2004 | 0.2093 |
| | 5 | 0.0246 | 0.0332 | 0.0432 | 0.0545 | 0.0668 | 0.0801 | 0.0939 | 0.1081 | 0.1222 | 0.1361 |
| | 6 | 0.0061 | 0.0091 | 0.0129 | 0.0177 | 0.0236 | 0.0305 | 0.0385 | 0.0474 | 0.0573 | 0.0680 |
| | 7 | 0.0012 | 0.0019 | 0.0030 | 0.0045 | 0.0065 | 0.0091 | 0.0124 | 0.0164 | 0.0211 | 0.0267 |
| | 8 | 0.0002 | 0.0003 | 0.0006 | 0.0009 | 0.0014 | 0.0022 | 0.0032 | 0.0045 | 0.0062 | 0.0084 |
| | 9 | 0.0000 | 0.0000 | 0.0001 | 0.0002 | 0.0003 | 0.0004 | 0.0006 | 0.0010 | 0.0015 | 0.0021 |
| | 10 | 0.0000 | 0.0000 | 0.0000 | 0.0000 | 0.0000 | 0.0001 | 0.0001 | 0.0002 | 0.0003 | 0.0004 |
| | 11 | 0.0000 | 0.0000 | 0.0000 | 0.0000 | 0.0000 | 0.0000 | 0.0000 | 0.0000 | 0.0000 | 0.0001 |

| | $p =$ | 0.21 | 0.22 | 0.23 | 0.24 | 0.25 | 0.26 | 0.27 | 0.28 | 0.29 | 0.30 |
|---|---|---|---|---|---|---|---|---|---|---|---|
| $x =$ | 0 | 0.0182 | 0.0146 | 0.0118 | 0.0094 | 0.0075 | 0.0060 | 0.0047 | 0.0038 | 0.0030 | 0.0023 |
| | 1 | 0.0822 | 0.0702 | 0.0597 | 0.0505 | 0.0426 | 0.0357 | 0.0299 | 0.0248 | 0.0206 | 0.0169 |
| | 2 | 0.1747 | 0.1584 | 0.1427 | 0.1277 | 0.1136 | 0.1005 | 0.0883 | 0.0772 | 0.0672 | 0.0581 |
| | 3 | 0.2322 | 0.2234 | 0.2131 | 0.2016 | 0.1893 | 0.1765 | 0.1634 | 0.1502 | 0.1372 | 0.1245 |
| | 4 | 0.2161 | 0.2205 | 0.2228 | 0.2228 | 0.2209 | 0.2170 | 0.2115 | 0.2044 | 0.1961 | 0.1868 |
| | 5 | 0.1493 | 0.1617 | 0.1730 | 0.1830 | 0.1914 | 0.1982 | 0.2033 | 0.2067 | 0.2083 | 0.2081 |
| | 6 | 0.0794 | 0.0912 | 0.1034 | 0.1156 | 0.1276 | 0.1393 | 0.1504 | 0.1608 | 0.1701 | 0.1784 |
| | 7 | 0.0332 | 0.0404 | 0.0485 | 0.0573 | 0.0668 | 0.0769 | 0.0874 | 0.0982 | 0.1092 | 0.1201 |
| | 8 | 0.0110 | 0.0143 | 0.0181 | 0.0226 | 0.0279 | 0.0338 | 0.0404 | 0.0478 | 0.0558 | 0.0644 |
| | 9 | 0.0029 | 0.0040 | 0.0054 | 0.0071 | 0.0093 | 0.0119 | 0.0150 | 0.0186 | 0.0228 | 0.0276 |
| | 10 | 0.0006 | 0.0009 | 0.0013 | 0.0018 | 0.0025 | 0.0033 | 0.0044 | 0.0058 | 0.0074 | 0.0095 |
| | 11 | 0.0001 | 0.0002 | 0.0002 | 0.0004 | 0.0005 | 0.0007 | 0.0010 | 0.0014 | 0.0019 | 0.0026 |
| | 12 | 0.0000 | 0.0000 | 0.0000 | 0.0001 | 0.0001 | 0.0001 | 0.0002 | 0.0003 | 0.0004 | 0.0006 |
| | 13 | 0.0000 | 0.0000 | 0.0000 | 0.0000 | 0.0000 | 0.0000 | 0.0000 | 0.0000 | 0.0001 | 0.0001 |

*(continued)*

**The Binomial Probability Distribution** *(continued)*

| | p = | 0.31 | 0.32 | 0.33 | 0.34 | 0.35 | 0.36 | 0.37 | 0.38 | 0.39 | 0.40 |
|---|---|---|---|---|---|---|---|---|---|---|---|
| x = | 0 | 0.0018 | 0.0014 | 0.0011 | 0.0009 | 0.0007 | 0.0005 | 0.0004 | 0.0003 | 0.0002 | 0.0002 |
| | 1 | 0.0139 | 0.0114 | 0.0093 | 0.0075 | 0.0060 | 0.0048 | 0.0039 | 0.0031 | 0.0024 | 0.0019 |
| | 2 | 0.0500 | 0.0428 | 0.0364 | 0.0309 | 0.0260 | 0.0218 | 0.0182 | 0.0151 | 0.0125 | 0.0102 |
| | 3 | 0.1123 | 0.1007 | 0.0898 | 0.0795 | 0.0701 | 0.0614 | 0.0534 | 0.0463 | 0.0398 | 0.0341 |
| | 4 | 0.1766 | 0.1659 | 0.1547 | 0.1434 | 0.1320 | 0.1208 | 0.1099 | 0.0993 | 0.0892 | 0.0796 |
| | 5 | 0.2063 | 0.2030 | 0.1982 | 0.1921 | 0.1849 | 0.1767 | 0.1677 | 0.1582 | 0.1482 | 0.1379 |
| | 6 | 0.1854 | 0.1910 | 0.1952 | 0.1979 | 0.1991 | 0.1988 | 0.1970 | 0.1939 | 0.1895 | 0.1839 |
| | 7 | 0.1309 | 0.1413 | 0.1511 | 0.1602 | 0.1685 | 0.1757 | 0.1818 | 0.1868 | 0.1904 | 0.1927 |
| | 8 | 0.0735 | 0.0831 | 0.0930 | 0.1032 | 0.1134 | 0.1235 | 0.1335 | 0.1431 | 0.1521 | 0.1606 |
| | 9 | 0.0330 | 0.0391 | 0.0458 | 0.0531 | 0.0611 | 0.0695 | 0.0784 | 0.0877 | 0.0973 | 0.1070 |
| | 10 | 0.0119 | 0.0147 | 0.0181 | 0.0219 | 0.0263 | 0.0313 | 0.0368 | 0.0430 | 0.0498 | 0.0571 |
| | 11 | 0.0034 | 0.0044 | 0.0057 | 0.0072 | 0.0090 | 0.0112 | 0.0138 | 0.0168 | 0.0202 | 0.0242 |
| | 12 | 0.0008 | 0.0010 | 0.0014 | 0.0018 | 0.0024 | 0.0031 | 0.0040 | 0.0051 | 0.0065 | 0.0081 |
| | 13 | 0.0001 | 0.0002 | 0.0003 | 0.0004 | 0.0005 | 0.0007 | 0.0009 | 0.0012 | 0.0016 | 0.0021 |
| | 14 | 0.0000 | 0.0000 | 0.0000 | 0.0001 | 0.0001 | 0.0001 | 0.0002 | 0.0002 | 0.0003 | 0.0004 |
| | 15 | 0.0000 | 0.0000 | 0.0000 | 0.0000 | 0.0000 | 0.0000 | 0.0000 | 0.0000 | 0.0000 | 0.0001 |

| | p = | 0.41 | 0.42 | 0.43 | 0.44 | 0.45 | 0.46 | 0.47 | 0.48 | 0.49 | 0.50 |
|---|---|---|---|---|---|---|---|---|---|---|---|
| x = | 0 | 0.0001 | 0.0001 | 0.0001 | 0.0001 | 0.0000 | 0.0000 | 0.0000 | 0.0000 | 0.0000 | 0.0000 |
| | 1 | 0.0015 | 0.0012 | 0.0009 | 0.0007 | 0.0005 | 0.0004 | 0.0003 | 0.0002 | 0.0002 | 0.0001 |
| | 2 | 0.0084 | 0.0068 | 0.0055 | 0.0044 | 0.0035 | 0.0028 | 0.0022 | 0.0017 | 0.0013 | 0.0010 |
| | 3 | 0.0290 | 0.0246 | 0.0207 | 0.0173 | 0.0144 | 0.0119 | 0.0097 | 0.0079 | 0.0064 | 0.0052 |
| | 4 | 0.0706 | 0.0622 | 0.0546 | 0.0475 | 0.0411 | 0.0354 | 0.0302 | 0.0257 | 0.0217 | 0.0182 |
| | 5 | 0.1276 | 0.1172 | 0.1070 | 0.0971 | 0.0875 | 0.0784 | 0.0697 | 0.0616 | 0.0541 | 0.0472 |
| | 6 | 0.1773 | 0.1697 | 0.1614 | 0.1525 | 0.1432 | 0.1335 | 0.1237 | 0.1138 | 0.1040 | 0.0944 |
| | 7 | 0.1936 | 0.1932 | 0.1914 | 0.1883 | 0.1841 | 0.1787 | 0.1723 | 0.1650 | 0.1570 | 0.1484 |
| | 8 | 0.1682 | 0.1748 | 0.1805 | 0.1850 | 0.1883 | 0.1903 | 0.1910 | 0.1904 | 0.1886 | 0.1855 |
| | 9 | 0.1169 | 0.1266 | 0.1361 | 0.1453 | 0.1540 | 0.1621 | 0.1694 | 0.1758 | 0.1812 | 0.1855 |
| | 10 | 0.0650 | 0.0733 | 0.0822 | 0.0914 | 0.1008 | 0.1105 | 0.1202 | 0.1298 | 0.1393 | 0.1484 |
| | 11 | 0.0287 | 0.0338 | 0.0394 | 0.0457 | 0.0525 | 0.0599 | 0.0678 | 0.0763 | 0.0851 | 0.0944 |
| | 12 | 0.0100 | 0.0122 | 0.0149 | 0.0179 | 0.0215 | 0.0255 | 0.0301 | 0.0352 | 0.0409 | 0.0472 |
| | 13 | 0.0027 | 0.0034 | 0.0043 | 0.0054 | 0.0068 | 0.0084 | 0.0103 | 0.0125 | 0.0151 | 0.0182 |
| | 14 | 0.0005 | 0.0007 | 0.0009 | 0.0012 | 0.0016 | 0.0020 | 0.0026 | 0.0033 | 0.0041 | 0.0052 |
| | 15 | 0.0001 | 0.0001 | 0.0001 | 0.0002 | 0.0003 | 0.0003 | 0.0005 | 0.0006 | 0.0008 | 0.0010 |
| | 16 | 0.0000 | 0.0000 | 0.0000 | 0.0000 | 0.0000 | 0.0000 | 0.0001 | 0.0001 | 0.0001 | 0.0001 |

*(continued)*

**The Binomial Probability Distribution** *(continued)*

$$n = 18$$

| | $p =$ | 0.01 | 0.02 | 0.03 | 0.04 | 0.05 | 0.06 | 0.07 | 0.08 | 0.09 | 0.10 |
|---|---|---|---|---|---|---|---|---|---|---|---|
| $x =$ | 0 | 0.8345 | 0.6951 | 0.5780 | 0.4796 | 0.3972 | 0.3283 | 0.2708 | 0.2229 | 0.1831 | 0.1501 |
| | 1 | 0.1517 | 0.2554 | 0.3217 | 0.3597 | 0.3763 | 0.3772 | 0.3669 | 0.3489 | 0.3260 | 0.3002 |
| | 2 | 0.0130 | 0.0443 | 0.0846 | 0.1274 | 0.1683 | 0.2047 | 0.2348 | 0.2579 | 0.2741 | 0.2835 |
| | 3 | 0.0007 | 0.0048 | 0.0140 | 0.0283 | 0.0473 | 0.0697 | 0.0942 | 0.1196 | 0.1446 | 0.1680 |
| | 4 | 0.0000 | 0.0004 | 0.0016 | 0.0044 | 0.0093 | 0.0167 | 0.0266 | 0.0390 | 0.0536 | 0.0700 |
| | 5 | 0.0000 | 0.0000 | 0.0001 | 0.0005 | 0.0014 | 0.0030 | 0.0056 | 0.0095 | 0.0148 | 0.0218 |
| | 6 | 0.0000 | 0.0000 | 0.0000 | 0.0000 | 0.0002 | 0.0004 | 0.0009 | 0.0018 | 0.0032 | 0.0052 |
| | 7 | 0.0000 | 0.0000 | 0.0000 | 0.0000 | 0.0000 | 0.0001 | 0.0001 | 0.0003 | 0.0005 | 0.0010 |
| | 8 | 0.0000 | 0.0000 | 0.0000 | 0.0000 | 0.0000 | 0.0000 | 0.0000 | 0.0000 | 0.0001 | 0.0002 |

| | $p =$ | 0.11 | 0.12 | 0.13 | 0.14 | 0.15 | 0.16 | 0.17 | 0.18 | 0.19 | 0.20 |
|---|---|---|---|---|---|---|---|---|---|---|---|
| $x =$ | 0 | 0.1227 | 0.1002 | 0.0815 | 0.0662 | 0.0536 | 0.0434 | 0.0349 | 0.0281 | 0.0225 | 0.0180 |
| | 1 | 0.2731 | 0.2458 | 0.2193 | 0.1940 | 0.1704 | 0.1486 | 0.1288 | 0.1110 | 0.0951 | 0.0811 |
| | 2 | 0.2869 | 0.2850 | 0.2785 | 0.2685 | 0.2556 | 0.2407 | 0.2243 | 0.2071 | 0.1897 | 0.1723 |
| | 3 | 0.1891 | 0.2072 | 0.2220 | 0.2331 | 0.2406 | 0.2445 | 0.2450 | 0.2425 | 0.2373 | 0.2297 |
| | 4 | 0.0877 | 0.1060 | 0.1244 | 0.1423 | 0.1592 | 0.1746 | 0.1882 | 0.1996 | 0.2087 | 0.2153 |
| | 5 | 0.0303 | 0.0405 | 0.0520 | 0.0649 | 0.0787 | 0.0931 | 0.1079 | 0.1227 | 0.1371 | 0.1507 |
| | 6 | 0.0081 | 0.0120 | 0.0168 | 0.0229 | 0.0301 | 0.0384 | 0.0479 | 0.0584 | 0.0697 | 0.0816 |
| | 7 | 0.0017 | 0.0028 | 0.0043 | 0.0064 | 0.0091 | 0.0126 | 0.0168 | 0.0220 | 0.0280 | 0.0350 |
| | 8 | 0.0003 | 0.0005 | 0.0009 | 0.0014 | 0.0022 | 0.0033 | 0.0047 | 0.0066 | 0.0090 | 0.0120 |
| | 9 | 0.0000 | 0.0001 | 0.0001 | 0.0003 | 0.0004 | 0.0007 | 0.0011 | 0.0016 | 0.0024 | 0.0033 |
| | 10 | 0.0000 | 0.0000 | 0.0000 | 0.0000 | 0.0001 | 0.0001 | 0.0002 | 0.0003 | 0.0005 | 0.0008 |
| | 11 | 0.0000 | 0.0000 | 0.0000 | 0.0000 | 0.0000 | 0.0000 | 0.0000 | 0.0001 | 0.0001 | 0.0001 |

| | $p =$ | 0.21 | 0.22 | 0.23 | 0.24 | 0.25 | 0.26 | 0.27 | 0.28 | 0.29 | 0.30 |
|---|---|---|---|---|---|---|---|---|---|---|---|
| $x =$ | 0 | 0.0144 | 0.0114 | 0.0091 | 0.0072 | 0.0056 | 0.0044 | 0.0035 | 0.0027 | 0.0021 | 0.0016 |
| | 1 | 0.0687 | 0.0580 | 0.0487 | 0.0407 | 0.0338 | 0.0280 | 0.0231 | 0.0189 | 0.0155 | 0.0126 |
| | 2 | 0.1553 | 0.1390 | 0.1236 | 0.1092 | 0.0958 | 0.0836 | 0.0725 | 0.0626 | 0.0537 | 0.0458 |
| | 3 | 0.2202 | 0.2091 | 0.1969 | 0.1839 | 0.1704 | 0.1567 | 0.1431 | 0.1298 | 0.1169 | 0.1046 |
| | 4 | 0.2195 | 0.2212 | 0.2205 | 0.2177 | 0.2130 | 0.2065 | 0.1985 | 0.1892 | 0.1790 | 0.1681 |
| | 5 | 0.1634 | 0.1747 | 0.1845 | 0.1925 | 0.1988 | 0.2031 | 0.2055 | 0.2061 | 0.2048 | 0.2017 |
| | 6 | 0.0941 | 0.1067 | 0.1194 | 0.1317 | 0.1436 | 0.1546 | 0.1647 | 0.1736 | 0.1812 | 0.1873 |
| | 7 | 0.0429 | 0.0516 | 0.0611 | 0.0713 | 0.0820 | 0.0931 | 0.1044 | 0.1157 | 0.1269 | 0.1376 |
| | 8 | 0.0157 | 0.0200 | 0.0251 | 0.0310 | 0.0376 | 0.0450 | 0.0531 | 0.0619 | 0.0713 | 0.0811 |
| | 9 | 0.0046 | 0.0063 | 0.0083 | 0.0109 | 0.0139 | 0.0176 | 0.0218 | 0.0267 | 0.0323 | 0.0386 |
| | 10 | 0.0011 | 0.0016 | 0.0022 | 0.0031 | 0.0042 | 0.0056 | 0.0073 | 0.0094 | 0.0119 | 0.0149 |
| | 11 | 0.0002 | 0.0003 | 0.0005 | 0.0007 | 0.0010 | 0.0014 | 0.0020 | 0.0026 | 0.0035 | 0.0046 |
| | 12 | 0.0000 | 0.0001 | 0.0001 | 0.0001 | 0.0002 | 0.0003 | 0.0004 | 0.0006 | 0.0008 | 0.0012 |
| | 13 | 0.0000 | 0.0000 | 0.0000 | 0.0000 | 0.0000 | 0.0000 | 0.0001 | 0.0001 | 0.0002 | 0.0002 |

*(continued)*

**The Binomial Probability Distribution** *(continued)*

| p = | 0.31 | 0.32 | 0.33 | 0.34 | 0.35 | 0.36 | 0.37 | 0.38 | 0.39 | 0.40 |
|---|---|---|---|---|---|---|---|---|---|---|
| x = 0 | 0.0013 | 0.0010 | 0.0007 | 0.0006 | 0.0004 | 0.0003 | 0.0002 | 0.0002 | 0.0001 | 0.0001 |
| 1 | 0.0102 | 0.0082 | 0.0066 | 0.0052 | 0.0042 | 0.0033 | 0.0026 | 0.0020 | 0.0016 | 0.0012 |
| 2 | 0.0388 | 0.0327 | 0.0275 | 0.0229 | 0.0190 | 0.0157 | 0.0129 | 0.0105 | 0.0086 | 0.0069 |
| 3 | 0.0930 | 0.0822 | 0.0722 | 0.0630 | 0.0547 | 0.0471 | 0.0404 | 0.0344 | 0.0292 | 0.0246 |
| 4 | 0.1567 | 0.1450 | 0.1333 | 0.1217 | 0.1104 | 0.0994 | 0.0890 | 0.0791 | 0.0699 | 0.0614 |
| 5 | 0.1971 | 0.1911 | 0.1838 | 0.1755 | 0.1664 | 0.1566 | 0.1463 | 0.1358 | 0.1252 | 0.1146 |
| 6 | 0.1919 | 0.1948 | 0.1962 | 0.1959 | 0.1941 | 0.1908 | 0.1862 | 0.1803 | 0.1734 | 0.1655 |
| 7 | 0.1478 | 0.1572 | 0.1656 | 0.1730 | 0.1792 | 0.1840 | 0.1875 | 0.1895 | 0.1900 | 0.1892 |
| 8 | 0.0913 | 0.1017 | 0.1122 | 0.1226 | 0.1327 | 0.1423 | 0.1514 | 0.1597 | 0.1671 | 0.1734 |
| 9 | 0.0456 | 0.0532 | 0.0614 | 0.0701 | 0.0794 | 0.0890 | 0.0988 | 0.1087 | 0.1187 | 0.1284 |
| 10 | 0.0184 | 0.0225 | 0.0272 | 0.0325 | 0.0385 | 0.0450 | 0.0522 | 0.0600 | 0.0683 | 0.0771 |
| 11 | 0.0060 | 0.0077 | 0.0097 | 0.0122 | 0.0151 | 0.0184 | 0.0223 | 0.0267 | 0.0318 | 0.0374 |
| 12 | 0.0016 | 0.0021 | 0.0028 | 0.0037 | 0.0047 | 0.0060 | 0.0076 | 0.0096 | 0.0118 | 0.0145 |
| 13 | 0.0003 | 0.0005 | 0.0006 | 0.0009 | 0.0012 | 0.0016 | 0.0021 | 0.0027 | 0.0035 | 0.0045 |
| 14 | 0.0001 | 0.0001 | 0.0001 | 0.0002 | 0.0002 | 0.0003 | 0.0004 | 0.0006 | 0.0008 | 0.0011 |
| 15 | 0.0000 | 0.0000 | 0.0000 | 0.0000 | 0.0000 | 0.0000 | 0.0001 | 0.0001 | 0.0001 | 0.0002 |

| p = | 0.41 | 0.42 | 0.43 | 0.44 | 0.45 | 0.46 | 0.47 | 0.48 | 0.49 | 0.50 |
|---|---|---|---|---|---|---|---|---|---|---|
| x = 0 | 0.0001 | 0.0001 | 0.0000 | 0.0000 | 0.0000 | 0.0000 | 0.0000 | 0.0000 | 0.0000 | 0.0000 |
| 1 | 0.0009 | 0.0007 | 0.0005 | 0.0004 | 0.0003 | 0.0002 | 0.0002 | 0.0001 | 0.0001 | 0.0001 |
| 2 | 0.0055 | 0.0044 | 0.0035 | 0.0028 | 0.0022 | 0.0017 | 0.0013 | 0.0010 | 0.0008 | 0.0006 |
| 3 | 0.0206 | 0.0171 | 0.0141 | 0.0116 | 0.0095 | 0.0077 | 0.0062 | 0.0050 | 0.0039 | 0.0031 |
| 4 | 0.0536 | 0.0464 | 0.0400 | 0.0342 | 0.0291 | 0.0246 | 0.0206 | 0.0172 | 0.0142 | 0.0117 |
| 5 | 0.1042 | 0.0941 | 0.0844 | 0.0753 | 0.0666 | 0.0586 | 0.0512 | 0.0444 | 0.0382 | 0.0327 |
| 6 | 0.1569 | 0.1477 | 0.1380 | 0.1281 | 0.1181 | 0.1081 | 0.0983 | 0.0887 | 0.0796 | 0.0708 |
| 7 | 0.1869 | 0.1833 | 0.1785 | 0.1726 | 0.1657 | 0.1579 | 0.1494 | 0.1404 | 0.1310 | 0.1214 |
| 8 | 0.1786 | 0.1825 | 0.1852 | 0.1864 | 0.1864 | 0.1850 | 0.1822 | 0.1782 | 0.1731 | 0.1669 |
| 9 | 0.1379 | 0.1469 | 0.1552 | 0.1628 | 0.1694 | 0.1751 | 0.1795 | 0.1828 | 0.1848 | 0.1855 |
| 10 | 0.0862 | 0.0957 | 0.1054 | 0.1151 | 0.1248 | 0.1342 | 0.1433 | 0.1519 | 0.1598 | 0.1669 |
| 11 | 0.0436 | 0.0504 | 0.0578 | 0.0658 | 0.0742 | 0.0831 | 0.0924 | 0.1020 | 0.1117 | 0.1214 |
| 12 | 0.0177 | 0.0213 | 0.0254 | 0.0301 | 0.0354 | 0.0413 | 0.0478 | 0.0549 | 0.0626 | 0.0708 |
| 13 | 0.0057 | 0.0071 | 0.0089 | 0.0109 | 0.0134 | 0.0162 | 0.0196 | 0.0234 | 0.0278 | 0.0327 |
| 14 | 0.0014 | 0.0018 | 0.0024 | 0.0031 | 0.0039 | 0.0049 | 0.0062 | 0.0077 | 0.0095 | 0.0117 |
| 15 | 0.0003 | 0.0004 | 0.0005 | 0.0006 | 0.0009 | 0.0011 | 0.0015 | 0.0019 | 0.0024 | 0.0031 |
| 16 | 0.0000 | 0.0000 | 0.0001 | 0.0001 | 0.0001 | 0.0002 | 0.0002 | 0.0003 | 0.0004 | 0.0006 |
| 17 | 0.0000 | 0.0000 | 0.0000 | 0.0000 | 0.0000 | 0.0000 | 0.0000 | 0.0000 | 0.0000 | 0.0001 |

*(continued)*

**The Binomial Probability Distribution** *(continued)*

$$n = 19$$

| $p =$ | 0.01 | 0.02 | 0.03 | 0.04 | 0.05 | 0.06 | 0.07 | 0.08 | 0.09 | 0.10 |
|---|---|---|---|---|---|---|---|---|---|---|
| $x = $ 0 | 0.8262 | 0.6812 | 0.5606 | 0.4604 | 0.3774 | 0.3086 | 0.2519 | 0.2051 | 0.1666 | 0.1351 |
| 1 | 0.1586 | 0.2642 | 0.3294 | 0.3645 | 0.3774 | 0.3743 | 0.3602 | 0.3389 | 0.3131 | 0.2852 |
| 2 | 0.0144 | 0.0485 | 0.0917 | 0.1367 | 0.1787 | 0.2150 | 0.2440 | 0.2652 | 0.2787 | 0.2852 |
| 3 | 0.0008 | 0.0056 | 0.0161 | 0.0323 | 0.0533 | 0.0778 | 0.1041 | 0.1307 | 0.1562 | 0.1796 |
| 4 | 0.0000 | 0.0005 | 0.0020 | 0.0054 | 0.0112 | 0.0199 | 0.0313 | 0.0455 | 0.0618 | 0.0798 |
| 5 | 0.0000 | 0.0000 | 0.0002 | 0.0007 | 0.0018 | 0.0038 | 0.0071 | 0.0119 | 0.0183 | 0.0266 |
| 6 | 0.0000 | 0.0000 | 0.0000 | 0.0001 | 0.0002 | 0.0006 | 0.0012 | 0.0024 | 0.0042 | 0.0069 |
| 7 | 0.0000 | 0.0000 | 0.0000 | 0.0000 | 0.0000 | 0.0001 | 0.0002 | 0.0004 | 0.0008 | 0.0014 |
| 8 | 0.0000 | 0.0000 | 0.0000 | 0.0000 | 0.0000 | 0.0000 | 0.0000 | 0.0001 | 0.0001 | 0.0002 |

| $p =$ | 0.11 | 0.12 | 0.13 | 0.14 | 0.15 | 0.16 | 0.17 | 0.18 | 0.19 | 0.20 |
|---|---|---|---|---|---|---|---|---|---|---|
| $x = $ 0 | 0.1092 | 0.0881 | 0.0709 | 0.0569 | 0.0456 | 0.0364 | 0.0290 | 0.0230 | 0.0182 | 0.0144 |
| 1 | 0.2565 | 0.2284 | 0.2014 | 0.1761 | 0.1529 | 0.1318 | 0.1129 | 0.0961 | 0.0813 | 0.0685 |
| 2 | 0.2854 | 0.2803 | 0.2708 | 0.2581 | 0.2428 | 0.2259 | 0.2081 | 0.1898 | 0.1717 | 0.1540 |
| 3 | 0.1999 | 0.2166 | 0.2293 | 0.2381 | 0.2428 | 0.2439 | 0.2415 | 0.2361 | 0.2282 | 0.2182 |
| 4 | 0.0988 | 0.1181 | 0.1371 | 0.1550 | 0.1714 | 0.1858 | 0.1979 | 0.2073 | 0.2141 | 0.2182 |
| 5 | 0.0366 | 0.0483 | 0.0614 | 0.0757 | 0.0907 | 0.1062 | 0.1216 | 0.1365 | 0.1507 | 0.1636 |
| 6 | 0.0106 | 0.0154 | 0.0214 | 0.0288 | 0.0374 | 0.0472 | 0.0581 | 0.0699 | 0.0825 | 0.0955 |
| 7 | 0.0024 | 0.0039 | 0.0059 | 0.0087 | 0.0122 | 0.0167 | 0.0221 | 0.0285 | 0.0359 | 0.0443 |
| 8 | 0.0004 | 0.0008 | 0.0013 | 0.0021 | 0.0032 | 0.0048 | 0.0068 | 0.0094 | 0.0126 | 0.0166 |
| 9 | 0.0001 | 0.0001 | 0.0002 | 0.0004 | 0.0007 | 0.0011 | 0.0017 | 0.0025 | 0.0036 | 0.0051 |
| 10 | 0.0000 | 0.0000 | 0.0000 | 0.0001 | 0.0001 | 0.0002 | 0.0003 | 0.0006 | 0.0009 | 0.0013 |
| 11 | 0.0000 | 0.0000 | 0.0000 | 0.0000 | 0.0000 | 0.0000 | 0.0001 | 0.0001 | 0.0002 | 0.0003 |

| $p =$ | 0.21 | 0.22 | 0.23 | 0.24 | 0.25 | 0.26 | 0.27 | 0.28 | 0.29 | 0.30 |
|---|---|---|---|---|---|---|---|---|---|---|
| $x = $ 0 | 0.0113 | 0.0089 | 0.0070 | 0.0054 | 0.0042 | 0.0033 | 0.0025 | 0.0019 | 0.0015 | 0.0011 |
| 1 | 0.0573 | 0.0477 | 0.0396 | 0.0326 | 0.0268 | 0.0219 | 0.0178 | 0.0144 | 0.0116 | 0.0093 |
| 2 | 0.1371 | 0.1212 | 0.1064 | 0.0927 | 0.0803 | 0.0692 | 0.0592 | 0.0503 | 0.0426 | 0.0358 |
| 3 | 0.2065 | 0.1937 | 0.1800 | 0.1659 | 0.1517 | 0.1377 | 0.1240 | 0.1109 | 0.0985 | 0.0869 |
| 4 | 0.2196 | 0.2185 | 0.2151 | 0.2096 | 0.2023 | 0.1935 | 0.1835 | 0.1726 | 0.1610 | 0.1491 |
| 5 | 0.1751 | 0.1849 | 0.1928 | 0.1986 | 0.2023 | 0.2040 | 0.2036 | 0.2013 | 0.1973 | 0.1916 |
| 6 | 0.1086 | 0.1217 | 0.1343 | 0.1463 | 0.1574 | 0.1672 | 0.1757 | 0.1827 | 0.1880 | 0.1916 |
| 7 | 0.0536 | 0.0637 | 0.0745 | 0.0858 | 0.0974 | 0.1091 | 0.1207 | 0.1320 | 0.1426 | 0.1525 |
| 8 | 0.0214 | 0.0270 | 0.0334 | 0.0406 | 0.0487 | 0.0575 | 0.0670 | 0.0770 | 0.0874 | 0.0981 |
| 9 | 0.0069 | 0.0093 | 0.0122 | 0.0157 | 0.0198 | 0.0247 | 0.0303 | 0.0366 | 0.0436 | 0.0514 |
| 10 | 0.0018 | 0.0026 | 0.0036 | 0.0050 | 0.0066 | 0.0087 | 0.0112 | 0.0142 | 0.0178 | 0.0220 |
| 11 | 0.0004 | 0.0006 | 0.0009 | 0.0013 | 0.0018 | 0.0025 | 0.0034 | 0.0045 | 0.0060 | 0.0077 |
| 12 | 0.0001 | 0.0001 | 0.0002 | 0.0003 | 0.0004 | 0.0006 | 0.0008 | 0.0012 | 0.0016 | 0.0022 |
| 13 | 0.0000 | 0.0000 | 0.0000 | 0.0000 | 0.0001 | 0.0001 | 0.0002 | 0.0002 | 0.0004 | 0.0005 |

*(continued)*

## The Binomial Probability Distribution *(continued)*

| | $p =$ | 0.31 | 0.32 | 0.33 | 0.34 | 0.35 | 0.36 | 0.37 | 0.38 | 0.39 | 0.40 |
|---|---|---|---|---|---|---|---|---|---|---|---|
| $x =$ | 0 | 0.0009 | 0.0007 | 0.0005 | 0.0004 | 0.0003 | 0.0002 | 0.0002 | 0.0001 | 0.0001 | 0.0001 |
| | 1 | 0.0074 | 0.0059 | 0.0046 | 0.0036 | 0.0029 | 0.0022 | 0.0017 | 0.0013 | 0.0010 | 0.0008 |
| | 2 | 0.0299 | 0.0249 | 0.0206 | 0.0169 | 0.0138 | 0.0112 | 0.0091 | 0.0073 | 0.0058 | 0.0046 |
| | 3 | 0.0762 | 0.0664 | 0.0574 | 0.0494 | 0.0422 | 0.0358 | 0.0302 | 0.0253 | 0.0211 | 0.0175 |
| | 4 | 0.1370 | 0.1249 | 0.1131 | 0.1017 | 0.0909 | 0.0806 | 0.0710 | 0.0621 | 0.0540 | 0.0467 |
| | 5 | 0.1846 | 0.1764 | 0.1672 | 0.1572 | 0.1468 | 0.1360 | 0.1251 | 0.1143 | 0.1036 | 0.0933 |
| | 6 | 0.1935 | 0.1936 | 0.1921 | 0.1890 | 0.1844 | 0.1785 | 0.1714 | 0.1634 | 0.1546 | 0.1451 |
| | 7 | 0.1615 | 0.1692 | 0.1757 | 0.1808 | 0.1844 | 0.1865 | 0.1870 | 0.1860 | 0.1835 | 0.1797 |
| | 8 | 0.1088 | 0.1195 | 0.1298 | 0.1397 | 0.1489 | 0.1573 | 0.1647 | 0.1710 | 0.1760 | 0.1797 |
| | 9 | 0.0597 | 0.0687 | 0.0782 | 0.0880 | 0.0980 | 0.1082 | 0.1182 | 0.1281 | 0.1375 | 0.1464 |
| | 10 | 0.0268 | 0.0323 | 0.0385 | 0.0453 | 0.0528 | 0.0608 | 0.0694 | 0.0785 | 0.0879 | 0.0976 |
| | 11 | 0.0099 | 0.0124 | 0.0155 | 0.0191 | 0.0233 | 0.0280 | 0.0334 | 0.0394 | 0.0460 | 0.0532 |
| | 12 | 0.0030 | 0.0039 | 0.0051 | 0.0066 | 0.0083 | 0.0105 | 0.0131 | 0.0161 | 0.0196 | 0.0237 |
| | 13 | 0.0007 | 0.0010 | 0.0014 | 0.0018 | 0.0024 | 0.0032 | 0.0041 | 0.0053 | 0.0067 | 0.0085 |
| | 14 | 0.0001 | 0.0002 | 0.0003 | 0.0004 | 0.0006 | 0.0008 | 0.0010 | 0.0014 | 0.0018 | 0.0024 |
| | 15 | 0.0000 | 0.0000 | 0.0000 | 0.0001 | 0.0001 | 0.0001 | 0.0002 | 0.0003 | 0.0004 | 0.0005 |

| | $p =$ | 0.41 | 0.42 | 0.43 | 0.44 | 0.45 | 0.46 | 0.47 | 0.48 | 0.49 | 0.50 |
|---|---|---|---|---|---|---|---|---|---|---|---|
| $x =$ | 0 | 0.0000 | 0.0000 | 0.0000 | 0.0000 | 0.0000 | 0.0000 | 0.0000 | 0.0000 | 0.0000 | 0.0000 |
| | 1 | 0.0006 | 0.0004 | 0.0003 | 0.0002 | 0.0002 | 0.0001 | 0.0001 | 0.0001 | 0.0001 | 0.0000 |
| | 2 | 0.0037 | 0.0029 | 0.0022 | 0.0017 | 0.0013 | 0.0010 | 0.0008 | 0.0006 | 0.0004 | 0.0003 |
| | 3 | 0.0144 | 0.0118 | 0.0096 | 0.0077 | 0.0062 | 0.0049 | 0.0039 | 0.0031 | 0.0024 | 0.0018 |
| | 4 | 0.0400 | 0.0341 | 0.0289 | 0.0243 | 0.0203 | 0.0168 | 0.0138 | 0.0113 | 0.0092 | 0.0074 |
| | 5 | 0.0834 | 0.0741 | 0.0653 | 0.0572 | 0.0497 | 0.0429 | 0.0368 | 0.0313 | 0.0265 | 0.0222 |
| | 6 | 0.1353 | 0.1252 | 0.1150 | 0.1049 | 0.0949 | 0.0853 | 0.0761 | 0.0674 | 0.0593 | 0.0518 |
| | 7 | 0.1746 | 0.1683 | 0.1611 | 0.1530 | 0.1443 | 0.1350 | 0.1254 | 0.1156 | 0.1058 | 0.0961 |
| | 8 | 0.1820 | 0.1829 | 0.1823 | 0.1803 | 0.1771 | 0.1725 | 0.1668 | 0.1601 | 0.1525 | 0.1442 |
| | 9 | 0.1546 | 0.1618 | 0.1681 | 0.1732 | 0.1771 | 0.1796 | 0.1808 | 0.1806 | 0.1791 | 0.1762 |
| | 10 | 0.1074 | 0.1172 | 0.1268 | 0.1361 | 0.1449 | 0.1530 | 0.1603 | 0.1667 | 0.1721 | 0.1762 |
| | 11 | 0.0611 | 0.0694 | 0.0783 | 0.0875 | 0.0970 | 0.1066 | 0.1163 | 0.1259 | 0.1352 | 0.1442 |
| | 12 | 0.0283 | 0.0335 | 0.0394 | 0.0458 | 0.0529 | 0.0606 | 0.0688 | 0.0775 | 0.0866 | 0.0961 |
| | 13 | 0.0106 | 0.0131 | 0.0160 | 0.0194 | 0.0233 | 0.0278 | 0.0328 | 0.0385 | 0.0448 | 0.0518 |
| | 14 | 0.0032 | 0.0041 | 0.0052 | 0.0065 | 0.0082 | 0.0101 | 0.0125 | 0.0152 | 0.0185 | 0.0222 |
| | 15 | 0.0007 | 0.0010 | 0.0013 | 0.0017 | 0.0022 | 0.0029 | 0.0037 | 0.0047 | 0.0059 | 0.0074 |
| | 16 | 0.0001 | 0.0002 | 0.0002 | 0.0003 | 0.0005 | 0.0006 | 0.0008 | 0.0011 | 0.0014 | 0.0018 |
| | 17 | 0.0000 | 0.0000 | 0.0000 | 0.0000 | 0.0001 | 0.0001 | 0.0001 | 0.0002 | 0.0002 | 0.0003 |

*(continued)*

## The Binomial Probability Distribution *(continued)*

### $n = 20$

| $p =$ | 0.01 | 0.02 | 0.03 | 0.04 | 0.05 | 0.06 | 0.07 | 0.08 | 0.09 | 0.10 |
|---|---|---|---|---|---|---|---|---|---|---|
| $x = $ 0 | 0.8179 | 0.6676 | 0.5438 | 0.4420 | 0.3585 | 0.2901 | 0.2342 | 0.1887 | 0.1516 | 0.1216 |
| 1 | 0.1652 | 0.2725 | 0.3364 | 0.3683 | 0.3774 | 0.3703 | 0.3526 | 0.3282 | 0.3000 | 0.2702 |
| 2 | 0.0159 | 0.0528 | 0.0988 | 0.1458 | 0.1887 | 0.2246 | 0.2521 | 0.2711 | 0.2818 | 0.2852 |
| 3 | 0.0010 | 0.0065 | 0.0183 | 0.0364 | 0.0596 | 0.0860 | 0.1139 | 0.1414 | 0.1672 | 0.1901 |
| 4 | 0.0000 | 0.0006 | 0.0024 | 0.0065 | 0.0133 | 0.0233 | 0.0364 | 0.0523 | 0.0703 | 0.0898 |
| 5 | 0.0000 | 0.0000 | 0.0002 | 0.0009 | 0.0022 | 0.0048 | 0.0088 | 0.0145 | 0.0222 | 0.0319 |
| 6 | 0.0000 | 0.0000 | 0.0000 | 0.0001 | 0.0003 | 0.0008 | 0.0017 | 0.0032 | 0.0055 | 0.0089 |
| 7 | 0.0000 | 0.0000 | 0.0000 | 0.0000 | 0.0000 | 0.0001 | 0.0002 | 0.0005 | 0.0011 | 0.0020 |
| 8 | 0.0000 | 0.0000 | 0.0000 | 0.0000 | 0.0000 | 0.0000 | 0.0000 | 0.0001 | 0.0002 | 0.0004 |

| $p =$ | 0.11 | 0.12 | 0.13 | 0.14 | 0.15 | 0.16 | 0.17 | 0.18 | 0.19 | 0.20 |
|---|---|---|---|---|---|---|---|---|---|---|
| $x = $ 0 | 0.0972 | 0.0776 | 0.0617 | 0.0490 | 0.0388 | 0.0306 | 0.0241 | 0.0189 | 0.0148 | 0.0115 |
| 1 | 0.2403 | 0.2115 | 0.1844 | 0.1595 | 0.1368 | 0.1165 | 0.0986 | 0.0829 | 0.0693 | 0.0576 |
| 2 | 0.2822 | 0.2740 | 0.2618 | 0.2466 | 0.2293 | 0.2109 | 0.1919 | 0.1730 | 0.1545 | 0.1369 |
| 3 | 0.2093 | 0.2242 | 0.2347 | 0.2409 | 0.2428 | 0.2410 | 0.2358 | 0.2278 | 0.2175 | 0.2054 |
| 4 | 0.1099 | 0.1299 | 0.1491 | 0.1666 | 0.1821 | 0.1951 | 0.2053 | 0.2125 | 0.2168 | 0.2182 |
| 5 | 0.0435 | 0.0567 | 0.0713 | 0.0868 | 0.1028 | 0.1189 | 0.1345 | 0.1493 | 0.1627 | 0.1746 |
| 6 | 0.0134 | 0.0193 | 0.0266 | 0.0353 | 0.0454 | 0.0566 | 0.0689 | 0.0819 | 0.0954 | 0.1091 |
| 7 | 0.0033 | 0.0053 | 0.0080 | 0.0115 | 0.0160 | 0.0216 | 0.0282 | 0.0360 | 0.0448 | 0.0545 |
| 8 | 0.0007 | 0.0012 | 0.0019 | 0.0030 | 0.0046 | 0.0067 | 0.0094 | 0.0128 | 0.0171 | 0.0222 |
| 9 | 0.0001 | 0.0002 | 0.0004 | 0.0007 | 0.0011 | 0.0017 | 0.0026 | 0.0038 | 0.0053 | 0.0074 |
| 10 | 0.0000 | 0.0000 | 0.0001 | 0.0001 | 0.0002 | 0.0004 | 0.0006 | 0.0009 | 0.0014 | 0.0020 |
| 11 | 0.0000 | 0.0000 | 0.0000 | 0.0000 | 0.0000 | 0.0001 | 0.0001 | 0.0002 | 0.0003 | 0.0005 |

| $p =$ | 0.21 | 0.22 | 0.23 | 0.24 | 0.25 | 0.26 | 0.27 | 0.28 | 0.29 | 0.30 |
|---|---|---|---|---|---|---|---|---|---|---|
| $x = $ 0 | 0.0090 | 0.0069 | 0.0054 | 0.0041 | 0.0032 | 0.0024 | 0.0018 | 0.0014 | 0.0011 | 0.0008 |
| 1 | 0.0477 | 0.0392 | 0.0321 | 0.0261 | 0.0211 | 0.0170 | 0.0137 | 0.0109 | 0.0087 | 0.0068 |
| 2 | 0.1204 | 0.1050 | 0.0910 | 0.0783 | 0.0669 | 0.0569 | 0.0480 | 0.0403 | 0.0336 | 0.0278 |
| 3 | 0.1920 | 0.1777 | 0.1631 | 0.1484 | 0.1339 | 0.1199 | 0.1065 | 0.0940 | 0.0823 | 0.0716 |
| 4 | 0.2169 | 0.2131 | 0.2070 | 0.1991 | 0.1897 | 0.1790 | 0.1675 | 0.1553 | 0.1429 | 0.1304 |
| 5 | 0.1845 | 0.1923 | 0.1979 | 0.2012 | 0.2023 | 0.2013 | 0.1982 | 0.1933 | 0.1868 | 0.1789 |
| 6 | 0.1226 | 0.1356 | 0.1478 | 0.1589 | 0.1686 | 0.1768 | 0.1833 | 0.1879 | 0.1907 | 0.1916 |
| 7 | 0.0652 | 0.0765 | 0.0883 | 0.1003 | 0.1124 | 0.1242 | 0.1356 | 0.1462 | 0.1558 | 0.1643 |
| 8 | 0.0282 | 0.0351 | 0.0429 | 0.0515 | 0.0609 | 0.0709 | 0.0815 | 0.0924 | 0.1034 | 0.1144 |
| 9 | 0.0100 | 0.0132 | 0.0171 | 0.0217 | 0.0271 | 0.0332 | 0.0402 | 0.0479 | 0.0563 | 0.0654 |
| 10 | 0.0029 | 0.0041 | 0.0056 | 0.0075 | 0.0099 | 0.0128 | 0.0163 | 0.0205 | 0.0253 | 0.0308 |
| 11 | 0.0007 | 0.0010 | 0.0015 | 0.0022 | 0.0030 | 0.0041 | 0.0055 | 0.0072 | 0.0094 | 0.0120 |
| 12 | 0.0001 | 0.0002 | 0.0003 | 0.0005 | 0.0008 | 0.0011 | 0.0015 | 0.0021 | 0.0029 | 0.0039 |
| 13 | 0.0000 | 0.0000 | 0.0001 | 0.0001 | 0.0002 | 0.0002 | 0.0003 | 0.0005 | 0.0007 | 0.0010 |

*(continued)*

## The Binomial Probability Distribution *(continued)*

| | p = | 0.31 | 0.32 | 0.33 | 0.34 | 0.35 | 0.36 | 0.37 | 0.38 | 0.39 | 0.40 |
|---|---|---|---|---|---|---|---|---|---|---|---|
| x = | 0 | 0.0006 | 0.0004 | 0.0003 | 0.0002 | 0.0002 | 0.0001 | 0.0001 | 0.0001 | 0.0001 | 0.0000 |
| | 1 | 0.0054 | 0.0042 | 0.0033 | 0.0025 | 0.0020 | 0.0015 | 0.0011 | 0.0009 | 0.0007 | 0.0005 |
| | 2 | 0.0229 | 0.0188 | 0.0153 | 0.0124 | 0.0100 | 0.0080 | 0.0064 | 0.0050 | 0.0040 | 0.0031 |
| | 3 | 0.0619 | 0.0531 | 0.0453 | 0.0383 | 0.0323 | 0.0270 | 0.0224 | 0.0185 | 0.0152 | 0.0123 |
| | 4 | 0.1181 | 0.1062 | 0.0947 | 0.0839 | 0.0738 | 0.0645 | 0.0559 | 0.0482 | 0.0412 | 0.0350 |
| | 5 | 0.1698 | 0.1599 | 0.1493 | 0.1384 | 0.1272 | 0.1161 | 0.1051 | 0.0945 | 0.0843 | 0.0746 |
| | 6 | 0.1907 | 0.1881 | 0.1839 | 0.1782 | 0.1712 | 0.1632 | 0.1543 | 0.1447 | 0.1347 | 0.1244 |
| | 7 | 0.1714 | 0.1770 | 0.1811 | 0.1836 | 0.1844 | 0.1836 | 0.1812 | 0.1774 | 0.1722 | 0.1659 |
| | 8 | 0.1251 | 0.1354 | 0.1450 | 0.1537 | 0.1614 | 0.1678 | 0.1730 | 0.1767 | 0.1790 | 0.1797 |
| | 9 | 0.0750 | 0.0849 | 0.0952 | 0.1056 | 0.1158 | 0.1259 | 0.1354 | 0.1444 | 0.1526 | 0.1597 |
| | 10 | 0.0370 | 0.0440 | 0.0516 | 0.0598 | 0.0686 | 0.0779 | 0.0875 | 0.0974 | 0.1073 | 0.1171 |
| | 11 | 0.0151 | 0.0188 | 0.0231 | 0.0280 | 0.0336 | 0.0398 | 0.0467 | 0.0542 | 0.0624 | 0.0710 |
| | 12 | 0.0051 | 0.0066 | 0.0085 | 0.0108 | 0.0136 | 0.0168 | 0.0206 | 0.0249 | 0.0299 | 0.0355 |
| | 13 | 0.0014 | 0.0019 | 0.0026 | 0.0034 | 0.0045 | 0.0058 | 0.0074 | 0.0094 | 0.0118 | 0.0146 |
| | 14 | 0.0003 | 0.0005 | 0.0006 | 0.0009 | 0.0012 | 0.0016 | 0.0022 | 0.0029 | 0.0038 | 0.0049 |
| | 15 | 0.0001 | 0.0001 | 0.0001 | 0.0002 | 0.0003 | 0.0004 | 0.0005 | 0.0007 | 0.0010 | 0.0013 |
| | 16 | 0.0000 | 0.0000 | 0.0000 | 0.0000 | 0.0000 | 0.0001 | 0.0001 | 0.0001 | 0.0002 | 0.0003 |

| | p = | 0.41 | 0.42 | 0.43 | 0.44 | 0.45 | 0.46 | 0.47 | 0.48 | 0.49 | 0.50 |
|---|---|---|---|---|---|---|---|---|---|---|---|
| x = | 0 | 0.0000 | 0.0000 | 0.0000 | 0.0000 | 0.0000 | 0.0000 | 0.0000 | 0.0000 | 0.0000 | 0.0000 |
| | 1 | 0.0004 | 0.0003 | 0.0002 | 0.0001 | 0.0001 | 0.0001 | 0.0001 | 0.0000 | 0.0000 | 0.0000 |
| | 2 | 0.0024 | 0.0018 | 0.0014 | 0.0011 | 0.0008 | 0.0006 | 0.0005 | 0.0003 | 0.0002 | 0.0002 |
| | 3 | 0.0100 | 0.0080 | 0.0064 | 0.0051 | 0.0040 | 0.0031 | 0.0024 | 0.0019 | 0.0014 | 0.0011 |
| | 4 | 0.0295 | 0.0247 | 0.0206 | 0.0170 | 0.0139 | 0.0113 | 0.0092 | 0.0074 | 0.0059 | 0.0046 |
| | 5 | 0.0656 | 0.0573 | 0.0496 | 0.0427 | 0.0365 | 0.0309 | 0.0260 | 0.0217 | 0.0180 | 0.0148 |
| | 6 | 0.1140 | 0.1037 | 0.0936 | 0.0839 | 0.0746 | 0.0658 | 0.0577 | 0.0501 | 0.0432 | 0.0370 |
| | 7 | 0.1585 | 0.1502 | 0.1413 | 0.1318 | 0.1221 | 0.1122 | 0.1023 | 0.0925 | 0.0830 | 0.0739 |
| | 8 | 0.1790 | 0.1768 | 0.1732 | 0.1683 | 0.1623 | 0.1553 | 0.1474 | 0.1388 | 0.1296 | 0.1201 |
| | 9 | 0.1658 | 0.1707 | 0.1742 | 0.1763 | 0.1771 | 0.1763 | 0.1742 | 0.1708 | 0.1661 | 0.1602 |
| | 10 | 0.1268 | 0.1359 | 0.1446 | 0.1524 | 0.1593 | 0.1652 | 0.1700 | 0.1734 | 0.1755 | 0.1762 |
| | 11 | 0.0801 | 0.0895 | 0.0991 | 0.1089 | 0.1185 | 0.1280 | 0.1370 | 0.1455 | 0.1533 | 0.1602 |
| | 12 | 0.0417 | 0.0486 | 0.0561 | 0.0642 | 0.0727 | 0.0818 | 0.0911 | 0.1007 | 0.1105 | 0.1201 |
| | 13 | 0.0178 | 0.0217 | 0.0260 | 0.0310 | 0.0366 | 0.0429 | 0.0497 | 0.0572 | 0.0653 | 0.0739 |
| | 14 | 0.0062 | 0.0078 | 0.0098 | 0.0122 | 0.0150 | 0.0183 | 0.0221 | 0.0264 | 0.0314 | 0.0370 |
| | 15 | 0.0017 | 0.0023 | 0.0030 | 0.0038 | 0.0049 | 0.0062 | 0.0078 | 0.0098 | 0.0121 | 0.0148 |
| | 16 | 0.0004 | 0.0005 | 0.0007 | 0.0009 | 0.0013 | 0.0017 | 0.0022 | 0.0028 | 0.0036 | 0.0046 |
| | 17 | 0.0001 | 0.0001 | 0.0001 | 0.0002 | 0.0002 | 0.0003 | 0.0005 | 0.0006 | 0.0008 | 0.0011 |
| | 18 | 0.0000 | 0.0000 | 0.0000 | 0.0000 | 0.0000 | 0.0000 | 0.0001 | 0.0001 | 0.0001 | 0.0002 |

# Appendix B

**The Proportion of the Area under the Normal Curve**

| Z | Area between −Z and +Z | Area beyond −Z or +Z | Z | Area between −Z and +Z | Area beyond −Z or +Z |
|---|---|---|---|---|---|
| 0.00 | 0.0000 | 0.5000 | 0.25 | 0.1974 | 0.4013 |
| 0.01 | 0.0080 | 0.4960 | 0.26 | 0.2051 | 0.3974 |
| 0.02 | 0.0160 | 0.4920 | 0.27 | 0.2128 | 0.3936 |
| 0.03 | 0.0239 | 0.4880 | 0.28 | 0.2205 | 0.3897 |
| 0.04 | 0.0319 | 0.4840 | 0.29 | 0.2282 | 0.3859 |
| 0.05 | 0.0399 | 0.4801 | 0.30 | 0.2358 | 0.3821 |
| 0.06 | 0.0478 | 0.4761 | 0.31 | 0.2434 | 0.3783 |
| 0.07 | 0.0558 | 0.4721 | 0.32 | 0.2510 | 0.3745 |
| 0.08 | 0.0638 | 0.4681 | 0.33 | 0.2586 | 0.3707 |
| 0.09 | 0.0717 | 0.4641 | 0.34 | 0.2661 | 0.3669 |
| 0.10 | 0.0797 | 0.4602 | 0.35 | 0.2737 | 0.3632 |
| 0.11 | 0.0876 | 0.4562 | 0.36 | 0.2812 | 0.3594 |
| 0.12 | 0.0955 | 0.4522 | 0.37 | 0.2886 | 0.3557 |
| 0.13 | 0.1034 | 0.4483 | 0.38 | 0.2961 | 0.3520 |
| 0.14 | 0.1113 | 0.4443 | 0.39 | 0.3035 | 0.3483 |
| 0.15 | 0.1192 | 0.4404 | 0.40 | 0.3108 | 0.3446 |
| 0.16 | 0.1271 | 0.4364 | 0.41 | 0.3182 | 0.3409 |
| 0.17 | 0.1350 | 0.4325 | 0.42 | 0.3255 | 0.3372 |
| 0.18 | 0.1428 | 0.4286 | 0.43 | 0.3328 | 0.3336 |
| 0.19 | 0.1507 | 0.4247 | 0.44 | 0.3401 | 0.3300 |
| 0.20 | 0.1585 | 0.4207 | 0.45 | 0.3473 | 0.3264 |
| 0.21 | 0.1663 | 0.4168 | 0.46 | 0.3545 | 0.3228 |
| 0.22 | 0.1741 | 0.4129 | 0.47 | 0.3616 | 0.3192 |
| 0.23 | 0.1819 | 0.4090 | 0.48 | 0.3688 | 0.3156 |
| 0.24 | 0.1897 | 0.4052 | 0.49 | 0.3759 | 0.3121 |

*(continued)*

**The Proportion of the Area under the Normal Curve** *(continued)*

| Z | Area between −Z and +Z | Area beyond −Z or +Z | Z | Area between −Z and +Z | Area beyond −Z or +Z |
|------|------|------|------|------|------|
| 0.50 | 0.3829 | 0.3085 | 0.90 | 0.6319 | 0.1841 |
| 0.51 | 0.3899 | 0.3050 | 0.91 | 0.6372 | 0.1814 |
| 0.52 | 0.3969 | 0.3015 | 0.92 | 0.6424 | 0.1788 |
| 0.53 | 0.4039 | 0.2981 | 0.93 | 0.6476 | 0.1762 |
| 0.54 | 0.4108 | 0.2946 | 0.94 | 0.6528 | 0.1736 |
| 0.55 | 0.4177 | 0.2912 | 0.95 | 0.6579 | 0.1711 |
| 0.56 | 0.4245 | 0.2877 | 0.96 | 0.6629 | 0.1685 |
| 0.57 | 0.4313 | 0.2843 | 0.97 | 0.6680 | 0.1660 |
| 0.58 | 0.4381 | 0.2810 | 0.98 | 0.6729 | 0.1635 |
| 0.59 | 0.4448 | 0.2776 | 0.99 | 0.6778 | 0.1611 |
| 0.60 | 0.4515 | 0.2743 | 1.00 | 0.6827 | 0.1587 |
| 0.61 | 0.4581 | 0.2709 | 1.01 | 0.6875 | 0.1562 |
| 0.62 | 0.4647 | 0.2676 | 1.02 | 0.6923 | 0.1539 |
| 0.63 | 0.4713 | 0.2643 | 1.03 | 0.6970 | 0.1515 |
| 0.64 | 0.4778 | 0.2611 | 1.04 | 0.7017 | 0.1492 |
| 0.65 | 0.4843 | 0.2578 | 1.05 | 0.7063 | 0.1469 |
| 0.66 | 0.4907 | 0.2546 | 1.06 | 0.7109 | 0.1446 |
| 0.67 | 0.4971 | 0.2514 | 1.07 | 0.7154 | 0.1423 |
| 0.68 | 0.5035 | 0.2483 | 1.08 | 0.7199 | 0.1401 |
| 0.69 | 0.5098 | 0.2451 | 1.09 | 0.7243 | 0.1379 |
| 0.70 | 0.5161 | 0.2420 | 1.10 | 0.7287 | 0.1357 |
| 0.71 | 0.5223 | 0.2389 | 1.11 | 0.7330 | 0.1335 |
| 0.72 | 0.5285 | 0.2358 | 1.12 | 0.7373 | 0.1314 |
| 0.73 | 0.5346 | 0.2327 | 1.13 | 0.7415 | 0.1292 |
| 0.74 | 0.5407 | 0.2296 | 1.14 | 0.7457 | 0.1271 |
| 0.75 | 0.5467 | 0.2266 | 1.15 | 0.7499 | 0.1251 |
| 0.76 | 0.5527 | 0.2236 | 1.16 | 0.7540 | 0.1230 |
| 0.77 | 0.5587 | 0.2206 | 1.17 | 0.7580 | 0.1210 |
| 0.78 | 0.5646 | 0.2177 | 1.18 | 0.7620 | 0.1190 |
| 0.79 | 0.5705 | 0.2148 | 1.19 | 0.7660 | 0.1170 |
| 0.80 | 0.5763 | 0.2119 | 1.20 | 0.7699 | 0.1151 |
| 0.81 | 0.5821 | 0.2090 | 1.21 | 0.7737 | 0.1131 |
| 0.82 | 0.5878 | 0.2061 | 1.22 | 0.7775 | 0.1112 |
| 0.83 | 0.5935 | 0.2033 | 1.23 | 0.7813 | 0.1093 |
| 0.84 | 0.5991 | 0.2005 | 1.24 | 0.7850 | 0.1075 |
| 0.85 | 0.6047 | 0.1977 | 1.25 | 0.7887 | 0.1056 |
| 0.86 | 0.6102 | 0.1949 | 1.26 | 0.7923 | 0.1038 |
| 0.87 | 0.6157 | 0.1922 | 1.27 | 0.7959 | 0.1020 |
| 0.88 | 0.6211 | 0.1894 | 1.28 | 0.7995 | 0.1003 |
| 0.89 | 0.6265 | 0.1867 | 1.29 | 0.8029 | 0.0985 |

*(continued)*

**The Proportion of the Area under the Normal Curve** *(continued)*

| Z | Area between −Z and +Z | Area beyond −Z or +Z | Z | Area between −Z and +Z | Area beyond −Z or +Z |
|------|------|------|------|------|------|
| 1.30 | 0.8064 | 0.0968 | 1.70 | 0.9109 | 0.0446 |
| 1.31 | 0.8098 | 0.0951 | 1.71 | 0.9127 | 0.0436 |
| 1.32 | 0.8132 | 0.0934 | 1.72 | 0.9146 | 0.0427 |
| 1.33 | 0.8165 | 0.0918 | 1.73 | 0.9164 | 0.0418 |
| 1.34 | 0.8198 | 0.0901 | 1.74 | 0.9181 | 0.0409 |
| 1.35 | 0.8230 | 0.0885 | 1.75 | 0.9199 | 0.0401 |
| 1.36 | 0.8262 | 0.0869 | 1.76 | 0.9216 | 0.0392 |
| 1.37 | 0.8293 | 0.0853 | 1.77 | 0.9233 | 0.0384 |
| 1.38 | 0.8324 | 0.0838 | 1.78 | 0.9249 | 0.0375 |
| 1.39 | 0.8355 | 0.0823 | 1.79 | 0.9265 | 0.0367 |
| 1.40 | 0.8385 | 0.0808 | 1.80 | 0.9281 | 0.0359 |
| 1.41 | 0.8415 | 0.0793 | 1.81 | 0.9297 | 0.0351 |
| 1.42 | 0.8444 | 0.0778 | 1.82 | 0.9312 | 0.0344 |
| 1.43 | 0.8473 | 0.0764 | 1.83 | 0.9328 | 0.0336 |
| 1.44 | 0.8501 | 0.0749 | 1.84 | 0.9342 | 0.0329 |
| 1.45 | 0.8529 | 0.0735 | 1.85 | 0.9357 | 0.0322 |
| 1.46 | 0.8557 | 0.0721 | 1.86 | 0.9371 | 0.0314 |
| 1.47 | 0.8584 | 0.0708 | 1.87 | 0.9385 | 0.0307 |
| 1.48 | 0.8611 | 0.0694 | 1.88 | 0.9399 | 0.0301 |
| 1.49 | 0.8638 | 0.0681 | 1.89 | 0.9412 | 0.0294 |
| 1.50 | 0.8664 | 0.0668 | 1.90 | 0.9426 | 0.0287 |
| 1.51 | 0.8690 | 0.0655 | 1.91 | 0.9439 | 0.0281 |
| 1.52 | 0.8715 | 0.0643 | 1.92 | 0.9451 | 0.0274 |
| 1.53 | 0.8740 | 0.0630 | 1.93 | 0.9464 | 0.0268 |
| 1.54 | 0.8764 | 0.0618 | 1.94 | 0.9476 | 0.0262 |
| 1.55 | 0.8789 | 0.0606 | 1.95 | 0.9488 | 0.0256 |
| 1.56 | 0.8812 | 0.0594 | 1.96 | 0.9500 | 0.0250 |
| 1.57 | 0.8836 | 0.0582 | 1.97 | 0.9512 | 0.0244 |
| 1.58 | 0.8859 | 0.0571 | 1.98 | 0.9523 | 0.0239 |
| 1.59 | 0.8882 | 0.0559 | 1.99 | 0.9534 | 0.0233 |
| 1.60 | 0.8904 | 0.0548 | 2.00 | 0.9545 | 0.0228 |
| 1.61 | 0.8926 | 0.0537 | 2.01 | 0.9556 | 0.0222 |
| 1.62 | 0.8948 | 0.0526 | 2.02 | 0.9566 | 0.0217 |
| 1.63 | 0.8969 | 0.0516 | 2.03 | 0.9576 | 0.0212 |
| 1.64 | 0.8990 | 0.0505 | 2.04 | 0.9586 | 0.0207 |
| 1.65 | 0.9011 | 0.0495 | 2.05 | 0.9596 | 0.0202 |
| 1.66 | 0.9031 | 0.0485 | 2.06 | 0.9606 | 0.0197 |
| 1.67 | 0.9051 | 0.0475 | 2.07 | 0.9615 | 0.0192 |
| 1.68 | 0.9070 | 0.0465 | 2.08 | 0.9625 | 0.0188 |
| 1.69 | 0.9090 | 0.0455 | 2.09 | 0.9634 | 0.0183 |

*(continued)*

**The Proportion of the Area under the Normal Curve** *(continued)*

| Z | Area between −Z and +Z | Area beyond −Z or +Z | Z | Area between −Z and +Z | Area beyond −Z or +Z |
|---|---|---|---|---|---|
| 2.10 | 0.9643 | 0.0179 | 2.50 | 0.9876 | 0.0062 |
| 2.11 | 0.9651 | 0.0174 | 2.51 | 0.9879 | 0.0060 |
| 2.12 | 0.9660 | 0.0170 | 2.52 | 0.9883 | 0.0059 |
| 2.13 | 0.9668 | 0.0166 | 2.53 | 0.9886 | 0.0057 |
| 2.14 | 0.9676 | 0.0162 | 2.54 | 0.9889 | 0.0055 |
| 2.15 | 0.9684 | 0.0158 | 2.55 | 0.9892 | 0.0054 |
| 2.16 | 0.9692 | 0.0154 | 2.56 | 0.9895 | 0.0052 |
| 2.17 | 0.9700 | 0.0150 | 2.57 | 0.9898 | 0.0051 |
| 2.18 | 0.9707 | 0.0146 | 2.58 | 0.9901 | 0.0049 |
| 2.19 | 0.9715 | 0.0143 | 2.59 | 0.9904 | 0.0048 |
| 2.20 | 0.9722 | 0.0139 | 2.60 | 0.9907 | 0.0047 |
| 2.21 | 0.9729 | 0.0136 | 2.61 | 0.9909 | 0.0045 |
| 2.22 | 0.9736 | 0.0132 | 2.62 | 0.9912 | 0.0044 |
| 2.23 | 0.9743 | 0.0129 | 2.63 | 0.9915 | 0.0043 |
| 2.24 | 0.9749 | 0.0125 | 2.64 | 0.9917 | 0.0041 |
| 2.25 | 0.9756 | 0.0122 | 2.65 | 0.9920 | 0.0040 |
| 2.26 | 0.9762 | 0.0119 | 2.66 | 0.9922 | 0.0039 |
| 2.27 | 0.9768 | 0.0116 | 2.67 | 0.9924 | 0.0038 |
| 2.28 | 0.9774 | 0.0113 | 2.68 | 0.9926 | 0.0037 |
| 2.29 | 0.9780 | 0.0110 | 2.69 | 0.9929 | 0.0036 |
| 2.30 | 0.9786 | 0.0107 | 2.70 | 0.9931 | 0.0035 |
| 2.31 | 0.9791 | 0.0104 | 2.71 | 0.9933 | 0.0034 |
| 2.32 | 0.9797 | 0.0102 | 2.72 | 0.9935 | 0.0033 |
| 2.33 | 0.9802 | 0.0099 | 2.73 | 0.9937 | 0.0032 |
| 2.34 | 0.9807 | 0.0096 | 2.74 | 0.9939 | 0.0031 |
| 2.35 | 0.9812 | 0.0094 | 2.75 | 0.9940 | 0.0030 |
| 2.36 | 0.9817 | 0.0091 | 2.76 | 0.9942 | 0.0029 |
| 2.37 | 0.9822 | 0.0089 | 2.77 | 0.9944 | 0.0028 |
| 2.38 | 0.9827 | 0.0087 | 2.78 | 0.9946 | 0.0027 |
| 2.39 | 0.9832 | 0.0084 | 2.79 | 0.9947 | 0.0026 |
| 2.40 | 0.9836 | 0.0082 | 2.80 | 0.9949 | 0.0026 |
| 2.41 | 0.9840 | 0.0080 | 2.81 | 0.9950 | 0.0025 |
| 2.42 | 0.9845 | 0.0078 | 2.82 | 0.9952 | 0.0024 |
| 2.43 | 0.9849 | 0.0075 | 2.83 | 0.9953 | 0.0023 |
| 2.44 | 0.9853 | 0.0073 | 2.84 | 0.9955 | 0.0023 |
| 2.45 | 0.9857 | 0.0071 | 2.85 | 0.9956 | 0.0022 |
| 2.46 | 0.9861 | 0.0069 | 2.86 | 0.9958 | 0.0021 |
| 2.47 | 0.9865 | 0.0068 | 2.87 | 0.9959 | 0.0021 |
| 2.48 | 0.9869 | 0.0066 | 2.88 | 0.9960 | 0.0020 |
| 2.49 | 0.9872 | 0.0064 | 2.89 | 0.9961 | 0.0019 |

*(continued)*

**The Proportion of the Area under the Normal Curve** *(continued)*

| Z | Area between −Z and +Z | Area beyond −Z or +Z | Z | Area between −Z and +Z | Area beyond −Z or +Z |
|---|---|---|---|---|---|
| 2.90 | 0.9963 | 0.0019 | 3.15 | 0.9984 | 0.0008 |
| 2.91 | 0.9964 | 0.0018 | 3.16 | 0.9984 | 0.0008 |
| 2.92 | 0.9965 | 0.0018 | 3.17 | 0.9985 | 0.0008 |
| 2.93 | 0.9966 | 0.0017 | 3.18 | 0.9985 | 0.0007 |
| 2.94 | 0.9967 | 0.0016 | 3.19 | 0.9986 | 0.0007 |
| 2.95 | 0.9968 | 0.0016 | 3.20 | 0.9986 | 0.0007 |
| 2.96 | 0.9969 | 0.0015 | 3.21 | 0.9987 | 0.0007 |
| 2.97 | 0.9970 | 0.0015 | 3.22 | 0.9987 | 0.0006 |
| 2.98 | 0.9971 | 0.0014 | 3.23 | 0.9988 | 0.0006 |
| 2.99 | 0.9972 | 0.0014 | 3.24 | 0.9988 | 0.0006 |
| 3.00 | 0.9973 | 0.0013 | 3.25 | 0.9988 | 0.0006 |
| 3.01 | 0.9974 | 0.0013 | 3.30 | 0.9990 | 0.0005 |
| 3.02 | 0.9975 | 0.0013 | 3.35 | 0.9992 | 0.0004 |
| 3.03 | 0.9976 | 0.0012 | 3.40 | 0.9993 | 0.0003 |
| 3.04 | 0.9976 | 0.0012 | 3.50 | 0.9995 | 0.0002 |
| 3.05 | 0.9977 | 0.0011 | 3.60 | 0.9997 | 0.0002 |
| 3.06 | 0.9978 | 0.0011 | 3.70 | 0.9998 | 0.0001 |
| 3.07 | 0.9979 | 0.0011 | 3.80 | 0.9999 | 0.0001 |
| 3.08 | 0.9979 | 0.0010 | 3.90 | 0.9999 | 0.0000 |
| 3.09 | 0.9980 | 0.0010 | 4.00 | 0.9999 | 0.0000 |
| 3.10 | 0.9981 | 0.0010 | | | |
| 3.11 | 0.9981 | 0.0009 | | | |
| 3.12 | 0.9982 | 0.0009 | | | |
| 3.13 | 0.9983 | 0.0009 | | | |
| 3.14 | 0.9983 | 0.0008 | | | |

# Appendix C

**Critical Values of the _Z_ Statistic**

| | | Level of significance | | | |
|---|---|---|---|---|---|
| | | *Two-tailed test* | | | |
| 0.20 | 0.10 | 0.05 | 0.02 | 0.01 | 0.001 |
| | | *One-tailed test* | | | |
| 0.10 | 0.05 | 0.025 | 0.01 | 0.005 | 0.0005 |
| **1.282** | **1.645** | **1.960** | **2.326** | **2.576** | **3.291** |

*Note:* To be significant, the observed value of Z must be greater than or equal to the value shown in the table.

# Appendix D

**Critical Values for the Chi-Square Statistic**

| Degrees of freedom | Level of significance | | | | |
|---|---|---|---|---|---|
| | *0.1* | *0.05* | *0.02* | *0.01* | *0.005* |
| 1 | 2.706 | 3.841 | 5.412 | 6.635 | 7.879 |
| 2 | 4.605 | 5.991 | 7.824 | 9.210 | 10.597 |
| 3 | 6.251 | 7.815 | 9.837 | 11.345 | 12.838 |
| 4 | 7.779 | 9.488 | 11.668 | 13.277 | 14.860 |
| 5 | 9.236 | 11.070 | 13.388 | 15.086 | 16.750 |
| 6 | 10.645 | 12.592 | 15.033 | 16.812 | 18.548 |
| 7 | 12.017 | 14.067 | 16.622 | 18.475 | 20.278 |
| 8 | 13.362 | 15.507 | 18.168 | 20.090 | 21.955 |
| 9 | 14.684 | 16.919 | 19.679 | 21.666 | 23.589 |
| 10 | 15.987 | 18.307 | 21.161 | 23.209 | 25.188 |
| 11 | 17.275 | 19.675 | 22.618 | 24.725 | 26.757 |
| 12 | 18.549 | 21.026 | 24.054 | 26.217 | 28.300 |
| 13 | 19.812 | 22.362 | 25.472 | 27.688 | 29.819 |
| 14 | 21.064 | 23.685 | 26.873 | 29.141 | 31.319 |
| 15 | 22.307 | 24.996 | 28.259 | 30.578 | 32.801 |
| 16 | 23.542 | 26.296 | 29.633 | 32.000 | 34.267 |
| 17 | 24.769 | 27.587 | 30.995 | 33.409 | 35.718 |
| 18 | 25.989 | 28.869 | 32.346 | 34.805 | 37.156 |
| 19 | 27.204 | 30.144 | 33.687 | 36.191 | 38.582 |
| 20 | 28.412 | 31.410 | 35.020 | 37.566 | 39.997 |
| 21 | 29.615 | 32.671 | 36.343 | 38.932 | 41.401 |
| 22 | 30.813 | 33.924 | 37.659 | 40.289 | 42.796 |
| 23 | 32.007 | 35.172 | 38.968 | 41.638 | 44.181 |
| 24 | 33.196 | 36.415 | 40.270 | 42.980 | 45.559 |
| 25 | 34.382 | 37.652 | 41.566 | 44.314 | 46.928 |

*(continued)*

**Critical Values for the Chi-Square Statistic** *(continued)*

| Degrees of freedom | Level of significance | | | | |
|---|---|---|---|---|---|
| | *0.1* | *0.05* | *0.02* | *0.01* | *0.005* |
| 26 | 35.563 | 38.885 | 42.856 | 45.642 | 48.290 |
| 27 | 36.741 | 40.113 | 44.140 | 46.963 | 49.645 |
| 28 | 37.916 | 41.337 | 45.419 | 48.278 | 50.993 |
| 29 | 39.087 | 42.557 | 46.693 | 49.588 | 52.336 |
| 30 | 40.256 | 43.773 | 47.962 | 50.892 | 53.672 |

*Note:* To be significant, the observed value of chi-square must be greater than or equal to the value shown in the table.

# Appendix E

**Critical Values of *D* in the Kolmogorov–Smirnov One-Variable Test**

| Sample size | Level of significance | | | |
|---|---|---|---|---|
| | *0.10* | *0.05* | *0.02* | *0.01* |
| 1 | 0.9500 | 0.9750 | 0.9900 | 0.9950 |
| 2 | 0.7764 | 0.8419 | 0.9000 | 0.9293 |
| 3 | 0.6360 | 0.7076 | 0.7846 | 0.8290 |
| 4 | 0.5652 | 0.6239 | 0.6889 | 0.7342 |
| 5 | 0.5095 | 0.5633 | 0.6272 | 0.6685 |
| 6 | 0.4680 | 0.5193 | 0.5774 | 0.6166 |
| 7 | 0.4361 | 0.4834 | 0.5384 | 0.5758 |
| 8 | 0.4096 | 0.4543 | 0.5065 | 0.5418 |
| 9 | 0.3875 | 0.4300 | 0.4796 | 0.5133 |
| 10 | 0.3687 | 0.4093 | 0.4566 | 0.4889 |
| 11 | 0.3524 | 0.3912 | 0.4367 | 0.4677 |
| 12 | 0.3382 | 0.3754 | 0.4192 | 0.4491 |
| 13 | 0.3255 | 0.3614 | 0.4036 | 0.4325 |
| 14 | 0.3142 | 0.3489 | 0.3897 | 0.4176 |
| 15 | 0.3040 | 0.3376 | 0.3771 | 0.4042 |
| 16 | 0.2947 | 0.3273 | 0.3657 | 0.3920 |
| 17 | 0.2863 | 0.3180 | 0.3553 | 0.3809 |
| 18 | 0.2785 | 0.3094 | 0.3457 | 0.3706 |
| 19 | 0.2714 | 0.3014 | 0.3369 | 0.3612 |
| 20 | 0.2647 | 0.2941 | 0.3287 | 0.3524 |

*Note:* To be significant, the observed value of *D* must be greater than or equal to the value shown in the table.

*Sources:* Leslie H. Miller, Table of Percentage Points of Kolmogorov Statistics, *Journal of the American Statistical Association,* v. 51 n. 273, March 1956, 111–121.

H. Leon Harter, Modified Asymptotic Formulas for Critical Values of the Kolmogorov Test Statistic, *The American Statistician,* v. 34 n. 2, May 1980, 110–111.

*(continued)*

## Critical Values of *D* in the Kolmogorov–Smirnov One-Variable Test *(continued)*

| Sample size | Level of significance | | | |
|---|---|---|---|---|
| | *0.10* | *0.05* | *0.02* | *0.01* |
| 21 | 0.2586 | 0.2872 | 0.3210 | 0.3443 |
| 22 | 0.2528 | 0.2809 | 0.3139 | 0.3367 |
| 23 | 0.2475 | 0.2749 | 0.3073 | 0.3295 |
| 24 | 0.2424 | 0.2693 | 0.3010 | 0.3229 |
| 25 | 0.2377 | 0.2640 | 0.2952 | 0.3166 |
| 26 | 0.2332 | 0.2591 | 0.2896 | 0.3106 |
| 27 | 0.2290 | 0.2544 | 0.2844 | 0.3050 |
| 28 | 0.2250 | 0.2499 | 0.2794 | 0.2997 |
| 29 | 0.2212 | 0.2457 | 0.2747 | 0.2947 |
| 30 | 0.2176 | 0.2417 | 0.2702 | 0.2899 |
| 31 | 0.2141 | 0.2379 | 0.2660 | 0.2853 |
| 32 | 0.2109 | 0.2342 | 0.2619 | 0.2809 |
| 33 | 0.2077 | 0.2308 | 0.2580 | 0.2768 |
| 34 | 0.2047 | 0.2274 | 0.2543 | 0.2728 |
| 35 | 0.2019 | 0.2243 | 0.2507 | 0.2690 |
| 36 | 0.1991 | 0.2212 | 0.2473 | 0.2653 |
| 37 | 0.1965 | 0.2183 | 0.2440 | 0.2618 |
| 38 | 0.1939 | 0.2154 | 0.2409 | 0.2584 |
| 39 | 0.1915 | 0.2127 | 0.2379 | 0.2552 |
| 40 | 0.1891 | 0.2101 | 0.2349 | 0.2521 |
| 41 | 0.1869 | 0.2076 | 0.2321 | 0.2490 |
| 42 | 0.1847 | 0.2052 | 0.2294 | 0.2461 |
| 43 | 0.1826 | 0.2028 | 0.2268 | 0.2433 |
| 44 | 0.1805 | 0.2006 | 0.2243 | 0.2406 |
| 45 | 0.1786 | 0.1984 | 0.2218 | 0.2380 |
| 46 | 0.1767 | 0.1963 | 0.2194 | 0.2354 |
| 47 | 0.1748 | 0.1942 | 0.2172 | 0.2330 |
| 48 | 0.1730 | 0.1922 | 0.2149 | 0.2306 |
| 49 | 0.1713 | 0.1903 | 0.2128 | 0.2283 |
| 50 | 0.1696 | 0.1884 | 0.2107 | 0.2260 |
| 51 | 0.1680 | 0.1866 | 0.2086 | 0.2239 |
| 52 | 0.1664 | 0.1848 | 0.2067 | 0.2217 |
| 53 | 0.1648 | 0.1831 | 0.2048 | 0.2197 |
| 54 | 0.1633 | 0.1814 | 0.2029 | 0.2177 |
| 55 | 0.1619 | 0.1798 | 0.2011 | 0.2157 |

*Note:* To be significant, the observed value of *D* must be greater than or equal to the value shown in the table.

*(continued)*

**Critical Values of *D* in the Kolmogorov–Smirnov One-Variable Test *(continued)***

| Sample size | Level of significance | | | |
|---|---|---|---|---|
| | *0.10* | *0.05* | *0.02* | *0.01* |
| 56 | 0.1604 | 0.1782 | 0.1993 | 0.2138 |
| 57 | 0.1591 | 0.1767 | 0.1976 | 0.2120 |
| 58 | 0.1577 | 0.1752 | 0.1959 | 0.2102 |
| 59 | 0.1564 | 0.1737 | 0.1943 | 0.2084 |
| 60 | 0.1551 | 0.1723 | 0.1927 | 0.2067 |
| 61 | 0.1539 | 0.1709 | 0.1911 | 0.2051 |
| 62 | 0.1526 | 0.1696 | 0.1896 | 0.2034 |
| 63 | 0.1514 | 0.1682 | 0.1881 | 0.2018 |
| 64 | 0.1503 | 0.1669 | 0.1867 | 0.2003 |
| 65 | 0.1491 | 0.1657 | 0.1853 | 0.1988 |
| 66 | 0.1480 | 0.1644 | 0.1839 | 0.1973 |
| 67 | 0.1469 | 0.1632 | 0.1825 | 0.1958 |
| 68 | 0.1459 | 0.1620 | 0.1812 | 0.1944 |
| 69 | 0.1448 | 0.1609 | 0.1799 | 0.1930 |
| 70 | 0.1438 | 0.1598 | 0.1786 | 0.1917 |
| 71 | 0.1428 | 0.1586 | 0.1774 | 0.1903 |
| 72 | 0.1418 | 0.1576 | 0.1762 | 0.1890 |
| 73 | 0.1409 | 0.1565 | 0.1750 | 0.1878 |
| 74 | 0.1399 | 0.1554 | 0.1738 | 0.1865 |
| 75 | 0.1390 | 0.1544 | 0.1727 | 0.1853 |
| 76 | 0.1381 | 0.1534 | 0.1716 | 0.1841 |
| 77 | 0.1372 | 0.1524 | 0.1705 | 0.1829 |
| 78 | 0.1364 | 0.1515 | 0.1694 | 0.1817 |
| 79 | 0.1355 | 0.1505 | 0.1683 | 0.1806 |
| 80 | 0.1347 | 0.1496 | 0.1673 | 0.1795 |
| 81 | 0.1339 | 0.1487 | 0.1663 | 0.1784 |
| 82 | 0.1331 | 0.1478 | 0.1653 | 0.1773 |
| 83 | 0.1323 | 0.1469 | 0.1643 | 0.1763 |
| 84 | 0.1315 | 0.1461 | 0.1633 | 0.1752 |
| 85 | 0.1307 | 0.1452 | 0.1624 | 0.1742 |
| 86 | 0.1300 | 0.1444 | 0.1614 | 0.1732 |
| 87 | 0.1292 | 0.1436 | 0.1605 | 0.1722 |
| 88 | 0.1285 | 0.1427 | 0.1596 | 0.1713 |
| 89 | 0.1278 | 0.1420 | 0.1587 | 0.1703 |
| 90 | 0.1271 | 0.1412 | 0.1579 | 0.1694 |

*Note:* To be significant, the observed value of *D* must be greater than or equal to the value shown in the table.

*(continued)*

**Critical Values of *D* in the Kolmogorov–Smirnov One-Variable Test *(continued)***

| Sample size | Level of significance | | | |
|---|---|---|---|---|
| | *0.10* | *0.05* | *0.02* | *0.01* |
| 91 | 0.1264 | 0.1404 | 0.1570 | 0.1685 |
| 92 | 0.1257 | 0.1397 | 0.1562 | 0.1676 |
| 93 | 0.1251 | 0.1389 | 0.1553 | 0.1667 |
| 94 | 0.1244 | 0.1382 | 0.1545 | 0.1658 |
| 95 | 0.1238 | 0.1375 | 0.1537 | 0.1649 |
| 96 | 0.1231 | 0.1368 | 0.1529 | 0.1641 |
| 97 | 0.1225 | 0.1361 | 0.1521 | 0.1632 |
| 98 | 0.1219 | 0.1354 | 0.1514 | 0.1624 |
| 99 | 0.1213 | 0.1347 | 0.1506 | 0.1616 |
| 100 | 0.1207 | 0.1340 | 0.1499 | 0.1608 |
| >100 | $\dfrac{1.224}{\sqrt{n + \Delta n}}$ | $\dfrac{1.358}{\sqrt{n + \Delta n}}$ | $\dfrac{1.518}{\sqrt{n + \Delta n}}$ | $\dfrac{1.628}{\sqrt{n + \Delta n}}$ |

$$\Delta n = \frac{\sqrt{n + 4}}{3.5}$$

*Note:* To be significant, the observed value of *D* must be greater than or equal to the value shown in the table.

# Appendix F

**Critical Values of the *t* Statistic**

| Degrees of freedom | Level of significance | | | | | |
|---|---|---|---|---|---|---|
| | *Two-tailed test* | | | | | |
| | 0.20 | 0.10 | 0.05 | 0.02 | 0.01 | 0.001 |
| | *One-tailed test* | | | | | |
| | 0.10 | 0.05 | 0.025 | 0.01 | 0.005 | 0.0005 |
| 1 | 3.078 | 6.314 | 12.706 | 31.821 | 63.657 | 636.619 |
| 2 | 1.886 | 2.920 | 4.303 | 6.965 | 9.925 | 31.599 |
| 3 | 1.638 | 2.353 | 3.182 | 4.541 | 5.841 | 12.924 |
| 4 | 1.533 | 2.132 | 2.776 | 3.747 | 4.604 | 8.610 |
| 5 | 1.476 | 2.015 | 2.571 | 3.365 | 4.032 | 6.869 |
| 6 | 1.440 | 1.943 | 2.447 | 3.143 | 3.707 | 5.959 |
| 7 | 1.415 | 1.895 | 2.365 | 2.998 | 3.499 | 5.408 |
| 8 | 1.397 | 1.860 | 2.306 | 2.896 | 3.355 | 5.041 |
| 9 | 1.383 | 1.833 | 2.262 | 2.821 | 3.250 | 4.781 |
| 10 | 1.372 | 1.812 | 2.228 | 2.764 | 3.169 | 4.587 |
| 11 | 1.363 | 1.796 | 2.201 | 2.718 | 3.106 | 4.437 |
| 12 | 1.356 | 1.782 | 2.179 | 2.681 | 3.055 | 4.318 |
| 13 | 1.350 | 1.771 | 2.160 | 2.650 | 3.012 | 4.221 |
| 14 | 1.345 | 1.761 | 2.145 | 2.624 | 2.977 | 4.140 |
| 15 | 1.341 | 1.753 | 2.131 | 2.602 | 2.947 | 4.073 |
| 16 | 1.337 | 1.746 | 2.120 | 2.583 | 2.921 | 4.015 |
| 17 | 1.333 | 1.740 | 2.110 | 2.567 | 2.898 | 3.965 |
| 18 | 1.330 | 1.734 | 2.101 | 2.552 | 2.878 | 3.922 |
| 19 | 1.328 | 1.729 | 2.093 | 2.539 | 2.861 | 3.883 |
| 20 | 1.325 | 1.725 | 2.086 | 2.528 | 2.845 | 3.850 |

*Note:* To be significant, the observed value of *t* must be greater than or equal to the value shown in the table.

*(continued)*

**Critical Values of the *t* Statistic** *(continued)*

| | Level of significance | | | | | |
|---|---|---|---|---|---|---|
| | *Two-tailed test* | | | | | |
| | 0.20 | 0.10 | 0.05 | 0.02 | 0.01 | 0.001 |
| | *One-tailed test* | | | | | |
| **Degrees of freedom** | 0.10 | 0.05 | 0.025 | 0.01 | 0.005 | 0.0005 |
| 21 | 1.323 | 1.721 | 2.080 | 2.518 | 2.831 | 3.819 |
| 22 | 1.321 | 1.717 | 2.074 | 2.508 | 2.819 | 3.792 |
| 23 | 1.319 | 1.714 | 2.069 | 2.500 | 2.807 | 3.768 |
| 24 | 1.318 | 1.711 | 2.064 | 2.492 | 2.797 | 3.745 |
| 25 | 1.316 | 1.708 | 2.060 | 2.485 | 2.787 | 3.725 |
| 26 | 1.315 | 1.706 | 2.056 | 2.479 | 2.779 | 3.707 |
| 27 | 1.314 | 1.703 | 2.052 | 2.473 | 2.771 | 3.690 |
| 28 | 1.313 | 1.701 | 2.048 | 2.467 | 2.763 | 3.674 |
| 29 | 1.311 | 1.699 | 2.045 | 2.462 | 2.756 | 3.659 |
| 30 | 1.310 | 1.697 | 2.042 | 2.457 | 2.750 | 3.646 |
| 40 | 1.303 | 1.684 | 2.021 | 2.423 | 2.704 | 3.551 |
| 60 | 1.296 | 1.671 | 2.000 | 2.390 | 2.660 | 3.460 |
| 120 | 1.289 | 1.658 | 1.980 | 2.358 | 2.617 | 3.373 |
| $\infty$ | 1.282 | 1.645 | 1.960 | 2.326 | 2.576 | 3.291 |

*Note:* To be significant, the observed value of *t* must be greater than or equal to the value shown in the table.

# Appendix G

## Critical Values of the F Statistic

| Degrees of freedom for the denominator | Degrees of freedom for the numerator |||||||||||||||||
|---|---|---|---|---|---|---|---|---|---|---|---|---|---|---|---|---|---|
| | 1 | 2 | 3 | 4 | 5 | 6 | 7 | 8 | 9 | 10 | 20 | 30 | 40 | 50 | 100 | 200 | ∞ |
| 1 | 161.45 | 199.50 | 215.71 | 224.58 | 230.16 | 233.99 | 236.77 | 238.88 | 240.54 | 241.88 | 248.01 | 250.10 | 251.14 | 251.77 | 253.04 | 253.68 | 254.31 |
| | **4,052** | **4,999** | **5,403** | **5,625** | **5,764** | **5,859** | **5,928** | **5,981** | **6,022** | **6,056** | **6,209** | **6,261** | **6,287** | **6,303** | **6,334** | **6,350** | **6,366** |
| 2 | 18.51 | 19.00 | 19.16 | 19.25 | 19.30 | 19.33 | 19.35 | 19.37 | 19.38 | 19.40 | 19.45 | 19.46 | 19.47 | 19.48 | 19.49 | 19.49 | 19.50 |
| | **98.50** | **99.00** | **99.17** | **99.25** | **99.30** | **99.33** | **99.36** | **99.37** | **99.39** | **99.40** | **99.45** | **99.47** | **99.47** | **99.48** | **99.49** | **99.49** | **99.50** |
| 3 | 10.13 | 9.55 | 9.28 | 9.12 | 9.01 | 8.94 | 8.89 | 8.85 | 8.81 | 8.79 | 8.66 | 8.62 | 8.59 | 8.58 | 8.55 | 8.54 | 8.53 |
| | **34.12** | **30.82** | **29.46** | **28.71** | **28.24** | **27.91** | **27.67** | **27.49** | **27.35** | **27.23** | **26.69** | **26.50** | **26.41** | **26.35** | **26.24** | **26.18** | **26.13** |
| 4 | 7.71 | 6.94 | 6.59 | 6.39 | 6.26 | 6.16 | 6.09 | 6.04 | 6.00 | 5.96 | 5.80 | 5.75 | 5.72 | 5.70 | 5.66 | 5.65 | 5.63 |
| | **21.20** | **18.00** | **16.69** | **15.98** | **15.52** | **15.21** | **14.98** | **14.80** | **14.66** | **14.55** | **14.02** | **13.84** | **13.75** | **13.69** | **13.58** | **13.52** | **13.46** |
| 5 | 6.61 | 5.79 | 5.41 | 5.19 | 5.05 | 4.95 | 4.88 | 4.82 | 4.77 | 4.74 | 4.56 | 4.50 | 4.46 | 4.44 | 4.41 | 4.39 | 4.36 |
| | **16.26** | **13.27** | **12.06** | **11.39** | **10.97** | **10.67** | **10.46** | **10.29** | **10.16** | **10.05** | **9.55** | **9.38** | **9.29** | **9.24** | **9.13** | **9.08** | **9.02** |
| 6 | 5.99 | 5.14 | 4.76 | 4.53 | 4.39 | 4.28 | 4.21 | 4.15 | 4.10 | 4.06 | 3.87 | 3.81 | 3.77 | 3.75 | 3.71 | 3.69 | 3.67 |
| | **13.75** | **10.92** | **9.78** | **9.15** | **8.75** | **8.47** | **8.26** | **8.10** | **7.98** | **7.87** | **7.40** | **7.23** | **7.14** | **7.09** | **6.99** | **6.93** | **6.88** |
| 7 | 5.59 | 4.74 | 4.35 | 4.12 | 3.97 | 3.87 | 3.79 | 3.73 | 3.68 | 3.64 | 3.44 | 3.38 | 3.34 | 3.32 | 3.27 | 3.25 | 3.23 |
| | **12.25** | **9.55** | **8.45** | **7.85** | **7.46** | **7.19** | **6.99** | **6.84** | **6.72** | **6.62** | **6.16** | **5.99** | **5.91** | **5.86** | **5.75** | **5.70** | **5.65** |
| 8 | 5.32 | 4.46 | 4.07 | 3.84 | 3.69 | 3.58 | 3.50 | 3.44 | 3.39 | 3.35 | 3.15 | 3.08 | 3.04 | 3.02 | 2.97 | 2.95 | 2.93 |
| | **11.26** | **8.65** | **7.59** | **7.01** | **6.63** | **6.37** | **6.18** | **6.03** | **5.91** | **5.81** | **5.36** | **5.20** | **5.12** | **5.07** | **4.96** | **4.91** | **4.86** |
| 9 | 5.12 | 4.26 | 3.86 | 3.63 | 3.48 | 3.37 | 3.29 | 3.23 | 3.18 | 3.14 | 2.94 | 2.86 | 2.83 | 2.80 | 2.76 | 2.73 | 2.71 |
| | **10.56** | **8.02** | **6.99** | **6.42** | **6.06** | **5.80** | **5.61** | **5.47** | **5.35** | **5.26** | **4.81** | **4.65** | **4.57** | **4.52** | **4.41** | **4.36** | **4.31** |
| 10 | 4.96 | 4.10 | 3.71 | 3.48 | 3.33 | 3.22 | 3.14 | 3.07 | 3.02 | 2.98 | 2.77 | 2.70 | 2.66 | 2.64 | 2.59 | 2.56 | 2.54 |
| | **10.04** | **7.56** | **6.55** | **5.99** | **5.64** | **5.39** | **5.20** | **5.06** | **4.94** | **4.85** | **4.41** | **4.25** | **4.17** | **4.12** | **4.01** | **3.96** | **3.91** |
| 20 | 4.35 | 3.49 | 3.01 | 2.87 | 2.71 | 2.60 | 2.51 | 2.45 | 2.39 | 2.35 | 2.12 | 2.04 | 1.99 | 1.97 | 1.91 | 1.88 | 1.84 |
| | **8.10** | **5.85** | **4.94** | **4.43** | **4.10** | **3.87** | **3.70** | **3.56** | **3.46** | **3.37** | **2.94** | **2.78** | **2.69** | **2.64** | **2.54** | **2.48** | **2.42** |
| 30 | 4.17 | 3.32 | 2.92 | 2.69 | 2.53 | 2.42 | 2.33 | 2.27 | 2.21 | 2.16 | 1.93 | 1.84 | 1.79 | 1.76 | 1.70 | 1.66 | 1.62 |
| | **7.56** | **5.39** | **4.51** | **4.02** | **3.70** | **3.47** | **3.30** | **3.17** | **3.07** | **2.98** | **2.55** | **2.39** | **2.30** | **2.25** | **2.13** | **2.07** | **2.01** |
| 40 | 4.08 | 3.23 | 2.84 | 2.61 | 2.45 | 2.34 | 2.25 | 2.18 | 2.12 | 2.08 | 1.84 | 1.74 | 1.69 | 1.66 | 1.59 | 1.55 | 1.51 |
| | **7.31** | **5.18** | **4.31** | **3.83** | **3.51** | **3.29** | **3.12** | **2.99** | **2.89** | **2.80** | **2.37** | **2.20** | **2.11** | **2.06** | **1.94** | **1.87** | **1.80** |
| 50 | 4.03 | 3.18 | 2.79 | 2.56 | 2.40 | 2.29 | 2.20 | 2.13 | 2.07 | 2.03 | 1.78 | 1.69 | 1.63 | 1.60 | 1.52 | 1.48 | 1.44 |
| | **7.17** | **5.06** | **4.20** | **3.72** | **3.41** | **3.19** | **3.02** | **2.89** | **2.78** | **2.70** | **2.27** | **2.10** | **2.01** | **1.95** | **1.82** | **1.76** | **1.68** |
| 100 | 3.94 | 3.09 | 2.70 | 2.46 | 2.31 | 2.19 | 2.10 | 2.03 | 1.97 | 1.93 | 1.68 | 1.57 | 1.52 | 1.48 | 1.39 | 1.34 | 1.28 |
| | **6.90** | **4.82** | **3.98** | **3.51** | **3.21** | **2.99** | **2.82** | **2.69** | **2.59** | **2.50** | **2.07** | **1.89** | **1.80** | **1.74** | **1.60** | **1.52** | **1.43** |
| 200 | 3.89 | 3.04 | 2.65 | 2.42 | 2.26 | 2.14 | 2.06 | 1.98 | 1.93 | 1.88 | 1.62 | 1.52 | 1.46 | 1.41 | 1.32 | 1.26 | 1.19 |
| | **6.76** | **4.71** | **3.88** | **3.41** | **3.11** | **2.89** | **2.73** | **2.60** | **2.50** | **2.41** | **1.97** | **1.79** | **1.69** | **1.63** | **1.48** | **1.39** | **1.28** |
| ∞ | 3.84 | 3.00 | 2.60 | 2.37 | 2.21 | 2.10 | 2.01 | 1.94 | 1.88 | 1.83 | 1.57 | 1.46 | 1.39 | 1.35 | 1.24 | 1.17 | 1.00 |
| | **6.63** | **4.61** | **3.78** | **3.32** | **3.02** | **2.80** | **2.64** | **2.51** | **2.41** | **2.32** | **1.88** | **1.70** | **1.59** | **1.52** | **1.36** | **1.25** | **1.00** |

*Note:* To be significant at the 0.05 level of significance, the observed value of $F$ must be greater than or equal to the value shown in lightface type in the body of the table. To be significant at the 0.01 level of significance, the observed value of $F$ must be greater than or equal to the value shown in boldface type in the body of the table.

# Appendix H

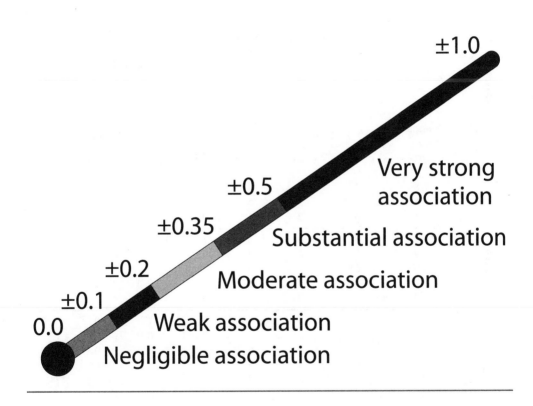

# Appendix I

**Critical Values of C in Fisher's Exact Probability Test**

| Sample size | Cell frequencies | | | Level of significance | | | |
|:-:|:-:|:-:|:-:|:-:|:-:|:-:|:-:|
| | | | | *Two-tailed test* | | | |
| | | | | 0.10 | 0.05 | 0.02 | 0.01 |
| | | | | *One-tailed test* | | | |
| *n* | *a + b* | *c + d* | *a* | 0.05 | 0.025 | 0.01 | 0.005 |
| 8 | 4 | 4 | 4 | 0 | 0 | | |
| 8 | 5 | 3 | 5 | 0 | 0 | | |
| 8 | 6 | 2 | 6 | 0 | | | |
| 9 | 5 | 4 | 5 | 1 | 0 | 0 | |
| 9 | 5 | 4 | 4 | 0 | | | |
| 9 | 6 | 3 | 5 | 0 | | | |
| 9 | 6 | 3 | 6 | 0 | 0 | | |
| 9 | 7 | 2 | 7 | 0 | | | |
| 10 | 5 | 5 | 5 | 1 | 1 | 0 | 0 |
| 10 | 5 | 5 | 4 | 0 | 0 | | |
| 10 | 6 | 4 | 6 | 1 | 0 | 0 | 0 |
| 10 | 6 | 4 | 5 | 0 | 0 | | |
| 10 | 7 | 3 | 7 | 0 | 0 | 0 | |
| 10 | 7 | 3 | 6 | 0 | | | |
| 10 | 8 | 2 | 8 | 0 | 0 | | |

*Note:* To be significant, the observed value of C must be less than or equal to the value shown in the table.

*Source:* After Ray Meddis, *Statistical Handbook for Non-Statisticians*. London: McGraw–Hill UK, 1991.

*(continued)*

**Critical Values of *C* in Fisher's Exact Probability Test *(continued)***

| Sample size *n* | Cell frequencies | | | 0.10 | 0.05 | 0.02 | 0.01 |
|---|---|---|---|---|---|---|---|
| | | | | 0.05 | 0.025 | 0.01 | 0.005 |
| | $a+b$ | $c+d$ | $a$ | | | | |
| 11 | 6 | 5 | 5 | 0 | 0 | | |
| 11 | 6 | 5 | 6 | 1 | 1 | 0 | 0 |
| 11 | 6 | 5 | 4 | 0 | | | |
| 11 | 7 | 4 | 6 | 0 | 0 | | |
| 11 | 7 | 4 | 7 | 1 | 1 | 0 | 0 |
| 11 | 7 | 4 | 5 | 0 | | | |
| 11 | 8 | 3 | 8 | 0 | 0 | 0 | |
| 11 | 8 | 3 | 7 | 0 | 0 | | |
| 11 | 9 | 2 | 9 | 0 | 0 | | |
| 12 | 6 | 6 | 6 | 2 | 1 | 1 | 0 |
| 12 | 6 | 6 | 5 | 1 | 0 | 0 | |
| 12 | 6 | 6 | 4 | 0 | | | |
| 12 | 7 | 5 | 6 | 1 | 0 | 0 | |
| 12 | 7 | 5 | 7 | 2 | 1 | 0 | 0 |
| 12 | 7 | 5 | 5 | 0 | | | |
| 12 | 8 | 4 | 6 | 0 | | | |
| 12 | 8 | 4 | 7 | 0 | 0 | | |
| 12 | 8 | 4 | 8 | 1 | 1 | 0 | 0 |
| 12 | 9 | 3 | 7 | 0 | | | |
| 12 | 9 | 3 | 8 | 0 | 0 | | |
| 12 | 9 | 3 | 9 | 1 | 0 | 0 | 0 |
| 12 | 10 | 2 | 10 | 0 | 0 | | |
| 12 | 10 | 2 | 9 | 0 | | | |

*Note:* To be significant, the observed value of *C* must be less than or equal to the value shown in the table.

*(continued)*

**Critical Values of C in Fisher's Exact Probability Test** *(continued)*

| Sample size *n* | \multicolumn{3}{c}{Cell frequencies} | | | Level of significance 0.10 (Two-tailed) / 0.05 (One-tailed) | 0.05 / 0.025 | 0.02 / 0.01 | 0.01 / 0.005 |
|---|---|---|---|---|---|---|---|
| | *a + b* | *c + d* | *a* | 0.05 | 0.025 | 0.01 | 0.005 |
| 13 | 7 | 6 | 4 | 0 | | | |
| 13 | 7 | 6 | 5 | 0 | 0 | | |
| 13 | 7 | 6 | 6 | 1 | 0 | 0 | 0 |
| 13 | 7 | 6 | 7 | 2 | 2 | 1 | 1 |
| 13 | 8 | 5 | 5 | 0 | | | |
| 13 | 8 | 5 | 6 | 0 | 0 | | |
| 13 | 8 | 5 | 7 | 1 | 0 | 0 | 0 |
| 13 | 8 | 5 | 8 | 2 | 1 | 1 | 0 |
| 13 | 9 | 4 | 6 | 0 | | | |
| 13 | 9 | 4 | 7 | 0 | 0 | | |
| 13 | 9 | 4 | 8 | 0 | 0 | 0 | |
| 13 | 9 | 4 | 9 | 1 | 1 | 0 | 0 |
| 13 | 10 | 3 | 8 | 0 | | | |
| 13 | 10 | 3 | 9 | 0 | 0 | | |
| 13 | 10 | 3 | 10 | 1 | 0 | 0 | 0 |
| 13 | 11 | 2 | 10 | 0 | | | |
| 13 | 11 | 2 | 11 | 0 | 0 | | |
| 14 | 7 | 7 | 4 | 0 | | | |
| 14 | 7 | 7 | 5 | 0 | 0 | | |
| 14 | 7 | 7 | 6 | 1 | 1 | 0 | 0 |
| 14 | 7 | 7 | 7 | 3 | 2 | 1 | 1 |
| 14 | 8 | 6 | 5 | 0 | | | |
| 14 | 8 | 6 | 6 | 0 | 0 | 0 | |
| 14 | 8 | 6 | 7 | 1 | 1 | 0 | 0 |
| 14 | 8 | 6 | 8 | 2 | 2 | 1 | 1 |
| 14 | 9 | 5 | 6 | 0 | | | |
| 14 | 9 | 5 | 7 | 0 | 0 | | |
| 14 | 9 | 5 | 8 | 1 | 1 | 0 | 0 |
| 14 | 9 | 5 | 9 | 2 | 1 | 1 | 1 |
| 14 | 10 | 4 | 7 | 0 | | | |
| 14 | 10 | 4 | 8 | 0 | 0 | | |
| 14 | 10 | 4 | 9 | 1 | 0 | 0 | 0 |
| 14 | 10 | 4 | 10 | 1 | 1 | 0 | 0 |
| 14 | 11 | 3 | 9 | 0 | | | |

*Note:* To be significant, the observed value of *C* must be less than or equal to the value shown in the table.

*(continued)*

**Critical Values of C in Fisher's Exact Probability Test** *(continued)*

| Sample size | Cell frequencies | | | Level of significance | | | |
|---|---|---|---|---|---|---|---|
| | | | | Two-tailed test | | | |
| | | | | 0.10 | 0.05 | 0.02 | 0.01 |
| | | | | One-tailed test | | | |
| *n* | *a* + *b* | *c* + *d* | *a* | 0.05 | 0.025 | 0.01 | 0.005 |
| 14 | 11 | 3 | 10 | 0 | 0 | | |
| 14 | 11 | 3 | 11 | 1 | 0 | 0 | 0 |
| 14 | 12 | 2 | 11 | 0 | | | |
| 14 | 12 | 2 | 12 | 0 | 0 | | |
| 15 | 8 | 7 | 5 | 0 | 0 | | |
| 15 | 8 | 7 | 6 | 1 | 0 | 0 | |
| 15 | 8 | 7 | 7 | 2 | 1 | 1 | 0 |
| 15 | 8 | 7 | 8 | 3 | 2 | 2 | 1 |
| 15 | 9 | 6 | 6 | 0 | 0 | | |
| 15 | 9 | 6 | 7 | 1 | 0 | 0 | |
| 15 | 9 | 6 | 8 | 2 | 1 | 0 | 0 |
| 15 | 9 | 6 | 9 | 3 | 2 | 1 | 1 |
| 15 | 10 | 5 | 6 | 0 | | | |
| 15 | 10 | 5 | 7 | 0 | 0 | | |
| 15 | 10 | 5 | 8 | 1 | 0 | 0 | |
| 15 | 10 | 5 | 9 | 1 | 1 | 0 | 0 |
| 15 | 10 | 5 | 10 | 2 | 2 | 1 | 1 |
| 15 | 11 | 4 | 8 | 0 | | | |
| 15 | 11 | 4 | 9 | 0 | 0 | | |
| 15 | 11 | 4 | 10 | 1 | 0 | 0 | 0 |
| 15 | 11 | 4 | 11 | 1 | 1 | 1 | 0 |
| 15 | 12 | 3 | 9 | 0 | | | |
| 15 | 12 | 3 | 10 | 0 | 0 | | |
| 15 | 12 | 3 | 11 | 0 | 0 | 0 | |
| 15 | 12 | 3 | 12 | 1 | 0 | 0 | 0 |
| 15 | 13 | 2 | 12 | 0 | | | |
| 15 | 13 | 2 | 13 | 0 | 0 | 0 | |

*Note:* To be significant, the observed value of *C* must be less than or equal to the value shown in the table.

*(continued)*

**Critical Values of C in Fisher's Exact Probability Test** *(continued)*

| | | | | Level of significance | | | |
|---|---|---|---|---|---|---|---|
| | | | | | Two-tailed test | | |
| | | | | 0.10 | 0.05 | 0.02 | 0.01 |
| Sample size | Cell frequencies | | | | One-tailed test | | |
| $n$ | $a + b$ | $c + d$ | $a$ | 0.05 | 0.025 | 0.01 | 0.005 |
| 16 | 8 | 8 | 4 | 0 | | | |
| 16 | 8 | 8 | 5 | 0 | 0 | | |
| 16 | 8 | 8 | 6 | 1 | 1 | 0 | 0 |
| 16 | 8 | 8 | 7 | 2 | 2 | 1 | 0 |
| 16 | 8 | 8 | 8 | 4 | 3 | 2 | 2 |
| 16 | 9 | 7 | 5 | 0 | | | |
| 16 | 9 | 7 | 6 | 0 | 0 | | |
| 16 | 9 | 7 | 7 | 1 | 1 | 0 | 0 |
| 16 | 9 | 7 | 8 | 2 | 2 | 1 | 0 |
| 16 | 9 | 7 | 9 | 3 | 3 | 2 | 2 |
| 16 | 10 | 6 | 6 | 0 | | | |
| 16 | 10 | 6 | 7 | 0 | 0 | | |
| 16 | 10 | 6 | 8 | 1 | 1 | 0 | 0 |
| 16 | 10 | 6 | 9 | 2 | 1 | 1 | 0 |
| 16 | 10 | 6 | 10 | 3 | 2 | 2 | 1 |
| 16 | 11 | 5 | 7 | 0 | | | |
| 16 | 11 | 5 | 8 | 0 | 0 | | |
| 16 | 11 | 5 | 9 | 1 | 0 | 0 | 0 |
| 16 | 11 | 5 | 10 | 1 | 1 | 0 | 0 |
| 16 | 11 | 5 | 11 | 2 | 2 | 1 | 1 |
| 16 | 12 | 4 | 8 | 0 | | | |
| 16 | 12 | 4 | 9 | 0 | 0 | | |
| 16 | 12 | 4 | 10 | 0 | 0 | 0 | |
| 16 | 12 | 4 | 11 | 1 | 0 | 0 | 0 |
| 16 | 12 | 4 | 12 | 1 | 1 | 1 | 0 |
| 16 | 13 | 3 | 10 | 0 | | | |
| 16 | 13 | 3 | 11 | 0 | 0 | | |
| 16 | 13 | 3 | 12 | 0 | 0 | 0 | |
| 16 | 13 | 3 | 13 | 1 | 1 | 0 | 0 |
| 16 | 14 | 2 | 13 | 0 | 0 | | |
| 16 | 14 | 2 | 14 | 0 | 0 | 0 | |

*Note:* To be significant, the observed value of C must be less than or equal to the value shown in the table.

*(continued)*

**Critical Values of C in Fisher's Exact Probability Test** *(continued)*

| Sample size *n* | Cell frequencies | | | Level of significance | | | |
|---|---|---|---|---|---|---|---|
| | | | | Two-tailed test | | | |
| | | | | 0.10 | 0.05 | 0.02 | 0.01 |
| | | | | One-tailed test | | | |
| | *a + b* | *c + d* | *a* | 0.05 | 0.025 | 0.01 | 0.005 |
| 17 | 9 | 8 | 5 | 0 | 0 | | |
| 17 | 9 | 8 | 6 | 1 | 0 | 0 | |
| 17 | 9 | 8 | 7 | 2 | 1 | 0 | 0 |
| 17 | 9 | 8 | 8 | 3 | 2 | 1 | 1 |
| 17 | 9 | 8 | 9 | 4 | 3 | 3 | 2 |
| 17 | 10 | 7 | 5 | 0 | | | |
| 17 | 10 | 7 | 6 | 0 | 0 | | |
| 17 | 10 | 7 | 7 | 1 | 0 | 0 | |
| 17 | 10 | 7 | 8 | 1 | 1 | 0 | 0 |
| 17 | 10 | 7 | 9 | 2 | 2 | 1 | 1 |
| 17 | 10 | 7 | 10 | 3 | 3 | 2 | 2 |
| 17 | 11 | 6 | 6 | 0 | | | |
| 17 | 11 | 6 | 7 | 0 | 0 | | |
| 17 | 11 | 6 | 8 | 1 | 0 | 0 | |
| 17 | 11 | 6 | 9 | 1 | 1 | 0 | 0 |
| 17 | 11 | 6 | 10 | 2 | 1 | 1 | 0 |
| 17 | 11 | 6 | 11 | 3 | 2 | 2 | 1 |
| 17 | 12 | 5 | 7 | 0 | | | |
| 17 | 12 | 5 | 8 | 0 | 0 | | |
| 17 | 12 | 5 | 9 | 0 | 0 | 0 | |
| 17 | 12 | 5 | 10 | 1 | 0 | 0 | 0 |
| 17 | 12 | 5 | 11 | 1 | 1 | 1 | 0 |
| 17 | 12 | 5 | 12 | 2 | 2 | 1 | 1 |
| 17 | 13 | 4 | 9 | 0 | | | |
| 17 | 13 | 4 | 10 | 0 | 0 | | |
| 17 | 13 | 4 | 11 | 0 | 0 | 0 | |
| 17 | 13 | 4 | 12 | 1 | 1 | 0 | 0 |
| 17 | 13 | 4 | 13 | 2 | 1 | 1 | 0 |
| 17 | 14 | 3 | 11 | 0 | | | |
| 17 | 14 | 3 | 12 | 0 | 0 | | |
| 17 | 14 | 3 | 13 | 0 | 0 | 0 | |
| 17 | 14 | 3 | 14 | 1 | 1 | 0 | 0 |
| 17 | 15 | 2 | 13 | 0 | | | |
| 17 | 15 | 2 | 14 | 0 | 0 | | |
| 17 | 15 | 2 | 15 | 0 | 0 | 0 | |

*Note:* To be significant, the observed value of *C* must be less than or equal to the value shown in the table.

*(continued)*

**Critical Values of C in Fisher's Exact Probability Test** *(continued)*

| Sample size *n* | Cell frequencies *a + b* | *c + d* | *a* | Two-tailed test 0.10 / One-tailed test 0.05 | 0.05 / 0.025 | 0.02 / 0.01 | 0.01 / 0.005 |
|---|---|---|---|---|---|---|---|
| 18 | 9 | 9 | 4 | 0 | | | |
| 18 | 9 | 9 | 5 | 0 | 0 | | |
| 18 | 9 | 9 | 6 | 1 | 1 | 0 | 0 |
| 18 | 9 | 9 | 7 | 2 | 1 | 1 | 0 |
| 18 | 9 | 9 | 8 | 3 | 3 | 2 | 1 |
| 18 | 9 | 9 | 9 | 5 | 4 | 3 | 3 |
| 18 | 10 | 8 | 5 | 0 | | | |
| 18 | 10 | 8 | 6 | 0 | 0 | | |
| 18 | 10 | 8 | 7 | 1 | 1 | 0 | 0 |
| 18 | 10 | 8 | 8 | 2 | 1 | 1 | 0 |
| 18 | 10 | 8 | 9 | 3 | 2 | 2 | 1 |
| 18 | 10 | 8 | 10 | 4 | 4 | 3 | 2 |
| 18 | 11 | 7 | 6 | 0 | 0 | | |
| 18 | 11 | 7 | 7 | 0 | 0 | | |
| 18 | 11 | 7 | 8 | 1 | 1 | 0 | 0 |
| 18 | 11 | 7 | 9 | 2 | 1 | 1 | 0 |
| 18 | 11 | 7 | 10 | 3 | 2 | 1 | 1 |
| 18 | 11 | 7 | 11 | 4 | 3 | 2 | 2 |
| 18 | 12 | 6 | 6 | 0 | | | |
| 18 | 12 | 6 | 7 | 0 | 0 | | |
| 18 | 12 | 6 | 8 | 0 | 0 | | |
| 18 | 12 | 6 | 9 | 1 | 0 | 0 | 0 |
| 18 | 12 | 6 | 10 | 1 | 1 | 0 | 0 |
| 18 | 12 | 6 | 11 | 2 | 2 | 1 | 1 |
| 18 | 12 | 6 | 12 | 3 | 3 | 2 | 2 |
| 18 | 13 | 5 | 8 | 0 | | | |
| 18 | 13 | 5 | 9 | 0 | 0 | | |
| 18 | 13 | 5 | 10 | 1 | 0 | 0 | |
| 18 | 13 | 5 | 11 | 1 | 1 | 0 | 0 |
| 18 | 13 | 5 | 12 | 2 | 1 | 1 | 0 |
| 18 | 13 | 5 | 13 | 2 | 2 | 1 | 1 |
| 18 | 14 | 4 | 9 | 0 | | | |
| 18 | 14 | 4 | 10 | 0 | 0 | | |
| 18 | 14 | 4 | 11 | 0 | 0 | | |
| 18 | 14 | 4 | 12 | 1 | 0 | 0 | 0 |

*Note:* To be significant, the observed value of *C* must be less than or equal to the value shown in the table.

*(continued)*

## Critical Values of C in Fisher's Exact Probability Test *(continued)*

| Sample size | Cell frequencies | | | Level of significance | | | |
|---|---|---|---|---|---|---|---|
| | | | | Two-tailed test | | | |
| | | | | 0.10 | 0.05 | 0.02 | 0.01 |
| | | | | One-tailed test | | | |
| n | a + b | c + d | a | 0.05 | 0.025 | 0.01 | 0.005 |
| 18 | 14 | 4 | 13 | 1 | 1 | 0 | 0 |
| 18 | 14 | 4 | 14 | 2 | 1 | 1 | 1 |
| 18 | 15 | 3 | 11 | 0 | | | |
| 18 | 15 | 3 | 12 | 0 | 0 | | |
| 18 | 15 | 3 | 13 | 0 | 0 | | |
| 18 | 15 | 3 | 14 | 0 | 0 | 0 | 0 |
| 18 | 15 | 3 | 15 | 1 | 1 | 0 | 0 |
| 18 | 16 | 2 | 14 | 0 | | | |
| 18 | 16 | 2 | 15 | 0 | 0 | | |
| 18 | 16 | 2 | 16 | 0 | 0 | 0 | |
| 19 | 10 | 9 | 5 | 0 | 0 | | |
| 19 | 10 | 9 | 6 | 1 | 0 | 0 | |
| 19 | 10 | 9 | 7 | 1 | 1 | 0 | 0 |
| 19 | 10 | 9 | 8 | 2 | 2 | 1 | 1 |
| 19 | 10 | 9 | 9 | 4 | 3 | 2 | 2 |
| 19 | 10 | 9 | 10 | 5 | 4 | 3 | 3 |
| 19 | 11 | 8 | 5 | 0 | | | |
| 19 | 11 | 8 | 6 | 0 | 0 | | |
| 19 | 11 | 8 | 7 | 1 | 0 | 0 | |
| 19 | 11 | 8 | 8 | 1 | 1 | 0 | 0 |
| 19 | 11 | 8 | 9 | 2 | 2 | 1 | 1 |
| 19 | 11 | 8 | 10 | 3 | 3 | 2 | 1 |
| 19 | 11 | 8 | 11 | 4 | 4 | 3 | 3 |
| 19 | 12 | 7 | 6 | 0 | | | |
| 19 | 12 | 7 | 7 | 0 | 0 | | |
| 19 | 12 | 7 | 8 | 1 | 0 | 0 | |
| 19 | 12 | 7 | 9 | 1 | 1 | 0 | 0 |
| 19 | 12 | 7 | 10 | 2 | 1 | 1 | 0 |
| 19 | 12 | 7 | 11 | 3 | 2 | 2 | 1 |
| 19 | 12 | 7 | 12 | 4 | 3 | 3 | 2 |
| 19 | 13 | 6 | 7 | 0 | | | |
| 19 | 13 | 6 | 8 | 0 | 0 | | |
| 19 | 13 | 6 | 9 | 1 | 0 | 0 | |
| 19 | 13 | 6 | 10 | 1 | 1 | 0 | 0 |

*Note:* To be significant, the observed value of C must be less than or equal to the value shown in the table.

*(continued)*

## Critical Values of *C* in Fisher's Exact Probability Test *(continued)*

| Sample size *n* | Cell frequencies *a + b* | Cell frequencies *c + d* | Cell frequencies *a* | Two-tailed test 0.10 / One-tailed test 0.05 | Two-tailed test 0.05 / One-tailed test 0.025 | Two-tailed test 0.02 / One-tailed test 0.01 | Two-tailed test 0.01 / One-tailed test 0.005 |
|---|---|---|---|---|---|---|---|
| 19 | 13 | 6 | 11 | 2 | 1 | 1 | 0 |
| 19 | 13 | 6 | 12 | 2 | 2 | 1 | 1 |
| 19 | 13 | 6 | 13 | 3 | 3 | 2 | 2 |
| 19 | 14 | 5 | 8 | 0 | | | |
| 19 | 14 | 5 | 9 | 0 | 0 | | |
| 19 | 14 | 5 | 10 | 0 | 0 | | |
| 19 | 14 | 5 | 11 | 1 | 0 | 0 | 0 |
| 19 | 14 | 5 | 12 | 1 | 1 | 0 | 0 |
| 19 | 14 | 5 | 13 | 2 | 1 | 1 | 0 |
| 19 | 14 | 5 | 14 | 2 | 2 | 1 | 1 |
| 19 | 15 | 4 | 10 | 0 | | | |
| 19 | 15 | 4 | 11 | 0 | 0 | | |
| 19 | 15 | 4 | 12 | 0 | 0 | 0 | |
| 19 | 15 | 4 | 13 | 1 | 0 | 0 | 0 |
| 19 | 15 | 4 | 14 | 1 | 1 | 0 | 0 |
| 19 | 15 | 4 | 15 | 2 | 1 | 1 | 1 |
| 19 | 16 | 3 | 12 | 0 | | | |
| 19 | 16 | 3 | 13 | 0 | 0 | | |
| 19 | 16 | 3 | 14 | 0 | 0 | | |
| 19 | 16 | 3 | 15 | 0 | 0 | 0 | 0 |
| 19 | 16 | 3 | 16 | 1 | 1 | 0 | 0 |
| 19 | 17 | 2 | 15 | 0 | | | |
| 19 | 17 | 2 | 16 | 0 | 0 | | |
| 19 | 17 | 2 | 17 | 0 | 0 | 0 | |
| 20 | 10 | 10 | 4 | 0 | | | |
| 20 | 10 | 10 | 5 | 0 | 0 | | |
| 20 | 10 | 10 | 6 | 1 | 0 | 0 | |
| 20 | 10 | 10 | 7 | 2 | 1 | 1 | 0 |
| 20 | 10 | 10 | 8 | 3 | 2 | 1 | 1 |
| 20 | 10 | 10 | 9 | 4 | 3 | 3 | 2 |
| 20 | 10 | 10 | 10 | 6 | 5 | 4 | 3 |
| 20 | 11 | 9 | 5 | 0 | | | |
| 20 | 11 | 9 | 6 | 0 | 0 | | |
| 20 | 11 | 9 | 7 | 1 | 1 | 0 | 0 |
| 20 | 11 | 9 | 8 | 2 | 1 | 1 | 0 |

*Note:* To be significant, the observed value of *C* must be less than or equal to the value shown in the table.

*(continued)*

**Critical Values of C in Fisher's Exact Probability Test** *(continued)*

| Sample size *n* | Cell frequencies *a + b* | Cell frequencies *c + d* | Cell frequencies *a* | 0.10 / 0.05 | 0.05 / 0.025 | 0.02 / 0.01 | 0.01 / 0.005 |
|---|---|---|---|---|---|---|---|
| 20 | 11 | 9 | 9 | 3 | 2 | 1 | 1 |
| 20 | 11 | 9 | 10 | 4 | 3 | 2 | 2 |
| 20 | 11 | 9 | 11 | 5 | 4 | 4 | 3 |
| 20 | 12 | 8 | 6 | 0 | 0 | | |
| 20 | 12 | 8 | 7 | 0 | 0 | | |
| 20 | 12 | 8 | 8 | 1 | 1 | 0 | 0 |
| 20 | 12 | 8 | 9 | 2 | 1 | 1 | 0 |
| 20 | 12 | 8 | 10 | 2 | 2 | 1 | 1 |
| 20 | 12 | 8 | 11 | 3 | 3 | 2 | 2 |
| 20 | 12 | 8 | 12 | 5 | 4 | 3 | 3 |
| 20 | 13 | 7 | 6 | 0 | | | |
| 20 | 13 | 7 | 7 | 0 | 0 | | |
| 20 | 13 | 7 | 8 | 0 | 0 | | |
| 20 | 13 | 7 | 9 | 1 | 0 | 0 | 0 |
| 20 | 13 | 7 | 10 | 1 | 1 | 0 | 0 |
| 20 | 13 | 7 | 11 | 2 | 2 | 1 | 1 |
| 20 | 13 | 7 | 12 | 3 | 2 | 2 | 1 |
| 20 | 13 | 7 | 13 | 4 | 3 | 3 | 2 |
| 20 | 14 | 6 | 7 | 0 | | | |
| 20 | 14 | 6 | 8 | 0 | 0 | | |
| 20 | 14 | 6 | 9 | 0 | 0 | | |
| 20 | 14 | 6 | 10 | 1 | 0 | 0 | |
| 20 | 14 | 6 | 11 | 1 | 1 | 0 | 0 |
| 20 | 14 | 6 | 12 | 2 | 1 | 1 | 0 |
| 20 | 14 | 6 | 13 | 2 | 2 | 1 | 1 |
| 20 | 14 | 6 | 14 | 3 | 3 | 2 | 2 |
| 20 | 15 | 5 | 9 | 0 | | | |
| 20 | 15 | 5 | 10 | 0 | 0 | | |
| 20 | 15 | 5 | 11 | 0 | 0 | 0 | |
| 20 | 15 | 5 | 12 | 1 | 0 | 0 | 0 |
| 20 | 15 | 5 | 13 | 1 | 1 | 0 | 0 |
| 20 | 15 | 5 | 14 | 2 | 1 | 1 | 1 |
| 20 | 15 | 5 | 15 | 2 | 2 | 2 | 1 |
| 20 | 16 | 4 | 10 | 0 | | | |
| 20 | 16 | 4 | 11 | 0 | | | |

Level of significance — Two-tailed test: 0.10, 0.05, 0.02, 0.01; One-tailed test: 0.05, 0.025, 0.01, 0.005.

*Note:* To be significant, the observed value of *C* must be less than or equal to the value shown in the table.

*(continued)*

**Critical Values of C in Fisher's Exact Probability Test** *(continued)*

| Sample size | Cell frequencies | | | Level of significance | | | |
|---|---|---|---|---|---|---|---|
| | | | | Two-tailed test | | | |
| | | | | 0.10 | 0.05 | 0.02 | 0.01 |
| | | | | One-tailed test | | | |
| *n* | *a + b* | *c + d* | *a* | 0.05 | 0.025 | 0.01 | 0.005 |
| 20 | 16 | 4 | 12 | 0 | 0 | | |
| 20 | 16 | 4 | 13 | 0 | 0 | 0 | |
| 20 | 16 | 4 | 14 | 1 | 0 | 0 | 0 |
| 20 | 16 | 4 | 15 | 1 | 1 | 0 | 0 |
| 20 | 16 | 4 | 16 | 2 | 1 | 1 | 1 |
| 20 | 17 | 3 | 12 | 0 | | | |
| 20 | 17 | 3 | 13 | 0 | | | |
| 20 | 17 | 3 | 14 | 0 | 0 | | |
| 20 | 17 | 3 | 15 | 0 | 0 | 0 | |
| 20 | 17 | 3 | 16 | 1 | 0 | 0 | 0 |
| 20 | 17 | 3 | 17 | 1 | 1 | 0 | 0 |
| 20 | 18 | 2 | 16 | 0 | | | |
| 20 | 18 | 2 | 17 | 0 | 0 | | |
| 20 | 18 | 2 | 18 | 0 | 0 | 0 | |
| 21 | 11 | 10 | 5 | 0 | 0 | | |
| 21 | 11 | 10 | 6 | 1 | 0 | 0 | |
| 21 | 11 | 10 | 7 | 1 | 1 | 0 | 0 |
| 21 | 11 | 10 | 8 | 2 | 2 | 1 | 0 |
| 21 | 11 | 10 | 9 | 3 | 3 | 2 | 1 |
| 21 | 11 | 10 | 10 | 4 | 4 | 3 | 2 |
| 21 | 11 | 10 | 11 | 6 | 5 | 4 | 4 |
| 21 | 12 | 9 | 5 | 0 | | | |
| 21 | 12 | 9 | 6 | 0 | 0 | | |
| 21 | 12 | 9 | 7 | 1 | 0 | 0 | |
| 21 | 12 | 9 | 8 | 1 | 1 | 0 | 0 |
| 21 | 12 | 9 | 9 | 2 | 2 | 1 | 0 |
| 21 | 12 | 9 | 10 | 3 | 2 | 2 | 1 |
| 21 | 12 | 9 | 11 | 4 | 3 | 3 | 2 |
| 21 | 12 | 9 | 12 | 5 | 5 | 4 | 3 |
| 21 | 13 | 8 | 6 | 0 | | | |
| 21 | 13 | 8 | 7 | 0 | 0 | | |
| 21 | 13 | 8 | 8 | 1 | 0 | 0 | |
| 21 | 13 | 8 | 9 | 1 | 1 | 0 | 0 |
| 21 | 13 | 8 | 10 | 2 | 1 | 1 | 0 |

*Note:* To be significant, the observed value of *C* must be less than or equal to the value shown in the table.

*(continued)*

**Critical Values of C in Fisher's Exact Probability Test** *(continued)*

| | | | | Two-tailed test | | | |
|---|---|---|---|---|---|---|---|
| | | | | 0.10 | 0.05 | 0.02 | 0.01 |
| Sample size | Cell frequencies | | | One-tailed test | | | |
| *n* | *a + b* | *c + d* | *a* | 0.05 | 0.025 | 0.01 | 0.005 |
| 21 | 13 | 8 | 11 | 3 | 2 | 1 | 1 |
| 21 | 13 | 8 | 12 | 4 | 3 | 2 | 2 |
| 21 | 13 | 8 | 13 | 5 | 4 | 3 | 3 |
| 21 | 14 | 7 | 7 | 0 | | | |
| 21 | 14 | 7 | 8 | 0 | 0 | | |
| 21 | 14 | 7 | 9 | 1 | 0 | 0 | |
| 21 | 14 | 7 | 10 | 1 | 1 | 0 | 0 |
| 21 | 14 | 7 | 11 | 2 | 1 | 1 | 0 |
| 21 | 14 | 7 | 12 | 2 | 2 | 1 | 1 |
| 21 | 14 | 7 | 13 | 3 | 2 | 2 | 1 |
| 21 | 14 | 7 | 14 | 4 | 3 | 3 | 2 |
| 21 | 15 | 6 | 8 | 0 | | | |
| 21 | 15 | 6 | 9 | 0 | 0 | | |
| 21 | 15 | 6 | 10 | 0 | 0 | 0 | |
| 21 | 15 | 6 | 11 | 1 | 0 | 0 | 0 |
| 21 | 15 | 6 | 12 | 1 | 1 | 0 | 0 |
| 21 | 15 | 6 | 13 | 2 | 1 | 1 | 0 |
| 21 | 15 | 6 | 14 | 2 | 2 | 1 | 1 |
| 21 | 15 | 6 | 15 | 3 | 3 | 2 | 2 |
| 21 | 16 | 5 | 9 | 0 | | | |
| 21 | 16 | 5 | 10 | 0 | 0 | | |
| 21 | 16 | 5 | 11 | 0 | 0 | | |
| 21 | 16 | 5 | 12 | 1 | 0 | 0 | |
| 21 | 16 | 5 | 13 | 1 | 0 | 0 | 0 |
| 21 | 16 | 5 | 14 | 1 | 1 | 0 | 0 |
| 21 | 16 | 5 | 15 | 2 | 1 | 1 | 1 |
| 21 | 16 | 5 | 16 | 3 | 2 | 2 | 1 |
| 21 | 17 | 4 | 11 | 0 | | | |
| 21 | 17 | 4 | 12 | 0 | 0 | | |
| 21 | 17 | 4 | 13 | 0 | 0 | | |
| 21 | 17 | 4 | 14 | 0 | 0 | 0 | |
| 21 | 17 | 4 | 15 | 1 | 0 | 0 | 0 |
| 21 | 17 | 4 | 16 | 1 | 1 | 0 | 0 |
| 21 | 17 | 4 | 17 | 2 | 1 | 1 | 1 |
| 21 | 18 | 3 | 13 | 0 | | | |

*Note:* To be significant, the observed value of *C* must be less than or equal to the value shown in the table.

*(continued)*

**Critical Values of C in Fisher's Exact Probability Test** *(continued)*

| Sample size *n* | Cell frequencies | | | Level of significance | | | |
|---|---|---|---|---|---|---|---|
| | | | | Two-tailed test | | | |
| | | | | 0.10 | 0.05 | 0.02 | 0.01 |
| | | | | One-tailed test | | | |
| *n* | *a + b* | *c + d* | *a* | 0.05 | 0.025 | 0.01 | 0.005 |
| 21 | 18 | 3 | 14 | 0 | | | |
| 21 | 18 | 3 | 15 | 0 | 0 | | |
| 21 | 18 | 3 | 16 | 0 | 0 | 0 | |
| 21 | 18 | 3 | 17 | 1 | 0 | 0 | 0 |
| 21 | 18 | 3 | 18 | 1 | 1 | 0 | 0 |
| 21 | 19 | 2 | 16 | 0 | | | |
| 21 | 19 | 2 | 17 | 0 | | | |
| 21 | 19 | 2 | 18 | 0 | 0 | | |
| 21 | 19 | 2 | 19 | 0 | 0 | 0 | 0 |
| 21 | 20 | 1 | 20 | 0 | | | |
| 22 | 11 | 11 | 4 | 0 | | | |
| 22 | 11 | 11 | 5 | 0 | 0 | | |
| 22 | 11 | 11 | 6 | 1 | 0 | 0 | |
| 22 | 11 | 11 | 7 | 2 | 1 | 0 | 0 |
| 22 | 11 | 11 | 8 | 3 | 2 | 1 | 1 |
| 22 | 11 | 11 | 9 | 4 | 3 | 2 | 2 |
| 22 | 11 | 11 | 10 | 5 | 4 | 3 | 3 |
| 22 | 11 | 11 | 11 | 7 | 6 | 5 | 4 |
| 22 | 12 | 10 | 5 | 0 | | | |
| 22 | 12 | 10 | 6 | 0 | 0 | | |
| 22 | 12 | 10 | 7 | 1 | 0 | 0 | 0 |
| 22 | 12 | 10 | 8 | 2 | 1 | 0 | 0 |
| 22 | 12 | 10 | 9 | 3 | 2 | 1 | 1 |
| 22 | 12 | 10 | 10 | 4 | 3 | 2 | 2 |
| 22 | 12 | 10 | 11 | 5 | 4 | 3 | 3 |
| 22 | 12 | 10 | 12 | 6 | 5 | 5 | 4 |
| 22 | 13 | 9 | 5 | 0 | | | |
| 22 | 13 | 9 | 6 | 0 | 0 | | |
| 22 | 13 | 9 | 7 | 0 | 0 | | |
| 22 | 13 | 9 | 8 | 1 | 1 | 0 | 0 |
| 22 | 13 | 9 | 9 | 2 | 1 | 0 | 0 |
| 22 | 13 | 9 | 10 | 2 | 2 | 1 | 1 |
| 22 | 13 | 9 | 11 | 3 | 3 | 2 | 1 |
| 22 | 13 | 9 | 12 | 4 | 4 | 3 | 2 |

*Note:* To be significant, the observed value of C must be less than or equal to the value shown in the table.

*(continued)*

**Critical Values of C in Fisher's Exact Probability Test** *(continued)*

| Sample size | Cell frequencies | | | Level of significance | | | |
|---|---|---|---|---|---|---|---|
| | | | | Two-tailed test | | | |
| | | | | 0.10 | 0.05 | 0.02 | 0.01 |
| | | | | One-tailed test | | | |
| *n* | *a + b* | *c + d* | *a* | 0.05 | 0.025 | 0.01 | 0.005 |
| 22 | 13 | 9 | 13 | 5 | 5 | 4 | 4 |
| 22 | 14 | 8 | 6 | 0 | | | |
| 22 | 14 | 8 | 7 | 0 | 0 | | |
| 22 | 14 | 8 | 8 | 0 | 0 | 0 | |
| 22 | 14 | 8 | 9 | 1 | 0 | 0 | 0 |
| 22 | 14 | 8 | 10 | 2 | 1 | 0 | 0 |
| 22 | 14 | 8 | 11 | 2 | 2 | 1 | 1 |
| 22 | 14 | 8 | 12 | 3 | 2 | 2 | 1 |
| 22 | 14 | 8 | 13 | 4 | 3 | 2 | 2 |
| 22 | 14 | 8 | 14 | 5 | 4 | 4 | 3 |
| 22 | 15 | 7 | 7 | 0 | | | |
| 22 | 15 | 7 | 8 | 0 | 0 | | |
| 22 | 15 | 7 | 9 | 0 | 0 | | |
| 22 | 15 | 7 | 10 | 1 | 0 | 0 | 0 |
| 22 | 15 | 7 | 11 | 1 | 1 | 0 | 0 |
| 22 | 15 | 7 | 12 | 2 | 1 | 1 | 0 |
| 22 | 15 | 7 | 13 | 2 | 2 | 1 | 1 |
| 22 | 15 | 7 | 14 | 3 | 3 | 2 | 2 |
| 22 | 15 | 7 | 15 | 4 | 4 | 3 | 3 |
| 22 | 16 | 6 | 8 | 0 | | | |
| 22 | 16 | 6 | 9 | 0 | 0 | | |
| 22 | 16 | 6 | 10 | 0 | 0 | | |
| 22 | 16 | 6 | 11 | 1 | 0 | 0 | |
| 22 | 16 | 6 | 12 | 1 | 1 | 0 | 0 |
| 22 | 16 | 6 | 13 | 1 | 1 | 0 | 0 |
| 22 | 16 | 6 | 14 | 2 | 1 | 1 | 1 |
| 22 | 16 | 6 | 15 | 3 | 2 | 2 | 1 |
| 22 | 16 | 6 | 16 | 3 | 3 | 2 | 2 |
| 22 | 17 | 5 | 9 | 0 | | | |
| 22 | 17 | 5 | 10 | 0 | | | |
| 22 | 17 | 5 | 11 | 0 | 0 | | |
| 22 | 17 | 5 | 12 | 0 | 0 | 0 | |
| 22 | 17 | 5 | 13 | 1 | 0 | 0 | 0 |
| 22 | 17 | 5 | 14 | 1 | 1 | 0 | 0 |
| 22 | 17 | 5 | 15 | 1 | 1 | 1 | 0 |

*Note:* To be significant, the observed value of *C* must be less than or equal to the value shown in the table.

*(continued)*

**Critical Values of C in Fisher's Exact Probability Test** *(continued)*

| Sample size | Cell frequencies | | | Level of significance | | | |
|---|---|---|---|---|---|---|---|
| | | | | \textit{Two-tailed test} | | | |
| | | | | 0.10 | 0.05 | 0.02 | 0.01 |
| | | | | \textit{One-tailed test} | | | |
| *n* | *a + b* | *c + d* | *a* | 0.05 | 0.025 | 0.01 | 0.005 |
| 22 | 17 | 5 | 16 | 2 | 2 | 1 | 1 |
| 22 | 17 | 5 | 17 | 3 | 2 | 2 | 1 |
| 22 | 18 | 4 | 11 | 0 | | | |
| 22 | 18 | 4 | 12 | 0 | | | |
| 22 | 18 | 4 | 13 | 0 | 0 | | |
| 22 | 18 | 4 | 14 | 0 | 0 | 0 | |
| 22 | 18 | 4 | 15 | 1 | 0 | 0 | 0 |
| 22 | 18 | 4 | 16 | 1 | 1 | 0 | 0 |
| 22 | 18 | 4 | 17 | 1 | 1 | 1 | 0 |
| 22 | 18 | 4 | 18 | 2 | 1 | 1 | 1 |
| 22 | 19 | 3 | 14 | 0 | | | |
| 22 | 19 | 3 | 15 | 0 | 0 | | |
| 22 | 19 | 3 | 16 | 0 | 0 | | |
| 22 | 19 | 3 | 17 | 0 | 0 | 0 | |
| 22 | 19 | 3 | 18 | 1 | 0 | 0 | 0 |
| 22 | 19 | 3 | 19 | 1 | 1 | 0 | 0 |
| 22 | 20 | 2 | 17 | 0 | | | |
| 22 | 20 | 2 | 18 | 0 | | | |
| 22 | 20 | 2 | 19 | 0 | 0 | | |
| 22 | 20 | 2 | 20 | 0 | 0 | 0 | 0 |
| 22 | 21 | 1 | 21 | 0 | | | |
| 23 | 12 | 11 | 5 | 0 | 0 | | |
| 23 | 12 | 11 | 6 | 1 | 0 | 0 | |
| 23 | 12 | 11 | 7 | 1 | 1 | 0 | 0 |
| 23 | 12 | 11 | 8 | 2 | 1 | 1 | 0 |
| 23 | 12 | 11 | 9 | 3 | 2 | 2 | 1 |
| 23 | 12 | 11 | 10 | 4 | 3 | 2 | 2 |
| 23 | 12 | 11 | 11 | 5 | 5 | 4 | 3 |
| 23 | 12 | 11 | 12 | 7 | 6 | 5 | 5 |
| 23 | 13 | 10 | 5 | 0 | | | |
| 23 | 13 | 10 | 6 | 0 | 0 | | |
| 23 | 13 | 10 | 7 | 1 | 0 | 0 | |
| 23 | 13 | 10 | 8 | 1 | 1 | 0 | 0 |
| 23 | 13 | 10 | 9 | 2 | 1 | 1 | 0 |

*Note:* To be significant, the observed value of *C* must be less than or equal to the value shown in the table.

*(continued)*

**Critical Values of C in Fisher's Exact Probability Test** *(continued)*

| | | | | Level of significance | | | |
|---|---|---|---|---|---|---|---|
| | | | | Two-tailed test | | | |
| | | | | 0.10 | 0.05 | 0.02 | 0.01 |
| Sample size | Cell frequencies | | | One-tailed test | | | |
| n | a + b | c + d | a | 0.05 | 0.025 | 0.01 | 0.005 |
| 23 | 13 | 10 | 10 | 3 | 2 | 1 | 1 |
| 23 | 13 | 10 | 11 | 4 | 3 | 2 | 2 |
| 23 | 13 | 10 | 12 | 5 | 4 | 3 | 3 |
| 23 | 13 | 10 | 13 | 6 | 6 | 5 | 4 |
| 23 | 14 | 9 | 6 | 0 | | | |
| 23 | 14 | 9 | 7 | 0 | 0 | | |
| 23 | 14 | 9 | 8 | 1 | 0 | 0 | |
| 23 | 14 | 9 | 9 | 1 | 1 | 0 | 0 |
| 23 | 14 | 9 | 10 | 2 | 1 | 1 | 0 |
| 23 | 14 | 9 | 11 | 3 | 2 | 1 | 1 |
| 23 | 14 | 9 | 12 | 3 | 3 | 2 | 2 |
| 23 | 14 | 9 | 13 | 4 | 4 | 3 | 3 |
| 23 | 14 | 9 | 14 | 6 | 5 | 4 | 4 |
| 23 | 15 | 8 | 6 | 0 | | | |
| 23 | 15 | 8 | 7 | 0 | | | |
| 23 | 15 | 8 | 8 | 0 | 0 | | |
| 23 | 15 | 8 | 9 | 1 | 0 | 0 | |
| 23 | 15 | 8 | 10 | 1 | 1 | 0 | 0 |
| 23 | 15 | 8 | 11 | 2 | 1 | 1 | 0 |
| 23 | 15 | 8 | 12 | 2 | 2 | 1 | 1 |
| 23 | 15 | 8 | 13 | 3 | 2 | 2 | 1 |
| 23 | 15 | 8 | 14 | 4 | 3 | 3 | 2 |
| 23 | 15 | 8 | 15 | 5 | 4 | 4 | 3 |
| 23 | 16 | 7 | 7 | 0 | | | |
| 23 | 16 | 7 | 8 | 0 | | | |
| 23 | 16 | 7 | 9 | 0 | 0 | | |
| 23 | 16 | 7 | 10 | 1 | 0 | 0 | |
| 23 | 16 | 7 | 11 | 1 | 1 | 0 | 0 |
| 23 | 16 | 7 | 12 | 1 | 1 | 0 | 0 |
| 23 | 16 | 7 | 13 | 2 | 1 | 1 | 1 |
| 23 | 16 | 7 | 14 | 3 | 2 | 1 | 1 |
| 23 | 16 | 7 | 15 | 3 | 3 | 2 | 2 |
| 23 | 16 | 7 | 16 | 4 | 4 | 3 | 3 |
| 23 | 17 | 6 | 8 | 0 | | | |
| 23 | 17 | 6 | 9 | 0 | | | |

*Note:* To be significant, the observed value of C must be less than or equal to the value shown in the table.

*(continued)*

**Critical Values of C in Fisher's Exact Probability Test** *(continued)*

| Sample size n | Cell frequencies a + b | Cell frequencies c + d | Cell frequencies a | Two-tailed test 0.10 / One-tailed test 0.05 | Two-tailed test 0.05 / One-tailed test 0.025 | Two-tailed test 0.02 / One-tailed test 0.01 | Two-tailed test 0.01 / One-tailed test 0.005 |
|---|---|---|---|---|---|---|---|
| 23 | 17 | 6 | 10 | 0 | 0 |   |   |
| 23 | 17 | 6 | 11 | 0 | 0 | 0 |   |
| 23 | 17 | 6 | 12 | 1 | 0 | 0 | 0 |
| 23 | 17 | 6 | 13 | 1 | 1 | 0 | 0 |
| 23 | 17 | 6 | 14 | 2 | 1 | 1 | 0 |
| 23 | 17 | 6 | 15 | 2 | 2 | 1 | 1 |
| 23 | 17 | 6 | 16 | 3 | 2 | 2 | 1 |
| 23 | 17 | 6 | 17 | 3 | 3 | 2 | 2 |
| 23 | 18 | 5 | 10 | 0 |   |   |   |
| 23 | 18 | 5 | 11 | 0 | 0 |   |   |
| 23 | 18 | 5 | 12 | 0 | 0 |   |   |
| 23 | 18 | 5 | 13 | 0 | 0 | 0 |   |
| 23 | 18 | 5 | 14 | 1 | 0 | 0 | 0 |
| 23 | 18 | 5 | 15 | 1 | 1 | 0 | 0 |
| 23 | 18 | 5 | 16 | 2 | 1 | 1 | 0 |
| 23 | 18 | 5 | 17 | 2 | 2 | 1 | 1 |
| 23 | 18 | 5 | 18 | 3 | 2 | 2 | 1 |
| 23 | 19 | 4 | 12 | 0 |   |   |   |
| 23 | 19 | 4 | 13 | 0 | 0 |   |   |
| 23 | 19 | 4 | 14 | 0 | 0 |   |   |
| 23 | 19 | 4 | 15 | 0 | 0 | 0 |   |
| 23 | 19 | 4 | 16 | 1 | 0 | 0 | 0 |
| 23 | 19 | 4 | 17 | 1 | 1 | 0 | 0 |
| 23 | 19 | 4 | 18 | 1 | 1 | 1 | 0 |
| 23 | 19 | 4 | 19 | 2 | 2 | 1 | 1 |
| 23 | 20 | 3 | 14 | 0 |   |   |   |
| 23 | 20 | 3 | 15 | 0 |   |   |   |
| 23 | 20 | 3 | 16 | 0 | 0 |   |   |
| 23 | 20 | 3 | 17 | 0 | 0 |   |   |
| 23 | 20 | 3 | 18 | 0 | 0 | 0 |   |
| 23 | 20 | 3 | 19 | 1 | 0 | 0 | 0 |
| 23 | 20 | 3 | 20 | 1 | 1 | 0 | 0 |
| 23 | 21 | 2 | 18 | 0 |   |   |   |
| 23 | 21 | 2 | 19 | 0 | 0 |   |   |

*Note:* To be significant, the observed value of $C$ must be less than or equal to the value shown in the table.

*(continued)*

**Critical Values of C in Fisher's Exact Probability Test** *(continued)*

| Sample size *n* | Cell frequencies | | | Level of significance | | | |
|---|---|---|---|---|---|---|---|
| | | | | Two-tailed test | | | |
| | | | | 0.10 | 0.05 | 0.02 | 0.01 |
| | | | | One-tailed test | | | |
| | $a+b$ | $c+d$ | $a$ | 0.05 | 0.025 | 0.01 | 0.005 |
| 23 | 21 | 2 | 20 | 0 | 0 | | |
| 23 | 21 | 2 | 21 | 0 | 0 | 0 | 0 |
| 23 | 22 | 1 | 22 | 0 | | | |
| 24 | 12 | 12 | 4 | 0 | | | |
| 24 | 12 | 12 | 5 | 0 | 0 | | |
| 24 | 12 | 12 | 6 | 1 | 0 | 0 | |
| 24 | 12 | 12 | 7 | 2 | 1 | 0 | 0 |
| 24 | 12 | 12 | 8 | 3 | 2 | 1 | 1 |
| 24 | 12 | 12 | 9 | 4 | 3 | 2 | 1 |
| 24 | 12 | 12 | 10 | 5 | 4 | 3 | 2 |
| 24 | 12 | 12 | 11 | 6 | 5 | 4 | 4 |
| 24 | 12 | 12 | 12 | 8 | 7 | 6 | 5 |
| 24 | 13 | 11 | 5 | 0 | | | |
| 24 | 13 | 11 | 6 | 0 | 0 | | |
| 24 | 13 | 11 | 7 | 1 | 0 | 0 | 0 |
| 24 | 13 | 11 | 8 | 2 | 1 | 0 | 0 |
| 24 | 13 | 11 | 9 | 3 | 2 | 1 | 1 |
| 24 | 13 | 11 | 10 | 3 | 3 | 2 | 1 |
| 24 | 13 | 11 | 11 | 4 | 4 | 3 | 2 |
| 24 | 13 | 11 | 12 | 6 | 5 | 4 | 3 |
| 24 | 13 | 11 | 13 | 7 | 6 | 5 | 5 |
| 24 | 14 | 10 | 5 | 0 | | | |
| 24 | 14 | 10 | 6 | 0 | 0 | | |
| 24 | 14 | 10 | 7 | 0 | 0 | 0 | |
| 24 | 14 | 10 | 8 | 1 | 1 | 0 | 0 |
| 24 | 14 | 10 | 9 | 2 | 1 | 0 | 0 |
| 24 | 14 | 10 | 10 | 2 | 2 | 1 | 1 |
| 24 | 14 | 10 | 11 | 3 | 3 | 2 | 1 |
| 24 | 14 | 10 | 12 | 4 | 3 | 3 | 2 |
| 24 | 14 | 10 | 13 | 5 | 4 | 4 | 3 |
| 24 | 14 | 10 | 14 | 6 | 6 | 5 | 4 |
| 24 | 15 | 9 | 6 | 0 | | | |
| 24 | 15 | 9 | 7 | 0 | 0 | | |
| 24 | 15 | 9 | 8 | 1 | 0 | 0 | |

*Note:* To be significant, the observed value of *C* must be less than or equal to the value shown in the table.

*(continued)*

**Critical Values of *C* in Fisher's Exact Probability Test** *(continued)*

| Sample size *n* | Cell frequencies | | | Two-tailed test 0.10 | 0.05 | 0.02 | 0.01 |
|---|---|---|---|---|---|---|---|
| | *a + b* | *c + d* | *a* | One-tailed test 0.05 | 0.025 | 0.01 | 0.005 |
| 24 | 15 | 9 | 9 | 1 | 1 | 0 | 0 |
| 24 | 15 | 9 | 10 | 2 | 1 | 0 | 0 |
| 24 | 15 | 9 | 11 | 2 | 2 | 1 | 1 |
| 24 | 15 | 9 | 12 | 3 | 2 | 2 | 1 |
| 24 | 15 | 9 | 13 | 4 | 3 | 2 | 2 |
| 24 | 15 | 9 | 14 | 5 | 4 | 3 | 3 |
| 24 | 15 | 9 | 15 | 6 | 5 | 4 | 4 |
| 24 | 16 | 8 | 7 | 0 | | | |
| 24 | 16 | 8 | 8 | 0 | 0 | | |
| 24 | 16 | 8 | 9 | 0 | 0 | 0 | |
| 24 | 16 | 8 | 10 | 1 | 0 | 0 | 0 |
| 24 | 16 | 8 | 11 | 1 | 1 | 0 | 0 |
| 24 | 16 | 8 | 12 | 2 | 1 | 1 | 0 |
| 24 | 16 | 8 | 13 | 3 | 2 | 1 | 1 |
| 24 | 16 | 8 | 14 | 3 | 3 | 2 | 2 |
| 24 | 16 | 8 | 15 | 4 | 3 | 3 | 2 |
| 24 | 16 | 8 | 16 | 5 | 4 | 4 | 3 |
| 24 | 17 | 7 | 8 | 0 | | | |
| 24 | 17 | 7 | 9 | 0 | 0 | | |
| 24 | 17 | 7 | 10 | 0 | 0 | 0 | |
| 24 | 17 | 7 | 11 | 1 | 0 | 0 | 0 |
| 24 | 17 | 7 | 12 | 1 | 1 | 0 | 0 |
| 24 | 17 | 7 | 13 | 2 | 1 | 1 | 0 |
| 24 | 17 | 7 | 14 | 2 | 2 | 1 | 1 |
| 24 | 17 | 7 | 15 | 3 | 2 | 2 | 1 |
| 24 | 17 | 7 | 16 | 3 | 3 | 2 | 2 |
| 24 | 17 | 7 | 17 | 4 | 4 | 3 | 3 |
| 24 | 18 | 6 | 9 | 0 | | | |
| 24 | 18 | 6 | 10 | 0 | 0 | | |
| 24 | 18 | 6 | 11 | 0 | 0 | | |
| 24 | 18 | 6 | 12 | 1 | 0 | 0 | |
| 24 | 18 | 6 | 13 | 1 | 0 | 0 | 0 |
| 24 | 18 | 6 | 14 | 1 | 1 | 0 | 0 |
| 24 | 18 | 6 | 15 | 2 | 1 | 1 | 0 |
| 24 | 18 | 6 | 16 | 2 | 2 | 1 | 1 |

*Note:* To be significant, the observed value of *C* must be less than or equal to the value shown in the table.

*(continued)*

**Critical Values of C in Fisher's Exact Probability Test** *(continued)*

| Sample size *n* | Cell frequencies $a+b$ | $c+d$ | $a$ | Two-tailed test 0.10 / One-tailed test 0.05 | 0.05 / 0.025 | 0.02 / 0.01 | 0.01 / 0.005 |
|---|---|---|---|---|---|---|---|
| 24 | 18 | 6 | 17 | 3 | 2 | 2 | 1 |
| 24 | 18 | 6 | 18 | 3 | 3 | 3 | 2 |
| 24 | 19 | 5 | 10 | 0 | | | |
| 24 | 19 | 5 | 11 | 0 | | | |
| 24 | 19 | 5 | 12 | 0 | 0 | | |
| 24 | 19 | 5 | 13 | 0 | 0 | | |
| 24 | 19 | 5 | 14 | 1 | 0 | 0 | |
| 24 | 19 | 5 | 15 | 1 | 0 | 0 | 0 |
| 24 | 19 | 5 | 16 | 1 | 1 | 0 | 0 |
| 24 | 19 | 5 | 17 | 2 | 1 | 1 | 0 |
| 24 | 19 | 5 | 18 | 2 | 2 | 1 | 1 |
| 24 | 19 | 5 | 19 | 3 | 2 | 2 | 2 |
| 24 | 20 | 4 | 12 | 0 | | | |
| 24 | 20 | 4 | 13 | 0 | | | |
| 24 | 20 | 4 | 14 | 0 | 0 | | |
| 24 | 20 | 4 | 15 | 0 | 0 | | |
| 24 | 20 | 4 | 16 | 0 | 0 | 0 | |
| 24 | 20 | 4 | 17 | 1 | 0 | 0 | 0 |
| 24 | 20 | 4 | 18 | 1 | 1 | 0 | 0 |
| 24 | 20 | 4 | 19 | 1 | 1 | 1 | 0 |
| 24 | 20 | 4 | 20 | 2 | 2 | 1 | 1 |
| 24 | 21 | 3 | 15 | 0 | | | |
| 24 | 21 | 3 | 16 | 0 | | | |
| 24 | 21 | 3 | 17 | 0 | 0 | | |
| 24 | 21 | 3 | 18 | 0 | 0 | 0 | |
| 24 | 21 | 3 | 19 | 0 | 0 | 0 | 0 |
| 24 | 21 | 3 | 20 | 1 | 0 | 0 | 0 |
| 24 | 21 | 3 | 21 | 1 | 1 | 0 | 0 |
| 24 | 22 | 2 | 19 | 0 | | | |
| 24 | 22 | 2 | 20 | 0 | 0 | | |
| 24 | 22 | 2 | 21 | 0 | 0 | | |
| 24 | 22 | 2 | 22 | 0 | 0 | 0 | 0 |
| 24 | 23 | 1 | 23 | 0 | | | |

*Note:* To be significant, the observed value of *C* must be less than or equal to the value shown in the table.

*(continued)*

**Critical Values of C in Fisher's Exact Probability Test** *(continued)*

| Sample size *n* | Cell frequencies *a + b* | *c + d* | *a* | Level of significance Two-tailed test 0.10 | 0.05 | 0.02 | 0.01 |
|---|---|---|---|---|---|---|---|
| | | | | One-tailed test 0.05 | 0.025 | 0.01 | 0.005 |
| 25 | 13 | 12 | 5 | 0 | 0 | | |
| 25 | 13 | 12 | 6 | 1 | 0 | 0 | |
| 25 | 13 | 12 | 7 | 1 | 1 | 0 | 0 |
| 25 | 13 | 12 | 8 | 2 | 1 | 1 | 0 |
| 25 | 13 | 12 | 9 | 3 | 2 | 1 | 1 |
| 25 | 13 | 12 | 10 | 4 | 3 | 2 | 2 |
| 25 | 13 | 12 | 11 | 5 | 4 | 3 | 3 |
| 25 | 13 | 12 | 12 | 6 | 5 | 5 | 4 |
| 25 | 13 | 12 | 13 | 8 | 7 | 6 | 5 |
| 25 | 14 | 11 | 5 | 0 | | | |
| 25 | 14 | 11 | 6 | 0 | 0 | | |
| 25 | 14 | 11 | 7 | 1 | 0 | 0 | |
| 25 | 14 | 11 | 8 | 1 | 1 | 0 | 0 |
| 25 | 14 | 11 | 9 | 2 | 1 | 1 | 0 |
| 25 | 14 | 11 | 10 | 3 | 2 | 1 | 1 |
| 25 | 14 | 11 | 11 | 4 | 3 | 2 | 2 |
| 25 | 14 | 11 | 12 | 5 | 4 | 3 | 3 |
| 25 | 14 | 11 | 13 | 6 | 5 | 4 | 4 |
| 25 | 14 | 11 | 14 | 7 | 6 | 6 | 5 |
| 25 | 15 | 10 | 6 | 0 | | | |
| 25 | 15 | 10 | 7 | 0 | 0 | | |
| 25 | 15 | 10 | 8 | 1 | 0 | 0 | |
| 25 | 15 | 10 | 9 | 1 | 1 | 0 | 0 |
| 25 | 15 | 10 | 10 | 2 | 1 | 1 | 0 |
| 25 | 15 | 10 | 11 | 3 | 2 | 1 | 1 |
| 25 | 15 | 10 | 12 | 3 | 3 | 2 | 2 |
| 25 | 15 | 10 | 13 | 4 | 4 | 3 | 2 |
| 25 | 15 | 10 | 14 | 5 | 5 | 4 | 3 |
| 25 | 15 | 10 | 15 | 6 | 6 | 5 | 5 |
| 25 | 16 | 9 | 6 | 0 | | | |
| 25 | 16 | 9 | 7 | 0 | 0 | | |
| 25 | 16 | 9 | 8 | 0 | 0 | | |
| 25 | 16 | 9 | 9 | 1 | 0 | 0 | |
| 25 | 16 | 9 | 10 | 1 | 1 | 0 | 0 |
| 25 | 16 | 9 | 11 | 2 | 1 | 1 | 0 |

*Note:* To be significant, the observed value of $C$ must be less than or equal to the value shown in the table.

*(continued)*

**Critical Values of *C* in Fisher's Exact Probability Test** *(continued)*

| Sample size *n* | Cell frequencies | | | Level of significance | | | |
|---|---|---|---|---|---|---|---|
| | | | | Two-tailed test | | | |
| | | | | 0.10 | 0.05 | 0.02 | 0.01 |
| | | | | One-tailed test | | | |
| | *a + b* | *c + d* | *a* | 0.05 | 0.025 | 0.01 | 0.005 |
| 25 | 16 | 9 | 12 | 2 | 2 | 1 | 1 |
| 25 | 16 | 9 | 13 | 3 | 2 | 2 | 1 |
| 25 | 16 | 9 | 14 | 4 | 3 | 3 | 2 |
| 25 | 16 | 9 | 15 | 5 | 4 | 3 | 3 |
| 25 | 16 | 9 | 16 | 6 | 5 | 5 | 4 |
| 25 | 17 | 8 | 7 | 0 | | | |
| 25 | 17 | 8 | 8 | 0 | 0 | | |
| 25 | 17 | 8 | 9 | 0 | 0 | | |
| 25 | 17 | 8 | 10 | 1 | 0 | 0 | |
| 25 | 17 | 8 | 11 | 1 | 1 | 0 | 0 |
| 25 | 17 | 8 | 12 | 2 | 1 | 1 | 0 |
| 25 | 17 | 8 | 13 | 2 | 2 | 1 | 1 |
| 25 | 17 | 8 | 14 | 3 | 2 | 2 | 1 |
| 25 | 17 | 8 | 15 | 3 | 3 | 2 | 2 |
| 25 | 17 | 8 | 16 | 4 | 4 | 3 | 2 |
| 25 | 17 | 8 | 17 | 5 | 5 | 4 | 3 |
| 25 | 18 | 7 | 8 | 0 | | | |
| 25 | 18 | 7 | 9 | 0 | 0 | | |
| 25 | 18 | 7 | 10 | 0 | 0 | | |
| 25 | 18 | 7 | 11 | 1 | 0 | 0 | |
| 25 | 18 | 7 | 12 | 1 | 0 | 0 | 0 |
| 25 | 18 | 7 | 13 | 1 | 1 | 0 | 0 |
| 25 | 18 | 7 | 14 | 2 | 1 | 1 | 0 |
| 25 | 18 | 7 | 15 | 2 | 2 | 1 | 1 |
| 25 | 18 | 7 | 16 | 3 | 2 | 2 | 1 |
| 25 | 18 | 7 | 17 | 3 | 3 | 2 | 2 |
| 25 | 18 | 7 | 18 | 4 | 4 | 3 | 3 |
| 25 | 19 | 6 | 9 | 0 | | | |
| 25 | 19 | 6 | 10 | 0 | | | |
| 25 | 19 | 6 | 11 | 0 | 0 | | |
| 25 | 19 | 6 | 12 | 0 | 0 | 0 | |
| 25 | 19 | 6 | 13 | 1 | 0 | 0 | |
| 25 | 19 | 6 | 14 | 1 | 1 | 0 | 0 |
| 25 | 19 | 6 | 15 | 1 | 1 | 0 | 0 |
| 25 | 19 | 6 | 16 | 2 | 1 | 1 | 0 |

*Note:* To be significant, the observed value of *C* must be less than or equal to the value shown in the table.

*(continued)*

**Critical Values of C in Fisher's Exact Probability Test** *(continued)*

| Sample size $n$ | Cell frequencies | | | Level of significance | | | |
|---|---|---|---|---|---|---|---|
| | | | | Two-tailed test | | | |
| | | | | 0.10 | 0.05 | 0.02 | 0.01 |
| | | | | One-tailed test | | | |
| | $a + b$ | $c + d$ | $a$ | 0.05 | 0.025 | 0.01 | 0.005 |
| 25 | 19 | 6 | 18 | 3 | 2 | 2 | 1 |
| 25 | 19 | 6 | 19 | 3 | 3 | 3 | 2 |
| 25 | 20 | 5 | 11 | 0 | | | |
| 25 | 20 | 5 | 12 | 0 | 0 | | |
| 25 | 20 | 5 | 13 | 0 | 0 | | |
| 25 | 20 | 5 | 14 | 0 | 0 | 0 | |
| 25 | 20 | 5 | 15 | 1 | 0 | 0 | 0 |
| 25 | 20 | 5 | 16 | 1 | 1 | 0 | 0 |
| 25 | 20 | 5 | 17 | 1 | 1 | 0 | 0 |
| 25 | 20 | 5 | 18 | 2 | 1 | 1 | 0 |
| 25 | 20 | 5 | 19 | 2 | 2 | 1 | 1 |
| 25 | 20 | 5 | 20 | 3 | 2 | 2 | 2 |
| 25 | 21 | 4 | 13 | 0 | | | |
| 25 | 21 | 4 | 14 | 0 | | | |
| 25 | 21 | 4 | 15 | 0 | 0 | | |
| 25 | 21 | 4 | 16 | 0 | 0 | 0 | |
| 25 | 21 | 4 | 17 | 0 | 0 | 0 | |
| 25 | 21 | 4 | 18 | 1 | 0 | 0 | 0 |
| 25 | 21 | 4 | 19 | 1 | 1 | 0 | 0 |
| 25 | 21 | 4 | 20 | 1 | 1 | 1 | 0 |
| 25 | 21 | 4 | 21 | 2 | 2 | 1 | 1 |
| 25 | 22 | 3 | 16 | 0 | | | |
| 25 | 22 | 3 | 17 | 0 | 0 | | |
| 25 | 22 | 3 | 18 | 0 | 0 | | |
| 25 | 22 | 3 | 19 | 0 | 0 | 0 | |
| 25 | 22 | 3 | 20 | 0 | 0 | 0 | 0 |
| 25 | 22 | 3 | 21 | 1 | 0 | 0 | 0 |
| 25 | 22 | 3 | 22 | 1 | 1 | 1 | 0 |
| 25 | 23 | 2 | 20 | 0 | | | |
| 25 | 23 | 2 | 21 | 0 | 0 | | |
| 25 | 23 | 2 | 22 | 0 | 0 | 0 | |
| 25 | 23 | 2 | 23 | 0 | 0 | 0 | 0 |
| 25 | 24 | 1 | 24 | 0 | | | |

*Note:* To be significant, the observed value of $C$ must be less than or equal to the value shown in the table.

*(continued)*

**Critical Values of C in Fisher's Exact Probability Test** *(continued)*

| Sample size | Cell frequencies | | | Two-tailed test | | | |
| | | | | 0.10 | 0.05 | 0.02 | 0.01 |
| | | | | One-tailed test | | | |
| *n* | *a + b* | *c + d* | *a* | 0.05 | 0.025 | 0.01 | 0.005 |
|---|---|---|---|---|---|---|---|
| 26 | 13 | 13 | 4 | 0 | | | |
| 26 | 13 | 13 | 5 | 0 | 0 | | |
| 26 | 13 | 13 | 6 | 1 | 0 | 0 | |
| 26 | 13 | 13 | 7 | 2 | 1 | 0 | 0 |
| 26 | 13 | 13 | 8 | 2 | 2 | 1 | 0 |
| 26 | 13 | 13 | 9 | 3 | 3 | 2 | 1 |
| 26 | 13 | 13 | 10 | 4 | 4 | 3 | 2 |
| 26 | 13 | 13 | 11 | 6 | 5 | 4 | 3 |
| 26 | 13 | 13 | 12 | 7 | 6 | 5 | 4 |
| 26 | 13 | 13 | 13 | 9 | 8 | 7 | 6 |
| 26 | 14 | 12 | 5 | 0 | | | |
| 26 | 14 | 12 | 6 | 0 | 0 | | |
| 26 | 14 | 12 | 7 | 1 | 0 | 0 | |
| 26 | 14 | 12 | 8 | 2 | 1 | 0 | 0 |
| 26 | 14 | 12 | 9 | 2 | 2 | 1 | 1 |
| 26 | 14 | 12 | 10 | 3 | 3 | 2 | 1 |
| 26 | 14 | 12 | 11 | 4 | 3 | 3 | 2 |
| 26 | 14 | 12 | 12 | 5 | 4 | 4 | 3 |
| 26 | 14 | 12 | 13 | 6 | 6 | 5 | 4 |
| 26 | 14 | 12 | 14 | 8 | 7 | 6 | 6 |
| 26 | 15 | 11 | 5 | 0 | | | |
| 26 | 15 | 11 | 6 | 0 | 0 | | |
| 26 | 15 | 11 | 7 | 1 | 0 | 0 | |
| 26 | 15 | 11 | 8 | 1 | 1 | 0 | 0 |
| 26 | 15 | 11 | 9 | 2 | 1 | 0 | 0 |
| 26 | 15 | 11 | 10 | 2 | 2 | 1 | 1 |
| 26 | 15 | 11 | 11 | 3 | 2 | 2 | 1 |
| 26 | 15 | 11 | 12 | 4 | 3 | 2 | 2 |
| 26 | 15 | 11 | 13 | 5 | 4 | 3 | 3 |
| 26 | 15 | 11 | 14 | 6 | 5 | 4 | 4 |
| 26 | 15 | 11 | 15 | 7 | 7 | 6 | 5 |
| 26 | 16 | 10 | 6 | 0 | | | |
| 26 | 16 | 10 | 7 | 0 | 0 | | |
| 26 | 16 | 10 | 8 | 1 | 0 | 0 | |
| 26 | 16 | 10 | 9 | 1 | 1 | 0 | 0 |

*Note:* To be significant, the observed value of *C* must be less than or equal to the value shown in the table.

*(continued)*

**Critical Values of C in Fisher's Exact Probability Test** *(continued)*

| Sample size *n* | Cell frequencies | | | Two-tailed test 0.10 | 0.05 | 0.02 | 0.01 |
|---|---|---|---|---|---|---|---|
| | *a + b* | *c + d* | *a* | One-tailed test 0.05 | 0.025 | 0.01 | 0.005 |
| 26 | 16 | 10 | 10 | 2 | 1 | 0 | 0 |
| 26 | 16 | 10 | 11 | 2 | 2 | 1 | 1 |
| 26 | 16 | 10 | 12 | 3 | 2 | 2 | 1 |
| 26 | 16 | 10 | 13 | 4 | 3 | 2 | 2 |
| 26 | 16 | 10 | 14 | 4 | 4 | 3 | 3 |
| 26 | 16 | 10 | 15 | 5 | 5 | 4 | 3 |
| 26 | 16 | 10 | 16 | 7 | 6 | 5 | 5 |
| 26 | 17 | 9 | 7 | 0 | | | |
| 26 | 17 | 9 | 8 | 0 | 0 | | |
| 26 | 17 | 9 | 9 | 1 | 0 | 0 | |
| 26 | 17 | 9 | 10 | 1 | 1 | 0 | 0 |
| 26 | 17 | 9 | 11 | 2 | 1 | 0 | 0 |
| 26 | 17 | 9 | 12 | 2 | 1 | 1 | 0 |
| 26 | 17 | 9 | 13 | 3 | 2 | 1 | 1 |
| 26 | 17 | 9 | 14 | 3 | 3 | 2 | 2 |
| 26 | 17 | 9 | 15 | 4 | 3 | 3 | 2 |
| 26 | 17 | 9 | 16 | 5 | 4 | 4 | 3 |
| 26 | 17 | 9 | 17 | 6 | 5 | 5 | 4 |
| 26 | 18 | 8 | 7 | 0 | | | |
| 26 | 18 | 8 | 8 | 0 | | | |
| 26 | 18 | 8 | 9 | 0 | 0 | | |
| 26 | 18 | 8 | 10 | 1 | 0 | 0 | |
| 26 | 18 | 8 | 11 | 1 | 0 | 0 | 0 |
| 26 | 18 | 8 | 12 | 1 | 1 | 0 | 0 |
| 26 | 18 | 8 | 13 | 2 | 1 | 1 | 0 |
| 26 | 18 | 8 | 14 | 2 | 2 | 1 | 1 |
| 26 | 18 | 8 | 15 | 3 | 2 | 2 | 1 |
| 26 | 18 | 8 | 16 | 3 | 3 | 2 | 2 |
| 26 | 18 | 8 | 17 | 4 | 4 | 3 | 3 |
| 26 | 18 | 8 | 18 | 5 | 5 | 4 | 4 |
| 26 | 19 | 7 | 8 | 0 | | | |
| 26 | 19 | 7 | 9 | 0 | | | |
| 26 | 19 | 7 | 10 | 0 | 0 | | |
| 26 | 19 | 7 | 11 | 0 | 0 | 0 | |
| 26 | 19 | 7 | 12 | 1 | 0 | 0 | |

*Note:* To be significant, the observed value of *C* must be less than or equal to the value shown in the table.

*(continued)*

**Critical Values of C in Fisher's Exact Probability Test** *(continued)*

| | | | | Level of significance | | | |
|---|---|---|---|---|---|---|---|
| | | | | Two-tailed test | | | |
| | | | | 0.10 | 0.05 | 0.02 | 0.01 |
| Sample size | Cell frequencies | | | One-tailed test | | | |
| *n* | *a* + *b* | *c* + *d* | *a* | 0.05 | 0.025 | 0.01 | 0.005 |
| 26 | 19 | 7 | 13 | 1 | 1 | 0 | 0 |
| 26 | 19 | 7 | 14 | 1 | 1 | 0 | 0 |
| 26 | 19 | 7 | 15 | 2 | 1 | 1 | 0 |
| 26 | 19 | 7 | 16 | 2 | 2 | 1 | 1 |
| 26 | 19 | 7 | 17 | 3 | 2 | 2 | 1 |
| 26 | 19 | 7 | 18 | 4 | 3 | 2 | 2 |
| 26 | 19 | 7 | 19 | 4 | 4 | 3 | 3 |
| 26 | 20 | 6 | 10 | 0 | | | |
| 26 | 20 | 6 | 11 | 0 | 0 | | |
| 26 | 20 | 6 | 12 | 0 | 0 | | |
| 26 | 20 | 6 | 13 | 0 | 0 | 0 | |
| 26 | 20 | 6 | 14 | 1 | 0 | 0 | 0 |
| 26 | 20 | 6 | 15 | 1 | 1 | 0 | 0 |
| 26 | 20 | 6 | 16 | 1 | 1 | 1 | 0 |
| 26 | 20 | 6 | 17 | 2 | 1 | 1 | 1 |
| 26 | 20 | 6 | 18 | 2 | 2 | 1 | 1 |
| 26 | 20 | 6 | 19 | 3 | 2 | 2 | 2 |
| 26 | 20 | 6 | 20 | 4 | 3 | 3 | 2 |
| 26 | 21 | 5 | 11 | 0 | | | |
| 26 | 21 | 5 | 12 | 0 | | | |
| 26 | 21 | 5 | 13 | 0 | 0 | | |
| 26 | 21 | 5 | 14 | 0 | 0 | | |
| 26 | 21 | 5 | 15 | 0 | 0 | 0 | |
| 26 | 21 | 5 | 16 | 1 | 0 | 0 | 0 |
| 26 | 21 | 5 | 17 | 1 | 1 | 0 | 0 |
| 26 | 21 | 5 | 18 | 1 | 1 | 0 | 0 |
| 26 | 21 | 5 | 19 | 2 | 1 | 1 | 1 |
| 26 | 21 | 5 | 20 | 2 | 2 | 1 | 1 |
| 26 | 21 | 5 | 21 | 3 | 2 | 2 | 2 |
| 26 | 22 | 4 | 13 | 0 | | | |
| 26 | 22 | 4 | 14 | 0 | | | |
| 26 | 22 | 4 | 15 | 0 | 0 | | |
| 26 | 22 | 4 | 16 | 0 | 0 | | |
| 26 | 22 | 4 | 17 | 0 | 0 | 0 | |
| 26 | 22 | 4 | 18 | 1 | 0 | 0 | 0 |

*Note:* To be significant, the observed value of *C* must be less than or equal to the value shown in the table.

*(continued)*

**Critical Values of *C* in Fisher's Exact Probability Test** *(continued)*

| Sample size *n* | Cell frequencies | | | Level of significance | | | |
|---|---|---|---|---|---|---|---|
| | | | | Two-tailed test | | | |
| | | | | 0.10 | 0.05 | 0.02 | 0.01 |
| | | | | One-tailed test | | | |
| *n* | *a* + *b* | *c* + *d* | *a* | 0.05 | 0.025 | 0.01 | 0.005 |
| 26 | 22 | 4 | 19 | 1 | 0 | 0 | 0 |
| 26 | 22 | 4 | 20 | 1 | 1 | 0 | 0 |
| 26 | 22 | 4 | 21 | 1 | 1 | 1 | 0 |
| 26 | 22 | 4 | 22 | 2 | 2 | 1 | 1 |
| 26 | 23 | 3 | 16 | 0 | | | |
| 26 | 23 | 3 | 17 | 0 | | | |
| 26 | 23 | 3 | 18 | 0 | 0 | | |
| 26 | 23 | 3 | 19 | 0 | 0 | | |
| 26 | 23 | 3 | 20 | 0 | 0 | 0 | |
| 26 | 23 | 3 | 21 | 0 | 0 | 0 | 0 |
| 26 | 23 | 3 | 22 | 1 | 0 | 0 | 0 |
| 26 | 23 | 3 | 23 | 1 | 1 | 1 | 0 |
| 26 | 24 | 2 | 20 | 0 | | | |
| 26 | 24 | 2 | 21 | 0 | | | |
| 26 | 24 | 2 | 22 | 0 | 0 | | |
| 26 | 24 | 2 | 23 | 0 | 0 | 0 | |
| 26 | 24 | 2 | 24 | 0 | 0 | 0 | 0 |
| 26 | 25 | 1 | 25 | 0 | | | |

*Note:* To be significant, the observed value of *C* must be less than or equal to the value shown in the table.

# Appendix J

**Critical Values of *U* in the Mann–Whitney Test**

### One-Tailed at the 0.005 level of significance or two-tailed at the 0.01 level of significance

| $n_2$ \ $n_1$ | 1 | 2 | 3 | 4 | 5 | 6 | 7 | 8 | 9 | 10 | 11 | 12 | 13 | 14 | 15 | 16 | 17 | 18 | 19 | 20 | 21 | 22 | 23 | 24 | 25 |
|---|---|---|---|---|---|---|---|---|---|---|---|---|---|---|---|---|---|---|---|---|---|---|---|---|---|
| 2 | — | — | — | — | — | — | — | — | — | — | — | — | — | — | — | — | — | — | — | — | 0 | 0 | 0 | 0 | 0 |
| 3 | — | — | — | — | — | — | — | — | 0 | 0 | 0 | 1 | 1 | 1 | 2 | 2 | 2 | 2 | 3 | 3 | 3 | 4 | 4 | 4 | 5 |
| 4 | — | — | — | — | — | 0 | 0 | 1 | 1 | 2 | 2 | 3 | 3 | 4 | 5 | 5 | 6 | 6 | 7 | 8 | 8 | 9 | 9 | 10 | 10 |
| 5 | — | — | — | — | 0 | 1 | 1 | 2 | 3 | 4 | 5 | 6 | 7 | 7 | 8 | 9 | 10 | 11 | 12 | 13 | 14 | 14 | 15 | 16 | 17 |
| 6 | — | — | — | 0 | 1 | 2 | 3 | 4 | 5 | 6 | 7 | 9 | 10 | 11 | 12 | 13 | 15 | 16 | 17 | 18 | 19 | 21 | 22 | 23 | 24 |
| 7 | — | — | — | 0 | 1 | 3 | 4 | 6 | 7 | 9 | 10 | 12 | 13 | 15 | 16 | 18 | 19 | 21 | 22 | 24 | 25 | 27 | 29 | 30 | 32 |
| 8 | — | — | — | 1 | 2 | 4 | 6 | 7 | 9 | 11 | 13 | 15 | 17 | 18 | 20 | 22 | 24 | 26 | 28 | 30 | 32 | 34 | 35 | 37 | 39 |
| 9 | — | — | 0 | 1 | 3 | 5 | 7 | 9 | 11 | 13 | 16 | 18 | 20 | 22 | 24 | 27 | 29 | 31 | 33 | 36 | 38 | 40 | 43 | 45 | 47 |
| 10 | — | — | 0 | 2 | 4 | 6 | 9 | 11 | 13 | 16 | 18 | 21 | 24 | 26 | 29 | 31 | 34 | 37 | 39 | 42 | 44 | 47 | 50 | 52 | 55 |
| 11 | — | — | 0 | 2 | 5 | 7 | 10 | 13 | 16 | 18 | 21 | 24 | 27 | 30 | 33 | 36 | 39 | 42 | 45 | 48 | 51 | 54 | 57 | 60 | 63 |
| 12 | — | — | 1 | 3 | 6 | 9 | 12 | 15 | 18 | 21 | 24 | 27 | 31 | 34 | 37 | 41 | 44 | 47 | 51 | 54 | 58 | 61 | 64 | 68 | 71 |
| 13 | — | — | 1 | 3 | 7 | 10 | 13 | 17 | 20 | 24 | 27 | 31 | 34 | 38 | 42 | 45 | 49 | 53 | 57 | 60 | 64 | 68 | 72 | 75 | 79 |
| 14 | — | — | 1 | 4 | 7 | 11 | 15 | 18 | 22 | 26 | 30 | 34 | 38 | 42 | 46 | 50 | 54 | 58 | 63 | 67 | 71 | 75 | 79 | 83 | 87 |
| 15 | — | — | 2 | 5 | 8 | 12 | 16 | 20 | 24 | 29 | 33 | 37 | 42 | 46 | 51 | 55 | 60 | 64 | 69 | 73 | 78 | 82 | 87 | 91 | 96 |
| 16 | — | — | 2 | 5 | 9 | 13 | 18 | 22 | 27 | 31 | 36 | 41 | 45 | 50 | 55 | 60 | 65 | 70 | 74 | 79 | 84 | 89 | 94 | 99 | 104 |
| 17 | — | — | 2 | 6 | 10 | 15 | 19 | 24 | 29 | 34 | 39 | 44 | 49 | 54 | 60 | 65 | 70 | 75 | 81 | 86 | 91 | 96 | 102 | 107 | 112 |
| 18 | — | — | 2 | 6 | 11 | 16 | 21 | 26 | 31 | 37 | 42 | 47 | 53 | 58 | 64 | 70 | 75 | 81 | 87 | 92 | 98 | 104 | 109 | 115 | 121 |
| 19 | — | — | 3 | 7 | 12 | 17 | 22 | 28 | 33 | 39 | 45 | 51 | 57 | 63 | 69 | 74 | 81 | 87 | 93 | 99 | 105 | 111 | 117 | 123 | 129 |
| 20 | — | — | 3 | 8 | 13 | 18 | 24 | 30 | 36 | 42 | 48 | 54 | 60 | 67 | 73 | 79 | 86 | 92 | 99 | 105 | 112 | 118 | 125 | 131 | 138 |
| 21 | — | 0 | 3 | 8 | 14 | 19 | 25 | 32 | 38 | 44 | 51 | 58 | 64 | 71 | 78 | 84 | 91 | 98 | 105 | 112 | 118 | 125 | 132 | 139 | 146 |
| 22 | — | 0 | 4 | 9 | 14 | 21 | 27 | 34 | 40 | 47 | 54 | 61 | 68 | 75 | 82 | 89 | 96 | 104 | 111 | 118 | 125 | 133 | 140 | 147 | 155 |
| 23 | — | 0 | 4 | 9 | 15 | 22 | 29 | 35 | 43 | 50 | 57 | 64 | 72 | 79 | 87 | 94 | 102 | 109 | 117 | 125 | 132 | 140 | 148 | 155 | 163 |
| 24 | — | 0 | 4 | 10 | 16 | 23 | 30 | 37 | 45 | 52 | 60 | 68 | 75 | 83 | 91 | 99 | 107 | 115 | 123 | 131 | 139 | 147 | 155 | 164 | 172 |
| 25 | — | 0 | 5 | 10 | 17 | 24 | 32 | 39 | 47 | 55 | 63 | 71 | 79 | 87 | 96 | 104 | 112 | 121 | 129 | 138 | 146 | 155 | 163 | 172 | 180 |

The table presents lower critical values $U_L$. To be significant for any given $n_1$ and $n_2$, the observed value of $U$ must be less than or equal to the critical value shown in the table or greater than or equal to $n_1 \cdot n_2 - U_L$.

### One-Tailed at the 0.01 level of significance or two-tailed at the 0.02 level of significance

| $n_2$ | $n_1$ 1 | 2 | 3 | 4 | 5 | 6 | 7 | 8 | 9 | 10 | 11 | 12 | 13 | 14 | 15 | 16 | 17 | 18 | 19 | 20 | 21 | 22 | 23 | 24 | 25 |
|---|---|---|---|---|---|---|---|---|---|---|---|---|---|---|---|---|---|---|---|---|---|---|---|---|---|
| 2 | — | — | — | — | — | — | — | — | — | — | — | — | — | 0 | 0 | 0 | 0 | 0 | 0 | 1 | 1 | 1 | 1 | 1 | 1 |
| 3 | — | — | — | — | — | — | 0 | 0 | 1 | 1 | 1 | 2 | 2 | 2 | 3 | 3 | 4 | 4 | 4 | 5 | 5 | 6 | 6 | 6 | 7 |
| 4 | — | — | — | — | 0 | 1 | 1 | 2 | 3 | 3 | 3 | 5 | 5 | 6 | 7 | 7 | 8 | 9 | 9 | 10 | 11 | 11 | 12 | 13 | 13 |
| 5 | — | — | — | 0 | 1 | 2 | 3 | 4 | 5 | 5 | 6 | 8 | 9 | 10 | 11 | 12 | 13 | 14 | 15 | 16 | 17 | 18 | 9 | 20 | 21 |
| 6 | — | — | — | 1 | 2 | 3 | 4 | 6 | 7 | 7 | 8 | 11 | 12 | 13 | 15 | 16 | 18 | 19 | 20 | 22 | 23 | 24 | 26 | 27 | 29 |
| 7 | — | — | 0 | 1 | 3 | 4 | 6 | 7 | 9 | 9 | 11 | 14 | 16 | 17 | 19 | 21 | 23 | 24 | 26 | 28 | 30 | 31 | 33 | 35 | 36 |
| 8 | — | — | 0 | 2 | 4 | 6 | 7 | 9 | 11 | 11 | 13 | 17 | 20 | 22 | 24 | 26 | 28 | 30 | 32 | 34 | 36 | 38 | 40 | 42 | 45 |
| 9 | — | — | 1 | 3 | 5 | 7 | 9 | 11 | 14 | -55 | 16 | 21 | 23 | 26 | 28 | 31 | 33 | 36 | 38 | 40 | 43 | 45 | 48 | 50 | 53 |
| 10 | — | — | 1 | 3 | 6 | 8 | 11 | 13 | 16 | 19 | -66 | 24 | 27 | 30 | 33 | 36 | 38 | 41 | 44 | 47 | 50 | 53 | 55 | 58 | 61 |
| 11 | — | — | 1 | 4 | 7 | 9 | 12 | 22 | 18 | 22 | 25 | 28 | 31 | 34 | 37 | 41 | 44 | 47 | 50 | 53 | 57 | 60 | 63 | 66 | 70 |
| 12 | — | — | 2 | 5 | 8 | 11 | 14 | 17 | 21 | 24 | 28 | 31 | 35 | 38 | 42 | 46 | 49 | 53 | 56 | 60 | 64 | 67 | 71 | 75 | 78 |
| 13 | — | 0 | 2 | 5 | 9 | 12 | 16 | 20 | 23 | 27 | 31 | 35 | 39 | 43 | 47 | 51 | 55 | 59 | 63 | 67 | 71 | 75 | 79 | 83 | 87 |
| 14 | — | 0 | 2 | 6 | 10 | 13 | 17 | 22 | 26 | 30 | 34 | 38 | 43 | 47 | 51 | 56 | 60 | 65 | 69 | 73 | 78 | 82 | 87 | 91 | 95 |
| 15 | — | 0 | 3 | 7 | 11 | 15 | 19 | 24 | 28 | 33 | 37 | 42 | 47 | 51 | 56 | 61 | 66 | 70 | 75 | 80 | 85 | 90 | 94 | 99 | 104 |
| 16 | — | 0 | 3 | 7 | 12 | 16 | 21 | 26 | 31 | 36 | 41 | 46 | 51 | 56 | 61 | 66 | 71 | 76 | 82 | 87 | 92 | 97 | 102 | 108 | 113 |
| 17 | — | 0 | 4 | 8 | 13 | 18 | 23 | 28 | 33 | 38 | 44 | 49 | 55 | 60 | 66 | 71 | 77 | 82 | 88 | 93 | 99 | 105 | 110 | 116 | 122 |
| 18 | — | 0 | 4 | 9 | 14 | 19 | 24 | 30 | 36 | 41 | 47 | 53 | 59 | 65 | 70 | 76 | 82 | 88 | 94 | 100 | 106 | 112 | 118 | 124 | 130 |
| 19 | — | 1 | 4 | 9 | 15 | 20 | 26 | 32 | 38 | 44 | 50 | 56 | 63 | 69 | 75 | 82 | 88 | 94 | 101 | 107 | 113 | 120 | 126 | 133 | 139 |
| 20 | — | 1 | 5 | 10 | 16 | 22 | 28 | 34 | 40 | 47 | 53 | 60 | 67 | 73 | 80 | 87 | 93 | 100 | 107 | 114 | 121 | 127 | 134 | 141 | 148 |
| 21 | — | 1 | 5 | 11 | 17 | 23 | 30 | 36 | 43 | 50 | 57 | 64 | 71 | 78 | 85 | 92 | 99 | 106 | 113 | 121 | 128 | 135 | 142 | 150 | 157 |
| 22 | — | 1 | 6 | 11 | 18 | 24 | 31 | 38 | 45 | 53 | 60 | 67 | 75 | 82 | 90 | 97 | 105 | 112 | 120 | 127 | 135 | 143 | 150 | 158 | 166 |
| 23 | — | 1 | 6 | 12 | 9 | 26 | 33 | 40 | 48 | 55 | 63 | 71 | 79 | 87 | 94 | 102 | 110 | 118 | 126 | 134 | 142 | 150 | 158 | 167 | 175 |
| 24 | — | 1 | 6 | 13 | 20 | 27 | 35 | 42 | 50 | 58 | 66 | 75 | 83 | 91 | 99 | 108 | 116 | 124 | 133 | 141 | 150 | 158 | 167 | 175 | 184 |
| 25 | — | 1 | 7 | 13 | 21 | 29 | 36 | 45 | 53 | 61 | 70 | 78 | 87 | 95 | 104 | 113 | 122 | 130 | 139 | 148 | 157 | 166 | 175 | 184 | 192 |

The table presents lower critical values $U_L$. To be significant for any given $n_1$ and $n_2$, the observed value of $U$ must be less than or equal to the critical value shown in the table or greater than or equal to $n_1 \cdot n_2 - U_L$.

| | **One-Tailed at the 0.025 level of significance or two-tailed at the 0.05 level of significance** | | | | | | | | | | | | | | | | | | | | | | | |
|---|---|---|---|---|---|---|---|---|---|---|---|---|---|---|---|---|---|---|---|---|---|---|---|---|
| | | | | | | | | | | | | $n_1$ | | | | | | | | | | | | |
| $n_2$ | *1* | *2* | *3* | *4* | *5* | *6* | *7* | *8* | *9* | *10* | *11* | *12* | *13* | *14* | *15* | *16* | *17* | *18* | *19* | *20* | *21* | *22* | *23* | *24* | *25* |
| **2** | — | — | — | — | — | — | — | 0 | 0 | 0 | 0 | 1 | 1 | 1 | 1 | 1 | 2 | 2 | 2 | 2 | 3 | 3 | 3 | 3 | 3 |
| **3** | — | — | — | — | 0 | 1 | 1 | 2 | 2 | 3 | 3 | 4 | 4 | 5 | 5 | 6 | 6 | 7 | 7 | 8 | 8 | 9 | 9 | 10 | 10 |
| **4** | — | — | — | 0 | 1 | 2 | 3 | 4 | 4 | 5 | 6 | 7 | 8 | 9 | 10 | 11 | 11 | 12 | 13 | 14 | 15 | 16 | 17 | 17 | 18 |
| **5** | — | — | 0 | 1 | 2 | 3 | 5 | 6 | 7 | 8 | 9 | 11 | 12 | 13 | 14 | 15 | 17 | 18 | 19 | 20 | 22 | 23 | 24 | 25 | 27 |
| **6** | — | — | 1 | 2 | 3 | 5 | 6 | 8 | 10 | 11 | 13 | 14 | 16 | 17 | 19 | 21 | 22 | 24 | 25 | 27 | 29 | 30 | 32 | 33 | 35 |
| **7** | — | — | 1 | 3 | 5 | 6 | 8 | 10 | 12 | 14 | 16 | 18 | 20 | 22 | 24 | 26 | 28 | 30 | 32 | 34 | 36 | 38 | 40 | 42 | 44 |
| **8** | — | 0 | 2 | 4 | 6 | 8 | 10 | 13 | 15 | 17 | 19 | 22 | 24 | 26 | 29 | 31 | 34 | 36 | 38 | 41 | 43 | 45 | 48 | 50 | 53 |
| **9** | — | 0 | 2 | 4 | 7 | 10 | 12 | 15 | 17 | 20 | 23 | 26 | 28 | 31 | 34 | 37 | 39 | 42 | 45 | 48 | 50 | 53 | 56 | 59 | 62 |
| **10** | — | 0 | 3 | 5 | 8 | 11 | 14 | 17 | 20 | 23 | 26 | 29 | 33 | 36 | 39 | 42 | 45 | 48 | 52 | 55 | 58 | 61 | 64 | 67 | 71 |
| **11** | — | 0 | 3 | 6 | 9 | 13 | 16 | 19 | 23 | 26 | 30 | 33 | 37 | 40 | 44 | 47 | 51 | 55 | 58 | 62 | 65 | 69 | 73 | 76 | 80 |
| **12** | — | 1 | 4 | 7 | 11 | 14 | 18 | 22 | 26 | 29 | 33 | 37 | 41 | 45 | 49 | 53 | 57 | 61 | 65 | 69 | 73 | 77 | 81 | 85 | 89 |
| **13** | — | 1 | 4 | 8 | 12 | 16 | 20 | 24 | 28 | 33 | 37 | 41 | 45 | 50 | 54 | 59 | 63 | 67 | 72 | 76 | 80 | 85 | 89 | 94 | 98 |
| **14** | — | 1 | 5 | 9 | 13 | 17 | 22 | 26 | 31 | 36 | 40 | 45 | 50 | 55 | 59 | 64 | 69 | 74 | 78 | 83 | 88 | 93 | 98 | 102 | 107 |
| **15** | — | 1 | 5 | 10 | 14 | 19 | 24 | 29 | 34 | 39 | 44 | 49 | 54 | 59 | 64 | 70 | 75 | 80 | 85 | 90 | 96 | 101 | 106 | 111 | 117 |
| **16** | — | 1 | 6 | 11 | 15 | 21 | 26 | 31 | 37 | 42 | 47 | 53 | 59 | 64 | 70 | 75 | 81 | 86 | 92 | 98 | 103 | 109 | 115 | 120 | 126 |
| **17** | — | 2 | 6 | 11 | 17 | 22 | 28 | 34 | 39 | 45 | 51 | 57 | 63 | 69 | 75 | 81 | 87 | 93 | 99 | 105 | 111 | 117 | 123 | 129 | 135 |
| **18** | — | 2 | 7 | 12 | 18 | 24 | 30 | 36 | 42 | 48 | 55 | 61 | 67 | 74 | 80 | 86 | 93 | 99 | 106 | 112 | 119 | 125 | 132 | 138 | 145 |
| **19** | — | 2 | 7 | 13 | 19 | 25 | 32 | 38 | 45 | 52 | 58 | 65 | 72 | 78 | 85 | 92 | 99 | 106 | 113 | 119 | 126 | 133 | 140 | 147 | 154 |
| **20** | — | 2 | 8 | 14 | 20 | 27 | 34 | 41 | 48 | 55 | 62 | 69 | 76 | 83 | 90 | 98 | 105 | 112 | 119 | 127 | 134 | 141 | 149 | 156 | 163 |
| **21** | — | 3 | 8 | 15 | 22 | 29 | 36 | 43 | 50 | 58 | 65 | 73 | 80 | 88 | 96 | 103 | 111 | 119 | 126 | 134 | 142 | 150 | 157 | 165 | 173 |
| **22** | — | 3 | 9 | 16 | 23 | 30 | 38 | 45 | 53 | 61 | 69 | 77 | 85 | 93 | 101 | 109 | 117 | 125 | 133 | 141 | 150 | 158 | 166 | 174 | 182 |
| **23** | — | 3 | 9 | 17 | 24 | 32 | 40 | 48 | 56 | 64 | 73 | 81 | 89 | 98 | 106 | 115 | 123 | 132 | 140 | 149 | 157 | 166 | 175 | 183 | 192 |
| **24** | — | 3 | 10 | 17 | 25 | 33 | 42 | 50 | 59 | 67 | 76 | 85 | 94 | 102 | 111 | 120 | 129 | 138 | 147 | 156 | 165 | 174 | 183 | 192 | 201 |
| **25** | — | 3 | 10 | 18 | 27 | 35 | 44 | 53 | 62 | 71 | 80 | 89 | 98 | 107 | 117 | 126 | 135 | 145 | 154 | 163 | 173 | 182 | 192 | 201 | 211 |

The table presents lower critical values $U_L$. To be significant for any given $n_1$ and $n_2$, the observed value of $U$ must be less than or equal to the critical value shown in the table or greater than or equal to $n_1 \cdot n_2 - U_L$.

| | | | | | | | | | | | | | $n_1$ | | | | | | | | | | | | |
|---|---|---|---|---|---|---|---|---|---|---|---|---|---|---|---|---|---|---|---|---|---|---|---|---|---|
| **One-Tailed at the 0.05 level of significance or two-tailed at the 0.10 level of significance** | | | | | | | | | | | | | | | | | | | | | | | | | |
| $n_2$ | 1 | 2 | 3 | 4 | 5 | 6 | 7 | 8 | 9 | 10 | 11 | 12 | 13 | 14 | 15 | 16 | 17 | 18 | 19 | 20 | 21 | 22 | 23 | 24 | 25 |
| **2** | — | — | 0 | 0 | 1 | 1 | 1 | 2 | 2 | 3 | 3 | 4 | 4 | 5 | 5 | 5 | 6 | 6 | 7 | 7 | 8 | 8 | 9 | 9 | 9 |
| **3** | — | — | 0 | 0 | 1 | 2 | 2 | 3 | 4 | 4 | 5 | 5 | 6 | 7 | 7 | 8 | 9 | 9 | 10 | 11 | 11 | 12 | 13 | 13 | 14 |
| **4** | — | — | 0 | 1 | 2 | 3 | 4 | 5 | 6 | 7 | 8 | 9 | 10 | 11 | 12 | 14 | 15 | 16 | 17 | 18 | 19 | 20 | 21 | 22 | 23 |
| **5** | — | 0 | 1 | 2 | 4 | 5 | 6 | 8 | 9 | 11 | 12 | 13 | 15 | 16 | 18 | 19 | 20 | 22 | 23 | 25 | 26 | 28 | 29 | 30 | 32 |
| **6** | — | 0 | 2 | 3 | 5 | 7 | 8 | 10 | 12 | 14 | 16 | 17 | 19 | 21 | 23 | 25 | 26 | 28 | 30 | 32 | 34 | 36 | 37 | 39 | 41 |
| **7** | — | 0 | 2 | 4 | 6 | 8 | 11 | 13 | 15 | 17 | 19 | 21 | 24 | 26 | 28 | 30 | 33 | 35 | 37 | 39 | 41 | 44 | 46 | 48 | 50 |
| **8** | — | 1 | 3 | 5 | 8 | 10 | 13 | 15 | 18 | 20 | 23 | 26 | 28 | 31 | 33 | 36 | 39 | 41 | 44 | 47 | 49 | 52 | 54 | 57 | 60 |
| **9** | — | 1 | 4 | 6 | 9 | 12 | 15 | 18 | 21 | 24 | 27 | 30 | 33 | 36 | 39 | 42 | 45 | 48 | 51 | 54 | 57 | 60 | 63 | 66 | 69 |
| **10** | — | 1 | 4 | 7 | 11 | 14 | 17 | 20 | 24 | 27 | 31 | 34 | 37 | 41 | 44 | 48 | 51 | 55 | 58 | 62 | 65 | 68 | 72 | 75 | 79 |
| **11** | — | 1 | 5 | 8 | 12 | 16 | 19 | 23 | 27 | 31 | 34 | 38 | 42 | 46 | 50 | 54 | 57 | 61 | 65 | 69 | 73 | 77 | 81 | 85 | 89 |
| **12** | — | 2 | 5 | 9 | 13 | 17 | 21 | 26 | 30 | 34 | 38 | 42 | 47 | 51 | 55 | 60 | 64 | 68 | 72 | 77 | 81 | 85 | 90 | 94 | 98 |
| **13** | — | 2 | 6 | 10 | 15 | 19 | 24 | 28 | 33 | 37 | 42 | 47 | 51 | 56 | 61 | 65 | 70 | 75 | 80 | 84 | 89 | 94 | 98 | 103 | 108 |
| **14** | — | 3 | 7 | 11 | 16 | 21 | 26 | 31 | 36 | 41 | 46 | 51 | 56 | 61 | 66 | 71 | 77 | 82 | 87 | 92 | 97 | 102 | 107 | 113 | 118 |
| **15** | — | 3 | 7 | 12 | 18 | 23 | 28 | 33 | 39 | 44 | 50 | 55 | 61 | 66 | 72 | 77 | 83 | 88 | 94 | 100 | 105 | 111 | 116 | 122 | 128 |
| **16** | — | 3 | 8 | 14 | 19 | 25 | 30 | 36 | 42 | 48 | 54 | 60 | 65 | 71 | 77 | 83 | 89 | 95 | 101 | 107 | 113 | 119 | 125 | 131 | 137 |
| **17** | — | 3 | 9 | 15 | 20 | 26 | 33 | 39 | 45 | 51 | 57 | 64 | 70 | 77 | 83 | 89 | 96 | 102 | 109 | 115 | 121 | 128 | 134 | 141 | 147 |
| **18** | — | 4 | 9 | 16 | 22 | 28 | 35 | 41 | 48 | 55 | 61 | 68 | 75 | 82 | 88 | 95 | 102 | 109 | 116 | 123 | 130 | 136 | 143 | 150 | 157 |
| **19** | — | 4 | 10 | 17 | 23 | 30 | 37 | 44 | 51 | 58 | 65 | 72 | 80 | 87 | 94 | 101 | 109 | 116 | 123 | 130 | 138 | 145 | 152 | 160 | 167 |
| **20** | — | 4 | 11 | 18 | 25 | 32 | 39 | 47 | 54 | 62 | 69 | 77 | 84 | 92 | 100 | 107 | 115 | 123 | 130 | 138 | 146 | 154 | 161 | 169 | 177 |
| **21** | — | 5 | 11 | 19 | 26 | 34 | 41 | 49 | 57 | 65 | 73 | 81 | 89 | 97 | 105 | 113 | 121 | 130 | 138 | 146 | 154 | 162 | 170 | 179 | 187 |
| **22** | — | 5 | 12 | 20 | 28 | 36 | 44 | 52 | 60 | 68 | 77 | 85 | 94 | 102 | 111 | 119 | 128 | 136 | 145 | 154 | 162 | 171 | 179 | 188 | 197 |
| **23** | — | 5 | 13 | 21 | 29 | 37 | 46 | 54 | 63 | 72 | 81 | 90 | 98 | 107 | 116 | 125 | 134 | 143 | 152 | 161 | 170 | 179 | 189 | 198 | 207 |
| **24** | — | 6 | 13 | 22 | 30 | 39 | 48 | 57 | 66 | 75 | 85 | 94 | 103 | 113 | 122 | 131 | 141 | 150 | 160 | 169 | 179 | 188 | 198 | 207 | 217 |
| **25** | — | 6 | 14 | 23 | 32 | 41 | 50 | 60 | 69 | 79 | 89 | 98 | 108 | 118 | 128 | 137 | 147 | 157 | 167 | 177 | 187 | 197 | 207 | 217 | 227 |

The table presents lower critical values $U_L$. To be significant for any given $n_1$ and $n_2$, the observed value of $U$ must be less than or equal to the critical value shown in the table or greater than or equal to $n_1 \cdot n_2 - U_L$.

# Appendix K

**Critical Values of *D* for the Kolmogorov–Smirnov Two-Variable One-Tailed Test**

| | | | | | | | | $n_1$ | | | | | | | |
|---|---|---|---|---|---|---|---|---|---|---|---|---|---|---|---|
| $n_2$ | *1* | *2* | *3* | *4* | *5* | *6* | *7* | *8* | *9* | *10* | *11* | *12* | *13* | *14* | *15* |
| 1 | — | — | — | — | — | — | — | — | — | — | — | — | — | — | — |
| | — | — | — | — | — | — | — | — | — | — | — | — | — | — | — |
| 2 | — | — | — | — | — | — | — | — | — | — | — | — | — | — | — |
| | — | — | — | — | — | — | — | — | — | — | — | — | — | — | — |
| 3 | — | — | — | — | 0.867 | 0.833 | 0.762 | 0.792 | 0.778 | 0.733 | 0.758 | 0.750 | 0.718 | 0.738 | 0.733 |
| | — | — | — | — | — | — | — | — | **1.000** | **0.933** | **0.939** | **0.917** | **0.872** | **0.881** | **0.933** |
| 4 | — | — | — | 1.000 | 0.800 | 0.750 | 0.750 | 0.750 | 0.694 | 0.700 | 0.659 | 0.750 | 0.635 | 0.679 | 0.633 |
| | — | — | — | — | — | **0.917** | **0.893** | **1.000** | **0.806** | **0.850** | **0.841** | **0.833** | **0.788** | **0.821** | **0.767** |
| 5 | — | — | 0.867 | 0.800 | 0.800 | 0.700 | 0.686 | 0.650 | 0.778 | 0.700 | 0.655 | 0.667 | 0.646 | 0.714 | 0.067 |
| | — | — | — | — | **1.000** | **0.867** | **0.829** | **0.825** | **0.800** | **0.800** | **0.745** | **0.767** | **0.738** | **0.729** | **0.800** |
| 6 | — | — | 0.833 | 0.750 | 0.700 | 0.833 | 0.595 | 0.688 | 0.667 | 0.633 | 0.727 | 0.597 | 0.615 | 0.607 | 0.067 |
| | — | — | — | **1.083** | **1.200** | **0.861** | **0.905** | **0.875** | **0.815** | **0.817** | **0.818** | **0.750** | **0.769** | **0.750** | **0.067** |
| 7 | — | — | 0.762 | 0.750 | 0.686 | 0.595 | 0.714 | 0.607 | 0.571 | 0.571 | 0.558 | 0.536 | 0.549 | 0.571 | 0.552 |
| | — | — | — | **0.893** | **0.829** | **0.738** | **0.857** | **0.750** | **0.730** | **0.714** | **0.688** | **0.679** | **0.648** | **0.714** | **0.667** |
| 8 | — | — | 1.000 | 0.813 | 0.750 | 0.708 | 0.714 | 0.625 | 0.611 | 0.600 | 0.591 | 0.552 | 0.558 | 0.536 | 0.067 |
| | — | — | — | **1.000** | **0.825** | **0.792** | **0.750** | **0.750** | **0.681** | **0.700** | **0.670** | **0.667** | **0.635** | **0.643** | **0.625** |
| 9 | — | — | 0.778 | 0.694 | 0.622 | 0.611 | 0.571 | 0.556 | 0.667 | 0.511 | 0.515 | 0.528 | 0.487 | 0.500 | 0.511 |
| | — | — | **1.000** | **0.806** | **0.800** | **0.778** | **0.730** | **0.681** | **0.778** | **0.678** | **0.626** | **0.639** | **0.624** | **0.611** | **0.622** |
| 10 | — | — | 0.733 | 0.700 | 0.700 | 0.633 | 0.571 | 0.550 | 0.511 | 0.600 | 0.518 | 0.500 | 0.477 | 0.486 | 0.500 |
| | — | — | **0.933** | **0.850** | **0.800** | **0.733** | **0.714** | **0.700** | **0.678** | **0.700** | **0.627** | **0.617** | **0.600** | **0.600** | **0.600** |
| 11 | — | — | 0.758 | 0.659 | 0.636 | 0.576 | 0.558 | 0.545 | 0.515 | 0.518 | 0.545 | 0.485 | 0.469 | 0.468 | 0.461 |
| | — | — | **0.939** | **0.841** | **0.745** | **0.742** | **0.688** | **0.670** | **0.626** | **0.627** | **0.727** | **0.583** | **0.594** | **0.578** | **0.576** |
| 12 | — | — | 0.750 | 0.750 | 0.600 | 0.667 | 0.536 | 0.542 | 0.528 | 0.500 | 0.485 | 0.500 | 0.455 | 0.464 | 0.467 |
| | — | — | **0.917** | **0.833** | **0.767** | **0.750** | **0.679** | **0.667** | **0.639** | **0.617** | **0.583** | **0.667** | **0.590** | **0.560** | **0.567** |

*(continued)*

| 13 | — | — | 0.718 | 0.635 | 0.615 | 0.551 | 0.549 | 0.510 | 0.487 | 0.477 | 0.469 | 0.455 | 0.538 | 0.429 | 0.441 |
| | — | — | **0.872** | **0.788** | **0.738** | **0.692** | **0.648** | **0.635** | **0.624** | **0.600** | **0.594** | **0.590** | **0.615** | **0.560** | **0.544** |
| 14 | — | — | 0.738 | 0.679 | 0.600 | 0.571 | 0.571 | 0.518 | 0.500 | 0.471 | 0.468 | 0.464 | 0.429 | 0.500 | 0.438 |
| | — | — | **0.881** | **0.821** | **0.729** | **0.714** | **0.714** | **0.643** | **0.611** | **0.600** | **0.578** | **0.560** | **0.560** | **0.571** | **0.529** |
| 15 | — | — | 0.733 | 0.633 | 0.667 | 0.567 | 0.533 | 0.500 | 0.511 | 0.500 | 0.461 | 0.467 | 0.441 | 0.438 | 0.467 |
| | — | — | **0.933** | **0.767** | **0.800** | **0.700** | **0.667** | **0.625** | **0.622** | **0.600** | **0.576** | **0.567** | **0.544** | **0.529** | **0.600** |

For any given $n_1$ and $n_2$, to be significant at the 0.05 level of significance, the observed value of $D$ must be greater than or equal to the value shown in lightface type in the body of the table. To be significant at the 0.01 level of significance, the observed value of $D$ must be greater than or equal to the value shown in boldface type in the body of the table. The symbol—means that the null hypothesis cannot be rejected regardless of the observed value of $D$. For larger sample sizes, the approximate critical value of $D$ is given by the equation:

$$D_{critical} = K \sqrt{\frac{n_1 + n_2}{n_1 \cdot n_2}}$$

where $K = 1.22$ at the 0.05 level of significance and $K = 1.52$ at the 0.01 level of significance.

*Sources:* F. James Rohlf and Robert R. Sokal. 1981. *Statistical Tables,* 2/e, W.H. Freeman and Mitchell H. Gail and Syklvan B. Green, "Critical Values for the One-Sided Two-Sample Kolmogorov-Smirnov Statistic, *Journal of the American Statistical Association,* v. 71 n. 355, September 1976.

## Critical Values of *D* for the Kolmogorov–Smirnov Two-Variable Two-Tailed Test

| $n_2$ | \| | | | | | | | $n_1$ | | | | | | | |
|---|---|---|---|---|---|---|---|---|---|---|---|---|---|---|---|
| | *1* | *2* | *3* | *4* | *5* | *6* | *7* | *8* | *9* | *10* | *11* | *12* | *13* | *14* | *15* |
| 1 | — | — | — | — | — | — | — | — | — | — | — | — | — | — | — |
|   | — | — | — | — | — | — | — | — | — | — | — | — | — | — | — |
| 2 | — | — | — | — | — | — | — | 1.000 | 1.000 | 1.000 | 1.000 | 1.000 | 1.000 | 0.929 | 0.933 |
|   | — | — | — | — | — | — | — | — | — | — | — | — | — | — | — |
| 3 | — | — | — | — | 1.000 | 1.000 | 1.000 | 0.875 | 0.889 | 0.900 | 0.909 | 0.833 | 0.846 | 0.857 | 0.800 |
|   | — | — | — | — | — | — | — | — | **1.000** | **1.000** | **1.000** | **1.000** | **1.000** | **1.000** | **0.933** |
| 4 | — | — | — | 1.000 | 1.000 | 0.833 | 0.857 | 0.875 | 0.778 | 0.750 | 0.750 | 0.750 | 0.750 | 0.750 | 0.733 |
|   | — | — | — | — | — | **1.000** | **1.000** | **1.000** | **1.000** | **0.900** | **0.909** | **0.917** | **0.923** | **0.857** | **0.867** |
| 5 | — | — | 1.000 | 1.000 | 1.000 | 0.800 | 0.800 | 0.750 | 0.778 | 0.800 | 0.709 | 0.717 | 0.692 | 0.657 | 0.733 |
|   | — | — | — | — | **1.000** | **1.000** | **1.000** | **0.875** | **0.889** | **0.900** | **0.818** | **0.833** | **0.800** | **0.800** | **0.800** |
| 6 | — | — | 1.000 | 0.833 | 0.800 | 0.833 | 0.714 | 0.708 | 0.722 | 0.667 | 0.652 | 0.667 | 0.667 | 0.643 | 0.633 |
|   | — | — | — | **1.000** | **1.000** | **1.000** | **0.857** | **0.833** | **0.833** | **0.800** | **0.818** | **0.833** | **0.769** | **0.762** | **0.767** |
| 7 | — | — | 1.000 | 0.857 | 0.800 | 0.714 | 0.857 | 0.714 | 0.667 | 0.657 | 0.623 | 0.631 | 0.615 | 0.643 | 0.590 |
|   | — | — | — | **1.000** | **1.000** | **0.857** | **0.857** | **0.857** | **0.778** | **0.757** | **0.766** | **0.714** | **0.714** | **0.786** | **0.714** |
| 8 | — | 1.000 | 0.875 | 0.875 | 0.750 | 0.708 | 0.714 | 0.750 | 0.639 | 0.600 | 0.602 | 0.625 | 0.596 | 0.571 | 0.558 |
|   | — | — | — | **1.000** | **0.875** | **0.833** | **0.857** | **0.875** | **0.764** | **0.750** | **0.727** | **0.708** | **0.692** | **0.679** | **0.675** |
| 9 | — | 1.000 | 0.889 | 0.778 | 0.778 | 0.722 | 0.667 | 0.639 | 0.667 | 0.589 | 0.596 | 0.583 | 0.556 | 0.556 | 0.556 |
|   | — | — | **1.000** | **1.000** | **0.889** | **0.833** | **0.778** | **0.764** | **0.778** | **0.700** | **0.707** | **0.694** | **0.667** | **0.667** | **0.667** |
| 10 | — | 0.900 | 0.900 | 0.750 | 0.800 | 0.667 | 0.657 | 0.600 | 0.589 | 0.700 | 0.545 | 0.550 | 0.538 | 0.529 | 0.533 |
|   | — | — | **1.000** | **0.900** | **0.900** | **0.800** | **0.757** | **0.750** | **0.700** | **0.800** | **0.700** | **0.667** | **0.646** | **0.643** | **0.667** |
| 11 | — | 0.909 | 0.909 | 0.750 | 0.709 | 0.652 | 0.623 | 0.602 | 0.596 | 0.545 | 0.636 | 0.545 | 0.524 | 0.532 | 0.509 |
|   | — | — | **1.000** | **0.909** | **0.818** | **0.818** | **0.766** | **0.727** | **0.707** | **0.700** | **0.727** | **0.652** | **0.636** | **0.623** | **0.618** |
| 12 | — | 0.917 | 0.833 | 0.750 | 0.717 | 0.667 | 0.631 | 0.625 | 0.583 | 0.550 | 0.545 | 0.583 | 0.519 | 0.512 | 0.517 |
|   | — | — | **1.000** | **0.917** | **0.833** | **0.833** | **0.714** | **0.708** | **0.694** | **0.667** | **0.652** | **0.667** | **0.609** | **0.619** | **0.600** |
| 13 | — | 0.923 | 0.769 | 0.692 | 0.600 | 0.615 | 0.615 | 0.596 | 0.556 | 0.538 | 0.524 | 0.519 | 0.538 | 0.489 | 0.492 |
|   | — | — | **1.000** | **0.923** | **0.846** | **0.769** | **0.714** | **0.692** | **0.667** | **0.646** | **0.636** | **0.609** | **0.692** | **0.571** | **0.590** |
| 14 | — | 0.857 | 0.786 | 0.696 | 0.614 | 0.619 | 0.643 | 0.571 | 0.556 | 0.529 | 0.532 | 0.512 | 0.489 | 0.571 | 0.467 |
|   | — | — | **1.000** | **0.857** | **0.857** | **0.762** | **0.786** | **0.679** | **0.667** | **0.643** | **0.623** | **0.619** | **0.571** | **0.643** | **0.586** |
| 15 | — | 0.867 | 0.733 | 0.700 | 0.600 | 0.600 | 0.590 | 0.558 | 0.556 | 0.533 | 0.509 | 0.517 | 0.492 | 0.467 | 0.533 |
|   | — | — | **0.933** | **0.867** | **0.867** | **0.767** | **0.714** | **0.675** | **0.667** | **0.667** | **0.618** | **0.600** | **0.590** | **0.586** | **0.600** |

For any given $n_1$ and $n_2$, to be significant at the 0.05 level of significance, the observed value of *D* must be greater than or equal to the value shown in lightface type in the body of the table. To be significant at the 0.01 level of significance, the observed value of *D* must be greater than or equal to the value shown in boldface type in the body of the table. The symbol — means that the null hypothesis cannot be rejected regardless of the observed value of *D*. For larger sample sizes, the approximate critical value of *D* is given by the equation:

$$D_{\text{critical}} = K \sqrt{\frac{n_1 + n_2}{n_1 \cdot n_2}}$$

where $K = 1.36$ at the 0.05 level of significance and $K = 1.63$ at the 0.01 level of significance.

# Appendix L

**Critical Values of *W* in the Wilcoxon Test**
 *N* = number of pairs of scores *N* = $n_1$ + $n_2$
 $n_1$ = number of signed ranks
 $n_2$ = number of unsigned ranks (pairs of scores having zero differences)

### One-Tailed at the 0.005 level of significance or two-tailed at the 0.01 level of significance

$n_1$

| $n_2$ | 1 | 2 | 3 | 4 | 5 | 6 | 7 | 8 | 9 | 10 | 11 | 12 | 13 | 14 | 15 | 16 | 17 | 18 | 19 | 20 | 21 | 22 | 23 | 24 | 25 |
|---|---|---|---|---|---|---|---|---|---|---|---|---|---|---|---|---|---|---|---|---|---|---|---|---|---|
| 2 | — | — | — | — | — | — | — | — | — | — | — | — | — | — | — | — | — | — | — | — | 3 | 3 | 3 | 3 | 3 |
| 3 | — | — | — | — | — | — | — | — | 6 | 6 | 6 | 7 | 7 | 7 | 8 | 8 | 8 | 8 | 9 | 9 | 9 | 10 | 10 | 10 | 11 |
| 4 | — | — | — | — | — | 10 | 10 | 11 | 11 | 12 | 12 | 13 | 13 | 14 | 15 | 15 | 16 | 16 | 17 | 18 | 18 | 19 | 19 | 20 | 20 |
| 5 | — | — | — | — | 15 | 16 | 16 | 17 | 18 | 19 | 20 | 21 | 22 | 22 | 23 | 24 | 25 | 26 | 27 | 28 | 29 | 29 | 30 | 31 | 32 |
| 6 | — | — | — | 10 | 16 | 23 | 24 | 25 | 26 | 27 | 28 | 30 | 31 | 32 | 33 | 34 | 36 | 37 | 38 | 39 | 40 | 42 | 43 | 44 | 45 |
| 7 | — | — | — | 10 | 16 | 24 | 32 | 34 | 35 | 37 | 38 | 40 | 41 | 43 | 44 | 46 | 47 | 49 | 50 | 52 | 53 | 55 | 57 | 58 | 60 |
| 8 | — | — | — | 11 | 17 | 25 | 34 | 43 | 45 | 47 | 49 | 51 | 53 | 54 | 56 | 58 | 60 | 62 | 64 | 66 | 68 | 70 | 71 | 73 | 75 |
| 9 | — | — | 6 | 11 | 18 | 26 | 35 | 45 | 56 | 58 | 61 | 63 | 65 | 67 | 69 | 72 | 74 | 76 | 78 | 81 | 83 | 85 | 88 | 90 | 92 |
| 10 | — | — | 6 | 12 | 19 | 27 | 37 | 47 | 58 | 71 | 73 | 76 | 79 | 81 | 84 | 86 | 89 | 92 | 94 | 97 | 99 | 102 | 105 | 107 | 110 |
| 11 | — | — | 6 | 12 | 20 | 28 | 38 | 49 | 61 | 73 | 87 | 90 | 93 | 96 | 99 | 102 | 105 | 108 | 111 | 114 | 117 | 120 | 123 | 126 | 129 |
| 12 | — | — | 7 | 13 | 21 | 30 | 40 | 51 | 63 | 76 | 90 | 105 | 109 | 112 | 115 | 119 | 122 | 125 | 129 | 132 | 136 | 139 | 142 | 146 | 149 |
| 13 | — | — | 7 | 13 | 22 | 31 | 41 | 53 | 65 | 79 | 93 | 109 | 125 | 129 | 133 | 136 | 140 | 144 | 148 | 151 | 155 | 159 | 163 | 166 | 170 |
| 14 | — | — | 7 | 14 | 22 | 32 | 43 | 54 | 67 | 81 | 96 | 112 | 129 | 147 | 151 | 155 | 159 | 163 | 168 | 172 | 176 | 180 | 184 | 188 | 192 |
| 15 | — | — | 8 | 15 | 23 | 33 | 44 | 56 | 69 | 84 | 99 | 115 | 133 | 151 | 171 | 175 | 180 | 184 | 189 | 193 | 198 | 202 | 207 | 211 | 216 |
| 16 | — | — | 8 | 15 | 24 | 34 | 46 | 58 | 72 | 86 | 102 | 119 | 136 | 155 | 175 | 196 | 201 | 206 | 210 | 215 | 220 | 225 | 230 | 235 | 240 |
| 17 | — | — | 8 | 16 | 25 | 36 | 47 | 60 | 74 | 89 | 105 | 122 | 140 | 159 | 180 | 201 | 223 | 228 | 234 | 239 | 244 | 249 | 255 | 260 | 265 |
| 18 | — | — | 8 | 16 | 26 | 37 | 49 | 62 | 76 | 92 | 108 | 125 | 144 | 163 | 184 | 206 | 228 | 252 | 258 | 263 | 269 | 275 | 280 | 286 | 292 |
| 19 | — | — | 9 | 17 | 27 | 38 | 50 | 64 | 78 | 94 | 111 | 129 | 148 | 168 | 189 | 210 | 234 | 258 | 283 | 289 | 295 | 301 | 307 | 313 | 319 |
| 20 | — | — | 9 | 18 | 28 | 39 | 52 | 66 | 81 | 97 | 114 | 132 | 151 | 172 | 193 | 215 | 239 | 263 | 289 | 315 | 322 | 328 | 335 | 341 | 348 |
| 21 | — | 3 | 9 | 18 | 29 | 40 | 53 | 68 | 83 | 99 | 117 | 136 | 155 | 176 | 198 | 220 | 244 | 269 | 295 | 322 | 349 | 356 | 363 | 370 | 377 |
| 22 | — | 3 | 10 | 19 | 29 | 42 | 55 | 70 | 85 | 102 | 120 | 139 | 159 | 180 | 202 | 225 | 249 | 275 | 301 | 328 | 356 | 386 | 393 | 400 | 408 |
| 23 | — | 3 | 10 | 19 | 30 | 43 | 57 | 71 | 88 | 105 | 123 | 142 | 163 | 184 | 207 | 230 | 255 | 280 | 307 | 335 | 363 | 393 | 424 | 431 | 439 |
| 24 | — | 3 | 10 | 20 | 31 | 44 | 58 | 73 | 90 | 107 | 126 | 146 | 166 | 188 | 211 | 235 | 260 | 286 | 313 | 341 | 370 | 400 | 431 | 464 | 472 |
| 25 | — | 3 | 11 | 20 | 32 | 45 | 60 | 75 | 92 | 110 | 129 | 149 | 170 | 192 | 216 | 240 | 265 | 292 | 319 | 348 | 377 | 408 | 439 | 472 | 505 |

The table presents lower critical values, $W_L$. To be significant for any given $n_1$ and $n_2$, the observed value of *W* must be less than or equal to the critical value shown in the table, or greater than or equal to $2\overline{W} - W_L$

L. R. Verdooren, "Extended Tables of Critical Values for Wilcoxon's Test Statistic," *Biometrika,* 50. 1 and 2, 1963. By permission.

## One-Tailed at the 0.01 level of significance or two-tailed at the 0.02 level of significance

$n_1$

| $n_2$ | 1 | 2 | 3 | 4 | 5 | 6 | 7 | 8 | 9 | 10 | 11 | 12 | 13 | 14 | 15 | 16 | 17 | 18 | 19 | 20 | 21 | 22 | 23 | 24 | 25 |
|---|---|---|---|---|---|---|---|---|---|---|---|---|---|---|---|---|---|---|---|---|---|---|---|---|---|
| 2 | — | — | — | — | — | — | — | — | — | — | — | — | 3 | 3 | 3 | 3 | 3 | 3 | 4 | 4 | 4 | 4 | 4 | 4 | 4 |
| 3 | — | — | — | — | — | — | 6 | 6 | 7 | 7 | 7 | 8 | 8 | 8 | 9 | 9 | 10 | 10 | 10 | 11 | 11 | 12 | 12 | 12 | 13 |
| 4 | — | — | — | — | 10 | 11 | 11 | 12 | 13 | 13 | 14 | 15 | 15 | 16 | 17 | 17 | 18 | 19 | 19 | 20 | 21 | 21 | 22 | 23 | 23 |
| 5 | — | — | — | 10 | 16 | 17 | 18 | 19 | 20 | 21 | 22 | 23 | 24 | 25 | 26 | 27 | 28 | 29 | 30 | 31 | 32 | 33 | 24 | 35 | 36 |
| 6 | — | — | — | 11 | 17 | 24 | 25 | 27 | 28 | 29 | 30 | 32 | 33 | 34 | 36 | 37 | 39 | 40 | 41 | 43 | 44 | 45 | 47 | 48 | 50 |
| 7 | — | — | 6 | 11 | 18 | 25 | 34 | 35 | 37 | 39 | 40 | 42 | 44 | 45 | 47 | 49 | 51 | 52 | 54 | 56 | 58 | 59 | 61 | 63 | 64 |
| 8 | — | — | 6 | 12 | 19 | 27 | 35 | 45 | 47 | 49 | 58 | 53 | 56 | 58 | 60 | 62 | 64 | 66 | 68 | 70 | 72 | 74 | 76 | 78 | 81 |
| 9 | — | — | 7 | 13 | 20 | 28 | 37 | 47 | 59 | 61 | 63 | 66 | 68 | 71 | 73 | 76 | 78 | 81 | 83 | 85 | 88 | 90 | 93 | 95 | 98 |
| 10 | — | — | 7 | 13 | 21 | 29 | 39 | 49 | 61 | 74 | 77 | 79 | 82 | 85 | 88 | 91 | 93 | 96 | 99 | 102 | 105 | 108 | 110 | 113 | 116 |
| 11 | — | — | 7 | 14 | 22 | 30 | 40 | 58 | 63 | 77 | 91 | 94 | 97 | 100 | 103 | 107 | 110 | 113 | 116 | 119 | 123 | 126 | 129 | 132 | 136 |
| 12 | — | — | 8 | 15 | 23 | 32 | 42 | 53 | 66 | 79 | 94 | 109 | 113 | 116 | 120 | 124 | 127 | 131 | 134 | 138 | 142 | 145 | 149 | 153 | 156 |
| 13 | — | 3 | 8 | 15 | 24 | 33 | 44 | 56 | 68 | 82 | 97 | 113 | 130 | 134 | 138 | 142 | 146 | 150 | 154 | 158 | 162 | 166 | 170 | 174 | 178 |
| 14 | — | 3 | 8 | 16 | 25 | 34 | 45 | 58 | 71 | 85 | 100 | 116 | 134 | 152 | 156 | 161 | 165 | 170 | 174 | 178 | 183 | 187 | 192 | 196 | 200 |
| 15 | — | 3 | 9 | 17 | 26 | 36 | 47 | 60 | 73 | 88 | 103 | 120 | 138 | 156 | 176 | 181 | 186 | 190 | 195 | 200 | 205 | 210 | 214 | 219 | 224 |
| 16 | — | 3 | 9 | 17 | 27 | 37 | 49 | 62 | 76 | 91 | 107 | 124 | 142 | 161 | 181 | 202 | 207 | 212 | 218 | 223 | 228 | 233 | 238 | 244 | 249 |
| 17 | — | 3 | 10 | 18 | 28 | 39 | 51 | 64 | 78 | 93 | 110 | 127 | 146 | 165 | 186 | 207 | 230 | 235 | 241 | 246 | 252 | 258 | 263 | 269 | 275 |
| 18 | — | 3 | 10 | 19 | 29 | 40 | 52 | 66 | 81 | 96 | 113 | 131 | 150 | 170 | 190 | 212 | 235 | 259 | 265 | 271 | 277 | 283 | 289 | 295 | 301 |
| 19 | — | 4 | 10 | 19 | 30 | 41 | 54 | 68 | 83 | 99 | 116 | 134 | 154 | 174 | 195 | 218 | 241 | 265 | 291 | 297 | 303 | 310 | 316 | 323 | 329 |
| 20 | — | 4 | 11 | 20 | 31 | 43 | 56 | 70 | 85 | 102 | 119 | 138 | 158 | 178 | 200 | 223 | 246 | 271 | 297 | 324 | 331 | 337 | 344 | 351 | 358 |
| 21 | — | 4 | 11 | 21 | 32 | 44 | 58 | 72 | 88 | 105 | 123 | 142 | 162 | 183 | 205 | 228 | 252 | 277 | 303 | 331 | 359 | 366 | 373 | 381 | 388 |
| 22 | — | 4 | 12 | 21 | 33 | 45 | 59 | 74 | 90 | 108 | 126 | 145 | 166 | 187 | 210 | 233 | 258 | 283 | 310 | 337 | 366 | 396 | 403 | 411 | 419 |
| 23 | — | 4 | 12 | 22 | 24 | 47 | 61 | 76 | 93 | 110 | 129 | 149 | 170 | 192 | 214 | 238 | 263 | 289 | 316 | 344 | 373 | 403 | 434 | 443 | 451 |
| 24 | — | 4 | 12 | 23 | 35 | 48 | 63 | 78 | 95 | 113 | 132 | 153 | 174 | 196 | 219 | 244 | 269 | 295 | 323 | 351 | 381 | 411 | 443 | 475 | 484 |
| 25 | — | 4 | 13 | 23 | 36 | 50 | 64 | 81 | 98 | 116 | 136 | 156 | 178 | 200 | 224 | 249 | 275 | 301 | 329 | 358 | 388 | 419 | 451 | 484 | 517 |

The table presents lower critical values, $W_L$. To be significant for any given $n_1$ and $n_2$, the observed value of $W$ must be less than or equal to the critical value shown in the table, or greater than or equal to $2\overline{W} - W_L$

| | | | | | | | | | | | | $n_1$ | | | | | | | | | | | | |
|---|---|---|---|---|---|---|---|---|---|---|---|---|---|---|---|---|---|---|---|---|---|---|---|---|
| $n_2$ | 1 | 2 | 3 | 4 | 5 | 6 | 7 | 8 | 9 | 10 | 11 | 12 | 13 | 14 | 15 | 16 | 17 | 18 | 19 | 20 | 21 | 22 | 23 | 24 | 25 |
| 2 | — | — | — | — | — | — | — | 3 | 3 | 3 | 3 | 4 | 4 | 4 | 4 | 4 | 5 | 5 | 5 | 5 | 6 | 6 | 6 | 6 | 6 |
| 3 | — | — | — | — | 6 | 7 | 7 | 8 | 8 | 9 | 9 | 10 | 10 | 11 | 11 | 12 | 12 | 13 | 13 | 14 | 14 | 15 | 15 | 16 | 16 |
| 4 | — | — | — | 10 | 11 | 12 | 13 | 14 | 14 | 15 | 16 | 17 | 18 | 19 | 20 | 21 | 21 | 22 | 23 | 24 | 25 | 26 | 27 | 27 | 28 |
| 5 | — | — | 6 | 11 | 17 | 18 | 20 | 21 | 22 | 23 | 24 | 26 | 27 | 28 | 29 | 30 | 32 | 33 | 34 | 35 | 37 | 38 | 39 | 40 | 42 |
| 6 | — | — | 7 | 12 | 18 | 26 | 27 | 29 | 31 | 32 | 34 | 35 | 37 | 38 | 40 | 42 | 43 | 45 | 46 | 48 | 50 | 51 | 53 | 54 | 56 |
| 7 | — | — | 7 | 13 | 20 | 27 | 36 | 38 | 40 | 42 | 44 | 46 | 48 | 50 | 52 | 54 | 56 | 58 | 60 | 62 | 64 | 66 | 68 | 70 | 72 |
| 8 | — | 3 | 8 | 14 | 21 | 29 | 38 | 49 | 51 | 53 | 55 | 58 | 60 | 62 | 65 | 67 | 70 | 72 | 74 | 77 | 79 | 81 | 84 | 86 | 89 |
| 9 | — | 3 | 8 | 14 | 22 | 31 | 40 | 51 | 62 | 65 | 68 | 71 | 73 | 76 | 79 | 82 | 84 | 87 | 90 | 93 | 95 | 98 | 101 | 104 | 107 |
| 10 | — | 3 | 9 | 15 | 23 | 32 | 42 | 53 | 65 | 78 | 81 | 84 | 88 | 91 | 94 | 97 | 100 | 103 | 107 | 110 | 113 | 116 | 119 | 122 | 126 |
| 11 | — | 3 | 9 | 16 | 24 | 34 | 44 | 55 | 68 | 81 | 96 | 99 | 103 | 106 | 110 | 113 | 117 | 121 | 124 | 128 | 131 | 135 | 139 | 142 | 146 |
| 12 | — | 4 | 10 | 17 | 26 | 35 | 46 | 58 | 71 | 84 | 99 | 115 | 119 | 123 | 127 | 131 | 135 | 139 | 143 | 147 | 151 | 155 | 159 | 163 | 167 |
| 13 | — | 4 | 10 | 18 | 27 | 37 | 48 | 60 | 73 | 88 | 103 | 119 | 136 | 141 | 145 | 150 | 154 | 158 | 163 | 167 | 171 | 176 | 180 | 185 | 189 |
| 14 | — | 4 | 11 | 19 | 28 | 38 | 50 | 62 | 76 | 91 | 106 | 123 | 141 | 160 | 164 | 169 | 174 | 179 | 183 | 188 | 193 | 198 | 203 | 207 | 212 |
| 15 | — | 4 | 11 | 20 | 29 | 40 | 52 | 65 | 79 | 94 | 110 | 127 | 145 | 164 | 184 | 190 | 195 | 200 | 205 | 210 | 216 | 221 | 226 | 231 | 237 |
| 16 | — | 4 | 12 | 21 | 30 | 42 | 54 | 67 | 82 | 97 | 113 | 131 | 150 | 169 | 190 | 211 | 217 | 222 | 228 | 234 | 239 | 245 | 251 | 256 | 262 |
| 17 | — | 5 | 12 | 21 | 32 | 43 | 56 | 70 | 84 | 100 | 117 | 135 | 154 | 174 | 195 | 217 | 240 | 246 | 252 | 258 | 264 | 270 | 276 | 282 | 288 |
| 18 | — | 5 | 13 | 22 | 33 | 45 | 58 | 72 | 87 | 103 | 121 | 139 | 158 | 179 | 200 | 222 | 246 | 270 | 277 | 283 | 290 | 296 | 303 | 309 | 316 |
| 19 | — | 5 | 13 | 23 | 34 | 46 | 60 | 74 | 90 | 107 | 124 | 143 | 163 | 183 | 205 | 228 | 252 | 277 | 303 | 309 | 316 | 323 | 330 | 337 | 344 |
| 20 | — | 5 | 14 | 24 | 35 | 48 | 62 | 77 | 93 | 110 | 128 | 147 | 167 | 188 | 210 | 234 | 258 | 283 | 309 | 337 | 344 | 351 | 359 | 366 | 373 |
| 21 | — | 6 | 14 | 25 | 37 | 50 | 64 | 79 | 95 | 113 | 131 | 151 | 171 | 193 | 216 | 239 | 264 | 290 | 316 | 344 | 373 | 381 | 388 | 396 | 404 |
| 22 | — | 6 | 15 | 26 | 38 | 51 | 66 | 81 | 98 | 116 | 135 | 155 | 176 | 198 | 221 | 245 | 270 | 296 | 323 | 351 | 381 | 411 | 419 | 427 | 435 |
| 23 | — | 6 | 15 | 27 | 39 | 53 | 68 | 84 | 101 | 119 | 139 | 159 | 180 | 203 | 226 | 251 | 276 | 303 | 330 | 359 | 388 | 419 | 451 | 459 | 468 |
| 24 | — | 6 | 16 | 27 | 40 | 54 | 70 | 86 | 104 | 122 | 142 | 163 | 185 | 207 | 231 | 256 | 282 | 309 | 337 | 366 | 396 | 427 | 459 | 492 | 501 |
| 25 | — | 6 | 16 | 28 | 42 | 56 | 72 | 89 | 107 | 126 | 146 | 167 | 189 | 212 | 237 | 262 | 288 | 316 | 344 | 373 | 404 | 435 | 468 | 501 | 536 |

The table presents lower critical values, $W_L$. To be significant for any given $n_1$ and $n_2$, the observed value of $W$ must be less than or equal to the critical value shown in the table, or greater than or equal to $2\overline{W} - W_L$

## One-Tailed at the 0.05 level of significance or two-tailed at the 0.10 level of significance

| $n_2$ | \| $n_1$ 1 | 2 | 3 | 4 | 5 | 6 | 7 | 8 | 9 | 10 | 11 | 12 | 13 | 14 | 15 | 16 | 17 | 18 | 19 | 20 | 21 | 22 | 23 | 24 | 25 |
|---|---|---|---|---|---|---|---|---|---|---|---|---|---|---|---|---|---|---|---|---|---|---|---|---|---|
| 2 | — | — | 3 | 3 | 4 | 4 | 4 | 5 | 5 | 6 | 6 | 7 | 7 | 8 | 8 | 8 | 9 | 9 | 10 | 10 | 11 | 11 | 12 | 12 | 12 |
| 3 | — | — | 6 | 6 | 7 | 8 | 8 | 9 | 10 | 10 | 11 | 11 | 12 | 13 | 13 | 14 | 15 | 15 | 16 | 17 | 17 | 18 | 19 | 19 | 20 |
| 4 | — | — | 6 | 11 | 12 | 13 | 14 | 15 | 16 | 17 | 18 | 19 | 20 | 21 | 22 | 24 | 25 | 26 | 27 | 28 | 29 | 30 | 31 | 32 | 33 |
| 5 | — | 3 | 7 | 12 | 19 | 20 | 21 | 23 | 24 | 26 | 27 | 28 | 30 | 31 | 33 | 34 | 35 | 37 | 38 | 40 | 41 | 43 | 44 | 45 | 47 |
| 6 | — | 3 | 8 | 13 | 20 | 28 | 29 | 31 | 33 | 35 | 37 | 38 | 40 | 42 | 44 | 46 | 47 | 49 | 51 | 53 | 55 | 57 | 58 | 60 | 62 |
| 7 | — | 3 | 8 | 14 | 21 | 29 | 39 | 41 | 43 | 45 | 47 | 49 | 52 | 54 | 56 | 58 | 61 | 63 | 65 | 67 | 69 | 72 | 74 | 76 | 78 |
| 8 | — | 4 | 9 | 15 | 23 | 31 | 41 | 51 | 54 | 56 | 59 | 62 | 64 | 67 | 69 | 72 | 75 | 77 | 80 | 83 | 85 | 88 | 90 | 93 | 96 |
| 9 | — | 4 | 10 | 16 | 24 | 33 | 43 | 54 | 66 | 69 | 72 | 75 | 78 | 81 | 84 | 87 | 90 | 93 | 96 | 99 | 102 | 105 | 108 | 111 | 114 |
| 10 | — | 4 | 10 | 17 | 26 | 35 | 45 | 56 | 69 | 82 | 86 | 89 | 92 | 96 | 99 | 103 | 106 | 110 | 113 | 117 | 120 | 123 | 127 | 130 | 134 |
| 11 | — | 4 | 11 | 18 | 27 | 37 | 47 | 59 | 72 | 86 | 100 | 104 | 108 | 112 | 116 | 120 | 123 | 127 | 131 | 135 | 139 | 143 | 147 | 151 | 155 |
| 12 | — | 5 | 11 | 19 | 28 | 38 | 49 | 62 | 75 | 89 | 104 | 120 | 125 | 129 | 133 | 138 | 142 | 146 | 150 | 155 | 159 | 163 | 168 | 172 | 176 |
| 13 | — | 5 | 12 | 20 | 30 | 40 | 52 | 64 | 78 | 92 | 108 | 125 | 142 | 147 | 152 | 156 | 161 | 166 | 171 | 175 | 180 | 185 | 189 | 194 | 199 |
| 14 | — | 6 | 13 | 21 | 31 | 42 | 54 | 67 | 81 | 96 | 112 | 129 | 147 | 166 | 171 | 176 | 182 | 187 | 192 | 197 | 202 | 207 | 212 | 218 | 223 |
| 15 | — | 6 | 13 | 22 | 33 | 44 | 56 | 69 | 84 | 99 | 116 | 133 | 152 | 171 | 192 | 197 | 203 | 208 | 214 | 220 | 225 | 231 | 236 | 242 | 248 |
| 16 | — | 6 | 14 | 24 | 34 | 46 | 58 | 72 | 87 | 103 | 120 | 138 | 156 | 176 | 197 | 219 | 225 | 231 | 237 | 243 | 249 | 255 | 261 | 267 | 273 |
| 17 | — | 6 | 15 | 25 | 35 | 47 | 61 | 75 | 90 | 106 | 123 | 142 | 161 | 182 | 203 | 225 | 249 | 255 | 262 | 268 | 274 | 281 | 287 | 294 | 300 |
| 18 | — | 7 | 15 | 26 | 37 | 49 | 63 | 77 | 93 | 110 | 127 | 146 | 166 | 187 | 208 | 231 | 255 | 280 | 287 | 294 | 301 | 307 | 314 | 321 | 328 |
| 19 | 1 | 7 | 16 | 27 | 38 | 51 | 65 | 80 | 96 | 113 | 131 | 150 | 171 | 192 | 214 | 237 | 262 | 287 | 313 | 320 | 328 | 335 | 342 | 350 | 357 |
| 20 | 1 | 7 | 17 | 28 | 40 | 53 | 67 | 83 | 99 | 117 | 135 | 155 | 175 | 197 | 220 | 243 | 268 | 294 | 320 | 348 | 356 | 364 | 371 | 379 | 387 |
| 21 | 1 | 8 | 17 | 29 | 41 | 55 | 69 | 85 | 102 | 120 | 139 | 159 | 180 | 202 | 225 | 249 | 274 | 301 | 328 | 356 | 385 | 393 | 401 | 410 | 418 |
| 22 | 1 | 8 | 18 | 30 | 43 | 57 | 72 | 88 | 105 | 123 | 143 | 163 | 185 | 207 | 231 | 255 | 281 | 307 | 335 | 364 | 393 | 424 | 432 | 441 | 450 |
| 23 | 1 | 8 | 19 | 31 | 44 | 58 | 74 | 90 | 108 | 127 | 147 | 168 | 189 | 212 | 236 | 261 | 287 | 314 | 342 | 371 | 401 | 432 | 465 | 474 | 483 |
| 24 | 1 | 9 | 19 | 32 | 45 | 60 | 76 | 93 | 111 | 130 | 151 | 172 | 194 | 218 | 242 | 267 | 294 | 321 | 350 | 379 | 410 | 441 | 474 | 507 | 517 |
| 25 | 1 | 9 | 20 | 33 | 47 | 62 | 78 | 96 | 114 | 134 | 155 | 176 | 199 | 223 | 248 | 273 | 300 | 328 | 357 | 387 | 418 | 450 | 483 | 517 | 552 |

The table presents lower critical values, $W_L$. To be significant for any given $n_1$ and $n_2$, the observed value of $W$ must be less than or equal to the critical value shown in the table, or greater than or equal to $2\overline{W} - W_L$

|       |    |    |    |    |    |    |    | $2\overline{W}$ |    |    |    |    |    |    |    |    |    |    |    |    |    |     |     |     |     |
|-------|----|----|----|----|----|----|----|----|----|----|----|----|----|----|----|----|----|----|----|----|----|-----|-----|-----|-----|
|       |    |    |    |    |    |    |    |    |   $n_1$  |    |    |    |    |    |    |    |    |    |    |    |    |     |     |     |     |
| $n_2$ | 1  | 2  | 3  | 4  | 5  | 6  | 7  | 8  | 9  | 10 | 11 | 12 | 13 | 14 | 15 | 16 | 17 | 18 | 19 | 20 | 21 | 22  | 23  | 24  | 25  |
| 2  | 4  | 10 | 12 | 14 | 16 | 18 | 20 | 22 | 24 | 26 | 28 | 30 | 32 | 34 | 36 | 38 | 40 | 42 | 44 | 46 | 48 | 50 | 52 | 54 | 56 |
| 3  | 5  | 12 | 21 | 24 | 27 | 30 | 33 | 36 | 39 | 42 | 45 | 48 | 51 | 54 | 57 | 60 | 63 | 66 | 69 | 72 | 75 | 78 | 81 | 84 | 87 |
| 4  | 6  | 14 | 24 | 36 | 40 | 44 | 48 | 52 | 56 | 60 | 64 | 68 | 72 | 76 | 80 | 84 | 88 | 92 | 96 | 100 | 104 | 108 | 112 | 116 | 120 |
| 5  | 7  | 16 | 27 | 40 | 55 | 60 | 65 | 70 | 75 | 80 | 85 | 90 | 95 | 400 | 105 | 110 | 115 | 120 | 125 | 130 | 135 | 140 | 145 | 150 | 155 |
| 6  | 8  | 18 | 30 | 44 | 60 | 78 | 84 | 90 | 96 | 102 | 108 | 114 | 120 | 126 | 132 | 138 | 144 | 150 | 156 | 162 | 168 | 174 | 180 | 186 | 192 |
| 7  | 9  | 20 | 33 | 48 | 65 | 84 | 105 | 112 | 119 | 126 | 133 | 140 | 147 | 154 | 161 | 168 | 175 | 182 | 189 | 196 | 203 | 210 | 217 | 224 | 231 |
| 8  | 10 | 22 | 36 | 52 | 70 | 90 | 112 | 136 | 144 | 152 | 160 | 168 | 176 | 184 | 192 | 200 | 208 | 216 | 224 | 232 | 240 | 248 | 256 | 264 | 272 |
| 9  | 11 | 24 | 39 | 56 | 75 | 96 | 119 | 144 | 171 | 180 | 189 | 198 | 207 | 216 | 225 | 234 | 243 | 252 | 261 | 270 | 279 | 288 | 297 | 306 | 315 |
| 10 | 12 | 26 | 42 | 60 | 80 | 102 | 126 | 152 | 180 | 210 | 220 | 230 | 240 | 250 | 260 | 270 | 280 | 290 | 300 | 310 | 320 | 330 | 340 | 350 | 360 |
| 11 | 13 | 28 | 45 | 64 | 85 | 108 | 133 | 160 | 189 | 220 | 253 | 264 | 275 | 286 | 297 | 308 | 319 | 330 | 341 | 352 | 363 | 374 | 385 | 396 | 407 |
| 12 | 14 | 30 | 48 | 68 | 90 | 114 | 140 | 168 | 198 | 230 | 264 | 300 | 312 | 324 | 336 | 348 | 360 | 372 | 384 | 396 | 408 | 420 | 432 | 444 | 456 |
| 13 | 45 | 32 | 51 | 72 | 95 | 120 | 147 | 176 | 207 | 240 | 275 | 312 | 351 | 364 | 377 | 390 | 403 | 416 | 429 | 442 | 455 | 468 | 481 | 494 | 507 |
| 14 | 16 | 34 | 54 | 76 | 400 | 126 | 154 | 184 | 216 | 250 | 286 | 324 | 364 | 406 | 420 | 434 | 448 | 462 | 476 | 490 | 504 | 518 | 532 | 546 | 560 |
| 15 | 17 | 36 | 57 | 80 | 105 | 132 | 161 | 192 | 225 | 260 | 297 | 336 | 377 | 420 | 465 | 480 | 495 | 510 | 525 | 540 | 555 | 570 | 585 | 600 | 615 |
| 16 | 18 | 38 | 60 | 84 | 110 | 138 | 168 | 200 | 234 | 270 | 308 | 348 | 390 | 434 | 480 | 528 | 544 | 560 | 576 | 592 | 608 | 624 | 640 | 656 | 672 |
| 17 | 19 | 40 | 63 | 88 | 115 | 144 | 175 | 208 | 243 | 280 | 319 | 360 | 403 | 448 | 495 | 544 | 595 | 612 | 629 | 646 | 663 | 680 | 697 | 714 | 731 |
| 18 | 20 | 42 | 66 | 92 | 120 | 150 | 182 | 216 | 252 | 290 | 330 | 372 | 416 | 462 | 510 | 560 | 612 | 666 | 684 | 702 | 720 | 738 | 756 | 774 | 792 |
| 19 | 21 | 44 | 69 | 96 | 125 | 156 | 189 | 224 | 261 | 300 | 341 | 384 | 429 | 476 | 525 | 576 | 629 | 684 | 741 | 760 | 779 | 798 | 817 | 836 | 855 |
| 20 | 22 | 46 | 72 | 100 | 130 | 162 | 196 | 232 | 270 | 310 | 352 | 396 | 442 | 490 | 540 | 592 | 646 | 702 | 760 | 820 | 840 | 860 | 880 | 900 | 920 |
| 21 | 23 | 48 | 75 | 104 | 135 | 168 | 203 | 240 | 279 | 320 | 363 | 408 | 455 | 504 | 555 | 608 | 663 | 720 | 779 | 840 | 903 | 924 | 945 | 966 | 987 |
| 22 | 24 | 50 | 78 | 108 | 140 | 174 | 210 | 248 | 288 | 330 | 374 | 420 | 468 | 518 | 570 | 624 | 680 | 738 | 798 | 860 | 924 | 990 | 1012 | 1034 | 1056 |
| 23 | 25 | 52 | 81 | 112 | 145 | 180 | 217 | 256 | 297 | 340 | 385 | 432 | 481 | 532 | 585 | 640 | 697 | 756 | 817 | 880 | 945 | 1012 | 1081 | 1104 | 1127 |
| 24 | 26 | 54 | 84 | 116 | 150 | 186 | 224 | 264 | 306 | 350 | 396 | 444 | 494 | 546 | 600 | 656 | 714 | 774 | 836 | 900 | 966 | 1034 | 1104 | 1176 | 1200 |
| 25 | 27 | 56 | 87 | 120 | 155 | 192 | 231 | 272 | 315 | 360 | 407 | 456 | 507 | 560 | 615 | 672 | 731 | 792 | 855 | 920 | 987 | 1056 | 1127 | 1200 | 1275 |

The table presents $2\overline{W}$. To be significant for any given $n_1$ and $n_2$, the observed value of $W$ must be less than or equal to the critical value, $W_L$, shown in the preceding tables, or greater than or equal to $2\overline{W} - W_L$.

# Appendix M

**Critical Values of Spearman's Rank Correlation Coefficient**

| Sample size $n$ | \multicolumn{4}{c}{Level of significance} | | | |
| --- | --- | --- | --- | --- |
| | \multicolumn{4}{c}{Two-tailed test} | | | |
| | 0.10 | 0.05 | 0.02 | 0.01 |
| | \multicolumn{4}{c}{One-tailed test} | | | |
| | 0.05 | 0.025 | 0.01 | 0.005 |
| 4 | 1.000 | | | |
| 5 | 0.900 | 1.000 | 1.000 | |
| 6 | 0.829 | 0.886 | 0.943 | 1.000 |
| 7 | 0.714 | 0.786 | 0.893 | 0.929 |
| 8 | 0.643 | 0.738 | 0.833 | 0.881 |
| 9 | 0.600 | 0.700 | 0.783 | 0.833 |
| 10 | 0.564 | 0.648 | 0.745 | 0.794 |
| 11 | 0.536 | 0.618 | 0.709 | 0.755 |
| 12 | 0.503 | 0.587 | 0.678 | 0.727 |
| 13 | 0.484 | 0.560 | 0.648 | 0.703 |
| 14 | 0.464 | 0.538 | 0.626 | 0.679 |
| 15 | 0.446 | 0.521 | 0.604 | 0.654 |
| 16 | 0.429 | 0.503 | 0.582 | 0.635 |
| 17 | 0.414 | 0.488 | 0.566 | 0.618 |
| 18 | 0.401 | 0.472 | 0.550 | 0.600 |
| 19 | 0.391 | 0.460 | 0.535 | 0.584 |
| 20 | 0.380 | 0.447 | 0.522 | 0.570 |

*Note:* To be significant at any given $n$ and level of significance, the observed value of the Spearman rank correlation coefficient must be equal to or greater than the critical value shown in the body of the table.

*Source:* Philip H. Ramsey, "Critical Values for Spearman's Rank Order Correlation," *Journal of Educational Statistics,* v. 14 n. 3 (Autumn 1989) 245–253.

*(continued)*

**Critical Values of Spearman's Rank Correlation Coefficient** *(continued)*

| | Level of significance | | | |
|---|---|---|---|---|
| | *Two-tailed test* | | | |
| | 0.10 | 0.05 | 0.02 | 0.01 |
| **Sample size** | *One-tailed test* | | | |
| **n** | 0.05 | 0.025 | 0.01 | 0.005 |
| 21 | 0.370 | 0.436 | 0.509 | 0.556 |
| 22 | 0.361 | 0.425 | 0.497 | 0.544 |
| 23 | 0.353 | 0.416 | 0.486 | 0.532 |
| 24 | 0.344 | 0.407 | 0.476 | 0.521 |
| 25 | 0.337 | 0.398 | 0.466 | 0.511 |
| 26 | 0.331 | 0.390 | 0.457 | 0.501 |
| 27 | 0.324 | 0.383 | 0.449 | 0.492 |
| 28 | 0.318 | 0.375 | 0.441 | 0.483 |
| 29 | 0.312 | 0.368 | 0.433 | 0.475 |
| 30 | 0.306 | 0.362 | 0.425 | 0.467 |
| 31 | 0.301 | 0.356 | 0.419 | 0.459 |
| 32 | 0.296 | 0.350 | 0.412 | 0.452 |
| 33 | 0.291 | 0.345 | 0.405 | 0.446 |
| 34 | 0.287 | 0.340 | 0.400 | 0.439 |
| 35 | 0.283 | 0.335 | 0.394 | 0.433 |
| 36 | 0.279 | 0.330 | 0.388 | 0.427 |
| 37 | 0.275 | 0.325 | 0.383 | 0.421 |
| 38 | 0.271 | 0.321 | 0.378 | 0.415 |
| 39 | 0.267 | 0.317 | 0.373 | 0.410 |
| 40 | 0.264 | 0.313 | 0.368 | 0.405 |
| 41 | 0.261 | 0.309 | 0.364 | 0.400 |
| 42 | 0.257 | 0.305 | 0.359 | 0.396 |
| 43 | 0.254 | 0.301 | 0.355 | 0.391 |
| 44 | 0.251 | 0.298 | 0.351 | 0.386 |
| 45 | 0.248 | 0.294 | 0.347 | 0.382 |
| 46 | 0.246 | 0.291 | 0.343 | 0.378 |
| 47 | 0.243 | 0.288 | 0.340 | 0.374 |
| 48 | 0.240 | 0.285 | 0.336 | 0.370 |
| 49 | 0.238 | 0.282 | 0.333 | 0.366 |
| 50 | 0.235 | 0.279 | 0.329 | 0.363 |

*Note:* To be significant at any given *n* and level of significance, the observed value of the Spearman rank correlation coefficient must be equal to or greater than the critical value shown in the body of the table.

*(continued)*

**Critical Values of Spearman's Rank Correlation Coefficient** *(continued)*

| Sample size *n* | Level of significance | | | |
|---|---|---|---|---|
| | *Two-tailed test* | | | |
| | 0.10 | 0.05 | 0.02 | 0.01 |
| | *One-tailed test* | | | |
| | 0.05 | 0.025 | 0.01 | 0.005 |
| 52 | 0.231 | 0.274 | 0.323 | 0.356 |
| 54 | 0.226 | 0.268 | 0.317 | 0.349 |
| 56 | 0.222 | 0.264 | 0.311 | 0.343 |
| 58 | 0.218 | 0.259 | 0.306 | 0.337 |
| 60 | 0.214 | 0.255 | 0.301 | 0.331 |
| 62 | 0.211 | 0.250 | 0.296 | 0.326 |
| 64 | 0.207 | 0.246 | 0.291 | 0.321 |
| 66 | 0.204 | 0.243 | 0.287 | 0.316 |
| 68 | 0.201 | 0.239 | 0.282 | 0.311 |
| 70 | 0.198 | 0.235 | 0.278 | 0.307 |
| 72 | 0.195 | 0.232 | 0.274 | 0.303 |
| 74 | 0.193 | 0.229 | 0.271 | 0.299 |
| 76 | 0.190 | 0.226 | 0.267 | 0.295 |
| 78 | 0.188 | 0.223 | 0.264 | 0.291 |
| 80 | 0.185 | 0.220 | 0.260 | 0.287 |
| 82 | 0.183 | 0.217 | 0.257 | 0.284 |
| 84 | 0.181 | 0.215 | 0.254 | 0.280 |
| 86 | 0.179 | 0.212 | 0.251 | 0.277 |
| 88 | 0.176 | 0.210 | 0.248 | 0.274 |
| 90 | 0.174 | 0.207 | 0.245 | 0.271 |
| 92 | 0.173 | 0.205 | 0.243 | 0.268 |
| 94 | 0.171 | 0.203 | 0.240 | 0.265 |
| 96 | 0.169 | 0.201 | 0.238 | 0.262 |
| 98 | 0.167 | 0.199 | 0.235 | 0.260 |
| 100 | 0.165 | 0.197 | 0.233 | 0.257 |

*Note:* To be significant at any given *n* and level of significance, the observed value of the Spearman rank correlation coefficient must be equal to or greater than the critical value shown in the body of the table.

# Appendix N

**Random Numbers**

|    | 1    | 2    | 3    | 4    | 5    | 6    | 7    | 8    | 9    | 10   |
|----|------|------|------|------|------|------|------|------|------|------|
| 1  | 7327 | 2445 | 5135 | 9596 | 9455 | 7409 | 0719 | 3525 | 4178 | 6815 |
| 2  | 0005 | 0824 | 7259 | 9204 | 5129 | 2728 | 5575 | 8724 | 0317 | 4337 |
| 3  | 7589 | 0097 | 6864 | 6862 | 4933 | 9877 | 7215 | 8269 | 7422 | 2676 |
| 4  | 6299 | 9901 | 4682 | 7957 | 0809 | 7717 | 9062 | 3337 | 9739 | 5985 |
| 5  | 5475 | 8080 | 2536 | 7341 | 4708 | 7121 | 9715 | 5078 | 8011 | 0123 |
| 6  | 1777 | 2238 | 6495 | 3344 | 8020 | 8025 | 4196 | 8824 | 9082 | 7812 |
| 7  | 1098 | 2926 | 5044 | 0870 | 4607 | 7040 | 8139 | 3330 | 3148 | 4486 |
| 8  | 2648 | 0911 | 4366 | 2791 | 2278 | 3108 | 2413 | 9018 | 9738 | 8584 |
| 9  | 9311 | 8811 | 5207 | 7221 | 5502 | 6256 | 8970 | 9499 | 9975 | 7190 |
| 10 | 3579 | 8245 | 0345 | 3160 | 7991 | 1199 | 0924 | 3587 | 1716 | 4784 |
| 11 | 1828 | 1633 | 7824 | 9360 | 1517 | 5571 | 9882 | 8436 | 8634 | 8585 |
| 12 | 9612 | 4021 | 2874 | 8234 | 4342 | 2145 | 6803 | 6992 | 5834 | 9945 |
| 13 | 9946 | 6669 | 3984 | 4389 | 6876 | 2272 | 1042 | 0497 | 5719 | 7532 |
| 14 | 8259 | 2972 | 8845 | 6935 | 4452 | 1638 | 1681 | 0684 | 6044 | 4167 |
| 15 | 1912 | 6387 | 3575 | 4544 | 8378 | 3968 | 4524 | 2411 | 5112 | 0534 |
| 16 | 1041 | 5024 | 2832 | 1980 | 4652 | 9684 | 3998 | 4563 | 9002 | 8387 |
| 17 | 6611 | 0794 | 1895 | 0625 | 9001 | 5537 | 2738 | 9794 | 2599 | 8755 |
| 18 | 2999 | 6055 | 4840 | 2505 | 0215 | 0236 | 0810 | 6908 | 0757 | 8966 |
| 19 | 6763 | 8028 | 8275 | 0108 | 7743 | 0162 | 0787 | 3283 | 0954 | 8042 |
| 20 | 3936 | 9203 | 0859 | 6638 | 3866 | 6856 | 9334 | 2550 | 5789 | 6506 |
| 21 | 1600 | 8966 | 9340 | 8722 | 4286 | 5115 | 7742 | 2333 | 6491 | 3550 |
| 22 | 2462 | 9153 | 2679 | 7352 | 3240 | 7299 | 3915 | 4045 | 8145 | 2609 |
| 23 | 2851 | 5711 | 0321 | 8187 | 1015 | 5624 | 7700 | 5816 | 3759 | 0677 |
| 24 | 8538 | 3313 | 2648 | 4649 | 6442 | 3927 | 0540 | 6472 | 4190 | 7189 |
| 25 | 6696 | 3123 | 4878 | 8676 | 1578 | 5358 | 2627 | 8563 | 8913 | 6568 |

*(continued)*

**Random Numbers** *(continued)*

|    | 1 | 2 | 3 | 4 | 5 | 6 | 7 | 8 | 9 | 10 |
|----|------|------|------|------|------|------|------|------|------|------|
| 26 | 1745 | 4412 | 5544 | 8626 | 3174 | 0528 | 2761 | 2735 | 1652 | 3055 |
| 27 | 7854 | 3172 | 8100 | 7654 | 3005 | 2129 | 0937 | 9232 | 3398 | 0522 |
| 28 | 5792 | 1046 | 1522 | 6959 | 0790 | 8247 | 1912 | 2470 | 9282 | 3423 |
| 29 | 9579 | 0869 | 4033 | 8351 | 8794 | 4708 | 4200 | 0279 | 4554 | 1828 |
| 30 | 0165 | 7347 | 7022 | 0687 | 4826 | 8309 | 9945 | 5067 | 5051 | 5652 |
| 31 | 0513 | 1929 | 8856 | 9456 | 4272 | 9999 | 5796 | 8915 | 2924 | 3116 |
| 32 | 3816 | 9486 | 9956 | 3307 | 0719 | 7674 | 8287 | 0625 | 4319 | 7013 |
| 33 | 5293 | 3002 | 8109 | 0819 | 2680 | 4981 | 7085 | 9577 | 4139 | 6254 |
| 34 | 9757 | 0732 | 0335 | 9070 | 1327 | 8943 | 6535 | 6126 | 4803 | 2636 |
| 35 | 1839 | 1510 | 7488 | 8511 | 4188 | 1719 | 3919 | 7758 | 9910 | 5286 |
| 36 | 9017 | 2102 | 9515 | 9293 | 2006 | 3653 | 3323 | 4315 | 3293 | 9422 |
| 37 | 2014 | 5802 | 7642 | 4144 | 1370 | 3460 | 1210 | 8170 | 4055 | 2875 |
| 38 | 3170 | 8367 | 0471 | 0096 | 7693 | 6579 | 0661 | 1732 | 9866 | 0654 |
| 39 | 2497 | 6740 | 7852 | 9444 | 1753 | 9119 | 9333 | 6292 | 0146 | 8904 |
| 40 | 8146 | 1978 | 3609 | 8657 | 9231 | 8206 | 5317 | 5701 | 6388 | 4334 |
| 41 | 0137 | 4590 | 1206 | 3708 | 9672 | 2432 | 5642 | 0404 | 1028 | 5453 |
| 42 | 4508 | 1294 | 2914 | 7190 | 3915 | 7132 | 2343 | 2521 | 3752 | 8084 |
| 43 | 2564 | 2500 | 5410 | 8334 | 4920 | 6826 | 8632 | 8512 | 9298 | 0802 |
| 44 | 1852 | 4966 | 1820 | 7557 | 5432 | 7784 | 6822 | 3041 | 6241 | 0217 |
| 45 | 1227 | 9386 | 0909 | 8142 | 1214 | 7064 | 7747 | 5298 | 2267 | 9742 |
| 46 | 4320 | 7770 | 4958 | 8078 | 2417 | 0792 | 8573 | 3160 | 5563 | 4654 |
| 47 | 1290 | 5275 | 2857 | 4117 | 2693 | 2027 | 2434 | 4317 | 1966 | 0405 |
| 48 | 6491 | 0357 | 9313 | 8595 | 8703 | 9372 | 4131 | 1596 | 8577 | 8047 |
| 49 | 0272 | 3340 | 6679 | 7726 | 4791 | 9832 | 6105 | 3963 | 0175 | 8598 |
| 50 | 3016 | 8970 | 4910 | 5740 | 6104 | 5583 | 8686 | 9370 | 9139 | 5367 |

# Index